CW01198354

ARMS FOR RUSSIA
& THE NAVAL WAR
IN THE ARCTIC
1941—1945

To all who served in the Arctic 1941–1945

'In the great epic of the sea war one of the most outstanding chapters was those magnificent exploits, the northern convoys.'
Ivan Maisky, Soviet Ambassador in London, April 1943

# Arms for Russia & the Naval War in the Arctic 1941–1945

## Andrew Boyd

Foreword by Andrew Lambert

**Seaforth**
PUBLISHING

Copyright © Andrew Boyd 2024
Foreword © Andrew Lambert
First published in Great Britain in 2024 by
Seaforth Publishing,
A division of Pen & Sword Books Ltd,
George House, Beevor Street, Barnsley S71 1HN

www.seaforthpublishing.com

British Library Cataloguing in Publication Data
A catalogue record for this book is available from the British Library

ISBN 978 1 3990 3886 7 (HARDBACK)
ISBN 978 1 3990 3887 4 (EPUB)

All rights reserved. No part of this publication may be reproduced or transmitted in any form or by any means, electronic or mechanical, including photocopying, recording, or any information storage and retrieval system, without prior permission in writing of both the copyright owner and the above publisher.

The right of Andrew Boyd to be identified as the author of this work has been asserted by him in accordance with the Copyright, Designs and Patents Act 1988.

Pen & Sword Books Limited incorporates the imprints of Atlas, Archaeology, Aviation, Discovery, Family History, Fiction, History, Maritime, Military, Military Classics, Politics, Select, Transport, True Crime, Air World, Frontline Publishing, Leo Cooper, Remember When, Seaforth Publishing, The Praetorian Press, Wharncliffe Local History, Wharncliffe Transport, Wharncliffe True Crime & White Owl

Typeset by Mac Style

Printed and bound in the UK by CPI Group (UK) Ltd,
Croydon, CR0 4YY

# Contents

| | | |
|---|---|---|
| List of Maps | | vi |
| List of Illustrations | | vii |
| Foreword | | 1 |
| Acknowledgements | | 3 |
| Abbreviations | | 5 |
| Glossary of Codenames | | 7 |
| Introduction | | 8 |
| Prelude: August 1941: Churchill and Roosevelt at Placentia Bay | | 14 |
| 1 | The Royal Navy in Autumn 1941: Brightening Prospects? | 39 |
| 2 | Barbarossa and the Reluctant Opening of an Arctic Theatre | 80 |
| 3 | The Case for Helping Russia: Ends, Ways and Means | 105 |
| 4 | The First Arctic Convoys and Their Impact | 143 |
| 5 | German Countermeasures | 185 |
| 6 | The Beginning of German Combined Arms Attacks | 213 |
| 7 | PQ 17: The Germans Seek a Decisive Victory | 251 |
| 8 | PQ 17: Catastrophe and Aftermath | 292 |
| 9 | Recovery: PQ 18 and the Impact of Torch | 335 |
| 10 | The Battle of the Barents Sea and its Impact | 373 |
| 11 | The Destruction of the German Battlefleet | 418 |
| 12 | Last Convoys and the Final Stand of the Kriegsmarine | 459 |
| Reflections | | 486 |
| Appendix 1: Arctic Convoys Summary | | 500 |
| Appendix 2: Arctic Aid Deliveries | | 502 |
| Notes | | 504 |
| Bibliography | | 544 |
| Index | | 561 |

# List of Maps

| | | |
|---|---|---|
| 1 | Shipments to Russia from the United States via different routes 1941–1945 | 146 |
| 2 | The Arctic Convoy routes 1941–1942 | 148 |
| 3 | British and German movements during Convoy PQ 12 6–9 March 1942 | 204 |
| 4 | Convoys PQ 17 and QP 13 3–6 July 1942 | 280 |
| 5 | The Defence of Convoy JW 51B 0830–1030 31 December 1942 | 382 |
| 6 | The Defence of Convoy JW 51B 1030–1200 31 December 1942 | 385 |
| 7 | The Sinking of the *Scharnhorst* Phase 1 0840–1500 26 December 1943 | 452 |

Distances on the maps: One minute of latitude equates to one nautical mile at the relevant latitude.

# List of Illustrations

*The plates sections are between pages 184–185 and 264–265*

*Prince of Wales* in Placentia Bay
Prime Minister Winston Churchill and Lord Beaverbrook at the Riviera Summit
Hurricanes at Vaenga, North Russia, September 1941
Matilda tanks for Russia being loaded at a British port
President Franklin Roosevelt with Churchill and Western military leaders at Casablanca
Soviet leader Josef Stalin with leading figures at Teheran
Rear Admiral Robert Burnett
Rear Admiral Louis Hamilton
Admiral of the Fleet Sir Dudley Pound
Admiral Sir John Tovey
Grand Admiral Erich Raeder
General Admiral Otto Schniewind
Vice Admiral Oskar Kummetz
Grand Admiral Karl Dönitz
Matilda tanks for Russia moving by rail to a British port
*King George V* viewed from *Victorious* while escorting PQ 12
Albacores launching from *Victorious*
German destroyer *Z 26* sinking after engagement with British cruiser *Trinidad*
PQ 17 sighted by German air reconnaissance
German heavy cruiser *Hipper* and destroyers viewed from *Tirpitz*
He 111 torpedo bomber
Battle of the Barents Sea
Ice-bound British cruiser
Bridge view of stormy seas from *Sheffield*

Liberty ship in an Arctic storm
*Tirpitz* in Altafiord
X6 bidding farewell to her towing submarine *Truculent*
Operation Tungsten
*Scharnhorst* leaving Altafiord viewed from *Tirpitz*
Fighters on the flight deck of escort carrier *Emperor*
British cruiser *Belfast* off Iceland
Second World War Arms for Russia poster

# Foreword

The Arctic convoys were the Royal Navy's most difficult and dangerous sustained commitment of the war at sea, indeed of any naval war in history. The sea and the weather, largely unknown to the Royal and Merchant Navies, could be lethal; sub-zero temperatures fractured welded ships, disabled weapons and killed men. The combination of extreme weather, a hostile ocean and powerful enemy forces attacking in three dimensions, challenged the capabilities and commitment of the men and ships of the Royal Navy, its allies, the merchant shipping they escorted, and the aircrew who supported them, but these challenges were met and overcome.

While there are many accounts of these operations, along with one major high-profile court case, an enduring fascination with the destruction of convoy PQ 17, and the threat posed by the German battleship *Tirpitz*, have obscured the strategic rationale for these operations. At the political level they helped bind the Allies, and stave off Stalin's demands for a second front, but they also served two critical strategic roles, equipping the Soviet Union to wage war, and distracting and degrading German naval and air forces, objectives which remained important through the last 18 months of the War. War materiel to sustain the Eastern Front, and German U-boats and aircraft destroyed, were the key indicators of success. This book focusses on the critical question: what was sent, from where, and what impact did it had on the Soviet war effort? The convoys delivered tanks and planes, trucks, radar, sonar, raw materials and even Soviet prisoners of war, some of whom may have served in German units. These quantities, tabulated and assessed, reveal the mechanics of global strategy. German forces, which had limited effect for much of the campaign, suffered heavy losses. The German Navy alone lost more men in the Arctic than the Royal and allied navies and merchant ship crews combined, while U-boat operations were less effective than in the Battle of the Atlantic and, with one exception, so were German air force attacks. In part this reflected the dysfunctional nature of German command structures, their poor naval-air co-ordination, with interference from the Führer increasing the difficulties of the task. Admiral Dönitz's view that the theatre was a waste of German U-boat resources was correct. Ultimately British/Allied success in the Battle of the Atlantic enabled the post-1941 Arctic convoys to carry predominantly American stores and exposed the vulnerability of U-boats operating in the Arctic, where they continued using the three-rotor Enigma encipherment long after the Atlantic boats switched to the four-rotor system. From January 1944 the British devoted increasing effort to degrading the U-boat arm, to prevent experienced crews combining with the anticipated Type XXI fast U-boats and exploiting Norwegian bases. The Germans, deliberately drawn into attritional battles against Battle of the Atlantic Escort Groups and Home Fleet escort carriers with access to 'Ultra' intelligence, suffered heavy losses.

While most convoys from spring 1942 were attacked by German naval and air forces, and some suffered serious losses, the tendency to focus on casualties and the controversy surrounding convoy PQ 17, which was ordered to scatter when it was believed it faced attack by the *Tirpitz*, has distracted attention from their purpose. Readers familiar with Andy Boyd's work will expect a new and challenging assessment of this complex campaign: they will not be disappointed. This book provides a broader and more nuanced context that situates the movement of ships and cargoes in the long process of balancing the strategic imperative to aid the Soviet Union against global naval operational requirements. German forces, drawn into the campaign by their inability to complete Operation Barbarossa, viewed the task as essentially defensive. These convoy operations were part of the global maritime war that linked the Allies, enabling them to deploy powerful forces across the world, rather than being restricted to a single major theatre. Major British and American warships that served in the Arctic also operated in the Indian Ocean, the Mediterranean and the Pacific. Furthermore, the Arctic convoys, unlike those in the Atlantic, were not a permanent commitment. They were suspended on several occasions to release naval resources for other campaigns, including re-supplying Malta, along with major amphibious landings – Torch and D-Day. The cruiser HMS *Belfast* took part in D-Day and the sinking of the *Scharnhorst*. Furthermore, the convoys were supplemented by longer, but less dangerous supply routes through Iran and the Soviet Far East for American deliveries. Overall, these supplies made a critical contribution to Allied victory.

*Professor Andrew Lambert*
*Kings College London*

# Acknowledgements

As ever, I am indebted to numerous fellow historians who helped me tackle the challenges posed by this book, especially in addressing the impact of Western aid on the Russian war effort.

In describing and reassessing the Arctic naval war and the management and contribution of the convoys, I have found the British and American official histories, notably Stephen Roskill's *War at Sea*, the Naval Staff volumes for the Arctic and Mediterranean edited by Malcom Llewellyn-Jones, Professor Harry Hinsley's *British Intelligence in the Second World War*, and relevant volumes of the United States Army in World War II, essential bedrock. The same is true of the multi-volume *Germany and the Second World War* for the German side of the story. The records and assessment of correspondence between Churchill and Roosevelt by Warren Kimball and of their interaction with Stalin by David Reynolds and Vladimir Pechnatov was invaluable in understanding the motives and perspectives of the top leaders as the war evolved. On the specific issue of the politics, policy, delivery and impact of Western aid to Russia via the Arctic, I am also greatly indebted to Joan Beaumont's groundbreaking 1980 study *Comrades in Arms*, the pioneering research exploiting Soviet and Russian archives undertaken over the last 30 years by Professor Mark Harrison of Warwick University and Professor Alexander Hill of Calgary University, Canada, and, for the Russian perspective, Mikhail Suprun, Boris Sokolov and Vladimir Kotelnikov. For making sense of overall Soviet defence production, equipment losses and evolving frontline strength, the work of Colonel General G F Krivosheev, Hugh Davie, Walter Dunn and David Glantz was especially important.

Professor Andrew Lambert not only kindly wrote the foreword, but his work continues to be an inspiration and model to which I can only aspire. I also owe particular thanks to Professors Mark Harrison, Nicholas Rodger, Richard Overy and Alexander Hill, and to Hugh Davie for reading parts of the manuscript, providing much helpful advice and comment, and steering me away from unjustified claims and judgements. I am also grateful to the daughters of Lieutenant Donald Cameron for permission to use a reproduction of one of their father's wonderful paintings of *X6* during Operation Source.

Researching and writing this book, in part through the Covid era, would have been much more difficult without the benefit of the extensive digitisation of archival records that has taken place over the last 20 years. This provides access, searching and the making of connections, unimaginable to earlier historians. The digital records of the National Archives at Kew, the wealth of material on American support to Russia in the Franklin D Roosevelt archive, and of the German Naval Staff Operations Division War Diary ONI translations in the US Naval Archives were especially useful.

It has once more been a joy to work with Julian Mannering at Seaforth Publishing. He has not only provided constant encouragement and outstanding support and advice but has somehow once again tolerated and accommodated repeated requests for both greater length and more time. I also thank Stephen Chumbley for his excellent and sensitive copy editing and accommodation of numerous revisions.

Finally, my wife Ginette has again not only endured my historical obsessions but provided constant encouragement and support.

# Abbreviations

| | |
|---|---|
| ABC-1 | American British Staff Conference No 1 |
| ACNS | Assistant Chief of the Naval Staff |
| ASV | Air to Surface Vessel Search Radar |
| CAS | Chief of the Air Staff |
| CIGS | Chief of the Imperial General Staff |
| C-in-C | Commander-in-chief |
| CNO | Chief of Naval Operations in the US Navy |
| COS | Chiefs of Staff |
| DCNS | Deputy Chief of the Naval Staff |
| D of P | Director of Plans |
| DMI | Director of Military Intelligence |
| DNI | Director of Naval Intelligence |
| FAA | Fleet Air Arm |
| FOPS | Future Operational Planning Section |
| Force H | RN Task Force established mid-1940 to guard Western Mediterranean |
| FSL | First Sea Lord and Chief of the Naval Staff |
| GAF | German Air Force |
| GC&CS | Government Code & Cypher School |
| GDP | Gross Domestic Product |
| HF/DF | High Frequency Direction Finding |
| IJN | Imperial Japanese Navy |
| JIC | Joint Intelligence Committee |
| JPC | Joint Planning Committee |
| JPS | Joint Planning Staff |
| KGV | *King George V* class battleships |
| NID | Naval Intelligence Division |
| NKVD | Soviet Intelligence Service |
| OIC | Operational Intelligence Centre |

| | |
|---|---|
| PM | Prime Minister |
| PVO | Soviet Home Air Defence Force |
| RAF | Royal Air Force |
| RN | Royal Navy |
| SIS | Secret Intelligence Service |
| SOE | Special Operations Executive |
| USN | US Navy |
| VCNS | Vice Chief of the Naval Staff |
| VVS | Soviet Air Force |

*Additional Abbreviations used in References*

| | |
|---|---|
| ADM | Admiralty |
| AIR | Air Ministry |
| ASE | Allied Supplies Executive |
| AT | Admiralty Telegram |
| CAB | Cabinet Office |
| CCA | Churchill College Archives, Cambridge |
| FO | Foreign Office |
| HW | GC&CS Records |
| IWM | Imperial War Museum |
| KV | Security Service Records |
| NMM | National Maritime Museum, Greenwich |
| NSOD | German Naval Staff Operations Division |
| PREM | Premier |
| PSF | President's Secretary's File, Franklin D Roosevelt Papers |
| TNA | The National Archives |
| UCI | University of California Irvine Libraries |
| WO | War Office |

(ADM, AIR, ASE, CAB, FO, HW, KV, PREM, and WO are categories in the British National Archives.)

# Glossary of Codenames

| | |
|---|---|
| **Ajax** | Autumn 1941 plan to attack Trondheim |
| **Anklet** | British raid on Norway December 1941 |
| **Arcadia** | Anglo-American Washington Summit December 1941/January 1942 |
| **Archery** | British raid on Norway December 1941 |
| **Aurore** | North Atlantic raiding cruise by *Lützow* planned for January 1943 |
| **Bagration** | Russian offensive against German Army Group Centre June 1944 |
| **Barbarossa** | German attack on the Soviet Union 22 June 1941 |
| **Blue** | German offensive in southern Russia June 1942 |
| **Bolero** | Build-up of American forces in Britain |
| **Cerberus** | Transit of German heavy ships via the Channel February 1942 |
| **Citadel** | German offensive at Kursk salient July 1943 |
| **Dervish** | Initial Arctic convoy August 1941 |
| **Gymnast** | Anglo-American invasion of North-west Africa – later Torch |
| **Halberd** | Malta convoy September 1941 |
| **Hardboiled** | British deception operation suggesting Norway landing spring 1942 |
| **Husky** | Allied invasion of Sicily July 1943 |
| **Jupiter** | Proposed British/Canadian attacks on northern Norway |
| **Marrow** | December 1941 Russian proposal for joint attack on Petsamo |
| **Modicum** | General Marshall's visit to London April 1942 |
| **Overlord** | Invasion of Normandy June 1944 |
| **Pedestal** | Major Malta convoy August 1942 |
| **Rankin** | Plan for unopposed occupation of post-conflict Western Europe |
| **Regenbogen** | German navy plan for surface attack on Arctic convoy winter 1942 |
| **Riviera** | Anglo-American summit at Placentia Bay August 1941 |
| **Rösselsprung** | German plan to attack convoy PQ 17 |
| **Roundup** | Anglo-American invasion of Western Europe – subsequently Overlord |
| **Sextant** | Anglo-American Cairo Conference November 1943 |
| **Sledgehammer** | Limited attack on Cotentin peninsula 1942 or 1943 |
| **Source** | Midget submarine operation against *Tirpitz* September 1943 |
| **Symbol** | Casablanca Conference January 1943 |
| **Torch** | Anglo-American invasion of North-west Africa November 1942 |
| **Trident** | Anglo-American Washington Conference May 1943 |
| **Tungsten** | Fleet Air Arm attack on *Tirpitz* April 1944 |
| **Typhoon** | German offensive against Moscow October 1941 |
| **Uranus** | Russian counter-offensive at Stalingrad |

# Introduction

The mid-point of 1941 saw three developments which fundamentally changed the dynamic of the European war that had broken out in September 1939, translating it into a true global conflict. The first, and ultimately most decisive, was the German attack on Russia, Operation Barbarossa, which began on 22 June. The second, just over a month later and partly influenced by the German action, was Japan's move into southern Indochina, triggering Western sanctions and the likelihood of early conflict between Japan and the Western Powers. These two developments triggered the third shift, pushing both Britain and the United States to view threats to their vital security through a global rather than essentially European focus. Importantly, it encouraged the United States' administration of President Franklin Roosevelt to accelerate support for Britain, including significant assistance in protecting Atlantic convoys, to initiate aid to Russia, and to adopt more forward defence in the western Pacific.

These events form the opening backdrop to the story in this book. Barbarossa led to political decisions in both London and Washington to provide aid to Russia which initially could be delivered most effectively by the Arctic Sea route round north Norway to the ports of Murmansk and Archangel (Map 2, p 148). Murmansk, located at the head of the Kola Inlet, 200 miles east of North Cape and just 60 miles from the Finnish border, was the more northerly port but ice free throughout the year. Archangel was located about 240 miles south-east on the White Sea and therefore less vulnerable to German attack but often icebound in winter. Both ports had rail connections southward. In early 1942, the de facto military alliance between the two Western Powers and Russia provoked German fears of an early British attack on Norway. This, along with the growing importance of the supply convoys, persuaded Germany to deploy substantial reinforcements to the Arctic theatre. By the spring, most of the major operational surface units of the German navy (Kriegsmarine) had relocated to Norway, joined by significant U-boat and air forces. The related requirements to supply Russia and counter these German forces ensured that, for the next three years, the Arctic became a major war theatre for the Royal Navy and the dominant focus of its Home Fleet.

Although the British and German commitment in Arctic waters from 1941–5 was considerable, the case for a new book on the topic requires explanation. From the 1950s onward, numerous works have addressed the more specific story of the Arctic convoys, albeit primarily from a British perspective.[1] These include a British naval staff history[2] and coverage in British and American official histories of both the naval war and Lend-Lease aid to Russia.[3] There are detailed accounts too of specific convoy operations, notably convoy PQ 17[4] and the Battle of the Barents Sea. There are many books covering the story of the German battleship *Tirpitz*[5] from her arrival in Norwegian waters in January 1942 until her final destruction in November 1944 and of the last fight of the battlecruiser *Scharnhorst*.[6] There are fewer works providing the German and Soviet perspectives on the Arctic naval war which have generally received less attention than they deserve.[7]

There are also important gaps in the existing coverage. To date, the story of the Royal Navy's war in the Arctic has focused either on the conduct of operations or the human endurance and courage displayed by the crews of warships and merchant vessels fighting both enemy and elements in one of the most inhospitable areas of the world. There has been less attempt to place the Arctic convoys and related German deployment in the wider political and strategic context of the war. Where such efforts have been made, conclusions often seem insufficient or unconvincing. Many historians, admittedly reflecting some contemporary views of Royal Navy leaders, have argued that the convoys, and by extension much of the support given to the Soviet Union, were effectively discretionary, that the aid commitment lacked a military rationale and was implemented primarily to meet Western political objectives. Their claimed purpose here was to show solidarity with the country bearing the brunt of German power, to discourage a separate peace, and reduce domestic pressure for a 'second front'. It follows that the convoys were never critical to the Western war effort which explains and justifies their suspension for extended periods. This attempt to distinguish political goals divorced from strategic necessity seems dubious, especially in wartime. The Arctic supply route was not only a constant preoccupation of British and American leaders, but over nearly four years from July 1941, it absorbed perhaps 20 per cent of Royal Navy resources and a significant share of

Allied merchant shipping badly needed in other theatres. Could this really be discretionary?[8]

There are important issues here, at best only partially answered to date. Why did Roosevelt and the British prime minister Winston Churchill quickly press for aid to Russia, after Barbarossa launched, in the face of more sceptical military advice? How did the perceived political and military benefits, costs, and risks in running the Arctic convoys evolve over the next 12 months? How did the convoys influence evolving relations between the Western Allies and Russia? What really motivated German reinforcement of Norway and the Arctic theatre from early 1942? Why were German countermeasures against the supply convoys slow to take effect? What were the trade-offs between the Arctic convoys and other theatres of war? What were the comparative advantages between the Arctic supply route to Russia and the alternative routes through Iran and the Far East and how did the latter two develop? Addressing these questions demonstrates that the Arctic theatre exerted more influence on the evolution of Allied, and to an extent German, grand strategy from mid-1941 onward than generally recognised.

A related objective of this book is to provide a comprehensive assessment of the value and impact of the Arctic convoys to the Russian war effort. Most histories of the Arctic theatre have offered lists of supplies delivered but lack context to make them useful or meaningful.[9] They also often failed adequately to distinguish aid delivered via the Arctic from that sent by other routes. During the Cold War, there was limited access to Russian records on how Lend-Lease supplies were used or their relationship to Russian domestic production. There was also a determined Russian effort to suggest that the overall impact of Lend-Lease aid was marginal.[10] Although much valuable research has appeared in the last 30 years, exploiting Russian archives and providing a different and more complex picture, this has received insufficient attention beyond a specialist audience and some narratives established in the Cold War era remain persistent.[11] Indeed flawed Cold War narratives have continued to influence attitudes in Vladimir Putin's Russia and much of the West through the first decades of the twenty-first century and thus resonate through the present war in Ukraine.

Other issues deserve more study than previous accounts of the Arctic theatre have offered. The Arctic war was not framed solely by the convoys, important though they were. For two years from August 1941, despite compelling and determined opposition from the British chiefs of staff, Prime Minister Winston Churchill pursued the idea of a landing in Norway to link up with the Russians and regain a foothold on the

Continent. In a striking parallel, the German leader, Adolf Hitler, was equally gripped by the prospect of a British descent on northern Norway, referring to it at the beginning of 1942 as the 'zone of destiny', 'of decisive importance for the outcome of the war'. This led to his insistence that the major units of the German Navy should concentrate in northern waters along with substantial air reinforcements. From this point both sides faced conflicting challenges. The Royal Navy Home Fleet had to balance protecting the supply convoys against formidable opposition with the need to counter a potential Atlantic raiding sortie by German heavy units. The German fleet and air forces had to reconcile the enduring priority of countering a British attack on Norway with the growing requirement to disrupt and destroy the convoys.

This context requires a clearer view of the comparative naval effort deployed by the combatants, the relative results achieved, and the implications posed for other theatres. Around 50 per cent of Royal Navy front-line units deployed to Arctic waters at some point over the four years from July 1941. The forces committed to any specific operation were naturally a much smaller fraction of overall strength but still at times substantial. Those deployed in support of convoy PQ 18 in September 1942 included two modern battleships, one escort carrier, seven cruisers, forty destroyers and ten submarines as well as numerous other specialist and smaller escort vessels. The overall Royal Navy Arctic commitment achieved the safe arrival of 89 per cent of the 811 merchant vessels, with 4.5 million tons of supplies convoyed to Russia, and 95 per cent of the 715 returning ships. It also destroyed Germany's only two capital ships operational after February 1942, sank one-third of the 110 U-boats assigned to the Arctic after July 1941, and inflicted significant damage on her available cruisers and heavy destroyers.

At first sight, the return to Germany for investing most of her heavy surface warships, 11 per cent of her deployable U-boats and significant air forces looks meagre. The surface units never sortied into the Atlantic. On the convoy route to Russia, they sank just three merchant vessels, none in convoy, one destroyer and one smaller escort. The average of twenty U-boats usually available in the Arctic theatre from early 1942 did better, sinking forty-one merchant ships along with a cruiser, four destroyers and six smaller escorts. However, only twenty-four of the merchant ships were sunk in convoy and the overall return for more than 500 U-boat patrols directed at seventy-five convoys was pitiful by North Atlantic standards. The campaign also cost forty-four U-boats, almost one for every Allied vessel sunk. Apart from a brief period in the summer of 1942, the impact of this major German naval effort on supplies to Russia was therefore negligible. Whether the Germans could and should have inflicted far more damage with the forces available is an important question. However, this record overlooks other critical German achievements; forcing the British leadership to suspend convoys for significant periods, thereby denying Russia vital supplies and incurring significant political damage; obliging the Royal Navy to deploy huge forces to the Arctic at the expense of other theatres where they were badly needed; and the deterrence of any major British action against Norway.

Another issue, which deserves more attention, is the exceptional operational challenge the Arctic posed for the Royal Navy in running large convoys, often in two directions at the same time, in relatively confined waters against an enemy able to deploy large attacking forces simultaneously across three dimensions. The problem here was exacerbated during 1942 by the need to mount parallel operations in broadly analogous circumstances in the Mediterranean, a point acknowledged in the naval staff history. There are again important questions. How well did the Royal Navy anticipate such convoy challenges and how well was it equipped to meet them? What had it learnt from Mediterranean experience in 1941? How good was cross-fertilisation between Mediterranean and Arctic in 1942 and later?

The final issue is the role of intelligence. From the mid-1970s, accounts of Arctic naval operations have emphasised the contribution of intelligence, especially Ultra decrypts of German naval and air communications from the Government Code and Cypher School (GC&CS) based at Bletchley Park, in shaping the outcome of both key engagements and the overall campaign. However, it was a further 20 years before there were substantial releases of the primary British intelligence records and, despite excellent work in recent years, significant parts of the vast archive now available remain under explored. Even where the ground has been well tilled,[12] there is scope for debate on how key reports were understood and exploited. The emphasis which most accounts give to the impact of Ultra decrypts on specific naval operations such as PQ 17 or the *Scharnhorst* engagement has perhaps also caused some distortion to the overall intelligence picture relevant to the Arctic theatre. First, the role of other sources such as SIS agents and aerial reconnaissance and the importance of intelligence relationships with the Russians and Swedes has been downplayed. Secondly, the origins and results of the various raiding operations in late 1941 targeted at capturing German cryptographic material merit more examination. Finally, insufficient account is taken of how intelligence shaped policy towards the Arctic convoys and the case for aiding Russia at the strategic level as well as understanding of German intentions. There is still scope therefore for significant reappraisal of the intelligence story.

Before now beginning the book, two obvious caveats require emphasis. First, this is a history focused on the naval war in the Arctic. That war was driven primarily, although not exclusively, by the requirement to deliver aid to Russia – hence *Arms for Russia* in the title. The focus is therefore the origin of that requirement, the benefits and costs involved in meeting it for the Allies, and in defeating it for the Germans. If the story is heavily weighted towards the Royal Navy, and at times veers into its experience in other theatres, that is because it was the dominant player in shaping events and those experiences are relevant. In describing specific operations, the book focuses heavily on those that remain controversial, notably PQ 17, but also seeks to break new ground rather than merely repeating what has been well covered elsewhere. Secondly, this is not a comprehensive history of the entire programme of Lend-Lease aid to Russia in the Second World War. Its focus is the contribution of the roughly 25 per cent which passed by the Arctic route between August 1941 and May 1945, in contrast to the same quantity sent through Iran and 50 per cent across the Pacific. Where the other routes are discussed, it is to provide essential context and not to assess their contribution in detail. As the book explains, the Arctic part was greatest in the 18 months leading up to February 1943. The book's content, ten chapters out of twelve, is therefore heavily weighted to that period. The Arctic carried the dominant share of weapons delivered in those months so there is more discussion of their role and impact than would be the case in any overall history of Western aid.

Finally, a word about terms and definitions. The Soviet Union, officially the Union of Soviet Socialist Republics (USSR), ceased to exist in 1991. Modern Russia occupies a quarter less territory and has a different sense of national identity. However, in the period covered by this book 'Russia' or 'Russian' and 'Soviet Union' or 'Soviet' were used interchangeably in Western circles and certainly in British and American government documents. I have therefore done the same. I have also occasionally used the term 'Red Army' for Soviet or Russian Army which was also common at the time and for long afterwards. I have also generally used English terms for German organisations and services, so 'German Air Force' rather than 'Luftwaffe' and 'German Navy' rather than 'Kriegsmarine'.

## Prelude
# August 1941: Churchill and Roosevelt at Placentia Bay

Saturday, 9 August 1941 brought a cold grey morning wreathed in mist to Placentia Bay, a vast inland sea on the south-east corner of Newfoundland which had not yet joined Canada and eight years earlier had reverted to the status of a British colony. It was normally a desolate place, comprising a 'wavering coastline of little beaches and coves, behind which the country rose in mournful hills clothed at the top with dense woods of fir and larch' with 'not a living soul to be seen'.[1] This was the bleak view that initially greeted Britain's newest battleship *Prince of Wales* as she steamed slowly into the bay accompanied by two American destroyers. The emptiness did not last. Rounding a headland, she found an array of United States Navy warships anchored off the settlement of Argentia, the cruisers *Augusta* and *Tuscaloosa*, the old battleship *Arkansas*, and a flotilla of destroyers. Meanwhile seaplanes from a nearby and new American airfield, established under the 'Destroyers for Bases' agreement signed between Britain and the United States a year earlier, patrolled overhead. Heading towards a buoy marked with a flag, *Prince of Wales* came abreast of *Augusta*, to see a tall man wearing a Palm Beach suit, President Franklin D Roosevelt, rise from his wheelchair positioned on her quarterdeck and raise his hat in salute. In the passing battleship, the pudgy figure of Prime Minister Winston Churchill, dressed in the uniform of an Elder Brother of Trinity House, stood to attention, his hand raised to the peak of his cap. The bosuns' pipes shrilled and the band of the Royal Marines crashed into *The Star Spangled Banner*. *Augusta* responded with *God Save the King* and at 0900 precisely *Prince of Wales* reached her allotted place and dropped anchor. There had been an unanticipated hitch in meeting her arrival time. When she met her escorting US Navy destroyers, the British learnt that the Americans were keeping a time zone 90 minutes behind

Newfoundland summertime. Much to the prime minister's annoyance *Prince of Wales* had therefore had to loiter in the outer bay.[2]

## *The Meeting*

Churchill and Roosevelt had met once before at a dinner in 1918 when the latter visited London as Assistant Secretary of the Navy, an occasion which Churchill, apparently to Roosevelt's irritation, had embarrassingly forgotten.[3] However, this was their first substantive face-to-face engagement as well as their first meeting as leaders of their respective countries. They would meet a further eight times, usually spread over several days, prior to Roosevelt's death in April 1945. Although Placentia Bay marked a new beginning in their relationship, in a sense they already knew each other well. They had begun an intense correspondence on 11 September 1939, a week after the start of Britain's war, which by the time they sighted each other at Placentia Bay comprised 170 telegrams and letters.[4] From the beginning there were regular phone calls too. As the dialogue developed following Churchill's accession to the premiership and they gained trust in each other, they expressed thoughts, ideas, hopes and fears, which they shared with few others and kept carefully guarded. They also studied each other closely through trusted intermediaries.

Perhaps surprisingly, given their respective status in 1939, it was Roosevelt who initiated the dialogue. Ostensibly, Roosevelt, who had been Navy Assistant Secretary throughout the crucial six years 1913–19, exploited Churchill's reappointment as First Lord of the Admiralty on the outbreak of war to remind the latter that they shared common naval experience and history and might therefore profitably engage on naval issues of interest. The naval bond here was genuine and, over his eight-month tenure as First Lord, Churchill did largely confine the dialogue, comprising only a dozen written messages in this period, to naval affairs. He was also careful not to tread on the territory of Prime Minister Neville Chamberlain or Foreign Secretary Lord Edward Halifax, who had both approved his contact with Roosevelt. This explains why Churchill adopted the title 'Naval Person' in the correspondence and, after becoming prime minister 'Former Naval Person'. However, on Roosevelt's part, there was also a characteristic element of political calculation. He had obtained a balanced picture of Churchill's strengths and weaknesses but recognised his commitment to confronting the German threat and his potential as a future leader. In December 1939, he told Joseph Kennedy, his ambassador to the United Kingdom and not a Churchill admirer: 'I'm giving him attention now because there is a strong possibility he will become the prime minister and I want to get my hand in now.'[5]

The Placentia Bay meeting, code-named 'Riviera' by the British, had been six months in the making. A Churchill–Roosevelt 'summit' was the logical endpoint to a series of initiatives which had steadily deepened the British–American relationship and the American material support which Britain increasingly saw as vital to containing Germany and ultimately winning the war. The first key milestone was the visit of Roosevelt's emissary and future head of the Office of Strategic Services (OSS), William J Donovan, in mid-July 1940 to assess Britain's real prospects against the defeatist view promoted by Kennedy. His favourable report was perhaps crucial in persuading Roosevelt to proceed with the destroyer–bases agreement.[6] This was followed by Rear Admiral Robert Ghormley's fact-finding mission to the British chiefs of staff a month later, and the first formal staff talks between the two countries, known as ABC-1, which began in Wahington the following January and proved prescient in shaping future British–American strategy with agreement on Germany as priority enemy. Most vital of all, was the passing of Lend-Lease legislation in March which facilitated aid to Britain without immediate payment.

However, perhaps the most important influence shaping Roosevelt's view of Churchill, Britain's situation, the best means of channelling American support, and the desirability of a meeting during 1941 was that of Harry Hopkins. Born in 1890, Hopkins came from a humble background in Sioux City, Iowa, and spent a career in welfare administration, initially in New York where he first came to the attention of Roosevelt when the latter was governor of New York State in the late 1920s. Roosevelt then gave him a central role in executing the New Deal before appointing him Secretary of Commerce in 1938. By then Hopkins was regarded as a future presidential candidate but failing health (the first symptoms of the stomach cancer that would kill him in 1946) obliged him to leave his Cabinet post in 1940 and settle for a more flexible role as presidential adviser, trouble-shooter and emissary, increasingly directed at foreign affairs. His loyalty to Roosevelt was absolute, from 1940 he lived with him in the White House, and he enjoyed his complete trust and confidence. His approach to international affairs was often somewhat simplistic but Roosevelt valued his ability to cut through protocol to essentials and get things done. 'When he (Harry) sees a piece of red tape, he just pulls out those old garden shears of his and snips it.'[7]

In early January 1941, Roosevelt despatched Hopkins to London. He was to explore Churchill's attitude to a meeting with the president, assess the prime minister's general outlook and of course Britain's overall prospects. Subsequently, he put his role more succinctly to the journalist Edward R Murrow – 'I suppose you could say that I've come here to be a catalytic agent between two prima donnas'. Hopkins spent exactly a month in Britain and was rarely out of the prime minister's company. Churchill recognised his importance and therefore put extraordinary effort into cultivating him, ordering 'the unrolling of any red carpets that might have survived the Blitz'.[8] He immediately spotted that ability to cut to the chase which made Hopkins so important to Roosevelt. Later in the war, Churchill gave Hopkins the 'two-thirds admiring, one-third satirical title of "Lord Root-of-the-Matter"'. This reflected his ability when future Anglo-American conferences became bogged down 'to throw a glass of fresh spring water in everyone's face' and say 'The issue we have to decide is this'.[9] With their different backgrounds, Hopkins was 'not a natural Churchill crony' but they rapidly developed an extraordinary rapport, genuinely enjoyed each other's company and created a lasting friendship. The closeness partly reflected the fact that 'like many of those whose company Churchill most enjoyed, he was a sophisticated outsider with a touch of loucheness'. Hopkins also had 'a mordant humour, he liked gambling and racetracks, and he was easily at home in any company where the tone was not too pious' – a good fit therefore for the late-night Churchill court.[10]

Churchill's doctor, Charles Moran, witnessed the result of Churchill's cultivation at a dinner in Glasgow on 17 January, given by the Regional Commissioner for Scotland, Tom Johnston. Moran sat next to Hopkins, 'an unkempt figure', who, after a while, got up and addressed the prime minister: 'I suppose you wish to know what I am going to say to President Roosevelt on my return. Well I am going to quote you one verse from that Book of Books in the truth of which Mr Johnston's mother and my own Scottish mother were brought up: "Whither thou goest, I will go; and where thou lodgest, I will lodge; thy people shall be my people, and thy God, my God."' Then he added very quietly: 'Even to the end'. Churchill was in tears. He knew what it meant. To the rest of the company, Moran added, 'the words seemed like a rope thrown to a drowning man'.[11]

If Churchill assumed Hopkins' words foreshadowed total American commitment to Britain's support and early entry into the war, he was to be disappointed. Through the first half of 1941, American commitment, valuable though it was, always lagged behind British hopes. Some in British leadership and political circles, although probably not Churchill, were frustrated by the outcome of Riviera, judging it still long on promises and short on practical delivery. This perception that Riviera was ultimately an anti-climax is echoed by many historians, including some writing recently, who emphasise its symbolism and emotional resonance but are restrained, even, downbeat on its results. This interpretation contrasts the image of two leaders, apparently united behind the shared values and common purpose of a new 'Atlantic Charter', with continuing lack of an American commitment to fight which it is claimed Roosevelt had no intention of giving.[12] Furthermore, the Charter's references to the right of self-government and to pursuit of free trade were difficult to square with the existing political and economic framework of the British Empire and therefore caused Britain discomfort later. There were more specific disappointments. Roosevelt, who had not consulted Churchill prior to imposing an oil embargo on Japan at the end of July, refused to provide any guarantee that the United States would provide military support to either Britain or the Dutch if Japan attacked their territories in South-east Asia, now a significantly enhanced risk. Even his promise to Churchill to deliver a severe warning to Japan was later broken. As regards war supplies, the Americans underlined the scale of their own needs in building up their forces and the need to accommodate requirements from China and Russia. British aspirations, especially regarding aircraft deliveries, must be curtailed.[13] Finally, the American military leaders were evidently unconvinced that Britain yet had a credible overall war strategy, although, at this point, they had no convincing alternatives to offer. The British chiefs of staff acknowledged that they had neither expected nor achieved startling results in the Riviera military talks.[14]

Churchill may have hoped for more from Roosevelt at Riviera. He told the Queen just before leaving: 'I do not think our friend would have asked me to go so far for what must be a meeting of world-wide importance, unless he has in mind some further forward step.' This accounts for the emphasis he gave to crafting the symbolism and choreography beforehand, along with elaborate rehearsals. The highlight here was the joint church service held on the quarterdeck of *Prince of Wales* on the Sunday morning. John Martin, Churchill's private secretary, vividly recorded this event:

> The PM had given much thought to the preparation of his Service (which he said should be fully choral and fully photographic), choosing the hymns (O God our Help in Ages Past, Onward Christian Soldiers and Eternal Father Strong to Save), and vetting the prayers. You would have had to be hard-boiled not to be moved by it all – hundreds of men from both fleets all mingled together, one rough British sailor sharing his hymn sheet with one American ditto. It seemed a sort of marriage service between the two navies, already in spirit allies, although the bright peace-time paint and spit and polish of the American ships contrasted with the dull camouflage of the *Prince of Wales*, so recently in action against the *Bismarck*.[15]

Following Royal Navy custom, Captain John Leach of *Prince of Wales* read the lesson, verses from Joshua, which, seemingly aimed directly at the president, echoed Hopkins' message of the previous January: 'There shall not any man be able to stand before thee all the days of thy life; as I was with Moses, so I will be with thee; I will not fail thee, nor forsake thee. Be strong and of good courage.'[16]

Churchill famously captured the emotion of the occasion in *The Grand Alliance*: 'We ended with "O God, Our Help in Ages Past", which Macaulay reminds us the Ironsides had chanted as they bore John Hampden's body to the grave. Every word seemed to stir the heart. It was a great hour to live. Nearly half those who sang were soon to die.'[17]

Roosevelt too was affected, describing Sunday morning as the 'keynote' of the meeting. Elliott Roosevelt reported his father saying: 'If nothing else had happened while we were here, that would have cemented us. "Onward Christian Soldiers." We are, and we will go on, with God's help.'[18] Symbolism therefore mattered more than those viewing events from a more cynical and secular vantage point 80 years onward may think.

## The Riviera Outcomes

Meanwhile Riviera promoted three important outcomes which deserve more emphasis. The first was agreement that the US Navy would implement western hemisphere Defence Plan No 4 from 1 September. Under this plan, the US Navy, with Canadian assistance, took responsibility for protecting most Atlantic convoys in the area west of 26° West, just short of the midway point between Liverpool and St John's. The only major exclusion was Canadian troop convoys, but American cover was extended to these under the subsequent Plan No 5 in October. In effect this represented a vast extension of the Pan-American Security Zone established in October 1939. The political and legal justification for the US Navy, representing a still-neutral power, to provide escort in these extended waters, was ensured by including at least one American-flagged ship in each convoy. Implementing Plan No 4 had two consequences. It released Royal Navy and Canadian escort resources. Churchill claimed both in his opening address at Riviera and to the War Cabinet on his return that this amounted to fifty-two destroyers and corvettes.[19] Admiralty calculations were more restrained. Sixteen Royal Navy destroyers and seven corvettes were available for immediate redeployment from the Newfoundland escort force. However, they also noted that Canadian escort of troop convoys would be doubled and existing Royal Navy escort forces in the eastern Atlantic further strengthened because they could be operated more efficiently over shorter distances.[20] American battleships also released four Royal Navy 'R' class battleships allocated to convoy escort against surface raiders, allowing them to be refitted for service in the Eastern theatre.

The introduction of US Navy escort also brought significant risk of an American clash with German U-boats or other forces. The continuing strength of isolationist sentiment had therefore caused Roosevelt to hesitate over convoy escort. Plan No 4, agreed in principle on 11 July, was more cautious than its predecessor but, even as Riviera began, it was uncertain that Roosevelt would finally implement even this revised version.[21] In the event, Riviera not only produced approval but remarkably robust instructions to the US Navy escort forces. These were authorised to destroy any German U-boat or surface raider which attacked shipping along the sea lanes between North America and Iceland or which approached sufficiently close to be deemed a threat to such shipping. As Churchill informed the War Cabinet, the Germans could either attack the convoys and be attacked by American naval forces or refrain which would be tantamount to victory in the western Atlantic. In six or eight weeks it might be desirable to provoke the enemy with exactly this choice.[22]

Churchill underestimated Roosevelt's continuing caution. In their private conversations around convoy escort, it is impossible to know whether Roosevelt literally said, as Churchill claimed, that 'he would wage war, but not declare it, and that he would become more and more provocative', that 'if the Germans did not like it, they could attack America first', and that 'he would look for an "incident" which would justify him in opening hostilities'.[23] Certainly, the president's orders conveyed to Admiral Harold Stark, his Chief of Naval Operations, and thence to the newly established Atlantic Fleet, regarding action against German surface raiders, did not allow much scope for ambiguity.[24] However, back in Washington, while preparations for Plan No 4 went ahead, Roosevelt stalled on confirming the final date for its implementation. It seemed he still did not know how he would explain convoy escort to Congress and the American public. The most convincing assessment of Roosevelt's position post-Riviera is that he wanted to do all he could to help Britain, but still preferred to keep the United States out of the war for as long as he could while recognising American involvement at some point was now inevitable.[25]

The president's problem in initiating Plan No 4 was solved by the first direct American–German naval clash which occurred on 4 September between *U-652* and the American destroyer *Greer*, albeit without damage to either side. In his most hawkish speech yet, delivered on 11 September and christened by the press 'shoot on sight', Roosevelt accused the Germans of 'piracy' and in vivid language argued the case for ensuring 'freedom of the seas', the safety of shipping and for protecting American waters. The US Navy would take all reasonable defensive measures and German or Italian warships entered waters necessary for American defence 'at their own peril'.[26] There were two further clashes before the end of October, both more serious than *Greer*. The destroyer *Kearney* was torpedoed on 17 October, suffering significant damage, and, on the last day of the month, the destroyer *Reuben James* was sunk by *U-552* with heavy loss of life while escorting a convoy near Iceland. The *Reuben James* appeared to qualify as the type of 'incident' triggering hostilities which Roosevelt had referred to at Riviera. However, compared to his stance following the *Greer* episode, the president's restraint was striking. He was evidently still not prepared to move from 'undeclared' Atlantic war to formal intervention. Three reasons are suggested for this. Roosevelt did not believe he would have Congressional support for war. Rearmament was still at an early stage and United States' forces therefore far from ready. Finally, deteriorating relations with Japan raised the unwelcome prospect of war on two fronts. As Roosevelt told his Secretary of the Interior, Harold Ickes, a few weeks before Riviera, 'it was terribly important for the control of the Atlantic for us to keep peace in the Pacific'. 'I simply have not got enough navy to go round.'[27]

There was perhaps a fourth factor which inclined Roosevelt to hold off. Despite the three clashes described, the German response to the extended American defence zone had so far been cautious. On 17 September, six days after Roosevelt's 'shoot to kill' speech, at one of the regular Führer conferences to discuss naval affairs held approximately monthly, Grand Admiral Erich Raeder, Commander-in-Chief of the German Navy, and Admiral U-boats, Rear Admiral Karl Dönitz, pressed the Führer, Adolf Hitler, to authorise an aggressive response. They proposed that Germany should only acknowledge a neutrality zone up to 20 miles from the coast of the American continent, north and south. If this was too drastic a reduction, the North America zone could be extended up to 60° West (running through the western tip of Newfoundland). U-boats would have free rein to attack without warning both merchant vessels and warships, unless positively identified as American, outside this new German-recognised neutrality zone. Hitler, however, was unwilling to risk confrontation, and possibly war, with the United States until the Russian campaign was successfully concluded, hopefully by mid-October. For the present, he insisted care was taken to avoid any 'incidents' involving American vessels.[28] Hitler's restrictions stayed in force at the next naval conference on 13 November, although he promised to review matters if the Americans repealed the Neutrality Acts, as they largely did four days later.[29]

Hitler's decision not to provoke America through the autumn reflected his preference for the present to deal with his enemies sequentially and avoid simultaneous major commitment on two fronts for as long as possible. Nevertheless, if, by autumn 1941, Roosevelt judged war with Germany as probably inevitable, Hitler more than reciprocated. For Hitler, antagonism to the United States, and more specifically Roosevelt, was not only rooted in the increasingly aggressive American support for Britain and potentially Russia, but also ideology. By this point, Roosevelt was firmly identified as the controlling agent of 'international Jewry', leading an all-embracing anti-German coalition.[30] Hitler was also aware, as Raeder and Dönitz continued to insist, that denying the growing U-boat force a free hand in the western Atlantic compromised his primary weapon against Britain, and perhaps the ultimate key to winning the entire war. With each week that passed, it was more evident that Germany was already in a de facto war with the United States in the Atlantic and that formalising this could only be a matter of time. From Hitler's viewpoint, the Japanese attack on Pearl Harbor on 7 December opened a window of opportunity and made the final decision easy. America would now be tied down in the Pacific with few resources to devote to Germany for at least a year. Meanwhile Britain would be undermined by cutting her supplies in the Atlantic and by Japanese attacks on her possessions and resources in the Far East. The U-boats were therefore unleashed on American waters immediately on 8/9 December. Germany's formal declaration of war followed two days later. Hitler's Propaganda Minister Joseph Goebbels was clear that the Atlantic tonnage war was the decisive factor driving the timing of this decision.

There has inevitably been much historical debate over the wisdom or necessity for a German declaration and the consequences if Hitler had held back, leaving the Americans to take the initiative. It is true Roosevelt might have faced difficulty getting Congressional support for an immediate declaration but the U-boat war in American waters would have gathered pace through December, making formal war inevitable within a month at most. The same U-boat offensive would have ensured that a weakening of the original British–American decision, reached at the ABC-1 staff talks the previous January, to give priority to the defeat of Germany was unlikely. Overall, therefore, the commitment to Hemisphere Plan No 4 at Riviera, by greatly increasing the likelihood of early American intervention, had a vital impact on the course of the war.[31]

The second important outcome of Riviera that requires more emphasis is the transformation of aid to Russia from hesitant aspiration to determined commitment. Russia receives surprisingly little attention in the formal Riviera records, yet the decisions made here proved far-reaching and can even be considered the meeting's most concrete achievement.[32] Indeed, Russia's prospects arguably underpinned every issue debated at Riviera. Both Churchill and Roosevelt arrived at the meeting instinctively convinced that Russia would survive at least the initial German offensive, which had begun on 22 June, and therefore deserved support. By early July, Churchill had made help for Russia a key war policy and, on 12 July, an Anglo-Soviet agreement was signed in Moscow pledging mutual assistance against Germany and no separate peace. Roosevelt was not only optimistic from the start that Russia would hold out but instinctively grasped that Hitler's opening of a new Eastern Front held a potential key to the entire war. As early as 24 June, in concert with the State Department, he announced that the United States would give all possible aid to Russia. On 10 July, responding to a list of urgent requirements from the Russian ambassador, Konstantin Umansky, Roosevelt assured him that the United States would ship supplies essential for Russia's defence by 1 October. Perhaps characteristically, Roosevelt failed to consult the War Department and to consider the impact of his promise on existing United States needs or those of Britain and other allies. This triggered acrimonious debate within the administration over what was feasible, especially in supplying aircraft. By the beginning of August, he was berating his advisers for not moving fast enough with aid. However, at this point, for both Churchill and Roosevelt, exactly what support to Russia should comprise, how it would be delivered and at what cost remained ill-defined. This reflected limited knowledge of Russian capability. Both leaders also faced strong resistance from unenthusiastic military advisers. Neither British nor American military leaders believed Russia would hold out for long. They therefore feared military aid would not only be wasted but would also divert scarce resources from their own urgent requirements.[33]

The catalyst for making Russian aid a firm commitment was Harry Hopkins. Roosevelt despatched him to London in mid-July to finalise arrangements for Riviera. When he learnt that Royal Air Force Coastal Command had opened a regular, if risky, air link to Archangel, he proposed that he immediately go to Moscow to solve the 'knowledge gap' with a first-hand view of Russian prospects and needs. Hopkins argued that, without such input, the Riviera summit would have limited usefulness. Roosevelt approved this enthusiastically. Churchill was more hesitant, fearing Hopkins would miss Riviera, but bowed to the inevitable and warmly commended Hopkins to the Russian leader Josef Stalin.[34] The latter was already well-informed on Hopkins' standing with the president and his powerful advocacy of aid to Russia from Umansky.[35]

Churchill had another anxiety. While committed to giving all possible support to Russia, he 'dreaded the loss of what we had expected and so direly needed' from the United States. Before departing for Riviera, he had therefore decided to include Lord Beaverbrook, newly appointed as Minister of Supply, in the second half of the meeting, fully briefed to ensure that American supplies to Russia took adequate account of British interests.[36] William Maxwell (Max) Aitken, First Lord Beaverbrook, was a successful Canadian multi-millionaire businessman, newspaper proprietor, international networker, and in his latter days considerable historian, who exerted important, if intermittent, influence in high-level British politics over five decades. He enjoyed a close, if erratic, friendship with Churchill and with David Lloyd George through the latter's premiership and beyond. He was judged by Churchill to have made a critical contribution as Minister of Aircraft Production the previous year, and thus a logical choice to shake up the Ministry of Supply, although some, notably Ernest Bevin, the Minister of Labour, and the future Chief of the Imperial General Staff, General Sir Alan Brooke, thought his talents over-rated and found him impossible to work with. Beaverbrook was a passionate advocate of aid to Russia, a long-standing confidant of the Russian ambassador in London, Ivan Maisky, and as will become evident, his role in implementing this over the next seven months was immensely important. Thereafter, he would become an ardent, although often unhelpful, promoter of an early 'second front'. His positive view of Russia, which long predated the war, veered between rational realpolitik and deluded romantic idealism and was undoubtedly often driven by self-promotion and political opportunism. But, for a while, as with aircraft production, he rendered valuable service that few others could have achieved.[37]

Hopkins' achievement during his Moscow visit, which included two sessions with Stalin, the second on 31 July lasting three hours and with the two alone save for an interpreter, has rightly been described as 'stunning'. Stalin admitted the Red Army had been caught off guard in a surprise attack but insisted that, although he did not underestimate German capability, he was confident they would be held before winter short of Moscow, Leningrad and Kiev. He provided details of Russian armaments and military production with a frankness which Laurence Steinhardt, the American ambassador, found 'astonishing'. Against this background, they discussed the help Russia needed, both immediate and longer term. The most urgent item was anti-aircraft weaponry, while for the future, Stalin stressed high-octane aviation fuel and aluminium for aircraft construction. Overall, while confident Russia could hold out, Stalin underlined that it needed help and by next spring the supply position would be serious. He admitted that, although evacuation of manufacturing equipment eastward had begun, if the Germans took Leningrad, Moscow and Kiev, Russia would lose 75 per cent of its industrial capacity. Tank losses on both sides were enormous, but the Germans could produce more this winter than Russia, hence the need for help. Hopkins returned in time to join *Prince of Wales* at Scapa Flow bringing ninety pages of notes and copious supplies of caviar and vodka.[38]

Some of Stalin's military predictions inevitably proved over-optimistic and supply priorities would need re-ordering although his early emphasis on aluminium was prescient. However, the importance of Hopkins' assessment lay in convincing Roosevelt and Churchill, despite the continuing doubts of their advisers, that Russia had the will and potential to resist, and that Western aid was therefore worth the investment. At Riviera, they accordingly took the easy decision to send a joint Anglo-American mission to Moscow to negotiate a supply agreement, to be led by Beaverbrook, who was well-known to Roosevelt, and Averell Harriman, Roosevelt's special envoy to Europe and Lend-Lease coordinator. (Harriman was chosen rather than Hopkins because of the latter's poor health.) They communicated this decision to Stalin on 12 August, stressing British–American cooperation 'to provide you with the very maximum of supplies you most urgently need' and that the Moscow meeting should reach 'speedy decisions' on 'apportionment of our joint (trilateral) resources'. They added: 'we want you to know that, pending decisions of the conference, we shall continue to send supplies and materials as rapidly as possible'.[39]

This message proved a hostage to fortune because it pre-empted the far more difficult task of deciding how Russian needs were to be met from current and future American production, already fully committed to meeting British and American war requirements. As Churchill told the War Cabinet on his return: 'we might have to make some sacrifices, but this would be well worthwhile so long as the Russian front remained in being'.[40] Judged as grand strategy, this perception was correct but Churchill did not yet appreciate that, for the next 10 months, most of the supply burden and its protection must come from British resources with important implications for the war in other theatres. Indeed, Britain despatched the first supplies, including forty Hurricanes for defence of Murmansk, and forty-eight crated American P-40 Tomahawk fighters, from Iceland on 21 August, 10 days after Riviera ended, in a convoy of seven ships code-named 'Dervish'.[41]

If the commitment to the Moscow meeting pre-empted hard decisions on resource allocation, it also accelerated processes already underway to reach a joint British–American assessment of their future war production requirements. This was therefore a third important outcome of Riviera. The concept of a joint production programme had its genesis in British–American exchanges during the second half of 1940 over how best to reconcile their respective armament requirements with available United States industrial capacity. Coordination then evolved against the background of the Lend-Lease agreement in March and the strategic principles separately endorsed at the ABC-1 staff talks concluded the same month. Lend-Lease potentially enabled Britain to maintain a significant share of hopefully growing American defence production but this still had to be integrated with United States' re-armament needs. The problem was that Lend-Lease removed the previous financial constraint on British demands and, in the first half of 1941, American production was insufficient to meet the requirements of both countries. The US Army initially tried to ensure that supplies to Britain did not interfere with its minimum essential rearmament programme. In practice, often under presidential pressure, it was forced to make concessions, with Britain receiving priority for some aircraft categories and tanks for the Middle East which undercut sensible forward planning. The situation was further exacerbated because of inadequate communication across the various United States government departments and agencies involved. Over the next four months, there was some progress towards an agreed joint allocation whereby 20 per cent of future defence production would be allocated to foreign aid, with Britain the main beneficiary. However, political caution and competing interests in Washington meant plans for increasing production still lacked coherence. Despite warnings from the War Department, Roosevelt hoped somehow to meet the growing defence needs without shifting to a war economy. The result was no substantial change in defence manufacturing output in the first half of 1941.[42]

Pressure from Henry Stimson, Secretary of War, to improve coordination, in which the president's desire to support Russia was influential, helped push Roosevelt to write formally on 9 July to Stimson and his naval counterpart, Frank Knox, ordering them to explore 'at once the overall production requirements required to defeat our potential enemies'. He appreciated that this exercise involved making 'appropriate assumptions as to our probable friends and enemies and to the conceivable theaters of operations which will be required'. Significantly, he wanted Hopkins to be closely involved.[43]

The president did not refer to British input but the British joint staff mission in Washington were kept well informed by their American contacts. The British chiefs of staff accordingly suggested the prime minister propose 'a joint study of our production programmes' in his next message to the president while carefully avoiding prior knowledge of Roosevelt's 9 July instruction. Churchill duly did so on 25 July. His decision to include Beaverbrook at Riviera and probably to send him on to Washington reflected this agenda. The need for a combined 'Victory production programme' was certainly subsequently discussed and endorsed in principle at the summit. Colonel Charles Bundy from the US Army War Plans Division showed an early draft of the emerging American study to Brigadier Vivian 'Dumbie' Dykes, Director of Plans at the War Office and a member of the British Joint Planning Staff while, immediately after the summit, Stimson asked the American embassy in London to obtain from the British a statement of their 'ultimate air and ground requirements'. Meanwhile Beaverbrook was despatched to Washington, armed with a new directive from Churchill, to pursue the 'joint production' agenda and to explore how Russian needs might be incorporated. (Dykes died tragically in an air crash in 1943 returning from the Casablanca summit conference, one of the losses therefore in Churchill's mind when later referring to the Riviera Sunday service.)[44]

Riviera did not just confirm that establishing the Victory programme should be a joint exercise with Britain, a point formally confirmed by Roosevelt and Churchill at the end of the month.[45] It also provoked Roosevelt, spurred by Hopkins, into issuing new instructions on 30 August which substantially reshaped his directive of 9 July. The new factor was Russia and the Moscow conference. Roosevelt now deemed it of 'paramount importance for the safety and security of America that all reasonable munitions help be provided for Russia, not only immediately but as long as she continues to fight the Axis powers effectively'. From this time onward, Roosevelt would regularly attach the words 'paramount importance' to the Soviet aid programme. Since early help must come from production already planned, he required the War and Navy Departments, by 10 September, to recommend how American war production should be allocated between the United States, Britain and Russia between now and 30 June 1942. He also wanted advice on the overall production effort to ensure munitions power was sufficiently superior to that of the Axis in the long term to ensure victory. An American–British meeting must be arranged in advance of the Moscow visit to agree the overall division of resources to mid-1942 and therefore the associated allocation to Russia.[46]

## The Military and Diplomatic Strands

Riviera was not just a summit meeting between Churchill and Roosevelt. There were parallel military and diplomatic strands. The first brought together the British and American chiefs of staff for the first time. Earlier joint military meetings, notably the ABC-1 staff talks, had been conducted at lower level. The diplomatic exchange was conducted by Sir Alexander Cadogan, permanent secretary at the Foreign Office, and Assistant Secretary Sumner Welles from the State Department. At Churchill's request, Cadogan wrote out from scratch the first draft of the Atlantic Charter, causing the prime minister to exclaim on the way home – 'Thank God I brought you with me!'. He would accompany Churchill to most of the future summits.[47]

There was a striking difference in approach between the two sides in preparing for the meeting. The British team knew each other well, with the chiefs of staff meeting daily and having almost daily contact with the prime minister who doubled as Minister of Defence. Two years into the war there was also a clear, effective, well-staffed structure under the War Cabinet and Defence Committee for resolving issues, agreeing policy and taking key decisions. The British accordingly arrived with a solid consensus on all major points. The American group knew each other less well, there were intense rivalries and suspicions between army and navy, joint structures for setting overall defence policy were embryonic, and, not least, Roosevelt's real intent on important strategic questions was opaque. Few reached into 'his heavily forested interior'.[48] General Harold H (Hap) Arnold, Chief of the US Army Air Corps, who had visited Britain earlier in the year, and had been impressed by 'the thoroughness with which the British prepare for such conferences' was especially frustrated at the lack of coherent American preparation for Riviera, judging that the Americans were 'going into this one cold'.[49] However, any judgement that their whole approach was 'slipshod' goes too far. The American Joint Board (comprising their three chiefs of staff) had commissioned important new strategy work to provide context for the production assessment sought by Roosevelt on 9 July. The staff input here was comparable in quality to that of their British counterparts although the thinking was not yet mature enough to be presented formally at Riviera.[50]

The military meetings provided the forum for reviewing the progress and prospects of what was still a European war and for debating strategic issues of common interest. Both parties also gained important insights into the personalities they would be working with in the future. The Chief of the Imperial General Staff, General Sir John Dill, soon to become Chief of the British Joint Staff Mission in Washington, initiated a close and lasting friendship with the US Army Chief of Staff, General George C Marshall. On the naval side, Admiral Ernest King, currently commanding the new Atlantic Fleet but within six months to be promoted Commander-in-Chief US Fleet and Chief of Naval Operations, made a powerful impression on the British. He was viewed in his own service as a brilliant, salty fighter, so flinty and tough, that he was said to 'shave with a blow torch'.[51] King himself played to this image. 'Once in war you have to have sons of bitches.' 'I was an SOB.' 'I didn't know what was right, but I knew we had to have decisions, so I made them.'[52] Captain Brian Schofield, present as Director of Trade Division, noted King's 'grim and sour' look while another British observer assessed him 'tough, ruthless, and unbending ... anti-British, and particularly anti-Royal Navy'. However, he responded well to those who stood up to him, notably Admiral Sir Andrew Cunningham, with whom he shared many qualities, and, at a different level, Commander Rodger Winn, who sold him the concept of the U-boat tracking room. The British perhaps did not yet appreciate how wide King's hates extended. It was true he had limited respect for the Royal Navy, but he hated the US Army more! As his daughter famously said – 'Father is the most even-tempered man I know ... he's always angry'! The present Chief of Naval Operations, Admiral Harold Stark, and opposite number of the First Sea Lord, Admiral of the Fleet Sir Dudley Pound, was the closest of the American military team to Roosevelt, who always called him 'Betty'. He was more cerebral than King, a planner and strategist more than fighting sailor, 'too much like a bishop to be a good admiral', and some felt he lacked strength and deferred too much to his Director of Plans, Rear Admiral Richmond (Kelly) Turner who the British knew from the ABC-1 talks. Nevertheless, Stark had been a powerful influence on the president, crafting the Plan 'Dog' national security strategy the previous November which powerfully foreshadowed the 'Germany first' strategy agreed at ABC-1. He was also a firm advocate of a forward strategy in the Middle East.[53]

The military agenda was framed by a British paper 'General Strategy', and the conclusions reached at the ABC-1 staff talks five months earlier.[54] The 'General Strategy' paper was in part an assessment of the present state of the war and part exposition of the strategic levers which the British hoped could ultimately deliver victory. On the state of the war, the paper stressed: a continuing risk of invasion of the United Kingdom although this was now unlikely in 1941 and not possible while Russia held out; maintaining control of sea communications with considerable improvement here recently evident in the North Atlantic; and the critical importance of holding the Middle East. The German attack on Russia which had been underway for six weeks provided Britain with breathing space, but the paper judged it did not affect Britain's core strategy. This strategy remained that of 'wear down', first defined by the chiefs of staff the previous September.[55] Germany would be weakened by the combination of blockade, bombing and subversion to the point where she either sued for peace or British invasion of the Continent became a feasible proposition. The paper touched briefly on American intervention which would 'revolutionise the whole situation'. At sea it would bring immediate relief and reduce shipping losses. Even if Japan intervened, the Western Allies would retain an advantage. American forces might prevent enemy penetration in Morocco and West Africa and take over the Atlantic islands. Annexes addressed this possibility in detail.[56]

The consensus of both contemporary records and most later historians is that the military talks allowed a frank exchange of views but produced no new concrete results beyond arrangements for implementing Plan No 4, with aid for Russia left waiting on the Moscow conference. The British believed that they had convinced the Americans that their emphasis on the Middle East was 'sound'. (Bundy, keeping the US Army record, judged that gaining American assistance in this theatre alongside help with Atlantic security were evidently Churchill's main priorities.[57]) That may have been over-optimistic although they had apparently already persuaded Hopkins of their strategic case during his recent London visit. The latter had written to Roosevelt on 25 July that the British 'were determined to fight it out' in that theatre with 'very convincing reasons to all of us for that determination'. Hopkins' support here would soon be important in protecting British claims on American supplies in the face of growing United States needs and those of Russia.[58] However, in general, the British found the Americans preoccupied with the defence of the western hemisphere, including the threat of Axis penetration into South America, and the problems of expanding their forces and ramping up arms production. There was a stark American warning that, even without new demands from Russia and China, the British must rein in their expectation of American supplies. Reflecting the references in the British strategy paper and American fears of Axis ambitions towards South America, substantial time was devoted to the implications of a German move into Spain and North-west Africa and contingency plans for securing the Atlantic islands. The American team were prepared to help on the latter but gave no encouragement on Africa.[59]

In recording their contemporary judgement that the Riviera military talks were little more than an exchange of views, British participants could not anticipate how far their strategic assessment would be endorsed by their American opposite numbers or indeed the president when he was fully briefed. The British strategy promoted at Riviera remained essentially defensive. At this stage, blockade, bombing and subversion were more 'containment' than 'wear down'. The big unknowns were Russian prospects and American intervention, with references to the latter always framed delicately by the British team. The Americans also concluded that British commitment to an ultimate land offensive to achieve Germany's defeat was half-hearted. Initial scene-setting comments from the prime minister, the rather sparse and conditional references in the strategy paper, and informal comments by the British chiefs all implied a belief that a land offensive on the scale of 1914–18 would not be necessary. Overall, the Americans detected no convincing route to victory. The perceived weaknesses in the British vision were confirmed in detailed studies of their 'General Strategy' paper undertaken by the American staffs for the Joint Board over the next month. These concluded that the British exaggerated both the likely impact of their 'wear down' elements and current United States military strength. Early United States intervention would not guarantee victory and would certainly not make it 'swift'. The Joint Board endorsed the American view that only minor attention had so far been given to the need for a land offensive. 'Naval and air power may prevent wars from being lost and, by weakening enemy strength, may contribute greatly to victory' but 'wars cannot be finally won without the use of land armies'.[60]

It is tempting to see this American analysis setting the scene for the fierce disagreements over an early landing on the Continent that dominated the first six months of 1942. It is true that American scepticism over British commitment to a major cross-Channel land offensive cast a long shadow then and later. However, in August and September 1941, debate about a land offensive was hypothetical. The United States was not in the war, there was no certainty of its early intervention and it could not contribute significant forces to land operations for at least a year. There are two further compelling reasons not to over-emphasise American post Riviera critiques of British strategy. First, and most important, there was nothing in the 'General Strategy' paper that conflicted with the strategic goals established at ABC-1, to which both parties remained firmly committed. The principle of a land offensive was not questioned. Its scale was for reasonable debate and dependent on factors not yet possible to foresee. Secondly, through September, as the Americans refined the strategic principles underlining the president's Victory programme, it became clear that a successful land offensive was impossible without substantial prior wearing down of German power. Put starkly, they judged the Axis powers would have 400 divisions by July 1943. By contrast, the Allies, without the United States and assuming Russian collapse, barely 100. A conventional 2:1 attack ratio would therefore require 700 American divisions, an impossible goal. Although superior technology might help compensate against greater Axis manpower, there was no substitute for prior wear-down on British lines. Europe would ultimately be the chief theatre but 'invasion by the United States of Germany will not be attempted until the air offensive against Germany has been successful and we can control the air over the area of the invasion in very large measure'. Thus, the American strategic assumptions underpinning the response to the president's directives of 9 July and 30 August ended up almost identical to those of their British counterparts.[61]

Meanwhile, the Riviera focus on the German threat to Iberia, North-west Africa and the Atlantic islands exerted lasting influence. British reference to the opportunities offered by gaining control of North-west Africa foreshadowed the more coherent Mediterranean-centric wear-down strategy the British would push with determination five months later at the Arcadia summit. Stark already understood this concept and Roosevelt, while giving little away, did so too. Even at this stage, the latter was inclining to an 'air/sea' way of war for the United States with Russia absorbing the bulk of German land power, underlining that any long-term American strategy involving land offensives was far from settled. The direction of travel towards the final commitment a year later to the 'Torch' landings in North-west Africa was therefore set at Riviera. The British commitment to bombing also found strong support in the American team. Arnold required no persuasion and, in the immediate run-up to Riviera, he and Marshall had decided that a strategic bombing force based in the Philippines was a key means of containing Japan.[62]

If Riviera effectively endorsed the joint British–American strategy already agreed at ABC-1 of wearing Germany down before any successful cross-Channel invasion directed at the German heartland could occur, the critical element that ultimately made 'wear down' successful was initially missing. None of the military leaders at Riviera in early August had much expectation of Russia. At most they saw Russia buying the two Western Allies some time to build up their strength. They recognised that giving her military supplies might extend this time but were sceptical whether quantities deliverable over the next few months could have much impact. By contrast the same resources applied in other theatres, notably in the Far East and Pacific, would make a real difference.[63] They did not yet see what both Roosevelt and Churchill perhaps already intuitively sensed, that, with the right support, Russia was the key to breaking German land power and limiting the Western blood price. However, by September, the attitude of the American military leadership was shifting. They too were beginning to recognise that sustaining an active front in Russia would be key to eroding superior Axis land power.

The Joint Board estimate for the Victory programme reached the president in its final form on 25 September.[64] As Roosevelt anticipated, it began with the obvious point that, to assess production needs, it was first necessary to identify America's enemies and how they could be defeated. This 'estimate' was not therefore merely a set of production requirements. It was also a strategy document, defining ends, ways and means, the enemies to be defeated, how this was to be done, and with what resources. The strategic overview with which it opened was an American parallel to the British 'General Strategy' document shared at Riviera. This has received insufficient recognition with attention invariably focused more on the Allied production programme that it spawned than the goals the United States military leadership intended this to achieve.[65]

The ultimate national goals defined in the estimate were: the security of the United States and the western hemisphere; preventing disruption of the British Empire; preventing further Japanese territorial aggression; promoting political stability in Europe and Asia; and, where possible, establishing regimes consistent with economic freedom and individual liberty. These goals rather neatly combined American national interest with the aspirations of the Atlantic Charter but with special status granted to Britain. The estimate saw Germany's current goal as the complete political and military domination of Europe and probably North and West Africa too. Thereafter she would pursue ambitions to the west and east which posed a fundamental threat to the United States. It assumed Germany's immediate aims were: the conquest of European Russia and overthrow of the Soviet regime, absorbing most of her land and air effort in the immediate future; destruction of British resistance through attrition of shipping and bombing, extending German control of the seaboard from Norway to French West Africa to achieve this; in concert with Italy the conquest of Egypt, Syria, Iraq and Iran; the occupation of Iberia, French West Africa and the Atlantic islands to make the shipping war against Britain more effective and to deny these areas to Germany's enemies. The estimate did not expect Germany to attempt an invasion of the United

Kingdom until her siege war was shown to fail. Turning to Japan, it saw her goal as securing effective control of Eastern Siberia, Eastern China, Indochina, Thailand, Malaya, the Philippines, and possibly Burma. This was an ambitious undertaking with Japan's limited resources, and she might have to make choices, but her aggressive intent was clear.

Most of this analysis was consistent with the British 'General Strategy' paper and the thrust of discussions at Riviera. So was the reaffirmation of Germany as primary enemy to be dealt with first as agreed at ABC-1. More striking was how the estimate then embraced the British strategy of 'wear down', but arguably with more clarity than the British had yet managed. Apart from Russia, it identified the principal strength of the Western Powers as their naval and air capability. Naval and air power prevented wars being lost and, by weakening an enemy, contributed to victory, but seldom alone delivered victory. Land armies were necessary to win. However, in a striking echo of recent British views, the estimate emphasised that the United States and its allies could not immediately undertake a sustained and successful land offensive against the centre of German power. It followed that, since defensive measures would obviously not defeat Germany, they must find alternative strategic offensive options. These included: economic blockade; prosecuting land offensives in distant regions where Germany could not easily deploy its full strength; air and sea offensives against German military, economic and industrial resources; and subversion operations in German-occupied territories. Options for containing Japan included: strong defence of Siberia and Malaya; blockade; raiding vulnerable points to stretch her resources; and Chinese action in Japanese occupied territory.[66]

The estimate anticipated key elements of Allied strategy over the next 18 months. First, the security of the United Kingdom was essential to effective prosecution of the current war against Germany and a potential war against Japan. This security ultimately rested on safe sea communications. This required American naval and air support in the Atlantic and large additional merchant ship tonnage. Secondly, preventing Axis penetration into French North-west Africa and the Atlantic islands was critical to the pre-eminent United States requirement of protecting the western hemisphere, to secure British sea communications, and as a potential base for a future land offensive. Thirdly, maintaining an active front in Russia offered the best prospect for a successful land offensive against Germany. Predicting the outcome of the present fighting was premature. But effective arming of Russian forces from outside and providing industrial capacity in the Volga basin and east of the Urals was an important opportunity for the Western Powers. Finally, retention of British control over the Red Sea, Iraq and Iran was also necessary to maintain options for decisive land action against Germany. The United States should therefore support Britain with munitions, raw materials, and shipping. The reference to industrial capacity east of the Urals reflected the huge American involvement in the first half of the 1930s in designing, constructing and equipping the vast automobile plants at Nizhniy Tagil near Sverdlovsk and Chelyabinsk which underpinned tank production. In 1932, two-thirds of American metalworking machinery exports went to Russia and there were 1000 Russians in the United States learning industrial techniques. When factories in Western Russia were hastily evacuated to the Urals in 1941, their standardised American design facilitated rapid incorporation in the existing Ural plants. Their previous American history also greatly enhanced the application of American aid during the war.[67]

This Joint Board view of future strategy, signed off by Marshall and Stark, undoubtedly reflected discussion with the president over the Riviera period. However, the political constraints facing Roosevelt in delivering such a strategy remained with key aspects hypothetical until the United States was at war with the Axis powers. The ambitious war production programme that followed the strategic overview, although highly detailed, was at this stage a combination of wish list and rough judgement of maximum American industrial output. Nevertheless, three key points stand out. First, in September 1941, the American military leadership was more closely aligned to current British strategy and more willing to support its key elements than generally recognised. Secondly, it recognised the crucial importance of shipping to the execution of a successful war against the Axis powers and made the first serious attempt to calculate the quantities needed. It argued that the United States must build 20.3 million tons of new merchant shipping by the end of 1944 including 6 million tons for Britain. This goal, involving a virtual trebling of the existing United States merchant marine, seemed ambitious that autumn but, given all the uncertainties, with one exception, the predicted requirements proved surprisingly accurate. The exception was the anticipated loss rate over these three years. American losses were 2.2 million tons more than the 3 million expected while British losses of 7.1 million were just covered by the combination of their own production and 4.5 million tons (compared to the originally-planned 6 million tons) supplied from the United States. In the event these greater Allied losses were more than covered by an additional 5.9 million tons of American shipping produced over the period.[68] Finally, the estimate demonstrated that the American military leaders had moved on in their attitude to

Russia since Riviera. They were now ahead of their British counterparts in recognising Russia's potential. The British still saw support for Russia primarily in terms of buying time to improve their strategic position. In contrast, the Americans now viewed Russia as vital to defeating German land power.

## First Aid to Russia

Even as United States strategy evolved, the British and American military ambivalence towards supporting Russia evident at Riviera was not allowed to survive for long. The power of the German advance, now threatening Moscow, Leningrad and Ukraine, meant that, through the second half of August, the Western Allies came under intense Russian pressure to deliver on their Riviera promise of 'speedy assistance'. As a current combatant, the British bore the brunt of this pressure which included demands for a major diversionary landing on the western boundary of German-occupied Europe. Meanwhile perceived American slowness in completing their overall war production estimate, then deciding what could be offered to Russia, and committing to a date for the promised Moscow conference, proved increasingly embarrassing to London.

By the end of the month, the British therefore resorted to stopgap measures, pending the conference. In addition to the Dervish delivery, they now confirmed the supply of a further 175 American P-40 Tomahawks (making 223 in all), fighters originally earmarked for the Middle East, and now, in addition, 200 more Hurricanes to be delivered as soon as possible. This did not satisfy Stalin who told Churchill on 3 September that, although welcome, these deliveries were but a drop in the ocean. He reiterated the need for a second front, sufficient to draw off thirty to forty German divisions, and monthly deliveries of 400 aircraft and 500 tanks, along with 30,000 tons of aluminium by October. Maisky underlined Russia's perilous position to Churchill and Eden, claiming the war was at a 'turning point'. If Russia were defeated, how could Britain win? Detecting 'an underlying air of menace' from Maisky, the prime minister responded sharply. Four months earlier, the British had not known whether Russia would fight against them on Germany's side. 'Whatever happens, and whatever you do, you of all people have no right to make reproaches to us.' Cadogan too thought 'Stalin's message lays it on a bit thick'. Current evidence did not suggest an imminent Russian break.[69]

Nevertheless, on 5 September, the War Cabinet decided immediately to offer half Stalin's requested monthly aircraft and tanks (in the hope the Americans would provide the other half) and subsequently added 5000 tons of aluminium with 2000 tons per month to follow. This new commitment reflected a Cabinet consensus, encouraged by representations from the newly-appointed ambassador to Moscow, Sir Stafford Cripps, that, if imminent Russian collapse was unlikely, it could not be ruled out. A greater risk was that Russia might seek a separate peace.[70] Meanwhile, 193 fighters, primarily Hurricanes but including some Tomahawks, of those promised prior to the end of August, and an initial batch of aluminium, along with twenty tanks and a further 15,000 tons of raw materials and assorted military stores, were embarked in convoy PQ 1, comprising ten ships, which left for Iceland two weeks later and thence to Archangel which it reached on 11 October.[71] This additional commitment was far short of Stalin's demands but, in concert with simultaneous British–Russian action to secure Iran, it probably provided sufficient reassurance against his immediate fear, mirroring that of Churchill, that Britain would reach separate terms with Germany.[72]

PQ 1 was the first of thirty-nine dedicated convoys on the North Russia route between September 1941 and May 1945, whose details are summarised in Appendix 1. The designation 'PQ' applied to the first eighteen of these convoys derived from the initials of the Admiralty officer responsible for their planning, Commander Philip Quellyn Roberts.[73] Returning eastbound convoys were designated 'QP'. The escort, comprising a single cruiser *Suffolk*, two destroyers, and several anti-submarine trawlers, for its ten merchant vessels, was distinctly modest compared to those required in the future. For the Royal Navy was now set to operate in a new theatre which would demand huge resources over the next four years and bring some of the hardest fighting of its war. It would apply lessons from the last two years and learn some harsh new ones too. Sustaining Russia and then improving her effectiveness would primarily drive this effort although at times the imperative behind operations would be political as well. The Arctic theatre would also influence and be influenced by all the other issues addressed at Riviera, the wider Battle of the Atlantic, the threats and opportunities presented by North-west Africa and the Mediterranean, and the challenge from Japan in the Far East.

## Chapter 1

# The Royal Navy in Autumn 1941: Brightening Prospects?

Following the Riviera conference, the battleship *Prince of Wales*, with the prime minister and British delegation aboard, returned to Scapa Flow on 18 August 1941. A month later, wearing the flag of Vice Admiral Alban Thomas Curteis, Second-in-Command Home Fleet, and accompanied by the cruisers *Edinburgh*, *Sheffield*, *Euryalus* and *Kenya*, and nine destroyers, she joined convoy WS 11X off the Clyde which initially comprised eleven freighters and four large naval auxiliaries. On reaching the Straits of Gibraltar on 24 September, the four auxiliaries and two freighters detached to Freetown. The remaining nine freighters, carrying 2600 troops and 81,000 tons of military equipment and civil supplies and designated convoy GM2, were bound for Malta. Simultaneously, three empty ships were to return from Malta to Gibraltar as MG2. The whole operation was code-named Halberd. This was the largest resupply effort to Malta of the war so far and, along with an earlier convoy in late July, it was critical to building up war stocks to enable Malta to play a key role in interdicting Axis supply lines between Italy and North Africa.

### *Evolving Royal Navy Capability: Operation Halberd*

The *Prince of Wales* group now joined the Gibraltar-based Force H to fight the convoy through against substantial opposition expected from Italian air, surface, and submarine forces. Force H, under Vice Admiral Sir James Somerville, comprised the battleship *Nelson*, the carrier *Ark Royal* (with twenty-seven Fulmar II fighters and twenty-seven Swordfish torpedo strike/reconnaissance (TSR) aircraft embarked), the cruiser *Hermione* and a further nine destroyers. For this operation it was also temporarily reinforced by *Nelson*'s sister battleship *Rodney*. The Halberd escort group, under Somerville's overall command, was thus a considerable force and comprised predominantly modern, state of the art ships with

Force H providing a battle-hardened core. The importance of the convoy and scale of escort required was rehearsed at length when Somerville visited London at the end of August. In addition to the escort group, nine Malta-based submarines were positioned off Sardinia, Sicily and southern Italy ready to intervene against any Italian surface forces, while aircraft from the Royal Air Force, based at Gibraltar and Malta, provided anti-submarine patrols, reconnaissance and fighter protection. To divert Italian attention, a sortie by the Eastern Mediterranean Fleet, under Admiral Sir Andrew Cunningham, from Alexandria was also planned.[1]

Halberd is relevant to the Royal Navy's coming war in the Arctic for four reasons. First, as the new Arctic theatre opened, it provides a benchmark for current Royal Navy ability, after two years of war, to mount a successful convoy operation in restricted geographical waters against a peer enemy operating in three dimensions. Secondly, it demonstrates the level of fighting capability, leadership, planning, tactics, sensors, weapons and skill in their application, that the Royal Navy had achieved by September 1941. Thirdly, it illustrates the level the Royal Navy had now reached in the operational exploitation of high-quality intelligence, primarily from signals intelligence (SIGINT), the intercept of radio signals, but also aerial reconnaissance, in a multi-threat environment. Finally, it reveals flexibility of deployment, the ability quickly to shift resources between theatres and yet create a new integrated force operating to common standards.

The Gibraltar–Malta convoys enjoyed several advantages over those on the Arctic route between Iceland and Murmansk or Archangel. The western passage to Malta, at about 1000 miles, was only half the distance of the Arctic route. The merchant vessels used on the Malta convoys were some 50 per cent faster, 13–15 knots compared to 8–9 knots. The Mediterranean weather was also far better. The western route to Malta could therefore be covered in three days with the main exposure to air attack limited to about 30 hours. By contrast the Arctic convoys took 10–12 days and were liable to heavy attack for at least half this period, posing obvious challenges for operational endurance and efficiency. Nevertheless, Halberd posed many of the same problems that would face the Royal Navy in the Arctic over the next 18 months. In both theatres the chief danger came from the air. The outward-bound Halberd convoy had to spend the last 400 miles within 150 miles of Sardinian and Sicilian airfields, exposed to bombing (both high level and dive-bombing) and torpedo attack covered by shore-based fighters. Submarine attack was possible throughout the convoy passage but especially in waters east of Sardinia where intervention by heavy Italian surface units was also likely. Two further threats, not present in the Arctic, were from motor torpedo boats (MTBs) and minefields in the Sicilian narrows and final approaches to Malta.[2]

Somerville and Cunningham were the Royal Navy's two outstanding fighting admirals of the war. Somerville, who held continuous senior operational command at sea for four years from mid-1940, was perhaps the more innovative of the two, a master of the new electronic sensors and the skilful exploitation of limited naval air resources for offensive and defensive effect. He was an inspirational leader and a fine seaman. Those who served with him found him a hard taskmaster, but they admired his professionalism, integrity and sheer humanity, while enjoying his wonderful sense of humour. His long front-line sea service overseas in this war, separated from wife and family, was reminiscent of Admiral Cuthbert Collingwood's lonely years in the Mediterranean after Trafalgar.[3] His first great wartime contribution after he was restored to service following unjustified medical retirement was to oversee the development of radar (or Radio Direction Finding (RDF) as it was known until 1943) in the Royal Navy. As a former communications specialist, and highly regarded flag officer at sea, he had the knowledge, drive, reputation and seniority to understand and promote radar's potential and then to mobilise the resources to ensure its speedy introduction. The credit for the remarkable speed with which ships were fitted in 1940–1 goes to him. The British pioneer of radar, Sir Robert Watson-Watt, rightly called Somerville the 'foster-father of naval radar'.[4]

Somerville's planning for Halberd reflected experience with previous western convoys to Malta, notably the most recent conducted between 21–24 July under Operation Substance, and the latest threat intelligence. Substance had successfully convoyed six merchant vessels and a troopship to Malta and six empty vessels in the westward direction with only one outbound ship damaged by MTB-launched torpedo. The escort, also composed from Force H and substantial Home Fleet reinforcements, was broadly comparable to that deployed for Halberd and suffered one destroyer sunk and one cruiser and destroyer damaged, all to aircraft torpedoes.[5]

For a year from July 1940, intelligence coverage of Italian naval dispositions and movements in the western Mediterranean was limited. The primary Italian naval codebooks and additive cipher systems could not be penetrated by the Government Code & Cypher School (GC&CS) codebreakers at Bletchley Park in this period or indeed through the rest of the Mediterranean war. For the last five months of 1940, Somerville was dependent on low-grade SIGINT, based on direction finding (D/F), traffic analysis and some reading of minor codes, limited air reconnaissance mainly out of Malta, and visual sightings. Matters improved somewhat by the turn of the year after GC&CS broke into the main Italian air force systems. This gave Somerville intelligence on Italian air force dispositions and reconnaissance operations, helping with evasive routing and providing some warning of air attacks. Intelligence coverage of air operations was then significantly increased through access to German air force Enigma traffic after Fliegerkorps X deployed to the central Mediterranean in January 1941. This provided excellent insights into German air operations relevant to the naval war and occasional insights into German strategic intent. However, in Somerville's area, this source waned as Fliegerkorps X moved eastward from early spring to support operations in Greece and Crete.[6]

While intelligence on Italian air force dispositions remained excellent through 1941, at the end of August, Somerville emphasised to the chiefs of staff that timely knowledge of Italian naval movements remained a critical gap which must be remedied. This reflected inadequate aerial reconnaissance forces at both Gibraltar and Malta and failure to share intelligence held in the United Kingdom (evidently a reference to high-grade SIGINT).[7] Somerville drew here on discussions with Lieutenant Commander Ian Fleming, personal staff officer to Director of Naval Intelligence Rear Admiral John Godfrey, who had visited Gibraltar two weeks previously.[8] Somerville's representations led to some improvements in air reconnaissance and intelligence management, but a more important source was also coming on stream in time for Halberd. This was an Italian navy encrypted traffic stream using a Swedish machine cipher, the Hagelin C38m. It had similarities to Enigma and GC&CS achieved full readability of the traffic it carried by July. Hagelin did not replace the book-based high-level Italian navy codes and was primarily used to carry communications regarding shipping movements, including all Axis supply convoys to North Africa. However, partly because it was easy to use, it frequently carried traffic relating to fleet movements too. Ironically, the Germans had pressed the Italians to use Hagelin for convoy communications because, as a machine system, they judged it more secure than hand cipher systems. The reverse was the case.[9] In the immediate run-up to Halberd, Hagelin decrypts, circulated by GC&CS using the same arrangements as for Enigma traffic and carrying the designation 'Ultra', confirmed that the Italians intended to intervene against the next Gibraltar–Malta convoy with their main fleet as well as by air attack. They also hinted (wrongly) at possible German air force support. Further decrypts just as the convoy sailed showed that the Italians had learnt from an agent that a large convoy was mustering in Gibraltar and that additional torpedo aircraft were deploying to Sardinia.[10]

Somerville could therefore make final plans for Halberd with good knowledge of the Italian air and surface threat. He knew, primarily from air reconnaissance, that the Italians had repaired the damage suffered at Taranto the previous November and Matapan in March and could therefore deploy up to three battleships, six cruisers and accompanying destroyers from Taranto, and their most modern and powerful battleships, *Vittorio Veneto* and *Littorio*, a cruiser and destroyers from Naples.[11] He anticipated that a substantial part of this force would concentrate south of Sardinia under fighter cover and attempt to draw off the British escort, enabling light forces then to destroy the convoy.[12] To date, the Italian surface fleet had operated cautiously and with varying competence but the strength they could mobilise ensured the British remained wary of their intervention.[13] Somerville also had a good knowledge of overall Italian air strength from air force decrypts and anticipated the main threat coming from the reinforced Sardinia torpedo group. In theory, there were seventy operational Italian strike aircraft in Sardinia and a further ninety in Sicily available to deploy against the Halberd convoys. Fighter numbers were 50 and 125 respectively. In numbers and capability, this Italian force in the central Mediterranean was comparable to that available to the Germans in Northern Norway in mid-1942. However, the Italians could not focus solely on the Halberd convoys. They also had to cover other requirements, not least ongoing operations against Malta. In practice, Sardinia deployed twenty-six torpedo bombers and fifty fighter escorts, in each case about 70 per cent of the available force. Numbers deployed from Sicily were proportionately lower, thirty-six strike aircraft, mainly high-level bombers, and only eighteen fighters.[14]

The projected Halberd air threat was broadly comparable to that encountered during Substance and Halberd planners could therefore draw lessons from this previous convoy. The primary conclusion, reflecting experience earlier in the year, was that Italian air attacks were effective, exploiting excellent reconnaissance, with bombing and torpedo strikes well synchronised and pressed home with determination. Although it is often suggested that the Royal Navy had a low opinion of Italian air capability in contrast to that of their German ally, this did not apply to Somerville or Cunningham. Four large Royal Navy cruisers had been damaged in torpedo attacks over the first year of the Mediterranean war and Cunningham judged Italian high-level bombing 'the best I have ever seen, far better than the German'. Substance experience suggested several observations for future convoy defence. First, shore-based fighters from Malta, now including twenty-two long-range Beaufighters and five Blenheims, and covering the final phase of the convoy's passage, required careful training and a clear understanding of the naval force requirements if they were to support it adequately. Secondly, Italian high-level bombing was accurate unless the formation was broken up by fighters. This required timely radar warning for fighters to gain sufficient height. Thirdly, although torpedo bombers had achieved one successful surprise attack, enabling them to drop their weapons at short range, they were also deterred by determined anti-aircraft barrages, which brought down four aircraft and persuaded them to drop at medium or long range, rendering attacks less accurate. Finally, *Ark Royal*'s fighters proved effective in breaking up incoming Italian strikes, destroying six bombers and two torpedo planes, and Somerville recorded that they had contributed 'in no small measure' to the safe arrival of the Substance convoy. Nevertheless, fighter attrition was heavy with six Fulmars lost during the operation, nearly a quarter of those embarked, although four crews were saved.[15]

The Italian fleet made no attempt to intervene against the Substance convoys. Somerville judged they may have been deterred by the presence of the Malta-based submarines which had been deployed across all exit and transit routes and had conducted sufficient attacks on enemy shipping to indicate their presence. The main surface threat came from three MTBs which attacked in the Sicilian narrows on the night of 23/24 July. These were detected on radar by the destroyer *Cossack* and driven off by concentrated fire from the escort force but not before they torpedoed and damaged the merchant ship *Sydney Star*. MTBs proved an abiding and dangerous threat to future convoys.

Italian submarines inflicted no damage during Substance although, on 22 July, *Diaspro* achieved near misses on the battlecruiser *Renown* and Australian destroyer *Nestor*, 140 miles south-west of Sardinia.[16] The British had more success. The cruiser *Hermione* sank the submarine *Tembien* in the approaches to Malta during a subsequent high-speed supply run in early August.[17] By this point, the British had concluded that the large Italian submarine force comprising about 100 boats at the start of the war was a 'paper tiger'. Partly by exploiting excellent intelligence, they had now destroyed at least one-third of the initial front-line boats and had suffered negligible damage in return.[18] Halberd would not change this assessment. The Italians deployed seven boats in the western approaches to the Sardinia–Tunisia gap but none mounted an effective attack on the outbound Halberd force, perhaps judging the threat from the constant daylight anti-submarine patrols by *Ark Royal*'s Swordfish and the large destroyer escort too great. They were more aggressive during the 36 hours from the evening of 28 September against elements of the Halberd force returning from Malta. Half a dozen attempted attacks, all unsuccessful, resulted in the sinking of the Italian submarine *Adua*, confirming that, by autumn 1941, taking on Royal Navy destroyers, if a submarine had technical, tactical, or training weaknesses, was a high-risk business. Also noteworthy was the radar detection of an Italian boat on the surface at a range of seven miles by *Prince of Wales* using the latest centimetric Type 273 surface-search set which had been fitted immediately after her return from Riviera.[19]

Even before Halberd, the successful delivery of the Substance convoy, boosting Malta's capacity as an offensive base, and the Italian failure to achieve any submarine interdiction, triggered a shift in German U-boat policy which was to have important consequences. By late August Axis shipping losses on the Africa supply route were becoming a serious concern and Hitler proposed to Raeder that six U-boats be transferred to the Mediterranean to counter the increasing British naval success. This would be the first U-boat deployment in that sea. Raeder, reluctant to reduce U-boat effort in the Atlantic, managed to stall a final decision. By mid-September losses on the Africa route were reaching one-third of those despatched and Raeder had to accept the despatch of six U-boats by the end of that month. The first of these, *U-371*, passed eastward at night on the surface through the Gibraltar Straits on 23 September. Twenty more followed by the end of the year, in all 30 per cent of the available front-line force. This brought a serious reduction in effort against Atlantic convoys and made it impossible to build up an effective force in the Arctic with only three boats allocated to North Norway before the end of the year.[20]

At 0900 on 25 September, the Halberd force departed the Gibraltar Straits in two groups. Somerville took 'Group I', comprising the usual Force H (*Nelson*, *Ark Royal*, *Hermione*, and six destroyers), along the North African coast, hoping to convince any Italian surveillance that this was a standard western Mediterranean sweep. The force was sighted and reported next morning some 250 miles south-west of the southern tip of Sardinia. Meanwhile, Curteis took 'Group II', comprising the convoy and the bulk of the escorts, north-east along the Spanish coast before turning south-east through the Balearic Islands, a route chosen to be clearer of shipping and potential aerial surveillance. Next morning his twelve destroyers refuelled in pairs from the accompanying tanker *Brown Ranger* which then returned to Gibraltar. This attempted deception and evasive routing brought some benefit as it would in several future Arctic operations. When the Italians spotted Group I, they initially judged its purpose was a repeat bombardment of Genoa, or a raid on Sardinian targets or the island of Pantellaria, 150 miles north-west of Malta. Although they later received reports of another British force from an Italian officer aboard a French mail plane overflying Group II on the afternoon of 26 September, the Commander-in-Chief Admiral Angelo Iachino, with two modern battleships (*Vittorio Veneto* and *Littorio*), three 8in and two 6in-gun cruisers, and fourteen destroyers, was ordered by the Chief of the Naval Staff, Admiral Arturo Riccardi, to concentrate east of Sardinia, ready to cover all options, against an assumed inferior Royal Navy force. Although Riccardi gave Iachino 'freedom of action', he qualified this by insisting he must not engage unless 'in decisive superiority'. In reality, the forces were about equal. The British had superior gunpower but the Italians had a significant speed advantage over the two *Nelson*s.[21]

Somerville's two groups met on the morning of 27 September about 70 miles south of the south-western tip of Sardinia. The three battleships took station either side of the merchant ships in two columns led by the cruisers, *Kenya* and *Edinburgh* with *Sheffield* following close astern, thus providing the convoy with good all-round protection against air attack. *Ark Royal*, with the two anti-aircraft cruisers *Euryalus* and *Hermione* as her dedicated protective screen, operated independently on the weather quarter, providing freedom for flying operations. *Hermione* executed another vital function for *Ark Royal*. The latter was never fitted with radar (or RDF as it was still known). *Hermione*, fitted with the latest Type 281 air-warning set, capable of detecting high-flying aircraft out to 100 miles, therefore acted as the Force H radar guardship, as had the cruiser *Sheffield* before her albeit using the less effective Type 79.[22] *Hermione* maintained the radar air and surface picture on behalf of *Ark Royal* and sometimes the whole force if no other ship was fitted. Radar contacts and tracks were exchanged with *Ark Royal* and the force command either by light, flag or VHF voice. Constant practice had brought this process to a high level of efficiency.[23] Sixteen destroyers were positioned in a wide semi-circular screen 6000 yards ahead of the convoy and its heavy escort with two more placed astern of the carrier group to protect it during flying manoeuvres. Although the primary role of the destroyer screen was anti-submarine, it had a valuable anti-aircraft role too. Not only was the firepower of eighteen destroyers significant but attacking aircraft had to penetrate 4000 yards beyond this screen to reach credible torpedo release range against the high-value targets during which they could expect concentrated fire from all directions. This cruising disposition was an expanded version of that perfected during Substance. Somerville's plan was for the battleships and *Ark Royal* to cover the convoy until it reached the Sicilian narrows. The heavy ships would then return westward leaving a close escort of the cruisers and nine destroyers for the final run to Malta. Long-range fighters from Malta would provide air cover in place of *Ark Royal*.

Italian air reconnaissance quickly reported the now-concentrated Halberd force, enabling an attack by thirty torpedo aircraft (a mixture of S.79s and S.84s based in Sardinia with a small reinforcement from Sicily) in the early afternoon, operating in three successive waves, and escorted by twenty CR.42 fighters. The first wave of eighteen aircraft, in two groups, twelve to the north and six to the east, were detected by *Hermione* at a range of 30 miles and broken up first by *Ark Royal*'s fighter patrol of eight Fulmars and then by gunfire. The Italians lost five aircraft but, regrettably, two Fulmars were also lost to barrage fire from *Prince of Wales* and *Rodney* respectively. The second wave, although comprising only seven aircraft and facing double the number of British fighters, was more successful, hitting *Nelson* with a single torpedo on her port bow, the only damage suffered by the ships of the Halberd escort throughout the operation. For this gain the Italians lost another three aircraft. The final group of five aircraft was reluctant to press home their attack in the face of fighters and heavy gunfire, most dropping their torpedoes outside the destroyer screen without result but still suffering two losses. Of the thirty aircraft attacking that afternoon, only eighteen got within effective torpedo firing range to achieve the single hit on *Nelson*. Six succumbed to gunfire and four to fighters, an overall loss rate of one-third, which was clearly unsustainable and a testament to the combination of radar directed fighter direction and barrage fire.[24]

While this air attack was underway, Iachino was loitering 70 miles north-east of the Halberd force and in a quandary. He now understood the British were running a convoy but still assumed the naval escort was essentially Force H, for him a manageable target, but his intelligence picture was becoming confused with muddled reports of other British forces in the area. Neither the torpedo strike force from Sardinia nor the reconnaissance aircraft he had launched himself had yet provided clarity. The fighter cover from Sardinia he had been promised had not appeared and it would be dangerous to proceed against a British carrier without this. He also knew he had been spotted by British reconnaissance from Malta. Between mid-afternoon and dusk he remained gripped by indecision in the face of further news, both positive and negative. Some CR.42 fighters did arrive and reports from the torpedo strike with inflated damage claims promised rich pickings. But visibility was deteriorating, and he received reports from his fighters that carrier reconnaissance aircraft (from *Ark Royal*) were searching for him, feeding his anxiety regarding a British air strike.

Somerville, well informed by the Royal Air Force scouting from Malta, meanwhile took aggressive countermeasures. He correctly judged that Iachino believed he only had to contend with one battleship and planned either to intercept the British force at the entrance to the Sicilian Narrows or to draw the heavy escort north-east, leaving the convoy vulnerable to light force attack in the Narrows after dark. At 1450, he launched two Swordfish to find and shadow the Italian force and, at 1530, exploiting the Royal Air Force reports of Iachino's position, detached *Prince of Wales*, *Rodney*, *Sheffield*, *Edinburgh*, and six destroyers, under Curteis, 'to close and drive off the enemy'. Simultaneously, he launched a strike force of twelve Swordfish, escorted by four Fulmars, from *Ark Royal*. These aircraft, and the earlier shadowers, were hampered by communication difficulties and both failed to find the Italian force, which was retreating northward at the time, putting them beyond the range of Swordfish radar. Somerville therefore recalled Curteis at 1700 when it was clear that Iachino could not reach the convoy before dark. Somerville later stressed that his measures were precautionary. He never felt that Iachino presented a serious threat, and his primary objective was the safe arrival of the convoy. Pursuit of Iachino was subordinate to this overriding goal.[25]

Ninety minutes later, soon after Curteis rejoined, the Halberd force reached the mouth of the Sicilian Narrows where it divided. Force A, comprising *Ark Royal*, the three battleships and half the destroyers, turned west back to Gibraltar, while Force X, under Rear Admiral Harold Burrough, comprising the five cruisers and the remaining nine destroyers, took the convoy on the last 250 miles to Malta. This avoided exposing the heavy ships to night attack in confined waters. The Force X cruisers positioned themselves ahead and astern of the merchant ships while the destroyers formed an outer circle for all-round protection. On the recommendation of Vice Admiral Malta, Burrough, with Somerville's approval, initially steered a northerly route via the Skerki Channel and nearer Sicily, judging that the enemy would expect him to take the shorter route along the coast of Tunisia. This route offered more sea room in the face of air or MTB attack and the convoy would be less silhouetted against the moon. The convoy was indeed heavily attacked after dark between 2000 and 2040 by small groups of torpedo aircraft which succeeded in hitting the merchant ship *Imperial Star*. After attempts to tow her failed, her personnel including 300 troops were evacuated and she was sunk by the destroyer *Oribi*. Although Italian aircraft continued searching for the convoy overnight, as did MTBs, there were no further attacks before it came under the protection of Malta-based fighters at dawn. The Italians were also distracted by an intense diversionary bombardment of Pantellaria by *Hermione*, although she failed to damage the airfield, her primary target. Halberd was over and proved the last Malta convoy of 1941.[26]

Halberd and Substance demonstrate tactics and capabilities perfected by the Royal Navy after two years of war for defending convoys under multiple forms of attack in contested waters. The two operations successfully passed twenty-five merchant ships between Gibraltar and Malta for one sunk and one damaged. The cost to the escort forces was one destroyer sunk and a battleship, cruiser and destroyer damaged. The Italians lost twenty-five aircraft and a submarine. Overall, this was a fine British achievement, securing Malta's defence and value as an attacking base for the rest of 1941. Somerville well deserved the award of a second knighthood, triggering Cunningham's famous signal – 'Fancy, twice a knight at your age'.

There were significant lessons, some transferable to the Arctic. Despite Somerville's late August criticisms, the intelligence picture of enemy strength and dispositions for Halberd, drawn from SIGINT and aerial reconnaissance, was generally excellent. It ensured the British allocated adequate escort forces and helped optimise the convoy route and timing. The staff work, not always a Royal Navy strength, for both Halberd and Substance was outstanding. Otherwise, the most important lesson from both operations was the critical contribution of a carrier. The Fulmar suffered in speed and manoeuvrability compared to the latest land-based fighters but proved competitive with the Italian CR.42. *Ark Royal*'s fighter group accounted for about half the Italian aircraft losses and disrupted many more attackers. Meanwhile *Ark Royal*'s Swordfish TSR squadrons posed a constant threat to Italian surface forces, significantly improved anti-submarine protection, and provided valuable reconnaissance options. *Ark Royal* offered Somerville capabilities that proved difficult to replicate in other British carriers for at least a year. She carried on average 40 per cent more aircraft than her *Illustrious* class successors. After a year with Force H, she had also reached a peak of combat efficiency in carrier operations spurred by the unique demands and opportunities of the western Mediterranean theatre. Despite her lack of radar, she had also established a benchmark for effective fighter direction at sea that would not be matched by the Royal Navy until Operation Pedestal the following August or reached by the US Navy before 1943.

The Royal Navy has been criticised for failing to develop and deploy a predictive tachymetric anti-aircraft fire-control system by 1939. By autumn 1941, it understood that its 'High-Altitude Control System' (HACS) could not deliver adequate controlled fire against either low-flying torpedo bombers or dive-bombers. However, Halberd demonstrates that, after two years of war, the Royal Navy compensated for HACS limitations through innovations in control and tactics and quantity of firepower which surpassed that in peer navies at this time. The most important tactical concept, evolved under Mediterranean air attacks through 1941, combined fire from destroyers in a circular screen of radius 6000 yards with a two-step barrage bursting at 4000 yards and 1500 yards from heavy ships of the main body. Battleship main armament could add to this barrage. The idea of exploiting radar ranges to predict the optimum barrage was raised in May 1940 during the Norwegian campaign and a practical system developed over the next year with an early version fitted in some Halberd ships including *Prince of Wales*. A precision ranging panel displaying 6000 yards and designated L.22 fed target range and range rate into a mechanical computer in an Auto Barrage Unit (ABU). This determined when to open fire to achieve the desired barrage range set on the shell fuzes when the target was predicted to pass through.[27]

Radar-assisted barrage fire proved highly effective against torpedo bombers which invariably approached low down to minimise their exposure to detection and had an optimum dropping point of 1000 yards. Indeed, aircraft were sometimes reluctant to penetrate the destroyer screen, preferring to drop their weapons outside. Those that did penetrate screen and barrages still faced mass fire from close-in weapons from individual ships. During Halberd, gunfire probably destroyed 15 per cent of the attacking force and damaged or disrupted many more.[28] Across 1941 as a whole, it is estimated that Italian S.79s attempted 260 attacks for fourteen aircraft lost and forty-six damaged.[29] By autumn 1941, the Royal Navy had taken a further measure to reinforce anti-aircraft firepower, especially for convoys. This was the commissioning of eight merchant ship conversions as auxiliary anti-aircraft ships. These ranged from 2000–5500 tons, had a minimum speed of 16 knots, were armed with six or eight 4in guns and multiple light weapons and equipped with the latest air-surveillance and fire-control radar. They were some of the most battleworthy conversions undertaken, offering almost the anti-aircraft firepower of a modern light cruiser. They would regularly operate in the Arctic.[30]

Halberd and Substance were important elements of a wider British effort through the summer and autumn of 1941 to establish Malta as a key operational base to contest control of the central Mediterranean. Air power was a vital component. Between April and November, 308

Hurricane IIs, eleven Albacores and two Swordfish were successfully delivered from carriers, primarily *Ark Royal*, in ten operations conducted from Gibraltar. Two-thirds of the Hurricanes were delivered by the end of June, the subsequent reduction caused by the requirement to supply Russia. Larger aircraft, the twin-engine Wellingtons, Blenheims, Beaufighters, and Marylands flew in direct from Gibraltar. By October, front-line Royal Air Force strength on the island averaged seventy-five Hurricanes, thirty each of Wellingtons and Blenheims for strike and reconnaissance, and ten Marylands for reconnaissance only.[31] There were also a dozen Fleet Air Arm torpedo bombers. Beaufighters supporting Substance and Halberd deployed temporarily for those operations. Malta's air strike capability, especially at night, was enhanced by fitting select aircraft with Air-Surface Vessel (ASV) radar. The Mark II version, deployed from early 1941, could detect a surfaced submarine at five miles and a medium-sized merchant vessel or warship at 15.[32] Initially only Swordfish and Albacores at Malta were ASV-fitted but Wellingtons equipped with longer-range sets able to detect ships at 40 miles arrived from September. These also carried a homing device called 'Rooster', enabling a Wellington conducting wide area reconnaissance to act as a beacon for a subsequent ASV-fitted strike force.[33] Meanwhile, in October, the strength of the 10th Submarine Flotilla at Malta reached ten boats, almost all the small 'U' class which proved well suited to Mediterranean waters.[34]

*Evolving Royal Navy Capability: Force K and the Destruction of the Beta Convoy*

The build-up of air and submarine forces, together with improved intelligence from the breaking of Hagelin and ASV aerial surveillance, enabled more effective attacks on Axis shipping between Italy and North Africa. Ultra targeting accounted for at least a third of shipping losses after mid-1941 and possibly 50 per cent on the Tunisian route.[35] Axis tonnage sunk rose nearly 20 per cent between the second and third quarters of 1941, and, in September alone, 28 per cent of cargo despatched was lost, hence the pressure from Hitler to transfer U-boats.[36] These results were not sufficient for the prime minister who saw substantial supplies still getting through (an average of 80 per cent of those shipped even in the third quarter) and too little naval effort to stop them. He therefore lobbied constantly through the summer for a surface strike force to be deployed to Malta. Pound resisted, partly because of demands elsewhere, including potentially in the Arctic, but he also doubted a small force of cruisers and destroyers could achieve much against the strength of escort the Italians could provide. They would also be vulnerable to air attack. These arguments were backed by Cunningham. Some of the prime minister's figures for Axis supplies were exaggerated and since submarines accounted for more than half the seventy-six Axis ships sunk in the second quarter, his criticism of the navy was overstated. Nevertheless, he ultimately wore Pound down and got his way. On 21 October, the light cruisers (6 x 6in guns) *Aurora* and *Penelope* and the new destroyers *Lance* and *Lively* arrived in Malta, designated as Force K. Pound still judged the risk/benefit equation adverse, and that submarines and aircraft were better suited to interdicting Axis shipping. His surrender reflected awareness that, if the forthcoming British 'Crusader' offensive in North Africa planned for mid-November failed, the navy would face lasting criticism for not attempting to cut Axis communications with surface forces.[37]

Despite its small size, Force K was well equipped for surface interdiction. All units carried torpedoes, the cruisers with six tubes and the destroyers eight. All were fitted with the latest radar, the cruisers had improved, more powerful, searchlights, and *Lance* had a trial version of shipborne High Frequency Direction Finding (HF/DF). The destroyers, uniquely for their class, carried eight 4in dual purpose guns, making them much better anti-aircraft platforms.[38] In contrast to Pound's low expectations, the Italians not only immediately detected Force K's arrival but judged it a 'considerable threat to our convoys and to the destroyers that are transporting troops'. Some convoys were immediately suspended, and the Force K ships targeted for air attack in Valletta while options for protecting the shipping routes were reviewed. Deploying a heavy escort of cruisers sufficient to combat Force K was initially judged unattractive because it would consume scarce fuel supplies and be vulnerable to night-time air attack at which the British were demonstrating proficiency. The initial Italian response was therefore to resort to smaller units, two transports and a single escort, which were less likely to be spotted. This tactic had mixed success. Most movements were identified by Ultra intercepts, enabling subsequent air attack with varying success, but initial sorties by Force K on 25 October and 1 November were frustrated.[39]

The reduction in Axis shipments in late October and the pressing need to build stocks for a planned attack on the British fortress of Tobruk caused the Italian Naval Staff to risk an unusually large convoy to Tripoli in the second week of November. The Beta convoy, as it was named, comprised five merchant vessels (including two German) and two tankers, carrying 400 vehicles, 30,000 tons of military supplies and 17,000 tons of fuel. Given its importance, and the known threat from Force K, it received a close escort of six destroyers and a distant escort of two heavy cruisers and a further four destroyers under Rear Admiral Bruno Brivonesi.

Two submarines provided further support. Daylight air cover was also arranged. The bulk of the ships left Naples early on 7 November and, once fully formed, the convoy passed through the Straits of Messina and was routed well to the east of Malta, beyond the estimated range of night torpedo attack and to pose what the Italians judged an almost impossible intercept challenge for Force K.

The Beta convoy, although not the distant escort, was spotted 40 miles south-east of Cape Spartivento by a Maryland returning to Malta from a patrol in the Ionian Sea in the early afternoon of 8 November. It provided an accurate position and course but underestimated the speed (11 knots as opposed to 8). Vice Admiral Malta, Wilbraham Ford, ordered Force K, under Captain William Agnew, in *Aurora*, to intercept and he sailed at 1730, expecting to hit Beta's estimated track around 0200 next morning. Contrary to most histories of the Beta operation, the Maryland sighting came by chance and was not triggered by Ultra intelligence. Nor did Ultra, or a patrolling ASV Wellington which suffered radar failure, deliver any other useful intelligence before Agnew found the convoy, by now as expected sailing south-south-east, at 0039 on 9 November. Indeed, the Italians were arguably better served. They not only spotted the initial Maryland, but their SIGINT intercepted its sighting report.

Agnew had carefully planned and rehearsed his tactics. His four simple rules were: maintain line ahead formation to avoid recognition problems and allow freedom for torpedo fire; disable escorts on the nearside of the convoy first; engage merchant ships systematically but be ready for rapid shift to any interfering escort; keep escorts on the bow until disabled. He instructed his ships to avoid illumination or star shell, and to fire steadily, stressing the importance of early and consistent hits. This preparation paid off handsomely. *Aurora* opened fire by radar at 0057 and then turned to parallel the convoy course. Within 15 minutes, the four Italian destroyers positioned ahead and astern and on the starboard wing of the convoy had been disabled, with *Fulmine* sunk and the leader *Maestrale* losing all ability to communicate. The British then commenced a ruthless and systematic destruction of the merchant ships by gunfire and torpedo as they executed a wide circle round the convoy before departing virtually on a reciprocal of their approach course. By 0200 it was all over. Force K headed west at 25 knots, having destroyed the entire convoy of seven ships and badly roughed up the close escort while suffering no damage in return, bar a few splinters to *Lively*. The Italians were taken by surprise, never adequately identified between own and enemy ships or indeed whether they primarily faced an air attack, and their response throughout was chaotic and ineffective. Brivonesi, initially positioned 8000 yards on the starboard quarter, never worked out what he was dealing with, and Italian misery was compounded when the submarine *Upholder* sank a second destroyer, *Libeccio*, next day. By contrast, Agnew, who was back in Malta by midday, had achieved a brilliant victory, perhaps the finest night action of the Second World War.[40]

The destruction of the Beta convoy deserves a place alongside Halberd as an important demonstration of Royal Navy capability in autumn 1941. It also established a benchmark for what a well-handled surface strike force from any navy might achieve against such a target even if powerfully escorted. Despite Pound's doubts about the wisdom of deploying Force K, this single engagement exerted a powerful psychological effect over both Italian and German leaderships and provoked some dissension between them. Nearly a month later, on 6 December, the German naval representative in Rome, Vice Admiral Eberhard Weichold, accused the Italian naval leadership of maintaining excessive caution in the face of the Force K threat and disregard of German advice. The Germans saw destruction of the cruisers as a priority.[41] The immediate result was the brief closure of Tripoli, severely disrupting supplies to Axis forces and their ability to meet the imminent British Crusader offensive. Overall, the surface threat now greatly complicated future supply operations since the only adequate counter was cruiser or battleship escort, expending scarce fuel supplies. Beta probably exerted wider strategic influence too, helping provoke further transfers of U-boats from the Atlantic, on which Ultra kept the Admiralty well informed, and the move of the German 2nd Air Fleet headquarters, under Field Marshal Albert Kesselring, along with one of his two air corps, from Russia to Italy from mid-November. The whole Mediterranean theatre now came under Kesselring's command. Fliegerkorps II, comprising about 200 bombers and 100 fighters, transferred from Russia to cover the central area, with the specific task of neutralising Malta, while the existing Fliegerkorps X covered the eastern Mediterranean.

The German rationale for these moves was defined in Führer Directive No 38 issued on 2 December.[42] The transfer of Fliegerkorps II reduced German air strength supporting Army Group Centre in the final drive on Moscow (Operation Typhoon) by at least one-third, thereby contributing significantly to the failure of this offensive.[43] By the end of December, there were 5.6 per cent more German combat aircraft deployed against Britain in the Western theatres than on the Eastern Front.[44] Nevertheless, the specific practical impact of Force K should not be overstated. Although Ultra ensured that the British maintained a devastating impact on Italian shipping over the last half of November, bringing cargo destroyed over the month to 62 per cent, only three of seventeen ships sunk in that fortnight were despatched by Force K. Furthermore, without Force K, the Beta group might well have sailed in smaller, more lightly-escorted units, and been picked off by submarine or air attack on either their outward or returning voyage, resulting in similar supply loss.[45]

The Germans had several opportunities to execute a Force K-style attack against British convoys in the Arctic theatre over the next two years, sometimes with a stronger force and against a weaker escort, yet never came close to matching the Beta success. Pound and other Royal Navy commanders clearly expected them to achieve more, and it is tempting to see Pound's attitudes and decisions in the Arctic, notably over PQ 17, as at least partly influenced by the Beta precedent. German inability to replicate Beta therefore requires explanation. As already noted, and contrary to long-standing belief, Force K's Beta victory did not reflect clear intelligence advantage. Interception was achieved based on an enemy position nearly 12 hours old and Agnew was unaware of the distant escort and its heavy ships. His two cruisers outmatched the close escort in gunpower, but the Italians had a numerical advantage. The British were helped by their radar but, in a confused engagement with multiple targets, it was not decisive. What gave Force K its critical edge with Beta and would be repeated by the Royal Navy in the Arctic, with the notable exception of PQ 17, was superior seamanship, tactical awareness, and leadership. These drew on long training, stretching back into the interwar period, including emphasis on night fighting, and the experience generated by sheer time at sea compared to its enemies.

However, perhaps more important, was the initiative, appetite for risk and willingness to accept responsibility which senior Royal Navy commanders instilled in their juniors through the 1930s and incorporated in the 'Fighting Instructions' issued at the end of that decade. The 1939 Fighting Instructions promulgated 'guiding principles' for all arms of the fleet in certain war operations and minor actions. The stress on 'guidance' was emphatic. The Instructions were not intended as 'orders'. The emphasis throughout was on officers exercising 'a strong offensive spirit', boldness and 'pressing the enemy' without remorse, while not being 'influenced by the possible damage their ships may receive'. Loss of ships to enemy action 'should be no deterrent' to carrying out an action. Initiative was essential since 'unforeseen circumstances' can 'always arise'. Commanders who found previous orders inapplicable 'must act as their judgement dictates'. Ships and aircraft were to maintain contact with the enemy in all but the direst circumstances and keep commanders informed of enemy strength and movements. Once in action it was better to give too much information than too little. The Instructions drew visibly on Nelson's famous precepts: 'no captain can do very wrong if he places his ship alongside that of the enemy' and 'engage the enemy more closely'. They represented a profound change in ethos from Jutland and foreshadowed the doctrine of 'mission command' embraced by the British military and others in the 1980s. Agnew acted entirely within their spirit during the Beta engagement.[46] The Fighting Instructions also directly influenced the framing of successive issues of 'Atlantic Convoy instructions' for escorts and escort commanders and their specific 'North Russian' section covering the Arctic convoys.[47]

## *Overall Royal Navy Strengths and Weaknesses in Autumn 1941*

Halberd and the Beta engagement illustrate how the Royal Navy could optimise fighting capabilities honed through two years of war to deliver outstanding results in a demanding context against a peer enemy. The other comparable peer navies, the US Navy and Imperial Japanese Navy (IJN), would have struggled to match the Halberd performance at this time and the former would soon discover it had much to learn about fighting a night engagement such as Beta. The remainder of this chapter now returns to the parallels raised earlier. How representative were these capabilities demonstrated in the Mediterranean and how far were they transferable to a new Arctic theatre? In doing so, it takes a wider look at Royal Navy strengths and weaknesses in the autumn of 1941.

### RESOURCES

The first issue is resources. Two years of attrition and multiple demands, including a potential new requirement to create an Eastern Fleet to counter Japan, as well as the Arctic commitment, had left the Royal Navy stretched. Pound had struggled to find ships for Force K. Producing simultaneously in a separate theatre in late September a second force of the scale and quality of the Halberd escort would have been difficult. In allocating resources, the Admiralty's main priority was the security of the United Kingdom home base and Atlantic communications. This then determined what forces could be deployed elsewhere. The German threat here at this time comprised three elements: a new attempt at invasion; the ongoing U-boat assault on transatlantic supplies; and raiding by her major surface units. By October, Britain was confident that Germany could not redeploy sufficient forces from Russia to mount an invasion before spring 1942 at the earliest, minimising the need to divert naval resources to home defence. The reduction in Atlantic shipping losses to U-boats, noted by Pound at Riviera, was also being sustained. Although

September was a poor month, losses in the second half of 1941 would be down 50 per cent on the first half, with a monthly average just one-third of that in the second quarter.

There were multiple reasons for this. Better intelligence, following the breaking of the German naval Enigma communications system, which was read nearly currently from the end of May, undoubtedly helped. So did the American assistance with convoy escort in the western Atlantic already discussed along with the parallel shift of U-boats to the Mediterranean. However, more, and better equipped, Royal Navy Atlantic escorts were critical too. In the two calendar years 1940–1, Britain and Canada completed 200 of these, primarily 'Flower' class corvettes. When various categories of destroyer escort and sloop, including ten 'Lake' class cutters transferred from the United States Coast Guard, are added, the overall Atlantic escort force under British control reached around 350 vessels by autumn 1941. With availability averaging about 80 per cent, this permitted an allocation of at least six escorts per convoy, and with steadily improving sensors and weapons. This pool of Atlantic escorts was now directed by Commander-in-Chief Western Approaches, Admiral Sir Percy Noble, based at Derby House in Liverpool. The creation of Western Approaches in February brought all anti-submarine naval and air escort together in one integrated command able to bring sound organisation and a clear strategy and doctrine to the Atlantic battle. Western Approaches would provide most of the anti-submarine vessels for the Arctic convoys.[48]

In autumn 1941, the German navy's potential surface raiders comprised: the battleship *Tirpitz*, still working up; the battlecruisers *Scharnhorst* and *Gneisenau*, both expected to be under repair at Brest until the end of the year; the pocket battleships *Lützow* and *Admiral Scheer*; and the heavy cruisers *Hipper* and *Prinz Eugen*. Of the last four, *Lützow* and *Prinz Eugen* were also known to be repairing action damage at Kiel and Brest respectively. Accepting that a significant part of this force would remain non-operational until 1942, the Admiralty judged that the minimum British force required in Atlantic waters comprised three fast, modern capital ships and two fleet carriers divided between Scapa Flow and Gibraltar with a further battleship and carrier in reserve. This requirement then determined the scale of force available to counter the five Italian capital ships, two *Littorio* and three *Cavour* class, currently operational in the Mediterranean.

Allowing for the contribution of the Gibraltar force to covering the western Mediterranean, the preferred minimum allocation to the Royal Navy Mediterranean Fleet at Alexandria was two modernised battleships and one, but preferably two, fleet carriers.[49] However, at the beginning of October, with the torpedoing of *Nelson*, three of eight modern or modernised capital ships, two of four modern fleet carriers, and one of two older fleet carriers, were under repair or in refit and unavailable before early 1942. A new battleship (*Duke of York*) and new carrier (*Indomitable*) would commission shortly but neither would be operational for some months.[50] Two further battleships (*Anson* and *Howe*) were within a year of completion but work on the last two *Illustrious* class carriers (*Indefatigable* and *Implacable*) was currently suspended so they would not complete before late 1943 at the earliest. The cruiser position was also tight. Of thirty-seven modern cruisers completed between 1928–39, only three had been lost to date. Ten more had commissioned since the start of the war, of which two had been lost, and a further eight were within a year of completion. Although this implied a current net gain of five vessels, action damage and wear and tear, especially severe in the Mediterranean during the first eight months of 1941, had reduced numbers serviceable from thirty-four at the outbreak of war to twenty-eight two years later. When pre-1925 ships were added, overall cruiser strength of fifty-eight remained well short of the target of seventy which the Admiralty judged the minimum to meet combined fleet and trade defence requirements.[51]

The most acute shortage was modern fleet destroyers, those completed from 1930 onward. Forty-four of these had been lost by October 1941 against twenty-seven completed since the outbreak of war.[52] This deficit partly reflected the temporary suspension in May 1940 of work on ten destroyers in build to free resources for construction of Atlantic escorts and merchant shipping but also attrition in the Mediterranean with eleven sunk there in the first eight months of 1941. In November that year, after taking account of the navy's new requirements in the Arctic and Far East, the Naval Staff estimated that 105 were required, of which only sixty-nine were in service with another twenty in refit. Although thirty new destroyers were expected to complete in 1942, projected losses suggested a net increase of only six.[53] Through the remainder of 1941 and then 1942, the deficit in fleet destroyers, not least for Arctic commitments, was made up by drawing on escort destroyers. These, as the name implied, were optimised for convoy escort and, in October 1941, they numbered about 135, falling into three categories. There were around thirty-five each of the new 'Hunt' class completed over the last 18 months and the old American destroyers acquired under the 1940 'destroyers for bases' agreement. The remaining sixty-five were older Royal Navy destroyers, mainly of the 'V and W' classes, completed at the end of the First World War, although modernised to varying degrees including the fitting of Anti-submarine detection sets (Asdic) later known as sonar. These would be joined by a further thirty-nine 'Hunts' in 1942. Although there were fleet tasks for which the better escort destroyers proved perfectly adequate, in general, their speed, sensors and armament did not match their fleet counterparts.

Royal Navy submarines would play a significant role in the Arctic theatre. At the start of the war, there were fifty-seven in commission, of which forty-six comprised front-line boats completed since 1927. The remainder dated from the First World War, were mainly small, and confined to training. There were only twelve building although a further nineteen were immediately ordered. By September 1941, twenty-four of the original front-line boats, just over half of the starting force, had been lost. These had been compensated by the commissioning of fifteen new 1090-ton 'T' class patrol submarines and fifteen smaller 545-ton 'U' class completed since the outbreak of war. The latter were initially envisaged as unarmed training boats but were redesigned with four torpedo tubes and proved well suited to the Mediterranean theatre. Of these thirty new boats, two 'Ts' and five 'Us' had been sunk, bringing total losses over two years of war to thirty-one, divided almost equally between those operating from the United Kingdom and those in the Mediterranean. Despite the high attrition, the building rate over the first two years of war was therefore just sufficient to maintain the initial front-line strength and the new boats brought a quality improvement. Allowing for refits, this meant that, through 1941, around twenty boats were based in home ports and the same number in the Mediterranean. A further ninety boats were on order or building in September 1941 (including thirty-six 715-ton 'S' class, a design resumed in mid-1940 after a four-year break) of which forty-two would complete by the end of 1942. This promised significant growth in the front line over that period.

The submarine loss rate during these first two years was greatest in the Mediterranean during the second half of 1940 following Italy's entry into the war. Nine Royal Navy submarines and two allied boats were sunk in this period for the rather meagre return of one Italian submarine and fifteen Italian merchant ships, amounting to 55,776 tons, although submarine minelaying added a further six ships of 23,600 tons. This costly and ineffective start to Mediterranean submarine operations provoked contemporary concern and questioning since Italian anti-submarine capability was judged poor. A favoured explanation was the unsuitability for Mediterranean conditions of the large and older 'O', 'P' and 'R' class submarines transferred from the China station which comprised the bulk of the losses. These were certainly too noisy and prone to oil leaks.[54]

Although other specific explanations have been advanced for these Mediterranean losses, including Italian reading of low-level British ciphers, those in home waters were only slightly less and the primary causes, mines and attacking patrol vessels in inshore waters, were little different in the two theatres. Furthermore, the German losses from a U-boat force, numerically almost identical in strength for the first 16 months of the war, were 30 per cent greater. A credible explanation for the common high loss rate in this period is that both sides were predominantly focusing their submarines in confined, shallow coastal waters where they were more vulnerable to detection and attack.

In contrast, 1941 was the most successful year for Royal Navy submarines in their tonnage war. An average strength of twenty Mediterranean boats, evenly divided between Malta and Alexandria, sank 140 Axis merchant and supply ships comprising 350,740 tons with a further 56,000 tons in home and Atlantic waters.[55] The Mediterranean flotillas also sank an Italian light cruiser and four submarines. This Mediterranean success reflected the value of Hagelin targeting in the second half of the year as already noted but also the deployment of more modern boats. Although the loss rate here reduced, it was still high with eleven boats sunk across the year. Comparing this success with the German record is again instructive. Over the year, the Germans deployed an average of three times the Royal Navy Mediterranean force in all theatres. The U-boat force suffered proportionately similar losses (thirty-five boats) but productivity was twice as high with 2.2 million tons of Allied shipping sunk. There is a case that superior overall submarine design, better fire control and torpedoes were factors but the major determinant was that the Germans were operating in a far richer target environment.

### Maritime Air Power

Resources for effective prosecution of a naval war were not confined to ships. Two years of war had emphasised to the Royal Navy the importance of air power whether delivered from carriers at sea or from land where the Royal Air Force had primary responsibility. The Admiralty only reacquired full control of its own air arm, soon designated the Fleet Air Arm, on 24 May 1939, when it assumed full responsibility from the Air Ministry for the procurement, administration and operation of all shipborne aircraft and personnel. Rebuilding the necessary policy, technical and logistic expertise successfully to implement this change would have been challenging in peacetime but was infinitely greater under the operational, deployment and expansion demands of war. In September 1939, the new Fleet Air Arm had only twelve strike and four fighter squadrons with 176 front-line aircraft supporting five fleet carriers and two light carriers. There were a further 433 aircraft in reserve and for training, four United Kingdom air stations transferred from the Royal Air Force and an overall personnel strength of 5300. Two years later front-line strength had almost doubled to 327 aircraft, deployed now in fourteen fighter and twenty-four strike squadrons to equip a potential force of five new and two old fleet carriers, two light carriers and a prototype merchant conversion escort carrier. There were now twelve air stations in the United Kingdom to provide initial and continuation flying and weapons training and to support disembarked squadrons. There was also a developing network of stations overseas, albeit so far of variable quality and some shared with the Royal Air Force. Aircraft stocks in reserve and for training were a healthy 1200.

The Fleet Air Arm had therefore made significant progress on the journey that would take it to eighty-one assorted carriers, seventy-one bases, 4024 planes and 84,000 personnel by August 1945.[56] Meanwhile, with the arrival of *Indomitable* in October, the Royal Navy briefly had five modern purpose-built fleet carriers in commission, all completed since mid-1938. The US Navy did not reach this number until mid-1943 and the IJN never achieved it. In theory, therefore, the Fleet Air Arm seemed well-placed this autumn to build on the important operational successes over the last 12 months, notably the night attack on the Italian fleet at Taranto, its contribution to Matapan, the crippling of the German battleship *Bismarck* and its valuable role in defensive operations such as Halberd. It had also proved an innovator, far ahead of competitors in the exploitation of ship and airborne radar for defence and offence and in night operations.

Nevertheless, at this time, the Fleet Air Arm also laboured under three major challenges that constrained its effectiveness until well into 1943. The most important was the obsolescence of its primary fighter and strike aircraft. The two-man Fulmar fighter lacked the performance to compete with the latest single-seat aircraft, whether land or carrier based, and even when dealing with bombers its speed and manoeuvrability advantages were limited. Robustness, four-hour endurance, ammunition capacity twice that of a Hurricane, reliability and crew skill partially compensated for these limitations, and radar-assisted fighter direction greatly improved its interception capability against bombers. These factors counted especially in the Mediterranean in 1940–1 where, remarkably, even in air to air combat against single seaters it achieved a five to three kill to loss ratio in its favour. Furthermore, although the figures are flattered by the quality of its opposition in the early period of the war, the Fulmar achieved more kills than any other Fleet Air Arm fighter, 122 for 40 losses.[57] The Swordfish and its derivative, the Albacore, were painfully slow for their primary torpedo strike role, making them highly vulnerable to modern fighters and gun defences and setting severe constraints in attacking fast-moving ships in adverse wind conditions. Low speed and structural limitations meant they were not credible as bombers against either land or warship targets, although they did prove effective anti-submarine aircraft. Exploitation of radar, good communications, carefully-chosen tactics, and flying skill could and did partly compensate for these aircraft limitations as was demonstrated in the final attack on *Bismarck*. The Swordfish/Albacore rank more competitively with contemporary peer strike aircraft when judged as an overall weapon system, taking account of their ASV II radar and an excellent torpedo. They were also uniquely capable of operating at night or in bad weather. Despite these various compensating factors, the limitations of Fleet Air Arm aircraft in the first half of the war have been aptly described as 'the first shock to the operational capability exercised by the Royal Navy'.[58]

There were multiple reasons for the failure to develop and introduce timely British successor aircraft. Of the three aircraft taken forward in 1940 (Firebrand interceptor, Firefly escort fighter and Barracuda strike aircraft) none reached service before 1943 and only the Firefly eventually proved operationally effective albeit not in its original role. The Naval Staff were too slow to recognise that the evolving air threat in the late 1930s demanded a carrier-based fighter fully competitive against the latest land-based types, including single-seat fighters. Without such an aircraft, defence of the fleet within range of enemy airfields would be inadequate and daylight strike operations within enemy air cover costly or impossible. By January 1940, the Naval Staff fully recognised the need for improved fighter performance but remained unwilling to dispense with an observer and therefore aimed to meet the requirement with a new two-seater aircraft.[59] The Norwegian campaign underlined the scale of the new air threat but also illuminated how new technology, namely radar fighter direction, lightweight VHF communications and radio homing made a high-performance single-seat fighter more viable. Unfortunately, the staff still struggled to reconcile the requirements of intercept and escort fighter, eventually concluding two aircraft were needed. This led to confused specifications to British suppliers, repeated design changes and therefore delay. The Fleet Air Arm also depended on the new Ministry of Aircraft Production (MAP) to allocate necessary resources, and during the initial war years, the Admiralty proved poor at protecting its interests and ensuring adequate industrial capacity. MAP prioritisation in May

1940 on five core aircraft, none of them naval, was especially detrimental and fatally compromised the Barracuda. Meanwhile over-dependence on a small number of naval suppliers meant production of existing types delayed development work.

The ultimate solution to Fleet Air Arm needs lay in American designs and production. As early as July 1940, the Grumman F4-F Wildcat, which the British designated the Martlet, was selected as an interim interceptor fighter pending development of a British aircraft. The British ordered over 500 Martlets in successive tranches over the 16 months to October 1941, easily enough to have equipped the Fleet Air Arm fighter front line by that autumn with ample reserves in the pipeline. By then, it was clear it was an excellent fighter, it had been adopted by the US Navy on British recommendation, and it would remain their primary fighter throughout 1942. Unfortunately, by the end of 1941, partly due to competing US Navy requirements and partly to wider prioritisation issues in the American aircraft industry, Grumman had delivered to the Fleet Air Arm less than half the numbers contracted and paid for. Crucially also, none had the folding wings which Grumman had promised to incorporate and were essential to British operation. To fill the gap, the Fleet Air Arm had to acquire modified Hurricanes and later Spitfires, both of which had limitations in operating from carriers.[60]

The second problem was carrier design. In conceiving its six *Illustrious* class fleet carriers in the mid-1930s, the Admiralty made a deliberate decision to prioritise protection over aircraft capacity and incorporated an armoured deck for the price of a reduced aircraft complement of thirty-six. This reflected the judgement, made prior to the arrival of radar, that there would invariably be insufficient warning time to position fighters to meet an air attack. Defence of capital units (battleships and carriers) must therefore rest primarily on armour and anti-aircraft gunpower. The trade-off between armour and aircraft capacity is a complex issue raising much historical debate.[61] There is an argument that armour proved less important to survival in wartime than other design factors such as isolation of hangars from hull spaces, although it demonstrated its value against kamikaze attack in the Pacific in 1945. Meanwhile war experience soon demonstrated that gunpower alone was quite insufficient against the intensity of air attacks suffered in Norway and the Mediterranean. The aircraft capacity cost was reduced as the war progressed by the introduction of outriggers and deck parking, and in the final three carriers by giving them additional hangar space. Nevertheless, it was almost a year, in August 1942, before another fleet carrier, *Indomitable*, undertaking another Malta convoy, Operation Pedestal, matched *Ark Royal*'s aircraft complement during Halberd. Otherwise, the four *Illustrious* class carriers completed by October 1941 rarely carried more than forty aircraft before 1943, two-thirds of *Ark Royal*'s Halberd strength. When added to the aircraft limitations described above, this severely constrained the power they could project in defence and attack. This was a factor in the Arctic theatre until 1943.[62]

In planning its new carrier fleet in 1936, the Naval Staff recognised that carriers were required for trade defence as well as fleet operations. However, resource limitations meant new construction concentrated on the large armoured carriers for fleet work. As these completed, they would release older carriers for trade defence. By late 1940, war losses combined with delays in the construction programme meant older carriers were now rarely available. Meanwhile the air threat, notably that posed by the German air force wing of Fw 200 Condor bombers operating from Bordeaux, was becoming significant. This wing sank 118 ships totalling 345,000 tons over the 12 months July 1940 to June 1941 as well as providing useful targeting support to U-boats.[63] One solution was conversion of suitable merchant ships of around 10,000 tons as 'escort carriers' to operate half a dozen fighter aircraft.[64] The prototype for the concept was an ex-German prize *Hannover*, formerly a refrigerated cargo ship. In the interests of speed, her conversion begun in January 1941 was rudimentary, razing her superstructure to provide a wooden flight deck from which six deck-parked aircraft could operate. Minimal defensive armament was provided and few other refinements apart from the latest single mast Type 279 air-warning radar, essential for effective interception. She was commissioned on 17 June as *Empire Audacity*, shortened the following month to *Audacity*.[65]

Well before *Audacity* commissioned, the Admiralty had decided on a substantial programme of escort carriers to be delivered with American assistance under Lend-Lease. The Americans were so enthused by the concept that they rushed ahead with a conversion of their own, *Long Island*, commissioned into the US Navy two weeks before *Audacity* on 2 June. By the middle of the year, the Admiralty had ordered nine additional escort carriers from the United States, all merchant conversions building on experience with *Audacity* and *Long Island*. Five further British conversions were also planned although four of these were much delayed due to problems acquiring suitable merchant ships. The first of the American carriers, *Archer*, arrived in Britain in November although machinery problems delayed her entry into service. Four others were completed to a similar design of which three were transferred to the Royal Navy by mid-1942. The *Archer*s, averaging 12,000 tons, were larger than

*Audacity* and a more elaborate conversion, with a longer flight deck fitted with a catapult, small island and importantly a hangar, allowing potentially fifteen aircraft to be carried. Once in Britain, they were given the latest radar, Types 279B air warning and 272 surface warning, and fitted with HF/DF. By the end of 1942, the Royal Navy had received eight escort carriers from the United States, with four of an improved *Tracker* class joining the four *Archer*s, and *Activity* converted in Britain. It received thirty more in 1943 and by the end of the war had operated a total of forty-five, of which only six, including *Audacity*, were British-built. More than half of the total were built as carriers from the keel up as opposed to conversions but had a C3 merchant hull form.[66]

Throughout her short life, spent primarily escorting Gibraltar convoys before she was sunk by *U-751* on 21 December, *Audacity* operated with six Martlets, reflecting the air defence role envisaged for her the previous November. Exploiting her radar, the Martlets were highly effective against the Condors, destroying five over the three months from 20 September and in Dönitz's rueful words providing a 'continuous air umbrella'. These losses represented almost 20 per cent of Condor operational strength over the year and 10 per cent of 1941 production. The Martlets were also good at spotting surfaced U-boats, engaging several with their gun armament, and assisted in the sinking of *U-131*.[67]

Through 1941, Naval Staff views on the role of escort carriers were evolving even before *Audacity* deployed. By early autumn, the ambition to attach an escort carrier to every important convoy was taking root and their task was to be more anti-submarine search and strike than anti-air. Four hundred additional Swordfish were accordingly ordered to equip the fourteen further carriers now on order. Nevertheless, no doubt reflecting experience with *Audacity*, there was evidently reluctance to dispense with a fighter role. On 30 November, Naval Air Division recommended that the nine American-built escort carriers, starting with *Archer*, should have a complement of nine Swordfish and six fighters, while the six British built carriers (including *Audacity*) would have six Swordfish only. The British carriers were so delayed that only *Activity* briefly operated with this complement before, like the others, receiving a combined strike/fighter group.[68] These aircraft allocations were approved in principle but, given the present difficulties with fighter procurement, the War Cabinet decreed that fighters for fleet carriers must take priority.[69] The entry of Japan into the war a week later and the demonstrable power of her naval air arm further underlined the need for and wider potential of escort carriers.[70] By early February 1942, the Fifth Sea Lord, Rear Admiral Lumley Lyster, in charge of the Fleet Air Arm, stated that, given the new commitments facing the Royal Navy especially in the East, more carriers able to operate with the fleet must be built as quickly as possible and need not be armoured. The navy could not afford a 'long term' build policy taking four years to reach fruition. The escort carrier or 'Woolworth carrier' could be most easily and quickly provided and Lyster now favoured their construction taking precedence over both armoured carriers and capital ships.[71]

Originally conceived by the Royal Navy to solve a specific problem, the potential role and capability of the escort carrier had therefore evolved greatly across 1941 and would continue to do so. By late 1943, these carriers were not only transforming convoy defence but had proved they could be an important multiplier to fleet air defence and strike operations. By then they could comfortably handle a mixed group of the latest (invariably American) fighter and strike aircraft and, exploiting a state-of-the-art British sensor fit, generate over a third of the fighting power of the fleet carriers. They count as one of the greatest innovations of the maritime war. The initial concept was British but American resources made its realisation possible. Without its escort carriers, and unable to complete the last two *Illustrious* class carriers until 1944 due to other priorities, the Royal Navy would have struggled to meet the demands facing it across multiple theatres. As will become evident, escort carriers played a critical role in the Arctic.

The third challenge facing the Fleet Air Arm in autumn 1941 was creating and growing the logistics necessary to support a front line that would soon be operating on a global basis. The dual control system under which the Royal Navy and Royal Air Force together managed the shipborne air force in the interwar period is traditionally judged responsible for two major failings: the poor quality of naval aircraft in 1939; and a lack of senior naval leaders with the skill and understanding to deploy air power at sea effectively. While there is some truth to these claims, both require important qualification. What is invariably overlooked in this debate is that aircraft maintenance in the interwar period was run entirely by the Royal Air Force. When the full transfer of the shipborne air force to the Royal Navy was agreed under the Inskip award in July 1937, there were few naval air engineers and no naval maintenance ratings at all. It was soon estimated that 8000 of the latter would be required to support a then projected front line of 450 aircraft in 1942. Clearly this required the creation of a demanding recruitment and training programme from scratch but, in the short term, the Fleet Air Arm was only viable with a substantial transfer of Royal Air Force personnel. One hundred and fifty officers and 2000 airmen were accordingly moved across, some voluntarily and some on loan. Furthermore, initial training of new naval recruits had to be undertaken by the Royal Air Force. Inevitably this complex transition process and the need rapidly to train a mass of new entrants meant an initial dilution of maintenance skills and to an extent of standards, although little criticism should apply to the Royal Air Force who were generally unstinting in their support. By autumn 1941, the new Fleet Air Arm had made significant progress on its journey to independence, but the relentless demands of wartime expansion meant many challenges were far from resolved. Importantly, and rarely acknowledged, the Fleet Air Arm was still heavily dependent on Royal Air Force support. Even in mid-1943, 12 per cent of maintenance staff were still on loan and much specialised training was still done by the Royal Air Force too.[72]

As explained above, the 1937 Inskip agreement which recommended the transfer of all shipborne aircraft to the Royal Navy also confirmed that land-based aircraft for naval tasks would remain under the control of and be provided by Royal Air Force Coastal Command or its relevant theatre commands overseas. The projection of British maritime air power did not therefore rest solely with the Royal Navy. Coastal Command began the war in a parlous state, some 20 per cent below its authorised strength with seventeen squadrons. Fifteen of these were tasked with maritime reconnaissance but only three were equipped with modern and effective aircraft, namely the Sunderland flying boat and American Lockheed Hudson. The rest had to make do with the totally inadequate Avro Anson with its limited armament and insufficient range even to patrol the width of the North Sea. The final two squadrons were dedicated to surface strike using obsolete Vildebeest biplane torpedo bombers inferior to the Swordfish. The condition of maritime reconnaissance and strike overseas was worse, with hardly any capability in the Mediterranean and two Vildebeest squadrons and a handful of other aircraft in the Far East. Coastal Command's deficiencies primarily reflected the greater emphasis the Air Ministry accorded to Fighter and Bomber Commands pre-war and like the Fleet Air Arm it suffered from the initial MAP prioritisation in May 1940. The following November, the First Lord, A V Alexander, described it as still the 'Cinderella of the RAF' and highlighted its continuing shortages in meeting the growing U-boat threat.[73]

Two years into the war the land-based component of maritime air power remained stretched and under-resourced but much improved. At home, the primary role of Coastal Command was now trade defence conducted under Admiralty operational control and as already noted, in close collaboration with Western Approaches command. There were more and better aircraft for convoy support and long-range reconnaissance, with Wellington bombers, additional Hudsons and American Catalina flying boats replacing most of the Ansons. Their effectiveness in countering U-boats in the North-west approaches was increased with the establishment of new bases in Northern Ireland, the Hebrides and Iceland, and with the fitting of ASV radar from late 1940. Over the year from autumn 1940, tactical inexperience, including with ASV, and the lack of a decent anti-submarine weapon prevented U-boat kills but increasing air cover kept U-boats dived in daylight, thereby reducing attack opportunities and productivity. The shift in U-boat operating areas to the mid-Atlantic from spring 1941 owed much to the increasing impact of Coastal Command cover.[74]

Surface strike capability had also improved if too slowly to meet growing commitments. In the United Kingdom, by 1941 the Vildebeests had been replaced by a new twin-engine torpedo bomber, the Beaufort, which had a performance comparable to the latest Japanese and Italian aircraft, although its range was less than the IJN Type 1. During 1941, Beauforts had significant operational successes. A torpedo attack on 6 April crippled the battlecruiser *Gneisenau* alongside in Brest, and a night operation on 13 June seriously damaged the pocket battleship *Lützow*. The latter attack off the Norwegian port of Egersund took place at a range of about 400 miles, only slightly less than the IJN strike on Force Z the following December. Unfortunately, the Beauforts suffered engine-reliability problems resulting in production delays in both the United Kingdom and Australia and there were only four squadrons available at the end of the 1941. The subsequent need to transfer most of this small force to the eastern Mediterranean and Indian Ocean meant there were no Beauforts available for the Arctic theatre the following year.

The shortage of Beauforts, the growth of the Fleet Air Arm Swordfish/Albacore force through 1941, and the availability of naval fighter and torpedo strike squadrons when carriers were damaged or in refit, meant that despite Inskip's division of responsibility, the Fleet Air Arm did often conduct operations from land bases during this period. Some units in the United Kingdom were formally attached to Coastal Command, usually in an anti-submarine role, while in the Mediterranean they remained under naval command but operated in close coordination with Royal Air Force units, often sharing their facilities. Operations were conducted from Port Sudan against Italian destroyers in the Red Sea, sinking two, from Egypt against land targets in the Western Desert, and from bases in Cyprus against Vichy French forces during the Syrian campaign.[75] 830 Squadron operated about a dozen Swordfish from Malta throughout the year, primarily conducting night attacks on Italian shipping which were increasingly effective after the aircraft were fitted with ASV II radar in June. Overall, it destroyed thirteen ships totalling 68,000 tons. 828 Squadron equipped with Albacores joined this Malta force in October.[76] The combined Royal Air Force and Fleet Air Arm maritime strike effort from Mediterranean land bases sank seventy ships comprising 150,000 tons in the theatre during 1941.[77]

An important development in Coastal Command that would exert influence on the Royal Navy was the appointment of Professor Patrick Blackett as Scientific Advisor with a specific brief to examine the exploitation of new technology, especially ASV radar, with which half the Command's aircraft were now fitted. However, it was only locating U-boats prior to visual contact in about 25 per cent of cases and not therefore delivering the anticipated additional U-boat kills. Blackett was a pioneer of operational research, the application of evidence-based analysis of past operations to improve the weapons and tactics in future operations, which he had applied successfully at Fighter Command. Blackett's team advised weaning crews off visual search since a U-boat invariably spotted the aircraft first. Instead, they should exploit cloud cover and use ASV search to catch U-boats by surprise, a tactic it was later calculated increased chances of a successful attack by a factor of five.[78] Blackett's work at Coastal Command encouraged the Admiralty to appoint him their chief adviser on operational research from January 1942, leading a small team reporting directly to the Vice Chief of the Naval Staff, Vice Admiral Henry Moore. Over the next two years, he produced one hundred papers for the Admiralty, of which 60 per cent addressed the anti-U-boat campaign. These were hugely valuable in identifying falling U-boat productivity, underlining the importance of ship-borne HF/DF and air support, both shore-based and from escort carriers, and in optimising convoy escort size and composition. Much of this work proved relevant to the Arctic theatre.[79]

*Transformational capabilities*

By autumn 1941, the Royal Navy was benefitting from two capabilities which were transforming its performance and a third was imminent. All three would have a major impact on operations in the Arctic theatre. The most important was radar whose contribution had been amply demonstrated during Halberd and the destruction of the Beta convoy. The development of naval radar, under the Signal School, was not initially prioritised over communications work and therefore moved slowly compared to the Royal Air Force. Nevertheless, a surge of effort in the 18 months before the outbreak of war produced an effective air-warning set, designated Type 79, which in trials and exercises rapidly demonstrated ability to detect high-flying aircraft at over 60 miles. To the designers' surprise, it also had some surface detection capability. Although this was somewhat erratic, it proved good enough to enable the cruiser *Sheffield* to shadow *Bismarck* on 26 May 1941. By September 1939, Type 79 was fitted in the battleship *Rodney* and the cruisers *Sheffield*, *Suffolk* and *Curlew* with four more ships due to receive it by the end of the year and a steady programme planned thereafter. At this point the Naval Staff saw its primary purpose as providing early warning for anti-aircraft gun crews and hence priority for fitting it was given to anti-aircraft cruisers. There was no immediate intent to fit it to carriers or create a radar-driven fighter direction system on the Royal Air Force model although airborne radar in naval aircraft was seen as desirable.[80] Meanwhile, the first radar-assisted wartime skirmish occurred on 26 September when *Rodney* detected three successive raids on units of the Home Fleet at about 80 miles. Although she tracked the attackers successfully, informing the Commander-in-Chief by flag signal, no fighters were flown off from the accompanying *Ark Royal* and *Rodney* felt her reports were not taken seriously.[81]

Two years later the situation had been transformed. All new-build ships down to corvette size were automatically fitted with radar and retrofitting to existing ships had the highest priority. By the end of September 1941, thirteen of sixteen capital ships (including *Duke of York* nearing completion), the four *Illustrious* class carriers (including *Indomitable*), *Audacity* and thirty-three cruisers had air-warning radar, either Type 279 (an upgraded Type 79) or the more advanced Type 281. Two capital ships and fourteen cruisers, primarily those newly completed, had surface or combined air-surface warning radar. Half the battleship force and sixteen cruisers also had Type 284 gunnery radar for their main armament and a growing number were fitted with Type 285 for their high-angle secondary armament. Gunnery radar could be used for search or shadowing as well as fire control, a facility demonstrated to great effect by the cruiser *Suffolk* which used her Type 284 to shadow *Bismarck* for 36 hours on 23–25 May. It was ironic that the German Fleet commander, Vice Admiral Günther Lütjens, was hugely impressed with *Suffolk*'s radar capability when it was operating outside its designed role and ships were already receiving the dedicated and superior centimetric Type 271 surface-warning set. Meanwhile, all destroyers, most sloops and twenty corvettes had the first mass-produced surface-warning radar, Type 286M, which was based on the aircraft-mounted ASV II. This was bulky, operated at 1.5m and had a heavy fixed aerial requiring the ship to be pointed at a target to get a solid return with obvious limitations operationally. Nevertheless, as it rolled out to more ships, it made U-boat night surface attacks riskier and it was responsible for the destroyer *Vanoc* sinking *U-100* commanded by the ace skipper Joachim Schepke on 17 March. Airborne ASV was common to both the Royal Air Force and Fleet Air Arm and its development was driven by the former. The initial version, which began trials as early as 1937, was insufficiently robust and production of the very effective Mark II slow to get underway. It did not therefore reach front-line naval aircraft until spring 1941 and it was first used in anger during the *Bismarck* operation.[82]

The scale of this radar programme implemented in two years with its vast potential to transform fighting effectiveness was a hugely impressive achievement. It not only owed much to the vision and drive of Somerville but also the naval scientific staff and, through 1941, a further revolution in its capability was underway, the introduction of centimetric radar. The Admiralty understood the importance of centimetric wavelengths from late 1938. The shorter the wavelength, the smaller and lighter the aerial needed to produce the narrow concentrated beam required for high definition surface echoes clear of sea clutter. It would make radar more viable for fitting in smaller vessels and was essential for an effective airborne radar. It was also more difficult for an enemy to detect and direction find (DF). Despite these theoretical advantages, centimetric radar was not judged technically feasible when war began. A triple breakthrough in early 1940 made it possible: development of the cavity magnetron, the reflex klystron valve and the crystal mixer. The first facilitated a radar transmitter and the second two a receiver, capable of operating at 10cm or less. By October, the Air Ministry research station at Swanage had an experimental 10cm system designed to provide an intercept set for night fighters. The results were shared with the Naval Staff who immediately recognised its potential in detecting surfaced U-boats or potentially periscopes. The following month the Royal Navy Signal School duplicated the technology for trial on ship targets and in early 1941 a trial system was at sea in a Western Approaches corvette. By the end of September 1941, the operational system, designated Type 271, now providing an all-round view as well as excellent discrimination, was at sea in twenty-three 'Flower' class corvettes, a sloop and two ex-American destroyers. That month the Director of Anti-Submarine Warfare, Captain George Creasey, stated that Type 271 rendered the Type 286M, with which most Atlantic escorts were still fitted, completely obsolete. Noting that current positive trends in the Atlantic battle might not continue, it was vital to install it as soon as possible. Meanwhile, a big-ship variant, Type 273, was also developed and first fitted in *Prince of Wales*, as already noted in time for Halberd. To the delight of Admiral Sir John Tovey, Commander-in-Chief Home Fleet, during pre-deployment exercises, she detected the battlecruiser *Repulse* and cruiser *Euryalus* at just under 20 miles range. Tovey noted that, apart from its range advantage, it was much easier to use than the Type 284 gunnery radar and he wanted it immediately installed across the fleet.[83]

The scale and speed with which radar was introduced over the two years to autumn 1941 posed extraordinary operational and personnel challenges which are rarely acknowledged. Since radar barely existed within the Royal Navy in September 1939, there was no dedicated radar branch and no organisation for training or maintenance. In the early months of the war, force commanders and captains of those ships fitted had to work out how to exploit it through intuition and experience. Exploitation was also complicated by initial caution over its use through fear that it would disclose the ship's whereabouts to the enemy. In a March 1939 exercise, the battleship *Rodney* had detected *Sheffield*'s Type 79 transmissions 100 miles away. This led to over emphasis on 'radar silence' and it took time to reach a sensible balance on benefit versus risk. The radar-informed fighter direction system deployed by *Ark Royal* in Force H and during Halberd had its origin in the Norwegian campaign and was developed through the initiative of a specialist Fleet Air Arm observer, Lieutenant Commander Charles Coke. Coke, then *Ark Royal*'s Air Signal Officer, began plotting radar reports from *Sheffield* and *Curlew* on a plotting board normally used by observers in the air. Initially he passed estimates of enemy position, course and speed to *Ark Royal*'s fighters, leaving them to plan an interception. He then realised he could monitor fighter movements too through the cruisers' radar and take the momentous step of directing them himself. Naval fighter direction was born and Coke subsequently founded the Royal Navy's Fighter Direction School at Yeovilton the following year. Meanwhile, from August 1940, *Illustrious*, with her own radar fitted, developed Coke's techniques further when she deployed to the eastern Mediterranean, using a more sophisticated plot. Although, through 1940, experience with radar was circulated formally within and between fleets in reports and despatches and informally through personal networking, sharing of knowledge was far from perfect. As late as February 1941, when Captain Robert Ellis took command of the cruiser *Suffolk*, three months before his brilliant radar shadowing of *Bismarck*, and found her newly fitted with the new 50cm Type 284 gunnery radar, he stated that 'not a soul could tell me a thing about its possible tactical applications. I had to figure that one out for myself, from such basic knowledge as I had, or could add to experimentally at sea.'[84]

Initially, radar operators were either junior ratings of the Telegraphist branch or bright young seamen chosen at random. Sets were maintained by Telegraphist senior rates. However, in September 1940, a new specialist radar branch was created for operators and a 'radio mechanic' branch for maintainers with appropriate induction and training systems then established. The earliest 'radar officers' were Royal Navy Volunteer Reserve (RNVR) officers selected either because they had radio experience or aptitude or were graduates in almost any subject in the hope this intellectual base would enable them to grasp the essential principles. This rather amateur approach might have constrained the operational exploitation of radar but for an inspired idea from the Canadian-born Charles Wright, the Director of Naval Scientific Research. He persuaded the Admiralty to ask the Canadian Government for the loan of engineering physicists for various duties, especially radar. The subsequent influx of talented Canadians was hugely successful and the radar in most larger Royal Navy warships was kept working at sea by Canadian radar officers until 1943. Radar officers, from whatever source, were expected to advise on the operational use of radar as well as supervise its maintenance, although by late 1941 radar courses were being introduced to enable general service officers to use it effectively.[85]

The second transformational capability enjoyed by the Royal Navy by autumn 1941 was SIGINT. The valuable naval intelligence acquired in the Mediterranean theatre through the reading of Italian Hagelin traffic and, to a lesser extent, German air force Enigma messages has been mentioned. GC&CS coverage of the primary German air force Enigma system known as Red was maintained throughout the war. It was helpful in guiding naval operations in the Atlantic through 1941 and would become critically important in assessing the German air threat in the Arctic theatre. Until 1943 it also provided the best window into German land operations on the Russian front including those in the far North. More important to the Royal Navy was the breaking by GC&CS of the German Navy's primary Enigma based communication system designated Dolphin. This had been broken for a brief period in mid-1940 albeit with long delays. But the capture of papers from the armed trawler *Krebs* on 4 March during a raid on the Lofoten Islands began a process which enabled GC&CS to read Dolphin consistently and usually with minimal delay from the beginning of June. From that point, Royal Navy commanders enjoyed a superb picture of the deployment and movements of German Navy surface and U-boat forces for the rest of the year.

GC&CS decrypts and any related comment and assessments were passed by teleprinter to an Operational Intelligence Centre (OIC) administered by the Naval Intelligence Division (NID) within the Admiralty in London. The OIC had been established in 1937 as what today would be described as an 'all source fusion centre'. The ambition was that it would bring together intelligence from every useful source and produce a comprehensive picture of own and enemy dispositions from which operational commanders could make decisions. By autumn 1941, the OIC had experienced a difficult four-year learning process but had become a powerful and effective asset. Along with the Operations and Trade Divisions and the war registry, it was now lodged in a new bombproof underground Citadel at the north-west corner of the Admiralty. It was linked by teleprinter to GC&CS at Bletchley, the Central Interpretation Unit (CIU) at Medmenham in Buckinghamshire, a tri-service unit generating intelligence from aerial photography, the Admiralty's global network of shore-based D/F stations, and to key naval commands. SIGINT and aerial photography were the OIC's most important sources but it also drew on human agents, prisoner of war (POW) intelligence, naval attachés and many others. This intelligence fed two main plots, one for surface and one for submarine operations, giving senior commanders at the Admiralty a complete picture of the war at sea. The submarine plot was duplicated at Western Approaches Command in Liverpool, constantly updated by teleprinter and secure telephone. Neither of the other British services, and certainly not its Axis enemies, had an intelligence organisation matching the power and capability of the OIC and its sources. In time, the US Navy would duplicate much of it but not all.[86]

The final capability, still under development in late 1941 but which would begin transforming anti-submarine performance over the next year, was shipborne HF/DF. The Royal Navy began experimenting with this before the war and a trial set installed in the cruiser *Southampton* detected a German U-boat in Cadiz harbour in March 1938. However, subsequent development and operational exploitation was hampered by two problems. First, the early sets had no 'sense' facility. Without this, DF provided a line through the receiver to give a bearing, for example, of 015 degrees or its reciprocal 195 degrees. Sense resolved the ambiguity. This was less important for shore stations because usually several stations took bearings to enable a fix. At sea, even if several ships in a force were fitted, they would invariably be too close together to obtain such a fix and communicating with more distant friendly vessels posed obvious problems of security and timeliness. Without sense therefore, shipborne HF/DF sets were almost useless for targeting an enemy at sea. Secondly, radar transmissions and the siting of radar aerials were difficult to reconcile with the fitting of HF/DF and radar had initial priority.

These sense and interference problems were solved mainly through the insight of Waclaw Struszynski, former head of D/F in the Polish state telecommunications department, who with a small team reached Britain in late 1940. He made several breakthroughs in the first half of 1941, producing an aerial which gave an indication of signal strength on the correct bearing and could be reconciled with radar. In modified form this aerial was still in use more than 40 years later. By May, trial results were promising enough for Commander-in-Chief Western Approaches to recommend urgently that at least one and preferably two escorts in every convoy should be HF/DF equipped. The production system known as FH3 was tried out alongside the new Type 271 centimetric radar in an ex-American sloop *Culver* in October. By January 1942, twenty-five FH3 sets were at sea in Atlantic escorts and by August seventy. By mid-year, FH3 was being replaced by the much superior FH4 which used a cathode ray tube to give the operator a visual display of a target signal instead of an aural tone and was more reliable. Seaborne HF/DF proved as important to Allied success in the Battle of the Atlantic as the reading of Enigma or employment of radar, contributing to perhaps a quarter of U-boat losses. It would prove a significant asset in the Arctic too.[87]

## WEAKNESSES

Some of the Royal Navy's weaknesses which hampered its operational effectiveness after two years of war have been addressed above, notably the limitations of its carrier aircraft and armoured carrier capacity and the lack of a tachymetric anti-aircraft fire-control system. There is an enduring popular belief that Royal Navy ships delivered under the late 1930s rearmament programme were inferior to foreign contemporaries, a claim especially focused on battleships, with the *King George V*s rated unfavourably against the *Bismarck*s which gain the aura of 'super-battleships'. This is particularly relevant to the Arctic given the prominent role played by *Tirpitz* in this theatre. Leaving aside the problem of comparing ships built within treaty limits against those which ignored them, most specialists now rate the *King George V*s a better overall design than the *Bismarck*s and fully competitive on a ship-to-ship basis. The additional German displacement contributed to a slightly higher speed but was also absorbed by the outdated twin-turret arrangement and a split secondary armament. The latter also required much higher manning than British ships.[88] Looking more widely, it is hard to find examples where Royal Navy warships laid down after 1930 were significantly inferior to foreign equivalents. This is true whether judged on paper specifications or, more important, comparative performance in battle. Royal Navy weapons were, with few exceptions, competitive although there were too many gun calibres and destroyers initially lacked a satisfactory high-angle weapon. There were no performance failures comparable to the torpedo problems suffered by US Navy and German submarines. British armour was the best in the world by the late 1930s, 25 per cent more effective for given weight than American. In the development and exploitation of modern electronic sensors, the Royal Navy was ahead of everyone else in 1939 and even further ahead in 1941.[89]

However, if there is unjustified focus on a perceived quality deficit in ships and weapons, this has diverted attention from important weaknesses in operational mobility and availability. As the Royal Navy gained increasing access to US Navy engineering practice and standards in 1941, partly through refit and repair work to its ships conducted in the United States, and partly through observation of American operations in the Atlantic, it became aware how much the evolution of its own machinery had atrophied in the interwar period. In terms of efficiency, the economical use of fuel, the weight and space occupied by machinery and boilers, and therefore space for fuel and weapons, and even in the workload to keep ships operational, the US Navy was 'light years ahead of the Royal Navy'. The discovery was galling to the rising generation of naval engineers because comparable technology to that deployed in American ships existed in the British power station industry which was equally ahead of the navy in both turbine and boiler design and water treatment. Turbine development suffered because of over-dependence on a single supplier, Parsons, and reluctance to innovate from machinery that had proved reliable. Meanwhile, in 1941, it was still a cardinal principle of Royal Navy engineering practice that boilers were opened and cleaned after 21 days steaming, a hugely laborious and time-consuming process with serious constraints on ship availability. Adopting the chemical treatment now standard in both the US Navy and British power industry would extend the period between cleaning by a factor of three. A further constraint was that Royal Navy furnaces were equipped to use premium-grade Persian fuel and the inevitable introduction of North American and Caribbean fuel in wartime produced excessive smoke, making ships easier to spot by an enemy.[90]

It has been claimed that a further factor constraining Royal Navy mobility at the beginning of the war was inability to refuel underway at sea and that this requirement was neither foreseen nor practised.[91] This seems an exaggeration. It is true that, through the interwar period, the

Admiralty assumed fleet mobility would be ensured primarily through its unparalleled global network of bases and the ability quickly to establish additional ones even if on a temporary basis. By 1941 new bases were in use at Hvalfjord in Iceland, Freetown in West Africa and Port T in the Maldive Islands in the Indian Ocean. Given this global network, refuelling at sea was not seen as essential and, before the 1930s, judged impractical. The Admiralty controlled a substantial tanker fleet of some fifty vessels in 1939 under the Royal Fleet Auxiliary, but most of these dated from the previous war and were employed primarily for transporting oil from one base to another. The development of flexible rubber hoses in the 1930s made replenishment at sea viable and the Royal Navy and US Navy developed two techniques: the astern method where the tanker streamed a hose to be picked up by the receiving vessel; and the trough method which provided refuelling abeam but demanded special equipment and more skilled ship handling. The Royal Navy certainly practised both methods, albeit infrequently. Prior to 1941 the abeam method was confined to naval vessels with battleships and carriers refuelling their escorts but, from this time, it was also adopted by the newer tankers such as the 'Ranger' class alongside the astern method so that they could refuel three ships simultaneously. As noted earlier, *Brown Ranger* did this during Halberd and by 1942 'Ranger' class RFAs and contemporary tankers were regularly replenishing escorts, three at a time, in Atlantic and Arctic convoys. However, it was assumed larger vessels would still rely on shore bases which caused embarrassment during the long high-speed pursuit of *Bismarck*. Even the modern RFA tankers were small compared to their US Navy counterparts and the Royal Navy would later struggle to cope with operations across the vast distances of the Pacific.[92]

## Brightening Prospects or False Dawn?

Had the Royal Navy leadership conducted a full review of the war at sea on the morning Force K reached Malta after destroying the Beta convoy, it might have judged that brighter days lay ahead. In the Mediterranean, the Malta-based strike forces had established a firm grip over the central part of the sea. As already noted, that month would see 62 per cent of Axis traffic to North Africa destroyed and there were notable successes still to come in early December.[93] The British were particularly successful in targeting fuel tankers. In November, 92 per cent of fuel shipped to North Africa was lost, forcing the Italian navy to use warships to resupply air and armoured units, but only 2500 tons of fuel reached their destination in this way. Warships acting as fuel tankers were equally exposed to Ultra targeting as happened to the cruisers *Da Barbiano* and *Di Giussano*, sunk off Cape Bon by a destroyer flotilla on the night of 12/13 December.[94]

Force H and the Mediterranean Fleet at Alexandria had also retained firm control at either end of the Mediterranean. On 1 December, the German Afrika Korps complained that 'the British fleet operates entirely unhindered off the Cyrenaica coast' a view accepted by the German Naval Staff. They judged the Italian fleet incapable of gaining control even when they enjoyed numerical superiority while U-boat numbers were still too small to achieve adequate impact. Given the 'tense situation at sea', the German High Command had therefore directed 'air transport as the main carrier across the Mediterranean'.[95] Meanwhile, November Allied shipping losses in the Atlantic declined to just fifteen ships, amounting to 76,056 tons, the lowest figure since May 1940. Losses remained low the following month which saw an outstanding victory in the face of an all-out attack by Dönitz on the homeward bound Gibraltar 76 convoy.[96] Thirty of thirty-two merchant vessels were safely delivered and three U-boats and two Condors destroyed for the loss of *Audacity* and the ex-American destroyer *Stanley*. The German battlecruisers were still bottled up in Brest. The newly-commissioned *Tirpitz* was a potential threat but, with the benefit of Ultra intelligence and improving air surveillance, the Home Fleet was better placed to cope with any Atlantic sortie than with *Bismarck* the previous May. With a new battleship and armoured fleet carrier commissioning, two more carriers soon returning from repair in the United States, and the transformational capabilities described above gaining traction, there was good reason to anticipate that the Royal Navy now had the upper hand against its German and Italian enemies. There was sufficient resource in hand to begin constructing a new Eastern Fleet to be based in Singapore by January to meet the prospect of Japan entering the war and *Prince of Wales*, the forerunner of this fleet, was already approaching Cape Town.

However, the Royal Navy was about to suffer a dramatic turn. On 14 November, five days after Force K's triumphant return, *Ark Royal*, the navy's most effective fleet carrier, was torpedoed and sunk by *U-81*, one of Hitler's Mediterranean reinforcements, off Gibraltar. Eleven days later, the battleship *Barham* was sunk in the eastern Mediterranean by *U-331* with heavy loss of life. On 10 December, *Prince of Wales* and the battlecruiser *Repulse* were sunk off Malaya by IJN torpedo bombers following Japan's entry into the war three days earlier. Over the next nine days there was a series of disasters in the Mediterranean. The light cruiser *Galatea* was sunk by another U-boat, *U-557*, off Alexandria and in the early morning of 19 December a reinforced Force K ran into a minefield off Tripoli, while attempting to intercept an Italian convoy, and suffered heavy losses, perhaps justifying Pound's original reservations. The biggest disaster was a successful attack by Italian human torpedoes on the battleships *Queen Elizabeth* and *Valiant* in Alexandria harbour putting them out of action for 18 and 8 months respectively. Five weeks earlier the Admiralty was planning for three armoured carriers in the Mediterranean in early 1942 (with one replacing *Ark Royal* for a much-needed refit) providing cover for the battlefleet to range into the central part of the sea. In the face of a surging Japanese threat, the Admiralty had drastically to re-orientate. After the Atlantic lifeline, defence of the Indian Ocean was now the overriding priority, consuming every available carrier and battleship.[97] The premier Mediterranean Fleet had almost ceased to exist, reduced to a handful of light cruisers, destroyers and submarines. British new construction entering service over the next year would alone substantially compensate for these losses and United States entry into the war offered the new allies seemingly endless resources to draw on, but mobilising these would take time. Meanwhile, despite the Royal Navy's residual strengths and resilience and for all the promise of new technology, 1942 was going to be a hard year with far fewer resources for a growing Arctic commitment.

# Chapter 2

# Barbarossa and the Reluctant Opening of an Arctic Theatre

Gaining control of Russian land, resources and labour for Germany's use, encapsulated in the term 'Lebensraum', was always fundamental to Hitler's vision for Germany as a future world power. It was a core part of the programme he developed and presented in the 1920s in *Mein Kampf* and *Hitler's Second Book* (also known as *Hitler's Secret Book*). How and when this new 'empire' in the East would be acquired was inevitably then influenced by Germany's evolving strategic situation, judgement of comparative military strength, and the actions of other powers, not least Russia herself. Through the 1930s, for Hitler and the wider Nazi leadership, there was also an increasing ideological and racial dimension – the elimination of Jewish Bolshevism.[1]

*The Genesis of Barbarossa*

There is broad agreement that the specific proposal to attack Russia in summer 1941, later code-named 'Barbarossa', was originated by Hitler at a meeting with the top leaders of the Oberkommando der Wehrmacht (OKW), Supreme Command of the Armed Forces, and those of the army and navy at Obersalzberg on 31 July 1940. The primary goal of this meeting was to decide on the feasibility and timing of the invasion of Britain, Operation Sealion. Raeder stressed the problems posed by British naval superiority and autumn weather. He saw some advantage in postponement until spring 1941 but judged an early operation possible, although not before 15 September. Hitler evidently judged the operation risky, noting that the German navy was 15 per cent of Britain's with a much worse ratio for destroyers and motor torpedo boats. Defence against surface attack would therefore rely on mining and air supremacy. Nevertheless, the prize was high, and he was not convinced delay until spring would improve the prospects of success. Preparations should therefore proceed but the coming air offensive would determine what was finally possible.[2] Hitler's reservations about the feasibility of Sealion were fully shared by the army leadership who had reviewed the operation in detail at a conference the previous day.[3]

Hitler then continued that, if the invasion could not take place, it was necessary to eliminate factors that might help Britain improve her situation. Submarine and air offensives might bring her defeat but not for a year or two. Britain's main hope lay in Russia and the United States. If Russia dropped out of the picture, Britain would lose America too because eliminating Russia would 'tremendously' increase Japan's power in the Far East. Russia was the 'Far Eastern sword of Britain and the United States pointed at Japan'. Russia was shaken by Germany's victory in the West. If she now hinted that a strong Germany was unwelcome, Britain would take heart. With Russia 'smashed', this last hope would be gone. Germany would be master of Europe and the Balkans. Russia's destruction must be part of 'this struggle' and Hitler's target date was spring 1941. The sooner Russia was crushed, the better. Hitler stressed that the attack would only achieve its purpose if Russia was shattered to its roots with one blow. Holding part of the country would not do. Standing still the following winter would be perilous. If the attack began next May there would be five months to finish the job before winter began. Tackling Russia in the present year would have been attractive but there was now insufficient time to prepare. It was better to wait a little longer but 'with resolute determination' proceed to eliminate Russia. Hitler added that a subsidiary motive was removing a rival power from the Baltic.[4]

The conference concluded that the objective was the destruction of Russian 'manpower' and that the operation would be divided into three 'actions'. First, a thrust to Kiev, securing flank protection on the Dnieper River. The German air force would destroy river crossings and Odessa would also be taken. Secondly, a thrust to the Baltic states followed by a drive on Moscow. Finally, these two thrusts would link up to be potentially followed by a drive to the Baku oil fields. The prospect of winning Finnish and Turkish support would be investigated. Germany was to take possession of Ukraine, White Russia, and the Baltics but Finland could be offered extension to the White Sea. The initial estimate of forces required was sixty divisions kept for the defence of Western Europe including Norway and 120 divisions for the proposed attack on Russia.[5]

The account of the 31 July meeting, which relies heavily on the diary kept by the army chief of staff, Colonel General Franz Halder, has posed questions over Hitler's motives, the attitude of the army leadership (Raeder had left before Russia was discussed), and whether a summer 1941 attack on Russia was now inevitable. For Hitler himself, there is ample evidence that a long-term aspiration to build a greater Germany in the East combined with ideology to make war with Russia inevitable at some point in the next few years. While Hitler was the driving force behind this eastern vision, support extended well beyond senior Nazi circles and embraced many military and business leaders too. However, according to Halder, the army leadership did not believe an early move against Russia was either necessary or desirable. His diary records his meeting with Field Marshal Walther von Brauchitsch, Army Commander-in-Chief, the day before the Obersalzberg conference, at which the two agreed it was preferable to keep on friendly terms with Russia and, if Sealion proved abortive, pursue a Mediterranean strategy from the coming autumn to weaken Britain.[6]

Nevertheless, by the end of July 1940, a combination of factors, not just Britain's refusal to reach terms, was pushing Hitler to implement his eastern programme sooner rather than later. A key factor, only briefly mentioned at Obersalzberg, was the role of the United States which, by now, Hitler evidently saw not just as a further source of aid to Britain but as an important growing enemy in her own right. If Germany was to meet this Western challenge successfully, through the mid-1940s, it must remove the last major threat on the European continent but also acquire more resources, not least oil, than Russia would ever supply under the 1939 Nazi–Soviet pact. Here the perception that the purges of the late 1930s had weakened the Red Army, a point apparently confirmed by its recent performance against Finland, was also important. Hitler and the army command were agreed Russia did not pose a threat to Germany at present but were also agreed that the Red Army was likely to improve and present a serious risk in the future. It followed that there was a window of opportunity to defeat Russia that outweighed the army's reluctance, aired the previous day, to contemplate war on two fronts. The rapid defeat of France had also instilled military confidence that Russia could be crushed quickly. For all these reasons, it seems that Hitler achieved a consensus at Obersalzberg that a turn to the east had considerable attractions over an invasion of Britain that looked problematic. If Halder and von Brauchitsch retained reservations, they did not voice them nor did they press their Mediterranean alternative.[7]

This consensus did not imply an irrevocable decision. If Germany had gained at least temporary air supremacy over southern England in August and September, Sealion might have been executed with unforeseeable consequences. Two alternative strategic options were also aired within the German leadership during autumn 1940: an Atlantic–Mediterranean–Africa strategy, now strongly advocated by the navy, to defeat Britain; and an anti-British Euro-Asia continental bloc proposed by Foreign Minister Joachim von Ribbentrop. The navy's concept comprised a comprehensive maritime strategy directed at Britain. Its Mediterranean element broadly aligned with the ideas aired by Halder and von Brauchitsch before the 31 July meeting and it may be assumed they remained receptive to it afterwards even if they apparently took no further steps to promote it as a direct alternative to an attack on Russia.[8] The navy's plan envisaged maximum support for Germany's ally Italy, persuading Spain to enter the war and at least passive support from Vichy France. Control of the Mediterranean would be ensured through the capture of Gibraltar and Suez and ejection of Britain from Egypt, to be followed by the establishment of bases in North-west Africa and the Atlantic islands to destroy British Atlantic trade and communications. Raeder promoted this strategy at meetings in September and November, gaining enough traction for it to dominate Führer Directive No 18 of 12 November. Raeder even argued that the Middle East would offer Germany a base from which to seize the Caucasus oil fields, rendering an attack on Russia in the north unnecessary.

There were problems with this naval strategy, some of which might have been overcome with sustained political, diplomatic and military commitment, but this was never forthcoming. Spain under General Francisco Franco was unwilling to commit to Germany unless she could guarantee benefits to outweigh the economic damage from any subsequent British blockade. Spanish aspirations in North Africa were in competition with French and Italian interests which Germany was reluctant to confront. Spain was also sceptical that British naval power could be easily dislodged from the Mediterranean. An attack on Gibraltar without Spanish support would be challenging. Meanwhile, displacing Britain from Egypt and the Middle East would be a complex operation, demanding substantial resources not readily available without discarding the option of a Russia operation. Any major German intervention in North Africa or the eastern Mediterranean would also cause tensions with Italy who saw this as her sphere. Ultimately, Raeder lacked the power base in the Nazi leadership and the naval capability to make his case convincing. Objectives such as the seizure of the Atlantic islands were not feasible in the face of British sea power.

In the autumn of 1940, Hitler probably saw the naval strategy as a useful complement to an attack on Russia if prosecuted at low political and resource cost. He certainly wanted to protect his southern flank, not least to ensure there was no threat to the vital Ploesti oil complex in Romania, and this dictated the limited German investment in a Mediterranean and North African campaign from early 1941. However, there is no evidence that he considered Raeder's proposition as a serious alternative to the Russia campaign that summer, now judged essential to his primary goals.[9] Nevertheless, the Atlantic–Mediterranean–Africa strategy articulated by the Naval Staff, and more briefly by Halder and von Brauchitsch, evolved through 1941 as a vision for how the war against Britain should be prosecuted after Russia had been defeated. This vision is evident in Führer Directive No 32 of 11 June 1941 and, more comprehensively, an OKW strategic survey dated 28 August.[10] The latter, which was approved by Hitler and issued to the three service chiefs, saw two options for defeating Britain: direct invasion or siege warfare. Invasion would involve a massive reallocation of resources not possible until late 1942. A successful siege meant sinking one million tons of shipping per month. This also required a large shift in resources but, to be effective, the acquisition of bases in Spain and North-west Africa too. In line with thinking the previous autumn, this ideally required a collaborative alliance with France, Spain, and Turkey but the survey recognised that the political and military challenges in achieving this remained formidable and depended on defeating Russia first.

The August survey was the final expression of an operational sequence which began at Obersalzberg a year earlier and achieved increasing definition over the following months: deal with Russia first; drive from the Caucasus into the Middle East; and then complete the conquest of North Africa through to the Atlantic coast. A conference held by the Assistant Chief of Staff Operations on 28 October 1941, by which time the Barbarossa offensive was stalling, concluded: 'Because of the course of the campaign in the east, the development of the supply situation in Africa, and the still unclear attitude of Turkey, of the three possible operational directions for attack on the Middle East (Egypt, Anatolia, Caucasus), at the present time the Caucasus is the obvious choice.' From this point, insistence that only decisive success against Russia could solve Germany's problems dominated the thinking of Hitler and the military leadership. The reference to the Caucasus foreshadowed the focus on a southern offensive, Plan Blue, the following summer.[11]

Two final points from the August 1941 OKW survey require emphasis. First, it was striking that, within two months of the opening of the Russian campaign, the German leadership had focused on the potential importance of the Iran supply route as a means for the Western Allies to keep Russia in the war. Secondly, there was remarkable parallelism between the British and American focus during their Riviera talks on the threat to Atlantic security posed by potential German moves into Spain and North-west Africa and the reality of German intent expressed two weeks later. Indeed, the overall German ambitions for the Middle East, Mediterranean and North Africa, and the specific linking of the last with successful prosecution of an Atlantic trade war, neatly matched the British vision for a Mediterranean-centric wear-down strategy that would emerge from Arcadia onward. Neither side could lose the war in the Mediterranean and Middle East theatre, but both perceived that, without holding it, the war might be impossible to win.[12]

The second strategic alternative to Barbarossa, Ribbentrop's Euro-Asian bloc, envisaged extending the Axis Tripartite Pact, between Germany, Italy and Japan signed on 27 September, into a quadripartite alliance including Russia. Such a combination would neutralise the United States and isolate Britain, undermining her position in the Mediterranean and Middle and Far East. Ribbentrop judged the three Axis partners had more to gain from long-term collaboration with Russia than competition. 'Living spaces' would touch but need not conflict, and the liquidation of the British Empire would offer rich pickings for all. Japan found this concept attractive since it would free her to pursue southern expansion.[13] Stalin probably saw conflict with Germany as inevitable, but he was desperate to postpone it. A report presented that December by his new Defence Commissar, Marshal Semyon Timoshenko, emphasised that the Russian military was in a dire state and unable to cope with war with Germany for at least two years. Stalin was therefore amenable to a deeper, more durable, agreement with Germany than that signed in August 1939 if it bought him time to strengthen Russia's economic and military strength while Germany and other 'capitalist powers' weakened themselves in internecine war.[14]

The prospect of a more ambitious pact was pursued during a three-day visit to Berlin by the Russian Foreign Minister Vyacheslav Molotov, beginning on 12 November. Here Molotov raised Russian interests and demands which Hitler found impossible. He emphasised that Russia still aspired to the annexation of Finland but also control of southern Bukovina, part of Romania. Russia also sought an alliance with Bulgaria, bases in the Dardanelles and Bosporus, and hinted at wider ambitions in the Persian Gulf and Sakhalin area in the East which inevitably cut across Japanese interests. Molotov's demands, under Stalin's direction, were probably a maximum opening bid, and were somewhat watered down later in the month. However, these November exchanges demonstrated a fundamental clash of security interests in Finland and Romania, and access to the Baltic region, on which neither side would ultimately concede. They also fostered increasing distrust. Importantly, the Russian maximum programme was inevitably seen by the German side as 'extortionist' and a long-term, if not immediate, threat. The Germans knew that a specific Russian objective regarding Finland was gaining control of Petsamo and its nickel supplies. Finnish nickel was essential to the German war effort and Russian annexation of this supply would be intolerable. The extension of Russian influence in Romania and Bulgaria was equally unacceptable since it would leave Germany's only reliable source of natural oil at Ploesti extremely vulnerable. Hitler therefore felt vindicated in his view that German and Russian interests were irreconcilable, that a clash was inevitable, and that it was in Germany's interest to attack as early as possible.[15]

It is difficult to judge whether a more conciliatory, even acquiescent, stance from Molotov, carefully crafted to minimise any potential clash of interests in the Balkans and Baltic, would have persuaded Hitler at a minimum to postpone Barbarossa. The available evidence suggests not and that, in his mind, the case for destroying Russia set out on 31 July had consolidated. A key influence here was the growing evidence of American commitment and support to Britain, signified by the 'destroyers for bases' deal in September and Roosevelt's post-election stance that would culminate in the 'arsenal of democracy' speech and launch of Lend-Lease in December. If Britain remained intransigent and the United States was preparing to intervene as in 1917, perhaps as early as 1942, then to meet this challenge, Germany must not only eliminate the potential threat from Russia but acquire its resources. Barbarossa was the only means of achieving a decisive strategic turn in Germany's favour. By contrast, the maritime strategy only offered limited gains in the short term while the quadripartite pact bought time without solving Germany's problem. On 18 December therefore, Hitler signed Führer Directive No 21 – Operation Barbarossa – directing the Wehrmacht to 'crush Soviet Russia in a rapid campaign'. Three weeks later, he expanded on his thinking at a meeting with the top military leadership at the Berghof on 9 January. Smashing Russia would leave Germany unassailable, while Russia's immeasurable wealth would provide the potential successfully to contest any future enemy alliance.[16]

At the end of 1940, Stalin certainly shared Hitler's assessment that German and Russian interests were ultimately irreconcilable, and conflict therefore inevitable. Despite this core perception, fully shared across the wider Russian political and military leadership, his policy over the next six months up to the launch of Barbarossa was shaped by two fundamental judgements. First, the condition of the Russian armed forces, still recovering from the disruption of the purges and undertaking an ambitious modernisation programme, meant they were not well placed to withstand a German attack before mid-1942 at the earliest. Everything possible would be done to prepare for the inevitable showdown but meanwhile it was vital to avoid any provocation that gave Hitler a pretext for an early attack. Secondly, Stalin was utterly convinced that Hitler would not risk a war on two fronts. He would therefore not attack Russia until the threat from Britain was eliminated. He also judged that, to prosecute the war with Britain and her American supporter, Germany was dependent on Russian economic supplies. Hitler would not risk disrupting these while the Western threat remained extant. Stalin held to this conviction until the bitter end, ignoring the growing volume of well-sourced intelligence through the spring warning of imminent attack. These warnings were also weakened by Russian overestimation of German strength in Western theatres which inevitably made their concentration in Eastern Europe less dramatic. Through the spring, Germany also appeared still heavily engaged in both an air war against the United Kingdom, operations in the Balkans and a new intervention in North Africa. Stalin's conviction that Hitler would avoid a two-front war also conditioned his attitude to Britain. He was suspicious of British warnings, seeing these as a blatant attempt to encourage German–Russian conflict. Every British move was also weighed for evidence of double-dealing, whether it presaged readiness to settle with Germany at Russia's expense.[17]

If it was essential to avoid provoking Germany, the maximalist demands made by Molotov in the Berlin talks demand explanation. The records suggest that, in floating the concept of a new quadripartite pact, Ribbentrop and Hitler kept to sweeping generalisations which Molotov found frustrating. His opening demands may have been partly a negotiating tactic but also an attempt to pin the German side down to specifics. The conviction, on which Stalin and Molotov were agreed, that Germany would not contemplate a two-front war, no doubt also persuaded them that there was nothing to lose by bidding high.

There is a risk that identifying a clear route from Hitler's presentation at Obersalzberg in July 1940 to the launch of Barbarossa 11 months later, through the tensions exposed in the Molotov visit and the issuing of Führer Directive No 21, reflects hindsight more than messy reality. If Hitler himself was decided following the postponement of Sealion, his commitment did not translate unambiguously to the army general staff. His Directive No 18 of 12 November, dominated by Raeder's Atlantic–

Mediterranean strategy, implied that Britain was the pressing priority and seemed to assign only subordinate influence to an Eastern campaign. For army planners the problems of Greece and a growing southern threat to the Balkans loomed large. Negotiations with Halder over the text of Directive No 21 were tortuous and, through January, there were significant doubts within the military leadership as to whether the emerging vision for Barbarossa would either deliver the desired blow against Britain or the anticipated resources to expand German war potential. Many still saw Barbarossa as an 'option' rather than an irrevocable commitment. Preparing the campaign plan exposed differences over priorities between Hitler and Halder and designated commanders that went unresolved.[18]

## British and American Perceptions of German Intent and Prospects

All this meant that, through the winter of 1940/41, the British and American leaderships found it difficult to gain an authoritative insight into real German intent. High-level discussion and planning for Barbarossa was closely held. Until March 1941, SIGINT was largely silent while reports from secret agents and diplomatic coverage were essentially speculative. Indications that did emerge were subject to alternative explanations and British intelligence effort naturally focused on the war underway rather than possible futures. A further factor was that speculation about a German attack on Russia, primarily initiated in the political as opposed to military domain, ran ahead of German preparations. Multiple rumours without foundation through the last half of 1940 meant genuine pointers in the early part of 1941 were viewed with scepticism.[19]

From the time that France collapsed through the remainder of 1940, both Churchill and Cripps consistently believed that, if Germany failed to invade the United Kingdom that year, she would turn against Russia in 1941. Their view was not based on authoritative intelligence. Throughout this period the Joint Intelligence Committee and service intelligence agencies remained convinced that defeating Britain, preferably through invasion, remained Germany's priority.[20] It rather reflected political and strategic intuition that German and Russian interests were ultimately incompatible, although by October the prime minister also judged that Germany would inevitably want to seize Russia's oil to underpin its war potential.[21] In the first three months of 1941, the British intelligence community noted a steady increase in German forces deployed in Eastern Europe, especially Poland. However, the deployment did not seem disproportionate, and it was logical that Germany should build up defensive forces to deter Russia while it mounted an offensive in Greece and the Balkans aimed at undermining British power in the eastern Mediterranean. The German move eastward was deliberately gradual and accompanied by well-crafted deception operations. Like Stalin, the British were convinced Germany would not undertake a war on two fronts and the evidence that Britain remained the priority appeared convincing.[22]

During April and May, there was a gradual shift in the British assessment driven primarily by a growing volume of high-quality intercepts by GC&CS of German Enigma traffic, circulated to a restricted readership, under the designation 'Ultra'. The impact of this intelligence, accompanied by separate insights from the Secret Intelligence Service (SIS) and diplomatic reporting, was cumulative and there were differences of view across the British leadership and intelligence communities not resolved until the end of May. Churchill and Cripps, not surprisingly, were rapidly convinced that Hitler was now committed to a summer attack on Russia and the former sent a warning to Stalin on 3 April, although, to the prime minister's fury, Cripps did not deliver this for two weeks, fearing it would be provocative. Churchill subsequently discovered that the message had also been presented to the Deputy Foreign Minister, Andrey Vishinsky, not Stalin, and that the latter might never have been informed. He judged Cripps obstinate and obstructive, preventing Churchill from establishing a personal relationship with Stalin three months before their first correspondence began.[23] The Foreign Office was also an early convert on German intent but, until well into May, Military Intelligence (MI) resisted the view that an attack was imminent. It still insisted that the German priority was defeating Britain and saw the build-up of forces in the East as partly defensive and partly coercive to win maximum economic support from Russia.[24]

Only on 23 May did the Joint Intelligence Committee draw together all available intelligence for its first specific assessment on 'Germany's intentions against the USSR'.[25] This judged that Germany could not attack Russia and simultaneously invade the United Kingdom. However, the evidence suggested that Sealion was on hold and that domination of Russia was now a fundamental German objective to be achieved as soon as possible. It concluded that 'Germany cannot fight a long war without obtaining greater economic help from Russia than she is now receiving. She can only obtain this by an effective agreement or war.' The assessment then weighed up the arguments for negotiation versus war and concluded that the advantages for Germany of an agreement were 'overwhelming'. This may have been true, but the suggestion that Germany was keeping its options open ignored important recent Ultra intelligence suggesting that she was now committed to war. An SIS report from the long-standing

Czech agent A54 provided further confirmation just as the assessment issued. A54 insisted that German–Russian negotiations were a 'delaying mechanism' and provided details of German occupation planning. The judgement that a negotiated settlement remained possible reflected continued MI doubt, not shared by GC&CS and Air Intelligence, that Germany would ultimately accept war on two fronts.[26]

By 30 May, reflecting more Ultra material and the A54 report, the Joint Intelligence Committee was convinced that Germany's next move was directed at Russia. All the evidence suggested she would 'enforce her demands on the Soviet by means of a threat of force which can immediately be turned into action'. The date for action, if taken, would probably be the end of June. The committee judged that, although it must be tempting for Germany to exploit the capture of Crete to mount a major drive into the eastern Mediterranean, she would not have sufficient forces for this unless she reached a rapid settlement with Russia.[27] The chiefs of staff endorsed this assessment but evidently accepted that Russian concessions remained possible because they proposed to stiffen Russian resistance by stressing that, if Germany received new oil supplies, Britain would bomb the Baku oilfields, rendering any Russian offer pointless.[28]

During the first 10 days of June, a huge volume of SIGINT material processed by GC&CS removed all doubt that Germany now intended to attack in the second half of the month.[29] This did not only derive from Enigma decrypts. GC&CS intercepted an important message from the Japanese ambassador in Berlin, General Hiroshi Ōshima, sent on 4 June recounting a meeting just concluded with Hitler. The latter stated that Russia, although outwardly friendly, was now habitually obstructive and must be eliminated. No date was mentioned for the start of hostilities, but the ambassador judged it imminent. The Berlin–Tokyo traffic was transmitted using a machine cipher designated Purple which had been broken by the Americans and shared with GC&CS in February.[30] On 9 June, Eden, referring directly to 'intelligence reports', commented to the prime minister that all information pointed to German concentrations against Russia being pressed 'with utmost speed and vigour'.[31]

As a result of this cumulative intelligence, on 12 June, the Joint Intelligence Committee stated categorically that 'fresh evidence' now showed that Hitler had made up his mind 'to have done with Soviet obstruction to Germany and intends to attack her'. Hitler was also reconciled to Japan not intervening against Russia for the present.[32] SIGINT not only revealed German intent but considerable detail on strength, dispositions, and probable lines of attack. This was incorporated in a comprehensive Joint Intelligence Committee assessment issued a week before Barbarossa commenced on 14 June.[33] With a German–Russian war now imminent, the War Cabinet instructed the chiefs of staff to prepare plans for a military mission to Moscow to discuss potential military cooperation.[34]

The 14 June assessment not only dealt with German intent and capability but included detailed analysis of Russian strength and ability to meet the anticipated attack. It therefore conditioned expectations within the British military leadership on both the course of the campaign and its likely outcome. Although its judgements were qualified, the Joint Intelligence Committee expected the Germans to capture Moscow, Leningrad, and the Ukraine within one to two months. This reflected knowledge of German expectations acquired through Ultra intercepts but also took account of the balance of forces.[35] Here the committee's estimates for Russian land forces deployed in the western theatres, at least 2.6 million men and 14,000 tanks, were broadly accurate. It was less good on Russian air strength, assuming barely 4000 combat aircraft available in the west, when reality was twice that. It correctly judged that the bulk of Russian equipment within both land and air forces was obsolescent although it was unaware that high-quality and competitive tanks (KVs and T-34s) and modern aircraft (Yak-1 and MIG-3 fighters, Su-2 and Il-2 Sturmovik ground attack planes with innovative weapon fits and Pe-2 dive-bombers) were coming into service, albeit so far in only small numbers. The committee also judged that the Russian military lacked initiative, with slavish adherence to doctrine and commanders afraid to accept responsibility, that it had little training in modern combined arms manoeuvre, and that maintenance standards and logistic support were poor. It would accordingly struggle to match the Germans in open warfare although its large number of tanks could cause them problems. Nevertheless, the Russian soldier was traditionally brave and patriotic, at his best in defence, and had large territories on which to fall back.[36]

The assessment did not devote much space to naval operations. It judged quite reasonably that the Soviet navy would 'be unlikely to take a great part in the operations', its role would be 'primarily defensive' and its bases were liable to capture by German land and air forces. Its appendix identified the current strength of the navy and its distribution between the four fleets, Baltic, Black Sea, Arctic and Far East. From this it was evident that the Arctic or Northern Fleet was by far the smallest, comprising just six destroyers and twenty submarines. The appendix also noted that the bulk of the navy and its equipment was 'obsolete or obsolescent'. Only four cruisers, about half the destroyers and most of the larger submarines could be classified as modern. This breakdown of Russian naval strength, drawn from NID records, was broadly accurate. This reflected well on NID's collection and assessment effort through the 1930s on a navy which was never seen as a primary potential enemy. Although it could devote very few staff to Russia, NID had drawn carefully on a wide range of sources, primarily overt and diplomatic, and only occasionally covert, to keep a good record of order of battle and reach sensible judgements on fighting capability.[37]

Contemporary American views of Russia's prospects in a war with Germany were similar to those of the Joint Intelligence Committee, no doubt reflecting exchanges between respective attachés in Moscow and the British embassy in Washington. The US Army attachés in Moscow, Major Ivan Yeaton and Major Joseph Michela, were impressed with Russian tanks and artillery but nevertheless concluded that they suffered overall weaknesses which compromised air power, fire power and mobility. Russia would not hold up against a hard-hitting, fast-moving army with modern equipment and armament.[38] Unfortunately, Yeaton allowed his virulent anti-communist stance to prejudice his reporting once war began and this undermined the quality of American assessments for some months. He quickly fell out with Hopkins during the latter's late July visit, partly because of his distrust of Soviet motives and partly his belief that the United States should seek a return for any aid provided. For similar reasons he was regarded with suspicion by Cripps. A combination of War Department frustration and Hopkins' lobbying led to his recall in the autumn with Michela taking over as senior attaché. Hopkins also got Yeaton's predecessor, Colonel Raymond Faymonville, appointed as 'Lend-Lease representative' reporting direct to him. This led to inevitable infighting between Michela and Faymonville which complicated American assessments of Russia's military capacity for the next three years.[39] It later transpired that Faymonville was possibly a Soviet agent. German assessments of Russian strength in June 1941 as Barbarossa opened were in some respects inferior to those of the Joint Intelligence Committee. They underestimated the overall trained manpower Russia could mobilise and their figures for overall tank strength were 50 per cent below reality. Estimates for Russian air force order of battle were worse, out by a factor of three for both overall strength and for that deployed in the western theatres.[40]

The 14 June assessment and the intelligence underpinning it, received over the preceding fortnight, contributed to discussion of the German–Russian confrontation at successive War Cabinet meetings on 9, 12 and 16 June.[41] Cripps, visiting London from Moscow, attended the last of these. He informed the Cabinet that the Russian leadership were aware of the scale of German force concentrating on their western border. The consensus in Moscow was that the Germans would now use the threat of invasion to extract maximum concessions, although they might be pitched so high as to be unacceptable, with the deliberate intent of forcing war. Cripps thought the Russian government was willing to appease Hitler with significant economic and military concessions provided they retained enough strength to recover when their relative strategic position improved. They would not therefore accept any disarmament measures or surrender control of their Ukrainian granary or Caspian oil. If lesser concessions did not suffice, they would fight. It was difficult to judge subsequent Russian military performance. They had manpower, considerable armoured forces, and a numerically strong air force. But he thought they would suffer from weak organisation and logistics. The prevailing view in Moscow diplomatic circles was that Russia would not hold out against a German attack for more than three to four weeks. By the end of that time, the Germans would be in Leningrad, Moscow, and Kiev. The prospects of staging a successful fallback to Siberia were hard to judge but consolidation there was possible.[42]

Cripps saw three possible results from a German ultimatum: Russian surrender and vassal status; defeat after a short campaign; and a peace deal short of military and economic subjugation. The first would be worst for Britain and the last best. He thought it unthinkable that any deal would grant Germany free passage to the Middle East. The Russians knew this would allow Germany to seize the Caspian oilfields en route. While acquiring oil was clearly a major German goal, Cripps thought they would struggle to extract significant quantities in the short term. He emphasised that in present circumstances, the Russians had to appear strictly neutral. There was no prospect of an approach to Britain. However, if war began, Britain should be ready with all possible help. The Foreign Secretary, Sir Anthony Eden, told the War Cabinet that he had been informed separately that the American ambassador in Moscow shared Cripps' assessment.[43] Two days later, when he dined with Ivan Maisky, the Russian ambassador in London, Cripps was no longer keeping options open. He told Maisky that Germany was now definitely set on invasion. While he may have spoken for effect to underline the seriousness of Russia's predicament, it is more likely that sight of all the latest intelligence had shifted his position.[44]

The growing consensus that Germany was now committed to attack Russia did not cause Britain's leadership immediately to reassess whether this might fundamentally alter the course of the war, to assess the prospects of a British–Russian strategic alliance, or urgently to consider how Russia might best be supported. Instead, the expectation that Russia would be defeated within weeks encouraged a focus on how Britain might take selfish advantage of a short breathing space to prepare against renewed risk of invasion or a German descent on the Middle East. It also discouraged any scoping of possible joint operations in the Arctic region or of what and how military and other material aid might be provided and delivered. The Foreign Office advised the chiefs of staff that, rather than contemplating any formal alliance with Russia, Britain would 'have a common enemy and common interest to do Germany all the harm we can'.[45]

Eden reflected the Foreign Office view to Maisky on 13 June. He emphasised the threat now posed by the German concentration on Russia's borders. If Germany attacked, Britain was prepared to provide help from its air force units in the Middle East, to send a military mission to share experience gained during the war, and to develop economic cooperation, exploiting access through the Persian Gulf and Far East. The first item referred to the plan for the Royal Air Force to bomb the Caspian oil fields which had been under discussion since the end of May while the proposal for a military mission had been agreed at the War Cabinet the previous day. The overall package certainly conveyed that British support would be less than wholehearted. However, while this neatly encapsulates the British attitude at this stage, it is doubtful it made any lasting impression in Moscow. Maisky apparently still fully shared Stalin's conviction that Germany would not invade, and he certainly shared Moscow's intense distrust of British motives.[46]

*The British and American Response to a Prospective German–Russian War*

The following day Churchill informed Roosevelt that trustworthy sources suggested a German attack on Russia was imminent. If war did break out, Britain would give all encouragement and any help it could spare to the Russians on the principle that 'Hitler is the foe we have to beat'.[47] However, at a subsequent meeting of the Defence Committee held on 17 June, which the prime minister used to update a gathering of commanders-in-chief on the overall state of the war, Russia received only brief reference despite the latest intelligence and, in priority, it evidently ranked well below the eastern Mediterranean and Middle East, the defence of the United Kingdom and the Battle of the Atlantic. The prime minister merely noted that the Germans were now focusing primarily on Russia and the acquisition of its oil and wheat. If war broke out, Britain must seize every opportunity this offered.[48] Russia did not merit mention at the next Defence Committee meeting on 19 June or, more surprisingly, the following one on 25 June, three days after the launch of Barbarossa, even though a key item for this second meeting was Britain's 'Future Strategy'.[49]

During the final week before Barbarossa launched, the chiefs of staff also hardly discussed Russia in their own daily meetings. The only initiative they took came on 20 June when, following the direction from the War Cabinet, they endorsed the advice of the Joint Planning Staff[50] on the despatch of a military mission to Russia.[51] The planners assumed the purpose of such a mission was to assist the British effort against Germany, directly or indirectly. They judged that its prime purpose would be to acquire intelligence on German and Russian capabilities, and in the event of war, the progress of operations. It would demonstrate British support, assist in coordinating British and Russian strategy, and perhaps maintain communications with residual Russian resistance forces in the East if European Russia disintegrated. The planners did not expect a mission to have any impact on Russian ability to withstand a German attack, although if Russian resistance lasted longer than currently expected, it would have increased value. Although they accepted the planners' recommendations, the chiefs acknowledged that further action required assurance that the Russians would accept a mission.[52]

Meanwhile, on 14 June, the planners completed their initial draft of the 'Future Strategy' paper which would be discussed 10 days later at the Defence Committee, and then, in its final form, shared with the Americans at Riviera in early August.[53] This paper was thus being written as the sheer scale of German preparations against Russia became increasingly evident to the British war leadership. Although the paper acknowledged Russia was now Germany's primary preoccupation, it gave the issue surprisingly little space. Despite the Joint Intelligence Committee's certainty that attack by the end of the month was probable, the planners evidently struggled to accept that this could be in Germany's interest and therefore still thought a coercive agreement would be reached. There was no suggestion in the paper that Russia would play a significant role in the war. In a commentary on the paper, which took account of feedback from the chiefs of staff and others, issued on 22 June, the day Barbarossa began, Russia did not feature in the recommendations.[54]

The planners' implication that Russia was almost peripheral was reflected in the reaction of the chiefs of staff the morning after the German attack. The record of their meeting conveys no sense that this was viewed as a turning point in the war. Instead, discussion concentrated on 'how we might turn German pre-occupation in Russia to our advantage'. The immediate focus was increased engagement with the German air force over northern France, an attrition battle the Royal Air Force had pursued with limited success since the spring. However, the chiefs also asked the Director of Combined Operations, Admiral of the Fleet Sir Roger Keyes, to prepare plans for a major raid at brigade strength, perhaps using Canadian forces, on the coast of northern France to 'kill Germans' and do as much damage as possible. Such an operation arguably foreshadowed the Dieppe raid in August the following year.[55] Both these initiatives stemmed from the prime minister who urged the chiefs, 'now the enemy is busy in Russia', to 'make hell while the sun shines'.[56] At this stage, they were evidently less about helping Russia than exploiting German distraction in the East. They are best viewed as elements of the long-standing 'wear-down' strategy. A Joint Planning Staff aide-memoire circulated next day confirmed that options for enhanced air effort against targets in western Germany and raids on the French coast were under investigation. Scope for sabotage activity in the Caucasus, managed by the Special Operations Executive (SOE), would also be examined and the planners stressed the importance of preventing Russian naval assets and shipping falling into German hands. Otherwise, the planners emphasised there was enough time before winter set in for the Germans to defeat Russia and switch forces back to mount an invasion of the United Kingdom. They accordingly cautioned against releasing more forces overseas.[57] On 25 June, the chiefs of staff directed that anti-invasion defences should be at maximum readiness by 1 September.[58]

Churchill's famous speech the evening that Barbarossa launched, delivered on the BBC, was a powerful and emotional declaration of common cause with Russia in fighting to destroy the Nazi regime, as Maisky fully recognised. However, Maisky noted that the promise to 'give whatever help we can to Russia and the Russian people' was easy to make. But what would the aid consist of? And would it be serious? He also observed widespread scepticism concerning the Red Army's survival. The War Office believed 'our resistance will last no more than four to six weeks'. Maisky might here have emphasised another revealing passage in the speech where Churchill noted that Hitler's invasion of Russia was 'no more than a prelude to an attempted invasion of the British Isles' which he hoped no doubt to accomplish 'before the winter comes' and before 'the United States may intervene'. The 'Russian danger' was therefore 'our danger' and 'the danger of the United States'. For all its powerful rhetoric, the speech fell short of proposing any formal alliance and nor did it make any specific commitments. More important was an underlying implication that existing British strategy and priorities remained intact.

This almost certainly reflected Churchill's expectation at this point that Russia would be defeated but that she might buy Britain time.[59]

Maisky was right about attitudes in the War Office. Harold Nicolson, a Parliamentary secretary working in the Ministry of Information, was informed that 80 per cent of War Office experts believed Russia would be defeated in 10 days.[60] When he learnt of the German attack on the morning of 22 June, the Director of Military Operations, Major General John Kennedy, also did not think the Russians would last long. However, he also judged that the attack 'would at least afford us a respite, extend the Germans, and dissipate their strength'. In his diary, he noted 'we shall have to try to keep it going'. His superior, Dill, was less objective in his immediate reaction. He regarded the Russians as 'so foul that he hated the idea of any close association with them'. Dill's sentiment was fully shared by his vice-chief, Lieutenant General Henry Pownall, who wrote in his diary for 29 June: 'I avoid the expression "Allies" for the Russians are a dirty lot of murdering thieves themselves, and double-crossers of the deepest dye.' He added: 'It is good to see the two biggest cut-throats in Europe, Hitler and Stalin, going for each other.'[61] These attitudes, common across the other two services too, partly reflected deep hostility to, and fear of, communism but also horror at the purges in the Russian army and navy from 1937. Senior British military leaders were well informed on the impact of the latter. In April 1938, Lieutenant Colonel Roy Firebrace, the army attaché in Moscow, had participated in a Foreign Office review of the purges at which he stated accurately that they had swept away about two-thirds of the highest-ranking officers. He therefore doubted Russia was any longer capable of conducting an offensive war, although, interestingly, he still judged the Red Army 'would be a formidable opponent' on the defensive.[62] Meanwhile Eden sought Kennedy's views on the despatch of a military mission. The latter summarised the views of the Joint Planning Committee from two days earlier. Kennedy saw no prospect of despatching supplies to Russia for some time, but a mission might be useful if it could influence Russian strategy or could help keep the war going. Eden consulted Maisky who confirmed the following day that a mission would be accepted in Moscow.[63]

The chiefs of staff approved a directive for this tri-service mission, led by Major General Noel Mason-Macfarlane, on 24 June. The objectives of '30 Mission', as it became known, were: to share British war experience in order to strengthen and prolong Russian resistance; to gain intelligence on both German and Russian operations; to provide a channel for the Russians to communicate requests for material assistance; to encourage the Russians to deny any economic assets to the Germans; and to help coordinate British and Russian strategy.[64] Macfarlane was assisted by a deputy for each service. The naval section was headed by Rear Admiral Geoffrey Miles, previously captain of the Home Fleet flagship *Nelson*, who would succeed Macfarlane the following May. Colonel E R Greer, the current army attaché in Moscow, took over the army section while Air Vice Marshal Alfred Collier, who had been air attaché in Moscow in the mid-1930s, headed the air section. It was originally planned that Roy Firebrace, Greer's predecessor in Moscow now promoted brigadier, would head the army section but he was appointed instead to lead a new multi-service Russia Liaison Group to liaise with the Russian military mission in London. These four, together with five assistants, joined Cripps on a flight around northern Norway to Archangel and thence to Moscow where they were introduced to Molotov. They had an initial meeting with the Russian Chief of the General Staff, General Georgy Zhukov, and Lieutenant General Filipp Golikov, head of the Russian Military Intelligence Directorate (GRU), on 28 June, just six days after the German attack. Zhukov, then little known to the Western Powers, would become the dominant Russian military leader of the war. Golikov would head delegations to Britain and the United States the following month.[65]

The 52-year-old Macfarlane was Dill's personal choice. At one level, he seemed well qualified. He had an outstanding fighting record, demonstrated by a DSO and three MCs, which might appeal to the Russians. He had held two attaché posts, to Hungary, Austria and Switzerland in the early 1930s and then to Germany in 1938–9. Following the outbreak of war, he became chief of intelligence staff in the British Expeditionary Force and, after the fall of France, deputy to the governor of Gibraltar. Apart from his unquestioned courage, he possessed great drive, energy and initiative, was immensely likeable and an excellent linguist, although he did not initially speak Russian. He was also eccentric and excitable, bordering on unstable, with a tendency to let a desire for the dramatic gesture cloud his judgement. He had famously proposed shooting Hitler during the 1939 birthday parade from the attaché residence in Berlin. However, Macfarlane was not convinced his new role was realistic and rightly concerned that his intelligence background would inevitably arouse suspicion in the paranoid Stalinist Russia of 1941. Dill rejected his pleas that someone else be chosen in his place, underlining that the core role of 30 Mission was to prolong Russian resistance for as long as possible. When that failed, the highest priority for him and Miles was to ensure the scuttling of the Red Fleet so that it did not fall into German hands. Once all was lost, Dill suggested the best chance of escape was then for Macfarlane to work his way south for a thousand miles and cross the Pamirs into India although he admitted this would be 'a very long walk'![66]

Macfarlane's concern about his intelligence pedigree probably had some justification but he would face a more fundamental problem in Moscow which was shared by the Russia Liaison Group in London which, although tri-service, was administered by the War Office and headed by an army officer and thus created the impression that it was army dominated. The senior Russian interlocutors in both Moscow and London soon made it clear that they had great respect for the Royal Navy and some for the Royal Air Force but had little more than contempt for the British Army. In early August, a Foreign Office official feared that 'our army does not impress or much interest the Soviet authorities'. Two weeks later, a Russian informed Firebrace as head of the Liaison Group that his embassy believed that the British Army and tactical sections of the Royal Air Force were 'on leave'![67] This low opinion of the Army deepened during 1942 with the fall of Singapore and Tobruk and the Soviet belief that they had nothing to learn from it persisted throughout the war.[68]

While 30 Mission established itself in Moscow, the war leadership in London waited to see whether the prevailing expectations of a rapid Russian collapse were borne out and considered the immediate threats and opportunities Barbarossa posed for Britain. For almost a month, the chiefs of staff broadly held to the view that the most that Russia could offer Britain was a breathing space in which to improve her defences, primarily at home, but also in the Middle East. They accordingly stuck to the objectives suggested by the joint planners. They were willing to make a limited investment in prolonging Russian resistance through enhanced air operations and raiding which aligned with British interests. Otherwise, the priority was to try and deny Germany assets that would follow a Russian collapse, notably Caucasian oil and naval units. The 'vital importance' of destroying the oil fields before 'the Hun push' reached them was stressed by the Minister of Economic Warfare, Hugh Dalton, also in charge of SOE, on 30 June.[69] The chiefs also saw no advantage in offering military supplies that were unlikely to make a difference and could end up being used by Germany against Britain.

*The Arctic Comes to the Fore*

Meanwhile it was immediately clear to Cripps and Macfarlane, on arriving in Moscow at the end of June, that the Russians had their own agenda. While not averse to any 'distraction operations' in the West, their priorities were material aid and securing the naval route from the west round northern Norway to their Arctic ports, soon dubbed the

'Murmansk operation'. In practice, they wanted disruption of German traffic in the northern Norwegian fiords, and flank protection of Russian forces defending against a German drive on the Murmansk region. Their immediate requests for material assistance, which were transmitted simultaneously to the United States government as well as to London, comprised: 3000 fighters and 3000 bombers; anti-aircraft guns and Asdic sets; and significant quantities of aluminium and rubber.[70]

The Admiralty were initially dismissive of any commitment to the Arctic, viewing it as a diversion from more important priorities and involving high risk to little benefit. Their sole interest was ensuring the Russian Northern Fleet did not fall into German hands although it is hard to see why it was judged that a force known to be small and ineffective would bring the Germans much advantage.[71] However, pressure from Cripps on the need for Britain to show more tangible support brought Murmansk on the agenda at the Defence Committee on 3 July, obliging the Admiralty to reconsider. Pound now proposed a carrier strike against German shipping supporting an offensive against Russia's Arctic ports and known to be present in the fiords near Petsamo, 65 miles north-west of Murmansk. However, his attitude to opening a sustained northern supply route to Russia or conducting regular operations in the Arctic theatre remained distinctly negative.[72]

In 1941, Petsamo was part of Finland which was cooperating with Germany against Russia. Strictly speaking, 'Petsamo' referred to a corridor approximately 120 miles by 30 miles which connected Finland to the Arctic Ocean between 1921 and 1944 when it was ceded to Russia. In 1941, the port referred to as 'Petsamo' by the British was known by the Finnish name Liinahaman and marked the north end of the Arctic Ocean Highway which ran 320 miles south to Rovaniemi which was connected by rail to the port of Kemi at the north end of the Gulf of Bothnia. Liinahaman now has the Russian name Liinakhamari. An operation against Petsamo could be mounted in the last half of the month.[73] The Defence Committee's support for this operation reflected their awareness that the proposed raid on the French coast was not feasible because of the need to allocate forces for the potential seizure of the Atlantic islands. The raid was formally abandoned the following day.[74] Meanwhile, with the prime minister's agreement, Eden hinted to Maisky on 7 July that unspecified 'naval action in the Arctic' to help the Russians had been 'agreed in principle'.[75]

Russian priorities were emphasised by a delegation to London between 8–12 July led by General Golikov. He was accompanied by Admiral Nikolai Kharlamov, who now became head of the Russian military mission in London and naval attaché until October 1944. In advising the chiefs of staff prior to the meeting, the Joint Planning Staff reiterated that the primary British objective was to keep Russia fighting. They also added – 'we are not allied with Russia and nor do we entirely trust that country'. Otherwise, they concentrated on protocol. There was no effort to identify likely Russian aims, despite useful insights provided by Cripps and Macfarlane, or how Britain might respond.[76] The prevailing mistrust towards the Russians and aversion to dealing with them was certainly evident in Golikov's subsequent meetings with the armed services. The Secretary for War, David Margesson, refused to shake hands and kept the delegation standing, while conveying the feeling that he neither believed in a Red Army victory or the viability of the communist system. Pound, chairing the meeting with the chiefs of staff, formally expressed admiration for the way the Russians were fighting, but gave his guests the impression that he was 'horrified' to be in their company, was in a rush, and had more important tasks than negotiating with 'Bolsheviks'.[77] This negative impression of Pound was underlined in his contacts with Maisky in the coming months.[78]

Golikov's priorities were recorded most clearly and coherently by Eden. After noting that Germany was now devoting 80 per cent of its forces against Russia, he stated that his mission had two basic objectives: joint military operations and material technical assistance. It was essential Britain undertake operations to reduce the weight of the German attack. Air attacks on Germany were welcome but his main interest was a combined operation in the Petsamo and Murmansk area to relieve pressure on the Central and Southern Fronts. He also repeated the supply priorities already flagged by Macfarlane, especially for fighter aircraft.[79]

On 9 July, Golikov expanded on the 'Murmansk operation' first with the chiefs of staff and then, in more detail, with the vice chiefs, chaired by the Vice Chief of the Naval Staff, Vice Admiral Sir Tom Phillips. He stated that German naval strength in the far north currently comprised four destroyers, at least five U-boats, and a dozen smaller craft. About 100 transport vessels were concentrated around Varanger fiord. German land forces in Scandinavia comprised 15–17 divisions, the bulk either in the extreme north or south, with four in the Petsamo area including two mountain divisions. The Petsamo force was supplied via the Arctic Ocean Road from Kemi in the Gulf of Bothnia. It was supported by 200 aircraft, mainly Me 109s and Ju 88s operating from airfields at Petsamo and Varanger. The Germans had a 50 per cent advantage in land force strength. Aircraft numbers were more equal but German aircraft were superior. German forces had crossed into Finland and were now pushing

Russian forces back from the Finnish frontier, posing a threat to the vital base of Murmansk. The Russians also feared an accompanying seaborne landing. Golikov overestimated German air strength. At this time their Norway based 5th Air Fleet, under Colonel General Hans-Jürgen Stumpff, comprised only 180 aircraft in total. Of these ninety-eight were based in the Arctic region and committed to Barbarossa on 22 June with eighty-two designated combat ready. The majority were based at Banak at the southern end of Porsanger Fjord, approximately 100 miles south of North Cape and 200 miles north-west of Murmansk, although the more primitive facilities at Kirkenes were also used.[80]

Golikov insisted the Russian request for help was not excessive. They hoped Britain could offer 200/300 aircraft, two or three cruisers and some lighter vessels to operate against the Germans in the Petsamo area. The initial joint objective would be to destroy the German air forces in the area, prevent any land offensive towards Murmansk and then conduct a counter-attack, including a landing on the German flank from the Ribachiy peninsula. These operations, if successful, would create the possibility for a British advance west and south-west along the Norwegian coastline, striking the enemy at a sensitive point, and laying a foundation for more ambitious operations in Scandinavia. The Russian team added that British air effort should be directed first against the German air force and its bases, then supply depots, and finally land and naval targets. Russian fighter forces could provide some cover in adjacent sea areas, but a carrier would probably be necessary. British aircraft would use Russian airfields with naval forces based at Murmansk. Russian defences were adequate and logistic support, not least fuel, could be managed.[81]

Pound informed the chiefs of staff the following day that the Naval Staff were studying the Russian proposals. However, the deployment of the suggested cruiser and destroyer force, once necessary oilers and minesweepers were added, was a considerable commitment. He doubted the effectiveness of Russian fighter support, especially out of sight of land. The initial Joint Planning Staff view was that the Russians underestimated the overall challenges in executing such a deployment. Pound proposed sending the Russians a questionnaire partly to elicit more information but also to 'educate' them. The clear implication of this discussion is that neither Pound nor his colleagues were willing to engage seriously with the Russian ideas for a joint northern operation. The Naval Staff were looking for problems not solutions and the questionnaire was not only a delaying mechanism but patronising.[82]

The attitude of the chiefs at this point is exemplified by a parallel message from Dill to Macfarlane, drawing on a brief drafted with breathtaking arrogance by his operations staff, and directing the latter on how to respond to Russian requests which risked drawing Britain into unsound military action for political reasons.

> It is the Russians who are asking for assistance: we are not. If they are going to fight, they will fight – but for their own lives and not to help us defeat Germany. Accordingly, I feel the line we should take is as follows: – 'We are doing quite nicely against Germany, particularly in view of ever-increasing American aid and the practical certainty that the USA will sooner or later come into the war. All our forces are now being devoted to the accomplishment of a definite strategy for winning the war without having allowed for Russian aid.'[83]

Macfarlane received a similar message four days later, this time from all the chiefs, after reporting that the Russians believed Britain 'was not pulling its weight'. The chiefs' sharp rejoinder was that 'our present difficulties are largely due to Russian action in 1939' and that Britain had been fighting alone against Germany the last 12 months. The Russians must now 'save themselves just as we saved ourselves in the Battle of Britain and in the Atlantic'.[84]

However, Pound was not permitted to bury Golikov's Murmansk proposal. The prime minister had seen the records of the relevant meetings and, on 10 July, the same day the chiefs considered the issue, he pushed for urgent action. It was essential to send a small naval squadron to the Arctic to 'operate with Russian naval forces'. This must be distinct from the already-agreed Petsamo carrier strike. The impact of such a force on the Russians 'might be of enormous value and spare a lot of English blood'. The advantage of keeping the Russians in the war at least until the winter was 'measureless'. A premature peace by Russia 'would be a terrible disappointment to great masses of people in our country'. If the Russians held out, it mattered much less where the actual front was. They had shown themselves worth backing and 'we must make sacrifices and take risks, even at inconvenience, which I realise, to maintain their morale'.[85] Later that day, the Defence Committee discussed the 'Murmansk operation'. Pound stated that the chiefs were sending by air a flag officer and senior air force officer to assess requirements and local conditions at first hand. Meanwhile, the Admiralty was readying a force of two cruisers and a few destroyers to operate with the Russians from the port. The prime minister reiterated his wish to see a Royal Navy force operating out of Murmansk and hoped there would be no delay.[86]

Not for the first or the last time Churchill grasped the big strategic picture better than his chiefs of staff. In doing so, he was not only drawing on his own instincts and reports from Cripps but his awareness that the Americans believed the Russians were holding well and that Roosevelt, encouraged by Hopkins, was inclined to respond favourably to the Russian requests for aid. On 9 July, Roosevelt directed Sumner Welles that substantial aid must be sent to Russia before 1 October and he confirmed this with the Russian ambassador the following day. He thought fighter aircraft could be delivered rapidly.[87]

## Chapter 3

# The Case for Helping Russia: Ends, Ways and Means

Before Pound's reconnaissance mission could report, two developments in mid-July influenced British attitudes and plans. The first was intelligence suggesting a favourable shift in Russia's prospects. The second was a Russian proposal, forwarded by Cripps and building on Golikov's 'Murmansk' proposal, for joint British–Russian action to occupy Spitzbergen, the largest island in the Svalbard archipelago, located nearly 500 miles north of North Cape, along with Bear Island, halfway between them. (The 1920 Svalbard Treaty had established full Norwegian sovereignty over the entire Svalbard archipelago but also granted specific commercial rights to signatory powers including Russia.)

*Intelligence Insights into Russia's Prospects*

The primary source of intelligence on German progress remained Ultra decrypts of German Enigma traffic. For the rest of 1941, the main line of traffic read was that in the Red key used by the German air force. This was supplemented by some material from a key designated Vulture by GC&CS which was used by the higher command on the Eastern Front and an army/air key called Kestrel. There were also some further decrypts from the Japanese ambassador in Berlin reporting to Tokyo. The Red key provided a comprehensive picture of air force operations which in turn enabled the identification of army unit designations down to division level. The German air force made frequent references to positions reached by the army which provided a good guide to the scale, objectives and progress of the German offensive.[1]

Intelligence sharing seemed an obvious means of fostering British–Russian trust and cooperation. Mason-Macfarlane 'always came back to intelligence as the best available method of aiding the Russians and demonstrating Britain's military prowess and importance'.[2] Ultra was judged too sensitive to be shared directly for fear that it would leak to the Germans, who Enigma decrypts revealed were reading several Soviet codes and ciphers. However, the gist of Ultra reports was shared, suitably 'paraphrased or massaged' or sometimes included where possible within other less sensitive material. By this means the British could still provide valuable intelligence on compromised Soviet ciphers, the location of German headquarters and supply dumps, and German operational planning and readiness. From early July therefore, once 30 Mission was in place, it received a daily intelligence signal prepared by the Joint Intelligence Committee which drew on all relevant material cleared for sharing and was approved by Sir Stewart Menzies, the Chief of SIS (or 'C'), who was ultimately responsible for the security of Ultra. This traffic went over a dedicated SIS secure wireless link. Despite all the precautions, Menzies still worried about security. Pressed by Churchill to send more Ultra-based material, he stressed that the immediacy of Ultra (its greatest strength) would jeopardise the source if sent too quickly. It would be impossible for any agent to have obtained the same degree of detail and transmitted it so quickly. He insisted on building in appropriate delay and had the Soviets tipped off that SIS had a well-placed source in Berlin. With occasional exceptions the return for this British investment was disappointing. Britain always got more information on Soviet dispositions and movements from Ultra decrypts of German traffic than from Soviet liaison personnel. The lack of a useful return from the Russians combined with continuing concern over German penetration caused the British to reduce the sharing of sanitised Ultra material from mid-1942.[3]

By mid-July, GC&CS reporting showed that, after making enormous gains, Barbarossa was faltering. The chiefs of staff reflected this in their weekly résumé for the War Cabinet of 17 July. The Germans had expected to reach Moscow in three weeks and to control all western Russia in six to eight. They appeared surprised by Russian resistance and concerned at their own losses. They had faced considerable air opposition and probably had insufficient fighter strength to cover both their forward armour units and troop concentrations and strategic positions in their rear. The calculus for the chiefs and War Cabinet was depth of Russian resistance versus German ability to maintain their offensives.[4] As Cadogan noted succinctly in his diary: 'Have the Russians got a strategic reserve? Can German transport keep the pace going?'[5] For, although the German advance was slowing, it continued. On 21 July, Kennedy recorded that, despite growing resistance, the Germans were still moving forward on a wide front, were east of Smolensk in the centre, and had reached Kiev in the south. In discussion with Macfarlane, the Russians were highly optimistic, but had provided no hard information on German progress or their own intentions. There were growing British hopes Germany would be preoccupied with Russia for a long time to come but there was still time for her to finish the campaign and turn on Britain before the winter.[6]

Britain was not solely dependent for intelligence on GC&CS SIGINT and whatever Macfarlane could glean. The military representatives of Allied governments in exile present in Moscow, especially the Czechs, Poles and Greeks, were valuable sources. The most important and prolific source on Russian operations and intentions was the Czech attaché, Colonel Heliodor Pika, who was in Moscow from early 1941 until the end of the war. The Czech intelligence mission in London began sharing his reporting well in advance of Barbarossa but he was also in regular contact with Macfarlane. The latter recognised his access, reporting in mid-August that the ability of the Czech and Polish representatives 'to get good information both official and unofficial is much better than mine'. Pika paid a terrible price for his loyalty to President Edvard Beneš despite constant pressure from the Russians to betray him. Following the 1948 communist coup in Czechoslovakia, he was arrested on trumped-up charges of spying for British military intelligence, convicted and executed.[7]

In September, Britain's Special Operations Executive (SOE) charged with fomenting resistance and subversion in occupied territories signed an agreement with the Soviet intelligence agency, the NKVD, to cooperate in subversive action in countries outside their respective 'spheres of influence'. An SOE mission was established in Moscow under Colonel George Hill, a long-standing Russia expert who had worked for SIS in the post-revolution period. Hill was declared to the NKVD but he also had an unavowed SIS officer in his mission who established a relationship with Colonel Leon Bortnowski, subsequently code-named 'Perch', who was the Polish intelligence service representative in Russia from August 1941 to September 1942. Although declared to the Russians, he offered to supply SIS with intelligence from his Polish network which included released prisoners of war. Although some of his insights proved useful, they did not match the quality of Pika's material.[8]

There were also more occasional sources in the autumn of 1941 that proved helpful. The American journalist, Ralph Ingersoll, who had founded the left-wing newspaper *FM* in mid-1940, gained an invitation to Russia following the outbreak of war. He was perceived as a useful lobbyist in winning American support, probably with the ear of Roosevelt, and apparently had several long talks with Stalin during September, although Cripps insisted his access here was overstated. He informed the US embassy in Moscow and then British representatives in Cairo on his route home that Russian morale was 'extremely high', that there was no evidence of political instability, and that Stalin was 'determined to fall back indefinitely if necessary'. He was probably the only observer at this time who judged that the transport system was working well and that evacuation of factories and workers to the East was 'orderly'. Ingersoll's observations were unusually positive at this date but in some respects prescient. They were judged sufficiently important to be shared with the War Cabinet.[9]

## Initial Plans for Operational Collaboration

Meanwhile, on 17 July, the chiefs of staff accepted Joint Planning Staff advice that there was some advantage to occupying both Spitzbergen and Bear Island, primarily to deny their use to the Germans, provided the Russians supplied the necessary occupying force. The British commitment would be limited to 'naval support'. In acquiescing, the chiefs probably saw this as an unwelcome but necessary 'political' investment to reduce pressure for a more ambitious commitment of British forces in the North.[10] This Spitzbergen operation now became a significant preoccupation over the next six weeks.

Simultaneously, Pound's Murmansk reconnaissance mission proceeded under the newly-promoted Rear Admiral Philip Vian, who undertook various northern operations over the next three months, pending his appointment in October to command the 15th Cruiser Squadron in the Mediterranean. Possessing 'a hard, long, hatchet face, the outward visor of a ruthlessly tough fighting sailor',[11] Vian had made his name as an aggressive destroyer commander and now began the trajectory that would make him perhaps the most famous fighting admiral of the war, although not always the most effective. Vian had powerful patrons, Pound, Admiral Sir John Tovey, the Commander-in-Chief Home Fleet, and especially Cunningham, all of whom had known him in the Mediterranean before the war. Others found him rude, arrogant, opinionated, lacking in judgement and impossible to work with. Admiral Sir Bertram Ramsay, his superior during the Normandy invasion, found Vian 'always apt to work against rather than with me' and at times thought him 'not quite normal'.[12] He was not therefore the most diplomatic choice for negotiations with the Russians and did not impress Admiral Arseni Golovko, the 35-year-old commander of the Northern Fleet and chief interlocutor on putative Arctic operations. Golovko found Vian 'brusque' and 'peremptory' and preferred dealing with Rear Admiral Miles.[13] Later in the year, Rear Admiral Harold Burrough, back in northern waters following Halberd, described Golovko, who retained his post throughout the war, as 'clever, far-seeing, and probably ruthless ... able to weigh up a situation very rapidly, but a man of the people. A rough diamond, quite unpolished and with poorish table manners. Rather scruffy but surprisingly well read. Keen to cooperate and undoubtedly a capable man.'[14] If Golovko had a problem with Vian, it was perhaps partly because they were too alike. However, Golovko's post-war memoirs, while admittedly written in the Cold War when he was Deputy Commander-in-Chief of the Soviet Fleet and subject to the ideological constraints of all Soviet memoirs, suggest a man rather more political, calculating and even deceitful, with an underlying attitude to his allies less friendly and supportive, than his various British interlocutors assumed.[15]

Burrough does seem to have established a good rapport with Golovko when he arrived in Vaenga Bay the following November with his flagship, the cruiser *Kenya*, and the destroyers *Bedouin* and *Intrepid*, after escorting convoy PQ 3 to Archangel. Their personal relationship, helped by Burrough having strong family links with Russia, resulted in what was possibly the only joint offensive operation conducted by the Royal Navy with its Russian ally, albeit one lasting barely 24 hours, on 24/25 November. It consisted of a search and destroy mission along the Norwegian coast to the vicinity of North Cape followed by a bombardment of the German base at Vardo, the port at the extreme north-east corner of Norway, during the return journey. Unfortunately, no shipping targets were found, possibly because excessive Russian radio traffic warning their deployed submarines of the movement of the force alerted the Germans. Burrough commended the Russian ships as smart and seamanlike.[16]

That operation lay in the future and meanwhile Vian was accompanied by Group Captain Frederick Pearce during his visit to Polyarnoe and Murmansk and they were joined by Rear Admiral Miles from Moscow on arrival. They reported back to the chiefs on 20 July after visiting Moscow, where Vian had an unproductive and evasive meeting with Navy Minister Admiral Nikolay Kuznetsov, and Archangel as well as Murmansk.[17] Their return coincided with the receipt the previous day of Stalin's first personal message to the prime minister. This stressed the importance of establishing a front against the Germans in the West, ideally in both France and the Arctic. Although he pressed the advantages of the former, he acknowledged the difficulties. By contrast a front in the Arctic was easier. In line with Golikov's earlier proposal, he emphasised Britain need only supply naval and air forces, although a light division of Norwegian forces to organise rebellion against the Germans would also be useful.[18]

Vian and Pearce reported that the Russians had six destroyers and twenty-one submarines at Murmansk facing a German naval force of six destroyers at the Norwegian port of Kirkenes, situated on the southern side of Varanger fiord and a few miles from the Russian border. This Russian naval strength was consistent with the Joint Intelligence Committee assessment of 14 June. The land forces in the Murmansk region were currently about equal, with two divisions on each side, deployed in depth. The front line was ill-defined, but it was unlikely the Germans would break through with their existing force, although a trickle of reinforcements was joining them by sea round North Cape to Kirkenes. In the air, the Russians were outnumbered two to one and the Germans enjoyed a quality advantage. (As already noted, this overestimated German numbers which barely matched the Russian total although the quality point was valid.) The Russian air strength of just over 100 aircraft included some modern fighters but their efficiency was low and poor flying weather a further challenge. German air attacks on Murmansk had so far been ineffective but it was within easy range of their airfields and the Russian warning system was almost non-existent and their anti-aircraft defences inadequate. Its wooden buildings later suffered severely from German incendiary bombs. Given this air threat and almost constant daylight in summertime, Vian did not think it feasible to base surface warships at the Kola ports, but submarines were possible. He also stressed that Murmansk and the Russian naval base at Polyarnoe, on the western side of the entrance to the Kola Inlet, had limited handling facilities. There was no crane with a lift of more than 11 tons, requiring a crane ship to be deployed before tanks could be unloaded. Cargo handling was further hampered by poor organisation. These constraints meant that ships waiting to unload would have to anchor in the exposed Vaenga Bay on the eastern side of the inlet, where holding ground was poor and they would be even more exposed to air attack. Furthermore, in both Polyarnoe and Murmansk, there was a severe lack of repair and docking facilities.[19]

The uncomfortable relationship between Vian and Golovko did not inhibit a positive naval intelligence exchange developing through July in Moscow, London, and even Murmansk although it would not last. This initial openness reflected the Russians' respect for the Royal Navy and their awareness they could gain from its greater experience and superior technology, the focus on specific and practical cooperation in the Arctic, and the determination of Rear Admiral John Godfrey, the Director of Naval Intelligence (DNI), to achieve a relationship outside the formal structures of 30 Mission and the War Office-supervised London Liaison Group. Godfrey had a low opinion of Macfarlane and briefly considered trying to make Miles's naval section totally independent of 30 Mission.

In July, he also wrote to Menzies about the possibility of embedding intelligence officers in Moscow who could work on acquiring information on the Soviet navy. It was a 'golden opportunity to obtain intelligence we have lacked for so long'. Menzies carefully deflected this request. While stressing to Godfrey that the present alliance against Germany had not altered the requirement to collect intelligence on the Soviet forces, SIS must move carefully. The ambassador and 30 Mission were 'most anxious' that nothing should 'impede' the successful collaboration with the Soviet authorities which could 'much influence' winning the war.[20] While Menzies' caution here was understandable, the subsequent establishment of the SOE mission and its embedded SIS officer noted earlier went some way to meeting Godfrey's proposal. Meanwhile, the Soviet Navy probably had another motive for pushing cooperation with their British ally to the limit of their political remit. They had only achieved independence from the Red Army four years previously and tensions and bitter jealousies continued between the two Russian services. Productive contact with the British was a potential means of strengthening their status within the Soviet politico-military hierarchy. This and the small size of the British naval mission, which initially consisted of Miles, his secretary, a Russian-speaking chief staff officer, and a small clerical and cipher team, enabled the naval relationship at least initially to circumvent much of the Soviet bureaucracy which hampered army and air force business.[21]

At the start of July therefore, Rear Admiral Miles passed the Russians intelligence on German mining techniques including specific mining operations off Murmansk, and guidance on minesweeping countermeasures and anti-submarine tactics. The Russians responded with documents on German U-boat construction and anti-aircraft defences at Kiel. The British also provided a sample Asdic set which delighted the Russians and this triggered an extensive working session on lessons from naval operations in the North Sea. In mid-July, Miles' team in Moscow received useful information on the *Bismarck* class battleships and detailed summaries of German minefields in the northern sea routes. Later in the month, the Russian navy passed an update on the location of German forces at Kirkenes and Petsamo, designed to assist the forthcoming carrier strike. Miles' team were also invited to visit Russian warships without waiting for reciprocal rights. Finally, during the last week of July, the Russians accepted the posting of British naval liaison officers to both the Northern Fleet and the Black Sea region, arrangements that remained in place for the rest of the war. On 29 July, Cripps noted, albeit rather tempting fate, that 'naval cooperation is excellent'.[22]

The Black Sea unit became arguably the most productive and enduring of these intelligence relationships. It was the only wartime liaison, naval, army or air, directly linked with, and at times embedded in, a front-line Soviet command. The posts in North Russia were different in that their role was to handle British operations alongside and in coordination with their Soviet counterparts. The Black Sea unit initially comprised Captain Barney Fawkes, a submariner who had commanded a flotilla in the Mediterranean, and Commander Geoffrey Ambrose, a Russian speaker fresh from active service. On arrival in Sevastopol in early August, they were introduced to the fleet commander, Vice Admiral Filip Oktyabrskii, by Miles' chief of staff, Commander Derek Wyburd. Ambrose joined the destroyer *Bodri* and became the first Western serviceman to participate in a Russian combat operation. Fawkes undertook three short submarine patrols including a war cruise off Romania. Both officers learnt much about Soviet naval practice and equipment. In general, they found ships and submarines well-handled and efficient but subject to rigid hierarchical attitudes regarding role and tactics and stifling bureaucracy. There was no appetite to explore Royal Navy ideas or war experience. Unfortunately, after barely six weeks, Fawkes and Wyburd were accused, quite unjustly, of inappropriate political remarks, and the issue escalated all the way to Molotov and Stalin who demanded their withdrawal. For the sake of wider relations at a difficult time and in the hope of keeping Ambrose in post, the British acquiesced, Churchill taking the attitude, 'They are far more dependent on us than we on them'. The calculation that Ambrose would be allowed to stay proved correct and, as described later, he produced valuable dividends through 1942, but the affair was also a warning of the perils in managing intelligence relations with a paranoid system.[23]

The officer appointed as Senior British Naval Officer (SBNO) North Russia was Rear Admiral Richard Bevan, a communications specialist who had retired in 1935 to become a farmer but was recalled to service in 1939 and had been naval attaché in Rome for the last 18 months. By early August, he had established his headquarters alongside that of the Northern Fleet at Polyarnoe where, despite the beauty of an Arctic summer, it was immediately apparent that working and living conditions were grim. In November, he was joined in the North by Captain Guy Maund who became SBNO Archangel. Bevan was not a good choice. He was temperamentally unsuited to the complex problems he soon faced and disliked the Russians whom he regarded as uncivilised and uncouth. Inevitably they never respected Bevan in the way they did his successors who came with more war experience. Golovko contemptuously dismissed him as 'an expert in agriculture who can discuss it until the cows come home'. Not surprisingly therefore, Bevan's initial professional assessment was negative although not necessarily unfair. He claimed the Northern Fleet staff were in a defensive mindset fixated on supplying the Red Army, especially the forces based on the Ribachiy peninsula. Air activity too was focused on defence, close support of the army and reconnaissance with no attempt to target German airbases in northern Norway. The two minelaying submarines were also not operating against German bases and supply routes. The rest of the submarine force seemed efficient and motivated compared to their surface counterparts but their equipment and tactics were rudimentary. Bevan also found Golovko unwilling to share relevant operational information, notably the movements of Russian submarines off the Norwegian coast. Mutual dislike no doubt played some part but this attitude was more a reflection of endemic Russian suspicion over real British motives and paranoia over 'spying'. Matters improved somewhat as Golovko recognised that, with the imminent arrival of two 'T' class submarines and the technical and intelligence assistance already provided, Bevan could bring him operational benefit. When 30 Mission, along with other foreign diplomatic missions, was withdrawn from Moscow in the face of the looming German threat in late October, Bevan became responsible for all matters relating to the Arctic supply convoys at the Russian end further obliging Golovko to make more effort.[24]

Against the background of Vian's report, the chiefs reviewed options for British assistance less from the viewpoint of its military advantage than the 'political and psychological effect' on the Russians. Norwegian army units available in the United Kingdom were currently too small to contribute usefully. British land forces allocated to the Atlantic islands could be diverted but were vulnerable to the superior German air forces able to exploit long hours of daylight. The chiefs were unwilling to deploy the naval force envisaged by the Russians without fighter protection both in harbour and at sea. An essential first step to achieve this was provision of radar, anti-aircraft guns, appropriate aviation and maritime fuel stocks and associated support services. Basing at Archangel would be too far from the action. The chiefs judged that the only immediate options were establishing a naval force at Spitzbergen and basing one or two submarines at Murmansk.[25] They also tasked the air staff to consider despatching three or four air squadrons to Murmansk with all the necessary support equipment and services to operate effectively.[26]

However, over the next few days, the prime minister pressed for faster and greater commitment to these putative northern operations. This reflected his response to Stalin's message. He had ruled out any major diversionary operation in France and was therefore obliged to emphasise potential help in the North. Here, the prime minister listed: the imminent Petsamo carrier strike; naval support for Spitzbergen; the deployment of a flotilla of submarines; and possibly the basing of British fighter squadrons at Murmansk.[27] However, at the Defence Committee on 21 July, he went further and asked the chiefs to prepare a British land force for despatch to Spitzbergen. The chiefs accordingly directed the joint planners to identify how a brigade could be sent without prejudicing commitments to the Atlantic islands.[28] When the prime minister met the chiefs on 23 July, he stressed the tremendous fight the Russians were making and the need to provide every possible assistance. Pound confirmed that the Petsamo carrier strike force would sail that evening and he subsequently ordered a reconnaissance of Spitzbergen by Vian, with the cruisers *Nigeria* and *Aurora* and three destroyers, to assess any German presence. The Admiralty also ordered two submarines, less than Churchill's promised 'flotilla', *Tigris* and *Trident*, to deploy to the Arctic and base at Polyarnoe. *Tigris*, which during her previous patrol in the Bay of Biscay had sunk the Italian submarine *Michele Bianchi*, departed north from Holy Loch on 26 July and reached Polyarnoe on 4 August. *Trident* returned from a war patrol off Brest on 23 July and departed north on 1 August, reaching Polyarnoe 10 days later.[29]

The Chief of the Air Staff, Air Chief Marshal Sir Charles Portal, hoped to send two or three squadrons of aircraft although this would be a 'political and moral gesture' with 'little strategical effect'. He was also investigating the supply of American P-40 Tomahawk fighters which had begun serving with the Royal Air Force in the Middle East the previous month. He subsequently confirmed availability of two squadrons of Hurricanes, Pound promised to allocate the old carrier *Argus* for their delivery, and, on 27 July, the prime minister instructed them to proceed. By 3 August it was agreed that forty Hurricanes (Mark IIBs), complete with pilots and ground staff, would be allocated to the defence of Murmansk and the Polyarnoe naval base. The British commander of the force would come under the operational control of the Soviet Northern Front command, in practice Major General A A Kuznetsov, Commander of the Air Force of the Northern Fleet. *Argus*, with six Grumman Martlets for self-defence, would fly off twenty-four Hurricanes once she was in range and the balance of sixteen would be delivered crated in the merchant vessel *Llanstephen Castle*, included in the initial Dervish supply convoy. Planned arrival was the third week of August, and the British personnel would operate the force until October when the aircraft and related ground equipment would be passed to the Russians.[30] By 11 August, 140 Tomahawks, eighty-six from stocks in the United Kingdom and fifty-four supplied direct from the

United States, had also been earmarked for Russia with an initial batch of forty-eight in crates added to the Dervish convoy of seven vessels sailing in parallel with *Argus* which reached Archangel on 31 August.[31]

This military support package was accompanied by the supply of significant raw materials and miscellaneous military equipment. During August, Britain shipped 17,700 tons of rubber (about 13.5 per cent of monthly global production), 5750 tons of lead, 1500 tons of tin, 5000 tons of wool, 5200 tons of jute and one million pairs of boots; 702,000 barrels of aviation fuel, 800 tons of tetraethyl lead (a key additive for manufacturing aviation fuel) and £90,000 of industrial diamonds were also sent. Most of these supplies were collected by Soviet merchant vessels and tankers which then sailed singly to the Russian Arctic ports. With few U-boats yet deployed in the Arctic and, for the present, limited German maritime air strike forces, the threat to these was minimal.[32] From late July, there were significant naval supplies, 200 standard mines and 1000 depth charges being despatched by the end of the month with 800 parachute mines and 3000 depth charges to follow in August. Some of these items, along with 100 magnetic mines, were embarked in the minelaying cruiser *Adventure* whose passage was coordinated with the Petsamo strike force. The depth charges were especially valuable given that the total Northern Fleet stock was currently less than 7000.[33] Meanwhile, in a striking of example of how the paranoid Russians could also be surprisingly cooperative, sample British aircraft including a Hurricane and Spitfire were also sent for the Russians to test while, in return, British test pilots sampled Russian aircraft.[34]

### Initial German Operations in the Arctic Theatre

Before further describing execution of the initial British military initiatives in the Arctic begun in late July, it is important to examine German intentions for this region. If the Germans seized Murmansk or decisively cut its railway and subsequently took or isolated Archangel, British operations in the area in support of Russia would be rendered pointless. Plans for a German offensive here as part of Barbarossa progressed slowly and were subject to considerable change and confusion. OKW initially saw Murmansk as an unnecessary diversion of effort given that Russia was expected to collapse quickly, a view that never entirely disappeared. Hitler was more committed but would sanction release of only limited forces from Norway due to his fears of British attack, exacerbated by the commando raid on the Lofotens in March. Deploying adequate German forces in the North and ensuring their long-term support required complex negotiations with Finland and potentially Sweden too. The possibility of Finland joining Germany as an 'ally' against Russia was explored through the first months of 1941 but the precise terms of Finnish military collaboration further complicated planning. The Finns were willing to offer Germany bases and transit rights and discuss joint military operations. However, their goals were primarily directed at recovering their own territory, especially Hanko and southern Karelia, lost in their recent war with Russia. They preferred to avoid an unlimited war to meet German aims. The Germans, for their part, would not disclose their overall intent. Even with conditional Finnish support, the logistic challenges in transporting German divisions to their start points, and then sustaining them, were formidable. Total German strength deployed in Finland by the start of Barbarossa was close to 100,000 men, more than two-thirds in the far north.[35]

Yet another critical issue complicated planning. Finland was a rich source of nickel, produced at Kolosjoki, 30 miles south-west of Petsamo port. Nickel was a vital component of high-quality steel and other vital war materials and, following a trade agreement in mid-1940, Germany had acquired 60 per cent of Kolosjoki's output. It was Germany's only reliable source and by 1944 contributed 80 per cent of its supplies. Strategically, certainly in Hitler's mind, Kolosjoki ranked not far behind the Ploesti oilfields in Romania and ultimately it acquired the most elaborate defences against air attack of any site in German-controlled Europe. The security of Kolosjoki therefore influenced the evolution of the putative Arctic offensive. Hitler regularly pronounced this more important than Murmansk. Planning required not only rapid occupation of the Petsamo region but sufficient forces to ensure it could be held against any feasible Russian pre-emptive move or counter-attack.[36] The British Ministry of Economic Warfare (MEW) was aware of Kolosjoki and its potential value to German war production, not least because it had been developed with substantial Canadian investment prior to 1939.[37] However, it is not clear they communicated its importance to the Admiralty. It certainly did not feature as a target for the forthcoming Fleet Air Arm Petsamo attack.

The final German plan, code-named Silver Fox, involved a three-pronged attack by three widely dispersed corps, each with two divisions, under the overall command of the German Army of Norway, headed by Colonel General Paul von Falkenhorst. In the far north, the German Mountain Corps under Lieutenant General Eduard Dietl would strike directly for Murmansk from Petsamo (Operation Platinum Fox). Dietl was a convinced Nazi and a long-standing friend and personal favourite of Hitler who had won military renown as the saviour of Narvik the previous year. His influence and standing with Hitler arguably led to his operation receiving resources better invested further south. One hundred and seventy-five miles in this direction, XXXVI Corps, with two German divisions was supposed to mount the main Silver Fox effort. This force would drive east (Operation Polar Fox) from the Finnish border along the railway route which originated at Kemi on the northern coast of the Gulf of Bothnia and ran via Rovaniemi and Salla to Kandalaksha, on the extreme north-western spur of the White Sea, where it joined the line from Murmansk. (In 1941, there were gaps in this rail route. On the Finnish side, the stretch from Rovaniemi to the border was not complete while, on the Russian side, parts of the branch from Kandalaksha were still under construction and it currently ended at Salla.) Seizing Kandalaksha would cut the Murmansk railway and trap Russian forces to the north. Sixty-five miles further south, the Finnish III Corps, incorporating one German division, would strike east to cut the Murmansk railway again at Loukhi, located 100 miles south of Kandalaksha. The Finns subsequently undertook a fourth thrust, a further 150 miles to the south, directed at Belomorsk where the Murmansk railway divided, one line proceeding to Leningrad, and the other veering east to join the line from Archangel to Moscow. The main Finnish effort was concentrated on recovering Hanko, the southern port Finland had been forced to lease to Russia under the Moscow Peace Treaty the previous year, and the Karelia territory around Lake Ladoga and north of Leningrad. The latter operation was intimately linked with German plans to capture that city.[38]

In their initial planning of naval support for Barbarossa in January 1941, the German Naval Staff stressed the strategic significance of the Russian bases at Murmansk and Polyarnoe. They judged it important to weaken these with massive air attacks, thus rendering British operations in the Arctic more difficult. However, anticipating the early capture of these ports by land attack, the staff saw no pressing need for offensive operations against the Soviet Northern Fleet. They assumed that once the ports ceased to be usable, surviving Northern Fleet units would probably head for Britain, mirroring British expectations here. Plans should therefore be made to destroy Russian surface units during their passage out. The staff nevertheless recognised the need to prevent the Northern Fleet harassing the German advance with coastal raids or interfering with seaborne supply lines. Five large destroyers of the 6th Destroyer Flotilla were accordingly deployed to Kirkenes which they reached on 10 July and two U-boats by the end of the month.[39] Despite this willingness to allow the Northern Fleet threat to be eliminated by land attack, at the Führer conference on 4 February Raeder still emphasised the importance of preventing the British gaining a foothold in Murmansk and Polyarnoe. He also stressed the need to destroy the locks in the White Sea Canal. He promoted these objectives regularly thereafter and they were incorporated in Barbarossa planning although in early July Halder referred to the 'dubiousness' of the Murmansk operation which he judged motivated by 'political' rather than operational imperatives.[40] It would be wrong to claim too much foresight for Raeder. There is little evidence that he anticipated the use of the Arctic route for a massive Western supply operation to Russia. He accepted the prevailing consensus that the Russian campaign would be complete by the autumn. His concern was rather that bases in Russia, even if temporary, would enable the Royal Navy to achieve substantial control over the Barents Sea, disrupting German coastal communications and threatening northern Norway.

None of the German thrusts under Silver Fox got even close to their primary objectives. Indeed, the story of this campaign deserves greater recognition as a corrective to the view that, for the first weeks of Barbarossa, the Germans swept all before them. In the far north, following the launch of Barbarossa on 22 June, Dietl's two divisions of German Mountain Corps Norway moved east (Operation Reindeer) without opposition into the Petsamo region where, within five days, they linked up with Finnish border units placed under German command and positioned on the Russian border. On 29 June, this force attacked across the border (now Operation Platinum Fox) with the aim of taking Murmansk, 70 miles away. After some initial success, the attack soon bogged down. The terrain proved more difficult than expected, Russian forces could not be dislodged from the Ribachiy peninsula on the northern flank, and Russian resistance was dogged. By the end of July, the Germans were stuck broadly on the line of the river Litza, just 20 miles from the border and barely one-third the distance to Murmansk. A breakthrough was no longer judged possible without reinforcements. At the Führer conference on 25 July, Raeder expressed concern at the stalling of this Arctic attack and the difficulties the failure to take Murmansk posed for German shipping and naval movements along the Arctic coastline. To help counter the growing threat from Russian and British naval units, two U-boats were now operating off the Ribachiy peninsula and the area around Kola and two more would shortly deploy from Trondheim.[41] Golikov's claim to the vice chiefs on 9 July that five U-boats were already present in the Far North was wrong. There were no U-boats in the area before the end of July. Lobbied by Dietl and in the face of determined opposition from Halder and Brauchitsch, Hitler now reluctantly agreed to add a third mountain division to the northern force, but this had to be redeployed from Greece and did not reach Petsamo until early October, hampered by British and Russian disruption of German sea communications round northern Norway. By this time, winter was setting in and Dietl's two initial divisions had taken 10,300 casualties, rendering them combat ineffective. Indeed, in percentage terms, they suffered the highest losses of any German unit on the entire Eastern Front up to December.[42] Vian's judgement that the Germans would not reach Murmansk in 1941 therefore proved accurate and indeed the northern front line remained the Litza until 1944 when the Russians finally moved forward.

Although XXXVI Corps was a stronger German formation, was supported by one of the best Finnish divisions, and enjoyed a more secure supply route by rail from Kemi, it too struggled to progress. The first objective, the town of Salla, was captured by 10 July but only after stiff fighting, heavy casualties and the partial collapse of the SS Division North whose leadership and training proved grossly inadequate. Thereafter the attackers renewed the advance but Russian resistance was skilful and dogged and, by the end of the month, they had moved only 10 more miles while losses reached 5500. Although the terrain was different to that in the north, it was no easier to navigate, the Russians exploited it to advantage with well-constructed defensive lines, the performance of SS North remained poor, and, in early August, Halder judged the attack must be called off. The operation was successfully revived with the help of Finnish forces but, by late September, the Germans were again stalled on the river Verman almost 50 miles short of their target and had now taken almost as many casualties as their northern counterparts. Nevertheless, OKW Supreme Command were keen to persist, reflecting growing concern over the British presence in Murmansk and the threat to the Petsamo nickel mines. On 10 October therefore, Führer Directive No 37 ordered von Falkenhorst to conduct a winter offensive for which he would receive two new mountain divisions. These never arrived and von Falkenhorst refused to move without them. Progress thus remained stalled through the winter of 1941/42 but, in contrast to the northern operation, the offensive was briefly resumed here the following spring albeit with no breakthrough. The Finnish attack towards Loukhi was maintained for longest, well into winter, and was the most successful, ultimately getting within 20 miles of the railway. The final phase was marked by growing tension between von Falkenhorst and the Finnish commander Major General Siilvarsuo and the latter may have been secretly instructed by Helsinki not to press for the railway. The Americans had warned Finland of serious consequences if American war materials for Russia were disrupted by specific Finnish action against the railway.[43] Although he did not refer directly to the railway, at the end of November, Churchill too warned the Finnish leader,

Field Marshal Carl Mannerheim, of the penalties Finland would suffer if she over-reached.[44]

The railway between Murmansk and the vital junction at Belomorsk was not seriously threatened by German or Finnish land forces for the rest of the war. Attempts by the German air force or by parachuted commando troops to disrupt the line by destroying bridges and other infrastructure, or even creating landslides, were equally unsuccessful. Although the Ju 88 force grew to sixty by February 1942 and over a hundred by the end of April, these aircraft were primarily targeted at the Arctic convoys and there were insufficient to inflict lasting disruption on the Kola ports or railway as opposed to occasional harassment. From September 1941, fighter defence at Murmansk was substantially reinforced with the arrival of British Hurricanes. A major raid there at the end of June 1942 did inflict significant damage to the town and port facilities but disruption was still temporary and Archangel was by then available. Five ships, three British and two American, were sunk in the harbour or while anchored in the Kola Inlet during the first half of 1942 but all their cargoes were successfully landed. The primary German strategic goal – destruction of the railway either completely or for a long time – was never achieved.[45]

There were multiple reasons for the failure of these northern operations in 1941. Apart from the Naval Staff, the German leadership, certainly the army but even Hitler himself, saw the objectives, including Murmansk, as desirable but not essential. Intelligence on Russian strength especially in artillery was poor, the overall German resources allocated were inadequate and compounded by dispersal across three distinct thrusts. That was especially true of air power with only ten Ju 88 medium bombers, thirty Stuka dive-bombers and twenty fighters available for these northern operations at the beginning of July. This air group received an impossible range of tasks in its operational directive: establish German air superiority over all combat areas and the coast of northern Norway; operations against hostile land and sea forces; operations against Russian supply routes, notably the White Sea canal, Murmansk, Archangel and Kandalaksha; and protection of German shipping from Allied attack.[46]

The difficulty of the terrain, especially in the drive from Petsamo, was also underestimated. So was the logistic challenge in supplying three distinct operations or shifting resources between them. Once it was clear more resources were needed, the problems in bringing new forces along tenuous sea and land communication lines from other theatres were almost insuperable. By contrast, the Russians could reinforce flexibly, not least exploiting the Murmansk railway which covered all three German targets. There is a popular view that the Germans should have held

Petsamo with a single division and maximised effort on Kandalaksha and cutting the railway. Murmansk could then have been taken more easily from the south. This ignores the perceived importance of holding Kolosjoki. A single division in the north might not have been enough to hold a Russian counter-attack. Finally, Silver Fox did not address the problem of Archangel. Even if Murmansk and its railway were taken, this provided an alternative connection to the Western Allies except for winter periods when it was ice bound.[47] Indeed, Admiral Golovko later claimed that Murmansk was not initially envisaged for receiving supplies as opposed to supporting naval operations. This reflected the perceived vulnerability of the southern section of the direct line to Leningrad which the Finns did indeed cut in the summer of 1941, first at the Svir river and then further south too.[48] However, once the link between Belomorsk and Obozerskaya on the Archangel–Moscow line was completed in November 1941, traffic could pass by this route to Moscow so long as the line north of Belomorsk remained intact.[49] Raeder stressed the importance of taking Archangel to Hitler on 17 September. Hitler responded that at least the railway line would be cut although it was not clear how this was to be achieved or even if Hitler understood what line was involved.[50]

*Operation EF – The Fleet Air Arm Attack on Petsamo*

The increasing difficulty the Germans experienced with their land operations from mid-July profoundly influenced how they perceived British and Russian naval activity in the Barents Sea. The carrier strike on Kirkenes and Petsamo port (30 miles south-east of Kirkenes), designated Operation EF, took place on 30 July. The Home Fleet task force commanded by Rear Admiral Frederick Wake-Walker, flying his flag in the heavy cruiser *Devonshire*, comprised two carriers, *Victorious* and *Furious*, escorted by a second heavy cruiser *Suffolk* and six destroyers. The intelligence underpinning the raid derived from Golikov's briefing to the vice chiefs on 9 July and Golovko's subsequent more detailed assessment shared with Vian and Miles. This was supplemented by some insights drawn from Ultra SIGINT but primarily the Red Enigma key used by the German air force. Unfortunately, although the Dolphin naval key was being read currently from the beginning of June, Bletchley faced problems picking up traffic in the Arctic from the middle of that month.[51] Wake-Walker's belief that there would be troop transports at both targets and a good chance of finding several destroyers at Kirkenes was not therefore based on recent intelligence. Nevertheless, the primary EF objective was indeed the destruction of transports and warships at the two ports, and any encountered in Varanger fiord while the aircraft were approaching the targets. SIGINT coverage of German air force dispositions was also patchy but Wake-Walker knew that there was a substantial presence in the area based at several airfields so the attackers could expect stiff opposition if they failed to achieve surprise. After sailing from Scapa Flow on 23 July, in company with *Adventure* carrying mines and depth charges to Archangel, the force refuelled in Iceland and, on reaching the operational area, split into two divisions. *Victorious* and *Devonshire* with three destroyers attacked Kirkenes, while *Furious* with *Suffolk* and three destroyers attacked Petsamo.

Admiral Tovey undertook EF, which he saw driven by political calculation rather than any worthwhile military benefit, with reluctance. He judged, presciently as it turned out, that the risk to the carriers, aircrew and supporting ships including oilers, was out of proportion to the most optimistic estimate of the results they could achieve. The slow Swordfish and Albacore strike aircraft were vulnerable to German land-based high-performance fighters which also outmatched escorting Fleet Air Arm Fulmars. Apart from these aircraft limitations, Tovey was also concerned that many aircrews lacked experience. Indeed, some of the pilots embarked in *Furious* had not previously conducted a deck landing. Meanwhile, the carriers and their escort would be exposed to counter-attack from German land-based bombers whose efficiency in attacking ships had been starkly demonstrated the previous year. Ultra SIGINT showed that the Germans conducted daily reconnaissance flights out to 40 miles from the coast. Given these risks, Tovey proposed attacking German coastal targets further south in Norway where a Royal Navy force was potentially less vulnerable, but this was rejected by the Admiralty as it would not serve the desired political purpose of cooperation with Russia.[52]

*Victorious* launched twenty torpedo-armed Albacores in two waves escorted by nine Fulmars. *Furious* despatched nine Swordfish, six with torpedoes and three with bombs followed by nine Albacores with a similar weapon mix. These were accompanied by six Fulmars armed with four 20lb bombs apiece in addition to their standard gun armament to use against targets of opportunity. Each carrier also launched a small combat air patrol for force defence. For both strike groups, the primary target was shipping but secondary targets were the iron ore plant at Kirkenes and oil storage tanks at Petsamo. There was no pre-strike reconnaissance. This could only be conducted from the carrier force and doing so would sacrifice surprise. Each group was dependent therefore on the prior intelligence provided by the Russians and estimates of German air strength and dispositions derived from Ultra SIGINT. They also lost the advantage of surprise after the carriers were spotted by German air reconnaissance shortly before the planned launch time, giving the defences at least an hour's warning. Tovey subsequently judged that the carrier force had moved too close to the coast despite the known risk of German aerial surveillance. Wake-Walker considered cancelling the operation but felt the political imperative justified continuing.

The immediate military benefits from the two strikes, as Tovey had feared, were negligible. There was no shipping of value in either port and the alerted German defences proved highly effective in disrupting the British attacks. A single small merchant vessel was destroyed in each port. Otherwise, there was slight damage to facilities at Kirkenes and several empty oil tanks were rendered inoperable at Petsamo. This did not mean the underlying intelligence was completely wrong. By this date, there were five large destroyers operating from Kirkenes and supply ships, supporting the German Mountain Corps, were regularly present in both ports. It appears the destroyers were out on a sweep and finding none on the actual day of the raid was sheer bad luck. The *Victorious* air group suffered heavily from German fighters (Me 109s, Me 110s and specially-adapted Stukas), losing eleven Albacores and two Fulmars, almost 50 per cent of the strike force and escort, with a further eight aircraft damaged. The Germans lost just two aircraft. The *Furious* group were more fortunate, losing only three aircraft in the face of much lighter fighter opposition.[53] The losses were especially severe given the small size of the German fighter force in the Kirkenes region at this time, just ten Me 109s, five Me 110s and perhaps ten modified Stukas.[54]

Wake-Walker did not consider a second strike practicable given the losses and therefore withdrew to the north. The force was not located again by German air surveillance, but heavy radio traffic was detected, probably from German destroyers, around Tana Fiord, 70 miles east of North Cape. A Fulmar was flown off next day to investigate but had to retreat in the face of heavy German air presence. Still keen to identify targets, Wake-Walker then commissioned an armed reconnaissance of Tromsø but this yielded nothing for the loss of a further aircraft and he departed for Scapa Flow, arriving on 7 August.

At nearly 2000 miles, EF was the longest-range multi-carrier strike against multiple shore targets yet undertaken by the Royal Navy. It also marked the first use of a significant fighter escort in support of the strike aircraft while maintaining a defensive screen over the carriers. Overall, it demonstrated strategic reach and brought out valuable lessons in planning and executing such operations in the future. Just under three years later, the same two carriers, albeit equipped with next-generation aircraft, would conduct the supreme carrier strike of the European war against the battleship *Tirpitz* in Kaafiord, 200 miles west of Petsamo. It is also noteworthy that the Royal Navy undertook EF while almost simultaneously demonstrating the power of a carrier in air defence of a convoy against shore-based attack during Operation Substance in the Mediterranean, 2500 miles to the south. Nevertheless, EF brutally exposed the limitations of current Fleet Air Arm aircraft which were discussed earlier. Whatever the merits of the Albacore or Swordfish as an overall weapon system, they could not survive in daylight against modern shore-based state-of-the-art fighters. Their only chance of results was if they enjoyed complete surprise. The Fulmar too, however well flown, was completely outmatched by the Me 109. There were valid suggestions for altering the strike package in favour of more fighters in future operations, but these would have limited effect without better aircraft. Both Tovey and Wake-Walker recognised the importance of accurate intelligence and achieving surprise. As the latter noted, German ships bringing supplies to the Arctic theatre front line could be strung out anywhere between Narvik and Kirkenes. Intelligence prior to sailing, or even from Ultra, could only be guaranteed up to date with aerial reconnaissance but this was difficult to reconcile with surprise.[55]

In his final report, Tovey emphasised to the Admiralty (and he no doubt hoped the prime minister) the deep reluctance with which he had undertaken EF. The material results were small and the losses heavy. There was no doubt that some survivors felt an attack on such poor targets against such heavy opposition was not justified and their morale was shaken until they understood the underlying political necessity. He could not resist adding, 'I trust that the encouragement to the morale of our Allies was proportionately great'.[56]

## Royal Navy Submarine Operations from Polyarnoe

Soon after EF, *Tigris* and *Trident* began operating from Polyarnoe. Each conducted three war patrols, mainly within 100 miles of North Cape, over the three months up to mid-November when they were replaced by *Sealion* and *Seawolf*, which conducted a further three patrols each up to mid-January. These patrols could exploit excellent intelligence, primarily drawn from Ultra, on German convoy patterns between Tromsø and Kirkenes. Between them the four submarines sank nine merchant and supply ships for an estimated 18,017 tons and damaged several more. They also sank two small anti-submarine vessels. *Trident* was the most successful boat, accounting for four of the merchant/supply ships, totalling 10,499 tons, and the two escorts. Her greatest achievement was sinking the troopship *Donau II* and severely damaging a second, *Bahia*

*Laura*, in Sørøysundet north-west of Hammerfest on 30 August. These were carrying vital reinforcements for the failing Litza river offensive and their loss was a severe setback. One report has 600 soldiers and seamen drowned although this seems excessive. Given the available intelligence, the overall results achieved by these boats were perhaps modest, but they had a useful deterrent effect on German coastal traffic, obliged the Germans to improve their anti-submarine defences, and possibly spurred the much larger Russian submarine force to operate more aggressively.[57] The Germans were soon aware from SIGINT coverage that several British submarines were operating alongside Russian boats in the Arctic area and on 2 December they also noted an Associated Press report that two British submarines in Arctic waters had sunk eight ships.[58] Meanwhile, any increased aggression by the Russian submarines delivered few results. Russian claims of forty-four ships sunk for nearly 200,000 tons over the six months to end December by a total of eighteen boats deployed in this period were grossly overstated. Post-war analysis suggests that only five of these Russian attacks were successful, sinking three supply ships, a German patrol boat, a barge and two fishing vessels.[59] Golovko offered grudging praise for the British performance in his memoirs.[60] On a lighter note, he also gifted the captain of *Trident*, Commander Geoffrey Sladen, with a reindeer, after the latter mentioned that his wife struggled to push a pram through the snow in England. Aware of the current sensitivities in British–Russian relations, Sladen, six and a half feet tall and a former England rugby player, felt it rude to refuse and the reindeer, named Pollyanna by the crew, was embarked in *Trident* through the torpedo loading hatch. She completed at least one war patrol, living on scraps from the galley, condensed milk and cigarettes, and allegedly sleeping under the captain's bunk, before returning with the submarine to her base at Blyth in Northumberland where she was gifted to London Zoo.[61]

The Home Fleet covering force for Dervish, Force M, again commanded by Wake-Walker, comprised *Victorious*, the cruisers *Devonshire* and *Suffolk* and three destroyers. The safety of the convoy and *Argus*, which travelled separately a week apart, each with their own close escort, was its primary objective but it was also to execute further shipping strikes, designated Operation EG, if circumstances permitted. A strike by two groups of six Albacores against shipping and oil tanks around Hammerfest, 140 miles north-east of Tromsø, prior to the arrival of the *Argus* group proved abortive, although it did alert the enemy to the presence of British forces, thus losing the surprise which should have conditioned Wake-Walker's conduct. Following the successful launch of *Argus*'s Hurricanes on 7 September, Force M refuelled in Spitzbergen before conducting a second strike on 12 September aimed at targets in Vest Fiord, which leads into Narvik, and Glomfjord 30 miles to the south, which was more successful. This again comprised two Albacore groups, one armed with torpedoes and the other with bombs. A medium-sized merchant ship was sunk in Vest Fiord and a quay and smaller vessel destroyed at Bodø while an aluminium works was hit and a D/F station destroyed in Glomfjord.[62]

Leaving aside the useful lessons it provided, there is a long-standing consensus that EF was a costly political gesture with no lasting impact. This needs qualification. EF, the subsequent Operation Dervish at the end of August and the EG strikes in September, along with the first patrols by *Tigris* and *Trident*, were seen as a serious threat by both Raeder and Hitler, albeit for slightly different reasons. Their view makes an interesting contrast with that of Churchill who, evidently drawing on Ultra decrypts, worried at the end of August that Murmansk was still under threat and that too much German shipping was moving freely along the Arctic coast.[63] Raeder presented a stark picture at the Führer conference on 17 September. The British understood the importance of the Arctic coast sea route for supplying German forces and were operating in the northern area with one or two carriers, several cruisers, destroyers, and submarines. German naval and air resources were slight. At present, troop transports were unable to proceed east of North Cape and supply steamers only at great risk. As the scope for German air operations was reduced by approaching winter, the British surface threat would increase. Hence capture of Murmansk remained essential but it would not alone stop British harassing operations. In expressing this view, Raeder evidently understood how easily the 6th Destroyer Flotilla might have been caught in Kirkenes. His gloominess over supply prospects must also have contributed to the decision to suspend Platinum Fox.[64] For Hitler, the growing British activity in the Arctic region apparent with EF, Dervish and Spitzbergen fed his increasing anxiety that northern Norway was being targeted for a major attack. As noted earlier, this worry stemmed from the British commando raid on the Lofoten Islands in early March and frequently re-surfaced thereafter. Through the last four months of 1941, the concern became a fixation, bordering on paranoia. By the end of the year, for Hitler, the region was 'of decisive importance for the outcome of the war' and Norway 'the zone of destiny'.[65]

## *The Spitzbergen Operation*

Meanwhile the Spitzbergen operation which the prime minister had initiated on 21 July proved a protracted affair, consuming more resources than it deserved. While Vian conducted his reconnaissance, the joint planners drew together what was known of the archipelago and their present population and the force required to take control of and deny the islands to the Germans. They judged any German response 'light and improbable'. The chiefs confirmed that the objectives of the operation were to eliminate any German presence, deny Spitzbergen's coal supplies to Germany and to establish a temporary naval refuelling base. It was quickly recognised that denial of coal could be achieved by destroying the mines and permanent occupation was not necessary. A problem arose when the Joint Intelligence Committee stated that, although the likelihood was low, the Germans could generate sufficient assets from their existing forces in northern Norway to overcome the two-battalion landing envisaged by the planners. They even raised the possibility of a German naval task force of one pocket battleship, two light cruisers and several destroyers.[66]

At the beginning of August, Vian reported that there was no German presence, Spitzbergen was under the control of a Norwegian military governor, and the ability of the Germans successfully to capture the islands was minimal. On 5 August, the Defence Committee, advised by the chiefs of staff, initially decided that a small occupying force of two Canadian battalions should still deploy to secure the desired refuelling base. The ostensible purpose of this base was to support naval forces 'operating in protection of the sea route to Archangel'. However, there were no agreed commitments yet requiring such protection and the chiefs evidently felt the Spitzbergen operation was essentially a political project to appease the Russians.[67] Two days later, the occupation was in doubt following a signal from Vian stating that it was unnecessary and advice from Tovey that the Home Fleet did not require a defended fuelling base.[68] On 11 August, following a full debrief of Vian, the Defence Committee endorsed the chiefs' revised view there was now no military purpose in occupying the islands but there was advantage in denying the Germans the 500,000 tons of coal per annum they had until now received from the Spitzbergen mines. The mines, along with the wireless and meteorological station, should therefore be destroyed, and the 700 Norwegian and 2000 Russian miners evacuated.[69]

Following discussion with the Russians and Norwegians, this destruction operation, again commanded by Vian and designated 'Gauntlet', received the final go-ahead from the chiefs on 14 August, employing around 650 troops embarked in the liner *Empress of Canada*, a smaller force than that envisaged for occupation.[70] It proved 'an exercise in diplomacy' or as Vian put it, 'the instalment of sweet reason' and 'demolition practice for the engineers' and was successfully completed by the end of the month.[71]

In addition to Spitzbergen, a small force was landed on Bear Island where there was a Norwegian-manned meteorological station. The Norwegians were evacuated and the station facilities destroyed.[72] A further success was that Vian's force, drawing on Admiralty provided intelligence, intercepted and sank the German escort destroyer *Bremse* in Hammer Fiord on 6 September, having diverted during their return journey, although the two troopships she was protecting, *Barcelona* and *Trautenfels* with 1500 embarked soldiers, managed to escape in thick fog. *Bremse* had been present at Kirkenes during Operation EF but had avoided damage.[73]

The Spitzbergen affair is usually judged an unnecessary distraction, at times bordering on farce. However, three points deserve emphasis. First, at the end of May, German Army Command Norway had briefly contemplated seizing Spitzbergen with an expeditionary force broadly on the lines suggested by the joint planners two months later. Given available resources, it was judged too high a risk for limited benefit. Secondly, the British naval activity associated with Vian's initial reconnaissance and then Gauntlet itself contributed to the German impression that the Royal Navy posed an increasing threat to its communications in the Arctic theatre and it fed Hitler's paranoia regarding an attack on northern Norway. Finally, when Barbarossa failed to achieve its objectives and the Germans were committed to a long war, their need to minimise Allied aid reaching Russia via the Arctic supply route brought renewed attention on Spitzbergen the following March. Drawing on the ideas raised the previous May, the Norway-based 5th Air Fleet headquarters suggested that Spitzbergen be occupied in the coming spring. An airfield could be constructed there to attack Allied convoys bound for Russia from the north as well as from Norway. A meteorological station would also provide valuable weather data. The Army of Norway believed a single battalion could be supplied to hold these facilities for a year. However, OKW judged that this operation would tie down considerable naval and air strength in defensive activity without offering any decisive advantage since, for most of the year, the ice boundary obliged convoys to keep within 300 miles of Norwegian airbases. Hitler therefore rejected the proposal.[74]

*The Occupation of Iran and the Opening of a New Supply Route*

In addition to the various operations in the North, including Spitzbergen, which followed the prime minister's directive to the chiefs of staff on 23 July, there developed a parallel operation in Iran with long-term consequences for the supply of aid to Russia. Iran was a neutral country in mid-1941 but of huge strategic importance to Britain because of its oil resources and the access it gave any hostile power to the Middle East from the north and to India from the west. In 1941, the Abadan refinery in Iran produced about 5.5 million tons of oil for the British Empire, 18 per cent of its overall consumption. However, it still underpinned the whole Empire fighting effort in the Middle East and its overall potential was more than twice 1941 output. The following year the chiefs of staff claimed that Abadan supported 25 per cent of the British war effort.[75] The journey that led to the joint British–Russian occupation of Iran at the end of August arguably began at the Defence Committee meeting on 25 June when the prime minister raised the probability that the Middle East war would soon extend to Iran and the Persian Gulf and called for plans to meet this.[76] Two days later the chiefs directed the joint planners to examine the issue.[77]

Several factors drove Churchill's new focus on Iran. There was a small but influential German community in Iran, businessmen and technicians, who had been encouraged by the monarch, Reza Shah, to participate in modernising the country and foster alternative trading links to those dominated by Britain. Until now this German element was not judged much threat but the pro-German risings in Iraq and Syria the previous month, requiring British intervention, had demonstrated what a German destabilisation operation might achieve. This risk to Britain's vital interests in Iran was greatly increased by the German attack on Russia and the prospect that the Germans might reach the Caucasus within weeks. A German 'fifth column' in Iran operating with the acquiescence of a 'friendly' Iranian government would greatly ease and speed a German descent on the Middle East from the north and certainly threaten Britain's oil interests. This perception of German subversion was hypothetical and never backed by compelling intelligence, but the strategic importance of Iran made British leaders disinclined to take risks.[78]

It took the joint planners two weeks to complete their report which was approved by the chiefs on 15 July. They concluded that, with a maximum rate of advance, the Germans might reach the Caucasus by mid-August. The constraints posed by geography, winter weather and logistics meant they could not then generate a credible land attack from there against either Iraq or Iran before April 1942. However, the German air force could mount a moderate air offensive from Caucasian bases against targets in Iraq and Iran from the coming autumn. That included strikes against the Iranian oil fields and Abadan. Air attacks would become more effective if Turkey or Iran collaborated and provided air bases. It followed that Britain should deploy air assets for both defence and counterstrike and have land forces ready to secure the oil fields if required.[79]

A week earlier on 8 July, Stalin had expressed concern to Cripps at the scale of the German presence in both Iran and Afghanistan. He feared the 6000–7000 Germans based in Iran (much higher than British estimates) might attempt to gain control of the oilfields both there and in Baku and suggested joint British–Russian action to forestall this. Maisky emphasised the same message to Eden the following day.[80] As a result, on 11 July, the Middle East Ministerial Committee agreed that the two governments would make parallel demands for Iran to expel all Germans. It also asked the chiefs of staff to examine joint military intervention if Iran refused. It is claimed that Stalin's request spurred Britain towards more pro-active intervention in Iran. Following the declaration of mutual assistance signed in Moscow on 12 July, it would compensate for the limited support provided to Russia in the Arctic and refusal to contemplate any landing in western Europe.[81] The timing of British decisions does not fit this interpretation. By mid-July, reflecting the advice of the planners and the new Commander-in-Chief India, General Sir Archibald Wavell, the chiefs were clear that the Germans must be removed, and Britain must prepare forces to secure the southern oilfields if necessary. They and the wider British leadership viewed Russian support as useful in pressuring Iran and in limiting the additional military resources Britain must otherwise find although they also wanted to avoid Iran falling entirely under Russian influence let alone occupation.[82] But, otherwise, there is little evidence that Russia's attitude or desire to appease her was a key determinant in British decisions. These were dictated by British strategic interests. Indeed, on 23 July, the joint planners underlined in stark terms the critical importance of Iranian oil. It was necessary 'to maintain our eastern lifelines' and 'if Abadan were ever lost the security of the East Indies oilfields would be vital to our existence'. 'With Japan sided with our enemies this source is not secure.'[83]

In judging the British attitude to Iran through July and August, a further factor is how far the British leadership anticipated its importance in providing an alternative supply route to Russia. The joint planners did not address this potential supply route when they considered the threat to Iran and Iraq in mid-July and nor did the chiefs.[84] In their subsequent 23 July paper considering 'the strategic necessity of holding our present Middle East position', the planners did note that this would provide a base from which to 'join hands with Russia through Iran'.[85] However, developing a land link to Russia did not feature in the 'real military requirements' for intervention in Iran which they listed three days later. These were the security of the oilfields and preventing Iran embarking on a policy hostile to British interests.[86] The value of the Trans-Persian railway, completed in the late 1930s, and running from the Persian Gulf to the Caspian and the need to ensure Iranian government support for its use in supplying Russia was apparently first raised at the Defence Committee on 1 August, chaired by the prime minister prior to his departure to Riviera. It was judged unlikely the Iranians would refuse and that troops would not therefore be required to ensure compliance. Maisky separately emphasised to Eden that Russia attached importance to accessing supplies via this route.[87]

Three weeks later, on 20 August, following his return from Riviera, and in the expectation that the Iranians would refuse to expel their German community, the prime minister was more emphatic. The time had come for military action. Delay in expelling Germans from Iran would be 'dangerous' and 'it was essential that we should have one clear channel by which we could send supplies to Russia'. He added that while removing the Germans was the immediate priority, any scaling up of military action could be justified by the need to keep open communications with Russia.[88] By 25 August, the War Cabinet were agreed that 'our ultimate object was to get a secure line of communication with Russia across Persia'.[89] On 1 September, Churchill told Roosevelt that Britain would 'double' the capacity of the Trans-Persian railway, 'opening a sure route by which long term supplies can reach the Russian reserve positions in the Volga basin'. He also used this objective to underline the importance of reinforcing Britain's position in the Middle East.[90] Two days later, by which time Britain and Russia had control of Iran, Churchill confirmed to the Defence Committee that the Trans-Persian railway was 'the big prize' which would create a front behind the natural barrier of the Caucasus Mountains and the Caspian.[91] In the War Cabinet he went further. It was now important that 'we should have complete control over Persia during the war' and especially of 'road and railway communications to Russia'. The previous day, reflecting his comments to Roosevelt, he had discussed how to develop the Middle East railway system not only to support British forces but to increase traffic to Russia. By the time the Anglo-American supply mission agreed at Riviera arrived in Moscow later in the month, it should be possible to offer deliveries through Iran as well as Vladivostok.[92] In sum, Iran's potential as a supply route to Russia did not initially influence the case for British intervention but the prime minister was quick to recognise its importance following the Riviera discussions. It probably accelerated the timing of intervention and made Britain determined to tighten its control of Iran.

## Russia's Prospects and Ways to Support Her

During the prime minister's absence at Riviera, there was a shift in Whitehall's assessment of Russia's prospects and their implications for the wider war. On 2 August, before his departure, the chiefs of staff informed him that the slower than expected German progress in Russia meant there was now no prospect of the Germans attempting an invasion of the United Kingdom before October. This reflected a Joint Intelligence Committee assessment received the previous day which effectively ruled out an invasion before winter set in. The chiefs therefore recommended that defence forces could safely step down to a lower level of readiness.[93] In addition to Ultra intercepts, a Swedish report stated that the Germans now expected to take at least three more months to subdue Russia. Macfarlane in Moscow also became more optimistic regarding Russia's chances, partly because of the greater willingness of his hosts to share information on the military situation. Indeed, late summer 1941 was one of the high points of the war in British–Russian intelligence cooperation.[94]

The growing optimism over Russian resistance was summarised in a Joint Intelligence Committee assessment issued on 8 August, the day before Riviera began. This both sharpened the judgements of the previous week and considered the wider implications for German strategy. It concluded that Germany had now been fighting in Russia for seven weeks yet there was no sign of a Russian collapse. The delay imposed by Russian resistance would now limit German options this year outside Russia to consolidation rather than full-scale offensive operations. An attempt to invade the United Kingdom this year was 'very unlikely' and the longer the Russian campaign lasted the more unlikely it became. For the rest of 1941, the German effort against Britain would therefore focus on air attacks, the shipping campaign, and perhaps a new offensive in North Africa. There might also be operations directed at Turkey, Iran or Spain but these would be limited in scope.[95] The Foreign Office reflected this view in a telegram to the Tokyo embassy on 14 August. Soviet resistance had upset the German timetable and the Germans were now expecting a longer campaign. A Soviet collapse was still possible but, even then, resistance would continue east of the Volga. Later in the month, an MI report anticipated that the Germans might be immobilised on the Soviet front when winter arrived.[96] An assessment of comparative aircraft losses on 29 August in response to a query from the prime minister, clearly relevant to the provision of British fighters, was more uncertain in its conclusions. Air Intelligence estimated German losses at around 1700, equivalent to 60 per cent of strength at the start of Barbarossa, which was fairly accurate. Assessing Russian losses was more difficult. They had admitted 4500 which was more than the British estimate of their initial strength, while German claims of more than 11,000 destroyed seemed grossly exaggerated. The Russians lost 11,500 aircraft in 1941 of which 8200 were combat types. A figure of 4500 lost in the first two months of the war was therefore reasonable.[97]

The prospect that Russia could survive until winter or, in the worst case, maintain strong resistance beyond the Volga line brought increased pressure from the prime minister and political leadership to find options to strengthen Russian resistance. Riviera had signalled British–American commitment to a long-term supply effort to be taken forward at the Moscow conference. Meanwhile the stand-down from invasion might give Britain more military options. On 23 August, the Joint Planning Staff completed a review of options for an attack on the Continent that might relieve the strain on Russia. This was the first serious appraisal of a potential 'second front', a concept relentlessly pushed from this time onward, first by the Russians, then the Americans, and significant elements of public opinion at home. The planners considered that a landing on the Cherbourg peninsula was the only operation that 'might prove feasible' but judged the risks and costs too great and, even if successful, it would not, with the resources available, achieve the aim of withdrawing German forces from the Eastern Front. In identifying Cherbourg, they initiated a preference that would be promoted in various forms for the next 12 months. The underlying assumption for all options was that available landing craft limited an initial assault force to one armoured and one infantry brigade with an additional small commando element. The maximum force ashore achievable in seven days, given the present state of trained manpower and equipment, was two armoured and three infantry divisions. Despite the advantages Cherbourg offered, including an easily accessible port and maximum deployment of British air power, the Germans could match this force in two weeks and far outweigh it in three without making any call on the East.[98]

The planners ruled out other options in France and the Low Countries but, reflecting pressure over the last six weeks from Golikov, Stalin and, not least, the prime minister, they examined the seizure of Kirkenes from Murmansk, and a landing around Narvik or Tromsø. A Kirkenes operation was rejected because: it was too distant from the United Kingdom to deploy and sustain a substantial force; four divisions would be needed to overcome the current German force of three; mountain troops would be required which Britain did not possess; and the terrain was extremely difficult. These were all valid points, but the planners overlooked that the Russians had never requested land forces, could certainly provide a major proportion of any offensive force and with relevant winter experience. It was naval and air support the Russians wanted for an attack on Kirkenes. Narvik/Tromsø was ruled out because: the Germans could quickly deploy overwhelming air power against a limited force deployable from carriers; a minimum of three divisions and an armoured brigade, all capable of winter warfare, would be required; and sustaining such a force would need 1.5 million tons of shipping.[99]

Although the planners' arguments appeared conclusive, reflecting political pressure the chiefs of staff commissioned further work into September. The possibility of a major deception or 'feint' operation to convince the Germans that Britain was planning an invasion of the Continent on a large scale was considered.[100] The consensus of the chiefs and Commander-in-Chief Home Forces, General Sir Alan Brooke, was that huge and disruptive preparations would be needed to make such a deception convincing and, even then, the Germans were unlikely to respond until the threat took effect. In short it would not divert German forces from the East.[101] The chiefs were undoubtedly correct that Britain had neither the resources nor the experience to implement a 'grand deception operation' in mid-1941. Nevertheless, the idea had potential and a variant would be implemented with great success in support of D-Day three years later. The planners also conducted a more detailed appraisal of an operation in northern Norway.[102] The chiefs concluded there was no chance of generating a force for the coming winter which would be large enough and sufficiently trained in Arctic warfare to overcome the known German garrison. Capturing a port would be essential and these were all strongly held. Mindful of the prime minister's enthusiasm for a Norway operation Pound, as chairman, directed the planners to consider whether a summer operation with more preparation time and avoiding use of a port was more viable.[103] The prime minister was not easily dissuaded. The chiefs were obliged to explore an operation to capture Trondheim (Operation Ajax) in collaboration, rather implausibly, with Sweden until well into October. This included a detailed planning study conducted by a sceptical and unenthusiastic Brooke, who as Commander-in-Chief Home Forces would have to resource much of the operation. Churchill was so enraged with Brooke's conclusion that a Trondheim operation was impractical for all the reasons already raised by the joint planners that he sent a note to Dill saying that Brooke was 'not again to be admitted to our counsels'. Characteristically, this did not stop him appointing Brooke as Dill's successor six weeks later![104]

The perceived impossibility of mounting a credible diversion operation in either western Europe or the Arctic, which the chiefs of staff now communicated at length to Maisky, inevitably drove a political imperative to provide more and earlier aid.[105] And, as explained previously, American slowness in confirming what they could provide meant Britain bore the brunt of Russian demands, especially those made by Stalin in his message to Churchill dated 3 September.[106] The War Cabinet's response, agreed two days later, immediately to meet half of Stalin's monthly demand for aircraft and tanks together with a significant contribution on aluminium, represented a substantial opportunity cost for Britain over the nine months October 1941 to June 1942. Two hundred fighters per month was about one-quarter of Britain's production over this period and 250 tanks one-third of combined British and Canadian output.[107]

However, two weeks later, the War Cabinet learnt that the cost was much greater. The British–American offer to be made at the Moscow supply conference agreed at Riviera was hammered out at a preparatory meeting of the national teams led by Beaverbrook and Harriman in London in mid-September. This London meeting was complicated because it effectively comprised two parallel strands with only limited crossover between them. While Beaverbrook and Harriman settled the Moscow approach, a separate American team led by Charles Bundy reviewed the British input into the Victory programme. This input comprised underlying strategic principles, which drew on ABC-1 and were therefore uncontroversial, estimates of overall British defence requirements and production, leading on to specific needs from the United States. Bundy's team validated the logic and data underpinning this British input but left decisions over allocations to be addressed in Washington once the overall Victory package was complete.[108]

The Victory programme was therefore still work in progress. Meanwhile, the Moscow aid offer would have to be drawn from existing American–British production allocations. Here, while Roosevelt had issued instructions on 30 August that it was of 'paramount importance' for America's security that 'all reasonable munitions help be provided for Russia', United States War Department planners inevitably sought to protect the requirements of the United States armed services. Meanwhile, the British approached the London meeting naively expecting that not only would the Americans match the War Cabinet offer to Stalin of 5 September but that their own projected supplies from the United States would be untouched. Indeed, Beaverbrook initially argued that the United States should begin with the maximum possible allocation to Britain. The London teams would then together agree what proportion could be reallocated to Russia. Beaverbrook insisted that this would protect existing British orders in the United States while providing Russia with essential supplies. However, while Harriman arrived with schedules of what could be exported in total from the United States, he insisted on deciding Russian needs first, ignoring the reasonable British argument that this was difficult without up-to-date Russian input. Although Beaverbrook achieved some compromise, it was clear that, if the United States was to match the British commitment to Stalin and adequately satisfy its own increasing requirements, previous commitments to Britain must be sharply cut. Britain was likely to receive 1600 fewer tanks and 1800 fewer aircraft from American production by the end of June 1942 than previously expected.[109] In practical terms, this meant delaying the formation of three new armoured divisions until late autumn and the loss over the next nine months, after including the aircraft transfers to Russia from British production, of twenty heavy and medium bomber squadrons, fifteen light bomber squadrons and fifteen fighter squadrons. This loss of aircraft would have serious consequences for Britain's position in the Middle and Far East in early 1942. Although Beaverbrook was a strong champion of aid to Russia, he felt the United States was selfishly focusing its supplies to Russia on what it could spare rather than what was needed. 'The sacrifice will fall almost entirely on us.'[110]

It is important to understand what underpinned the War Cabinet's grim acceptance of this price.[111] Stalin's 3 September message stated that the 'stabilisation' of the front achieved by mid-August had been overturned by the arrival of strong German reinforcements and the active participation of Finnish and Romanian forces. As a result, most of the Ukraine was now lost and Leningrad was coming under siege. Key war production sites had also been lost and although some facilities had been evacuated to the East, their reconstitution would take time. Russia was now in 'mortal peril'. Without an operation in the West to divert significant German forces and substantial aid, Russia must either be defeated or cease to be active in confronting the German threat.[112] As noted earlier, the seriousness of this message was reinforced by Cripps from Moscow and Maisky in London. However, British acquiescence in the consequences of their new supply commitment was also helped by Roosevelt's message to Churchill of 17 September, stating that he intended to increase American tank production by 25 per cent by May 1942, and his subsequent promise to double it, in comparison to the figures deployed by Harriman with Beaverbrook. As Churchill said, this was cheering news 'when we were feeling very blue about all we have to give up to Russia'.[113] Churchill's anxiety was doubtless further assuaged when he learnt early next month that British aircraft production in September had reached 2000 and that intelligence showed that British front-line air strength was now greater than Germany's.[114] This intelligence was correct. By mid-1942, British strength was over 20 per cent ahead, a margin that would steadily increase for the rest of the war.[115]

Stalin's representations in early September, including a further meeting with Cripps when he refused to guarantee that Russia could survive until the spring even with the newly-promised Western aid, did not persuade the British war leadership that Russia now faced imminent collapse. Through September, the Joint Intelligence Committee held to the view established the previous month. The Germans were still advancing but faced strong resistance and were unlikely to achieve all their main goals before winter. It was rather three other factors that drove Britain towards more substantial aid than hitherto contemplated. First, as Churchill and Eden informed the War Cabinet, and the prime minister subsequently told Roosevelt, they sensed that behind Stalin's message lay the threat of a separate peace.[116] At a minimum he evidently harboured doubts that Western aid would materialise and needed reassurance.[117] Secondly, there was growing recognition by the War Cabinet and chiefs of staff that it was in Britain's interest to strengthen and extend Russian resistance as much as possible. This was the logic of the Joint Intelligence Committee judgement a month earlier: every week of Russian survival was a week more of security for Britain. The British leadership was clear that no military operation that Britain could mount would divert German effort from Russia, so aid was the only tool available. As Churchill said to Roosevelt, 'If they keep fighting, it [aid] is worth it; if they don't, we do not have to send it'. He added, 'We are hitting ourselves very hard in tanks, but this argument decided me'.[118] Finally, as noted earlier, the United States was moving too slowly. Only Britain could immediately appease Stalin.

The War Cabinet decision on 5 September to commit to significant ongoing aid to Russia coincided with an effort by the Joint Intelligence Committee in collaboration with MEW to assess how the steady loss of territory would affect Russia's war potential (essentially combined economic and military strength). An early draft assessment was available by 6 September and probably shared with the Americans at that time. A more developed version was shared with the chiefs of staff and other Whitehall customers a week later and a complete one in early October. It did not therefore affect the initial response to Stalin's demands but probably exerted some influence on British and American attitudes at the London conference and the subsequent Moscow supply conference at the end of September. The committee examined how much war potential would remain along four different front lines, labelled A, B. C and D. 'A' was the front line on 6 September and the remainder were projections following successive German advances. The 'B' line was broadly that reached by the Germans by the beginning of December before the Moscow counter-offensive. The 'C' and 'D' lines were the Volga and the Urals and were never reached. The committee assessed that the present line (A) could support 95 per cent of war potential falling to about 75 per cent after three to four months. This would initially support 225 divisions on the active front and 40 more in the Far East. The other lines would see war potential drop to 70, 40 and 35 per cent respectively. Their paper argued therefore that, if the Germans reached the B line, sustainable divisions would drop to 210.[119]

There were inevitably many gaps and uncertainties in this assessment. However, conceptually it was on the right lines and its overall conclusions reasonable. Contemporary wartime Soviet government statistics estimated that the area occupied by Germany in autumn 1942 had contributed one-third of Soviet industrial production in 1940.[120] The British assessment was six months ahead of comparable German studies. To date, these had focused less on how the Soviet economy underpinned its war potential and more on the economic benefit, especially in agriculture and raw materials, oil above all, which Germany would derive from captured territory.[121] Only in spring 1942 did Germany conduct a serious review of Soviet war potential in the circumstances then prevailing.[122] In influencing British–American judgements on initiating aid, the most important Joint Intelligence Committee conclusions related to armaments production and the raw materials feeding this. The area already lost to the Germans primarily focused on agricultural and raw materials production and the loss of direct arms manufacturing was not significant. However, it did include the Krivoi Rog iron ore fields, producing 60 per cent of Russia's output, the Nikopol manganese fields with 35 per cent, and the major Zaporozhye aluminium refinery delivering 44 per cent. Krivoi Rog and the lost aluminium capacity were emphasised by Stalin in his 3 September letter. It was the loss of these vital raw materials which would turn the initial reduction of 5 per cent in war potential to perhaps five times that within three months. If the Germans reached line B, the assessment estimated that direct arms manufacturing capacity remaining in Russian hands would still be approximately 70 per cent (about 80 per cent for aircraft, 60 per cent for tanks, 90 per cent for artillery, 70 per cent for small arms, but under 20 per cent for shipbuilding). There would be important further losses in raw materials, notably the Donetz which produced 50 per cent of Russia's coal and steel and in aluminium, taking output here to less than half pre-war levels. However, the assessment argued these new raw material losses would be less important than they seemed. Most of the Donetz coal was consumed locally or in territory already occupied while the steel plants depended on the Krivoi Rog supplies of ore no longer available. Overall, a German advance to line B would bring remaining Russian manufacturing capacity more into line with available raw materials. Hence war potential would only drop another 5 per cent bringing the overall loss from occupation up to line B to 30 per cent.[123]

Meanwhile, on 18 September, the chiefs of staff asked the Joint Intelligence Committee to review an appreciation of Russia's situation by General Wladyslaw Sikorski, the prime minister of the Polish government in exile in London. Sikorski stated that the Russian economy had suffered serious losses from the German advance to date, but he judged the manpower, food and oil situation manageable. If the Germans surrounded Leningrad, reached Moscow and, above all, took the Donetz, there would be severe problems. In this scenario, it was unlikely the Red Army could cope through the coming winter without foreign help. The Joint Intelligence Committee judged that Sikorski's view was broadly in accord with their assessment. Churchill and Eden saw both these papers.[124]

## The Moscow Supply Conference

Following the London conference between Beaverbrook and Harriman, the prime minister prepared a 'directive' to guide Beaverbrook at the forthcoming Moscow supply conference. This was approved by the Defence Committee on 19 September. It confirmed the British pledges of tanks and aircraft for the nine months October 1941 to June 1942 made to Stalin on 5 September. It then gave Beaverbrook maximum discretion over what other equipment and material could be offered in this period. He was also encouraged to promise increased aid over the year from 1 July 1942 in line with Britain's increased war production. The limitations of shipping and ports on the Arctic route were to be stressed along with the consequent importance of developing alternative routes through Iran and across the Pacific to Vladivostok. Beaverbrook was also to emphasise the obvious point that the United States was not a belligerent and Britain had to balance help to Russia with the numerous other war commitments it faced. However, in a potential hostage to fortune, Beaverbrook was permitted to say that Britain had 'every intention of intervening on land next spring, if it could be done'. All possibilities were being studied here, including action on the northern and southern flanks of the Russian front. Norway was specifically mentioned but not France. Two further qualifications on such intervention were the small force available (no more than six or seven divisions including two armoured) and the need to guard against the hostility of Spain and a German move into North-west Africa.[125]

Beaverbrook therefore enjoyed considerable latitude and he understood that his role in Moscow was as much political as military. The British and Americans had to establish what arms and other supplies were most needed and then negotiate what could be provided. But it was also vital to convince the Russian leadership of Western commitment and sincerity. In the event, the Moscow discussions, which began on 29 September and coincided with the start of the German drive on Moscow, Operation Typhoon, after a frosty start ended amicably. There were arguments over aircraft type (the Russians wanted Spitfires rather than Hurricanes) and composition (the Russians wanted a higher proportion of bombers but had to settle for fighters in lieu), and it was impossible to meet their full demand for tanks. Beaverbrook dealt with these problems skilfully. The Allied delegations increased their offer of raw materials and non-military supplies to compensate for deficiencies in the military deliveries. Beaverbrook did not press the Russians to justify their demands but looked for compromises or alternatives. He avoided demanding information which the Russians regarded as sensitive and steered clear of strategic and military exchanges which he recognised would inevitably provoke argument, misunderstanding and distrust to no purpose. Importantly, he also got on well with Stalin, winning his confidence in so far as anyone could. Harriman reported that 'Beaverbrook has been a great salesman. His personal sincerity was convincing. His genius never worked more effectively.'[126]

In general, both Beaverbrook and Harriman sought to offer all they could without demanding any payment or benefit in return. Both seem to have been genuinely convinced that, without substantial aid, Russia would not stay in the war. The agreement signed after four days incorporated an agreed British–American supply programme over the nine months ending 30 June 1942 and became known as the 'First Protocol'. The breakdown of deliveries demonstrates that Britain was the senior partner in the provision of this first batch of aid to Russia. Many early deliveries came from Britain with the United States making up the balance later, the bulk of the raw materials came from British and Canadian stocks, and Britain would play the dominant role in delivery. Britain would also end up compensating for initial shortfalls in American production although the balance would be restored later. For example, she agreed to provide fifty extra tanks per month on top of her allocation of 250 until the end of the year.[127]

Beaverbrook's handling of the Moscow talks encountered heavy criticism from parts of Britain's war leadership both at the time and later. Cripps felt his advice was ignored and was furious to be shut out of key meetings including those with Stalin. Cadogan, perhaps fed by Cripps, dismissed Beaverbrook's mission as a 'newspaper stunt'. Beaverbrook pre-empted the ambassador's anticipated complaints by getting his account to Churchill first on 8 October. Cripps and the other critics, notably Brooke, currently Commander-in-Chief Home Forces but soon to be Chief of the Imperial General Staff, felt Beaverbrook had not asked the Russians to justify their needs, had failed to press for an assessment of the state of operations and had refused to sanction the 'strategic discussions' for which Major General Sir Hastings Ismay, the prime minister's chief military adviser,[128] and Lieutenant General Gordon Macready, Assistant Chief of the Imperial General Staff, were also in Moscow. While these complaints appear compelling, Ismay was later adamant that initial military discussions with Soviet officials 'were frustrating and achieved nothing'. Overall, he was unimpressed by what he saw. He detected no real higher war direction and felt the Russians lacked the mobility, flexibility and power of concentration of the Germans. It was certainly impossible to establish any clear rationale for the numerous military equipment demands. Beaverbrook was almost certainly correct therefore that the objectives sought in any strategic talks were undeliverable and that pursuing them would foster dissension and lack of trust to no purpose. A brief exchange between Ismay and Stalin was not only gratuitously disparaging of Britain's overall war contribution but amply demonstrated that opening such a dialogue would inevitably trigger Russian demands for action which the British had already ruled out. Nor were the Russians ever likely to offer political concessions, for example on post-war borders, in return for supplies. The Russians did provide some information on comparative strength in tanks and aircraft and on their own production, including loss of aluminium supplies. The data was limited but was indicative of underlying reality.[129]

Churchill was quick to send Beaverbrook his 'heartiest congratulations'. He was equally quick to advise Stalin of the rapid pace of deliveries, providing details of the first two post-protocol convoys, PQ 2 and PQ 3, which would sail in October. Three hundred fighters, fully meeting the October protocol commitment, and 280 tanks would arrive in Russia by 6 November. The balance of British-supplied tanks would be made up during November and other British-supplied armaments would arrive on schedule. Churchill's convoy dates were somewhat optimistic since the first two convoys did not reach Archangel until 30 October and 28 November respectively but thereafter a fortnightly schedule was broadly maintained over the next six months.[130]

The signing of the First Protocol represented the end of a three-month journey undertaken by the British chiefs of staff since the launch of Barbarossa. They had started sceptical that Russia would survive more than a few weeks, with their pessimism exacerbated by ingrained hostility towards the Soviet regime. They initially responded reluctantly to the initiatives for supporting Russia promoted primarily by Churchill and Eden but later Beaverbrook. They judged these driven by political rather than military imperatives. However, the strength of Russian resistance gradually overcame the chiefs' reservations and by mid-September there was consensus across the British leadership that keeping Russia in the war was a critical strategic interest justifying significant sacrifice of resources. It is tempting to argue that, if the chiefs had responded more positively and pro-actively to the Arctic options aired by Golikov in early July, German difficulties in prosecuting Silver Fox could have been exploited by Britain and Russia to gain control over northern Norway, avoiding much political and military pain later. This is almost certainly an illusion. If the joint planners' assessments of putative Arctic operations in autumn 1941 sometimes seemed self-serving, their arguments were nevertheless compelling. Given the constraints of distance, terrain and climate, Germany could always redeploy sufficient force to defeat any British attack. Instead, as October opened, Britain was committed to an ambitious nine-month supply programme. The impact of this and the challenges in delivering it had yet to be discovered.

# Chapter 4

# The First Arctic Convoys and Their Impact

The Dervish convoy and PQ 1, which left Hvafiord in Iceland on 29 September 1941, were in effect both one-off deliveries of urgent aid to Russia, together providing 50,000 tons and initiated while any long-term provision of support remained under discussion. It was the signing of the First Protocol in Moscow on 1 October that committed Britain and America to a firm programme of supplies for the next nine months ending 30 June 1942. The headline requirements sought by Stalin in his message of 3 September, 400 aircraft and 500 tanks per month and 30,000 tons of aluminium, of which 5000 tons was already in transit with PQ 1, were agreed. But these represented only the highest-profile items in a list of some seventy categories of aid comprising not just weaponry, including considerable naval equipment, but 85,000 trucks, manufacturing equipment and machine tools, communications equipment, oil, raw materials, clothing and medical items, amounting to an estimated 1.8 million tons of cargo over the full period, or 200,000 tons per month. The protocol also undertook to provide food, 200,000 tons of wheat and 70,000 tons of sugar per month.[1]

## The First Protocol until February 1942: Successes and Shortfalls

The scale and composition of the First Protocol supplies demonstrates that, right from the start of the Western aid programme, the Soviet leadership had three broad goals in view. First, they needed urgently to boost their firepower to compensate for heavy ongoing weapon losses and to help buy time while defence production ramped up – hence the emphasis on aircraft and tanks. Secondly, they wanted additional resources, such as aluminium, specialised steel and machine tools, to support key defence industries and boost long-term war potential. Finally, they would take any supplies that would ease the acute squeeze on the civilian sector of the population – hence the emphasis on food. From the Soviet perspective, the role of aid was never solely to plug gaps in products, materials or technology, although all these existed, but also to extend economic and indeed military choices. Western supplies helped them to concentrate domestic resources where they enjoyed greatest comparative advantage.

Those choices make assessing the impact of Western aid complex. The availability of Western weapons probably encouraged the Soviet leadership to pursue offensive operations in the first half of 1942 beyond what was wise. Western aluminium enabled far greater aircraft output than would have been possible otherwise. Aid also allowed specialisation in armoured vehicle production at the expense of trucks which could be imported. It enabled the civilian sector to be squeezed more in 1942 than would have been feasible without it. However, there was nothing immutable about these choices. Without Western aid or with less of it, the Soviet leadership would have been obliged to allocate resources differently and pursue alternative strategies. It could have pursued a more defensive war for longer, traded more territory, produced less tanks and more trucks etc. Furthermore, there was never a neat framework of Soviet economic policy and planning into which aid seamlessly fitted. The Soviet war economy had strengths and weaknesses like those of the other combatants. For the first year of the war economic management veered between the chaotic and the inspirational. As the war progressed, priorities changed with events and this was reflected in aid demands. Expediency and what was on offer ruled as much as planning.[2]

The Moscow conference recognised that transporting the agreed supplies would be a formidable challenge: 1.5 million tons of shipping would be required of which the Soviet Union could offer less than one-tenth, with one-third of this located in the Pacific. Importantly, the Western Allies did not commit to delivering the supplies to Soviet ports. They undertook rather to make them available and 'help with their delivery'. They accepted that transport would fall largely to them but providing necessary shipping must be balanced against numerous commitments elsewhere. Nevertheless, in November, Roosevelt instructed Admiral Emory Land, then Chairman of the United States Maritime Commission but soon to take over War Shipping Administration, to make every effort to provide ships for delivering Soviet aid and only 'insurmountable difficulties' should interfere.[3]

At the outset, three supply routes to the Soviet Union were identified: Archangel, which the Russians claimed could handle 300,000 tons of cargo per month; Vladivostok, capable of 140,000 tons; and the Persian Gulf estimated at 60,000 tons. In theory, this covered all the First Protocol commitments including the food imports. However, in autumn 1941, each of these routes posed problems. The Russians were initially unwilling to use Murmansk, certainly not for military supplies, because of its perceived vulnerability and convoys were not run there until December when, despite Russian promises that it could be kept open, Archangel was closed by ice. Even then, they required considerable persuasion.[4] The Admiralty had anticipated the need to shift to Murmansk a month previously although they too worried about its vulnerability and also its limited capacity.[5] Archangel never offered more than ten berths for unloading during the First Protocol period and Murmansk only eight. British and American port experts soon estimated that the true capacity of Archangel was therefore a maximum of 90,000 tons and Murmansk about the same, although the Archangel to Moscow railway could easily handle three times this quantity. These port limitations inevitably restricted processing of supplies especially once larger convoys began from PQ 11 onward. At the end of October, the Joint Intelligence Committee did not believe Archangel was in imminent danger of German attack but a more realistic target was cutting the railway at Vologda, situated about 250 miles east of the present front line on the Svir river and the same distance north of Moscow. If this occurred, supplies delivered through Archangel could only use the newly completed branch running east from Konosha, some 50 miles north of Vologda, but its capacity was unknown.[6]

Vladivostok was used extensively before Japan entered the war for the import of raw materials from the Far East and Australia, mainly tin, lead, rubber and wool. The Russians used their own ships for these imports because British vessels were not permitted to sail in Japanese-controlled waters north of Hong Kong. In addition to these Far East imports, there were some shipments by American vessels direct from the United States, mainly oil, before Japan entered the war. Overall, the Pacific route handled just over 160,000 tons over the last five months of 1941. Thereafter the route was vulnerable to disruption by Japan. However, Russia and Japan had signed a neutrality pact in April 1941 and it was evident early the following year that Japan would not interfere with Russian-flagged vessels carrying Lend-Lease supplies from North America. The Pacific route made only a small contribution to the First Protocol but it became increasingly important from mid-1942 although, to avoid antagonising Japan, initially no military supplies were included. To begin with, Vladivostok also suffered from poor cargo handling facilities and the long rail transit with limited traffic capacity to the western war zones was a further constraint. The modest initial estimates for the capacity of the Persian route proved ambitious given the poor state of its inland road and rail communications. Over the first six months of the protocol, it carried just 36,500 tons. However, the Moscow conference agreed that, with development, it might ultimately offer the best route of the three for delivering supplies. Harriman informed Roosevelt on 29 October that the likely overall cost of the First Protocol package was USD one billion. The Soviet Union had financed October shipments but it was impossible for them to keep funding thereafter, making Lend-Lease provision 'most desirable'. Harriman's estimate soon proved insufficient and, by the following February, it was clear the cost would be closer to USD two billion.[7]

These three supply routes with comparative American quantities shipped through the entire war are displayed in Map 1 below. 0.9 million tons from Britain and Canada must be added to the 3.7 million tons of American supplies which actually reached the North Russian ports and 0.1 million tons to American Persian Gulf arrivals. However, constraints facing the Pacific and Persian routes until mid-1942 made the Arctic the preferred delivery route throughout the First Protocol. It carried two-thirds of these supplies, including all military equipment, across the full nine months and three-quarters in the first six months. It had the further advantage that it was by far the shortest sea route and, so long as the rail links from Murmansk and Archangel southward remained under Russian control, it provided easiest access to key military fronts and industrial centres. Although there were some independent sailings on the route by Russian ships, the bulk of supplies were carried by British and American vessels in Royal Navy-escorted convoys. Beginning with PQ 2 which left Scapa Flow on 17 October, with a cargo including 140 medium

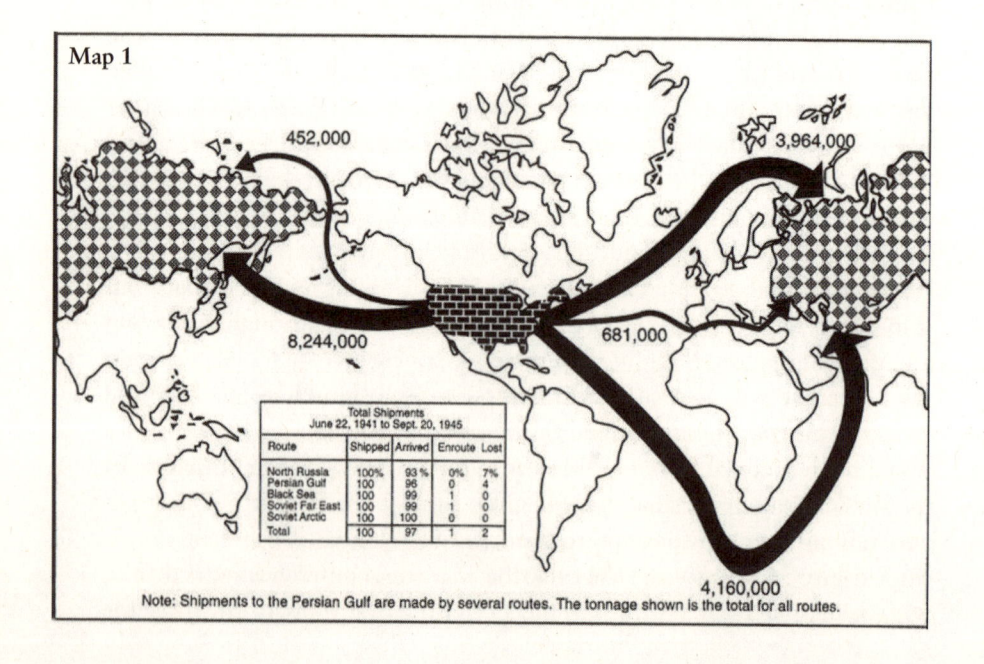

Map 1

| Route | Shipped | Arrived | Enroute | Lost |
|---|---|---|---|---|
| North Russia | 100% | 93% | 0% | 7% |
| Persian Gulf | 100 | 96 | 0 | 4 |
| Black Sea | 100 | 99 | 1 | 0 |
| Soviet Far East | 100 | 99 | 1 | 0 |
| Soviet Arctic | 100 | 100 | 0 | 0 |
| Total | 100 | 97 | 1 | 2 |

Total Shipments June 22, 1941 to Sept. 20, 1945

Note: Shipments to the Persian Gulf are made by several routes. The tonnage shown is the total for all routes.

tanks, 100 Hurricanes and 200 Bren carriers, these departed at roughly fortnightly intervals for the first six months. This rate of two convoys per month was a third less than the convoy every 10 days which Churchill, perhaps unwisely, promised Stalin on 6 October, immediately after the Moscow signing.[8] Two-thirds of the convoyed supply ships were British in this period.[9]

Admiralty planners and Tovey, as Commander-in-Chief Home Fleet the responsible front-line commander, well understood the challenges in successfully convoying supplies via the Arctic route shown in Map 2 overleaf. The post-war naval staff history succinctly stated the problem facing Tovey here:

> He had to provide for their safety on passage to and from a destination some 2000 miles distant. The route which was open to U-boat attack throughout its entire length, was limited to the westward and northward by ice and to the eastward and southward by an enemy occupied coast, well provided with anchorages whence surface forces could operate at will, and airfields from which aircraft could dominate 1400 miles of its furthest east, and therefore most vulnerable, waters. The whole route, moreover, including the terminal ports at each end, lay within the range of enemy air reconnaissance, for which he was not lacking in resources, and at two points was crossed by German routine meteorological flights. British shore-based air support was confined to what could be given from Iceland and Sullom Voe in the Shetlands.[10]

As an assessment of the potential threat, this was all true enough and it would be amply confirmed by events in the summer of 1942. However, despite these German advantages, the first ten convoys carrying First Protocol supplies, numbers PQ 2 to PQ 11 over the period to the end of February, encountered little difficulty. Seventy-seven ships sailed in these outbound convoys with only one loss to a U-boat from PQ 7 and one early return due to weather damage from PQ 3. The PQ 7 loss was the merchant vessel *Waziristan* sunk by *U-134* on 2 January 1942 with 3700 tons of supplies, including 1000 tons of copper and 410 Ford trucks. This convoy had divided in two parts with *Waziristan* sailing in company with *Cold Harbor* and escorted by two anti-submarine trawlers as PQ 7A five days earlier than the main convoy. *Waziristan*, which was one of the first British ships to load supplies for Russia in the United States, had separated from the others in bad weather. Two weeks later, on 17 January, one merchant vessel in PQ 8 was damaged by *U-454* but was

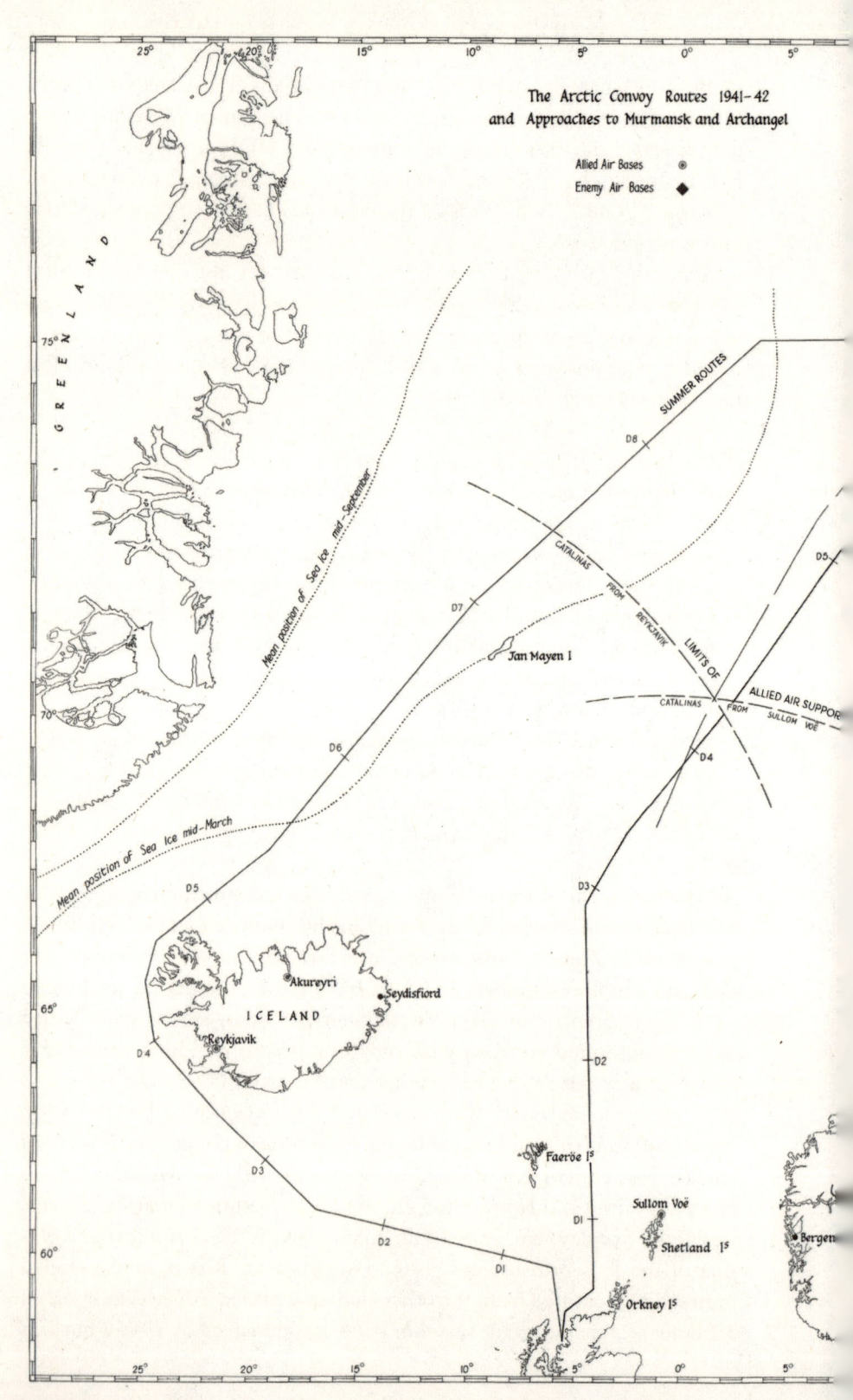

Map 2

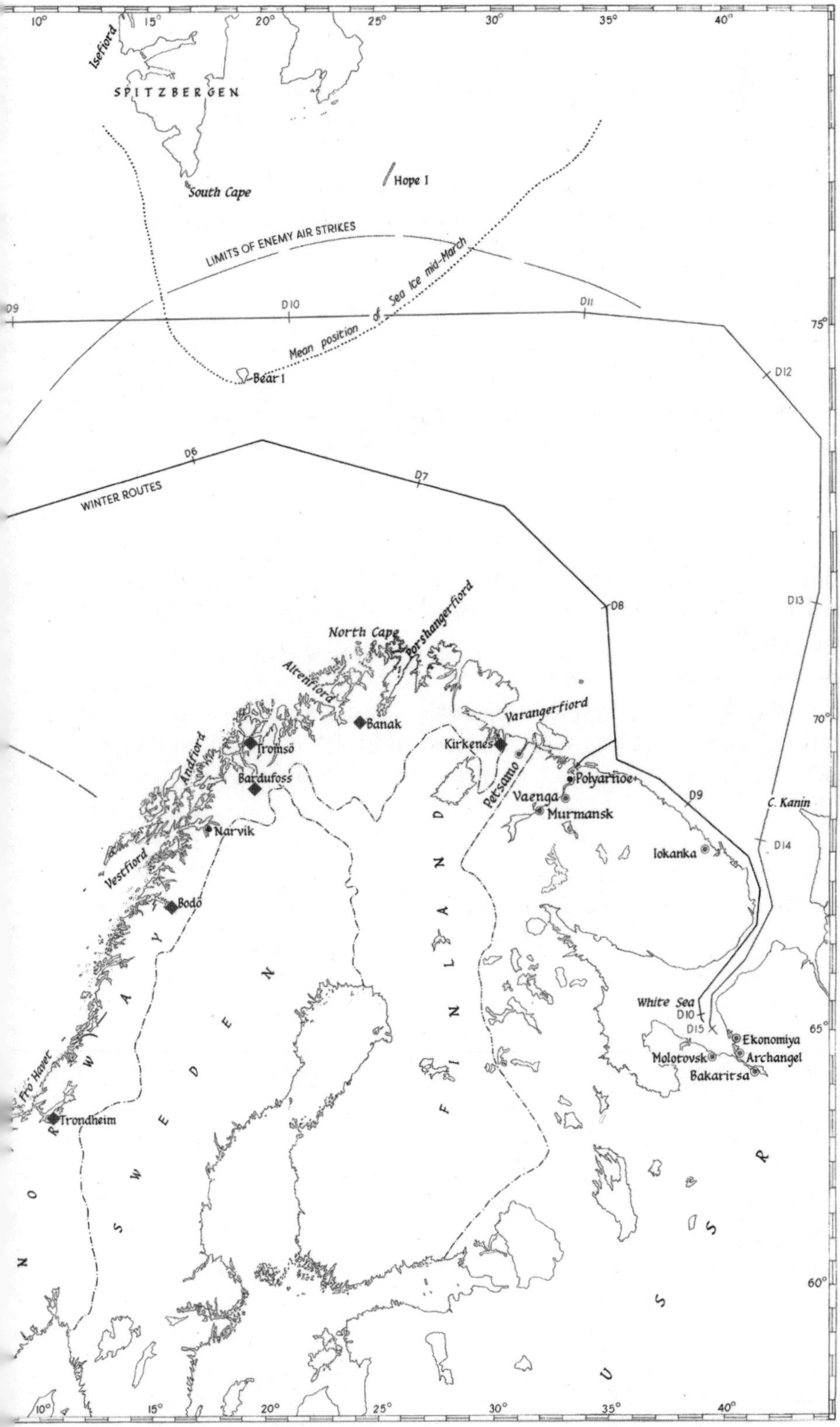

SPITZBERGEN
Isefiord
South Cape
Hope I
LIMITS OF ENEMY AIR STRIKES
Mean position of Sea Ice mid-March
Bear I
D9
D10
D11
D12
D13
D14
D15
WINTER ROUTES
D6
D7
D8
North Cape
Porshangerfiord
Altenfiord
Banak
Varangerfiord
Kirkenes
Tromsö
Andfiord
Bardufoss
Narvik
Vestfiord
Bodö
Petsamo
Polyarnoe
Vaenga
Murmansk
Iokanka
C. Kanin
White Sea
Ekonomiya
Archangel
Molotovsk
Bakaritsa
Frö Havet
Trondheim
NORWAY
SWEDEN
FINLAND
USSR
10°
15°
20°
25°
30°
35°
40°
75°
70°
65°
60°

successfully towed on to Murmansk but the destroyer *Matabele* from the escort was sunk by the same U-boat with only two survivors. In the same period, six convoys, QP 2 to QP 7, comprising fifty-one ships returned westward. These suffered no losses to enemy action although four ships returned to Russian ports due to weather damage.[11]

There were several reasons for the lack of effective German intervention. Contrary to what is often suggested, the German leadership quickly appreciated the potential threat posed by Western supplies delivered through the Arctic ports. They also recognised that powerful British escort ships returning from Murmansk posed a considerable danger to the poorly-defended German supply ships moving along the north Norwegian coast. Even before the arrival of PQ 1, Hitler's Directive No 37 of 10 October accordingly ordered the navy 'to attack enemy supplies going by sea to Murmansk and to protect our own traffic in the Arctic Ocean within the limits of its forces'.[12] However, prior to January 1942, when they began to reinforce, German air and naval forces deployed in the Arctic theatre were, as already described, limited, with barely a dozen Ju 88 bombers available to interdict convoys if they could find them, with the larger Stuka force lacking the necessary range and heavily committed to supporting the army with Silver Fox. This small air force was further hampered by primitive airfield facilities, tenuous logistics and poor communications. More widely, although it would partially recover, the German air force overall was in a poor state by the end of December. Total losses of combat aircraft in all theatres from the launch of Barbarossa were 5730 against production in the second half of the year of 5417. The nominal Eastern Front air strength had fallen to 1900 of which only 775 were ready for action. Finding resources for the Arctic was therefore difficult.[13]

Naval forces averaged five destroyers, initially belonging to the 6th Flotilla but replaced by the 8th, comprising Z 23–Z 27 inclusive, in December, and four U-boats all mainly based at Kirkenes, with perhaps a maximum of two of the latter at sea at any time. The destroyers were tasked with protecting the Germans' own coastal traffic as well as conducting offensive operations and therefore moved frequently between Kirkenes and Tromsø. In January, the 8th Flotilla suffered a series of mishaps. At the beginning of the month, Z 26 and Z 27 had to return to Germany with defects and two weeks later Z 23 and Z 24 had a serious collision, leaving just one operational destroyer. Shortage of fuel was also a continuing limitation on operations as stressed in numerous references in the Naval Staff war diaries for the months December to February. Meanwhile, in mid-December, General Admiral Hermann

Boehm, the Commanding Admiral Norway, complained that the Arctic U-boat force was totally inadequate given the area to be covered, the almost complete absence of aerial reconnaissance and the inexperience of the assigned boats, most of which had no combat experience. To put his comments in perspective, at the end of that month, the German Naval Staff recorded that, of ninety-eight operational U-boats, only thirty-eight were at sea or immediately available for action. Three each were in the Arctic and American waters, five off western Norway and twenty-three in the Mediterranean or on passage there. German submarine resources were, for the present, therefore tightly stretched, forcing difficult choices. The impact of Britain's autumn naval successes in the Mediterranean was especially striking.[14]

The capability of these small German forces was further hampered by winter darkness and often appalling weather. Enigma decrypts of the German air force Red key and German navy Dolphin key, which were read by Bletchley usually within 12 hours and rarely with more than 36 hours delay, ensured Tovey was well informed of German dispositions and their weakness.[15] In these circumstances, the convoys could sail with a minimal escort, normally a cruiser, a couple of destroyers and some anti-submarine trawlers. The Russians provided additional escort forces, albeit not very efficient, at the eastern end of the voyage.[16] The demands on Home Fleet resources until February were therefore modest which explains how two cruisers could be released to form Force K and the battleship *Prince of Wales* for deployment to the Far East.

If the impact of German interference up to the arrival of PQ 11 at Murmansk on 23 February was negligible, the record of supplies delivered was disappointing. Five months in, the First Protocol was well behind schedule. Excluding PQ 1 deliveries, 917 aircraft and 929 tanks were delivered by the end of February against the promised targets by that date of 2000 and 2500 and 7023 vehicles against 47,000 expected. The protocol anticipated overall monthly cargo deliveries of 200,000 tons but the average over these months barely exceeded 50,000. Admittedly it was clear that the Russians had overestimated the capacity of the northern ports. As noted above, the onset of winter ice obliged convoys from PQ 6 onward to use Murmansk and it would remain the destination port until June. For this six-month period this reduced the maximum capacity of the northern route to 90,000 tons per month, all that Murmansk could handle. However, in the first six months of the protocol, no month got close to this tonnage limit. The loading of individual ships was also wasteful with many taking around 50 per cent of their cargo capacity.[17]

The bulk of the supply shortfall lay with deliveries from the United States. Britain provided well over 80 per cent of the tanks and aircraft delivered to the end of February and it met 70 and 90 per cent respectively of its monthly commitments for these categories. They represented about eight weeks of her tank and six weeks of her fighter production. Britain had also shipped 12,000 tons of aluminium, 2000 tons more than its monthly commitment and on top of 5000 tons already supplied prior to the start of the protocol. Britain had been expected to provide a quarter of the anticipated 200,000 tons monthly of protocol supplies and had managed an average of 30,000 tons with a good record against most of the aid categories to which she had committed. The United States was supposed to provide three times the British quantity but had delivered less.[18]

*Initial British Deliveries: Relative Success*

The positive British delivery record was both a huge management achievement and a sacrifice to its other, often pressing, war goals. To meet the demands of the First Protocol, the prime minister established an inter-departmental committee, the Allied Supplies Executive (ASE), which Beaverbrook chaired as Minister of Supply and signatory to the Moscow agreement. The ASE included the Foreign Secretary, Secretaries of State for War and Air, the Parliamentary Under-Secretary of State for War Transport and often Admiralty representation too. It had ultimate authority over the shipment of all supplies to the Soviet Union, approving lists and loading programmes coordinated by the War Office which were then passed to the Ministry of War Transport to allocate the necessary shipping. It was in frequent contact with Soviet representatives and, unless vital strategic priorities were involved, decided whether to approve new requests. Britain therefore had a single body coordinating overall policy, cargo schedules and the shipping required for delivery.[19]

The ASE enjoyed power and system but could not have met the demanding schedule of the first months of the protocol without the overwhelming political commitment provided by the prime minister and War Cabinet along with the single-minded drive of Beaverbrook, for meeting the protocol commitments became more taxing than anticipated as the strategic situation deteriorated through the last quarter of 1941. Britain had to balance the risk of Russian collapse as the Germans renewed their drive on Moscow, the potential requirement to defend the Middle East from German attack from the North, replacing heavy losses incurred in the Western Desert Crusader offensive, and, finally, substantial resources to meet the Japanese onslaught in the East. The situation was further exacerbated by the need to cover some gaps in agreed American supplies at short notice and endless Russian demands for modifications, for more spare parts and replacements for goods damaged in transit.

Nevertheless, despite the changes in the strategic situation, disappointments in production and Russian discrimination, Britain gave the protocol overriding precedence. The Middle East remained her first priority but the ASE avoided choosing between the Middle East and the protocol largely by postponing or drawing down resources earmarked for home defence, although the Far East also suffered. Political determination to keep to the protocol reflected the sensitive state of British–Soviet relations through the autumn and winter. Stalin showed little gratitude for aid and instead demanded agreement on joint war aims, recognition of Russia's post-war borders and immediate British declarations of war on Finland, Romania and Hungary. Above all, he wanted more active British participation in the war, preferably an imminent 'second front' to reduce the German pressure. As Cripps warned, the Russians were increasingly convinced that the British would fight to 'the last drop of Russian blood'. A British proposal to deploy troops and aircraft to bolster the defences of the Caucasus only then to withdraw the offer, inevitably further fed Soviet annoyance and suspicion. So did American failure to deliver their share of the promised aid. For their part, the British still feared a Russian collapse or some compromise peace. The brutal reality was that the protocol was the only direct support Britain could offer and, over its first six months, nothing was allowed to threaten it. Churchill put it well. While he forgave the Russians for their past 'in proportion to the number of Huns they kill', they forgave him 'in proportion to the number of tanks I send'.[20]

Beaverbrook was the driving and essential force behind this strong British delivery record. He had the prime minister's solid support and usually, although not always, that of Eden. However, the service ministers were inevitably inclined to minimise equipment losses to British forces and the chiefs of staff even more so. During his first eight months as Chief of the Imperial General Staff, Brooke was a consistent sceptic over aid to Russia and critical both of Beaverbrook's negotiation of the original First Protocol package and of his determination to meet its terms whatever the perceived damage to other British interests. He was emphatic that Beaverbrook was the decisive voice on supplies to Russia, on which issue 'he controls the PM'. Brooke later claimed that the more he saw of Beaverbrook through the war, the more he disliked and distrusted him. He was an 'evil genius' exercising 'the very worst of influence' on Churchill.[21] Given this opposition, fully shared by Pound, without Beaverbrook's firm commitment, supplies would probably have reduced sharply in the three months following Japanese entry into the war, as happened with those from the United States. Furthermore, his contribution was not confined to political impetus. The future prime minister, Harold Macmillan, who was then Beaverbrook's deputy, later emphasised the latter's effectiveness as an administrator and problem solver in driving the delivery schedule.[22]

The motives behind Beaverbrook's ardent support for Russia, first with the protocol and then promotion of the 'second front', have aroused much speculation. Although he had a long-standing interest in Russia, this did not extend to ideological sympathy with Stalin or his regime. As the sponsor of the protocol, he had a vested interest in its success and Maisky no doubt regularly stressed the importance of his role. His claim that aid was crucial to Russia's survival probably reflected genuine conviction. However, some contemporaries detected political opportunism. Lieutenant General Sir Henry Pownall, the Vice Chief of the Imperial General Staff, thought the reason Beaverbrook was 'quite barmy' over aid to Russia was that it was a useful stick with which to beat the prime minister whom he wanted to replace.[23] Eden's private secretary, Oliver Harvey, also wondered whether Beaverbrook was deliberately weakening the prime minister by using Russia to strike down his lieutenants.[24] While there is no convincing evidence that Beaverbrook harboured ambitions to replace Churchill at this time, with some encouragement from Macmillan, he may have hankered after the role of 'Home affairs supremo'. Another plausible motive is that by exploiting unconditional support for Russia, he could position himself as leader of the radical left, displacing Cripps, Bevin and the Labour leader and deputy prime minister Clement Attlee. But it has also been suggested that 'his primary purpose in life was to combat boredom', in which case the protocol was a compelling temporary project with no defined purpose beyond that. Whatever the truth of Beaverbrook's ambitions, the second half of 1941 arguably marked the peak of his political influence. By the end of the year, even Churchill was tiring of his prima donna behaviour and finding it impossible to provide a position where he could contribute effectively. Many contemporaries never understood the strength of Churchill's relationship with Beaverbrook. Bevin offered a memorable explanation – 'Well, you see it's like this; it's as if the old man had married an 'ore. He knows what she is but he loves her.'[25]

There is little sign that intelligence influenced British supply decisions in the initial months of the protocol although it did illuminate the limits to German military power. There were three relevant areas where intelligence could potentially shed light: the overall progress of the Eastern war and Russia's prospects for survival; the evolution of comparative military strength; and Russian war production and its outlook. During the last quarter of 1941, the most valuable source on military operations and comparative strength, albeit from the German viewpoint, remained Ultra. Decrypts of the German air force Red Enigma key remained important but the major change in this period was more regular coverage by GC&CS of the Vulture key used for the German army high command network in the Eastern theatre. This provided detailed operational reports, occasional high-level appreciations, statements of intent and some logistic information. Vulture decrypts provided excellent warning of and then coverage of the German drive on Moscow, Operation Typhoon, which began on 2 October and, within three weeks, got within 65 miles of the capital. It showed that this was the greatest German offensive yet mounted, deploying two-thirds of available armoured divisions. At least eight warnings of what was coming were transmitted to the Russians via 30 Mission in the last days of September.[26] However, it appears these warnings were either lost somewhere in the Soviet system or else ignored.[27]

The Russian decision in mid-October to evacuate most government departments, including 30 Mission, to Kuibyshev, 500 miles east of Moscow, suggested doubt the latter would hold. Several Soviet leaders evidently did believe Moscow would fall. On the evening of 19 October, Lavrentiy Beria, Stalin's notorious Chief of State Security, told Molotov 'We should abandon Moscow. Otherwise, they will wring our necks like chickens.' Molotov wisely kept his mouth shut given that minutes later Beria was the first to agree with Stalin that Moscow should not be abandoned![28] By the last week of the month, 30 Mission was convinced Moscow would fall before the end of the year. Churchill, drawing on Ultra, put the odds at 'even' with Dill and the Director of Military Intelligence, Major General Francis Davidson, slightly more pessimistic. Only Ismay was confident Moscow would hold, quoting odds of ten to one and reflecting well on his powers of observation and judgement the previous month.[29] Beaverbrook had been an Ultra recipient since the previous year and was thus privy to the same intelligence, as were most ministers in the ASE.[30] The gloomy outlook revealed by Ultra SIGINT possibly underpinned his somewhat intemperate paper demanding more effective support for Russia put to the Defence Committee on 22 October.[31] He pushed for a British landing in northern Norway or in Murmansk. The prime minister responded that this had been thoroughly investigated and was not feasible. Beaverbrook did, however, get his firm support against any dilution or change to the agreed First Protocol commitments at least until the end of the year.[32]

On 8 November, the Joint Intelligence Committee assessed that Germany was making 'a supreme effort' to capture Moscow, and possibly Leningrad, and cut the northern supply route before winter set in. Thereafter it would aim to stabilise the northern and central fronts to rest and refit forces but might continue to press forward in the south. The capture of Moscow might encourage Germany to push for a peace settlement although she would want to secure control of Caucasian oil. For the first time the committee hinted that German forces were becoming severely stretched, although with time for recuperation, it expected them to be well capable of resuming the offensive in 1942 not only in Russia but also the Mediterranean and Atlantic.[33] By the middle of the month, Ultra increasingly showed that Typhoon was slowing due to bad weather, logistic difficulties, especially shortage of fuel, and effective Russian resistance. There was also evidence the Russians were gaining air superiority.[34] By 2 December, just before the Russian Moscow counter-offensive began, of which the British were unaware, the Joint Intelligence Committee emphasised that the German army was now 'stretched to its utmost'. While it did not rule out a final successful push on Moscow, it did not expect it and judged that consolidation along the existing front line for the winter was now their intent. The exception was the south where they still hoped to press into the Caucasus but, even here, they had already been pushed back from Rostov. Not surprisingly, given excellent Ultra coverage, the committee noted a sharp decline in German combat air strength which it now correctly put at 1800 compared to 2600 at the start of Barbarossa. This reflected losses but also withdrawals to Germany and the Mediterranean.[35]

Ultra was comparatively slow to reveal the scope of the Russian counter-offensive in the Moscow region which began on 6 December. This probably reflected German surprise and initial confusion. On 10 December, the prime minister told the War Cabinet that, given the 'enormous service' Russia was providing 'hammering the German army on her western front', he would not ask her to declare war on Japan since this would prevent her exploiting reinforcements from Siberia.[36] However, he did not refer specifically to an offensive and in an assessment issued the following day the Joint Intelligence Committee did not refer to it either. This instead reiterated the theme of German defensive consolidation and otherwise concentrated on the significant German air force withdrawals, notably of the 2nd Air Fleet to the Mediterranean.[37] It was only over the following week that the impact of the offensive emerged with Ultra revealing that Fourth Panzer Group, the formation most threatening Moscow, had collapsed with severe losses. Thus, on 18 December, the chiefs of staff weekly assessment stated that, at the beginning of the month, the Germans had evidently planned to establish a defensive line short of Moscow over the winter. However, their recent offensives had exhausted their fighting capacity, leaving them vulnerable to Russian counter-attack. They had been driven back across the whole central sector, in places up to 60 miles. The Russians now held the initiative.[38] The insights here reflected the last regular Ultra reporting from the Vulture Enigma key which from mid-December dried up for at least a year due to the widespread introduction of landlines by the German army.[39]

Stalin provided additional information on the operational situation and Russia's improving prospects when Eden and Lieutenant General Archibald Nye, the newly appointed Vice Chief of the Imperial General Staff, visited Moscow in the second half of December. He thought the Germans would take at least two months to recover their equilibrium after being driven back by the Russian counter-offensive. The Russians would exploit this breathing space to maintain the pressure. They had slight superiority in the air and could offset Germany's marked superiority in tanks with better winter equipment and superior morale. Stalin thought it probable that Germany's fighting efficiency had been permanently impaired. He did not offer detail on Russian arms production although he admitted this had slumped for a period with aircraft output down to thirty per day. However, the war industries were fast recovering with the implication that output was at least back to levels he had given to Beaverbrook and Harriman during the Moscow conference at the beginning of October.[40] Stalin had then claimed that aircraft output was seventy per day, or roughly 25,000 per year, while tank production was 1400 per month. British and American experts had been sceptical of these earlier figures although information from a variety of sources during the autumn suggested they were possible.[41] Real overall 1941 output was about half that implied in Stalin's October figures but they would be broadly achieved over 1942.[42] Stalin's reference to a continuing German tank advantage on the central front may have been partly designed to bolster the need for Western aid in this category but Soviet records giving an average ratio of 1000:670 in the Germans' favour suggest the claim was genuinely believed. Real tank strength here was about equal, with 1000 the absolute maximum the Germans could muster across the whole Eastern Front.[43]

## 'Wear Down' versus 'Containment' and the Arcadia Conference in Washington

Even before the full impact of the Russian counter-offensive was clear, their success in stalling Typhoon had shifted British leadership thinking.

This was apparent in briefing provided by the chiefs of staff to support Eden during his visit. It demonstrated that the chiefs now saw Russia as a key component in the British strategy of containment and wear down. They argued that the British Empire and Russia together held Germany within an 'iron ring'. This stretched from Petsamo in the north along the Russian battlefront, then through Iran and Syria to North Africa where Britain was fighting at the end of a 12,000-mile supply route. The remainder of the ring through the Mediterranean, Atlantic and Arctic was held by British sea power. Russia was inflicting major damage on Germany's land power. Britain was not engaged in land operations on an equivalent scale but provided the only base from which German industry and communications could be directly targeted, primarily through air power which was increasingly exposing the German population to attack. Meanwhile the British blockade was starving Germany of key resources and Britain and Russia could together deny her the oil she required to maximise her war potential.[44]

In a strategic overview prepared for the chiefs of staff on 16 December in preparation for the British–American summit in Washington beginning just over a week later, the Joint Planning Staff developed this theme further, emphasising the failure of the German army to defeat the Russians. Russian resistance was 'an immense contribution' to 'wearing down' the enemy's forces and 'lowering his morale'. More was possible. If the Russian effort could be sustained, the Allies would possess 'for the first time a front on land' from which to mount a direct assault on the frontiers of Germany. Continuation of Russian resistance was of 'primary importance' to the defeat of Germany.[45]

Six weeks later, a Joint Intelligence Committee assessment which examined German intentions for 1942 emphasised Russia's achievement in wearing down German strength, stating that Russia still retained the initiative on the Eastern Front while German forces continued to fall back. Until the present Russian offensive was exhausted, Germany would be unable to refit and regroup for new offensive operations of its own either in Russia or elsewhere. Two other factors constrained Germany's options. She was short of oil and the German air force had reduced to an overall front-line strength of 4000 combat and 1400 transport aircraft. This reduction in air strength meant Germany could not mount a major operation elsewhere if she was successfully to contain Russia although she had already strengthened air and naval forces in the Mediterranean to safeguard communications with North Africa, to neutralise Malta and counter a British advance towards Tunisia. The committee therefore judged that, once the Russian offensive petered out and the front stabilised,

Germany would probably focus on a major operation through Ukraine to the Caucasus to obtain oil. In addition, she would consolidate control over the central and eastern Mediterranean and exploit her position in North Africa. It was unlikely she could find sufficient resources for a more general offensive across the whole Russian front. This was an impressive analysis on two counts. It correctly recognised the limits to German power after the major losses in 1941 and it anticipated the southern offensive, Plan Blue, which Germany would begin executing almost five months later. However, the committee arguably understated the precipitate decline in German air power. Its figure for nominal front-line strength of 4000 was correct. However, between 21 June 1941, immediately before the launch of Barbarossa, and 24 January 1942, serviceable combat strength in fighters and bombers had fallen by exactly 50 per cent from 2720 aircraft to 1362. Numbers would recover by the summer but the quality of the force was never the same.[46]

There were important gaps in this evolving intelligence picture over the four months from October to the end of January. Coverage of German strength, movements and intentions, drawn primarily from Ultra, was far better than that on Russia. There was little reliable insight into Russian losses of personnel and equipment although they had clearly been heavy. Nor was there any fresh study of Russia's war potential updating that provided by the Joint Intelligence Committee in September. It was accordingly difficult to judge whether the shift in Russia's favour with the December counter-offensive would prove permanent or temporary. Despite these gaps, it is tempting to argue that intelligence encouraged a shift over the last quarter of 1941 in the underlying rationale for aid to Russia, moving it from ensuring Russian survival to strengthening her potential as a key component of 'wear down' as suggested by the joint planners in mid-December. Churchill, Beaverbrook, and perhaps Eden, were beginning to think in these terms. On the same day the joint planners presented their paper, Churchill completed his own grand strategy overview, while on passage to the United States in the new battleship *Duke of York*, and which he shared with Roosevelt the following week. In the opening section, he stated that Hitler's failure and losses in Russia were 'the prime fact of the war at this time'. It was not yet possible to judge the impact of the latest winter fighting and the only role for Britain and the United States was to send, 'without fail and punctually', the supplies 'we have promised'. This alone would exert influence over Stalin and permit 'the mighty Russian effort' to be woven into the overall war.[47] However, this perception of Russia's central role did not yet translate into formal British or indeed American policy.

For, at the British–American Arcadia summit in Washington which opened on 23 December and ran until 14 January, Russia's role and prospects received surprisingly little attention given the huge proportion of German military power she was currently engaging. The American and British grand strategy agreed at Arcadia, known as WW1 and based on a British joint planners' draft, built logically on the conclusions reached at ABC-1 and Riviera. It therefore confirmed that Germany was the primary enemy, to be tackled initially through a strategy of 'wear down' while 'safeguarding vital interests in the Eastern theatre' from Japan. The components of 'wear down' were the familiar bombing, blockade and subversion, but these were now joined by 'assistance to Russia's offensive by all available means'. The strategy judged it unlikely that any major land offensive could be undertaken against Germany in 1942 except by Russia. However, although it promoted 'wear down', it also had a strong defensive cast. This was most obvious in the East, but it also stressed the need to secure production centres and maritime communications and to construct a solid ring around German-occupied Europe. Here it was essential to assist the Russians in holding Leningrad, Moscow and the Caucasus oilfields and maintain their war effort. This emphasis on defence, influenced by the dire position in the Far East theatre, made the strategy closer to 'containment' than 'wear down' and little different to the British approach at Riviera.[48]

The emphasis on containment was evident in Roosevelt's own strategic overview which opened the formal summit sessions on 23 December and drew on a memorandum prepared by Secretary Stimson. Extraordinarily, given the scale of the Russian counter-attack currently underway and the potential opportunities the British joint planners thought this might offer, the only brief mention of Russia by either Roosevelt or Churchill in his response was to Stalin's reluctance to attack the Japanese at this time. Stimson's memo did not mention Russia at all.[49] The American–British joint planners subsequently produced an Arcadia report on 'Immediate Assistance to China' but no equivalent for Russia. Nor was there any substantive discussion of Russia's requirements and prospects at any of the thirteen meetings of the combined chiefs of staff. Overall, the focus of summit debate was on containing Japan, the movement of limited American forces to Britain, and a potential joint landing in North-west Africa, designated Super-Gymnast. Even this landing had a defensive cast, being motivated primarily to forestall an expected German move into Spain and thence southward.[50]

The summit did acknowledge awkward trade-offs between shipping now required for Far East reinforcements and the initial movement of

American forces to Britain while maintaining sufficient to meet the Russia supply schedule. Marshall, as US Army Chief of Staff, and King, now Commander-in-Chief US Fleet, were evidently prepared to accept a 30 per cent cut in American supplies to Russia over the next four months. Marshall stressed this would be on top of the existing American deficiency that could not therefore be made up in this period. While Marshall's willingness to countenance this cut was no doubt driven primarily by the urgent demands in other theatres, he was also receiving intelligence advice that the Russians might not survive the winter. He may accordingly have felt aid would be wasted. None of the British team opposed this cut on military grounds and Portal, the British Chief of the Air Staff, was anxious that supplies for Russia did not reduce those destined for the Middle East. Field Marshal Dill, speaking for the Army in the absence of Brooke left in London, noted that any cuts would meet political resistance. King argued that, since the Russians could not process a full schedule of deliveries, the proposed cuts had little practical consequence. The British chiefs were in fact entirely in accord with their American counterparts and would have liked a similar diversion, taking advantage of an escape clause in the protocol which allowed for consultation between the signatories if the overall war situation fundamentally changed. Two weeks after Arcadia Brooke tried unsuccessfully to remove 283 tanks from the Soviet Union's allocation for redeployment to India and Australasia. Reflecting Stalin's recent comments to Eden and Nye in Moscow, he noted that Russian tank production was apparently steadily increasing while Britain had already shipped them more tanks 'than to all other theatres of war'.[51]

Churchill and Roosevelt did indeed reject any cut in promised Russian aid. The latter stated that supplies to Russia were an unavoidable 'moral obligation'. Any reduction might bring 'awkward consequences later on'. The potential for awkward consequences was certainly true but justifying aid on moral grounds was not likely to persuade the Western military leadership that the sacrifices incurred elsewhere were necessary. Hopkins suggested that only seven ships per month were required to meet the Russian schedule and felt these could be found. Subsequent investigation forced him to recognise that fifty ships were required in January to restore the schedule of which only twenty could be found for the Arctic route with another four going to Vladivostok. Oddly, the British team did not challenge Hopkins' initial estimate although they must have known that the shipping requirement over the last three months averaged out at twice this number which would inevitably increase to meet the growing shortfall in promised deliveries. The summit concluded that immediate Far East demands could be met by reducing planned American reinforcements to

Iceland and Northern Ireland. However, there was an implicit assumption that maintaining the First Protocol schedule to Russia would mean postponing the proposed 'Super Gymnast' by several months.[52]

## The Initial American Record: Managing a Deficiency

By contrast with the positive British delivery record, there were many reasons for the American difficulties that autumn. The commitments Harriman had signed in Moscow on 1 October were in many categories more aspirational than practical and several were subject to presidential authorisation. The financing of supplies to Russia was uncertain until the end of the month when, in formally approving the First Protocol deliveries and in line with Harriman's advice, Roosevelt decreed that the Soviet Union would be eligible for Lend-Lease with an initial allocation of USD one billion. This began a Soviet aid programme second only to Britain in scale. On 7 November, Roosevelt also declared the defence of the Soviet Union vital to that of the United States, emphasising again determined political commitment. However, for the War Department, the primary agency involved in implementing it, the new Soviet aid programme brought to the fore three linked problems. First, the need to bring system and order to the hitherto chaotic way in which Lend-Lease production was planned. Existing and future commitments to Britain, China, and the Dutch for the defence of the Netherlands East Indies, had to be properly identified and prioritised alongside the new demands of the First Protocol. Secondly, there was no prospect in the next six months of meeting burgeoning Lend-Lease demands and the minimal needs of American war preparation and rearmament. Until mid-1942 therefore, allocation involved dividing a deficiency. New demands further hindered management of this shortfall. The British complained that the Americans reneged on promised military deliveries to them but did not hesitate to inflict new demands. In the case of tanks, urgent British requests for help in the Middle East at the beginning of November absorbed the entire three months of medium tank production previously destined for the US Army. Finally, there were presidential complications. Roosevelt not only wished to avoid visible signs of a 'war economy' but seemed to prefer that America's contribution to defeating the Axis should be weapons not armies.[53] It is striking that as late as 23 December, he thought it 'a mistake to send United States troops into England or Scotland'.[54]

Although, despite all the constraints, there was significant improvement in the planning and prioritisation of Lend-Lease supplies in the last months of 1941, there were still other problems to resolve. There were unforeseen production bottlenecks in defence industries that, for all their vast potential, were still embryonic compared to those of Britain. American suppliers, geared to meeting the demands of their own forces, struggled to adapt to foreign requirements. There were problems in packing, crating, provision of spare parts and relevant ammunition, timely transport to ports and efficient cargo handling and stowage. Shipping was poorly coordinated. All this created delay, even to Britain, a primary defence customer since 1939 with well-established delivery systems. In 1941, a mere 11.5 per cent of British war supplies came from the United States and only 2.4 per cent from Lend-Lease.

For Russia, a new and unfamiliar customer and with many new items required, the problems were worse. Despite pressure to deliver, the War Department could not get supplies to the ports in keeping with the protocol schedule for October and November. Furthermore, what was delivered brought numerous complaints from Soviet representatives checking supplies before they were loaded. They insisted that too many items were delivered incomplete or defective or inadequately packed for a long and difficult sea voyage. Key paperwork was missing. They refused to accept items until problems were remedied, adding further delay often by as much as six weeks. A note from the Soviet embassy dated 25 November, which reached the president, recorded these failings, revealing that only one-third of aircraft, tanks and trucks scheduled for October had so far departed, compounded by the inadequacy of shipping. Of forty-one ships promised by the Maritime Commission for October and November, only twelve had been made available and one of these returned to port due to its unseaworthy condition. The War Department did its utmost to resolve these early errors and hoped, rather optimistically, to recover much of the initial delays in December. The outbreak of war and the inevitable disruption and shifting priorities made this impossible.[55] At the end of December, providing an update on supplies to Russia over the last three months, the War Department admitted that 298 of the promised 750 tanks had neither been delivered nor were in transit. Later records suggest that the only American tanks reaching Russia in 1941 were thirty-one Stuart M3 light tanks included in PQ 6 which arrived in Murmansk on 20 December. For fighters and light bombers, the shortfall in delivery/transit was much worse, 780 out of 900 and 747 of 828. Harriman acknowledged that, while Britain was 100 per cent on schedule in meeting its commitments, the United States had to date only shipped 25 per cent of agreed supplies.[56]

The Soviet assessment was equally grim. In a report to Stalin and Molotov on 9 January, Anastas Mikoyan, the Politburo member responsible for war supplies and transport, reviewed First Protocol deliveries for the three months October to December. He stated that, while Britain had fulfilled its obligations 'more or less accurately and carefully', which, as explained later, was generous in regard to tanks, this was not true of the United States. The Americans claimed they had delivered 395 of the 600 aircraft promised in this quarter. However, only 204 had so far been shipped and of these only 95 had arrived in the Soviet Union. The American government had now recalled almost all the 457 aircraft awaiting shipment to Russia in its ports for redeployment to other war theatres. The large build-up in the ports reflected aircraft arriving without propellers, armament or spares and insufficient allocated shipping. The shortfall in tanks was similar. The Americans claimed to have provided 673 tanks over the quarter. In reality, only 182 had been supplied and of these only 27 had reached the Soviet Union (clearly the PQ 6 M3s referred to above). The Russians would find there was no early improvement in American performance. No further American aircraft arrived before PQ 12 reached Murmansk on 12 March and, at most, only seventy more tanks, all M3 Lee medium tanks, were delivered before the end of March. There were no more Stuarts until 201 arrived with PQ 15 on 5 May.[57]

Stalin was well aware of the continuing American shortfall. On 29 March, when he received the new British Ambassador, Sir Archibald Clark Kerr, Stalin expressed thanks, and surprise, that the British had fulfilled their supply commitments, comparing this favourably with the behaviour of the Americans. This followed 'a good man-to-man chat about pipes, sex and China' (Clark Kerr's previous post). Stalin undoubtedly came to enjoy Clark Kerr's company with the latter deliberately spicing their exchanges with racist and sexist banter. Few others would have dared tease Stalin as Clark Kerr did at the Teheran summit the following year. Seeing Stalin puffing on a cigarette, he insisted this habit was 'cissy' since real men smoked pipes. To the surprise of a horrified Churchill, Stalin complied, put out his cigarette and sheepishly reached for his pipe! How far this rapport delivered real diplomatic benefit is more debatable, but Clark Kerr certainly became a shrewd reader of Stalin and the Soviet system and therefore an invaluable adviser to Churchill and Eden.[58] Meanwhile, Stalin was meticulous in tracking Mikoyan's reports on Western aid. As early as November, he was totting up the number of planes delivered (432) in red pen on Mikoyan's notes.[59] The figure 432 clearly comprised deliveries by Dervish, PQ 1 and PQ 2, the last reaching Archangel on 30 October.

As noted earlier, the United States' entry into the war following the Japanese attack on Pearl Harbor and German declaration of war four days later provoked a suspension of Lend-Lease supplies as material and shipping was diverted to meet immediate and critical American needs. Shipments to Russia inevitably fell even further into arrears. While, in mid-December, a week after Pearl Harbor, Marshall favoured continuing aid to the Soviet Union 'to the maximum extent possible', he and Stimson felt the First Protocol commitments must be revised downward to meet the pressing new war requirements of the American military. The president flatly refused, stressing on 28 December that the Russian programme was 'vital to our interest' and decreeing that the existing protocol schedule must be re-established from 1 January and deficits made up by 1 April. Stimson insisted there would have to be some modifications. No anti-aircraft or anti-tank guns could be supplied before the end of March. Nor could schedules for tanks, aircraft and trucks be made up by 1 April although they probably could be by 30 June. The president reluctantly approved these recommendations as 'minimum schedules' but reiterated he wanted the protocol commitments restored as soon as possible.[60]

This presidential insistence had limited immediate effect. As already described, it did not stop Marshall and King again attempting sharply to reduce the pace of aid to Russia during the Arcadia discussions on 12 January. Hopkins' best efforts found less than half the shipping necessary to recover the schedule in January. On 16 January, four days after the Arcadia meeting, Roosevelt told Admiral Land that he was 'terribly disturbed' by the Russian supply situation and that he 'simply must find some ships that can be diverted at once'. Despite this outburst there were even fewer sailings in February and not many more in March. On 11 March, when Henry Morgenthau, his Treasury Secretary, briefed him on the scale of the continuing backlog, Roosevelt declared:

> I do not want to be in the same position as the English. The English promised the Russians two divisions. They failed. They promised them help in the Caucasus. They failed. Every promise the English have made to the Russians, they have fallen down on.... The only reason we stand so well with the Russians is that up to date we have kept our promises. I suppose the reason we are behind on our deliveries to Russia is because we got into the war ourselves.... Nothing would be worse than to have the Russians collapse.... I would rather lose New Zealand, Australia or anything else than have the Russians collapse.[61]

In authorising Morgenthau to expedite shipments to Russia, he stressed that the United States must keep its word because at this point in the war Russian resistance mattered most.[62] This was an extraordinary insight into the value Roosevelt placed on Russia's contribution and his commitment to helping her. Also extraordinary was his assessment of Britain's contribution, in part selective and misleading and in part downright dishonest, while the portrayal of Russia's present attitude to the United States was naïve. For his part, Morgenthau was clear that the aid backlog reflected management failings rather than the new demands of war, although he seems not to have told the president this.[63] A week later, Roosevelt sent an equally strong directive to Admiral Land telling him to find shipping to meet the protocol, if necessary from South American and Caribbean routes, 'regardless of other considerations'. Hopkins commented that this meant 'the protocol must be completed in preference to any other phase of our war program'. These presidential interventions, possibly spurred by a growing intelligence consensus that Russia would struggle to meet the expected German summer offensive, did have a major impact. In April, sixty-three ships departed from the United States for Iceland and the start of the Arctic convoy supply route. Six more headed for the Persian Gulf and ten across the Pacific to Vladivostok. These April shipments totalled 450,000 tons compared with 375,000 tons shipped from the United States over the whole of the previous six months. Furthermore, the president now proposed to adopt Hopkins' fifty ships per month target until November. Unfortunately, the fruits of this April surge did not reach the Russians for many months because, by the time they arrived in Iceland, for reasons discussed later, the Royal Navy was obliged sharply to reduce onward convoy capacity.[64]

## The Consequences of Shortfall

There were four important consequences from this shortfall of supplies, primarily from the United States, over the first six months of the First Protocol. First, it produced a reduction of perhaps 5 per cent in Russia's tank and combat aircraft strength over the seven months from December 1941 until June 1942. This loss estimate compares actual American deliveries in these categories against those possible if the original Moscow agreement schedule had been kept. The December start date for the loss reflects an inevitable lag in supplies reaching the Russian front line while the surge in April shipments which began to recover the deficit was not felt at the front before the end of June. With the benefit of hindsight, it may be argued that this loss had no practical impact on either the Moscow counter-offensive or the execution of the disastrous Russian spring offensive at Kharkov. However, at a time when comparative strength on the Eastern Front was finely balanced, this margin could have helped slow the German summer offensive in the south and might even have proved critical had events taken a slightly different course. The impact of the shortfall in non-military items and raw materials is harder to gauge but a loss of 5 per cent in Russia's overall war potential in these months again seems reasonable.

The second consequence was the damage to relations between the Western Allies and Russia. The perceived failure to deliver on promises fed the distrust and suspicion which was never absent for long with Stalin and other members of the Soviet leadership group. The belief that the United States and Britain would happily leave Russia to bleed while pursuing their own interests was deeply entrenched. There was ample scope for further tension during 1942 but it was amplified by perceived failure to support Russia when she needed it most. A third consequence was that the delay in executing the main American supply effort until well into 1942 meant that the Western Allies failed to take maximum advantage of the period when German ability to interdict the Arctic convoys was at its weakest. The American surge from April to make up the shortfall coincided with the arrival of substantial German air and naval reinforcements, making the Arctic route far more dangerous and therefore more demanding of defensive resources not easily spared from other theatres. The surge supplies therefore took far longer to reach the Russian front line and factories. This led to the final consequence. From mid-1942, the opportunity costs of persisting with Arctic route, given the shipping and escort demands posed by operations in the Atlantic and Mediterranean became unfavourable for extended periods. These final two factors inevitably further fed Soviet distrust and doubt over Western commitment.

### *The Impact of the First Convoys on the Soviet War Effort*

While there were numerous items on the First Protocol list, for Stalin and the Soviet leadership, three priorities dominated not only in its early months but throughout the period it was in force and indeed the rest of 1942. These were aircraft, tanks, and aluminium and specialised steel products for aircraft and armour production. Machine tools and related industrial equipment also became significant as 1942 progressed. These items absorbed about 30 per cent of the tonnage of Western deliveries via the Arctic until the end of that year.[65]

#### AIRCRAFT

The most visible early contribution of British aid to Russia was the wing of Hurricane IIB fighters delivered at the end of August 1941. 151 Wing Royal Air Force, under Wing Commander Henry Ramsbottom-

Isherwood, comprised two squadrons totalling forty aircraft. Twenty-four were accommodated in the carrier *Argus* which reached Murmansk on 28 August although the fighters were not flown off to Vaenga, the airfield from which they would operate, until 7 September. Two unfortunately wrecked their undercarriage on take-off necessitating belly landings at Vaenga. There were supposed to be sixteen further aircraft embarked in crates in the merchant vessel *Llanstephen Castle*, part of the Dervish convoy which reached Archangel on 31 August, but one was damaged beyond repair in transit. Due to lack of suitable handling facilities at the port, the assembly and transit of these crated fighters was protracted and they did not reach Vaenga, after flying from a makeshift air strip at Archangel, until 10 days after arrival. 151 Wing, which arrived with a full outfit of pilots and ground crew, had two main tasks, as 'Operation Benedict': to assist in the defence of Murmansk under the Northern Fleet Air Force; and to train a nucleus of Russian personnel to take over and operate not only the Vaenga-based wing but the many Hurricanes expected to follow.[66]

Meanwhile, a small batch of the forty-eight crated P-40 Tomahawk fighters which had also arrived with Dervish were assembled under British instruction and, from 10 September, were flown by pilots of the Soviet air force testing unit from Archangel to an airbase near Kadnikov, 25 miles north-east of Vologda which was in turn 250 miles north-east of Moscow. The 27th Reserve Air Regiment at Kadnikov was one of two units now charged with the acceptance, assembly and induction of foreign aircraft into the Soviet air force. The other unit, the 21st Reserve Air Regiment, was situated at Kineshma, 230 miles south-east of Vologda on the River Volga. Initially, Kadnikov handled the introduction of P-40s and Kineshma Hurricanes. After unloading at Archangel, aircraft were usually delivered in their crates by rail, either direct to Kineshma or to Sokol, which was on the line to Moscow and just 11 miles from Kadnikov. Unfortunately, the introduction of the Tomahawks into service was hampered by Soviet reluctance to allow foreign personnel into these bases. Five weeks passed before, in late October, twenty-two British specialists from 151 Wing reached Kadnikov. By then a first batch of Soviet pilots and ground crew had trained themselves and departed south for the front line with their new P-40s on 12 October. The British team did their best to support future aircraft batches until February when they were withdrawn but Soviet willingness to accept technical and operational advice proved erratic. A separate British team reached Kineshma on 9 November to assist with the Hurricanes arriving with PQ 1. They too faced diminishing Russian cooperation until they were summarily ordered to depart at minimal notice. The introduction of the American P-39 Airacobra in early 1942 faced similar delay and obstruction with the Russians only reluctantly accepting help after crashing the first aircraft they erected.[67]

The Hurricanes of 151 Wing almost doubled the Northern Fleet's fighter strength. Although their performance was inferior to the latest marks of German single-seat fighters, that did not matter in the Murmansk region in the last quarter of 1941. The Hurricanes were superior to the current Soviet Northern Fleet fighters, comprising obsolescent I-15s, I-16s and I-153s, and competitive against the small German air group currently based in the Arctic. Despite later Soviet claims of inferiority, the Hurricane IIB's overall performance was broadly equivalent to their latest fighters although its lack of cannon made it under-armed for late 1941. The Northern Fleet anyway had low priority for the newest Soviet types (LaGG-3, MiG-3 and Yak-1) and even by the following July it had only acquired four MiG-3s. 151 Wing began operations on 11 September and enjoyed their first combat success the following day, catching a German reconnaissance mission by surprise and shooting down three German fighters for the loss of one Hurricane, whose pilot, Sergeant 'Nudge' Smith, was killed. This was the only pilot loss suffered by 151 Wing during its six weeks of operation. Although defensive operations were hampered by the lack of radar and an effective early warning system, on 20 September three German aircraft were shot down during an attempted raid on Murmansk, a success which Portal brought to Churchill's attention. By 20 October, with winter fast setting in, 151 Wing had flown 365 sorties, primarily in a defensive role but also including thirty attack missions escorting Soviet bombers. Overall, they had destroyed about fifteen German aircraft, suitable revenge for the Fleet Air Arm casualties suffered at Petsamo in July. They had also trained sufficient Soviet pilots to permit the handover of twenty-eight operational aircraft to form 78th Fighter Air Regiment. The British team then withdrew to the United Kingdom although it was late November before shipping was available. Hurricanes remained the principal Northern Fleet fighter for the next year. Through the winter they continued to compose 50 per cent of its fighter strength and by July it was 75 per cent.[68]

By the end of December, the Russians had received 790 fighters (including the Dervish deliveries) from the Western Allies, of which 700 (484 Hurricanes and 216 P-40s) had been provided from Britain. Four hundred and eight more Hurricanes arrived from Britain in January and February with no arrivals from the United States in those months.[69] The Western aircraft supplied to the end of December represented 13.1 per cent of new aircraft added to Soviet fighter stock during the second half of 1941, 8.2 per cent of fighter losses in the same period, and equated to about 10 per cent of Russia's nominal fighter stock remaining at the outset of 1942 although front-line fighter strength was a maximum of 2000.[70] The British aircraft represented 10 per cent of United Kingdom 1941 single seat fighter production and the same proportion of Soviet fighter production.[71]

Apart from the Arctic region, P-40s began operating with the Moscow air defence forces in mid-October although they did not record any 'kills' until December. By November, Hurricanes were operating on the Karelian front near Leningrad, losing a first aircraft on the last day of the month but then claiming three aircraft destroyed for the loss of one of their own on 4 December. By then, twenty P-40s were operating in defence of the 'road of life' across the frozen Lake Ladoga to Leningrad. Western fighters were prominent in the defence of Leningrad for the next 18 months.[72] Meanwhile, on 16 November, a squadron of eleven Hurricanes flew from Kineshma to join P-40s in the defence of Moscow. From mid-November, German intelligence reports in Army Groups North and Centre made increasing reference to the presence of Western fighters although at this stage numbers reported and aircraft whereabouts were often inaccurate. For example, on 14 November, Third Panzer Group's war diary reported that 136 British and American planes had been identified at an airfield along with British radio transmissions.[73]

Through the winter, most of the Western fighters were deployed in the various regions of the Soviet Home Air Defence Force (PVO), one of the four distinct branches of the Soviet air force (VVS). At the beginning of January, in addition to some seventy Hurricanes serving with the Northern Fleet Air Force (part of the Naval Fleet Air Force, another branch of the VVS) to protect the northern ports, there were ninety-nine Hurricanes and thirty-nine P-40s in service with the PVO, making up just over 9 per cent of a strength of 1470 aircraft. The most powerful element of the PVO at this time was the Moscow air defence region, 6th Air Defence Corps, which Stalin ensured was always well-resourced and, from the beginning of December, in addition to protecting the capital, also provided the fighter support for the Moscow counter-offensive. At the start of this, there were only ten Hurricanes and eleven P-40s included in its strength of 472 aircraft but a month later this had doubled to nineteen Hurricanes and twenty P-40s in a total strength of 480 and the proportion of Western fighters steadily increased. By 1 February, three regiments of 6th Air Defence Corps (roughly equating to Royal Air Force squadrons) had Hurricanes and a month later six. In mid-February,

German observers were staggered to see up to fifty Hurricanes operating above the fierce fighting around Rzhev, 140 miles north-west of Moscow.

By 1 March, 6th Air Defence Corps had 112 Hurricanes and 16 P-40s out of a total nominal strength of 492, representing 26 per cent, although serviceability for all its aircraft was much lower. If older Russian fighters are omitted, the strength of 6th Air Defence Corps in these winter months was comparable to that of 11 Group defending London and the South-East during the Battle of Britain although the fighting and attrition in that battle was on a vastly greater scale than the air campaign in the Moscow region. Out of seventy-five raids on the capital over the nine months from July 1941, fifty-nine had less than ten aircraft and only nine more than fifty. About 1000 tons of bombs were dropped while London received 16,000 tons in the equivalent period the previous winter. The air campaign against Moscow was thus a pale shadow of that against London and other British cities and had negligible military and economic effect.[74] This renders a recent claim that the Russians could deploy fighters over Moscow in numbers the Royal Air Force 'could not match' somewhat surprising. Nor is it true that Moscow anti-aircraft guns vastly outnumbered those in London during the Blitz the previous winter.[75]

The average 10 per cent proportion of Western fighters at the start of 1942 downplays their real value over the next year since a high proportion of the Russian aircraft were older types, completely outclassed by the German opposition. Only about half the Russian total in the PVO strength at the beginning of January were competitive modern aircraft and a more accurate gauge of the Western contribution is therefore 17 per cent. Furthermore, the three new Russian types all suffered production and teething problems. Eight serious defects were identified in the first batches of LaGG-3s, only 263 existed at the start of the Moscow counter-offensive, its wooden construction proved unsuited to winter conditions, its hydraulics were unreliable and it was difficult to maintain, with operational availability barely 25 per cent. The MiG-3 was poorly armed and optimised for high-altitude interception which was rarely relevant on the Eastern Front. In late December, Stalin, who took a close but not always well-grounded interest in aircraft design, therefore ordered production to cease in favour of the Il-2 Sturmovik ground attack aircraft which had a similar engine. The Yak-1 was the best of the three modern fighters but its performance was not optimised until well into 1942 when it was competitive with the latest marks of the German Me 109. However, even then, the Yak-1 and its successive evolutions through the Yak-3, Yak-7 and Yak-9 faced constant quality-control problems. There are claims that each Yak-1 was almost unique with different-length landing gear and in 1943 there were problems with aircraft shedding their skin due to unauthorised and inappropriate camouflage paint. As a result of these problems, during March and April, the Western fighters, predominantly Hurricanes, made up a third of the overall modern fighter force in 6th Air Defence Corps. By that time deployment of Hurricanes was underway across the Soviet air force with eight regiments receiving the type during the second quarter of the year. On 1 May, there were 249 Western fighters in a total PVO strength of 1757 or 14 per cent. Throughout 1941–2, twenty-nine PVO and VVS regiments were equipped with Hurricanes.[76]

Numbers aside, the Soviet view promoted during the Cold War that the Western aircraft supplied under Lend-Lease, especially under the First Protocol, were obsolescent 'cast-offs' and often in poor condition retains considerable traction. The main complaints levelled against the Hurricane IIB were its inadequate armament, poor armour protection and lack of power, the latter compounded by shortage of 100-octane petrol in Russia. Soviet pilots and ground crew also had difficulty handling it when taxiing, with many aircraft damaged on rough airstrips. Shortage of spares, intense cold weather and poor servicing meant operational availability in Hurricane units was often very low. On the positive side, Soviet pilots acknowledged the Hurricane was robust and easy to fly and its radio and navigational equipment were highly prized. They also recognised that lack of speed was compensated by its tight turning circle. Soviet pilots apparently preferred the P-40 which they judged as easy to fly and with better performance. However, its armament and protection were no better than the Hurricane, it was more sensitive to cold weather and poor maintenance and there were similar problems with spares. Furthermore, criticism of the Hurricane invariably overlooks the substantial modification programme which the Russians undertook from March onward. By the end of 1942, 925 Hurricanes had been rearmed and put into service with Soviet cannons and machine guns and in many cases equipped for delivering bombs and rockets too. Thus, from mid-year, the Hurricane was often used as a fighter-bomber and to considerable effect, in the same way as the Royal Air Force was using it in North Africa.[77]

As already noted, the latest Soviet fighters had their own troubles. More important, during the winter of 1941/42 German pilots did not rate the Western fighters inferior to their Russian counterparts. They treated the Hurricane with respect, remembering that its turning circle was 'much smaller than that of the Me 109'. Overall, they judged they held a distinct advantage in air combat but that this was 'tactical' not 'technical'. In performance the Western fighters were a fair match for the Me 109. This view is confirmed by the surviving records, especially Soviet war diaries. The operational results achieved by Western fighters within the Moscow air defence region, where records are most accessible, during the five months December 1941 to April 1942 were broadly consistent with their proportionate strength within the 6th Air Defence Corps' modern fighter force. 6th Air Defence Corps units claimed 233 German aircraft destroyed within this period, of which fifty-one, or 22 per cent, were down to Hurricanes and P-40s, thirty-four and seventeen respectively. German records reveal actual losses to fighters of about 100. For perspective, this compares with seventy-five German aircraft lost on the single day of 15 August 1940 during the Battle of Britain. Russian recorded losses were about eighty, including twenty-eight Hurricanes and three P-40s, the latter a suspiciously low number. If December, when there were few Western aircraft operationally active in this region, is excluded from the figures, then their share of claimed kills rises to 32 per cent, a significant contribution in the most important sector of the air war at this time. The impact of the Western fighters in Karelia, around Leningrad, and along the front north-west of Moscow, at a time when the Russian fighter force was suffering steady attrition, was similar. The commander of the 29th Fighter Air Regiment arrived at Kuvshinovo, 175 miles north-west of Moscow, on 12 March with thirty-six Hurricanes, joining sister regiments with just seven MiG-3s and eight LaGG-3s. Over the next three weeks they flew three sorties a day and by April had only thirteen aircraft left.[78]

### TANKS

If Western aircraft made a valuable contribution to Russian effectiveness in this first winter of the war, so did tanks. British records state that the United Kingdom delivered 481 tanks during the last quarter of 1941 and a further 468 by the end of February following the arrival of convoy PQ 11. All of these were medium tanks, either Matilda IIs or Valentines, with an increasing number of the latter now built in Canada. Their categorisation as medium is justified by scale of armour, both greater than a T-34, and weight. At 29 tons, the Matilda II was almost as heavy as a T-34 and the lighter Valentine at 17.6 tons still 70 per cent heavier than a T-70, the latest Soviet light tank, which only began production in March 1942. They were the most effective tanks the British had widely available in late 1941. A successor tank, the Churchill, at 40 tons almost as heavy as a KV-1, was just being introduced and, in early December, the possibility of supplying 100 of these to Russia next spring was discussed.[79] A first batch of these was sent in May and eighty-four delivered by the end of 1942. The total of 949 tanks over the five months to February compared with a commitment under the First Protocol to deliver 1250 in this period

(250 per month). The British had also promised to deliver 50 extra tanks per month until early 1942, while American production built up, with the United States compensating in the latter part of the protocol. However, this 300 per month figure was not reached until February and March when Britain was already well behind the formal 250 schedule. If British supplies were in deficit, the American record, as noted earlier, was woeful. Of the initial batch of 182 tanks the Russians believed were in transit at the beginning of January, less than 100 had arrived by the end of February, not even a single fortnight's supply. Deliveries did ramp up in the second quarter of the year so that a total of 796 American tanks had arrived by the end of June, divided almost equally between Stuart light and Lee medium categories. As a result of the slow American build-up, over the 15 months to the end of 1942, Britain and Canada delivered 2050 tanks to Russia compared to 1825 from the United States. More surprisingly, in numbers, British/Canadian deliveries still far outstripped American in 1943, with 2102 tanks compared to 1180, although American tanks were now predominantly much higher-quality Shermans.[80]

Russian sources differ slightly from British records, claiming receipt of 466 tanks by the end of December, 187 Matildas and 259 Valentines, of which 145 and 216 had already been supplied to the Russian Army. Total Russian army tank stocks at the end of December were 7700, of which 1400 were medium or heavy models represented in the Soviet inventory by the new T-34 and KV-1. British deliveries represented nearly 15 per cent of new medium/heavy tanks added to the Soviet inventory in the second half of 1941 and following the huge losses over that period equated to 6 per cent of overall Russian tank stocks and one-third of the medium/heavy category remaining by the start of 1942.[81] The first twenty Valentines from convoy PQ 1 apparently reached the tank training school at Kazan, 450 miles east of Moscow, on 28 October, at which time a further 120 were approaching Archangel in PQ 2. By 20 November, ninety-seven Valentines and twenty Matildas were deployed with front-line units, almost all in the Moscow region, with some in action for the first time a week later with General Konstantin Rokossovsky's 16th Army in the battles around Istra and Klin north-west of Moscow. British intercepts of German Enigma traffic indicated that German units had encountered British tanks operated by Soviet units on 26 November.[82]

Russian records suggest that the Soviet army had about 1700 tanks deployed in front-line units at the beginning of December, of which 500 were medium/heavy types. When the ninety British tanks which 30 Mission reported had seen action by 9 December are added, they therefore represented 15 per cent of the total Soviet medium/heavy force. Although there is some dispute over how many Soviet medium/heavy tanks were deployed on the Moscow fronts at the beginning of December, the probable figure is just over 200, out of a total tank force of 650–750, with the British tanks therefore contributing here about 30 per cent of overall medium/heavy strength. In tank numbers the British contribution through December easily matched that of the two armoured formations which arrived as reinforcements from the Far Eastern Army Group and Siberia. Soviet production of T-34s, their best tank in this category, ramped up slowly in 1941 and inevitably suffered considerable disruption, with 765 delivered in the final quarter from a low point of 185 in October. This compares with the 361 British tanks in Russian army hands by the end of the same period of which 182 had been committed to combat by late December and seventy-seven lost. Although these losses along with serviceability issues apparently reduced the operationally available British tank force to about fifty by the beginning of January, their proportion of the Soviet medium/heavy front-line force was probably still a minimum of 20 per cent and there were at least 150 now in reserve.[83]

As with Western aircraft, the Russians criticised the quality of the British tanks they received. The Matilda and Valentine were certainly inferior to the T-34 and KV-1 on most criteria but far superior to the light tanks in the Soviet inventory and, importantly, competitive with most German tanks they faced this first winter of the Eastern war. Furthermore, as the much-vaunted T-34 moved into mass production, quality control suffered. By mid-1943, only 7.7 per cent of output met quality control standards. When American experts examined the single T-34 handed over, they discovered a catalogue of shoddy engineering. The main Russian criticisms of the British tanks were their light main armament, a 2-pounder or 40mm anti-tank gun which also lacked high explosive ammunition compared to the Russian 76mm, their narrow track plates which were unsuitable in snow, ice and mud, and lack of engine power translating into significantly lower speed than most contemporary tanks. More positively, the Russians liked the armour, which was impervious to most German anti-tank weapons, the radio, and found the British tank engines quiet and reliable. During tests in autumn 1942, they also found that the Valentine was equal to the T-34 in crossing wet marshy ground and 'overcoming roadside ditches'. The Russians attempted some upgrading, including rearming, but given other demands and the pressing need to use every available tank operationally, a minimum was done.

To the surprise of the British who regarded the Valentine as obsolete by mid-1941, the Russians preferred it to all other British tanks including the larger, more modern and heavily-armed Churchill and Centaur. This obliged the British to keep Valentine production going both in the United Kingdom and Canada through 1943, solely to meet Russian demand. Over the three years 1941–3, Canada produced 1420 Valentines of which 1388 were shipped to Russia while Britain provided 2302 by mid-1944. By 1943, the latest marks of Valentine had been upgraded with a 6-pounder gun capable of firing a high explosive round, making them a more attractive proposition. The appeal of the Valentine lay in its power to weight ratio, sound armour and acceptable armament when uprated. The Russians judged it an excellent substitute for their domestic light tanks, including the latest T-70, which they began phasing out in 1943. The Valentine was ideal for the reconnaissance role where it served until the end of the war. By contrast, the Russians disliked the American tanks shipped in 1942, comprising a mix of Stuart light tanks and medium Lee/Grants, because they had petrol engines and caught fire easily. Sitting in these was described as being in a 'coffin'.[84]

Criticism of British tank armament in the early deliveries was not universal. During a visit to the Gorkiy tank centre in May 1942, 30 Mission officers were informed that the 2-pounder was 'very good indeed, accurate, easy to handle with good penetration'. Lack of high explosive ammunition was not mentioned. As with aircraft there were problems with spares and damage in transit from poor stowage. Reliability also suffered in Russian winter conditions compounded by limited time to train Russian crews. Given these limitations, the Russians were inclined to use the British tanks in an infantry support rather than anti-tank role. The Germans were familiar with the Matilda from the Western Desert and less deprecatory of its qualities. They were impressed with, and feared, its armour which made it difficult to kill and its gun in an anti-tank role was broadly comparable to that of the Panzer III, the mainstay of German armour at this time. However, they agreed with the Russians that it was too slow, lacked range and was hampered by the lack of HE ammunition.[85]

Another measure of the contribution of the British tanks on the Moscow front from late November onwards is by comparison with German tank strength. Soviet sources claim the Germans retained a 50 per cent tank advantage at the start of their counter-offensive on 6 December. This is undoubtedly an exaggeration. Maximum tank strength in Army Group Centre in late November was 900 but many of these were no longer combat ready. A more realistic assessment is that by 6 December there was parity between Germans and Russians in both overall tank numbers and the proportion of medium/heavy types. The arriving British tanks therefore provided a slight but growing edge. It is telling that Zhukov, now commander of an enlarged Western Army

Group, assured Stalin in late November that Moscow could be held so long as he received two more armies and 200 tanks. In general, Russian success through December reflected neither grand strategic design nor numerical superiority but rather surprise against an exhausted opponent, skilful exploitation of local advantage, and better adaptation to winter conditions. As regards the balance of resources, for the Russians the margins were 'fearfully narrow'.[86]

Against this context, the value of the British tanks, as with Western aircraft, lay not just in useful numbers added but moral impact against an increasingly tired and discouraged opponent. The Germans were aware of the arrival of British tanks by 4 November when 'Foreign Armies East', their Eastern Front intelligence service, reported the movement of 'over 100 English tanks' from Archangel to Yaroslavl (located on the railway midway between Vologda and Moscow) which it assumed were destined for the front line. These tanks presumably derived from convoy PQ 2. The report reached German leadership circles two days later, provoking some surprise and alarm. Foreign Armies East subsequently assessed that several new armoured groups equipped with British and American tanks could be anticipated. On 23 November, 2nd Panzer Division stemmed a major Russian armoured attack, reporting destruction of thirty-four enemy tanks including five British models factory stamped 'September 1941'. Over the next fortnight there were numerous further sighting reports of British tanks and the number apparently now present in Soviet forces in the Moscow area made a growing impression on both front line German units and senior officers of Army Group Centre. On 4 December Halder noted that two-thirds of the tanks in a new Russian armoured brigade attacking south-west of Moscow were British.[87]

*ALUMINIUM*

Apart from fighters and tanks, the most important item delivered in these early months, again mainly from Britain, was aluminium. Aluminium, as Stalin recognised in his first conversation with Hopkins, was an exceptionally valuable material for the Second World War combatants. It is light but with a high strength-to-weight ratio, non-corrosive, has high thermal conductivity, and is very malleable, capable of easy fabrication into almost any shape. It is also nontoxic and nonmagnetic. Its main military use from the late 1930s was in the construction (and repair) of aircraft where its role and ubiquity soon equated to that of wood in the age of sail. Aluminium itself is comparatively weak but its alloys, such as duraluminum and hiduminium, have high tensile strength and could be used not just in airframes but also aircraft engines. For most

Second World combat aircraft aluminium-derived content was probably a minimum of 80 per cent, two tons in an early Spitfire or Me 109 and eight times more in a heavy four-engine bomber such as the Lancaster. There were some exceptions such as the British Mosquito light bomber which made extensive use of wood, as did many Soviet aircraft. However, from 1942, the major combatants were generally devoting at least 70 per cent of their aluminium supplies to aircraft production. The Russians used aluminium alloys widely in their tank as well as aircraft engines, notably for the T-34, which substantially boosted their requirement for the metal. Aluminium was also an important component in explosives and prefabricated construction of all types. Overall, as a warfighting material, by 1941, it was as important as steel.[88]

There is a consensus that Soviet aluminium production in 1940 was between 60,000 and 66,000 tons and that, by the end of 1941, about 60 per cent of this capacity was lost when the major plants at Volkhovsky, near Leningrad, and Dnepropetrovsk, near Zaporozhye in the Ukraine, together with the Tikhvin alumina refinery (120 miles east of Leningrad), either fell into German hands or were at unacceptable risk. Although much equipment at these plants was dismantled and moved east beyond the Urals, it was not possible to exploit this for renewed production, and initially only on a small scale, until mid-1943. A loss of 60 per cent production in the second half of 1941 equated to 19,000 tons, reducing overall 1941 production to 45,000 tons although possibly less with Maisky later claiming that Russia had lost three-quarters of its aluminium capacity. Production then recovered from a reduced capacity of about 25,000 tons per year at the start of 1942 to achieve 52,000 tons across the year as a whole. The deficit in 1942 compared to 1940 capacity was therefore about a further 12,000 tons. This revived 1942 production was initially centred primarily on the Uralsk Aluminium complex which had a theoretical capacity of 25,000 tons per year by 1941.[89]

Soviet military aircraft production in 1941 was 15,735 units of which 40 per cent were twin-engine bombers and transport aircraft. Allowing for 5000 tons required for the 6500 tanks built this year, this output was therefore apparently achieved with a maximum of 50,000 tons of aluminium if the British 5000 tons despatched from September is included. Britain built 25 per cent more aircraft this year, split across broadly similar categories, yet used three and a half times as much aluminium. One obvious explanation is that Britain produced three times as many multi-engine aircraft, rising to four times in 1942–3. A second is that most Soviet aircraft produced at this time and for much of the war used far less aluminium in their construction than those of other major combatants, relying on wood and in the case of the mass-produced Il-2 Sturmovik significant quantities of steel. Lower aluminium content contributed to the poorer quality and performance of many Soviet aircraft compared to other combatants.[90] Nevertheless, aluminium was still a critical component and the capacity lost in the autumn contributed to a halving of aircraft and 20 per cent reduction in medium tank output between the third and fourth quarters of 1941. Although tank production thereafter increased rapidly, third quarter output in aircraft did not recover until the second half of 1942.[91] General industrial dislocation that autumn undoubtedly contributed to this production fall in the final quarter, partially acknowledged by Stalin's admission when Eden saw him in Moscow in December, that aircraft output had dropped to thirty a day (equivalent to just under 11,000 annually).[92] However, a sustained loss of 1500 tons of aluminium per month would have delayed recovery of aircraft and tank output for a much longer period. This dependence on aluminium was the context for Stalin's original plea to Hopkins for urgent supplies, the initial 5000 tons committed by the British War Cabinet on 5 September and included with PQ 1, and the subsequent British promise to deliver 2000 tons per month under the First Protocol with the Americans investigating additional supplies.

Britain shipped 17,817 tons of the 18,000 tons to which she had committed under the First Protocol by 12 May 1942, but, as of 30 June, only 13,388 tons had arrived with 3513 tons still in transit and 916 tons sunk. This shipment ahead of schedule reflected Russian pressure for the earliest possible delivery, causing supplies from both Britain and Canada to be 'greatly accelerated' in January and February. These 17,817 tons were additional to the 5000 tons committed the previous September. By 30 September 1942, deliveries had risen to 14,980 tons with 2189 tons sunk and 648 tons of the original allocation still in transit. The quantity sunk was also being replaced.[93] Thus, by mid-1942, Russia had received just over 18,000 tons of aluminium from Britain and Canada, including the pre-protocol 5000 tons. This replaced at least half of the estimated production shortfall up to mid-1942 from the loss of Russia's western aluminium plants the previous autumn. It probably raised aircraft and medium tank output by 25 per cent over over the nine months of the First Protocol period.

The United States also promised 2000 tons per month of aluminium under the First Protocol along with 500 tons per month of duraluminum. These quantities were subsequently adjusted to a total of 15,580 tons of aluminium and 7716 tons of duraluminum. However, as with other American supplies, deliveries ran well behind schedule with only 4451 tons of aluminium and 1914 tons of duraluminum reaching Russia by 31 May 1942. Most of the outstanding balance had by then been shipped but, even by the end of October, there was still a shortfall of 1500 tons in the combined total of American aluminium and duraluminum arriving.[94] The United States also committed to 2000 tons of aluminium and 500 tons of duraluminum per month under the Second Protocol covering the 12 months from 1 July 1942, with the overall quantities promised subsequently raised in October by 13 and 58 per cent respectively.[95] About 40 per cent of the original American commitment under the Second Protocol reached Russia by the end of the year, by which time Britain had shipped a further 12,000 tons to which it had separately committed under the new protocol. Some of this, sourced in Canada, went via the Pacific to Vladivostok rather than by the Arctic route.[96] Over the first 18 months of the war therefore, the period of its greatest need, Russia received around 62,000 tons of aluminium and duraluminum, of which Britain provided about half. This was almost sufficient to cover both the capacity lost in the second half of 1941 and to double the supplies available to Russia in 1942. No simple formula translates aluminium supplies into weapons production. However, if Russia produced 15,735 military aircraft and 3135 heavy tanks with a domestically produced supply of 50,000 tons of aluminium in 1941, then a significant proportion of the additional 9,700 aircraft and 11,500 heavy/medium tanks produced in 1942 can be attributed to Western-supplied aluminium.[97]

In December 1942, Maisky, doubtless reflecting perceptions in Moscow, evidently still saw Britain as the most reliable and rapid source of urgently needed aluminium and pressed for a further 1000 tons a month to be delivered via the Arctic route during the first half of 1943. This request was turned down by the War Cabinet due to the low level of British reserves.[98] The scale of Britain's aluminium contribution through 1942 has nevertheless been under-recognised. Lend-Lease histories traditionally emphasise American supplies, often quoting figures of around 250,000 tons supplied through the war, with the British and Canadian share painted as marginal.[99] This overlooks the relatively slow growth in American deliveries. Supplies actually reaching Russia only overtook those of Britain and Canada in January 1943. At the end of September 1943, two years from the beginning of the First Protocol, the cumulative total of American aluminium and duraluminum delivered was still just under 70,000 tons and, at the end of the Third Protocol on 30 June 1944, it was 130,000 tons. If British and Canadian supplies are added, then overall Western supplies of 165,000 tons since the start of the war exactly equalled Soviet domestic production in the same period. By mid-

1944, the value of Western aluminium had been further boosted by the commissioning of an entire rolling mill shipped from the United States for production of aluminium sheet for the Soviet aircraft industry. American supplies then accelerated sharply in the last 10 months of the European war but too late to make a major difference to front-line armaments.[100]

The Soviet aircraft industry did not only benefit from Western aluminium. By the end of January 1943, the United States had delivered 31,500 tons of special hot rolled aircraft steel. By the end of the Second Protocol on 30 June, 43,000 tons had arrived and a year later over 160,000 tons, matching therefore aluminium deliveries at that time. Overall, Soviet aircraft production benefited significantly from Western metal supplies.[101]

*Munitions and Explosives*
By the autumn of 1941, the Soviet leadership and military high command recognised that they faced interlocking problems in sustaining an adequate supply of munitions to front-line forces. The Soviet munitions industry had developed significantly through the 1930s but, in June 1941, it was too small to support the existing Red Army deployed at the start of Barbarossa let alone the vast expansion required in wartime. The shortfall was soon compounded by the loss of production facilities in occupied territory, the destruction or capture of a large proportion of ammunition reserves located too near the fronts, poor logistic management and transport limitations. Although great strides were made through the war in replacing lost capacity and expanding production, the Soviet munitions industry could never meet the overall operational needs of its forces. Soviet munitions output across the five years 1941–5 was only 88 per cent of Britain's and dwarfed by that of the United States. Compared with Britain alone, the Soviet Union deployed nearly three times the military manpower but with 12 per cent less munitions. And even this lesser output was hugely dependent on Western support.[102]

By the Moscow Conference, not only was there a desperate shortage of ammunition stocks but also of toluene, the crucial component of TNT, to maintain munitions production in 1942. Soviet representatives therefore pressed the Western Allies to provide 4000 tons of toluene per month. Over the First Protocol period, this would underpin production of 80,000 tons of TNT, almost two-thirds of that needed to meet estimated Red Army requirements in 1942. The Americans only committed to supply 1250 tons per month from November with the further promise of 10,000 tons of TNT as soon as possible.[103] As with other American supplies at this time, deliveries fell well short with just over 3000 tons of toluene and a similar quantity of TNT reaching Russia by the end of June although the British added 6000 tons of cordite propellant. Significant losses during shipment (1000 tons of toluene, 1600 tons of TNT and 800 tons of cordite) suggest most of these supplies went via the Arctic route.[104] Together, the supplies arriving met about 7.5 per cent of Soviet high explosive requirements in this period. While this initial contribution was distinctly modest, the Americans were determined to make up the backlog and boost supplies. At the end of July, a further 9000 tons of toluene and 6000 tons of TNT were en route. By mid-1943, America had successfully delivered 28,000 tons of toluene, 25,000 tons of TNT and 22,000 tons of cordite with Britain adding 8000 tons to the latter. At least half this total went via the Arctic route where a further 10,000 tons of these items were lost.[105] By this point, American supplies of toluene and TNT were sufficient to support about 50 per cent of Red Army firepower, a proportion that held for the rest of the war.[106] This enormous Western contribution is rarely emphasised in the history of the Eastern Front. Both Western Allies also added considerable quantities of ready-use ammunition to the weapons they provided with the British adding 4000 depth charges by June.

*Overall Assessment of the Impact of the First Convoys*

The first twelve Arctic convoys (including Dervish) up to PQ 11, which arrived in Murmansk on 23 February, made four important contributions. As explained, the supplies enabling these contributions derived predominantly from Britain in this period, were carried mainly by British ships and were protected by the Royal Navy. The first was providing a sufficient force of modern fighters to the Murmansk region to ensure that, from the autumn of 1941, the risk of lasting damage to the Arctic ports and railway communications south from German air attack was minimal. The second was the support provided by British-supplied aircraft and tanks to bolstering Russian forces in the Moscow and Leningrad regions from the beginning of December. British aid did not save Moscow, nor did it play more than a marginal role in the initial Soviet counter-offensive. The German attack had culminated by early December. By this time, the German air force, with nominal strength supporting Army Group Centre reduced to barely 600 aircraft, lacked the resources for meaningful strikes on the city, although Britain had contributed here by encouraging the transfer of a significant portion of the German 2nd Air Fleet to the Mediterranean.[107] However, over the winter, British tanks and aircraft around Moscow became important in two respects. The added strength they provided helped the Russians push the Germans further back than might have been possible otherwise and, in January and February, their growing numbers gave the Russians an important cushion against any German counter-attacks when their own reserves were increasingly stretched. Russian criticism of the quality of British aircraft and tanks, especially when delivered after the war, requires perspective. During Eden's December visit to Moscow, Stalin and other senior Soviet personnel praised the performance of both Hurricanes and Valentines. Matildas were acknowledged to be less effective in snow but expected to give good service in summer conditions.[108]

The third contribution lay in support to Russia's long-term war potential. The importance of aluminium to aircraft and medium tank production has been stressed. The 17,000 tons Britain supplied by the end of March broadly compensated for the production Russia lost over the six months beginning in October. However, significant quantities of other raw materials, vital to the Soviet war effort, were also shipped in these early convoys, notably 10,000 tons each of copper and rubber, the latter in addition to supplies collected by Soviet vessels in the Far East prior to the Japanese attack on Malaya. These were accompanied by a vast range of smaller items, both military and non-military. Radar and Asdic equipment deserve emphasis here. The former facilitated important improvements in anti-aircraft defence while the latter made Soviet defence of the Arctic ports more effective. The final contribution lies in timing. Russia had held and exhausted the Barbarossa offensive by early December but, in doing so, had suffered enormous losses in military personnel and equipment and significant parts of her war industries were now in German hands. Replacing industrial capacity in safe space to the east would take many months and, in the meantime, current military expenditure was outrunning production. The value of Western aid, delivered primarily by Britain through the Arctic, in this first winter of the war lay in bridging the gap between current deficit and future potential. Unfortunately, the Germans were recognising this too and, by February 1942, had plans to shut down the Arctic supply route.

In theory, the opportunity cost to Britain from these contributions in terms of resources lost to the Middle and Far East theatres was considerable. If even a quarter of the 700 fighters and nearly 500 tanks Britain delivered to Russia by the end of 1941 had deployed to Malaya instead their impact might have transformed that campaign. However, for these resources to have translated into military effect, they had to be transported at the right time and be accompanied by the right personnel and logistic support. That implied timely decisions by Britain's war leadership on relative benefits and costs and logistic feasibility. To achieve any realistic impact in Malaya, a decision to deploy reinforcements in lieu of Russia would have been required in early September. Leaving aside the consequences for Russia, for many reasons addressed elsewhere that was never likely.[109]

It is nevertheless striking that no comprehensive cost/benefit assessment was ever commissioned by the chiefs of staff on behalf of the war leadership during the period of these initial convoys or indeed later. Instead, the justification for a major Western but, at this stage primarily British, commitment evolved from buying time against a full-scale German assault in the West to viewing Russia as a key component in containment and wear down. Insurance against a sudden Russian collapse or separate peace was also a constant factor. These rationales were all valid, even if British and American military leaders were invariably more sceptical than their political masters, but they were never subjected to formal critical analysis. Stalin's apparent confidence, during his mid-December sessions with Eden and Nye, in both the progress of his counter-offensive and recovery in arms production surely justified such an appraisal even if it concluded change was too difficult within the First Protocol period. If some of the comments made by Marshall and King at Arcadia were self-serving, they were certainly right about shipping limitations and the need to address difficult choices. Brooke's questioning over tanks was reasonable and he certainly had the authority to ask the joint planners to conduct a full cost/benefit study into aid to Russia but he did not do so. While American supplies declined sharply for three months after Pearl Harbor, the British programme continued despite increasingly dire risks in the Far East.

*Prince of Wales* in Placentia Bay for the Riviera summit, August 1941. (US Navy, Naval History and Heritage Command NH 67194A)

Prime Minister Winston Churchill and Lord Beaverbrook at the Riviera summit. (Alamy RW3MCE)

Hurricanes at Vaenga airfield in North Russia, September 1941. (Alamy 2T1KTS)

Matilda tanks bound for Russia being loaded at a British port. (Alamy 2NC9DRD)

President Franklin Roosevelt with Prime Minister Winston Churchill and key Western military leaders at the Casablanca summit January 1943. Standing behind from the left: Admiral Ernest J King, General George C Marshall, Admiral of the Fleet Sir Dudley Pound, Air Chief Marshal Sir Charles Portal, Field Marshal Sir Alan Brooke, Field Marshal Sir John Dill and Vice Admiral Lord Louis Mountbatten. (US Navy, Naval History and Heritage Command NH 80-G 35135)

Soviet leader Josef Stalin with leading figures at the Teheran summit in November 1943. General George C Marshall shakes hands with the British Ambassador to Russia, Sir Archibald Clark Kerr, with the American Ambassador Averell Harriman next to the right, looking towards Stalin. (Alamy 2R9M8KK)

Rear Admiral Robert Burnett, Flag Officer Destroyer Flotillas, and later the commander of the 10th Cruiser Squadron, Home Fleet. He played a central role in the defence of convoy PQ 18, the Battle of the Barents Sea and sinking of the *Scharnhorst*. (Alamy 2X07HYP)

Rear Admiral Louis Hamilton, who commanded the 1st Cruiser Squadron in the Home Fleet during 1942–3 and played a critical role in the PQ 17 disaster. (Alamy 2WYB5PB)

Admiral of the Fleet Sir Dudley Pound, First Sea Lord from June 1939 until immediately before his death in October 1943. Although blamed for the convoy PQ 17 disaster, he led the Royal Navy through the most difficult period of the war until victory was within sight everywhere. (Alamy 2HX5JJ3)

Admiral Sir John Tovey, Commander-in-Chief Home Fleet from November 1940 until May 1943. He commanded Arctic convoy operations during their most critical period.
(Alamy 2T1KGWW)

General Admiral Otto Schniewind, Commander German Fleet from December 1941 until July 1944. He simultaneously held the post of Commander Group North from February 1943 until July 1944. (Alamy C45M0D)

Vice Admiral Oskar Kummetz, Admiral Battleships and Commander Northern Task Force June 1942 until February 1944. He led the German force at the Battle of the Barents Sea. (Official German Navy portrait)

Grand Admiral Erich Raeder, Chief of the German Naval Staff and head of the German Navy from 1928 until January 1943.
(Alamy 2C23NTE)

Grand Admiral Karl Dönitz. Admiral commanding U-boats until January 1943 when he replaced Raeder as Chief of the German Naval Staff.
(Alamy BKFGBH)

British Matilda tanks bound for Russia moving to their embarkation port in the United Kingdom, April 1942. (Alamy 2HX4MJ5)

*King George V* viewed from the starboard forward 4.5in gun battery of the fleet carrier *Victorious* while escorting PQ 12, early March 1942. (Alamy 2X02J51)

## Chapter 5
## German Countermeasures

The stalling of Barbarossa and Russia's Moscow counter-offensive heightened Hitler's fear that Britain, with support from her new American ally, would exploit Germany's present difficulties to undertake a landing in northern Norway and link up with Soviet forces in the Arctic. In his view, such an operation offered Britain several advantages. It would remove a potential threat on her northern flank; supplies could be conveyed via the Arctic Ocean to Russia's northern ports without interference; and the northern end of Germany's Eastern Front and the interests of its Finnish ally would be threatened, as would ore deposits in Sweden and Petsamo vital to the German armaments industry.[1] This broadly mirrored Churchill's thinking in regard to the abortive Operation Ajax. Hitler's attitude was based partly on personal conviction and the special place Norway had long held in his strategic vision, and partly on British action, but also intelligence reports of varying reliability.

*British Raids on Norway and their Consequences*
The potential British threat appeared more imminent following British commando raids on the Norwegian coast on 26 and 27 December 1941. Remarkably, on 25 December, the German Supreme Command (OKW) issued a warning that Britain and the United States were preparing a large-scale operation in the Scandinavian area, most likely to gain a foothold in northern Norway. This reflected information from various sources including the Finnish envoy in Washington, the latter perhaps drawing on loose talk in the margins of the Arcadia gathering. OKW thought the objective would be to disrupt the German supply route on the polar coast and divert forces from the Russian front in northern and central Finland. The target might be the area between Varanger and Alta fiords which was less well defended than the Petsamo and Narvik regions. OKW stressed that resource limitations meant a landing would be limited

to acquiring a 'foothold' but this would still boost enemy prestige and disrupt iron and nickel supplies. Falkenhorst, as commanding general Norway, was accordingly advised to alert his forces and report on what defensive improvements were required.[2]

OKW was broadly right on British intent but not on specifics. Several factors influenced the form and execution of these December raids. The abandonment of Ajax in mid-October led to prime-ministerial demands for a raiding programme against suitable targets on the occupied coast of Western Europe, partly to help relations with Stalin but also pursuing the 'subversion' element of 'wear down'. Meanwhile the fading requirement to seize the Canary Islands (Operation Pilgrim) following a German capture of Gibraltar released assault forces for deployment elsewhere. Finally, the appointment of Commodore Lord Louis Mountbatten as Director of Combined Operations in October, in place of Admiral of the Fleet Sir Roger Keyes, brought fresh drive and initiative to raiding. The chiefs of staff therefore endorsed a programme of small raids on France and a larger one of 700–800 men in Norway, drawing on the precedent of Operation Claymore, the Lofoten Islands raid the previous March. The Norwegian government in exile here sought two caveats: a new raid should avoid the mainland and premature encouragement of the population to revolt which would invite reprisals.[3]

Despite these caveats, the first Norwegian operation proposed, codenamed Ascot, was ambitious and risky. Nine thousand men would seize and hold the Bodø peninsula, 110 miles south-west of Narvik, for several weeks. Light naval forces would then operate from the occupied port to cut sea communications between northern and southern Norway and hopefully disrupt Swedish iron ore traffic heading south from Narvik. A simultaneous diversionary raid would target Tarven Island, subsequently changed to Vågsøy, 100 miles north of Bergen. The Lofoten islands on the other side of Vest Fiord were soon substituted for Bodø as the proposed base since they were lightly garrisoned and difficult to reinforce. Tovey, who would command the operation, now designated Anklet, as Commander-in-Chief Home Fleet, then suggested that the primary goal of disrupting German sea traffic could be achieved from ships using the Lofotens as a temporary anchorage and that a large landing was unnecessary. Churchill viewed Tovey's attitude as negative but the chiefs backed him.[4] Tovey's version of Anklet went ahead on 26 December under Rear Admiral Louis 'Turtle' Hamilton and proved an almost exact replica of Claymore. Hamilton's force, comprising the light cruiser *Arethusa*, seven destroyers, two assault ships and several smaller vessels, destroyed several German communication stations, some coastal craft found in the area and fish oil facilities. They also took some prisoners and gained 260 Norwegian recruits. There were no British losses. However, the primary goal of cutting the north/south sea route was never implemented. An obviously alert German air force and a warning from Tovey, drawing on Enigma decrypts, that heavy air reinforcements were on their way from France persuaded Hamilton to withdraw within 48 hours.[5]

The diversion operation, Archery, targeted at the island of Vågsøy and town of Måløy began the day after the start of the Anklet raid. It has some claim to be the first true tri-service combined operation and was under the joint command of Rear Admiral Harold Burrough, commander of Force X during Halberd three months earlier, and Brigadier Charles Haydon. The Archery force was slightly smaller than that for Anklet, reflecting the anticipated shorter duration of the operation. It comprised the cruiser *Kenya*, four destroyers and two assault ships with about 600 men, mainly Commandos, embarked. There was also a Norwegian contingent from the Norwegian Independent Company of the SOE led by its founder Captain Martin Linge. There was further support from a significant air group operating from Scotland with Hampden and Blenheim bombers and Beaufighters. The Archery objectives included fish oil and canning factories and any vessels in the sound. But they were also targeted at the substantial German garrison and their strong coastal defences including a fortress at Holvik. Overall, the aim was to put on a display of raiding strength, create a sense of mayhem and do as much damage as possible. This goal was achieved but German resistance was stronger than anticipated and German fighter aircraft were quickly on the scene. The British force lost eight aircraft and twenty men killed ashore while German casualties were about 120 killed and a similar number taken prisoner. Tragically Linge was one of those killed.[6]

Given the resources expended, the immediately visible results of these two raids looked meagre. They had created 'sound and fury' and provided some useful experience in executing combined operations but the damage inflicted on German forces and interests was negligible. Anklet had completely failed to meet its primary objective. There was political damage too. The Norwegian government was angry not to have been properly consulted, not least about the inclusion of Norwegian personnel, and felt the results did not justify the costs to the local population in terms of lost livelihoods and German reprisals. The loss of Linge, who was hard to replace, was a heavy blow to SOE capability in Norway. There was also bitterness within his company who felt exploited as word of German reprisals against their own people filtered back and they became a target for hostility from their own government.[7]

However, the raids had two further important consequences largely hidden from the view of most British and German observers. These justified Pound's insistence to Churchill, who had heavily criticised Tovey and Hamilton for premature abandonment of Anklet, that, taking the two operations together, 'we certainly were up on the deal'.[8] The earlier raid on the Lofotens, Operation Claymore, in March had featured the capture of vital cryptographic material from the German armed trawler *Krebs*. This enabled the first sustained reading by GC&CS of the primary German Enigma-based naval cipher known as Dolphin. Bletchley Naval Section were briefed on the forthcoming Anklet and Archery raids and their travelling expert, Lieutenant Allon Bacon, carefully researched the prospects for further 'pinches' which would be invaluable in maintaining coverage against cryptographic changes. The respective force commanders were also aware that 'pinches' were important subsidiary objectives. Drawing on intelligence from a Norwegian fisherman, John Sigurdson, Bacon decided to focus on Vågsøy and deployed there personally. He was rewarded by a substantial haul of cryptographic material from the German armed trawlers *Foehn* and *Donner*. Meanwhile, the previous day, the destroyer *Ashanti* achieved an equally valuable capture from the trawler *Geier* in the Lofotens during Anklet. These successful 'pinches' ensured Bletchley could continue using Dolphin, which was used by almost all German navy surface units and Arctic-based U-boats, more or less currently for the rest of the war.[9]

The second consequence of the raids was to underline the perception of both Hitler and OKW that Germany's position in Norway was both threatened and vulnerable. As already described, the German air force response was rapid and effective given its limited resources. By contrast, the naval reaction not only exposed inadequate strength, but a confused command structure, excessive caution and poor skills, and achieved nothing. Only two destroyers of the 8th Flotilla and three torpedo boats of the 8th PT Boat Flotilla, all of which were at Tromsø on 26 December, and three U-boats in the area of Vest Fiord were potentially able to intervene. Commanding Admiral Norway, General Admiral Boehm, was initially reluctant to move the 8th Destroyer Flotilla to Narvik because of the 'uncertain enemy situation', 'inadequate training' and 'navigational difficulties'. One torpedo boat did subsequently ground near Harstad. It is inconceivable that a Royal Navy commander would have raised these factors to excuse inaction but they continued to trouble the German navy throughout the Arctic war.[10] Even Dönitz was uncharacteristically passive and determined to avoid increasing U-boat support in the Arctic, informing Group North naval command on 28 December that using

U-boats to defend against further British raids was impractical. Group North, under General Admiral Rolf Carls, was responsible for all German navy operations in the German Bight, the northern parts of the North Sea and North Atlantic, and the Arctic. Dönitz insisted that U-boats would rarely reach a threatened area in time and would be ineffective against fast-moving, elusive targets. Norwegian deployment would divert U-boats from the war against merchant shipping in the Atlantic to which they were best suited. There had been no U-boats in the Atlantic for several weeks. Promising opportunities in American waters had not been exploited while the British had concentrated anti-submarine forces at vulnerable points, increasing U-boat losses. Norwegian operations would also consume a lot of fuel needed to support the new effort in the Western Atlantic.[11] Leaving aside the validity of these arguments in regard to Norway, they underlined how stretched the front-line U-boat force was at the end of 1941 following the transfers to the Mediterranean.[12]

Meanwhile, at a meeting with Hitler at the Wolfsschanze Eastern Front Headquarters in East Prussia on 29 December, Raeder and the Naval Staff delivered an accurate assessment of the recent British raids, albeit carefully avoiding reference to German naval shortcomings. British perceived objectives were: to destroy German coastal defences; harass and disrupt merchant shipping; reconnoitre terrain and defences for the later establishment of bridgeheads in order to disrupt and destroy supply routes; and propaganda and prestige. No comprehensive large-scale operation was yet apparent but shortage of German operational naval forces emphasised the need for strong air forces in the Norwegian area to repel future attacks.[13] Hitler commented that, if the British did things 'properly', they would attack northern Norway at several points. They would try to displace Germany, take Narvik and exert pressure on Sweden and Finland. 'This might be of decisive importance for the outcome of the war.' The German fleet should therefore concentrate on the defence of Norway and that included the transfer of all its battleships and heavy units. It implied the early deployment of the newly-completed *Tirpitz*, sister ship of *Bismarck* and the largest battleship in European waters, and the pocket battleship *Admiral Scheer* which were both ready for action. Hitler also viewed the return of the Brest Group (battlecruisers *Scharnhorst* and *Gneisenau* and heavy cruiser *Prinz Eugen*) as 'most desirable'. This would best be accomplished by a surprise breakout through the Channel without prior movements for training or work-up as the Naval Staff were currently proposing. Hitler was convinced that any prior moves would be spotted by excellent British intelligence, leading to torpedo and bombing attacks which would soon damage the ships.

Precedent from earlier in the year suggested that Hitler was right about the vulnerability of the Brest ships once they left the protection of the inner harbour, at least during daylight. However, the Naval Staff were evidently reluctant to dispense with training they judged essential to operational efficiency and they were equally reluctant to forsake other deployment options. Hitler was persuaded to defer final decisions pending further study. Nevertheless, to the obvious concern of the Naval Staff, he suggested that, if a breakout via the Channel was impossible, the Brest ships should be decommissioned and their guns and crews added to Norway's fortifications. This scepticism over the value of battleships foreshadowed a fundamental clash on this issue with Raeder exactly a year later. Throughout this debate, Hitler's focus was the defence of Norway. The possibility of using the heavy ships against the Arctic convoys was mentioned in passing but, for the moment, this was a subsidiary issue.[14]

Hitler's perception of how Britain might follow up the latest raids came surprisingly close to the proposal aired by Stalin to Eden and Nye in Moscow 10 days earlier. On 18 December, Stalin had suggested a joint operation initially against Petsamo and thence northern Norway. Its goals would be establishing a new centre of resistance against the Germans and securing the Arctic sea route. Russia would provide the bulk of the land forces. Britain would supply naval and air support, some troops if possible, and also facilitate the introduction of Norwegian volunteers. For Stalin, this was an alternative to the so far abortive attempts to establish a 'second front' or to deploy British forces alongside the Russians in the East. It was essentially a revival of the Russian proposal raised back in July and, as Eden recognised, probably deliberately aimed more at exerting political leverage rather than credible military benefit. Nevertheless, it was agreed Nye and Marshal Boris Shaposhnikov, who had succeeded Zhukov as Chief of the Soviet Army General Staff at the end of July, should develop a detailed plan for presentation to their respective military leaderships.[15]

According to Nye, Shaposhnikov envisaged a joint seaborne attack on Petsamo followed by a drive on Kirkenes to deny the enemy bases 'from which he could operate against our northern convoy route' and 'the mineral resources in the area'. Shaposhnikov promised three Soviet divisions and half the 200 aircraft required. Britain would provide the balance of the aircraft, the Norwegian forces based in Britain and all the naval support. Ideally the operation would launch at the end of January or early February. Nye was cautious, given his awareness of how stretched Britain now was in the Middle and Far East and the obvious difficulty of mounting a complex combined operation involving two countries with no history of such cooperation. However, Shaposhnikov's enthusiasm and insistence that difficulties were not 'insuperable' persuaded Nye to advise Brooke that it was politically 'most desirable' to agree to this operation unless military objections were 'overwhelming'.[16]

Russian enthusiasm did not last. When Macfarlane tried to follow up in early January, he was told that the Finnish general staff had learnt of 'our combined operation' and 'Marrow', as the proposal was known, was now cancelled. Macfarlane did not believe the Finnish leak story and judged the Soviet leadership had changed its mind for unknown reasons. It is certainly plausible that Stalin was never serious or that more detailed study convinced the Russian military leadership that they lacked sufficient resources. However, in the first week of January, the German Naval Staff received a series of reports suggesting further British action against Norway was imminent. One 'reliable agent report' stated that 'Great Britain and Russia have agreed to launch a joint offensive against Finland'.[17] The Finnish compromise therefore was also plausible. The prospect of an increased threat to the Arctic convoys from German reinforcements caused Macfarlane to seek London's permission to raise Marrow again with the Russians at the end of January. The chiefs of staff agreed so long as he made no British commitment. They also advised Churchill that, while they subscribed to the desirability of Marrow, the necessary naval, air and shipping resources were currently beyond British capacity. In the event, the Russians were no longer interested and the specific Marrow proposal now faded from view. However, the core concept of an attack on northern Norway soon returned to the table in London.[18]

*German Naval Reinforcement and its Limitations*

Hitler's desire to redeploy the Brest Group met strong resistance when the German naval leadership reviewed options in Paris at the beginning of January. The three Commanding Admirals, for Groups North and West and Battleships, were all bitterly opposed to redeployment via the Channel, Operation Cerberus[19] as it was eventually designated. In their view, transferring the ships from the Atlantic, and the inevitable losses entailed, would undermine 'our strategic and political position'. The independent-minded Commanding Admiral Group West, General Admiral Alfred Saalwächter, who was no fan of Hitler, even stated that, given the choice between withdrawal and dismantlement of the ships, he would opt for the latter. As one of the key naval commanders during the 1940 invasion, Saalwächter had a good grasp of the Norwegian theatre and his advice always carried influence. Although genuinely committed to the continued possibilities of Atlantic raiding, his assessment of Cerberus was defeatist and gloomy and unlikely to appeal to Hitler. By contrast, Raeder and Naval Staff Operations Division were more positive about concentration in Norway. Raeder emphasised the Führer's scepticism that the ships could ever deploy in the Atlantic and his fear of losing them without a fight. Raeder himself saw great scope for operations in the North and strategic advantage in tying down large enemy forces. In no circumstances should the navy permit dismantlement which meant irrevocable loss. The key issue was whether Cerberus was possible. Given the positive case that Raeder made for concentration in Norway, his subsequent recommendation to Hitler on 8 January was oddly ambivalent, indeed he sat on the fence. After expressing suitable enthusiasm for prioritising Norway, of 'decisive importance to the war', he advised that Cerberus was too risky and commended the strategic benefits of leaving the ships in Brest, although *Tirpitz* would move to Trondheim in mid-January as already planned.[20]

The same day Raeder submitted his report, General Admiral Boehm provided a detailed assessment of the strategic situation in Norway and the implications for the German navy. He argued that a Russian offensive via Finland combined with a British seaborne attack, probably in the Narvik area, could easily undermine Germany's whole position in Scandinavia with serious political and economic consequences and must be an attractive proposition for her enemies. The forces currently available to meet this threat and the objectives in the Führer's Directive No 37 of the previous October were totally inadequate. He concluded that the defence of Norway had reached a 'critical stage' and an attack need not be very strong to break it.[21]

Meanwhile, Hitler's fears regarding Norway intensified. A meeting on 12 January, convened to consider Raeder's report and which included OKW, the Naval Staff and air force representation, took the decision in principle to redeploy the Brest Group to Norway. Hitler stated that, if it could be guaranteed the ships would remain undamaged in France over the next few months and that new circumstances would allow valuable employment in the Atlantic, he might reconsider. However, he had growing evidence of a large-scale British–Russian offensive in Norway with Swedish collaboration. (Although he echoed Boehm here, it is unlikely he had yet seen the latter's report.) Hitler therefore stressed his determination to have the main strength of the navy, backed by strong air forces, protecting Norway. Based in Brest the ships had the 'flypaper effect' of tying down enemy forces but this applied equally in Norway and he feared their survival in Brest was time limited. He was confident that Cerberus could exploit surprise and he doubted British ability to make and execute lightning decisions. He added that the situation of the Brest Group was comparable to a cancer patient, doomed without an operation. An operation, even if drastic, offered some hope of saving the patient. The passage of the ships through the Channel was such an operation and must be attempted.[22]

Hitler further reinforced these views at the next conference with the Naval Staff 10 days later. He was now 'thoroughly convinced' Britain and the United States would attack northern Norway, probably at several points between Trondheim and Kirkenes. He had proof (not shared with the Naval Staff) of Sweden's collaboration (of which Raeder was privately sceptical) and expected her to be rewarded with Narvik and the Petsamo ore deposits. Anglo-Saxon domination of the 'Swedish area' would threaten Germany's position in the Baltic and surviving heavy ships would then have to be scrapped to extract their nickel, an obvious reference to the perceived importance of the Petsamo supply. It followed that events in Norway might bring 'catastrophic consequences', it was the 'zone of destiny' in this war and must be heavily and speedily reinforced with forces from all three services, but the navy had prime responsibility for immediately countering any British attack. It must also take over reconnaissance from the air force in poor flying weather. For the navy therefore, Norway took priority over every other theatre bar the Mediterranean and Hitler demanded that all available vessels be deployed there. To the concern of the Naval Staff, this order evidently included redeployment of all U-boats to Norway to ensure adequate reconnaissance of an approaching enemy and then to attack his landing forces. However, when Hitler was briefed the following day on recent U-boat successes off the American coast, he agreed these boats should remain on station for an indefinite period. Raeder chose to interpret this as agreement that the present pattern of U-boat operations overall should remain unchanged although there would be a modest reinforcement in the Arctic. He emphasised to the Naval Staff that it was impossible to relocate all U-boats to Norway due to lack of suitable bases and it made no sense confining the whole submarine force to a defensive role.[23]

The U-boat issue aside, at the end of January, Raeder now had to rally the Naval Staff and his senior commanders behind Hitler's determined emphasis on Norway and to establish what this meant in practical terms. With Cerberus decided, he argued that the vulnerability of French bases to air attack and the lack of carrier support, which he claimed essential for successful Atlantic raiding, had brought fleet operations conducted out of France to a strategic dead end. By contrast, concentrating on Norway was not only essential for Germany's successful prosecution of the war but offered the navy wider strategic and operational opportunities which had so far gone unexploited, although Raeder did not spell out exactly what these were. The Commanding Admiral Battleships, Vice Admiral Otto Ciliax, who conducted the Cerberus breakout, recorded views here that, in several respects, proved prescient. Until now the role of German surface forces, despite numerical inferiority, had always been offensive, with the threat of a surprise move occupying substantial enemy resources. A defensive role in Norway meant losing the initiative. The vast coastline made it impossible to guarantee timely warning of invasion or even a raid and the enemy could always bring superior force to bear, making it difficult to intervene decisively against a landing. Operating out of bases such as Trondheim or Narvik, which lacked the significant repair facilities and the protection against air attack available in Brest, would be demanding. Any return to Germany for repairs would be a complex and high-risk operation given the forces the British could mobilise.[24] Ciliax, who moved to Norway after Cerberus, was well qualified for his role, having commanded *Admiral Scheer* from 1936–8, including deployment in the Spanish Civil War, before being appointed the first captain of *Scharnhorst*. British pre-war reports emphasised his 'strength' and 'keenness' but many who served under him saw a notorious martinet and reluctant delegator, nicknamed within the fleet 'the Black Czar'.[25]

Against this background, Cerberus went ahead on 11/12 February. Despite the doubts of the Naval Staff and Group West, superb planning and the commitment of huge naval and air resources, including almost all available operational destroyers, together with some luck, brought the three heavy ships successfully through to Germany. Overall, the operation, which has been well described elsewhere, was an undoubted tactical success and humiliation for Britain. But it also proved a strategic defeat for Germany. First, Britain did not have to contend with a surface raiding threat from two widely separated geographic locations. Secondly, neither *Gneisenau* nor *Scharnhorst* made it to Norway in 1942 and *Prinz Eugen* only briefly. Both battlecruisers were damaged by mines dropped by the Royal Air Force along the latter part of their Cerberus escape route which had been revealed by Ultra decrypts. *Gneisenau*, only lightly damaged, was moved into dry dock at Kiel and it was anticipated that she would be ready to depart for Norway on 6 March. Repairs were almost complete when she was attacked by Royal Air Force bombers over the night of 26/27 February. Her forward section up to and including 'A' turret was comprehensively wrecked and burnt out. She was moved to Gotenhafen (modern Gdynia) where it was hoped she could be repaired but she never went to sea again. In 1943, some of her guns did make it to Norway where they were installed as part of the Trondheim defences. *Scharnhorst* was more severely damaged by the mines and repairs and subsequent mechanical problems kept her out of action for almost a year. She finally deployed to Norway in March 1943.[26]

It is extraordinary that during the January debates regarding redeployment to Norway, between Hitler and the naval leadership and within the naval leadership itself, there was almost no reference to operations against the British Arctic supply convoys. This had been the pre-eminent task placed on the navy in the northern theatre under Führer Directive No 37 the previous October and remained extant. In planning the onward deployment of the Brest group to Norway in the third week of February, the Naval Staff and Group North recognised that, on arrival, they would conduct 'both offensive and defensive operations in the northern area'.[27] However, the dominant preoccupation in the first quarter of the year was the threat to Norway with the convoys a less pressing issue. The single exception in the early weeks of 1942 was a proposal from Group North on 2 January to deploy *Tirpitz* on a four-day raid against the 'PQ' route immediately after leaving the North Sea for Norway. The implication was that she would detach her escorting destroyers to Trondheim while continuing northward herself and then drawing on the support of the existing Arctic Ocean destroyer force. The Naval Staff endorsed the concept but judged that in winter darkness, with no effective air reconnaissance, the prospects of success were negligible. Furthermore, without a destroyer escort *Tirpitz* would be at risk from the British cruiser and destroyer force escorting the convoy. The idea was thus abandoned and, following Hitler's agreement, *Tirpitz* deployed direct from Wilhelmshaven to Trondheim which she reached without incident on 16 January. It was soon clear that lack of destroyers, due to the demands of Cerberus, and shortage of fuel would confine her there until at least mid-February.[28]

Trondheim, re-named Drontheim by the Germans and initially the primary base for their new northern fleet, had special symbolic status in Hitler's vision and fears for Norway. Following the 1940 invasion, Hitler developed ambitious plans with both Raeder and Albert Speer, then Hitler's chief architect but later his armaments minister, to make Trondheim Germany's largest naval base, equipped with the most modern shipyards and defences, a 'Super-Singapore'. The shipyards were to be capable of constructing the largest warships, regardless of draught. Alongside the base and separate from the existing town, a new city was to be built, incorporating quarter of a million Germans and becoming Germany's northernmost cultural centre, a grand showcase for the new

Reich. Trondheim would be linked by a four-lane autobahn and network of vast bridges through Sweden to Germany while a new road to Kirkenes would also be constructed. Swedish acquiescence in transit rights would be achieved by offering equivalent access rights to Narvik. Although, in theory, this grand concept remained alive, in early 1942 little practical work had yet been done in creating more than rudimentary naval operating facilities although, in May, Hitler was still pressing for early completion of a dock capable of accommodating vessels larger than the *Tirpitz* class. The most significant development actually underway was the construction of concrete covered U-boat pens, similar to those in France, which began in autumn 1941 with the first phase Dora 1 complete in mid-1943.[29] NID provided an accurate progress assessment in mid-June 1942.[30]

The questions posed by Ciliax and others were valid enough, but given Hitler's unambiguous orders, the naval transfers of heavy ships to Norway progressed steadily over the next few months even if the battle group which resulted was less than Hitler hoped. Five weeks after *Tirpitz*, the pocket battleship *Admiral Scheer* and the heavy cruiser *Prinz Eugen*, the latter fresh from the Cerberus dash through the Channel, also moved from Kiel to Trondheim under Operation 'Sportpalast'. Thanks to Dolphin Enigma decrypts and SIS coast-watching agents, the British Admiralty were well sighted on the Sportpalast route, enabling the submarine *Trident*, still commanded by Geoffrey Sladen of reindeer fame, to torpedo *Prinz Eugen* on the morning of 23 February. Although this was a far from perfect attack due to drill errors which meant only three torpedoes were fired instead of the planned seven, *Prinz Eugen* lost 10m of her stern. After being patched up in Trondheim fiord, she returned to Germany for permanent repair in mid-May, narrowly avoiding further intelligence-led air strikes en route. She was out of action for the rest of 1942, demonstrating the validity of Ciliax's earlier concerns over Norway operations. *Prinz Eugen*'s sister ship, *Hipper*, deployed in March and the pocket battleship *Lützow* in May, bringing the total of heavy ships to four.[31]

However, two factors severely constrained the operational deployment of this new Trondheim battlegroup during the first half of 1942, shortage of destroyers and fuel. On 16 January, the German navy nominally had eighteen destroyers capable of ocean-going operations, but only seven were fully operational and assigned to the 5th, 6th and 8th Flotillas. Two more were expected to become operational at the end of the month and a further four between the beginning of March and end of May.[32] Four destroyers of the 5th and 6th Flotillas escorted *Tirpitz* to Trondheim but were then immediately reassigned to the control of Group West to provide the Cerberus escort. Meanwhile, the 8th Flotilla permanently assigned to Norway had already been reduced to three ships and the collision between Z 23 and Z 24 on 19 January left only one destroyer, Z 25, fully operational by the end of the month and she had to be withdrawn and loaned to the 5th Flotilla for Cerberus.[33] Following Cerberus, five destroyers of the 5th Flotilla escorted *Prinz Eugen* and *Scheer*, reaching Trondheim on 24 February where three of them remained permanently based while the other two later escorted the damaged *Prinz Eugen* to Germany.[34] A month later they were joined by three destroyers of the 8th Flotilla escorting *Hipper*. Group North then ordered the three destroyers 'with the best engines and best trained crews' of the eight now in Trondheim to transfer north to Kirkenes under the control of Admiral Arctic Ocean for deployment against convoy PQ 13, an operation described below. At the end of March therefore there were eight destroyers in Norway with only five available to support the three operational heavy ships at Trondheim. In addition, there were three 'torpedo boats' at Trondheim, two more at Bergen and about ten E-boats and numerous other assorted patrol vessels and anti-submarine trawlers spread more widely across Norwegian bases. However, these light vessels were essentially restricted to the defence of coastal waters and traffic.[35]

As regards fuel, Raeder had informed Hitler in mid-November that German navy oil reserves were down to 380,000 tons, monthly consumption was 100,000 tons, with the same quantity required to support the Italian navy, while allocated monthly supplies were just 84,000 tons. By the end of February, reserves had dropped to 150,000 tons and the monthly allocation to 50,000 tons, with Operation Cerberus alone consuming 20,000 tons. A month later the dire fuel position made 'fleet operations of any importance absolutely out of the question'. The shortage of supplies and the need to support the Italians with critical escort duties to North Africa made reductions to German navy provision inevitable. For the present operations by heavy forces must be halted except in emergency when necessary to counter enemy attack. The situation deteriorated further at the beginning of April when the Naval Staff learnt that only 8000 tons of fuel would be supplied from Romania that month instead of the promised 46,000 tons. This produced even more restrictive instructions to discontinue all operations including those by light forces.[36] By early January, British naval intelligence, drawing primarily on Ultra, was tracking this fuel shortage and its impact in considerable detail.[37]

At the beginning of 1942, there were still only four U-boats permanently allocated to Norway, normally based at Kirkenes and tasked with targeting the PQ convoys. Raeder had diluted Hitler's initial order to transfer all boats but some reinforcement was inescapable and, by the end of April, the Norway force had increased to twenty-three, with two additional boats arriving in January, seven in February, nine in March and one in April. A strength of about twenty-three boats was maintained for the rest of the year. In mid-1942, this represented nearly 20 per cent of the overall front-line force.[38] While this build-up was in progress, and against strong resistance from Dönitz, eight boats were allocated to patrol the Iceland–Faeroes–Scotland area, refuelling as necessary in Norway.[39] In theory, this initial force might have been effective against PQ traffic transiting between Iceland and the United Kingdom. However, the combination of prevarication by Dönitz, lack of aerial reconnaissance, and confused objectives meant little was achieved by this deployment which lasted from mid-February to mid-April. Meanwhile, the primary role of the growing Norway and Arctic U-boat force, as with the heavy surface units, was to counter Allied raids and landings, a task Dönitz insisted was impractical. He also argued that the returns achieved by the initial four-boat force against the PQ convoys did not justify the effort expended, let alone reinforcement. Raeder disagreed, ordering that eight U-boats should be available for deployment against every convoy and potentially along the whole route from Iceland to Murmansk. They would find and shadow convoys for the benefit of the reinforced German air force, establish patrol lines for interception, finish off ships damaged by air attack and rescue downed airmen. This requirement for eight boats on patrol dictated that an overall force of twenty-three was required.[40]

It was one thing to deploy extra U-boats to Norway but another creating adequate infrastructure to support them. The new force was divided between Bergen, Trondheim, Narvik and Kirkenes but, even at the first two, base facilities were primitive during 1942. U-boats requiring battle-damage repairs or overhauls therefore had to return to Germany. Shore-based support with operational planning and direction was equally inadequate. A first combat flotilla, the 11th, was formed at Bergen in early June but it was not fully operational until the late summer. A second flotilla, the 13th at Trondheim, did not form until mid-1943. Command of the force was confused with responsibility shifting between Group North in Kiel, Boehm, as admiral commanding Norway and Rear Admiral Hubert Schmundt, commanding Arctic waters from Narvik.[41]

At the start of 1942, Stumpf's 5th Air Fleet still had barely 150 combat aircraft which reached about 225 in February following the transfer of two groups from Holland, one bomber and one fighter, and eight Condors moved from Bordeaux to Trondheim. The Arctic force now comprised sixty long-range bombers, thirty dive-bombers, forty-five fighters and twenty long-range reconnaissance aircraft. Serviceability was about 60 per cent for the strike aircraft, less for the fighters. There were also fifteen He 115 torpedo float planes belonging to the German Navy's small air arm.[42] This remained a tiny force to cover a huge territory and, in theory, three distinct commitments: protection from raids and invasion; support of the land forces on the Eastern Front; and interdiction of the PQ convoys. Not surprisingly, Raeder emphasised that air power was a vital pre-requisite both for successful defence of Norway and the protection of his new battlefleet whether in harbour or on operations. The present shortage of aircraft was therefore 'deplorable'.[43] The 22 January Führer conference promised some improvement when Hitler directed Reichsmarschall Hermann Göring to strengthen the 5th Air Fleet alongside the naval reinforcements he had ordered. Göring pleaded shortage of both aircraft and suitable airfields but, by the end of the month, had reluctantly agreed to deploy a new bomber group comprising three squadrons of torpedo-equipped He 111s.[44] Unfortunately, from Raeder's point of view, the German air force had been slow to invest in torpedo strike, partly from obstruction by the navy, and a serious programme only started in the last months of 1941, first at Grossenbrode in the Baltic and then at Grosseto in Italy. By July 1942, an overall combat strength of seventy-seven torpedo-capable aircraft was achieved, divided equally between Ju 88s and He 111s. However, the first unit did not reach the Arctic until late April with the first successful attack conducted on convoy PQ 15 on 3 May. Meanwhile torpedo strike was limited to the much less effective He 115.[45]

### Tirpitz Deploys against PQ 12

Shortage of destroyers and fuel did not prevent Group North proposing and Raeder and Hitler approving a sortie by *Tirpitz* in early March against convoy PQ 12. Group North was the driving force for this operation and it seems that Raeder acquiesced against the advice of the Naval Staff Operations Division who judged it high risk and incompatible with the primary task of guarding against invasion. However, Group North and Raeder were aware of some ambiguity in Hitler's current priorities. In a conversation with Vice Admiral Theodor Krancke, Raeder's permanent representative at Führer headquarters, on 21 February, Hitler both expressed doubts over British commitment to an attack on Norway and his desire to see a successful attack on the Murmansk convoys.[46]

Essentially, this latest attack proposal was a resurrection of the operation suggested by Group North two months earlier before *Tirpitz* left German waters but now with the advantages of longer daylight and greater availability of aerial reconnaissance. By this time, German naval commanders had a good understanding of the frequency and routes of the PQ convoys and a communications intercept on 24 February brought news that PQ 12 had left Scotland for Iceland. Air searches by Fw 200 Condors then commenced on 1 March to locate the convoy once it left Iceland bound for the Russian ports and it was finally sighted four days later. It was correctly reported to comprise fifteen merchant vessels escorted by a cruiser, two destroyers and several smaller vessels, but errors in its estimated position and speed placed it further west than it actually was. Nevertheless, with every prospect of more sightings from either aircraft or U-boats positioned across the convoy's predicted track, the prospects for a successful interception by the Trondheim battlegroup looked good. Ciliax, who had arrived with *Scheer* and *Prinz Eugen* to take command of the battlegroup, accordingly sortied with *Tirpitz* and three destroyers at 1100 on 6 March, hoping to hit the convoy at around 1500 next day when it would be about 500 miles due north of Trondheim.

Insufficient thought was apparently given to the possibility raised by Operations Division that the British Home Fleet might be covering the convoy and the risks this would pose to the *Tirpitz* group in open waters more than 200 miles off the north Norwegian coast. Air reconnaissance of Scapa Flow was planned but abandoned due to bad weather. Establishing the definite whereabouts of the Home Fleet was evidently not seen by Group North as a pre-requisite. Instead, the lack of anything unusual in aerial sweeps along the projected PQ route was taken to mean no major British units were at sea. Group North did direct Ciliax to avoid engagement with superior enemy forces although he could tackle a force of equal strength if this was necessary to destruction of the convoy. In addition, *Scheer* was left in Trondheim so that her lower speed did not hamper the German force. Presumably, it was judged that superior speed and protection would keep *Tirpitz* out of trouble although the *Bismarck* experience suggested that was a bold assumption. Ciliax's underlying caution was evident when he warned his force against any belief that German 'superior training' would provide an edge against an enemy of equal strength. The British would always quickly draw on carriers, cruisers and destroyers whereas German escorts, because of 'low fuel capacity and bad seakeeping', would become 'a burden' in any extended operation.[47]

PQ 12 had in fact sailed from Reykjavik on 1 March and comprised fifteen merchant vessels and a tanker. Its military cargo included 200 aircraft (144 Hurricanes, 44 P-40s and 20 Airacobras), 162 tanks (75 Matildas, 43 Valentines, 44 American M3s), 53 Bren Gun Carriers, and 3500 lorries and reconnaissance vehicles. Other key items comprised nearly 3500 tons of aluminium and duraluminum, 15,000 miles of telegraph cable, 300 radio sets and 312 machine tools. Its destruction would therefore be a significant prize.[48] The German estimate of the close escort, centred on the cruiser *Kenya* and destroyers *Offa* and *Oribi*, was correct and it would pose little threat to the *Tirpitz* group so long as it was well handled. What the Germans did not know was that the British Home Fleet was indeed at sea and, at the moment Ciliax sailed, was cruising some 50 miles south of PQ 12, providing distant support. The strength of the fleet compared to the *Tirpitz* force was overwhelming. It comprised the modern battleships *King George V* and *Duke of York*, the modernised battlecruiser *Renown*, the aircraft carrier *Victorious*, heavy cruiser *Berwick* and nine destroyers. It reflected the present (arguably pessimistic) British calculation that *Tirpitz* equated to one and a quarter KGVs, while the German pocket battleships and heavy cruisers each equated to one and a quarter British 8in cruisers. Interestingly, Ciliax appears to have rated *Tirpitz* and a KGV as equal.[49]

The presence of the Home Fleet reflected excellent British intelligence on the arrival of German heavy units in Norway, along with the accompanying U-boat and air reinforcements, and a sound assessment of their likely role, including the potential threat they posed to the PQ convoys. This intelligence drew primarily on Ultra intercepts but also a developing SIS agent network and aerial and submarine surveillance of Trondheim and other Norwegian bases.[50] The British correctly judged that the main motive driving German reinforcement was defensive, aimed at countering a British or Russian attack on Norway. However, they also recognised that the combination of a surface strike force at Trondheim, new air units including torpedo aircraft deploying to northern bases and an increased U-boat force operating from Narvik and Kirkenes, might herald a more determined German effort than hitherto against the PQ convoys. They thought it unlikely that German heavy units would venture west of the Iceland–Faeroes line until reinforced by *Scharnhorst* and *Gneisenau*. Whatever the ultimate motivation, the presence of *Tirpitz* and other heavy units in Norway offered the Germans new advantages and options. The constant threat of a breakout into the Atlantic, even if it was not imminent, would alone tie down major British resources while protection of the PQ convoys would become more difficult. Apart from direct attack on a convoy, the Germans might also lure British heavy units into waters where they were vulnerable to U-boat and air attack.[51]

Tovey, as Commander-in-Chief Home Fleet, in planning for PQ 12 and subsequent convoys, expected the Germans to concentrate their enhanced U-boat and air forces on the eastern section of the PQ route between Bear

Island (located halfway between Norway's North Cape and Spitzbergen) and the Russian ports. German surface forces would then operate to the westward, probably posing the greatest threat over the 500-mile stretch of water east of Jan Mayen Island (located 300 miles north-east of the north-east tip of Iceland), about two and a half days for the average convoy to transit. Providing protection for convoys running on the present 14-day cycle would now be a major commitment for the Home Fleet. Countering the surface threat alone would require heavy forces to be in northern waters for five days in every fourteen posing demands for screening destroyers difficult to meet. Tovey therefore intended to synchronise outbound and inbound convoys to maximise protection from available resources. The inbound QP 8, also comprising fifteen ships, therefore left Murmansk on 1 March, the same day PQ 12 left Reykjavik. The two convoys passed each other at midday on 7 March, some 200 miles south-west of Bear Island. Tovey and the Admiralty accepted that deploying the Home Fleet northward also increased the risk of an enemy raiding force breaking out into the Atlantic further south. However, set against these various challenges and risks was the prospect of successfully engaging and destroying any German heavy units, including *Tirpitz*, which targeted the PQ route.[52]

The respective movements of British and German forces over the four days 6–9 March are shown on Map 3 on pages 204–5. By the morning of 7 March, Ciliax had received no update on PQ 12's position from either air search or U-boats, both hampered by poor weather. At 0850, he therefore detached his three destroyers to sweep towards the 1500 position estimated from the 5 March Fw 200 sighting while *Tirpitz* searched further to the north-west. All Ciliax's units followed a strict communications and electronic emissions policy, including radar silence. Search was therefore essentially visual although all ships including *Tirpitz* slowed occasionally for a listening scan on sonar although sea and ice noise rendered this ineffective. On a day when fog and mist predominated, the visual search area even with high definition rangefinder optics was small.[53] At this point PQ 12 was about 100 miles directly ahead of the destroyers, heading north-east at 8 knots, and at Admiralty insistence keeping to the edge of the icefield. The Germans therefore were sweeping too far astern to achieve an interception without fresh intelligence. They had a much better prospect of finding QP 8, heading south-west and on a converging course with the searching German destroyers. With only a light anti-submarine escort of two corvettes and two trawlers, QP 8 was an easy target. Meanwhile, unknown to Ciliax, Tovey was only 100 miles to his west and also on a converging course. Tovey did know *Tirpitz* was at sea because she had been sighted heading north from Trondheim the previous evening by the submarine *Seawolf* and Tovey correctly assessed her objective was PQ 12. Both sides were now hampered by icy conditions and poor visibility. These prevented *Victorious* conducting an air search of the area south of the convoys which would probably have located *Tirpitz*, while one of Ciliax's destroyers possibly passed 10 miles from QP 8 without detecting it. Bad weather similarly prevented a search by *Tirpitz*'s two reconnaissance aircraft. However, the Germans did encounter a straggler from QP 8, the Russian merchant vessel *Ijora*, which was sunk by the destroyer *Friedrich Inn* at 1715, although not before she transmitted a distress signal with an accurate position.[54]

Ciliax, who had received no reports on QP 8's progress and proximity, now reasoned that *Ijora* was part of PQ 12 and that his best chance of interception was to shift rapidly eastward ahead of the convoy and intercept it to the south of Bear Island. His intentions were again constrained by bad weather. This prevented him refuelling his destroyers from *Tirpitz* and he was obliged to detach them to Tromsø, leaving the battleship to sweep eastward alone through the night of 7/8 March. Meanwhile, Tovey, confident that the weather would protect PQ 12, had loitered well to the west, partly to cover QP 8 and partly to avoid hazarding his major units in waters where U-boats were operating. Until early afternoon on 7 March, delays in decrypting Enigma traffic and the weather constraints on flying meant Tovey faced the same dearth of intelligence as Ciliax, with *Seawolf*'s report the last definitive news of *Tirpitz*. However, between 1400 and 0700 the following morning, a series of Ultra decrypts should have convinced Tovey that the balance of probability suggested *Tirpitz* was continuing to search for PQ 12 immediately south and west of Bear Island. Unfortunately, the Ultra picture was clouded by misinterpretation of two D/F intercepts, originating from U-boats but thought to be *Tirpitz*, and garbled receipt of the *Ijora* distress signal. These inputs briefly convinced Tovey that *Tirpitz* was returning to Trondheim and to despatch destroyers southward to intercept her while he followed with the heavy ships. By daybreak on 8 March, he was convinced that both convoys were safe, that one way or another, *Tirpitz* had eluded him, and, with his destroyers short of fuel, he began heading for Iceland.[55] In reality, at 0700, PQ 12 was now 60 miles south-west of Bear Island, with *Tirpitz* 100 miles south-east of the convoy but heading north at an average of 20 knots and still in determined search mode. *Tirpitz* closed to within 80 miles of Bear Island by mid-morning when she turned west, confident she was now ahead of the convoy if it was still heading for Russia and had not been ordered back. Shortly afterwards, she rendezvoused with a patrolling

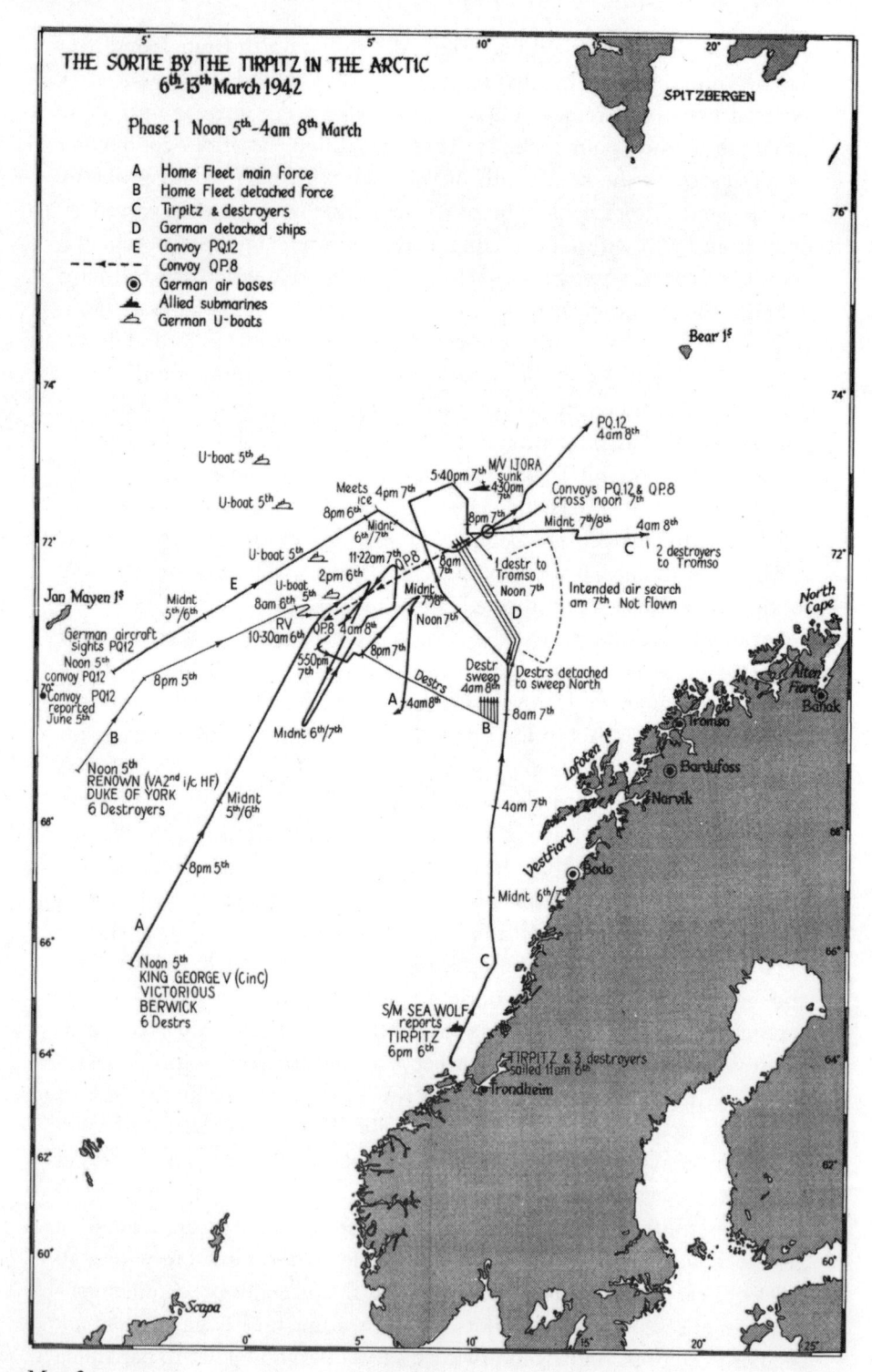

Map 3

# GERMAN COUNTERMEASURES

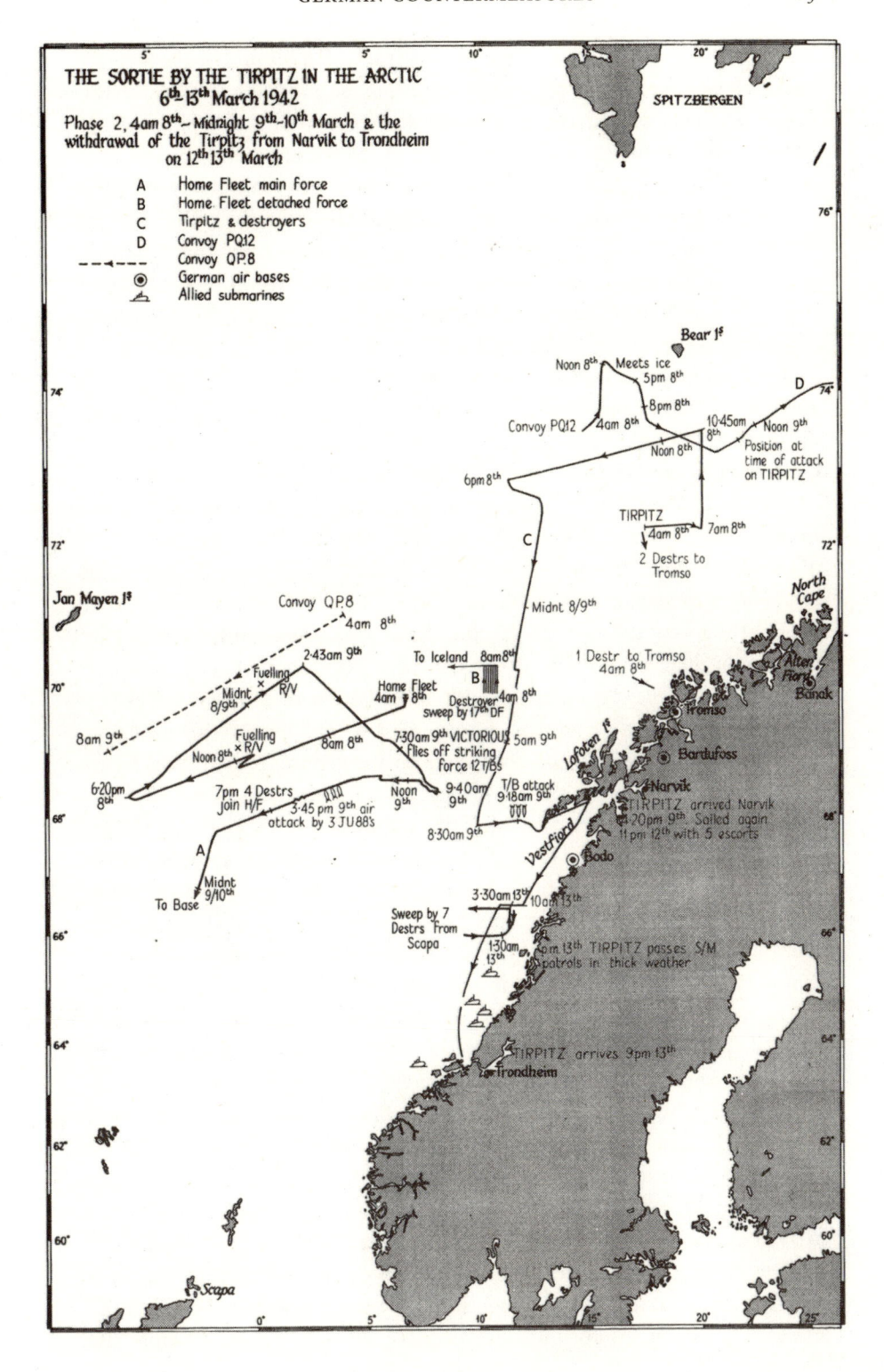

## THE SORTIE BY THE TIRPITZ IN THE ARCTIC
### 6th–13th March 1942

Phase 2, 4am 8th – Midnight 9th–10th March & the withdrawal of the Tirpitz from Narvik to Trondheim on 12th–13th March

- A — Home Fleet main force
- B — Home Fleet detached force
- C — Tirpitz & destroyers
- D — Convoy PQ.12
- ---◁--- Convoy Q.P.8
- ⊙ German air bases
- ⚓ Allied submarines

Fw 200 which she asked to sweep westward. Either *Tirpitz* or the aircraft might then have found the convoy, despite indifferent visibility, if the Admiralty had not ordered it on a precautionary jink north, skirting the extreme edge of the icefield, with directions to pass north of the island if possible. This Admiralty instruction reflected superb analysis by the OIC of *Tirpitz*'s probable whereabouts drawing on the latest Enigma decrypts. Although a north transit was not feasible, given the state of the ice which had already damaged the destroyer *Oribi*, the jink which took the convoy just 40 miles south of the island fortunately kept it about 50 miles clear of *Tirpitz* as she raced westward.[56]

While Ciliax searched the waters south and west of Bear Island, he had already decided to break off the mission if there was no sign of PQ 12 by dusk on 8 March and had ordered his destroyers to communicate this to Group North on their arrival in Tromsø. He judged it possible the convoy had turned back either as a result of the 5 March sighting or the *Ijora* sinking. It was also feasible that the latter had triggered the sailing of the Home Fleet, bringing a risk that *Tirpitz* would be intercepted while returning to Narvik or Trondheim. Group North was initially keen to extend the mission a further day but ultimately conceded the possibility the convoy had retreated and left Ciliax to decide whether to continue searching. For Ciliax the growing risk of British interception was decisive. At 2025, he therefore advised Group North that he was returning to Trondheim and ordered his destroyers to meet him west of Vest Fiord early the following morning, 9 March.[57]

This debate with Group North had generated rather too much signals traffic, not least because several changes had to be made in orders to the destroyers. Poor reception requiring repeats was a further problem. Bletchley Park therefore intercepted and decrypted most of the messages, this time with minimal delay. At 1500, the Admiralty informed Tovey that *Tirpitz* was still searching in the vicinity of Bear Island and that the Germans seemed unaware he was at sea. Tovey, then 300 miles southwest of the island, broke radio silence to give his position and brought his force round to a north-east intercept heading. He also explained that he had no destroyer screen and that communication difficulties, not unusual in Arctic waters, were hampering his control of detached forces. He therefore asked the Admiralty to operate the cruisers and destroyers of the Home Fleet. The Admiralty kept him informed as new intelligence arrived and at 0137 the next morning instructed him to steer course 120 degrees at maximum speed. Shortly after they followed up with an Ultra signal summarising Group North's acknowledgement of Ciliax's 2025 message which helpfully had included the full text of the original. At

0248, a further signal gave detail of *Tirpitz*'s route back to Trondheim after picking up his destroyers. Tovey now had the information necessary to mount an air strike from *Victorious* and just sufficient time to get in range.[58]

At dawn, four hours later, *Victorious* flew off six Albacores, briefed to search a 40-degree arc to the south-east out to 150 miles. These were followed by a strike force of twelve torpedo-armed Albacores which began taking off at 0735, spurred on by a signal from Tovey – 'A wonderful chance, which may achieve most valuable results. God be with you.' One of the searchers found *Tirpitz* shortly after 0800 and began shadowing, soon joined by a second aircraft. *Tirpitz* identified her shadowers as carrier aircraft and, having intercepted their reports, knew an attack was imminent. Accompanied at this stage by just one distantly-placed destroyer, she turned east to close the coast and increased speed to 29 knots. She also launched an Arado seaplane in an attempt to down the shadowers. Although the strike force was successfully guided to *Tirpitz*, its approach was made difficult because pursuing a 29-knot ship into a 30 knot headwind reduced its closing speed to barely 30 knots. The protection and surprise offered by cloud cover also had to be balanced against the risk of icing. Despite these challenges, the strike leader had intended to climb through cloud and exploit ASV radar to gain the classic position ahead of his target before the force dived to attack simultaneously from multiple directions. However, a sudden gap in the cloud, revealing an apparently unalerted *Tirpitz*, persuaded him to attack short of the optimum position. This proved a critical error and led to a poorly coordinated attack, allowing *Tirpitz* time to outmanoeuvre successive waves of aircraft and thus avoid all torpedoes. Although *Tirpitz*'s war diary acknowledges that one torpedo passed 'within ten metres', it insists it did so in parallel to the ship's track and not across her stern as often claimed. At the close of the attack, *Tirpitz* was about 30 miles west of the Lofotens and the entrance to Vest Fiord which she reached two hours later, thence proceeding to Bogen Bay in Ofotfjord where she remained for four days.[59]

*Tirpitz*'s escape reverberated at the highest level. Churchill demanded that Pound explain why twelve aircraft had obtained no hits in comparison with the 'extraordinary efficiency' of the Japanese attack on *Prince of Wales* and *Repulse* three months earlier.[60] Henry Bovell, the captain of *Victorious*, expressed huge disappointment that *Tirpitz* had survived unscathed. The conditions for a torpedo attack were 'almost ideal' and he feared (rightly as it turned out) that it was an opportunity 'which may never recur'. He ascribed the failure, somewhat brutally, to poor execution. Tovey, aware of how hard the aircrews had tried, was more forgiving but stressed the need to learn lessons in operations and training. Naval Air Division put considerable effort into driving such improvement. A torpedo attack trainer, incorporating advanced simulation techniques, was established at Crail while larger and faster ships were provided in the Firth of Forth exercise area for practice attacks with emphasis on new pilots coming through training. Not all the criticisms made by Bovell and Tovey were necessarily valid. They suggested many aircraft had dropped their weapons at too great a range, possibly more than 2000 yards. Observers in *Tirpitz* did not agree, judging the attackers 'daring' and determined, and claiming that most weapons were dropped between 450 and 1300 yards, but with a few either side of this bracket.[61] British criticisms also failed to emphasise how the low speed of the Albacore constrained attack options. *Tirpitz* was steering south-east until the attack was imminent. The strike force could not reasonably assume she would then alter to the east, thus enabling them to cut the corner and get ahead of *Tirpitz*. They could not therefore have easily avoided the laborious stern chase into the wind. The contemporary Japanese B5N2 (Kate) carrier torpedo bomber was at least 50 knots faster than the Albacore, while the Barracuda and American Avenger, which would re-equip the Fleet Air Arm in 1943, had an advantage of 80–100 knots. Deployment of such aircraft by *Victorious* in March 1942 would have transformed attack prospects.

Both sides drew important conclusions from the PQ 12 operation with consequences later in the summer. Both recognised that luck, chance and bad weather had influenced the outcome. Beyond that, for the British, apart from the specific lessons of the *Victorious* strike, the main issues concerned effective exploitation of intelligence and command and control. Post-operation analysis showing how close *Tirpitz* was to PQ 12 off Bear Island on 8 March was sobering. Tovey complained about Admiralty interference and insufficient clarity and context in providing intelligence. Here he underestimated the difficulties posed for the Admiralty by uncertainty over his whereabouts and intent caused by the demands of radio silence and then communication difficulties. With hindsight, the OIC could have helped Tovey more, but their failings were minor, reflecting inexperience in handling real-time intelligence in a fast-moving situation, and they learnt quickly. They deserve great credit for identifying and convincing Admiralty operations staff of the risks posed by *Tirpitz*, especially on 8 March, so that PQ 12 was directed away from danger. However, while Admiralty interventions were undoubtedly correct on this occasion, they probably encouraged Pound and others towards excessive confidence in intelligence-led direction from the Admiralty.[62]

For the German naval leadership, the operation underlined their present naval and air weakness in the northern theatre. The Royal Navy could counter every move by deploying strong forces, especially carriers, the most dangerous opponent. German air weakness allowed the enemy to approach the coast while lack of destroyers and other escorts left German heavy ships insufficiently protected against air and surface attack. Group North provided a damning assessment of the German air force – not even 'roughly up to requirements', leading to 'the grotesque picture of the enemy chasing us in our own coastal waters, while himself sailing there unchallenged'. Ciliax too complained that the preparation and execution of the operation had been amateur and he saw no purpose in deploying a single warship in an area where the enemy inevitably dominated. The German Naval Staff acknowledged that British forces were skilful. They maintained radio silence, aerial surveillance and subsequent torpedo strikes were highly effective, as were submarine operations, and overall command and control and cooperation between different combat elements were excellent.

It followed that strong air support (comprising reconnaissance, bomber and torpedo aircraft), to provide timely intelligence and determined targeting of enemy carriers, was an essential pre-requisite for the future success of German naval operations. Given the crucial role of the navy in countering an enemy landing, its heavy units should only deploy when enemy whereabouts and strength were precisely determined and adequate air cover guaranteed. Unless these conditions were met, the risks were too great. Meanwhile, the construction of Germany's own carrier, *Graf Zeppelin*, should be accelerated. The goal for successful Arctic operations should be a fast, powerful task force comprising *Tirpitz*, *Scharnhorst*, a carrier, two heavy cruisers and a dozen destroyers.[63] Hitler endorsed these conclusions at his meeting with Raeder on 12 March and apparently agreed to press Göring on improving air support. Hitler's oral support for the 'super' task force was easy to make but meaningless unless the necessary resources were allocated. By this point in the war there was little prospect of this as Raeder should have recognised. His concept was utopian. Although Hitler made no specific comment regarding the carrier strike on *Tirpitz*, it evidently made a powerful impression. The risk of a repeat would condition his attitude to operations against PQ 17 three months later.[64]

The reviews of the *Tirpitz* sortie conducted by the German naval leadership made no reference to disruption of PQ convoys receiving increased priority or urgency. Nor is it apparent that Hitler addressed this with Raeder on 12 March. Indeed, Raeder subsequently informed the Naval Staff that the Führer was content to combat the PQ convoys for the present with 'light forces' and U-boats. The implication was that the dominant threat remained an Allied attack on Norway, with the convoys essentially still a target of opportunity. This misjudged Hitler's true thinking. By now, he clearly saw the supply convoys, and a potential British/Russian attack on Norway and seizure of vital war resources, notably the Petsamo nickel mines, as a combined threat. This was underlined on 14 March, just two days after Raeder's meeting with Hitler, when OKW Supreme Command issued a directive with a potentially transformative effect on Arctic operations. On Hitler's authority, 'Operations in the North' called for massive reinforcement of naval and air forces in northern Norway in order to 'cut the previously undisturbed sea link between the Anglo-Saxons and the Russians in the Arctic, and to eliminate enemy naval supremacy, which reaches even into our own coastal waters'. U-boats were fully included in this demand, once again potentially compromising Dönitz's Atlantic strategy. The same day Göring informed the 5th Air Fleet that attacks on PQ convoys now had 'prime importance' and that it was to execute this task in the 'closest' cooperation with the navy.[65]

Although Raeder's lobbying for more air resources in Norway may have influenced the new OKW directive, the primary factor driving this new focus on the PQ convoys lay in the emerging plans for Germany's summer offensive in Russia, to be known as Operation Blue. On 5 April, Führer Directive No 41 established that this would centre on the southern front with the aim of breaking through into the Caucasus and seizing its oilfields. Two aspirations underpinned Blue, especially in Hitler's mind. First, acquisition of the oil of the Caucasus would solve Germany's shortage and underpin its future war potential. Secondly, denial of the oil to Russia along with the resources of the eastern Ukraine would deal a catastrophic blow to her economy and thus her ability to continue the war. As this rationale for Blue evolved over the first quarter of 1942, it became apparent that increased Anglo-American supplies delivered via the Arctic route had the potential to mitigate at least some of the economic losses Russia might suffer. As noted earlier, the Germans were increasingly aware of British tanks and aircraft on the Russian front, especially in the Moscow area, from the previous November. Through the winter, the intelligence picture of these supplies, drawn primarily from Russian prisoners and convoy survivors, remained fragmentary but the scale of support was increasingly apparent.

In German eyes, the perceived impact of Western aid was heightened further because in spring 1942 they seriously underestimated Soviet war production. In March, they assessed armoured vehicle output at no more than 500 per month and aircraft at 550, compared to actual monthly totals averaging 1800 and 1600 respectively over the first half of the year.

Meanwhile, Colonel Reinhard Gehlen, who took over Foreign Armies East on 1 April, estimated that by July the Western Allies had delivered 2800 tanks, sufficient to equip some thirty Russian armoured brigades. This broadly accurate figure almost equalled the German estimate for six months of Soviet output and helps explain why cutting off Western supplies through the Arctic was now judged an essential accompaniment to Blue, especially given the likelihood of intensified deliveries through the summer and autumn. Nevertheless, during the first half of 1942, Gehlen and others focused mainly on Western-supplied armaments and probably underestimated the impact of non-military items including strategic raw materials such as aluminium.[66] Germany continued to underestimate Soviet war potential until 1944 when its figures for output of key raw materials became more accurate.[67]

Whatever balance of factors drove the March OKW directive, it certainly led to substantial air reinforcement. Within a month 5th Air Fleet strength was almost double that at the start of the year. The primary strike force comprised 120 medium bombers (Ju 88s and He 111s) including an initial batch of He 111 torpedo bombers working up at Stavanger. There were also still forty Ju 87 dive-bombers primarily allocated to army support. The long-range reconnaissance force now comprised about twenty-five Fw 200 aircraft with much of the Bordeaux force transferred to Trondheim in the last week of March. Hitler justified this on the basis that, with Atlantic U-boat operations now concentrated in American and Caribbean waters, ocean reconnaissance over the eastern Atlantic could be reduced. The Fw 200s were supported by fifty Ju 88s and He 111s adapted for reconnaissance and some seventy coastal aircraft, He 115s and BV 138s. Meanwhile the fighter force had grown to 100 aircraft, mainly Me 109s. Overall, by the end of April, the reinforced 5th Air Fleet comprised about 8 per cent of German Air Force combat strength.[68]

It was also now grouped in three main forces, under commands 'North-east' at Kirkenes, 'Lofotens' at Bardufoss, located halfway between Narvik and Tromsø, and 'North-west' at Sola, near Stavanger. The largest force with most of the strike aircraft was concentrated under the 'North-east' command and was tasked with targeting the convoys, army support, and raids on Murmansk and Archangel. Kirkenes was its main base but there were also airfields at Petsamo, Banak and Billefiord, the last two located near Porsangerfiord running south from North Cape. Each of these 5th Air Fleet commands had a role in PQ convoy operations. Once an inbound convoy was expected, either through specific intelligence or by the predicted fortnightly cycle, North-west command would reconnoitre out towards Scotland and Iceland. Lofotens command would then conduct initial attacks until the convoy crossed the line between North Cape and Spitzbergen. From this point, North-east command took over and was directed to concentrate solely on convoy attack and forsake all land support operations unless given express permission by Stumpff, as 5th Air Fleet commander. Once a convoy crossed into North-east region, Lofotens command continued to provide support, deploying aircraft from Bardufoss to Kirkenes and Petsamo as required.[69] For the 'frictionless' collaboration with the navy demanded by Göring, 5th Air Fleet had to maintain tight uniform control over its separate commands and to guarantee faultless communications with area naval commanders. The necessary structures and reporting systems between naval and air staffs were therefore discussed at a special conference which produced binding agreements and appointment of liaison officers.[70]

Arctic air operations were demanding due to poor and unpredictable weather, with long periods of minimal visibility, the difficult terrain in which airbases were situated and their primitive infrastructure. Take-offs and landings on cement and wooden runways in narrow valleys enclosed by hills and ridges over a thousand metres high – often lashed by extremely hazardous crosswinds – would 'normally be regarded as lunacy'. The initial attacks in April were hampered by the spring thaw which wreaked havoc on the northern airfields while those in May faced abysmal weather. It was difficult to coordinate or concentrate attacks which therefore too often comprised only half a dozen aircraft and were much easier for a well-drilled convoy escort defence to counter.[71]

As described earlier, the new focus on the convoys and related air reinforcement resurrected the idea of establishing a base on Spitzbergen. Hitler had decided on 22 March that this project would not proceed since 'it would bear no relation to the expense necessary to acquire and maintain it'. However, he revisited the issue in mid-May, apparently now convinced it would after all permit more effective disruption of the PQ convoys but he also now wanted to exploit its coal supplies. It was agreed that options would be explored although OKW and other military leaders evidently hoped the issue would be forgotten.[72] Meanwhile, by the third week of March the British were aware from Ultra of the renewed German interest in establishing a presence on Spitzbergen and possibly Bear Island and considered options to counter this. The favoured solution was to establish a small Norwegian party to maintain a permanent watch, including a floatplane unit for reconnaissance and capable of reaching out to Bear Island.[73] Ultimately the British investment was more modest and confined to a Norwegian-manned meteorological station which coexisted with a similar German site elsewhere in the archipelago for most of the war.

## Chapter 6

# The Beginning of German Combined Arms Attacks

The first opportunity for the Germans to put the new OKW directive into practice came with PQ 13, comprising nineteen merchant ships, which left Reykjavik on 20 March 1942, while the parallel inbound convoy QP 9 left Murmansk a day later. German reinforcements were still building but they had sufficient forces in place to mount the first serious combined arms attack on a PQ convoy. Thanks mainly to Ultra, British knowledge of German aircraft order of battle, including the arrival of torpedo bombers and extending now to fuel and weapon stocks at airfields, remained extraordinarily detailed.[1] The British dispositions to cover the two convoys were almost identical to those for PQ 12 and QP 8. Although the PQ 12 experience together with shortage of fuel had caused the Germans to put strict constraints on the deployment of heavy ships, the British did not know this and the arrival of the heavy cruiser *Hipper* in Trondheim late on 20 March potentially provided another fast, powerful unit they could bring into play. The full Home Fleet, under Tovey's second-in-command, Vice Admiral Curteis, accordingly sailed to meet any surface attack in the western part of the convoy route.

*German Operations against Convoys PQ 13/QP 9 and their Impact*
The first four days of PQ 13's passage were uneventful but, on 25 March, it encountered a violent storm which, after three days, left its ships scattered over an area stretching 150 miles westward from a point 80 miles north of North Cape. By the morning of 28 March, the weather had cleared and the close escort, led by the cruiser *Trinidad*, had shepherded the merchant vessels into two main groups, albeit still 100 miles apart. However, clear weather brought a German shadower followed by successive air attacks for the rest of the day which sank two ships and damaged others.[2] Drawing on Ultra intercepts, the Admiralty provided

some warning of these air attacks along with details of U-boat patrol areas. Although the Atlantic U-boat force had from February moved to the Enigma four-rotor Shark system which GC&CS could not read, the Arctic boats continued to use the familiar Dolphin three-rotor system and did so until September 1944.[3]

Meanwhile, three German destroyers sortied from Kirkenes at 1330 the same day. These comprised the 8th Flotilla which had escorted *Hipper* to Trondheim. Group North had then ordered them onward to Kirkenes where they had arrived two days earlier, specifically to target PQ 13.[4] They headed north-east until they hit the probable track of PQ 13 predicted by air reconnaissance and began sweeping westward. Shortly after midnight, they sighted the merchant vessel *Bateau*, one of the orphans of the storm sailing alone, and promptly sank her, which proved their sole success. The movements of this destroyer force were covered in detail by Ultra decrypts enabling the Admiralty to give the escort commander effective warning of the threat. During the night of 28/29 March, *Trinidad* and the destroyer *Fury* therefore positioned south of and between the two groups of merchant vessels to cut off the German destroyers before they could intervene. Early the next morning, the two forces ran into each other almost head on with *Trinidad* picking up the Germans on her Type 281 radar at 0845 at about 12,000 yards. A running fight followed over the next two hours with short sharp engagements punctuated by periods of mist and snow, rendering identification difficult as other British and Russian warships appeared. The German flotilla leader, *Z 26*, was badly damaged by *Trinidad*'s second salvo, using Type 284 radar-directed fire, at the beginning of the action and was later finished off by the destroyer *Eclipse* so that she sank just before 1100. After inflicting some damage on *Eclipse*, the other two German destroyers, *Z 24* and *Z 25*, judged the opposition was too great to achieve any useful result and headed back to Kirkenes. The British were the undoubted winners of this surface action but, unfortunately, victory was marred by severe damage to *Trinidad* from one of her own torpedoes which malfunctioned probably due to icing in its mechanism.[5]

The final act in the PQ 13 story came on 30 March with the loss of the merchant vessels *Induna* and *Effingham* to *U-376* and *U-456* respectively during the final run into Murmansk. Set against these successes, the Germans lost *U-655* which was rammed by the minesweeper *Sharpshooter* between Bear Island and North Cape on 23 March while she was escorting QP 9. This was the only German attempt against QP 9 which reached Reykjavik on 3 April unscathed. The Germans also lost *U-585*, sunk by a drifting mine off the Ribachiy peninsula on 30 March.[6]

The loss of five ships out of nineteen inevitably provoked concern for both Tovey and the Admiralty. Tovey assessed that the Germans were now determined to stop the PQ traffic. This view reflected a comprehensive NID assessment of the overall German operation against PQ 13 and QP 9, remarkable not just for its detail but also its clear understanding of the shift to a combined arms approach.[7] The British recognised that the dispersal of PQ 13 caused by the weather had arguably helped the Germans on this occasion and it was notable that the ships lost had all been sailing independently without protection when they were sunk. In losing a large destroyer and a U-boat to the Royal Navy, the Germans had also paid a high price for their successes. Nevertheless, this first combined arms targeting of a PQ convoy and the further reinforcements which Ultra revealed the Germans would soon deploy underlined to the British naval command the growing dangers facing future convoys. German prospects would also be enhanced by longer daylight and better weather, bringing advantages for aerial reconnaissance and strike while convoy routes were still constrained by ice. If the British were concerned, German satisfaction was muted. The Naval Staff did not feel that sinking five ships made up for the loss of *Z 26* and much of her crew considering how few destroyers were available. However, without a clearer picture of enemy dispositions and an improvement in the fuel position, there was no prospect of deploying heavy units in support. The Germans were also disturbed at how quickly *Trinidad* had disabled *Z 26* with her radar-directed fire. *Trinidad*'s captain recorded that her Type 284 had been critical in the destroyer engagement and did all that was asked of it.[8]

The experience of PQ 13 and QP 9 also underlined the shortage of vessels available to Tovey for close escort. Once he had met the requirement for screening his heavy ships, there were few destroyers available to contribute to a close escort which it was now agreed must be at least ten ships per convoy. Western Approaches Command had until now provided support on an ad hoc basis but the Admiralty now agreed that this arrangement must be formalised and from PQ 14 onward Western Approaches provided the bulk of close escorts. This meant that, for a fortnightly cycle, at least 10 per cent of the Western Approaches escort strength was diverted to the Arctic commitment and every Arctic convoy pair broadly implied the loss of a transatlantic pair.[9]

Tovey's concerns were echoed by Pound and resurrected doubts across the wider British military leadership over whether the benefits of supplying Russia justified the risks not only in running the convoys but in resources lost to other theatres. On 10 April, two days after the next convoy, PQ 14, left Reykjavik, Pound told the chiefs of staff that there was no precedent for running convoys against the current scale of air opposition on the northern route. Geographical conditions so greatly favoured the Germans that losses in both convoyed ships and escorts could render the whole aid operation uneconomical. Implicit here were four key differences from Mediterranean experience with convoys such as Halberd: convoy frequency with one sailing ever fortnight; duration of exposure to air and surface attack; distance from friendly bases; and lack of land-based air support. The Russian Northern Fleet Air Force never matched the Royal Air Force contribution to convoy defence through fighter and strike aircraft from Malta. Pound stressed that, if the supplies were essential, every effort should be made to deliver them. If, as Mason Macfarlane had recently implied, they were a mere drop compared to what Russia herself was now producing, then the serious drain on resources and shipping should be avoided. Pound's points were all valid as far as they went but he could have acknowledged that the Germans faced problems too. German ships operating in Arctic waters were equally far from docking and sophisticated repair facilities and, as Pound well knew from Ultra, they were desperately short of fuel. Brooke agreed that Britain was undertaking considerable risks but with little information on whether Western aid was deployed effectively. He reminded his colleagues that Britain had never committed to delivering supplies to Russia as opposed to making them available.[10] Brooke was evidently more frustrated with Russia than the official record acknowledged. The previous day he complained to Cadogan that Russia was getting everything she asked for while offering nothing in return.[11]

Pound's concerns must also be viewed against the wider battle he was fighting within Britain's political and military leadership at this time to divert air resources from bombing to protection of sea communications. Despite American entry into the war, Britain's maritime position was now at its nadir. Ultra coverage of the Atlantic U-boat force had been lost with the introduction of the four-rotor Enigma Shark system on 1 February. U-boat inflicted shipping losses on the American eastern seaboard were reaching appalling levels. The Royal Navy had lost control of the central Mediterranean and the fleet at Alexandria was reduced to a handful of cruisers and destroyers. There was little to stop the Japanese sweeping all before them in the Indian Ocean if they chose to do so. It was no wonder therefore that Pound began his presentation on air resources to the Defence Committee on 5 March with the dramatic words – 'If we lose the war at sea, we lose the war. We lose the war at sea when we can no longer maintain those communications which are essential to us.' A month later Pound inevitably saw the prospect of steady attrition in the Arctic for, as he saw it, ill-defined gain with grave concern.[12]

Four days after the chiefs' discussion, the War Cabinet noted that the convoy challenges were exacerbated by the acceleration in American supplies, with potentially forty ships per month arriving in Iceland which the Royal Navy would have to convoy. If twelve British ships currently being prepared were added, this implied a convoy of twenty-five every fortnight, the absolute maximum Pound judged the Home Fleet could manage, although he would prefer a single convoy per month. The Cabinet agreed that Oliver Lyttleton, the Minister of Production replacing Beaverbrook, would produce a rapid report on the maximum supplies, taking account of shipping and escorts as well as production, which Britain could send to Russia after the First Protocol expired at the end of June. Following significant losses, two ships to aircraft bombing and two to U-boats, to the westbound QP 10 which had left Murmansk on 10 April, they also agreed to emphasise to the Russians the increasing risks facing the PQ convoys.[13]

The apparent reluctance of the chiefs of staff to endorse the value of the Russian aid programme and therefore the PQ convoys which were the only current means of delivering significant supplies is partly understandable. Whatever Russia's real needs, the opportunity costs in supplying her were currently acute. The Imperial Japanese Navy had just raided Ceylon, British control of the Indian Ocean was in doubt, north-east India threatened by land attack and there were setbacks in the Middle East. It was also true that getting the Russians to account in detail for their use of Western supplies or to provide a consistent and useful picture of their own production of war materials had proved impossible. Nevertheless, the intelligence picture, drawn from multiple if fragmentary sources, of Russia's prospects through the balance of 1942, which was available to British and American leaders by the beginning of April, was broadly consistent. It suggested that Russia's ability to withstand an expected German summer offensive was finely balanced. Germany was perceived to have recovered well from winter setbacks, to have suffered far less losses, and to be outproducing Russia in key war materials. There were some differences between British and American views, with the former slightly more optimistic, but these were not significant. Neither ruled out a Russian collapse or separate peace.[14]

*Continental Operations Revisited: The Rise of 'Sledgehammer'*
It followed that Western support had the potential to tip the balance in Russia's favour. This was certainly still Churchill's view as expressed to Roosevelt on 1 April. All depended on the vast Russo–German struggle, in which 'we are doing all we can to help and also to take the weight

off'. That included fighting every convoy through to Murmansk.[15] It was also the position of the British joint planners when they again considered the option of establishing a 'bridgehead' in France, probably at either the Pas de Calais or the Cherbourg peninsula, under the new codeword 'Sledgehammer' during March. Reflecting Joint Intelligence Committee views, they stated that Germany's need for oil would require a decisive offensive against Russia, probably in the south and beginning in May. Russia's survival was crucial to future British (and by implication American) strategy and present Allied help, supply of material, Mediterranean operations and the air offensive, was 'not enough'. Hence the need for a major diversion operation. The chiefs of staff did not demur on the desirability of additional supportive action although they questioned whether the Sledgehammer concept could deliver useful benefit at acceptable cost.[16] Oddly they appear to have seen no contradiction between exploring a Sledgehammer option and questioning the necessity for the PQ supply programme.

The British variant of Sledgehammer developed in March and early April differed somewhat from the options for a diversionary landing on the continent considered the previous August. Its starting point was that the German air force was under acute strain and therefore a weak link in German power. The objective of Sledgehammer was therefore to force Germany into protracted air fighting in the West in an area where Britain enjoyed advantage, thus reducing her air power on the Eastern Front. By mid-March, German total serviceable strength in combat aircraft in all theatres had risen from its January low point but was still 40 per cent below that of June 1941. The Sledgehammer goal was therefore logical. Five options to achieve it were considered: a major raid on the French coast; a series of linked raids; a deception operation suggesting a major landing was imminent; seizing a bridgehead in force to be held for several weeks; and air action alone. By early April just prior to the questioning over the convoys, the choice had narrowed to the last two. The chiefs judged the risks and costs of the bridgehead option, which could only be contemplated if Russia faced existential pressure, were unacceptable. But they were also unconvinced that air action alone would achieve the desired goal of destroying an additional 200 German fighters a month. Here, the joint planners had claimed that losing 100 fighters per month would pose an 'intolerable strain' on Germany. This misinterpreted Air Intelligence advice that such a loss rate would prevent Germany recovering to its mid-1941 strength from its present low point. Portal thought a loss of 200 per month would be required to prevent recovery but doubted this could be sustained for long enough to inflict serious pain.[17] (German fighter losses in March, single and twin engine, from all causes, were about 210 aircraft, representing 10.5 per cent of a total strength of 2000 at this time.[18] Portal's figure would thus double present monthly losses and would certainly have a serious impact if sustained over say six months. But none of the Sledgehammer options were envisaged to last that long. Most anticipated an operation lasting weeks.)

The initial British conclusions regarding Sledgehammer and the growing convoy concerns coincided with a visit to London by General Marshall and Harry Hopkins to discuss future war strategy which began on 8 April. Marshall unveiled American plans for the next 12 months comprising three linked elements: a variant of Sledgehammer to be implemented this year, and deploying eight divisions, should it become essential to relieve pressure on Russia; a full-scale American–British landing with forty-eight divisions and nearly 6000 aircraft to establish a 'second front' in Western Europe in 1943, code-named Roundup; and the build-up of American forces, land and air, to support these operations, code-named Bolero. In his initial presentation, Marshall stressed two primary considerations: ensuring Russian resistance continued and the need to give American forces arriving in Britain early battle experience. His first point meant the subsequent debate with the British political and military leadership focused more on Sledgehammer than Roundup. Marshall constantly reverted to the potential requirement for an 'emergency operation' should things go badly for Russia in the coming summer or conceivably, if the German offensive failed, to exploit opportunities offered by any collapse in their morale. Marshall's problem with his version of Sledgehammer, which he evidently saw as a significant 'bite and hold' 'bridgehead' operation, was that the United States could offer little support before September when Britain would still provide 75 per cent of the forces and bear the bulk of the risk. Marshall's second point carried an implicit threat, not lost on the British, 'use them or lose them'. 'Germany first' might be official American policy but there were voices in Washington, notably Admiral King, who felt the Pacific should have greater priority. If Germany first and Bolero were to survive, Marshall must assure the American leadership that Britain supported early action.[19]

The British therefore faced two problems. To safeguard Germany first and Bolero, they must not only support Roundup in 1943, a relatively straightforward commitment at this distance, but also show adequate enthusiasm and commitment to Marshall's variant of Sledgehammer, a concept which their March studies had convinced the chiefs of staff was unacceptably risky and probably impossible to resource in the timescale. It was also clear that American commitment to Sledgehammer and Roundup along with their Pacific priorities would leave Britain with minimal help in the Indian Ocean, Mediterranean and Middle East. Britain could not possibly find the naval and shipping resources to support Marshall's plans, meet existing critical commitments in the Atlantic and Arctic and stave off looming defeat in other theatres. Given all the complexities posed by a global war, inevitable differences in American and British priorities, and the challenges involved in executing combined operations on the scale of Sledgehammer, let alone Roundup, misunderstandings were inevitable. Marshall left London convinced he had full British support for his agenda and either ignored or played down British qualifications. For their part, the British were not sufficiently honest about their reservations and implied commitments they knew they might find difficult to keep. Ismay later admitted that, when Marshall's proposals were discussed at the Defence Committee on 14 April, everyone seemed to agree with the American proposals in their entirety. 'No doubts were expressed; no discordant note struck.' He was convinced that much future American suspicion and misunderstanding over British attitudes and motivation would have been avoided if the British leadership had only set out its reservations frankly.[20]

Nevertheless, the story of Sledgehammer over the two months following Marshall's visit and the related differences in British and American attitudes and perceptions is more complicated than either Ismay or many recent historical accounts suggest. The British chiefs of staff were certainly sceptical that Sledgehammer as envisaged by Marshall was viable and should have said so. However, the claim that they and the prime minister were deceitful in that they agreed to an operation they were determined not to execute under any circumstances goes too far. The British continued to study the benefits, risks and feasibility of Sledgehammer, along with a range of alternatives, until the War Cabinet agreed conditions on 11 June that effectively ruled it out. The insurmountable problem that finally killed Sledgehammer and persuaded Roosevelt of the need to look at alternatives was shortage of landing craft.[21]

That said, it seems that, in contrast to Marshall, Roosevelt was never persuaded by British promises. On 21 April, two days after Marshall's return, Roosevelt told the Soviet ambassador, Maxim Litvinov, who had replaced Umansky in December, that, while Churchill and the War Cabinet had called for a 'second front', the British chiefs of staff were against it because of the overextended British position. He went on to disparage British war performance before stressing that, while the British wanted postponement until 1943, the Americans insisted on a second front straightaway. Whether this disparagement exemplified Roosevelt's genuine opinion or was primarily tactics aimed at establishing himself as Stalin's preferred Western counterpart while blaming second front collapse on Britain is hard to judge. Probably it was a combination of all these elements. The ignominious fall of Singapore, the simultaneous embarrassment of Cerberus and setbacks in the Middle East had undoubtedly damaged Britain's reputation in Washington and Roosevelt knew Churchill was facing increasing domestic criticism for his conduct of the war. Stalin was well aware of this too through Maisky.[22]

Meanwhile, against the background of the Marshall visit and the Sledgehammer debate, PQ 14 was making its way to Murmansk and the next outbound convoy was planned to depart Iceland at the end of the month, thus maintaining the current fortnightly schedule. These two convoys were the largest yet, comprising twenty-four and twenty-five ships respectively, with the second convoy PQ 15 including two icebreakers. In line with the increased German threat, the first convoy PQ 14 received an enhanced close escort, comprising the cruiser *Edinburgh*, a veteran of Operation Halberd which was carrying vital parts for the repair of *Trinidad*, five destroyers and four corvettes, under Rear Admiral Stuart Bonham-Carter, while Tovey provided heavy cover from the battlefleet as before. The Germans fully intended a strong combined arms attack, including deployment of the 8th Destroyer Flotilla, back up to three vessels with *Hermann Schoemann* moving from Trondheim on 5 April to replace the sunk *Z 26*. However, on this occasion, the key determinant was appalling weather. Three days into its voyage, on 11 April, the convoy encountered a combination of gales, minimal visibility and thick drifting ice which forced two-thirds of the ships to return to Iceland. Eight ships continued and, after being sighted by German air reconnaissance on 15 April, suffered intermittent but largely ineffective air and U-boat attack when weather conditions permitted over the next three days. The only casualty was the Commodore's ship, *Empire Howard*, which blew up after being hit by two torpedoes from the newly commissioned *U-403*. Her lost cargo included twenty fighters, twenty-five Matilda tanks, eighty-two lorries, and one million rounds of ammunition. An attack on *Edinburgh* by another new boat, *U-376*, failed. The Germans had more success against the parallel inbound convoy QP 10, although it was also strongly escorted by *Edinburgh*'s sister ship *Liverpool* and five destroyers, demonstrating that when weather allowed their combined forces were increasingly efficient. Two of sixteen ships were lost to air attack with a third badly damaged and *U-435* sank a further two. Nevertheless, the Germans paid a price, losing six aircraft to escort anti-aircraft fire. The 8th Flotilla also sortied against QP 10 on 13 April but poor visibility convinced its commander there was no chance of finding the convoy and shortage of fuel was a constant constraint.[23]

On 17 April, as Marshall and his team prepared to depart for Washington and before the results of PQ 14 and QP 10 were fully known, the Vice Chief of the Naval Staff, Vice Admiral Henry Moore, defined for Lyttleton's forthcoming report the maximum protection the Royal Navy could provide for future PQ convoys. The combination of German reinforcements and the prevailing ice conditions, which made convoys easier to find, meant that stronger escort forces were now required between Bear Island and Murmansk. Given other naval commitments, adequate escorts could only be achieved if the convoy cycle was reduced to three every two months and size restricted to twenty-five ships since otherwise the demands on anti-submarine vessels would become prohibitive.[24] Although PQ 14 had only lost one ship to enemy action, when the returnees were discounted and the QP 10 casualties added, the real loss rate to this pair of convoys was over 20 per cent. There was little comfort here for the Admiralty. They had to assume that with better weather and a full convoy to target, losses were likely far to exceed this figure, as Bonham-Carter emphasised starkly in his report: 'Under present conditions with no hours of darkness, continually under air observation for the last four days, submarines concentrating in the bottlenecks, torpedo attack to be expected, our destroyers unable to carry out proper hunt or search owing to the oil situation, serious losses must be expected in every convoy.'[25] There was no doubt about German intent. On 13 April, a week before Bonham-Carter drafted his report, Hitler emphasised to Raeder that 'attacks on the Murmansk convoys are most important at the moment'.[26]

The new Admiralty view on convoy limits soon reached the Americans, provoking concern up to presidential level. This reflected the scale of the American backlog described earlier which was at last being made up but also the quantity of idle shipping accumulating in Iceland, now including the PQ 14 returnees. Sixty-three ships had left the United States for Iceland in April. It was awkward for the Western Powers that only seven ships had arrived in Russia in April compared to forty in March. The Americans had anticipated that 107 ships would be convoyed forward from Iceland in May alone. American concern also reflected the president's intense personal commitment to maintaining supplies to Russia and desire to avoid embarrassment with Stalin. On 18 March, Roosevelt had informed Churchill that he could handle Stalin better than either the Foreign Office or his own State Department. Given that he had never met Stalin and had exchanged only a handful of messages, this claim was decidedly arrogant.

Three weeks later, on 11 April, Roosevelt followed up with a rare (at this time) message to Stalin suggesting a personal meeting in the summer but, in the meantime, a visit by Molotov to discuss 'a very important military proposal'. It was not difficult for Stalin to establish from Litvinov that this referred to an early landing in France.[27] This initiative was not only taken without informing Churchill but pre-empted the Marshall discussions then underway in London.

The proposed reduction in convoying thus came at an awkward moment and the last days of April consequently saw forceful exchanges between Roosevelt and Churchill, with the former pleading for maximum effort and the latter trying to assuage while respecting Admiralty advice. Tensions were temporarily reduced with a promise to raise convoy size to thirty-five ships if PQ 15, which left Iceland on 26 April, passed satisfactorily. Meanwhile, Admiralty figures showing that seventy-five ships, sailing over two months, could still meet current commitments if efficiently loaded were deceptive since they took no account of probable losses. The Americans thus had no alternative but to scale down their ambitions for deliveries through the Northern ports and only twenty-one left the United States for Iceland over the two months May and June. Some of the supplies destined for delivery to Russia by the Arctic route were now diverted to the Persian Gulf but some shipping was also released to the US Army for Bolero.[28]

The interaction of Marshall's visit and British insistence on reducing the convoy flow now brought further consequences. It encouraged Roosevelt, with what was probably guarded support from Marshall, to promise Molotov, still the Soviet Foreign Minister, during his visit to Washington at the end of May that there would be a second front in Europe in the present year. This was inevitably damaging to relations with the Soviet Union when this commitment was shortly shown to be false. Soviet distrust was then compounded when Roosevelt and Marshall suggested that the mounting of a second front operation was complicated by the scale of shipping required for the Murmansk convoys and sought Molotov's help in getting this reduced by keeping Russian demands to those that were essential.[29] Roosevelt had already proposed using Bolero as an excuse to reduce supplies with Churchill a month earlier.[30] Molotov was well aware convoy frequency was reducing and, in the second half of the year, they would almost cease on the Arctic route. From the Soviet perspective, instead of trading a reduction in supplies for a second front, Western duplicity had ensured they lost both. There was a reverse trade-off here which the British leadership, and certainly the chiefs of staff, should have recognised back in March. If Russia's survival was crucial as all agreed, and Sledgehammer was not viable, then maximising convoy deliveries surely became more important.

## PQ 15 and the Loss of the Cruiser Edinburgh

Meanwhile, PQ 15 and its inbound counterpart QP 11 sailed at the end of April. The arrangements for close escort and distant cover were broadly similar to those for the two previous convoy pairs but there were three innovations in the close escort of the outbound convoy that became a standard feature in future. The first was inclusion of a Catapult Aircraft Merchant Ship (CAM Ship), in this case the *Empire Morn*. CAM Ships were merchant vessels fitted with a rocket-propelled catapult capable of launching a single Hurricane, intended to shoot down a shadowing aircraft such as a Fw 200. The Hurricane could not be recovered so the pilot would bail out or ditch near the convoy and hope for rescue. The second addition was a specialist Anti-Aircraft Ship, for PQ 15 the converted merchant vessel *Ulster Queen*. She displaced nearly 4000 tons and was armed with six high-angle 4in guns in twin turrets, mounted on the centreline for all-round coverage, two four-barrelled 2pdr pom poms and ten single 20mm guns. She was fitted with a warship bridge and the latest air-warning radar. This anti-aircraft capability equated to that of a converted *Capetown* class cruiser. Given the scale of the new air threat, convoys from PQ 15 onward would have benefitted from having at least one, and ideally two, modern *Dido* class cruisers as had supported Halberd the previous autumn. However, of the seven survivors of the class completed by this time, one was working up and the other six fully committed in the Mediterranean. PQ 18 in September was the first convoy to receive one.[31]

The final innovation was inclusion of a submarine, in this instance *Sturgeon*. This reflected a wider change in submarine dispositions. Since the arrival of *Tirpitz* in January, a permanent patrol of two submarines was maintained in the Frohavet Channel north-west of Trondheim through which German heavy ships set on attacking the PQ route must pass. It was here that *Seawolf* spotted *Tirpitz* when she sortied against PQ 12. By the end of April, extended daylight meant the risk of boats being sighted when they surfaced to charge their batteries became unacceptably high. New patrol areas were accordingly established further north which were at least 100 miles from the Norwegian coast but protected the flank of the PQ route. Although Ultra might in theory help with the optimum positioning of available submarines, there was a vast threat area for the few available boats to cover. There were only ten submarines based in home waters at the start of 1942 and, although numbers were slowly increasing, it was rarely possible to allocate more than five to protection of the PQ route which would leave many gaps for German heavy ships to slip through undetected. Adding a boat to the close escort gave some extra assurance although *Sturgeon* only stayed with PQ 15 for the first four days before moving to one of the new patrol areas. These new arrangements had problems. Two of PQ 15's escorts detected a submarine and attacked, forcing it to the surface, when they found to their horror it was the Polish submarine *Jastrzab*. She was one of the boats allocated to the new areas but 95 miles out of position because she had been unable to get a navigational fix for a week. She was so badly damaged she had to be sunk after the surviving crew were taken off.[32]

PQ 15 also marked the arrival of US Navy support for the PQ convoys although it only lasted a limited period. An American squadron, Task Force 39 (later redesignated 99), under Rear Admiral Robert Giffen, comprising the new battleship *Washington*, the carrier *Wasp*, heavy cruisers *Wichita* and *Tuscaloosa*, and six destroyers had joined the Home Fleet on 3 April. In some respects, this American contribution was a logical extension of the US Navy battlefleet cover in the Western Atlantic which had first been negotiated in the ABC-1 staff talks in early 1941 and then implemented later in the year. However, the specific trigger was a request on 14 March from Churchill to Roosevelt for the US Navy to replace Force H at Gibraltar, enabling the British ships to deploy to the Indian Ocean to support the seizure of Madagascar (Operation Ironclad). Roosevelt responded two days later that the Americans preferred to reinforce the Home Fleet, thus releasing British resources to Gibraltar. Subsequent correspondence confirmed that the force would be more powerful than the British had sought.[33] The rapid American response was not driven solely by Ironclad. It reflected American recognition of the importance of the PQ convoys, the potential wider risks to Atlantic security posed by the German navy redeployment, and the limits to Royal Navy resources, all the subject of discussion between Pound and King since mid-February.[34] *Wasp* did not stay with the Home Fleet. On 9 April, she left Scapa Flow for the Clyde where she picked up a load of Spitfires which she subsequently flew off to Malta from the western Mediterranean. She then conducted a second Malta reinforcement operation before being transferred to the Pacific.

The PQ 15 operation began with a serious accident when Tovey's flagship *King George V* collided with the destroyer *Punjabi* in thick fog, cutting her in half. The destroyer's primed depth charges then exploded, compounding damage to the battleship. *King George V* was under repair at Birkenhead for two months and not fully operational again until the autumn. She was replaced by her sister battleship *Duke of York* and, with *Washington* available from Task Force 39, the heavy covering force remained adequate against any German sortie. Meanwhile, the convoy itself was picked up by German air search late on 30 April when 250 miles south-west of Bear Island. Thereafter it was under regular observation by aircraft or U-boat for the next four days but frequent bouts of poor visibility hampered the Germans in translating this surveillance into successful attacks. A bombing attack by six Ju 88s late on 1 May was 'ragged and very poorly executed' in the face of intense anti-aircraft fire and cost the Germans one aircraft for nil return. However, early on 3 May, an attack by six He 111 torpedo aircraft, sweeping in low during twilight, when the convoy was about 100 miles due south of Bear Island, achieved surprise and sank three supply ships for the loss of three aircraft. The lost cargo included seventy-three tanks, twenty-one aircraft, 101 lorries, two million rounds of ammunition, 600 tons of tin and 175 tons of machine tools. This was the first operational success by the new German air force torpedo-strike unit which had been training assiduously for the last six weeks. It was also the only successful German strike on PQ 15. Thereafter the escort kept air and U-boat attackers at bay and the weather helpfully deteriorated to cover the convoy in the last phase of its passage.[35]

Meanwhile, the parallel inbound convoy, QP 11, left Kola Inlet on 28 April with thirteen merchant ships and a close escort under the command of Bonham-Carter, who was returning after delivering PQ 14. The escort included the cruiser *Edinburgh*, six destroyers and four corvettes. *Edinburgh* was carrying 465 gold ingots, weighing about 4.5 tons, representing a partial Russian payment to the United States government for pre-Lend-Lease war supplies. On the afternoon of 30 April, while patrolling 15 miles ahead of the convoy and about 250 miles north-west of Murmansk, *Edinburgh* suffered two successive torpedo hits from *U 456*, the first portside amidships and the second blowing off her stern as far as 'Y' turret. This was an outstanding attack by Max-Martin Teichart of *U-456* who was down to his last two torpedoes and faced a target zigzagging at high speed. A spread of four torpedoes fired almost simultaneously by *U-88* all missed. Good damage control and heroic efforts by her crew kept *Edinburgh* afloat and she could still steam at slow speed although steering with two remaining outboard screws was erratic. Supported by two destroyers, *Foresight* and *Forester*, detached from the convoy, and joined shortly by the two Russian destroyers, *Gremyaschi* and *Sokrushitelni*, she began the long journey back to Murmansk. Although other vessels, British and Russian, arrived from Murmansk to aid her recovery and help keep further

U-boats at bay, her progress, sometimes under tow and sometimes under her own power, was painfully slow.

On learning of *Edinburgh*'s predicament, Schmundt, who remained German Admiral Arctic Ocean, initially decided to deploy the 8th Destroyer Flotilla in the early hours of 1 May to finish her off. He judged that this prize outweighed current fuel restrictions. However, on reflection, he then re-directed them instead to attack QP 11 with its now depleted escort. The three German destroyers caught up with the convoy in the early afternoon. It was then skirting the icefield 80 miles south-east of Bear Island after successfully evading four U-boats detected by HF/DF and an attack by four torpedo bombers in the course of the morning. The German destroyers made five successive attempts to get at the convoy over four hours between 1345–1745 but were beaten off by the escort in a series of short sharp engagements amidst the ice floes, in which both sides deployed guns and torpedoes, some of the latter exploding against icebergs, adding to the chaos of battle. Although the British ships were far inferior in gunpower and suffered some damage, the only German success was the torpedoing and sinking of a Russian straggler. The remainder of QP 11's voyage to Iceland was relatively untroubled.[36]

German records are not clear whether the 8th Flotilla decision to break off the convoy attack, which had exhausted at least half their ammunition, in favour of targeting *Edinburgh*, now 200 miles to the east, was made locally or by higher command orders. Over the previous 20 hours, there had been debate and some dissension, not for the first or last time, between Admiral Arctic, Group North and the Naval Staff over whether QP 11, the cruiser, or even PQ 15 was the priority for the destroyers. There was concern that taking on *Edinburgh* if her armament was undamaged would be risky. It was. When the Germans found the *Edinburgh* group at 0630 on 2 May, the cruiser disabled *Hermann Schoemann* with her second salvo despite firing in local control and being almost unmanoeuvrable. Thereafter there was a confused and violent fight between the two forces, involving hide and seek in the midst of snow squalls and smokescreens. *Edinburgh* received a further torpedo hit amidships putting her in a sinking condition while *Forester* and *Foresight*, in the absence of the Russian destroyers which had returned to Kola to refuel after less than 24 hours at sea, were both badly damaged by their more heavily armed opponents, Z 24 and Z 25. The Germans achieved a definite advantage with the potential to finish off the three main British units and then despatch the smaller British and Russian vessels assisting *Edinburgh* at their leisure. Instead, the Germans chose to focus on helping the sinking *Hermann Schoemann* before retreating to Kirkenes. This decision to break off the action may have been influenced by a now-acute shortage of ammunition and torpedoes. Overall, the Germans had achieved their objective in sinking *Edinburgh* albeit at the cost of one of their number. The British could claim a moral victory with *Edinburgh*'s firepower and the determination of the destroyers discouraging the Germans from pressing home their attack. Bonham-Carter found it inexplicable they had not despatched the whole British *Edinburgh* recovery force. For their part, in assessing the entirety of their operations against PQ 11, the German Naval Staff judged the results 'excellent'. This reflected their belief that they had sunk *Edinburgh*, damaged two destroyers and probably sunk five transport vessels, more than compensating for the loss of *Hermann Schoemann*.[37]

Given the scale of force the Germans could now deploy against the PQ route, the merchant ship losses suffered by this latest pair of convoys, at 12 per cent for PQ 15 and 8 per cent for QP 11, were not disproportionate when set against Atlantic and Mediterranean convoys subjected to similar levels of attack. Four Atlantic convoys in September 1941 lost more than six ships with Slow 42 losing nineteen out of sixty-five, representing nearly 30 per cent. Convoy MW 10 to Malta in March had all four of its ships sunk, if those finished off on arrival in the Island are included. Losses to the escort included two destroyers sunk and two cruisers and three destroyers damaged.[38] The latest PQ losses were also not prohibitive against available shipping resources. However, the price paid by the escorts was high, a cruiser sunk and four destroyers heavily damaged without taking account of the *King George V* and *Punjabi* incident. *Edinburgh*, one of two expanded 'Town' class, was a valuable fighting unit, by displacement if not armament qualifying as a heavy cruiser, while, in 1942, the gold she was carrying broadly equated to the cost of a replacement. Most of this shipment would eventually be recovered from the bottom of the Barents Sea nearly 40 years later in 1981.

The circumstances of *Edinburgh*'s loss posed questions only partly addressed by Tovey and the Admiralty. From the start of the PQ convoys, Tovey had usually deployed a cruiser in support, primarily to counter the threat posed by the German destroyers at Kirkenes, but generally with considerable freedom to patrol areas adjacent to the convoys while they transited east of Bear Island rather than sticking rigidly within the confines of the escort screen. This freedom contrasted with the approach adopted by Somerville in the Mediterranean. It had advantages in terms of scouting intelligence and creating uncertainty for the Germans. But the *Edinburgh* incident underlined that a lone cruiser was also vulnerable and that high speed and zigzagging did not guarantee immunity to U-boat attack. In this case, Bonham-Carter hoped that his high-speed dash ahead of the convoy would catch one or more surfaced U-boats which HF/DF intercepts showed were gathering in the area. *Edinburgh* had an excellent radar fit, similar Asdic to the destroyers and depth charges. In theory therefore she was as well equipped to hunt U-boats as a destroyer but her value was much greater, rendering the cost/benefit questionable.

*Both Sides Take Stock*

Apart from conclusions specific to PQ 15, both sides now reviewed their wider strategy towards the PQ convoys. The British assessment was initially framed by the completion of Lyttleton's review on 26 April and its subsequent discussion at the Defence Committee three days later.[39] Cripps, now back from Moscow and appointed Lord Privy Seal, attended this meeting. Lyttleton's recommendations drew on five premises. First, Russia would face Germany's main offensive power in 1942. To maintain her confidence and morale and avoid a separate peace, Britain must deliver the maximum possible weaponry. Secondly, Britain faced the choice of either promising 'a large-scale invasion of the continent in 1942' (presumably Sledgehammer) or maintaining a high rate of supply to Russia even at the risk of damaging Britain's own armament programmes. The second option was preferable. Thirdly, supplies should comprise the most effective weapons Britain produced and be delivered in time for the coming summer campaign. Fourthly, any slackening of aid to Russia would undermine the enthusiasm of the British workforce. Finally, the case for increasing tank deliveries was stronger than aircraft deliveries. British-produced tanks could not be deployed against Germany except by invasion of the Continent whereas aircraft could (although this argument rather overlooked significant demands in North Africa and India).

The first two premises were critically important but controversial. This appears to be the only high-level document in this period addressing the linkage between Continental operations and aid and the potential requirement to choose between them. It is not clear how far Lyttleton consulted on these two assumptions or whether he judged they commanded consensus. They were probably a fair reflection of the prime minister's attitude and that of Eden, Attlee and Bevin. However, it is doubtful the chiefs of staff ever accepted that renouncing Sledgehammer in 1942 should necessarily translate into a higher rate of supply to Russia and they certainly resisted consequent damage to Britain's own requirements. Given this lack of consensus across the overall war leadership, it is therefore surprising that these fundamental premises apparently provoked no significant debate in the Defence Committee, the War Cabinet or in the meetings of the chiefs. Instead, discussion focused almost entirely on two points: whether to impose a reduction of 40 per cent in fighter deliveries due to Russia in May and June under the First Protocol; and how far Britain could meet a 50 per cent increase in fighter and tank deliveries sought by the Russians for the first six months of a Second Protocol beginning 1 July. The May/June reduction to meet urgent British requirements in India and the Middle East would follow a current shortfall of 136 aircraft for the period to the end of April. The Defence Committee judged that, given the threat facing Russia from the forthcoming German summer offensive, it was vital to meet First Protocol commitments and the Air Ministry should find other means of meeting the shortfall. Lyttleton judged that tank production was sufficient to support a 50 per cent increase in deliveries from July which would make it easier for the Russians to accept aircraft deliveries staying at their present level. However, Brooke successfully argued that substantial reserves were required for Sledgehammer and the committee therefore deferred any increase for the present.

Apart from the trade-off between 'invasion' and 'supplies', Lyttleton's review made other major assumptions which the Defence Committee and War Cabinet might have tested but did not. The Russians had identified 10.5 million tons of requirements under the proposed Second Protocol covering 12 months from 1 July, of which the United States was prepared in theory to cover 8.3 million tons. However, the Americans calculated that real Russian import capacity was half this, three million tons through the Northern ports and one million via the Persian Gulf. Allowing for 10 per cent losses, this implied a lift requirement of 4.4 million tons. Lyttleton noted that, if the Admiralty convoy limit for the Arctic route, three convoys of twenty-five ships every two months, was accepted and a target of 6000 tons per ship achieved, then 2.7 million tons could be delivered to the Northern ports. If larger convoys became feasible, as the Admiralty had hinted, then the shortfall could be covered as the year progressed.

There were three issues for the British in these projections. First, they did not include British supplies which Lyttleton seemed to feel could be easily absorbed in the larger American total. However, even if these remained at their present level, that would still add a further 10 per cent to the lift requirement. Secondly, if viewed against the delivery record over the last six months, let alone the potential challenges posed by the rising German threat, the projections for the Arctic route looked wildly optimistic. Total tonnage so far reaching the Arctic ports in this period was 320,000 tons, so Russian ability to handle three million tons per year had not been remotely tested. In addition, the average load per ship to date was barely half the American assumption of 6000 tons. Finally, and most important, Britain would bear the major, if not entire, burden and risk in organising and protecting the convoys to deliver these predominately American supplies. Reduced convoy frequency did not greatly reduce this burden since bigger convoys combined with the higher German threat demanded more escorts. The Admiralty currently assessed that each PQ convoy pair now already absorbed three times the anti-submarine escort resources allocated to any Atlantic convoy.[40] The Defence Committee could therefore have questioned whether the escort demands were sustainable in the face of multiple demands elsewhere, not least convoys to Malta. They would soon discover they were not. Furthermore, while for the present, the dominant naval commitment was the Arctic route, protection of the route from North American ports to the Persian Gulf would also fall primarily to the Royal Navy. For the first half of 1942, Britain also had the main responsibility for organising and upgrading transport capacity from the Persian ports into Russia.

Although the Defence Committee appeared at least provisionally to have settled policy on British aid to Russia for the balance of 1942, the subsequent fate of the cruiser *Trinidad* now raised fresh doubts about the viability of the PQ convoys through the next three months. Throughout April, the cruiser *Trinidad* had undergone temporary repairs at Murmansk following her self-inflicted torpedoing during PQ 13. Facilities at Murmansk were primitive but vital parts along with a Royal Navy constructor officer were brought in by *Edinburgh* in the next convoy. Following her undocking in early May, the plan was to make a fast passage to Iceland at the best speed she could manage and then to proceed to the United States for permanent repairs. Tovey planned her extraction as a major operation, positioning four cruisers and four destroyers west of Bear Island under Burrough while the battlefleet provided further cover to the south-westward against any German interference from Trondheim. *Trinidad* duly left Murmansk on the evening of 13 May accompanied by four destroyers, the whole force commanded by Bonham-Carter. The group came under German air surveillance early next day and heavy bombing raids commenced that evening. Numerous attacks were successfully evaded but *Trinidad* was finally hit and set ablaze by a Ju 88 dive-bomber while she was distracted fending off torpedo aircraft. NID subsequently circulated an Ultra intercept describing the sophisticated combined tactics deployed by the six He 111s and three Ju 88s deployed in this attack. Despite valiant efforts to save the cruiser, the fires were soon out of control and she was sunk by the destroyer *Matchless* after taking off her crew. Relentless attacks continued on the destroyers out to a range of 350 miles from the German airfields but they made it to Iceland without further damage.[41]

Bonham-Carter again provided a grim appraisal, fully endorsed by Tovey. He was convinced that until the airfields in North Norway were 'neutralised' and there were 'some hours of darkness', the convoys 'should be stopped'. If they must continue 'for political reasons', 'serious and heavy losses must be expected'. German attacks would 'increase not diminish'. While the Royal Navy were 'paid to do this sort of job', it was arguably asking 'too much' of the Merchant Navy. Warships could use their speed to avoid bombs and torpedoes but a 6- or 8-knot ship could not.[42] Pound needed no persuading of this analysis and must have viewed the loss of *Trinidad* as reinforcing the lesson of Crete and sinking of *Trinidad*'s sister *Fiji* the previous year. Even the best-fought warships could not survive in waters where the enemy enjoyed total air supremacy.

Bonham-Carter's reference to 'political reasons' underlines how deeply embedded was the view among senior officers that the purpose of the convoys was political rather than directly benefitting the British and American war effort. This clearly demonstrated the failure of Britain's war leadership to agree a clear rationale for aiding Russia, and more specifically delivery through the PQ convoys, and then to communicate it. Without this there was a risk that Pound and Tovey, as the officers tasked with implementing the convoys, would focus more on problems than solutions. It was here that Russian attitudes, the constant demands for more, ingratitude for what was delivered at considerable cost, and perceived failure to make a reasonable contribution to convoy protection, were potentially corrosive. If the Russians could not be bothered to help protect the convoys, or at least explain convincingly why they could not, the obvious conclusion seemed that aid was less important than they claimed.

The belief that Tovey over-emphasised the difficulties in running the PQ convoys spurred a deterioration in his relationship with the prime minister during the early months of 1942, although perceived lack of offensive spirit in mounting Anklet and Archery and opposition to Churchill's wider ambitions for Norway were also factors. The result was a determined effort by the prime minister through May and June to replace Tovey, described as a 'stubborn and obstinate man' with 'a naturally negative and unenterprising attitude of mind', with Cunningham. These comments were hardly fair. Tovey had proved himself a fine fighting admiral, at his best combining aggression, determination, personal charm and utter integrity which few others matched. He was a superb leader, able to inspire subordinates, delegate responsibility, and win the respect and confidence of all who served with him. Where perhaps Churchill had a point was that as a 'thinking admiral' he was less impressive. He lacked the mental agility and the technical insight of Somerville. Churchill was also certainly right that he was obstinate. When he was Flag Captain to Admiral Sir John Kelly in the Atlantic Fleet in the early 1930s, the latter famously noted in Tovey's confidential report: 'Captain Tovey shares a characteristic with myself. In my case, I call it tenacity of purpose and in his obstinacy.' However, if Churchill found Tovey stubborn, he was not likely, as he must have known, to find Cunningham easier! Nor, for all his fine qualities would Cunningham have provided deep thinking. In any case, firm resistance from Pound and the First Lord, A V Alexander, ultimately forced the prime minister to back down and Tovey stayed.[43]

Russian assistance to the passage of the PQ convoys was therefore important not only for operational reasons but also strategically and presentationally. Tovey considered that the Russians could support the convoys in five ways. First, by making the Kola Inlet and White Sea approaches unusable by U-boats which Ultra revealed were regularly targeting these areas. The British liaison teams in Murmansk and Archangel were clear the Russians had sufficient local resources to do this. The Royal Navy had also provided Asdic sets and considerable anti-submarine advice. Secondly, the Soviet submarines based at Polyarnoe could take up patrol areas off the north Norwegian coast and help intercept German surface units moving against the convoys. Thirdly, it was essential to have fighter cover to protect the Kola Inlet and the eastern end of the convoy route, ideally out to 200 miles. The Russians had regularly promised this but rarely delivered although pressure from 30 Mission secured the deployment of twenty twin-engine fighters and thirty additional Russian Hurricanes to Vaenga and other northern airfields at the end of February. Fourthly Russian escort vessels were required to supplement Royal Navy forces as far out along the convoy route as their endurance would permit. The Russians appeared to have sufficient ships to allocate three or four to each convoy. Finally, it was essential for Russian bombers to execute interdiction missions against forward German airfields in Norway and Finland when convoy operations were underway.[44]

These requirements had been raised regularly by British liaison staff in the Arctic ports and by 30 Mission since the start of regular convoys in October. The Russian response on all points had been grudging, unreliable and ineffective. Under pressure from Pound, Churchill now raised them directly with Stalin on 9 May before the loss of *Trinidad*.

While emphasising continued British commitment to the convoys, he stressed the growing German threat and the resource burden on the Royal Navy which dangerously weakened Atlantic escorts. He then set out starkly that, if Russia was to receive a 'fair proportion' of material despatched from Britain and the United States, it was essential for Soviet naval and air forces to take prime responsibility for protecting convoys in the area east of 28° East. This was a line running due north from the western tip of Varanger fiord, approximately 100 miles north-west of the mouth of Kola Inlet. Stalin sent an emollient reply to Churchill, promising to implement 'all possible measures' while stressing the limited Soviet resources available in this theatre. He then separately applied pressure on Roosevelt to expedite the delivery of supplies which were of the 'utmost urgency'.[45]

Stalin's attitude to British representations was inevitably influenced by reporting from Golovko and the Russian Naval Staff. This grossly exaggerated the successes of the Northern Fleet and criticised, even disparaged, the performance of the Royal Navy. Golovko claimed that, during the first year of the war in the Northern theatre, the Russians sank 135 enemy ships amounting to 583,400 tons and destroyed 412 aircraft.[46] Post-war analysis reveals that Russian submarines sank twenty-eight ships for about 40,000 tons in this period and it is doubtful either surface ships or aircraft added significantly to this total.[47] Of forty-four U-boats sunk in Arctic waters between June 1941 and May 1945, the Russians were responsible for just two. Both were sunk in the Kara Sea, *U-639* by the submarine *S101* in August 1943 and *U-362* by the minesweeper *T116* in September 1944. Of the remaining forty-two, one sank in an accident, one remains missing fate unknown, two were sunk by American aircraft, and the other thirty-eight were sunk by British ships or aircraft.[48] The British investment in anti-submarine support for the Russian navy therefore delivered little. As to Golovko's aircraft claim, given the small size of the German Arctic air group before March, it seems unlikely the Russians accounted for more than 10 per cent of Golovko's figure. Golovko also accused the Royal Navy of abandoning *Edinburgh* and her gold unnecessarily rather than tow her to a Russian port. Had the British known of this claim, it would have particularly rankled. *Gremyaschi* and *Sokrushitelni* had apparently been ordered to return to *Edinburgh*'s assistance after refuelling and could have rejoined her before her last fight on the morning of 2 May but they failed to appear. Indeed, Rear Admiral Miles provided a stark assessment of Soviet naval performance three days later. On the positive side he noted that personnel were young, well disciplined, tough and good fighters. But they were held back by lack of any sea tradition and a system that discouraged initiative and disparaged foreign help and advice. In operations, the spectacular took precedence over the useful. Routine patrols in support of convoys were therefore disliked. Seamanship and navigation were far below British standards and weapon efficiency only adequate in fair weather. Sea time was the exception rather than the rule, destroyers never refuelled on return to harbour, and paid little attention to readiness.[49]

There was one element of Soviet support that Churchill did not mention in his message to Stalin, no doubt partly because it was working well but also awareness that it was vulnerable to suspicion and misunderstanding. This was the naval intelligence exchange. Uniquely within the overall British–Soviet intelligence relationship, this continued to flourish in the first half of 1942. The most important development was the establishment at the beginning of the year of a SIGINT intercept site as part of the Royal Navy liaison unit at Polyarnoe naval base which was given the rather odd cover name 'Wye Cottage'. This was soon collecting large quantities of German naval and air traffic from northern Norway and the Arctic which was outside the coverage of intercept sites based in the United Kingdom. It was accordingly especially valuable to GC&CS in monitoring the German threat to the PQ convoys. This was initially a local initiative brokered with Golovko but, on 10 February, Rear Admiral Miles briefed Navy Minister Kuznetsov who raised no objection.[50]

Apart from Wye Cottage, another intelligence source of great value in the first half of 1942 was the British Naval Liaison Officer in the Black Sea, Commander Geoffrey Ambrose, who had remained in post despite the difficulties of the previous autumn and enjoyed unique and regular access to Soviet front-line units. He provided insights into Soviet navy capability, comprising doctrine, tactics, competence, manning practices and equipment that were all potentially relevant in understanding the strengths and weaknesses of the Northern Fleet in the Arctic. His geographical location meant he was also in a superb position to report on wider developments on the crucial southern front during the spring and summer of 1942. Once the Germans cut off the Crimea and the Black Sea Fleet withdrew to bases on the eastern shore, Ambrose moved from Sevastopol to Tuapse in November 1941. In January, reflecting his good standing with his Soviet navy counterparts, he was permitted an assistant and, in March, he was joined by a Royal Navy Volunteer Reserve Special Branch officer, Sub Lieutenant Hugh Veysey. The same month Ambrose was promoted acting captain. Their primary role now became the provision of SIGINT material to the Black Sea Fleet, on Axis shipping movements through the Bosphorus and in the western Black Sea, using special communications links to the British naval attaché in Istanbul and Mediterranean Fleet headquarters in Alexandria. This was of high value to the Russians who responded with operational and intelligence summaries on a regular basis as well as technical material on German equipment including acoustic and photomagnetic mines.[51]

The naval mission in Moscow also gleaned some valuable information in this period. This included new detail on the German naval building programme including the status of the fourth *Hipper* class cruiser *Seydlitz* which the Russians had been negotiating to buy before the war. At the beginning of the year, following the outbreak of the Far East war, the Russians contributed some insights on Japanese naval building and, in April, eyewitness accounts of the American 'Doolittle' bombing raid on Tokyo. There were also details of German operations in northern and southern Russia, apparently deriving from SIGINT. A Russian navy report handed over in mid-June provided the text of a German navy signal from Wilhelmshaven to the U-boat base at Kirkenes, raising the possibility that the Russians were reading some high-grade German cipher traffic.[52]

On 15 May, Pound drew on *Trinidad*'s loss to emphasise to the chiefs of staff and the prime minister the risks now facing the PQ convoys. He insisted that the arrival of PQ 15 with only three ships lost was deceptive. *Trinidad*'s sinking demonstrated that, unless bad weather prevented flying, the chances of even a highly manoeuvrable ship, steaming at 18 knots with substantial anti-aircraft armament, avoiding and surviving attack were remote in prevailing daylight and ice conditions. Although increasing the number of escorts had reduced losses to U-boats to an acceptable level, these escorts could not offer similar security against air attack from a substantially increased German strike and reconnaissance force. The low speed of a convoy exposed it to air attack for at least seven days and it was impossible to provide either fighter cover or sufficient anti-aircraft firepower to reduce the threat to an acceptable level. Given this scale and duration of attack, it seemed inevitable that only a small proportion of ships could reach their destination. Pound therefore advocated informing Stalin that, rather than risk losing a whole convoy, it would be better to defer sailings until early July by which time the ice would have receded northward and convoys could be routed further from German airbases. This meant missing the convoys currently planned to depart Iceland on 18 May and 3 June. Pound also emphasised the potential German threat to Spitzbergen and the desirability of establishing a strong deterrent force there.[53] (Over the next three weeks, the chiefs thoroughly reviewed the options for Spitzbergen but ultimately concluded, as they had previously, that the difficulties of establishing and then supporting a substantial military force there outweighed any conceivable benefits. They correctly expected the Germans to reach the same view.[54]) In proposing representations to Stalin, Pound was possibly influenced by Mason Macfarlane's claim made a month earlier that, if the convoys got into trouble, Stalin would be open to arguments for a temporary suspension. On this, Macfarlane's judgement was definitely wrong![55]

Pound aired similar thoughts with Admiral King three days later on 18 May, referring to the Russian convoys as a 'regular millstone round our necks' causing 'steady attrition in both cruisers and destroyers'. They were a 'most unsound' operation with 'the dice loaded against us in every direction'. He acknowledged the necessity of helping the Russians but expressed frustration at not knowing the real impact of aid. If it was not time sensitive, there was an overwhelming case to delay convoys until ice conditions were better. King sympathised and promised to support whatever arguments Pound put forward but emphasised the 'political' imperative and offered no practical support.[56]

The War Cabinet addressed Pound's case for postponement, now endorsed by his fellow chiefs of staff, the same day he wrote to King. Two arguments against deferral were stressed. It would be difficult to make up the deficit from not running two convoys. Even if post-July convoys were increased to fifty ships, this would create handling problems and further delay in Russian ports. It would also be difficult to convince either Stalin or Roosevelt that suspension was justified. It was pointless asking Stalin if the supplies were essential. He was bound to say yes and demand the convoys were fought through whatever the cost. The decision was for Britain to make. The prime minister confirmed a consensus that the May convoy, PQ 16, should sail that night as planned. The Russians were engaged in a 'life or death struggle' against a common enemy. It was Britain's duty to support them. Cancellation would do serious damage to relations with both of Britain's main allies. He added that, as with PQ 15, the results might prove better than feared. Brief consideration was given to restricting the convoy to fast ships but Pound's advice was that all thirty-five ships might as well sail. However, Stalin would be asked to provide air support and specifically to conduct strikes against German airfields.[57]

Churchill duly wrote to Stalin the following day. He confirmed that PQ 16, comprising thirty-five ships, had now departed but faced determined attack from about 100 German bombers. Unless bad weather constrained flying operations, 'we must expect' that 'a large proportion' of ships and supplies 'will be lost'. Much therefore depended on Soviet interdiction of German airfields. He coupled this plea with a warning. If the convoy did suffer heavy losses, it might prove necessary to suspend further convoys until the ice receded northward in July. Stalin responded on 23 May, promising that Soviet air and naval forces would 'to their utmost' protect PQ 16. Twenty Il-4 bombers had accordingly been deployed to the Arctic and would execute 'systematic strikes against enemy airfields in Bardufoss, Svartnesse, Tromsø and Hammerfest from 25 to 29 May'.[58]

Meanwhile, the Germans were also re-assessing options against their experience with the latest convoys. On 12 May, the German Naval Staff assessed that the Western Allies recognised the vital importance of aid to Russia at this time and would therefore increase shipments through the Arctic route. There were already intelligence reports of forthcoming 'super convoys'. Increased convoy traffic would probably be accompanied by a landing or raids in northern Norway in order to prevent German disruption of these supplies. Given Allied shipping constraints, raids were most likely, possibly aimed at specific military targets such as submarine bases. At the beginning of May, the operational surface fleet in Norway potentially capable of operating against either the convoys or an Allied attack comprised *Tirpitz*, *Admiral Scheer*, *Hipper*, six destroyers and six torpedo boats (effectively light destroyers suitable for coastal work). *Scheer*'s sister ship, *Lützow*, was expected in Trondheim in the middle of the month and most of the remaining destroyer force (ten vessels) which was under repair or working up in German waters would become deployable by early June.

The first basing of a heavy unit away from Trondheim began on 9 May when *Scheer* moved with two destroyers to Narvik so as to have a combat force, albeit a 'weak one' in the view of the German Naval Staff, nearer the PQ route, although due to the strength of enemy escorts, it would only deploy if conditions were 'particularly favourable'. Schmundt, as Admiral Arctic Ocean, also now moved from Kirkenes to Narvik, bringing his surviving destroyers, *Z 24* and *Z 25*. A week later it was agreed that *Scheer* would be joined by *Lützow*, with a further two destroyers, to provide a strike force against PQ convoys under the command of Vice Admiral Oskar Kummetz and the overall direction of Group North. Short-range operations as far east as 18° East (approximately a line due north from Tromsø) were envisaged although the ships would avoid engagement with equally strong or superior enemy forces. No action was yet anticipated against the next convoy, PQ 16. The constraints imposed on the new Narvik force provoked some bemusement among its senior officers as to its purpose. Kummetz's chief operations officer, Commander Hansjürgen Reinicke, who had served in the same role under Ciliax through Operation Cerberus, did not see how the pocket battleships, even with their six destroyers, could achieve anything useful in the Arctic in the face of current British power. The pocket battleships' speed was inadequate, their medium-calibre armament 'feeble' and anti-aircraft firepower 'pitiful'. The force could therefore expect a 'severe hammering'.[59]

While the Naval Staff were moving towards more pro-active use of the surface fleet, their expectations of the U-boat force reduced. Looking at recent operations, they concluded that U-boats could only operate on a limited scale during the Arctic summer. Night-attack tactics which had enjoyed so much success in the Atlantic were clearly not feasible. Meanwhile, continuous daylight made it difficult to maintain contact and avoid counter-attack, and the enemy was adept at exploiting the cover of bad weather. Time and again during recent convoys, boats were sighted before they achieved an attack position and were driven off by the escort. Until August, only 'minor and purely accidental' successes were likely. Given these constraints, increasing U-boat numbers offered no advantage.[60] Needless to say, Dönitz was again lobbying hard for redeployment of the Arctic boats. On 3 May, he quoted statistics showing that the Arctic boats had sunk 40,000 tons of shipping in the two months of March and April. An equivalent force in the Atlantic could have sunk 216,000 tons, more than five times as much.[61]

However, the Naval Staff did not favour reduction. Given the importance of the PQ convoy target, sinking even the occasional ship was worthwhile and ten to twelve U-boats must therefore remain in the Arctic Ocean. The case for keeping boats at Trondheim and Bergen was more open since, as Dönitz stressed, their anti-invasion value was negligible and they were needed in the Atlantic. In reaching their conclusions, the Naval Staff did not quote statistics either from Dönitz or elsewhere but these were certainly compelling. During the 10 months up to the beginning of May, thirty-two U-boats had operated in the Arctic theatre, between them conducting about sixty patrols. Twenty-seven PQ convoys had been run since late August (sixteen outbound including Dervish and eleven inbound) comprising 309 merchant and supply ships. Of these, U-boats had sunk just six, one ship every ten patrols and a loss rate less than 2 per cent, with the addition of a cruiser (*Edinburgh*) seriously damaged and a destroyer (*Matabele*) sunk. These gains had cost two U-boats. By the standards currently being set in American waters, these were pitiful results. Here, over the first four months of 1942, an average force of twenty-five boats on station had sunk 336 ships totalling 1.8 million tons. The comparison fully justified Dönitz's argument that the Arctic deployment was a waste of precious U-boat resources.[62]

## The Ordeal of PQ 16

PQ 16 left Hvalfiord in Iceland on 21 May, three days after the War Cabinet decided it should sail. Its cargo included 468 tanks, 201 aircraft and 3277 motor vehicles.[63] The delay in departure reflected the need to assess the implications of the presence of *Scheer* and her destroyers in Narvik, which Ultra revealed on 10 and 11 May, and then uncertainty over *Lützow*'s movements and intentions. In fact, the latter moved in stages up the Norwegian coast arriving in Narvik on 26 May, disclosed by Ultra the previous day and then confirmed by photographic reconnaissance.[64] As agreed by Pound, and in line with the promise to the Americans, PQ 16 comprised thirty-five merchant supply ships, making it easily the largest convoy to date. To speed cargo unloading once it reached Russia, one-quarter of the ships was to proceed to Archangel, now becoming free of ice. In a new innovation, all the merchant ships could stream balloons to hamper low-flying aerial attackers. Warship support was also correspondingly heavy. The close escort covering the convoy for its entire journey, under Commander Richard Onslow in the 'Tribal' class destroyer *Ashanti*, comprised the Anti-Aircraft Ship *Alynbank* (one-third larger than *Ulster Queen* and carrying two more 4in guns), six destroyers, five corvettes, four anti-submarine trawlers and two submarines, all supported by two oilers. Onslow, a future admiral, was one of the outstanding destroyer officers of the war, serving in every major theatre and winning four DSOs. Rear Admiral Burrough with four cruisers and a further three destroyers provided close support as far as Bear Island with the primary task of protecting against any sortie by the German surface units now established at Narvik. Tovey, as usual, provided distant support from a position north-east of Iceland with *Duke of York*, the American *Washington*, *Victorious*, two heavy cruisers and thirteen destroyers, aimed particularly at countering any foray by *Tirpitz* and *Hipper* from Trondheim. Finally, four flying boats from Iceland provided some additional anti-submarine protection for the initial two-thirds of the distance to Bear Island and, as with PQ 15, five submarines were positioned in moving patrol areas designed to keep between the convoy and the German naval bases. Three Soviet boats extended this flank guard eastward.[65]

PQ 16 also introduced an intelligence innovation, the deployment of a small unit in the escort commander's ship *Ashanti* tasked with intercepting and reading German low-grade radiotelephone traffic. This technique, developed between NID and Air Intelligence over the last year, was known as 'Headache'. Headache operators drawn from both services received specialist training and were German speakers. They listened in to aircrew chatter both in the air and on the ground before and after operations, often gleaning valuable warning of forthcoming attack.[66]

PQ 16's parallel inbound convoy QP 12 also sailed on 21 May, leaving the Kola Inlet with fifteen ships including the CAM-fitted *Empire Morn* which had arrived with PQ 15. Its close escort comprised *Ulster Queen*, six destroyers and four anti-submarine trawlers for the entire journey to Iceland but was joined by two Russian destroyers until the convoy reached 30° East, approximately 250 miles due north of Kirkenes. Although the weather was generally good during the first four days of its passage, QP 12 was not sighted by German reconnaissance until the morning of 25 May, by which time the convoy was 280 miles south-west of Bear Island and about to pass the outbound PQ 16. *Empire Morn* catapulted her Hurricane which shot down a shadowing Ju 88 although its pilot, Pilot Officer J B Kendell, was tragically killed when he subsequently bailed out and his parachute malfunctioned. Although more aircraft appeared and shadowed the convoy for a while, no attacks followed and the convoy was also untroubled by U-boats. It therefore arrived intact at Reykjavik on 29 May.[67]

German aerial reconnaissance over Reykjavik and Hafnarfiord on 2 May, which had spotted at least twenty-one merchant ships and three tankers, and subsequent radio traffic, persuaded Group North that PQ 16 would follow the normal fortnightly schedule and reach the vicinity of Jan Mayen Island about the middle of the month. It accordingly began deploying U-boats to this area which it intended then to place under command of Admiral Arctic. A request to 5th Air Fleet to allocate a force to locate and attack any heavy units of the Home Fleet providing distant escort was rejected because there were no aircraft to spare. Group North felt this underlined the present weakness of the German air force which was clearly inadequate to meet even essential commitments. Meanwhile it also asked Admiral Arctic to consider the feasibility of deploying *Scheer* and *Lützow* from Narvik against the convoy but stressed this must only be contemplated if air reconnaissance guaranteed no enemy battleships, carriers or cruisers providing remote or close escort. The failure of PQ 16 to appear on schedule provoked some puzzlement compounded by failure to find any sign of a westward convoy either. In the event, it was only on the morning of 25 May therefore that the two convoys were finally sighted in close proximity and their respective size and escort strength correctly reported. However, German commanders were initially uncertain whether they were seeing a cross-over between inbound and outbound convoys or the coming together of an anticipated 'super convoy'. The latter possibility confused the German picture over the next few days and helped feed inflated claims by the 5th Air Fleet.[68]

PQ 16 suffered its first two air attacks by a total of thirty-three aircraft during the evening of 25 May, beginning 12 hours after the first German sighting. These foreshadowed a running fight with successive waves of aerial attackers over the next five days. The initial attacks were beaten off with only one merchant ship suffering minor damage although it obliged her return to Iceland. The defence was assisted by Burrough's cruiser force which had joined the close escort that morning after scouting forward to a position midway between Iceland and Bear Island. A Hurricane was also launched by the CAM Ship *Empire Lawrence* and brought down at least one Ju 88. Despite 5th Air Fleet plans for a concentrated assault on 26 May, there was only one ineffective attack that day by thirteen aircraft in the evening after Burrough's force had departed. The main threat on this day came from multiple U-boat attacks conducted by the six boats deployable out of nineteen currently based in Norwegian waters. These sank one merchant ship but were otherwise kept at bay by the escort. *U-591* fired a three-torpedo spread at Onslow's *Ashanti* but missed while *U-436* was badly damaged by depth charges and had to limp back to Narvik. Group North again stressed to 5th Air Fleet that the pocket battleships would only deploy from Narvik if air reconnaissance gave an absolute guarantee of no enemy battleships or carriers in the vicinity.

The main damage to the convoy began at 1115 on 27 May when it was skirting the edge of the ice field 80 miles south-east of Bear Island. Over the next ten hours, 108 aircraft (ninety-five Ju 88s, eight He 111s and five He 115s) executed dive-bombing and torpedo attacks in successive waves and sank six ships, including *Empire Lawrence*, while three were damaged along with the Polish-manned destroyer *Garland*. These successes cost the Germans just three aircraft. Meanwhile, the five remaining U-boats in the vicinity of the convoy also attempted attacks but found it difficult to get close enough in the generally excellent visibility and calm sea and were again driven off. One boat was also attacked by dive-bombers and lucky not to be hit. At the end of this day, with 20 per cent of the convoy ships and a quarter of the overall cargo lost, including 147 tanks, 37 aircraft and 770 vehicles, several ships damaged, three more days to run, and ammunition running short, prospects looked grim. However, the next morning brought the welcome reinforcement of three Russian destroyers, Group North withdrew the U-boats to meet a possible invasion threat, and the Germans did not maintain the tempo or intensity of their air attacks. The reduced German air effort probably reflected the impact of Soviet air support in line with Stalin's promise to Churchill. The Russians claimed to have mounted 1055 sorties against Banak, Petsamo and Kirkenes between 21 and 31 May, the vast majority from 28 May onward. From early on 30 May, they also provided fighter cover over both convoy arms, deploying a total of sixteen Pe-3s and seventy-six Hurricanes. Russian estimates of twenty-three German bombers and twelve fighters destroyed in these operations were undoubtedly much exaggerated. German records acknowledge only limited strikes on the airfield at Kirkenes and 'Pe 2 fighter-bombers' covering the convoys in their final approach. Nevertheless, at a minimum, Russian activity was evidently a significant distraction. Despite generally good flying conditions, the Germans mounted only ninety-six sorties against PQ 16 over the three days 28–30 May which inflicted no further damage. On the evening of 29 May, the convoy divided with six ships along with *Alynbank* and one destroyer proceeding to Archangel and the rest to Murmansk.[69]

Commander Onslow made several recommendations, mainly related to countering the air threat, most of which were applied to future convoys, although some took time to implement. He stressed the importance of more fighters, provided either in an auxiliary carrier or a large number of CAM Ships, to eliminate shadowers and disrupt raids. *Alynbank* had proved her worth against dive-bombers but more specialist anti-aircraft ships were needed and as many destroyers as possible should be capable of high-angle fire. Once Burrough's cruisers departed, PQ 16 had just two ships fitted with long-range search radar, with only *Alynbank* able to provide this cover after *Empire Lawrence* was sunk. More sets were needed. The duration of exposure to air attack risked ammunition stocks running dangerously low so ways must be found to carry more reserves. Finally, he suggested including specialist rescue ships and a salvage tug equipped for fire-fighting. In supporting Onslow's recommendations, Tovey was agreeably surprised that, given the scale of attack, four-fifths of PQ 16 ships had got through, a success 'beyond expectation'. He rightly praised an outstanding performance by the escort and the courage and determination of the merchant ships.[70]

If Tovey was surprised, the Germans, initially at least, were euphoric. 5th Air Fleet grossly overestimated the damage inflicted, claiming thirteen merchant ships sunk, a further five together with a destroyer (*Garland*) probably sunk, and up to twenty-five damaged, with two more ships sunk and another set on fire during a raid on Murmansk. The overestimation partly reflected the conviction, stemming from the original first sighting of PQ 16 and QP 12 together, that PQ 16 was a super convoy of fifty ships. Ships missing from this total as the convoy neared the Russian ports were therefore chalked up as 'sunk'. The Naval Staff, although they suspected these claims might be too high, judged the action against PQ 16 an 'outstanding success' which would have considerable impact, direct and indirect, on future PQ traffic. It would also relieve the threat to Norway since the enemy had learnt the risk of bringing even a strong expeditionary force within range of the German air force.[71]

Meanwhile, four factors had conditioned German decisions regarding PQ 16 of which the British were not aware, at least not immediately. These all exerted influence over the next convoy, PQ 17. The first was the continuing German fear of invasion. On 26 May, the Naval Staff were informed by OKW Supreme Command that an 'agent' report suggested an imminent enemy landing in Norway. By the following day, Hitler had personally ordered all U-boats outbound from German ports to be redirected to Narvik. The Naval Staff advised OKW that, out of nineteen U-boats currently based in Norway, only seven were immediately operational, the five deployed against PQ 16 and two more at Trondheim. They also assumed that, if a large-scale British operation was underway, the entire Home Fleet would be at sea. It made no sense for German forces to risk battle against a superior enemy and all forces in the invasion area must therefore remain on the defensive. Group North accordingly reaffirmed that the Narvik surface group should not deploy against PQ 16 for the present but come to three hours' notice. If it became certain British heavy units had withdrawn westward, this group would move via inshore waters up to Altafiord, south-west of North Cape, and sortie against the convoy from there.[72] The inflated German air force claims of the destruction wreaked on PQ 16 on 27 May persuaded both Hitler and OKW that any immediate invasion risk had ended and that U-boat deployment could revert to normal. Almost simultaneously, the Abwehr advised that agents radioing in from England confirmed the abandonment of the invasion plan.[73] The air successes also persuaded Group North that deploying the Narvik force was unnecessary. In any case, the presence of British heavy forces had not been categorically ruled out. The 'invasion scare' certainly provoked confusion, briefly disrupted some Atlantic U-boat movements and effectively prevented a surface sortie which was always unlikely. Otherwise, the only practical result was the suspension of U-boat operations against PQ 16 by Group North on the morning of 28 May but by then the chances of further sinkings was low.

The agent report referred to by OKW derived from Germany's military intelligence service, the Abwehr. On 19 May, it reported that, at Dunfermline on the Firth of Forth, strong commando forces were being embarked, with artillery and technical units. On the following day, a further report stated that a landing would take place in Norway three days later.[74] These reports derived from a British deception operation executed by a unit known as 'Future Operational Planning Section' (FOPS) of the Joint Planning Staff led by Colonel Oliver Stanley with a small team including the future thriller writer Denis Wheatley. Stanley had worked up a scheme, code-named 'Hardboiled', designed to suggest a landing in Norway notionally timed for early May which the chiefs of staff authorised on 28 February. The plans for this fictitious landing were developed in considerable detail. The apparent objective was to seize the port of Stavanger and the adjacent airfields of Forus and Sola. The assault force supposedly comprised two armoured regiments and three infantry brigade groups which would be followed up by three divisions and appropriate supporting forces including a major air group. The choice of Stavanger reflected earlier guidance from the chiefs that the fictitious landing must be sited south of Trondheim so as not to conflict with possible genuine raids in the North, following up Archery and Anklet.[75]

Hardboiled was allowed to exploit the Royal Marine Division based in Scotland to inject realism, there was extensive contact with Norwegian forces in the United Kingdom and, crucially, some use made of double agents under the control of the Security Service MI5. However, Stanley was not told of the existence of double agents, let alone of the double agent network, by now known as the 'Double-Cross System' and operated by the 'Twenty Committee'. Nor did he know that much Abwehr communications was monitored by GC&CS. He knew only that MI5 had 'special means' to convey information to enemy intelligence if required. This was a pity because greater awareness of Double-Cross and its limitations might have made Hardboiled more effective. Although much Abwehr traffic, both in hand cipher and using Enigma, could now be read, it was invariably hard to judge what influence or impact a specific double agent report generated. Assessment within Abwehr headquarters was rarely visible and onward dissemination to OKW and then to senior military commands was usually by landline which could not be intercepted by GC&CS.[76]

There is no evidence that Hardboiled was directed specifically at assisting PQ operations and it is unlikely Stanley was even aware of convoy timings. It seems that the operation was viewed as a potentially useful and wider deception complement to genuine Continental raiding operations or bigger projects like Sledgehammer, although at this time there was no shortage of sceptics regarding its benefits. The link to PQ 16 provoked by the 'agent' reports initiated on 19 May was thus almost certainly fortuitous. It is unclear why the supposed invasion was both 'launched' by double agents and then reported 'abandoned' all within the space of a week. Perhaps FOPS decided this specific deception, which absorbed significant resources, could not be sustained for longer. For it seems that Hardboiled had become effectively a 'rolling operation' from mid-March to late May with FOPs sowing reports of imminent landings at regular intervals. In a review of strategic deception produced by the joint planners in mid-June, they claimed that Hardboiled had achieved 'considerable success', convincing the Germans that a landing in Norway was probable and provoking significant reinforcement.[77] However, it is not clear what evidence the planners had to justify this claim. As already described, Hitler's fears for Norway and German reinforcement preceded the launch of Hardboiled although it is plausible it made the perceived threat more credible. Certainly, German naval records have several references to 'agent warnings' across this period. An invasion alarm issued by Group North on 30 March deriving from the Finnish military attaché in Stockholm, apparently reporting from contacts on London, was probably initiated by FOPS although on this occasion it had no visible impact on subsequent German actions.[78] The number of Abwehr warnings also provoked scepticism in senior German naval circles. Ciliax, his successor Admiral Otto Schniewind, Rear Admiral Gerhard Wagner, Head of Operations in the Naval War Staff, and Vice Admiral Kurt Assmann, Head of the Historical Section in the Naval High Command and an important confidant of Raeder, were all suspicious of British 'deception'. However, there was reluctance to push these doubts for fear of questioning the Führer's judgement.[79]

Equally unclear is how much the Admiralty and Tovey engaged with Hardboiled and whether it exerted any influence on a quite separate deception operation they were sponsoring by the last week of April. Both were copied the original Hardboiled proposals and asked to play their part in making the invasion appear credible. The naval member of Double-Cross, Commander Ewen Montagu, was privy to the operation and would have briefed the DNI, still Rear Admiral John Godfrey, who may in turn have mentioned it to Ultra-cleared senior members of the Naval Staff. Pound was already aware from the February discussion with the chiefs of staff. It would be logical if this triggered thoughts on how deception might be applied more specifically in support of the PQ convoys. What is certain is that, by 25 April, the Admiralty, represented by Godfrey and Rear Admiral Arthur Power, the Assistant Chief of the Naval Staff (Home), together with Tovey had approved a plan proposed by MI5 and Montagu and designated 'Spider' to exploit Abwehr radio sets and agents captured at Iceland with the trawler *Arctic* and following a landing from *U-252* early on 6 April. (*U-252* survived only another eight days. En route to France, she ran into a convoy outbound from Gibraltar which she reported. Her signal was D/Fd and she was destroyed by the 36th Escort Group led by the famous Commander Johnny Walker.[80]) The aim of 'Spider' was to lure the German naval command into a false sense of security regarding the whereabouts of the Home Fleet covering force during the transit of PQ 16 from mid-May.[81] For various reasons this was not implemented but, by the last week of May, it had translated into a more ambitious deception plan to suggest an imminent landing in Norway, which also exploited Double-Cross agents in Iceland, and was to be implemented in parallel with the next convoy, PQ 17.[82]

The second factor bearing on German decisions was the patchiness of their air force reconnaissance. They missed the sailing of QP 12 and then failed to pick this convoy up, despite generally good weather, as it navigated round northern Norway. The initial ambiguity caused by sighting QP 12 and PQ 16 in close proximity early on 25 May was never satisfactorily resolved. Subsequent sightings produced a muddled picture leading to a conviction that PQ 16 comprised at least fifty ships but had also divided into at least two parts by the end of that day. This contributed to the exaggerated claims for ships sunk. When twenty-eight ships were correctly counted on 28 May, it was assumed twenty-two had probably been destroyed. The belief that 50 per cent of PQ 16 had been destroyed, after adding ships believed sunk in Murmansk, fed a German ambition now to destroy an entire convoy and thus effectively end the PQ traffic. The Germans also failed to pinpoint the whereabouts of the Home Fleet. The hard reality they faced here was that, if Tovey remained more than 200 miles from Bear Island, the sea area to be swept was too large for the limited air resources to have much hope of finding him. If the British had recognised these reconnaissance failings, they might have taken encouragement from increasing scope for convoy evasion as the ice receded and have focused more effort on additional CAM Ships to despatch shadowers. They might also have seen advantage in 'showing' the Home Fleet closer to Bear Island.[83]

The third factor concerned U-boat performance where once again Dönitz offered a scathing assessment. PQ 16 had confirmed the limited prospects for success against the Arctic convoys especially in summer conditions. In addition to constant daylight, Dönitz noted the variable weather and visibility, abnormally strong escorts, clever handling of the convoy, and the appearance of Russian aircraft which obliged U-boats to dive on sighting German aircraft too. Despite effective shadowing and determined attack efforts, the net result for six U-boats deployed had been one ship sunk and four probable hits (in reality none). These meagre results had resulted in depth-charge damage to five boats, all of which would probably require considerable time in dockyard hands. The success of these British anti-submarine measures was exacerbated by limited repair facilities both in Norway and Germany which meant more than 50 per cent of U-boats operating in Arctic waters were likely to be unfit for service if the PQ campaign continued.[84]

The German Naval Staff insisted, however, that the now paramount importance of the PQ target required a continuing U-boat effort of at least eight boats per convoy despite the unfavourable conditions. The staff reiterated that even occasional sinkings made a useful contribution while the U-boats also played an essential role in shadowing convoys and guiding the air force to targets. This requirement justified the inevitable loss to Atlantic operations. Three additional U-boats were being despatched from Germany to bring total strength in Norwegian waters to twenty-two and ensure the desired aim of eight boats per convoy. To conserve effort, U-boats would also now only operate against the empty QP convoys sailing westward when this could be linked with PQ operations. Further reinforcement up to forty or fifty boats was ruled out because of the inevitable impact on other theatres. Figures for overall U-boat deployment on 29 May, as the PQ 16 operation was coming to an end, underline the opportunity cost for Dönitz of maintaining the Arctic force. There were twenty boats in the Mediterranean, the same as the Arctic, and fifty-six in the Atlantic. However, although in theory the Atlantic had nearly three times the number in each of the other theatres, half of these Atlantic boats were in transit, with just twenty-two actually on patrol off the American coast and in the South Atlantic and only six operating against the crucial North Atlantic lifeline.[85]

The final factor brought to the fore during the PQ operation was the use of Altafiord as a forward operational base for heavy surface units to operate against the PQ convoys. The centre of this fiord was located about 180 miles north-east of Narvik and 100 miles south-west of North Cape. Altafiord offered the Germans several operational advantages. Facing north, it was significantly closer to the PQ route than Narvik, where it was necessary to exit south-west through Vest Fiord. Situated on approximately the same longitude as Bear Island, it was also ideally sited to interdict convoys while they were proceeding to the east of that line. The fiord itself provided a large expanse of protected water, about 24 miles by 5, ringed by mountains and covered at its mouth by islands offering multiple exit routes. Fighter protection from Banak and Kirkenes was within easy reach. Its potential was spotted in February and, on 4 March, Group North ordered berths to be prepared for two heavy ships and a destroyer flotilla, although at this time its role was apparently to support a potential landing operation on the Rybachiy peninsula rather than PQ interdiction.[86]

The idea of using Altafiord as a base from which to target the PQ convoys was first suggested by Ciliax, still Commanding Admiral Battleships, at the end of April. He favoured moving *Scheer* and her destroyers, together with the supply ship *Dithmarschen*, to Alta via Narvik. Once there, she would come under the tactical command of Admiral Arctic Ocean. The intent was evidently to reinforce the 8th Destroyer Flotilla at Kirkenes with *Scheer* providing a counter to Royal Navy cruiser escorts. In the event, shortage of fuel confined *Scheer* to Narvik.[87] A month later on 22 May, Group North and Fleet Commander Admiral Otto Schniewind agreed that Alta was a better base than Narvik for operations against the PQ convoys. This followed staff analysis which showed that, during convoy operations, the Home Fleet distant heavy covering force generally operated along the Faeroes–Bear Island line and, importantly, had never yet crossed east of the Spitzbergen–Lofoten line. The east and westbound convoys were directed so that they could enjoy simultaneous protection from the same distant covering force. There were thus good prospects for success if the German heavy units were moved as far north as possible in good time for interception but also with minimum risk of detection. From there, they could reach a convoy in the Barents Sea in a few hours, especially as ice conditions in June meant convoys must pass at a range of 220–240 miles from German air and naval bases. June would be especially suitable for a surprise attack, partly because continuous daylight facilitated reconnaissance but also because the frequency of fog was low compared with July.[88]

*A Watershed Moment*

These factors conditioning the German perspective on PQ 16 now combined with other developments to make the completion of this operation a watershed moment for all parties involved in the PQ traffic. The arrival of PQ 16 coincided with the conclusion of the Battle of Kharkov, an overwhelming Russian defeat which lost them perhaps thirty divisions, 1200 armoured vehicles, 540 aircraft and 2000 guns.[89] Allied supplies were needed more than ever to fill the material deficit. The continuing significance of Allied tank supplies in particular is demonstrated by over 21 per cent of Russian armour at Kharkov comprising British Matilda IIs and Valentines. The Matildas participated in some nasty surprises for the Germans in the initial Russian attacks over 12–14 May. Kharkov also marked the operational debut of the American Lee medium tank which now equipped 114th Tank Brigade. As usual, Soviet assessments of the Lee were mixed. They found the design distinctly odd and the profile far too tall. It was inferior to the T-34 in armour but more durable and reliable and its 75mm gun comparable.[90] The importance of Western tanks at this time was also shown when the Russians created their first two 'Tank Armies' at the beginning of June, which were designed to underpin future offensive operations. 5th Tank Army had eighty-eight Matilda IIs in an overall strength of 439 tanks. If the 159 'near useless' light T-60s are excluded, the Matilda share of medium/heavy strength was just over one-third, even if this substantial presence of slow and under-armed tanks in a premier unit also demonstrated that the Red Army had some way to go in creating an effective 'Deep Battle' force. Perhaps not surprisingly therefore, 5th Tank Army lost three quarters of its tanks, including fifty-one Matildas, during the fierce battle around Voronezh six weeks later.[91]

For the Germans, Kharkov left them ideally placed to mount their own summer offensive, Plan Blue, whose launch was now just four weeks away. They accordingly had every incentive to cut the northern aid route once and for all – hence the increasing priority OKW placed on this task in directives to the Naval Staff and 5th Air Fleet. The British not only remained gloomy about unacceptable losses but were struggling to find escort resources for three convoys every two months in the face of demands to meet a dire situation in the Mediterranean and adequately to resource the Indian Ocean where they had just mounted a major effort (Operation Ironclad) to seize Madagascar. The Americans, for their part, were beginning to recognise that current promises to the Soviets would be hard to reconcile with continuing ambitions for Sledgehammer. All of these issues influenced the visits of Soviet Foreign Minister Molotov to London and Washington which occurred almost simultaneously with the passage of PQ 16.

## Chapter 7

# PQ 17: The Germans Seek a Decisive Victory

Molotov's visit to the Western capitals originated with Roosevelt's invitation to Stalin of 11 April 1942 with its veiled hint that the primary purpose was to discuss a 'second front'. Promoting this was certainly a key Soviet objective but Stalin well understood that it required British support which looked distinctly doubtful. Stalin also had a second goal, the conclusion of the comprehensive Anglo–Soviet political treaty which had been under negotiation for six months and which he hoped would incorporate recognition of Russia's June 1941 borders. By early May, Churchill and the Cabinet were reluctantly willing to concede Soviet control of the Baltic states, subject to a right of emigration, but were refusing concessions over Poland's borders which effectively acknowledged Russia's gains under the Nazi-Soviet Pact. Stalin recognised these issues might only be resolved face to face. London therefore became as important a focus for Molotov as Washington and, in any case, the logistics of wartime air travel virtually demanded stopovers in the United Kingdom in both directions.

*The Politics of Molotov's Visit and Russia's Prospects Reassessed*
Molotov, flying in a new Russian TD-7 four-engine bomber, landed in Dundee on 20 May and then travelled to Chequers, meeting Maisky, whom he cordially disliked, en route. The previous day Churchill had notified Stalin of the imminent departure of PQ 16, stressing again the importance of Soviet assistance and warning that heavy losses would mean suspension of further convoys until the ice receded. The continuing provision of supplies through the Arctic was therefore an abiding theme in the background as treaty talks progressed. After four days, these were completely stalled. The British refused further concessions and produced a new draft treaty which provided for a wartime alliance and 20-year pact of mutual assistance and post-war collaboration while avoiding territorial

issues. Molotov forwarded this to Stalin, describing it as 'unacceptable', 'an empty declaration', which rendered returning to the United Kingdom after Washington pointless. He did not get the expected response. Instead of endorsing Molotov's advice, Stalin told him to accept the British offer subject to trivial amendments, claiming that the territorial demands were not essential since these would ultimately be settled by force. Several factors probably drove this shift in Stalin's position. He calculated that further pressure on the territorial issue would be counterproductive, undermining trust not only in London but even more in Washington where the Roosevelt administration was resolutely opposed to such concessions. Given the emerging collapse at Kharkov and in the Crimea, this was no time to risk undermining Western support and the prospects of the all-important second front. Churchill's latest message was also a sharp reminder that continuation of the PQ convoys was not a given. He may also have judged that the new treaty ended any prospect of a separate Anglo–German peace. At any rate, Molotov now left for Washington with Anglo-Soviet relations on a more positive footing than at any time since the start of Barbarossa. This was underlined in a cordial exchange between Churchill and Stalin on 27/28 May with the latter promising to do all possible to protect the convoys.[1]

In Washington, Roosevelt began with a pitch for a post-war 'international police force' of the victor powers, which he hinted the United States and Russia would dominate, another transparent attempt to promote a special relationship with Stalin which sidelined Churchill. Molotov was encouraging but non-committal, focusing instead on his priority – a second front in 1942, sufficient to draw off forty German divisions. Roosevelt in return offered the six to ten-division Sledgehammer which he acknowledged posed risks with 'no guarantee of success'. However, it was necessary to make sacrifices to help Russia in 1942 even if it meant another 'Dunkirk' and the loss of 120,000 men. He omitted the obvious point that most of those sacrificed would be British Empire forces. Harriman later admitted this concept of Sledgehammer as 'a sacrifice for the common good' had some traction. It reflected Roosevelt's sensitivity that the Red Army lost 'eight Ivans for every Allied soldier killed in battle'.[2] However, Molotov was not impressed by Sledgehammer which in Roosevelt's telling had anyway departed significantly from the original concept. Pressed to make a more ambitious commitment, Roosevelt, with reluctant acquiescence from a worried Marshall, authorised Molotov to tell Stalin that 'we expect the formation of a second front this year'. In the final communiqué, this became 'full understanding was reached' on 'the urgent task of creating a second front in Europe in 1942'. This was deliberately ambiguous. It could be interpreted to mean that either the task was urgent or that an invasion would be mounted.[3]

Roosevelt undoubtedly saw Russia's survival as critical, emphasising again to Morgenthau on 16 June that 'whether we win or lose the war depends upon the Russians'.[4] He also knew that a full-scale invasion in 1942 was impossible but apparently judged that 'encouragement, even when based on false premises, would stiffen the Soviet will'. Unfortunately, given the fate of the PQ convoys over the coming months, he now compounded the deception. At the beginning of May, King expressed doubt over whether the proposed Second Protocol goal of delivering 4.4 million tons of aid to Russia over the year from 1 July was feasible and got the American–British Joint Staff Planners to conduct a review. No doubt reflecting input from Pound who visited Washington at the end of April, King noted the general shortage of shipping, the increasing difficulties on the PQ route and the demands of Bolero. The joint planners not only absorbed these points but also the growing loss rate on the PQ route and the impossibility of increasing escorts without robbing those needed elsewhere. Their stark conclusion was that the allocation of shipping 'to transport 4.4 million tons of shipping to Russia will, of necessity, curtail some other war effort'. King and Marshall briefed the president on this on 31 May, the day after Molotov's arrival.[5]

Roosevelt accordingly now proposed to Molotov that non-military supplies under the Second Protocol be reduced from 2.3 million tons to just 700,000 tons to accelerate supplies to the second front. As Hopkins recorded the meeting, Roosevelt repeated that 'we expected to set up a second front in 1942', but every ship shifted to 'the English run' made the second front 'much closer to being realised'. 'Ships could not be in two places at once' and the Soviets 'could not have their cake and eat it'.[6] Roosevelt's proposed reduction in supplies appeared plucked from thin air but, surprisingly, Stalin did not demur and seems, at least briefly, to have viewed it as a signal that commitment to an early second front was genuine. By contrast, Molotov was sceptical, rightly fearing there would be neither a second front nor sufficient supplies. When Roosevelt argued that reducing supplies would bring the 'second front' closer, Molotov retorted that the 'second front' would be stronger if the 'first front' stood fast. He hoped that non-military items in particular would not be cut. Metals, factory machinery of all types and railway materials were essential to sustaining the present Russian front line.[7] Molotov's scepticism was borne out when he returned to London. Mentioning Roosevelt's reference to a 'second Dunkirk' to Churchill provoked an explosive response – 'we shall not win the war by doing such stupid things'. The prime minister would resign rather than undertake an operation with no chance of success which would not help the Russians.[8]

At the end of their meetings on 10 June, Churchill presented Molotov with an 'aide-memoire', largely drafted by Ismay but with input from the chiefs of staff. This emphasised how Britain was already taking the weight off Russia, thus putting the role of a future second front in better perspective. It made four core points. First, it reaffirmed Britain's commitment to providing aircraft, tanks and other vital war supplies via the Arctic and Persian routes. Britain was also willing to enhance the security of the Arctic route by deploying fighter and bomber units to the Murmansk region and to review options for a joint operation against Petsamo. Secondly, Britain was already engaging substantial German forces. Across the various war theatres, Britain currently contained one-half of Germany's fighter strength and one-third of her bombers. Bombing German cities and industries and air operations over occupied France would pull further German air resources from the Eastern Front. Meanwhile, in Libya, Britain confronted eleven Axis divisions including two German armoured divisions and a German motorised division while, for the last four months, Malta had absorbed 400 front-line German aircraft. Thirdly, there would be a programme of raids at various points on the Continent during the summer designed to keep the Germans under pressure and prevent any reduction in the current thirty-three divisions garrisoning Western Europe. Finally, the paper dampened the expectations aroused by Roosevelt for a 'second front' in 1942, mainly by emphasising preparation for an ambitious invasion in 1943, 'unlimited' in scope. Preparations for a landing in the current year would continue but its viability depended on sufficient specialised landing craft, the overall military situation in late summer, and whether its prospects were 'sound and sensible'. No promises could therefore be made.[9]

In stressing how much Britain was tying down German air strength, the paper highlighted a key component of the 'wear-down' strategy which Britain had begun to articulate in September 1940 and then evolved at the Riviera and Arcadia summits. Given the constant Soviet pleas for more fighter aircraft that emerged over the rest of the year, it could have argued more forcefully that this already amounted to a 'second front'. Over the remaining seven months of the year German aircraft losses in the West exceeded those on the Eastern Front by 6.7 per cent.[10] The case was even stronger when the growing potential of the bombing campaign was added, with the first 1000-bomber raid by the Royal Air Force upon Cologne taking place 10 days previously. The demands of air defence were now impacting significantly on German arms production priorities. The share of fighters in her military aircraft production, one-quarter in 1940, was now one-third and outstripping bombers with obvious implications for offensive power in the East. Another telling statistic is that, of 19,713 88mm and 128mm dual purpose anti-aircraft and anti-tank guns that Germany produced between 1942 and 1944, all but 3,172 were allocated to air defence, thereby sharply reducing supplies of a critical weapon for the Eastern Front ground war. By 1944 anti-aircraft arms production equalled that of all arms produced in 1941.[11] Furthermore, while it is doubtful the paper's references to the North African campaign cut much ice with Molotov and Stalin, in mid-1942 the British contribution was significant. Not only did the Mediterranean now absorb about 18 per cent of German fighter strength but North Africa absorbed a disproportionate share of German armour including some of their latest tank models. Germany lost 2480 tanks on the Eastern Front in 1942 but 563 in North Africa or 18.5 per cent of total armour losses. That armour expended in North Africa would have made a huge difference in Russia this year.[12]

The paper could also have emphasised the overall scale and value of the military equipment transfers Britain had already made as the First Protocol drew to a close. With the arrival of PQ 16, Britain had shipped around 1500 Hurricanes of which 1300 had arrived. This transfer represented about 16 per cent of British fighter production over the year to end June 1942. One thousand five hundred fighters were a slightly higher proportion of Soviet production in this period, perhaps 21 per cent, with the 1300 arrivals adding about 18 per cent to domestic production. The attrition rate for the Hurricane force was colossal and, on 1 July, their front line within the Soviet air force was just 200 aircraft although there were many more in the PVO air defence regions and serving with the Northern Fleet. July probably marked the peak of Hurricane deployment in the air force front line where they now equipped eight regiments. That month Hurricanes made a significant contribution on the southern front in the battles approaching the river Don where they furnished four regiments, nominally eighty-eight aircraft at full strength. With two regiments of P-39 Airacobras, Western fighters comprised about 15 per cent of Russian fighter strength on the entire southern front at the start of the German Blue offensive. Although outclassed by the latest German fighters, the Hurricanes destroyed twenty-nine enemy aircraft in the first five days of July and over the whole month achieved a kill to loss rate of at least 2:1. The value of Western fighters here is demonstrated by the scale of Soviet fighter losses in the first two months of Blue with the force reduced to just 172 when the Stalingrad assault commenced at the end of August – hence the desperate pleas from Stalin for more fighters.[13] Medium tank shipments up to PQ 16 were about 1800 of which 1400 had arrived. This transfer was 25 per cent of British and 22.5 per cent of Soviet heavy/medium tank production over the same period, with the 1400 arrivals adding at least 17 per cent to domestic production. Importantly, Soviet production of fighters and heavy/medium tanks only just balanced losses in this period. Lend-Lease supplies therefore provided a vital surplus, enabling front-line strength to grow, albeit slowly.[14]

The aide-memoire coincided with the circulation of a Joint Intelligence Committee assessment on the future course of the Russian campaign and its implications. It was the most comprehensive study of the Eastern Front produced in 1942 to date and read closely by Churchill who made numerous comments in red pen but judged it overall 'a very good appreciation'. He ordered it to be circulated to all War Cabinet ministers, members of the Defence Committee and for the fullest version possible to go to overseas commanders. He regarded all prophecy as dangerous but the committee were right to attempt it.[15] As usual, Ultra gave the committee a more accurate picture of the German than the Soviet order of battle. Their breakdown of German army units was almost exactly right but they overestimated German air strength in the East by 25 per cent which the prime minister queried.[16] Overall, they correctly judged that Germany could not generate the same overall strength as she had the previous year and would therefore focus her effort in the south. Despite her losses, she remained a formidable fighting machine, superior to the Russians in the practice of armoured warfare and combined operations. However, the Russians probably had greater numbers, were at least adequately equipped from their eastern industries, had grown in experience and could afford to trade space. The committee therefore expected the Germans to make initial gains but, by late August, to be held broadly on the line Voronezh to Rostov, 200 miles short of Stalingrad and the Volga and well short of the Caucasus oilfields they were targeting. They anticipated a climatic struggle between August and October, by which time both sides would have experienced heavy losses, with a result that could go either way. The paper was arguably over-optimistic on Russian capability and certainly in suggesting a sudden collapse in German morale if they judged the Eastern war unwinnable. The chiefs of staff picked up on this. They felt the assessment painted 'rather too rosy a hue for Russia' and they questioned whether the Germans could be held on the Voronezh–Rostov line.[17] Through the spring most American assessments were more pessimistic than British over Soviet capabilities and prospects. However, they expressed 'broad agreement' with the conclusions in this June study.[18]

The paper made little reference to the role of Western supplies to Russia. It suggested that Allied provision of tin, rubber, ferro-alloys and tooled steel was important to Soviet war production although, oddly, aluminium was not mentioned. So long as these materials were available, it judged the net loss in war potential over the last year would not exceed 15 per cent. This was a smaller loss than the committee had projected the previous autumn for the present front lines and post-war analysis suggests it was reasonably accurate. Although Soviet Gross Domestic Product (GDP) fell by one-third and industrial production only slightly less between 1940 and 1942, ruthless resource transfers nearly quadrupled defence industry production while more than halving civilian industrial output. Thus, although the Soviet economy was 30 per cent smaller than Germany's in 1942, Russia significantly outproduced Germany in every major category of land weapons and in aircraft. The paper's quoted figures of 2000 per month for Soviet production of both aircraft and tanks were therefore about right but caused Churchill to ask whether these included Allied supplies. In fact, Molotov, during his visit, had apparently provided Churchill with aircraft figures consistent with these estimates. He stated that Soviet output of combat aircraft had dropped to 700 per month over the winter but was 1500 in April and steadily increasing. Seeing these figures must certainly have again caused both the British and American chiefs of staff to wonder whether the continuing transfers in these categories planned for the Second Protocol, at considerable opportunity cost, were justified. Soviet production of both tanks and aircraft was only 10 per cent below American output in 1942 and Russian medium/heavy tanks were of superior quality.[19]

The combination of the increasing threat to the Arctic convoys underlined in the War Cabinet debate over sailing PQ 16, the impetus given to Sledgehammer by the Molotov visit, and the political desirability of some new action of direct value to Russia, all now encouraged the prime minister to revisit his pet project for a major landing in Norway. This bubbled away in the background during May, with passing mention to Roosevelt and Molotov,[20] but, now re-christened Operation Jupiter, it was launched more formally at the chiefs of staff on 2 June. The Jupiter proposal gave full rein to the prime minister's military imagination while skating over issues of harsh practicality. It inevitably drew heavily on the Ajax concept of the previous autumn but was more directly focused on securing the Arctic sea route by capturing the northern airfields. In Churchill's mind, the concept was straightforward. The initial landing force need only be large enough to subdue the airfields and 10,000–12,000 German troops based in the region. It would be self-contained, carrying sufficient supplies for four months and using the transport ships for accommodation. Surprise would be achieved because the Germans would not know until the last moment that the invasion convoy was not a normal PQ convoy. British aircraft would be landed in Murmansk in support and assistance from Russian land forces was probable. If all went well, this would become a small-scale 'second front', capable of steady expansion southward thus 'unrolling the Nazi map of Europe from the top'. For the prime minister, this was a cheaper, less risky, alternative to Sledgehammer, requiring far fewer resources and thus less impact on other commitments. It was also perhaps 'all we have to offer the Russians' at this time.[21]

Not surprisingly, given the studies the previous autumn, an initial appreciation by the joint planners convinced the chiefs of staff when they discussed it on 5 June that the prime minister's concept for Jupiter was not feasible. The key point was that the Germans were using around ten airfields across the whole arc of northern Norway from the front line with Russia in the east to Narvik in the west. Eliminating the air threat to the PQ convoys and preventing the German air force inflicting unacceptable damage on the Jupiter landing forces meant that most, if not all, these bases must rapidly be seized and then held. That meant taking control of the whole northern region including the Narvik area, with its difficult terrain and climate and limited communications. German land forces were stronger than the prime minister suggested and therefore a substantial force, probably four divisions, would be required just to secure the area around Petsamo and Banak which, in turn, demanded major shipping resources and continuous protection from the bulk of the Home Fleet. In the initial stages, air cover would be dependent on Fleet Air Arm fighters operating from carriers which all wartime experience to date showed could not compete with land-based equivalents. Furthermore, it was unlikely that Jupiter could be mounted before the autumn when the risks posed by weather increased while the benefits began to decline as German air operations against the convoys also became increasingly constrained by bad weather and darkness. In any case, the overall naval and shipping commitment might make it impossible to continue the PQ convoys, thereby defeating a primary purpose of Jupiter.[22] This assessment was bleak enough but probably underestimated the scale of force required even for a limited version of Jupiter given that intelligence showed that the Germans were moving two new mountain divisions into Finland, together with tank landing craft up the coast of Norway, possibly with a view to mounting a new offensive against Murmansk at the end of June.[23]

The chiefs were nevertheless careful to demonstrate that they had explored all possible options so that the prime minister could be worn down with reasoned argument. Through June, the joint planners therefore examined a more limited operation to seize Petsamo in concert with the Russians, essentially an updated version of Marrow, and the impact of deploying a significant fighter force to Murmansk to increase air cover for any landings. For his part, the prime minister emphasised that, if Sledgehammer was abandoned, it became more important to pursue Jupiter as an alternative. For the next three months, he doggedly kept it on the table, attempting to recruit Roosevelt, Stalin, Mountbatten and Lieutenant General Andrew McNaughton, commander of Canadian forces in Britain, as allies, albeit with little success. He also mounted several determined counter-attacks against the planners and what he perceived as a negative and defeatist attitude across the British military leadership to any proposals for offensive operations on the Continent. All this consumed staff time which would have been better spent elsewhere because the fundamental constraints identified by the chiefs in early June could never be overcome. In the end, it was only the demands of the November Torch landings in North-west Africa that persuaded Churchill that Jupiter must be abandoned at least in 1942.[24]

*Mediterranean Parallels: Convoys Harpoon and Vigorous*
Meanwhile, on 1 June, the day that the last part of PQ 16 reached Archangel, and before the Jupiter debate got underway, the War Cabinet agreed to delay the departure of the next PQ convoy for up to two weeks to release sufficient escorts for a convoy carrying essential supplies to Malta.[25] Operation Harpoon would sail six supply ships to Malta from the west, while a parallel operation, Vigorous, delivered eleven ships from eastern Mediterranean ports. This effort was crucial to provide food and war supplies to enable Malta's survival beyond the end of the month. The chiefs of staff judged this essential for three reasons, including one directly relevant to Russia. First, Malta was a crucial air staging point in moving forces to India and Ceylon. Secondly, it was a vital base for interdicting enemy supplies to North Africa as well as a staging point for British forces in the Middle East. Finally, it currently absorbed significant German air power that might otherwise be directed at Russia.[26]

Only one earlier convoy, MG 1, had reached Malta in 1942, delivering three out of four ships to the island in late March following the defensive action known as the Second Battle of Sirte. Unfortunately, less than one-third of the cargo from these ships was successfully unloaded before they were all destroyed in harbour.[27] Furthermore, despite the undoubted bravery and boldness displayed in the face of a superior enemy, the image of Sirte, an action conducted by Vian and for which he received a knighthood, owes more to myth than reality. It was not the dramatic victory claimed at the time and frequently embellished since. Nor does it merit its reputation as an ideal model for convoy defence by implying that light forces, applying the right tactics with skill and determination, might invariably hold off a battlefleet.[28]

Harpoon had many similarities to Halberd the previous September. Its six ships left the Clyde on 5 June and Vice Admiral Curteis again commanded the escort detached from the Home Fleet, comprising the cruisers *Kenya* and *Liverpool* and eight destroyers. Passing the Gibraltar Straits on the night of 11/12 June, Curteis was reinforced by ships of the North Atlantic Station, including the unmodernised battleship *Malaya* and the older carriers *Eagle* and *Argus*, along with the anti-aircraft cruiser *Cairo* and a further nine destroyers. The carriers had sixteen Hurricanes, six Fulmars and eighteen Swordfish between them, a less numerous and less cohesive force than *Ark Royal* deployed for Halberd. The eleven Vigorous ships left Beirut and Port Said almost simultaneously, initially split into three separate groups before joining together with their escort on the afternoon of 13 June. Thirteen submarines were also deployed in support of the two convoys in patrol areas chosen to maximise their chances of intercepting sorties by the Italian fleet. The air, surface and submarine threat faced by both convoys was similar in scale to that now facing PQ planners in the Arctic. Their preparation and execution therefore brought lessons directly relevant to PQ 17 and subsequent convoys.[29]

To deal with the Harpoon convoy, which they detected on the morning of 12 June, the Italian Naval Staff counted on about 150 Italian and German strike aircraft based between Sardinia and Sicily, comprising a mixed force of torpedo, high-level and dive-bombers, with numerous fighter escorts in support. There were about twenty submarines disposed in the western basin and off Malta. They also planned to deploy a surface strike force of two 6in cruisers and five destroyers from Cagliari in southeast Sardinia and motor torpedo boats in the Sicilian Channel. The bulk of the Italian fleet, then at Taranto was earmarked to attack the larger, and apparently more important, Vigorous convoy identified on 13 June. The overall forces confronting Curteis's Harpoon group were alone somewhat larger than any combined strike the Germans had yet mustered against a PQ convoy.

Although the Harpoon convoy was continuously shadowed through 13 June, there was no attack until the following morning when it was 80 miles south-west of Sardinia. Curteis adopted a similar formation to

Somerville during Halberd, deploying a destroyer screen at 7000 yards from the heavy warships and merchantmen which were in two columns, thus facilitating all-round anti-aircraft fire. The carriers manoeuvred independently, each with a dedicated anti-aircraft ship and destroyer escort. Through 14 June, as the convoy transited past Sardinia, it was attacked by at least 150 aircraft in successive waves. These sank one merchant ship and badly damaged the cruiser *Liverpool*, a sister ship to *Edinburgh*, for the loss of twenty-five aircraft. The carrier fighters accounted for eleven of these, damaged many more and disrupted attacks while losing seven of their own, mainly to enemy fighter escorts. The Director of Naval Air Division subsequently judged this fighter performance 'outstanding'.[30]

At 2100 that evening, on reaching the Sicilian Narrows, Curteis turned back with his heavy ships while the convoy altered south-east, hugging the Tunisian coast. With 250 miles to run, the remaining close escort comprised the anti-aircraft cruiser *Cairo*, nine destroyers and four fleet minesweepers. There was also now some long-range air cover from Malta-based Beaufighters. Meanwhile, Malta air surveillance tracked the move of the Italian Cagliari cruiser force to Palermo in Sicily which they reached that evening. Vice Admiral Ralph Leatham, Flag Officer Malta, judged they would now head east to join the rest of the Italian fleet targeting the Vigorous convoy. In fact, they headed south to intercept the western convoy and the Harpoon escort only learnt of their presence from a patrolling Beaufighter at 0620 next morning, 15 June, when they were 15 miles away. In a running fight over the next three hours, in which both sides suffered significant damage, the British managed, with skilful use of smokescreens and some assistance from Malta strike aircraft, to prevent the superior Italian force getting to the merchantmen. However, the price for this success was to leave the merchant ships without adequate protection from air attack to which three ships were now lost, as was the heavily-damaged destroyer *Bedouin*. After the Italian surface force withdrew, the two remaining merchant ships were successfully shepherded to Malta where they landed enough supplies to keep the island going until August. The escort was less fortunate, losing the Polish destroyer *Kujawiak* to mines in the final approaches with four other destroyers damaged.[31]

The planning and execution of Harpoon closely followed the pattern established with Substance and Halberd the previous year. But Vigorous posed greater challenges given the high probability of intervention from the Italian main fleet, including two powerful modern battleships, *Vittorio Veneto* and *Littorio*, each comparable in firepower and speed to *Tirpitz*, and up to ten cruisers, a far superior force therefore to that currently disposed by the Germans in the Arctic. With no Royal Navy heavy units now available in the eastern Mediterranean, it could potentially annihilate the entire convoy with ease. The initial solution to this problem, promoted by the prime minister and agreed by the Defence Committee at the end of April, was for the Eastern Fleet to detach from the Indian Ocean via the Suez Canal during the June dark period for the two weeks necessary to cover a Malta convoy. The key units would be the battleship *Warspite* and three *Illustrious* class carriers.[32] However, further study by the Naval Staff and joint planners convinced the chiefs of staff that securing Malta did not justify the risk of serious damage from air or submarine attack to one or more heavy units of the Eastern Fleet, thereby prejudicing control of the western Indian Ocean.[33] The Naval Staff alternative which the chiefs agreed was for the Eastern Fleet to detach its light forces only, leaving its heavy ships in the Red Sea where the risk of submarine attack was negligible. The loan of a dozen destroyers would give the Vigorous escort a total of twenty-five, providing a two-to-one advantage over the maximum destroyer force likely to accompany the Italian battlefleet. This, along with probable equality in cruisers, would provide a sufficient torpedo-strike threat to deter the Italian heavy ships. The staff accepted that the lack of carrier fighters for Vigorous risked greater loss to air attack but this could be reduced by prior Royal Air Force strikes on enemy airfields and would also be offset by better anti-submarine protection from the additional destroyers.[34]

The final Vigorous escort, again under the command of Vian, now Rear Admiral Sir Philip, comprised seven cruisers (including two borrowed from the Eastern Fleet), the former battleship *Centurion*, unarmed apart from a limited anti-aircraft suite but masquerading as a capital ship (which did not fool the Italians), an anti-aircraft cruiser, twenty-six destroyers and four corvettes. Submarines were placed across the Italians' most likely intercept route from Taranto but they would also adopt a moving protective screen on the northern flank of the convoy as it transited the area between Crete and Malta. As an additional counter to Italian surface attack, the Royal Air Force mounted the maximum possible reconnaissance effort and contributed some forty strike aircraft based in Malta and Egypt, mainly Beauforts and Wellingtons but also some American Liberator bombers. There was also some long-range fighter support. The overall commander was Admiral Sir Henry Harwood, Cunningham's successor as Commander-in-Chief Mediterranean, who had only taken up his post on 20 May. In a new innovation which recognised the complexity of the supporting air operation, he joined the Air Commander Middle East, Air Marshal Sir Arthur Tedder, in a special combined operations room.[35]

The Vigorous plan was risky considering the scale of the surface threat but well-constructed given the resources available with reasonable prospects of success if executed with determination. Nothing done by the Germans and Italians as the convoy transited 'bomb alley' south of Crete on 14 June should have been a surprise. The air attacks that afternoon and E-boat attacks overnight were predictable and inflicted some damage but were manageable. News of a Malta aircraft sighting at 1845 that evening of an Italian force comprising two battleships, four cruisers and eight destroyers steering south from the Gulf of Taranto was also predictable. When they learnt this at 2230, with the convoy now 100 miles south-west of Crete, Harwood and Vian knew that, at the convoy's present course and speed, the Italians would intercept it at about 0900 the following morning with 250 miles still to run to Malta. This was the critical decision point. Did Vian stand on and use his destroyer and cruiser superiority to hold the Italians at bay or did he retreat temporarily in the hope the Italian threat could be reduced by air strikes? If he retreated, consuming time, fuel and ammunition as he ran back into 'bomb alley', when and how, given the inevitable 'fog of war', would it be judged sensible to resume progress westward?[36]

What now became clear was that both Harwood and Vian ultimately lacked confidence in the plan conceived in May to hold the Italians off with destroyer superiority. Both suggested later that it was never credible to conduct such an action across an entire day, yet this had always seemed a likely requirement. Harwood therefore ordered Vian to reverse course temporarily at 0200, but now became hostage to the hope of successful Royal Air Force air strikes, inevitably fragmentary intelligence, and the difficulty of sharing a complex picture and decision-making with Vian across radio links often subject to significant delay. In the event, the British air attacks had little impact. They disabled the heavy cruiser *Trento* which was later sunk by the submarine *Umbra* but *Littorio* brushed off a bomb hit. This was not enough to break Italian pursuit of the Vigorous convoy. Meanwhile, it is hard to avoid a judgement that, through the morning of 15 June, Harwood dithered, unable firmly to commit to either pressing on or to retreat, although Vian too showed uncharacteristic irresolution, possibly through illness. Over the ten hours from 0200, on Harwood's orders, Vian reversed course four times, no mean feat with fifty ships involved. By the afternoon Harwood was forced into abandonment. Although the Italians had given up the chase, the convoy had now lost an entire day of passage and the escort was too short of fuel and anti-aircraft ammunition to continue. Vigorous had failed and at significant cost, a cruiser, three destroyers and two merchant vessels sunk, with three cruisers, a corvette and two more merchant vessels damaged.[37]

A comparison of the four Arctic convoys PQ 13 to PQ 16, their matching returns QP 9 to QP 12, with the three Malta convoys MG1/Harpoon/Vigorous is instructive. All eleven faced actual or potential combined arms attack from enemy air, submarine and surface forces and the scale of attack the enemy could potentially deploy against any individual convoy was comparable. Not surprisingly, the overall resources deployed in their defence were also generally similar. 103 ships sailed in convoys PQ 13 to 16, of which sixteen were lost and seventy arrived, an overall success rate of 70 per cent. In the four return convoys, sixty-three sailed, five were lost and fifty-six arrived, a success rate of nearly 90 per cent. These eight convoys cost the British two cruisers lost to enemy action while the Germans lost two destroyers and two U-boats. Both sides had several more warships damaged. Meanwhile, twenty-one ships sailed in the three Malta convoys, seven were sunk and only five ships arrived with three of those sunk before unloading much of their cargo, an effective success rate therefore of 11 per cent. The three convoys cost the British a cruiser and seven destroyers while the Italians lost two cruisers and two destroyers (the latter due more to storm damage than British action). As in the Arctic both sides had many vessels damaged.

Several points may be drawn from MG1/Harpoon/Vigorous which were directly relevant to handling the growing combined threat in the Arctic. First, these statistics did not support an assessment that summer convoys in the Arctic were uniquely problematic, as Pound rather implied. The risks and costs in running Mediterranean convoys were fully comparable. Secondly, Harpoon again underlined the huge contribution that a carrier-borne fighter force, even in relatively small numbers, contributed to effective air defence. This contribution promised to be even greater in the Arctic because the attackers would not have the benefit of escorting fighters. Thirdly, it is noteworthy that, for most of their passage, these Mediterranean convoys were protected by a closely integrated group of warships. Cruisers and destroyers and, in the case of Harpoon, the battleship and carriers, formed a single close escort under a flag officer. This facilitated easier command and control, brought greater concentration of fire against air attack, and made anti-submarine screening more efficient, while still allowing the flexibility to detach escort elements for specific tasks. It is striking that the destroyer forces made available to support the Mediterranean convoys were both more numerous and composed of more modern vessels than Tovey could call on, at least in the first half of 1942.

Albacores launching from *Victorious* to attack *Tirpitz* on the morning of 9 March 1942. (Alamy 2X07WT3)

German destroyer *Z 26* sinking on 29 March 1942 after her engagement with the British cruiser *Trinidad* during the German operation against convoy PQ 13. (Public domain)

Convoy PQ 17 sighted by German air reconnaissance, probably on the afternoon of 2 July 1942. (US Navy, Naval History and Heritage Command NH 71382)

The German heavy cruiser *Hipper* and destroyers viewed from the battleship *Tirpitz* probably during Rösselsprung, the operation to attack PQ 17 in early July 1942. (US Navy, Naval History and Heritage Command NH 71393)

German He 111 torpedo bomber, armed with two torpedoes, as deployed in the Arctic theatre from May to November 1942. (Alamy 2PYW8KB)

Painting by Charles Pears showing the British destroyer *Onslow* in action at the Battle of the Barents Sea, 31 December 1942. It beautifully conveys the poor light conditions in which the engagement took place. (National Maritime Museum BHC0682)

Ice-bound British 'County' class 8in cruiser in Arctic waters. (Alamy 2NE1K0K)

Bridge view of stormy seas from the British cruiser *Sheffield*. (Alamy 2T1MJ62)

Liberty Ship in an Arctic storm. (Alamy 2T1MK2J)

The German battleship *Tirpitz* in berthed in Altafiord. (US Navy, Naval History and Heritage Command NH 71390)

Lieutenant Donald Cameron, commander of the midget submarine *X6*, bidding farewell to his towing submarine *Truculent* prior to setting off for Altafiord on the evening of 20 September 1943. (From a painting done by Cameron while a prisoner of war, kindly shared by the Cameron family.)

Painting by Charles Pears of the Fleet Air Arm attack on *Tirpitz* (Operation Tungsten), 3 April 1944. (National Maritime Museum BHC0687)

The German battlecruiser *Scharnhorst* viewed from *Tirpitz* leaving Altafiord on 6 September 1943 for Operation Zitronella, the raid on Spitzbergen. (Courtesy Maritime Quest)

Hellcat fighters of Fleet Air Arm 800 Squadron on the flight deck of the escort carrier *Emperor* preparing to attack *Tirpitz* (Operation Tungsten) early on 3 April 1944. (Alamy 2X010C)

The British cruiser *Belfast* leaving Iceland on 21 February 1943 to escort convoy JW 53. (Alamy 2T1K57H)

British government 1943 propaganda poster created by Frederick Donald Blake.

**ARMS FOR RUSSIA** ... A great convoy of British ships escorted by Soviet fighter planes sails into Murmansk harbour with vital supplies for the Red Army.

Finally, all three Mediterranean convoys incorporated new ideas for managing the threat posed by a much superior Italian surface threat able to operate with the advantages of geography and significant air protection. Yet Vigorous emphasised that this problem remained unsolved. If the 'fighting destroyer escort' represented the answer, its credibility had not yet been tested under real combat and Harwood had demonstrated little faith in it. He placed the blame for retreat on an air strike force that lacked 'the weight required' to stop a fast, powerful enemy force and failed to compensate for 'lack of heavy ships'. The chiefs of staff too apparently judged that any renewed attempt to supply Malta from the east would depend on significant air reinforcement, even temporarily 'packing Malta with an overwhelming air striking force' sufficient to 'nullify' Italian capital ships. The chiefs also evidently felt that if, despite such air support, a convoy was in danger of interception, it must 'turn around'. In the event, assurance that the surviving Harpoon ships enabled Malta to survive until the end of August allowed re-supply to be deferred. The need to avoid further delay to PQ 17 was also a factor.[38]

*Rösselsprung and its Implications*

As described earlier, the idea of exploiting Altafiord as an advance base from which to target a PQ convoy with heavy surface units as it transited east of Bear Island emerged in discussions between the staffs of Group North, Fleet and Arctic commands during the last half of May. These discussions coincided with changes in German naval command structure. The post of Commanding Admiral Battleships, held by Ciliax, was abolished at the end of May with its role and supporting staff absorbed by the Fleet Commander Admiral Schniewind. This abolition was initially planned to be temporary, driven by Ciliax's illness, but it became permanent. It also coincided with the formal creation of the new post of Admiral Commanding Cruisers, filled by Oskar Kummetz, who took responsibility for the two pocket battleships and their supporting destroyers at Narvik. At one level this change was cosmetic since Schniewind retained a vice admiral as his deputy and had merely changed the latter's area of responsibility. However, the fact that Schniewind now took direct responsibility for the Trondheim force, comprising *Tirpitz* and *Hipper* and their escorts, brought two consequences. It meant Schniewind would inevitably go to sea himself with the Trondheim force if it sortied and, as overall fleet commander, take charge of the Narvik group too if the two forces operated jointly. Secondly, as a full admiral, Schniewind had the confidence and authority to take decisions that Ciliax might have reserved to Group North. He was also more offensively minded. This had an impact on operations against PQ 17.[39]

In late May, Group North still doubted that air reconnaissance, even in good weather, would be adequate to pinpoint the British 'remote escort' of heavy ships and carriers supporting a PQ convoy. The sea area to be swept as the ice receded was simply 'too great'. Locating the remote escort was essential before the two pocket battleships could safely deploy against a convoy. They could only be used if it was certain they would only encounter the close escort of light forces and that attack could be broken off at any time. However, even if these conditions were met, escorting cruisers and destroyers could still prevent them reaching their primary target, the convoy. They would then have consumed precious fuel oil needlessly. There was also the risk of damage requiring long periods of repair. The logic of providing them with heavy support from the Trondheim force was obvious.[40]

By 1 June, Group North's view had therefore evolved. This partly reflected lobbying by Schniewind who had met with Raeder in Trondheim two days earlier. Schniewind emphasised that, with Germany's summer offensive imminent, the Western Allies would make a maximum effort to deliver supplies. This called for a decisive demonstration of German naval superiority against the next convoy. June with continuous daylight and the promise of clear weather was the optimum month for this, fuel was available, and his fleet had been strengthened in destroyers and torpedo boats. He accordingly advocated 'simultaneous attack by all naval units in northern waters, including *Tirpitz* and *Hipper*'. Total destruction of a PQ convoy would have immense impact on the war at sea.[41] Schniewind's view that the navy should make a more prominent contribution to Germany's Eastern war was already shared by the Operations Division of the Naval Staff and Schmundt as Admiral Arctic, whom Raeder saw on 3 June. It was not surprising that it also now found echoes in Group North staff although Carls remained cautious. Less voiced, but prevalent across the whole naval leadership, was the feeling that the heavy ships must earn their keep and that, if they did not do so, their future was in jeopardy.[42]

Group North now advocated that, once the next convoy PQ 17 had been located, the Trondheim group should transfer north and make a joint attack with the pocket battleships while U-boats tracked the convoy. The plan would be to close with the convoy as rapidly as possible while avoiding all engagement with enemy forces save with the immediate escort. The close escort would be destroyed by *Tirpitz* and *Hipper* while the pocket battleships and their destroyers annihilated the merchant ships. It was unnecessary to waste time sinking every vessel. So long as they were disabled, they could be finished off by U-boats. This would permit the surface forces to make a rapid withdrawal. A successful operation on these lines fully justified the fuel expenditure. The danger from enemy submarines now invariably accompanying convoys was judged no greater than that posed by torpedo attack from destroyers. The Naval Staff supported this plan and undertook to brief the Führer whose approval was required for any operational use of *Tirpitz*. Hitler was duly briefed on 5 June by Vice Admiral Krancke, Raeder's permanent representative at Führer headquarters. Hitler withheld approval but was content for planning to proceed. Two days later, in further support for decisive intervention against PQ 17, the German Naval Staff provided an assessment of supplies delivered to Russia along the northern route by the first sixteen PQ convoys. This estimated that 250 to 300 merchant vessels had sailed carrying a potential 1.5 million tons of cargo. Forty ships had been sunk with eighty-six damaged, suggesting therefore delivery of 1.25 million tons to Russian ports. In reality, subtracting early returns, only 189 ships had sailed of which only seventeen were lost. These carried about 950,000 tons of cargo of which about 70,000 tons was lost. The German estimate was not only nearly 25 per cent out on actual deliveries, if reasonably accurate on cargo composition, but they grossly exaggerated both the number of ships involved and their sinking rate. Nevertheless, the overall weight of supplies they correctly judged to have reached Russia were a powerful argument for a new initiative to stop the flow.[43]

By 8 June, Schniewind's original proposal for targeting PQ 17 with all available heavy units was therefore formally approved by both Group North and the Naval Staff with the operation allocated the codeword Rösselsprung (Knight's Move). The same day Group North confirmed that Admiral Arctic had been ordered to position three experienced U-boats in the north-east of the Demark Strait and that further boats should deploy in the area of Jan Mayen. Discussions had also opened with 5th Air Fleet on providing a maximum air reconnaissance effort. Given the area to be swept, the Naval Staff accepted this would reduce the number of available strike aircraft but this was justified by a successful naval attack. The Naval Staff also confirmed command arrangements. For the Trondheim group, Group North, under General Admiral Carls, had strategic command with tactical command delegated to Schniewind as Fleet Commander. Schmundt as Admiral Arctic had strategic command of the Narvik group with tactical command passed to Vice Admiral Kummetz. Two days later, it was evident that 5th Air Fleet would resist any diversion of its bombers to a reconnaissance role, insisting that the experience of PQ 16 demonstrated that, in summer months, air attack was the optimum means of attacking PQ convoys. Group North feared this 'negative attitude' would jeopardise Rösselsprung which depended on adequate reconnaissance. Naval liaison to the Air Force High Command confirmed that the Chief of Staff, Colonel General Hans Jeschonnek, had been briefed on the operation but doubted he would approve the diversion of bombers to reconnaissance. The Naval Staff accordingly recognised that their argument that naval attack was the only means of achieving complete destruction of a convoy, which in turn depended on adequate reconnaissance, would only be won through direct appeal to the Führer.[44]

In addition to these problems in gaining adequate reconnaissance support, the Naval Staff worried that current communications between Group North based in Sengwarden, near Wilhelmshaven, 5th Air Fleet headquarters at Oslo, and their respective subordinate units, were inadequate to support an operation of the complexity of Rösselsprung where timely delivery of all relevant operational information to front-line commanders was critical. Group North insisted present arrangements were sufficient. This overlooked the fact that command of both naval and air forces in Norway and the Arctic was simultaneously highly fragmented and rigidly hierarchical, with only limited channels of communication between the two services. All requests for aerial reconnaissance by naval commanders had to be channelled through Group North and from there to Oslo with decisions and results passed back along the same route. Radio and landline links between Sengwarden and Oslo were poor and links to the Arctic area were hampered by difficult geographic and atmospheric conditions. These problems compounded the limited resources allocated to reconnaissance support for Rösselsprung.[45]

Raeder now formally presented the Rösselsprung plan to Hitler at the Berghof on the afternoon of 15 June. He stressed the objective, the destruction of an entire PQ convoy, and outlined the composition of the two task groups and command arrangements. Once PQ 17 had been located, the two groups would rendezvous off Altafiord and await the executive signal to proceed from Group North. The move north would be made as late as possible to avoid alerting the enemy. The operation would be executed at maximum speed, giving enemy heavy forces no opportunity to intervene. He assured Hitler that action with superior forces would be avoided and the close escort only engaged when essential to the primary task of destroying the merchant vessels. Raeder then stressed the importance of aerial reconnaissance, both in tracking the convoy and ensuring than any enemy heavy covering force was located. Given the potential prize of destroying the whole convoy, reconnaissance should take precedence over air force participation in the battle. Finally, he stressed that twelve destroyers were now available for the operation, six with each task group, there was sufficient fuel, and June weather was especially favourable, while the ice edge still kept the convoy in German-controlled air space. Raeder only won partial approval from Hitler and many of his fellow senior officers subsequently believed he failed to press his case with either determination or conviction. He was given authority to move the task groups north in good time but their deployment from Altafiord required Hitler's further specific permission. This would depend on assurance that enemy aircraft carriers had been located and that they had been neutralised by air attack if they presented any threat. Raeder also failed to persuade Hitler to intervene with Göring over ensuring additional reconnaissance effort.[46]

## British Awareness of Rösselsprung and Dispositions for PQ 17

Prior to this meeting the British had no significant insight into the emerging Rösselsprung operation. NID spotted Schniewind's meeting with Raeder in Trondheim through Ultra coverage of their flight details but with no indication of what was discussed. Rather surprisingly, NID was uncertain of the responsibilities of the 'Fleet Commander', suggesting that Schniewind's role was analogous to that of the First Sea Lord and that he exercised 'control' over Groups North, West and South. In reality, a better, if not precise, British analogue was Tovey.[47] Beyond that, Ultra provided no substantive clues on German intent towards PQ 17 apart from what seemed standard U-boat and air reconnaissance deployment.[48]

The first substantive intelligence on Rösselsprung came not from GC&CS but the naval attaché in Stockholm, Captain Henry Denham. Denham had a professional relationship with the Chief of the Foreign Section of Swedish military intelligence, Colonel Carl Björnstjerna, a strong anglophile who had served as military attaché in London in the mid-1930s. Through the first months of 1942, they established a close friendship within which Denham gradually coaxed Björnstjerna to exceed his professional brief and share highly classified Swedish intelligence, including intercepted German naval signals traffic covering operations and intentions in Norway. Swedish access to German military and diplomatic traffic reflected two factors. Following their invasion of Norway, the Germans rented extensive access to telegraph lines crossing Swedish territory to ensure communications to all major sites in Norway including Trondheim and Narvik. Sensitive German traffic was naturally encrypted and used a teleprinter-based cipher system, the Geheimschreiber, which GC&CS later designated 'Fish', and which, as with Enigma, the Germans believed unbreakable. Given the potential German threat to their sovereignty, the Swedes had a powerful motive to read this traffic, they had ready access to it through their landlines, and they had a cryptographic genius, Arne Beurling. In what was 'possibly the finest feat of cryptanalysis performed during the Second World War',[49] Beurling broke the Geheimschreiber in June 1940, more than two years before GC&CS, and the Swedes read it continuously until May 1943. Decrypted messages were distributed on an industrial scale, 7100 in 1941, 41,400 in 1941, and 120,800 in 1942. On one day in October 1943, a record 678 messages were distributed. By comparison, in that year, GC&CS rarely managed more than 300 per month.[50]

Björnstjerna was either unwilling or unable for security reasons to give Denham physical copies of intercepted signals, nor would he permit Denham to make notes in his office where their meetings generally occurred. Instead, he provided an oral summary of recent decrypts relying on memory which Denham too had to remember until he reached his embassy. Björnstjerna's summaries were not necessarily verbatim recall of raw decrypts but more often assessed collations of several decrypts. Furthermore, there was usually a time lag in his intelligence since he could rarely credibly see Denham more than once a week. Nevertheless, over the six months from March 1942 until September when Björnstjerna came under suspicion and was forced to resign, he provided a treasure trove of intelligence drawn from German naval and air force communications traffic between Norway and Germany. In addition to insights on naval movements and operations, this included a comprehensive picture of 5th Air Fleet deployment and the results of air attacks on convoys reported back to Berlin. Following the attacks on PQ 16, he noted an acute shortage of torpedoes. Because Björnstjerna could deliver insights gleaned from communication between senior German naval and air commanders which were rarely confided to the airwaves, his intelligence often complemented rather than duplicated GC&CS interception of radio-borne Enigma traffic. Its importance is under-recognised in the history of the Arctic theatre, with reference often confined to a single report originating on 13 June.[51]

That day, Denham briefed DNI on intelligence he had just received from Björnstjerna summarising the attack plan against the next PQ convoy, drawn from decrypted German naval messages transmitted over the previous week. The plan anticipated detecting the convoy once it reached the vicinity of Jan Mayen when air attacks would commence. In parallel, the two pocket battleships would move from their Bogen Bay anchorage, 12 miles north-west of Narvik, to Altafiord accompanied by six destroyers and probably anchor at the mouth of the fiord in Sørøy Sound. Meanwhile, *Tirpitz*, *Hipper*, two destroyers and three torpedo boats would transit from Trondheim to the now vacant Bogen Bay anchorage. These two forces would sortie from their new positions once the convoy reached 5° East (midway between Jan Mayen and Bear Island). They would rendezvous on the Bear Island longitude (75 miles west of the Altafiord longitude) and conduct a simultaneous attack on the convoy supported by U-boats and air units. Given the delicate fuel situation, the forces would be supported by the tanker *Ditmarschen* which would arrive in Altafiord as late as possible to avoid warning of its use as an operational base. To assist covert transit of the forces, a new buoyed channel was also being established between the Lofotens and the mainland.[52]

Denham's report, which was issued by NID the following morning and passed to Tovey as well as Admiralty recipients, is a crucial part of the PQ 17 story.[53] It correctly conveyed the German intent to attack the next convoy with the combined weight of all their heavy ships. It made this threat the dominant preoccupation for Tovey and the Admiralty in planning for PQ 17 over the rest of the month. However, while right on intent, as so often the way with intelligence, the report not only had important omissions but was also misleading. This was partly because German plans were still evolving, with Schniewind only issuing his operation order for Rösselsprung on 14 June, the day after Denham reported, but also because Björnstjerna had to assess many different and sometimes conflicting items of traffic. These errors and omissions exerted influence on British planning and the later fatal decision to scatter the convoy. Traditional accounts emphasise the failure of Denham's report to mention that any German sortie required Hitler's final approval which in turn depended on precisely locating British carriers. But even more important was its implication that the combined German surface force would attack in the area 250 miles west of Bear Island following the rendezvous on its longitude. In reality, Schniewind's operation order was clear that the two German forces would meet at the head of Altafiord and that the preferred attack area was the sector 150 miles east of Bear Island. Later it was decided the two forces would anchor well inside the fiord rather than outside in Sørøy Sound. Denham's report thus reinforced rather than challenged the long-standing British assumption that the Germans would focus any surface force attack in the area from Bear Island westward targeted by *Tirpitz* with PQ 12, leaving the Barents Sea to U-boat and air attack. This inevitably shaped their countermeasures.[54]

Given this British perspective on the increased surface threat, the arrangements for protecting PQ 17 which sailed from Reykjavik on

27 June broadly followed those for its PQ 16 predecessor. However, there were important enhancements which made the overall escort and support forces the strongest yet given to an Arctic convoy. The close escort, under Commander Jack Broome, with six destroyers, two anti-aircraft ships (*Palomares* and *Pozarica*), four corvettes and two submarines (*P614* and *P615*), was similar to that allocated to PQ 16 but the second anti-aircraft ship was a valuable addition and Broome could also call on three dedicated rescue ships to pick up survivors. To keep the escorts topped up with fuel, Broome also had a tanker, the modern 17,500-ton *Aldersdale*. A second tanker, *Gray Ranger*, escorted by the destroyer *Douglas*, was positioned near Jan Mayen to support Tovey's destroyers and the escort of the westbound QP 13.[55] As was now customary, Broome and most of the destroyers and corvettes allocated to the close escort were seconded from Western Approaches Command, with the Home Fleet and other commands providing the rest. The 41-year-old Broome was one of the Royal Navy's great characters, highly professional but with an iconoclastic streak, albeit softened by great charm and wit. He was a wonderful cartoonist although this inevitably did not endear him to all his targets. A former submariner, he had made a successful transition to U-boat hunter and, as commander 1st Escort Group, was highly regarded by his Commander-in-Chief, Admiral Sir Percy Noble.[56]

There were again two distinct covering forces. Four heavy 8in cruisers (two British and two American) and three destroyers, under Rear Admiral Louis 'Turtle' Hamilton, who had succeeded Frederick Wake-Walker in February in command of the 1st Cruiser Squadron, were allocated to provide close support at least as far as Bear Island. This force was sufficiently powerful to deter Kummetz's two pocket battleships. Together the cruisers could deliver a slightly higher weight of main armament broadside at a higher rate of fire and they were 5 knots faster. Broome evidently admired Hamilton, describing him as a 'brilliant destroyer officer', promoted rear admiral 'over many heads', 'a little human terrier', a 'troubleshooter' any convoy would want in its support, and 'a bachelor, wedded to the Royal Navy, courteous, unflappable and popular'. The distant cover force, under Tovey, comprised the battleships *Duke of York* and American *Washington*, the carrier *Victorious*, two cruisers and twelve destroyers. This would cruise to the north of the convoy track in an area centred roughly 150–200 miles north-west of Bear Island, ready to counter the Trondheim force should they intervene anywhere west of that island.[57] Finally, no less than nine submarines were deployed in patrol areas between Bear Island and the Norwegian coast to maximise their chances of intercepting the pocket battleships deploying from Altafiord or the Trondheim group moving up from the south. Seven of these deployed from the United Kingdom while the remaining two, *Seawolf* and *Trident*, joined after escorting QP 13 from Polyarnoe. The deployment of eleven boats in total, including the two within the close escort, was achieved partly through a small increase in Home Flotilla strength reflecting the increased build rate, partly by coordinating patrol schedules with convoy transits, and partly by drawing on boats for a single northern patrol before they deployed to the Mediterranean. Once PQ 17 moved east of Bear Island, patrol areas would also shift east to provide a continuing screen against any German force moving up from the Norwegian coast. This British submarine effort was carefully coordinated with a significant Russian deployment of seven boats across the north Norwegian coast.[58]

One further potential source of protection was ruled out by the Admiralty for PQ 17 although it would be implemented for the next convoy in September. In the light of experience with PQ 16, on 2 June, the Commander-in-Chief Coastal Command, Air Chief Marshal, Sir Philip Bennet Joubert de la Ferté, suggested investigating Russian willingness to have a force of land-based torpedo aircraft based near Murmansk to operate against any German heavy forces venturing into the Barents Sea. The Russians were duly consulted and on 11 June, Rear Admiral Miles, who had just replaced Mason Macfarlane as head of 30 Mission, confirmed their agreement in principle. However, there were currently only two torpedo squadrons in the United Kingdom, one with Beauforts and one with Hampdens, and the Admiralty felt none of this small force could be spared at this time. Joubert later argued that the deployment of one squadron to Vaenga would have avoided the tragedy that was now to overtake PQ 17.[59]

In making these dispositions, which represented a substantial naval investment, Tovey and the Admiralty remained acutely aware that the Germans enjoyed crucial advantages. Their Arctic air and U-boat forces, on which Ultra-generated intelligence was excellent, had reached a new peak. Good summer weather and constant daylight would inevitably aid their aerial reconnaissance and strike. German surface units could operate under a protective air umbrella out to 300 miles from the Norwegian coast between Kirkenes and Narvik. Royal Navy covering forces entering these waters had no shore-based air cover, save the so far limited and ineffective Soviet support, were exposed to U-boat as well as air attack, were a thousand miles from their nearest base, and destroyers would be too short of fuel to escort a damaged ship to safety. These distance factors, combined with the lack of air support comparable to that provided by the

Royal Air Force from Malta, made the protection of PQ 17 far more challenging than Harpoon and Vigorous.

There were also two weaknesses in Tovey's dispositions. Broome's close escort, with its core of Western Approaches vessels, was well equipped to deal with the U-boat threat. However, it lacked both the numbers and armament to provide a convoy of this size with adequate defence against the scale of air threat it was known it would face. Still less could it credibly hold off more than a minimal surface attack force for long. Broome had barely one-third the destroyer force covering the six Harpoon ships up to the Sicilian Narrows, two of his destroyers were more than 20 years old, two were 'Hunt' class (Type II) which lacked torpedo armament, while his two anti-aircraft ships hardly substituted for the firepower of the Harpoon battleship and four cruisers let alone the contribution of two carriers. Furthermore, about half Broome's ships were new to him and he had no time to work them up into a cohesive force and perfect anti-surface tactics. Tovey was aware of the limitations of the close escort and proposed that the convoy be split into two sections, an option rejected by Pound. Not only was the latter under political pressure to move the supplies backing up in Iceland but it is not clear how Tovey's solution would have resolved a fundamental shortage of warships.[60]

The second problem was a potential blurring and overlap in command arrangements. The Admiralty reserved the right to intervene directly with operational instructions. This was partly because it inevitably had a fuller intelligence picture, and partly because experience showed that, once Tovey was at sea, his communications would be constrained by atmospheric conditions as well as any requirement for radio silence. It also reflected Pound's centralising tendency. A second issue was how much Hamilton as a rear admiral, whose cruiser force was meant to provide close support to both PQ 17 and the parallel incoming convoy QP 13 west of Bear Island, should exercise direct control over the convoys and their respective escorts led by comparatively junior officers. Partly because it was judged unwise to confine valuable cruisers within a convoy that moved 5 knots slower than its Mediterranean counterparts, and partly because of the requirement to cover both outbound and inbound convoys, Hamilton adopted a roving brief.[61] This meant his contact with and therefore his practical ability to direct PQ 17 was intermittent. Normally, this would only matter if Hamilton issued orders from a distance that Broome judged unwise or impractical and, for the second half of PQ 17's voyage, it was always planned that Broome would be on his own anyway. However, the potential ambiguity in Hamilton's remit over the convoy and close escort was liable to be exposed in an unforeseen crisis.

To help counter the growing German advantages and the specific threat of a strike by heavy surface ships, Tovey planned deception and evasion measures. An obvious evasion option was to route the convoy further north, ideally north of Bear Island, taking advantage of the receding ice. This increased its range from German airfields and added to the area they must sweep with air searches. It also increased the exposure of their surface units. Tovey knew from Ultra that the Germans were monitoring the ice boundary although they apparently underestimated how far it had receded. Nevertheless, the shift was enough to worry Schniewind who commented to his staff that it would inevitably influence Rösselsprung and that the radius of action of the Trondheim group could not be indefinitely extended.[62]

The first deception action was the despatch of a substantial dummy convoy from Scapa Flow designed to suggest a major raid or landing in Norway. The convoy comprised five ships of the 1st Minelaying Squadron and four colliers, escorted by the new cruiser *Sirius*, currently working up, the old light cruiser *Curacoa* and several destroyers and trawlers, enough to be convincing to any German reconnaissance flight. It made two attempts to gain German attention in the waters east of the Shetlands in the four days after PQ 17 sailed from Iceland but without any success. This operation was an expansion of the Hardboiled concept involving significant resources although without apparently using the Double Cross network.

Tovey's second deception proposal was for the convoy to turn back for 12 to 18 hours on reaching 10° East, approximately 180 miles south-west of Bear Island, unless there was clear evidence the German heavy units remained in harbour or poor weather prevented enemy air shadowing. His aim was either to tempt the Germans west, allowing interception by the Home Fleet, or to force them to loiter in the vicinity of Bear Island where they were vulnerable to the British submarine screen. The Admiralty rejected this option. They judged that, in summer conditions, the Germans were unlikely to lose the convoy for long, there was no reason to risk their ships outside protective air cover, and they could wait in safe waters longer than the convoy could stall. Pound was probably also conscious of the recent Vigorous experience. Once a reversal took place, there were always reasons not to resume the advance and there was obvious reluctance to see two critical convoys abandoned in quick succession. With the benefit of hindsight, it is clear that, as Tovey himself later acknowledged, his reversal would never have worked because the Germans always planned to intercept east of Bear Island.[63]

The debate over reversal was part of a wider telephone discussion between Pound and Tovey of which no formal record exists. Its content must be gleaned from Tovey's sparse post-war references and the Admiralty instructions that followed the phone call. During negotiation with the Admiralty in 1948 over the wording of his Arctic Convoys despatch, Tovey stated that he was 'in considerable disagreement' with Pound's 'proposed method of carrying out the operation' but was finally 'instructed' to implement Pound's plan. He added that their exchange ended with Pound remarking – 'We can always order the convoy to scatter' – to which Tovey replied – 'That will be just plain bloody murder'.[64]

This final exchange is another element indelibly established in the PQ 17 story, interpreted to display prescience on the part of Tovey and fatalistic defeatism by Pound. However, there are problems with the emphasis traditionally given to it and the implication that Pound approached the operation already predisposed to scatter, having ruled out Tovey's 'reversal'. The main disagreement between Pound and Tovey was not 'reversal', splitting the convoy into two parts, or even the possibility of 'scattering'. It was about who had ultimate control over PQ 17 in managing the threat from enemy surface forces identified in Denham's intelligence. Here the lessons drawn by Pound from PQ 12 were decisive and framed the opening paragraph of the Admiralty directive issued to Tovey on 27 June, the day PQ 17 sailed. Since the Admiralty would have better and earlier intelligence (a clear reference to Ultra) on the movement of enemy surface forces than Tovey and his subordinate commanders, and that Tovey might not wish to break radio silence, the Admiralty would control the convoy when a surface risk materialised. The directive allowed latitude to commanders at sea to qualify Admiralty orders to take account of weather or other local factors but emphasised that any decision on 'reversal' or return to Iceland should generally be taken by London. In principle, surface attack west of Bear Island would be met by the covering forces and eastward of that point by the submarine screen. Hamilton's cruisers should not proceed east of Bear Island unless the convoy was threatened by a force the cruisers could fight and, even then, they were not expected to venture more than 100 miles.[65]

The directive did not employ the term 'scatter' but envisaged circumstances arising east of Bear Island where it might be best for the convoy to 'disperse' and proceed independently to Russian ports. Implicit here was the prospect of overwhelming surface attack. Within the Royal Navy, 'disperse' and 'scatter' had different meanings. The former meant allowing ships to break convoy formation and adopt the optimum individual course and speed to reach their destination. It implied that most ships would inevitably remain in close proximity for a while. 'Scatter' meant the convoy immediately breaking up with ships initially sailing in multiple directions according to prior convoy instructions. It is impossible to know whether Pound definitely used the term 'scatter' rather than 'disperse' in his conversation with Tovey and, if he did, whether he was using it in a general or precise technical sense.

Whatever Pound said and meant during this discussion, the subsequent notorious fate of PQ 17, together with Tovey's claim of disagreement and emotive reference to 'murder', have entrenched two claims. First, that all previous experience demonstrated that a convoy was better off sticking together even when a superior enemy hove over the horizon. Secondly, that this was embedded Royal Navy doctrine. By implication therefore, Pound was suggesting an option both inappropriate and never previously contemplated. The sole example of the deliberate and successful scattering of a convoy in the face of surface threat usually quoted is Halifax convoy HX84 attacked by *Admiral Scheer* on 5 November 1940. Valiant defence by the sole escort, the armed merchant cruiser *Jervis Bay*, enabled the convoy to scatter behind a smokescreen and *Scheer* could only find and sink five of thirty-seven ships. The argument runs that this was an exceptional case reflecting the lack of a warship escort. Three months later, the sinking of seven out of nineteen ships from the unescorted Freetown convoy SLS64 by the heavy cruiser *Hipper* on 11 February 1941 certainly demonstrated what happened to a convoy that did not immediately scatter when attacked. But the existence of a powerful escort did not guarantee a convoy's protection, as the British showed with Beta the following November. As regards doctrine, it is true that both Atlantic Convoy Instructions and Tovey's standing instructions for Arctic convoys both stressed the importance of keeping a convoy together. However, they also stressed the need for escort commanders to exercise judgement since it was impossible to anticipate every operational situation that could arise. As with the 1939 Fighting Instructions, they should comply with the spirit of the directions rather than follow rules slavishly. Furthermore, there were examples where senior Royal Navy commanders had resorted to dispersal. Cunningham had done so for MG1's final run to Malta in March following Vian's engagement with the Italian fleet. During Vigorous, Harwood had even ordered Vian to 'sacrifice' the convoy and extricate his escort forces if cornered by a superior Italian force. The message is that neither experience nor doctrine provided cast-iron rules here. Whether a convoy held together or dispersed/scattered required a sensible assessment of risk/benefit.[66]

## PQ 17: Composition, Value and Initial Progress

PQ 17 sailed from Hvalfiord, Iceland, on 27 June, the day before the German summer offensive, Plan Blue, kicked off. Its route, British escort and support forces and the key events in its passage are shown in Map 4 on p 280. Like its immediate predecessor, the convoy initially comprised thirty-five merchant ships. Eight were British, two Russian, two Panamanian, one Dutch and the rest American. This time the bulk of the ships were to proceed to Archangel which was now completely ice free although eight American ships were planned to detach to Murmansk. Recent heavy German bombing dictated that this was the maximum group Murmansk could handle. The convoy carried a total cargo of 140,606 tons, averaging just over 4000 tons per vessel or two-thirds the desired figure used by the Anglo-American planners. Included in the cargo were 594 tanks (195 British), 297 fighters (215 British), twelve American bombers, and 4246 assorted vehicles (508 British). The tanks and fighters each equated to about 10 days of Russian output at this time while the vehicles were worth about seven weeks. The British-supplied tanks and fighters represented about one month of her First Protocol commitment, 40 per cent of combined British/Canadian monthly tank production and one-quarter of British monthly fighter production. When the American supplies are included, a surplus of 94 tanks over the joint First Protocol Anglo-American monthly target of 500 compensated for a shortfall of 91 in their aircraft target of 400.[67] Captain Harry Hill, commanding the American cruiser *Wichita*, part of Hamilton's covering force, told his officers that PQ 17's cargo was valued at USD 700 million. It is not clear where he got this figure because it was a sevenfold exaggeration.[68] In any case, the real value of the convoy did not lie in monetary accounting. At this stage of the Eastern war, Russia was losing more war material each month than it was gaining from domestic production despite the impressive mobilisation of industry in the Urals. Over the six months beginning 1 May, the deficit between production and losses averaged 7 per cent for tanks and 18 per cent for combat aircraft. In the first month of the German Blue offensive alone, the Russians lost 2436 tanks and 783 aircraft. Lend-Lease was currently bridging this gap and allowing some front-line growth.[69]

Although PQ 16 and 17 had between them moved seventy ships, and the Americans had scaled back deliveries on the Arctic route following the Admiralty reduction to three convoys every two months, PQ 17's departure still left a backlog of twelve, primarily American, ships waiting in Iceland with First Protocol supplies. Meanwhile, on 22 June, a further eight British-controlled and three Soviet ships carrying June quotas were either already on their way to Iceland or still being loaded in British ports. In addition, a further twenty-eight American-controlled ships were expected to reach Iceland in time to join PQ 18 currently due to depart on 18 July. If PQ 18 was limited to thirty-five ships, the backlog would increase to at least sixteen and PQ 19 was not scheduled to leave until 30 August. A major effort was now going into improving the Persian route with 200,000 tons despatched to the Gulf by thirty-two ships over the last three months, including 400 each of aircraft and tanks. However, not only was this still barely one-third of deliveries via the Arctic in the same period but very little on this southern route had yet reached the Soviet front line. Overall, therefore, there was both a significant deficit still in First Protocol deliveries and a growing risk that those under the Second Protocol would start more than a month in arrears. Molotov's fear that Russia would receive neither a second front nor supplies was becoming reality.[70]

Given the German commitment to an all-out surface attack, the fate of PQ 17, and potentially its westbound pair convoy QP 13 also with thirty-five ships, now rested heavily on the intelligence available to the two sides. For the British, the challenge was to confirm how, when and where the German intent identified by Denham would be implemented. For their part, the Germans had to locate and track the convoy, which was sailing later than they anticipated, taking it into a month when visibility was less predictable and enabling it to transit further north. They also had to convince Hitler there was minimal risk of interference from British heavy ships and, above all, carriers.

By far the most valuable source available to the British was Ultra drawn from continuing coverage of the Enigma Red key used by the German air force and the naval home waters key Dolphin. When PQ 17 sailed, this provided excellent coverage of German air and U-boat strength and dispositions across the Arctic region, including German air force plans for finding and shadowing the convoy and their reports on the position of the ice edge. It is not clear why the Arctic U-boats never adopted the more sophisticated four-rotor Shark key which their Atlantic and Mediterranean counterparts had been using since February and which the British could not read until November. Possibly the Germans just saw some security advantage in using different keys for different theatres but, in this case, it was an unexpected windfall for GC&CS. German surface units in Norway also used Dolphin and the British could anticipate this giving valuable insights on the movements and intent of the Trondheim and Narvik forces once they sailed, as had been the case with *Tirpitz*'s foray in March. There was a brief moment of anxiety on

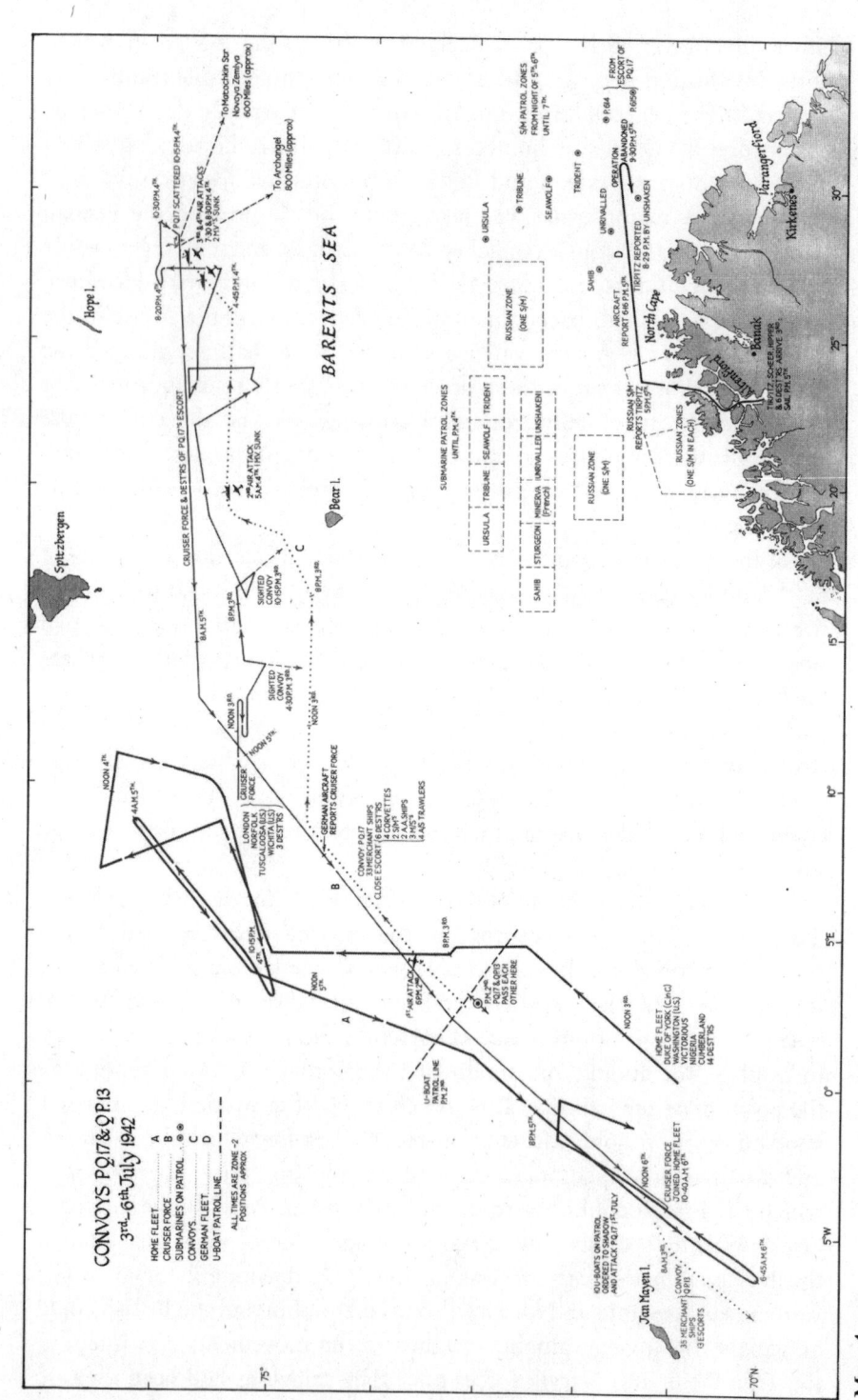

Map 4

the morning of 3 July when GC&CS was unable to decrypt two signals which it feared suggested German use of a new four-rotor system for flag officers which the British had designated Barracuda. Fortunately, this was not the case and apart from these signals all traffic remained readable. Swedish SIGINT updates from Denham were also possible but, given the constraints around his meetings with Björnstjerna, unlikely to be timely. In the event, Denham did provide one important report late on 3 July.

Although GC&CS had been reading Dolphin continuously for a year, its coverage was not seamless. The Germans changed settings at noon every day so that the key had to be effectively broken afresh every 24 hours, requiring considerable input from Bletchley's electro-mechanical computers or 'bombes'. During PQ 17's passage, shortage of bombe capacity at Bletchley required difficult decisions over the relative priority given to decrypting traffic for the Arctic theatre and the Western Desert where the final German drive for Cairo was underway. The chiefs of staff ruled in favour of the Arctic. For technical reasons, breaking the second 24-hour period of changes in settings was easier than the first, so that delays in decryption generally occurred every 48 hours, to be followed by 48 hours of increasingly current reading until the next major change. This 'decryption cycle' had important consequences for PQ 17. A further important source of intelligence available to the British was aerial photographic reconnaissance (PR). By this time, the Royal Air Force's United Kingdom reconnaissance group, No 1 PRU, had two-engine Mosquitos capable of covering Trondheim and Narvik and the latest PR Spitfires could reach the former. In addition, for the PQ 17 operation, the Russians agreed to the basing of eight Coastal Command Catalinas at Grasnaya, on the Kola near Vaenga, and Lake Lakhta near Archangel which it was planned would monitor the area east from the longitude of Altafiord once the convoy had passed Bear Island.[71] A final intelligence source was the network of coast-watching stations established by SIS. During the spring this had contributed useful information on the Trondheim group and in May the first site in the far north, near Tromsø, became active but its capability at this time was limited and it could provide no regular coverage of Altafiord. Although there have been persistent claims of an agent reporting from Altafiord itself, many of these originated as a cover story for Ultra. The evidence for an agent in the area at this time, possibly working for the Norwegian resistance, is tenuous and, if one did exist, there was no reporting relevant to PQ 17.[72]

The OIC, the NID section in the 'Citadel', the Admiralty's purpose-built underground headquarters, which collated and assessed all intelligence relating to the war at sea has been described earlier. By mid-1942, co-located with key elements of the Naval Staff, this had matured into a highly effective organisation which enjoyed a uniquely close relationship with GC&CS Naval Section at Bletchley Park, its most important source. By this time too, GC&CS Naval Section was much more than a provider of raw decrypts. Like the OIC, it received copies of all naval intelligence collected from every source and had the resources and expertise to conduct deep long-term research complementing the immediate operational focus of the OIC. Whilst in harbour, Tovey and his staff officers cleared for Ultra were in regular contact with the OIC by telex and scrambler telephone, providing a constantly updated intelligence picture. Once at sea, sensitive intelligence was conveyed by Ultra signals using one-time encryption pads available only to flag officers. During PQ 17, in accordance with established practice, only Tovey and Hamilton were Ultra recipients. The OIC was permitted to originate intelligence signals without staff clearance but was required carefully to distinguish fact from assessment and comment. It was also now standard practice to keep Ultra recipients at sea informed on the breaking of daily settings, using phrases such as 'Information from 1200/1 to 1200/3 not yet available. Expected time uncertain but probably by 0800/3.'[73]

Although the German naval SIGINT division, B-Dienst, was also enjoying significant success in reading British and Allied naval traffic during 1942, contrary to recent claims this provided only limited help in monitoring PQ convoys.[74] B-Dienst's chief success this year lay in breaking British Naval Cipher No 3, also known as the Combined Cipher, which it began reading 'currently and extensively' from March. This cipher was used for communication between British, American and Canadian naval forces and was the dominant cipher used in managing Atlantic convoy operations. This achievement was supplemented by similar readability of the Merchant Navy Code. These penetrations gave U-boat Command a valuable intelligence advantage at a time when GC&CS could not read Shark. There was little call to use the Combined Cipher in controlling the PQ convoys but the Merchant Navy Code provided useful intelligence as did occasional plain-language intercepts. B-Dienst penetration of the Royal Navy's primary cipher in use at this time, Naval Cipher No 4, which would have yielded more relevant and valuable intelligence, was limited and usually only achieved with a significant time lag. For example, on 26 June, B-Dienst provided decrypts of Admiralty signals sent on 21 April, 7 and 17 May, covering respectively losses to QP 10, PQ 16, and the air attack on *Prinz Eugen* while on passage back to Germany. But even the most recent of these messages was more than a month old. Fortunately for the security of Ultra, the Flag Officers' Cipher was never broken. Overall, B-Dienst could only provide occasional insights on the progress of PQ 17.[75]

Given this limited help from SIGINT, the Germans were dependent for news of PQ 17's sailing and progress on aerial reconnaissance and U-boat sightings. Although the Abwehr had achieved occasional agent reporting on shipping movements in Iceland, this was rarely reliable and timely, subject as noted earlier to British intervention and deception, and it did not contribute to PQ 17. 5th Air Fleet began sweeping for PQ 17 in mid-June but the first circumstantial evidence for its departure was only acquired on 30 June when the westward-bound QP 13 was briefly sighted 180 miles north north-west of North Cape before the weather closed in. The likelihood that PQ 17 had also sailed was consistent with the brief sighting of a naval force including an American battleship north-east of Iceland two days earlier.[76] However, bad weather hampered effective air searches of the area between Iceland and Jan Mayen between 28 June and 2 July and the first definite sightings of PQ 17 were therefore made by *U-255* and *U-406* on the afternoon of 1 July and by *U-456* early the following morning. An air sighting on the afternoon of 2 July confirmed that the convoy comprised up to thirty-seven merchant ships and sixteen escorts. Meanwhile intermittent sightings of QP 13 the same day, backed by intercepts from B-Dienst, confirmed correctly that the two convoys had passed each other roughly midway between Jan Mayen and Bear Island. The initial U-boat sightings were sufficient for Group North to initiate Rösselsprung and order the Trondheim and Narvik groups, also known as 'Task Forces I and II', to move to their advance bases, respectively the southern entrance to Gimsøystraumen and Altafiord. (Gimsøystraumen was a strait, about 100 miles west of the Bogen Bay anchorage, in the south-west Lofotens connecting Vest Fiord with the Atlantic. Contrary to Denham's report, Schniewind had chosen it in preference to Bogen Bay.) The German Naval Staff did not demur over these moves but worried that poor July visibility would render the operation more difficult.[77]

The Trondheim and Narvik groups accordingly deployed the evening of 2 July at 2000 and midnight respectively. *Lützow* ran aground in fog near the Storbøen lighthouse, while negotiating the narrow channel west of Bogen Bay between the Lofoten chain and the mainland. This channel had been selected to keep the task group close inshore and hopefully away from British eyes. *Lützow* was sufficiently damaged to oblige her return to Bogen Bay and she took no further part in the operation. *Scheer* and her accompanying destroyers reached Altafiord in the late afternoon. Shortly after the two German forces departed, 5th Air Fleet spotted a substantial enemy force, comprising a carrier, two battleships, three cruisers and five destroyers, 150 miles south-east of Jan Mayen. Group North assumed correctly this was the customary British heavy covering force. It was currently positioned about 275 miles south-west of the convoy and judged unlikely to pose a significant threat unless it moved further east. If it did so, Group North planned to move both German task groups to Altafiord and reassess options. Subsequent sightings, before contact was lost at 0430, raised the possibility of two enemy groups but Group North was confident the sightings were of the same force. To provide warning of a British move east towards the Norwegian coast, four Fw 200s flew an extensive search between northern Norway and Jan Mayen over the night of 3/4 July which found nothing. However, this was false reassurance. Tovey had moved beyond this search to the north-east and was well placed to cover the convoy then passing north of Bear Island.[78]

Later in the day, 5th Air Fleet speculated that the unusual strength of the enemy naval forces suggested not a PQ operation but a major raid on either Norway or Spitzbergen. However, both Group North and the Naval Staff insisted this was PQ 17 and enemy strength reflected the threat from German heavy units. There were sightings of another enemy force mid-afternoon of 3 July by *U-457* and at 2245 that evening by 5th Air Fleet. Both reported a battleship, two or three cruisers and three destroyers cruising close to the convoy.[79] This was clearly Hamilton's squadron and Group North correctly judged the 'battleship' was probably a cruiser and part of a separate close covering force distinct from that sighted earlier in the day, although Schmundt, who as Admiral Arctic was controlling U-boats, apparently believed there was also a carrier in the area.[80] Contact with the convoy itself was intermittent during the day but there were sufficient air and U-boat sightings to keep German commanders abreast of its progress and B-Dienst intercepts confirmed its speed averaged 8 knots.[81]

At 1600 on 3 July, when the convoy was 60 miles due west of Bear Island, Group North decided that the *Tirpitz* group, which had reached Vest Fiord two hours earlier, should now transfer to Altafiord by the following morning rather than sortieing directly from Gimsøystraumen. This reflected desire to persist with Rösselsprung balanced with continuing uncertainty over the status of the enemy covering forces. Locating the whole German force in Altafiord minimised the time for executing the operation once it was judged safe to proceed. Raeder agreed, as did Vice Admiral Krancke in Hitler's absence, on the understanding there would be no subsequent move from Altafiord without specific Führer approval. Schniewind accordingly departed soon after 1700, although he seems to have pre-empted official authorisation. Three of his five destroyers were almost immediately damaged after they grounded on apparently uncharted rocks when entering the Gimsøystraumen channel and were forced to return to Trondheim. This incident, along with *Lützow*'s mishap, reduced the total force allocated to Rösselsprung by 25 per cent and reflected poorly on German seamanship.

That night the German Naval Staff judged that the concentration in Altafiord would soon become known to British commanders (presumably from their air or submarine reconnaissance), giving the latter four options. They could turn the convoy back, bring up their heavy covering force to fight it through, strengthen convoy defence and bring up a separate carrier force to threaten the Lofotens and Alta area, or, finally, keep their heavy forces out of range of air attack and leave convoy defence to the standard PQ close escort. The first two would render German surface attack impossible but impose costs on the British, abandonment of or serious delay to PQ 17 or damage to valuable units from German air or U-boat attack. The third option would probably put a German sortie at unacceptable risk. Only the last British option allowed Rösselsprung to be successfully and safely executed. All would now depend on determining the status and intent of the force detected close to the convoy at 2245 (Hamilton's cruisers). If air reconnaissance confirmed this group was no longer heading east or contained no battleship, an attack by the combined force now concentrating at Altafiord on the morning of 4 July would become possible either later that day or the next.[82]

Meanwhile, from a British perspective, despite all the foreboding created by Denham's warning, for the first week of its passage, PQ 17 advanced steadily and largely untroubled by enemy intervention although one ship was damaged by ice in the Denmark Strait and forced to return to Iceland. U-boats were sighted on 1 July and intermittently thereafter but were driven off without difficulty. German air surveillance began that day and their shadowing was regular thereafter, facilitating an initial attack by nine torpedo bombers on the evening of 2 July. This did not penetrate the escort screen and achieved no hits while the Germans lost one aircraft. The convoy lost no ship until 0500 on 4 July, when a single aircraft torpedoed the American merchant ship *Christopher Newport* through a hole in the fog as PQ 17 was skirting the ice 60 miles north of Bear Island and the *Tirpitz* group was approaching Altafiord, 300 miles to the south.[83]

Ultra provided no intelligence on German surface movements before 0500 on 3 July when the settings for the period 1200 1 July to 1200 3 July were broken and the most important decrypts from this period reached the OIC over the next five hours. By 1030, the OIC had informed Tovey and Hamilton that PQ 17 was being closely shadowed subject to weather, that *Tirpitz*, *Scheer* and *Lützow* were all at sea since late the previous evening, although the latter two were apparently not in company, and that their movements were associated with Operations 'Concert' and 'Knight's Move'. In addition, at 2100 on 2 July, the Home Fleet battle group had not been sighted by the Germans for 24 hours.[84] Overall, although the Admiralty did not say so, this intelligence suggested that a combined attack on PQ 17 by the two German task groups was now unlikely before it reached the longitude of Bear Island. The *Tirpitz* group would require 36 hours at 20 knots to reach the convoy before it passed the island and one decrypt put the *Scheer* group only just north of the Lofotens at 0500. Overall, this initial intelligence package lent credence to Hamilton's view the previous evening that *Tirpitz* might head for the westbound QP 13 and lure Tovey southwards while the pocket battleships made for PQ 17 to the east of Bear Island. Until now he had shadowed the convoy 40 miles to the north, hoping not to be spotted by air reconnaissance and allowing him then to take the pocket battleships, if they attacked, by surprise. Now, on the morning of 3 July, with the knowledge the *Scheer* group was definitely at sea, he decided to close the convoy and disclose his position in case the Germans attacked in thick weather and escaped unscathed. In the event, despite his efforts, the Germans did not spot his force until midafternoon. Meanwhile, that forenoon, after learning from the Admiralty that the ice edge was further north than anticipated, Hamilton used his flagship *London*'s Walrus aircraft to order Broome to take the convoy well north of Bear Island and adopt a course keeping at 400 miles range from Banak airfield. Anxious to keep moving eastward, Broome only partially complied but, at 1700, he received a direct order from the Admiralty to pass at least 50 miles north of Bear Island while Hamilton underlined his instructions regarding Banak next day. Overall, this northward shift cost the convoy about four hours of eastward movement but added about the same time to German interception from Altafiord.[85]

Poor weather had prevented aerial reconnaissance of Trondheim and Narvik for several days but a PR Spitfire succeeded in photographing the former at 1400 on the afternoon of 3 July and confirmed *Tirpitz* and *Hipper* were at sea.[86] It was this intelligence which caused the Admiralty to insist that Broome pass well north of Bear Island. Tovey now steered for a position 150 miles north-west of the island to bring him within air strike range of the convoy if the Germans intervened up to midday on 4 July. Hamilton, judging that the pocket battleships had now reached Altafiord, decided to exercise the discretion available to him in the Admiralty's 27 June orders and stay with the convoy until it reached longitude 25° East, approximately 100 miles beyond Bear Island in the afternoon of 4 July. Meanwhile, the Admiralty informed both flag officers that Catalinas operating from Iceland, supported by B-24 Liberators, would sweep the coastal strip from Altafiord to North Cape from mid-afternoon 3 July until early on 5 July to give early warning when any German force exited.[87]

The remainder of 3 July passed without significant incident for both convoy and covering forces. *U-88*, *U-456*, and *U-255* all attempted attacks but were driven off by the escorts or frustrated by poor visibility.[88] A long Ultra signal to Tovey and Hamilton at 1745 confirmed that all traffic up to noon on 3 July, when the latest readable settings expired, had been studied but added no significant new information other than an assessment that the *Tirpitz* group had left Trondheim by midnight the previous evening. It added ominously that no further Ultra traffic was expected until 2359 on 4 July. A further Admiralty signal at 2220 sent to all Home Fleet forces confirmed that the enemy was moving heavy ships northward, thus threatening the convoy, but assessed there was no imminent danger. The Admiralty was therefore taking no further action but awaiting developments.[89]

The established PQ 17 intelligence story for 3 and 4 July focuses primarily on Ultra Enigma coverage, especially the consequences of the gap before traffic for the period 1200 3 July to 1200 5 July became available from 1900 on 4 July. However, early on 4 July, the OIC now transmitted another piece of intelligence to Tovey and Hamilton with implications generally neglected. This drew on a report from Denham transmitted from Stockholm the previous afternoon but received just before midnight. It stated that the westbound QP 13 had been spotted near North Cape the afternoon of 2 July but then lost in fog. Sighting of PQ 17 was at that time anticipated shortly and would trigger the German plan reported by Denham on 13 June. However, the attack on the convoy would now occur in the area between longitudes 15° and 30° East, from roughly 50 miles west of Bear Island to 150 miles east of it. The OIC indicated to Tovey and Hamilton that the source was the same as the mid-June report which they knew was Swedish intercept of German navy landline communications. It was the first hard intelligence that the Germans might focus their attack well east of Bear Island. The report was shared with the US Navy liaison office in London which passed it to Washington in the late afternoon.[90]

When the OIC relayed this intelligence, PQ 17 was already about to pass due north of Bear Island. It therefore implied the attack would come in the next 150 miles and 18 hours. This had obvious implications for

Hamilton's cruisers which would reach their ordered turnaround point of 25° East at about 1400, well short of the eastern limit of the new surface-attack zone specified in the report. Through the subsequent forenoon, the Admiralty had enough D/F indications to know the convoy and Hamilton were being closely shadowed while Broome had ample visual evidence too.[91] The key question for the senior British commanders was therefore the deterrent value of the cruisers. This was the key topic at a staff conference called by Pound mid-morning. If the German attack option was confined to the pocket battleships and their destroyers sortieing from Altafiord (and the British had no evidence at this stage that *Lützow* was absent), Hamilton's force might well be seen as posing them too high a risk. On the other hand, if *Tirpitz* and *Hipper* and their destroyers were also available, the equation changed radically. They could attack the convoy, confident of destroying Hamilton if he stood in the way. This worst case possibility apparently caused Pound to reconsider the option of 'scattering' because he called Captain Gordon Allen, Deputy Director Trade, to the staff meeting to ask if PQ 17 merchant vessels carried one-time pads which would permit communication with the Admiralty if the convoy was dispersed. Allen confirmed this was the case.[92] (In 1947, Allen was appointed Churchill's naval research assistant for his post-war Second World War history and in this capacity investigated the whole background to PQ 17 two years later.[93])

At 1230, the Admiralty signalled Hamilton that he could proceed east of 25° E 'should situation demand it' although they were not urging him to do so against his 'discretion'.[94] Subsequent accounts of PQ 17 invariably struggle to reconcile this new 'permission' with the firm policy established on 27 June. They also present it as the initiation of Admiralty interference over the head of Tovey which would dictate events for the rest of the day. However, the signal makes sense if Pound's Admiralty meeting had concluded that two pocket battleships at Altafiord were currently the only German force capable of executing the attack foreshadowed in the new 0230 intelligence originating from Denham, and that these could be deterred or countered by Hamilton. Although the available evidence suggests this was indeed the Admiralty view, they could have explained their thinking to Tovey and Hamilton rather than assuming they could work it out. In the event, it is clear Hamilton shared the implicit Admiralty assessment and was keen to stay with the convoy. By contrast, Tovey apparently feared that *Tirpitz* might already be in the Barents Sea, subsequently insisting that he knew of no information justifying a reversal of the principles set out on 27 June. He therefore ordered Hamilton at 1512 to withdraw when he reached 25° E unless the

Admiralty was certain he would not meet *Tirpitz*. The Admiralty did not address Tovey's stipulation which probably persuaded Pound to visit the OIC in late afternoon to ask when *Tirpitz* could reach PQ 17 if she had moved direct from Trondheim. Rear Admiral Patrick Brind, the Assistant Chief of the Naval Staff (Home), suggested she could already be in striking range but Commander Norman (Ned) Denning, who headed the surface plot in the OIC, thought this unlikely, arguing that her destroyers would need a stop at Narvik or Tromsø to refuel. Pound apparently accepted this. Meanwhile, poor Hamilton was left with contradictory instructions. However, he remained convinced that he should stick with the convoy at least for the rest of the day and used the need to refuel his destroyers to stall Tovey.[95]

The Admiralty judgement that the Germans would be deterred by the presence of Hamilton's cruisers was correct. Perhaps surprisingly, the deterrence effect continued to apply even after *Tirpitz* and *Hipper* joined *Scheer* in Altafiord at 0900 on 4 July. German caution was probably influenced by ongoing doubt as to whether the Allied close covering force comprised four heavy cruisers or included a battleship[96] and, following an apparent sighting of two suspected British torpedo bombers at 1830,[97] the possibility of a carrier in the vicinity. (These supposed 'torpedo aircraft' were probably Walruses catapulted from Hamilton's cruisers.) There was also concern that, without *Lützow* and three of Schniewind's destroyers, the British covering force and close escort was now competitive enough to inflict serious damage on the German force even if they were eventually overwhelmed. In the forenoon, the German Naval Staff accordingly informed Vice Admiral Krancke at Führer headquarters and OKW that the presence of heavy forces near the convoy made it impossible to execute Rösselsprung unless air and submarine forces could degrade them. Schmundt separately directed his U-boats that heavy enemy forces were their major target when encountered.[98] By 1700, Group North set a final deadline of 1700 the following day, 5 July, for implementing the operation, otherwise the Trondheim group should be withdrawn to Narvik.[99]

On the British side, shortly after 1800, no doubt to appease Tovey, Hamilton reported that he intended leaving the convoy and retiring westward at 2200 once refuelling of his destroyers was complete. By that point, as the Admiralty and Tovey could easily calculate, he would be at least 60 miles east of the original 25° East limit. This time the Admiralty did respond with an Ultra signal nearly an hour later instructing Hamilton to stay with the convoy pending further instructions. This terse signal carried two implications. First, that the latest Dolphin settings had been broken. GC&CS had in fact achieved this at 1837, over five hours earlier than originally feared, and the first decrypts reached the OIC at 1900. Secondly, at this point the Admiralty evidently still believed that any German surface attack would be confined to the pocket battleships, which Hamilton and Broome could deter or combat, and that *Tirpitz* was not an imminent threat.[100]

While the Admiralty assessed the new decrypts, PQ 17 was preoccupied with two successive air attacks, the first conducted in strength for 48 hours. This long pause was primarily down to poor visibility with long periods of fog and low cloud hampering operations at the airfields as well as over the Barents Sea. It is also possible 5th Air Fleet held back operations on the morning of 4 July in the expectation that a fleet sortie from Altafiord was imminent. However, by 1530, Fliegerführer Lofoten was preparing a substantial strike for 2000, suggesting that no surface operations were now expected that day.[101] The first attack to hit the convoy at 1930 was a half-hearted affair inflicting no damage. A handful of Ju 88s bombed ineffectively, hampered by low-lying cloud while six He 115 torpedo bombers proved reluctant to press home their attack against intense anti-aircraft fire and released their weapons outside the screen to no effect. Broome commended the performance of the American destroyer *Wainwright*, part of Hamilton's force present because she was fuelling from *Aldersdale*. Armed with five 5in high-angle guns and the latest fire control, she delivered highly effective long-range fire. The second attack, detected on *Palomares*' radar at 2020, nearly an hour later, comprised twenty-three He 111 torpedo bombers from Banak which approached in two successive waves, fast and very low on the starboard quarter and from astern. The leader, Leutnant Konrad Hennemann, who late received a posthumous Knight's Cross, drove in with great determination to the middle of the convoy and put two torpedoes into *Navarino* before crashing in flames ahead of *Keppel*. The fate of the leader discouraged the remainder who proved reluctant to brave the intense anti-aircraft barrage and hit only two more ships. One of these, the Russian tanker *Azerbaidjan* was not seriously damaged and eventually reached harbour. The other vessel, *William Hooper*, had to be sunk along with *Navarino*. The Germans, who claimed they had sunk five ships and damaged the same number, lost three aircraft.[102]

At 2100, having beaten off these air attacks, the convoyed ships, Broome's close escort and Hamilton's cruisers visible in the distance could be well satisfied with PQ 17's progress. They were now 130 miles north north-east of Bear Island and had covered a good part of the most dangerous stretch of the passage for the loss of only three ships. Every

U-boat attempt to close the convoy had been firmly countered. Now two air assaults had been beaten off with little damage to the convoy and significant attrition inflicted on the attackers, operating the closest they would ever be to their main airfield and in near perfect conditions. Captain Don Moon of the *Wainwright*, which had made a valuable contribution in fighting off both attacks, commended the performance of the close escort under Broome to Hamilton as 'particularly impressive'.[103] The official staff history also judged convoy discipline and shooting 'admirable' with a substantial toll on the enemy. Broome sensed high morale bordering on elation. His impression 'on seeing the resolution displayed by the convoy and its escort was that, provided the ammunition lasted, PQ 17 could get anywhere'.[104] Broome's euphoria was short lived. At 2040, soon after the final German aircraft disappeared, he received a terse signal from Hamilton – 'Due to proximity surface forces report when convoy is on 045 degrees'. This confirmed an order from Hamilton just prior to the second attack to make this course change. Unknown to Broome, Hamilton had received an Ultra signal an hour earlier advising that *Tirpitz* had reached Altafiord at 0900 that morning. PQ 17 was now only 20 miles from the eastern limit revealed in Denham's intelligence, and the range from Altafiord was steadily increasing. The Admiralty had ordered him to await instructions, but he must now have been feeling less comfortable with his decision to stick with the convoy against Tovey's wishes. Meanwhile Broome could only speculate on what Hamilton meant by 'proximity'. He considered launching the convoy's Hurricane aboard the CAM Ship *Empire Tide* to search the threat sector to the south-west and take down any aerial shadower. He also ordered his two submarines to stay in the vicinity of the convoy if it was attacked, seeking opportunities to counter-attack at their discretion. This led to a famous but amusing exchange when the senior submarine commander signalled – 'In the event of attack by heavy enemy surface forces propose to remain on the surface' and Broome responded – 'So do I'. Broome's growing sense of looming threat was compounded by a report from *Pozarica* at 2147 exploiting her superior radar – 'Suspected formation, 230 degrees, 29 miles'. That implied something coming from Norway. However, neither Hamilton nor Broome were prepared for what was actually coming next.[105]

## Chapter 8

# PQ 17: Catastrophe and Aftermath

The news that Bletchley had broken the Dolphin daily settings for the period beginning midday on 3 July was telephoned to Ned Denning in the Admiralty OIC at 1837 by Harry Hinsley, Deputy Head of GC&CS Naval Section. The 23-year-old Hinsley had been recruited to GC&CS as a Cambridge undergraduate historian at the start of the war and rapidly demonstrated extraordinary aptitude for intelligence work. He not only possessed outstanding analytical skills but had the rare ability to present complex technical issues in terms operational officers, including the most senior, could understand. He had an excellent eye for an opportunity and had planned the key 'pinches' of cryptographic material which had made the breaking of naval Enigma possible. Despite his youth, his self-confidence and sheer mastery of every aspect of SIGINT capability ensured that he was given a key role in sensitive negotiations with the Americans later in the summer. But, for the present, he was the key interpreter of GC&CS intercepts relevant to PQ 17.[1]

*The Impact of New Ultra Intelligence on the Evening of 4 July*
Denning passed the news to Captain John Eccles, Director of Operations (Home), who was present in the OIC talking to its Director, Rear Admiral Jock Clayton. Eccles left to brief Pound and his own immediate superior, Brind, but before doing so drafted the holding signal on awaiting instructions to Hamilton, copied to Tovey, sent at 1858. Meanwhile Bletchley began decrypting the new traffic, concentrating first on those German signals which from outward appearance (addressees and precedence) seemed the most urgent operationally. Following the receipt of the two indecipherable signals the previous day, Bletchley was relieved that all traffic was still encrypted with the Dolphin system.[2] The first two signals to be teleprinted through to the OIC were in 'officer' cipher and could not be read, the next two had limited significance but the fifth

and sixth were potentially important and the eighth, arriving at 1859, crucial. The fifth advised two U-boats in the vicinity of the convoy on the afternoon of the previous day that their main task was to shadow. The sixth reported an aerial sighting of what was clearly Hamilton's force at 0015 the previous morning but stated that it included a battleship. This was the first of several decrypts revealing German uncertainty over the composition of the cruiser group but unfortunately the next ones did not reach the OIC until after 2000, more than an hour later. Meanwhile, the vital eighth signal was addressed to Kummetz from Schniewind in *Tirpitz* at 0612 that morning. It stated that the Trondheim group would arrive in Altafiord at 0900 and Kummetz was requested to allot an anchorage to *Tirpitz* in outer Vagfiord. Accompanying destroyers and torpedo boats were also to be immediately refuelled.[3]

The issue was now what this important new intelligence, likely soon to be supplemented by further decrypts, signified. Denning began drafting an Ultra signal to Tovey and Hamilton giving the facts but also adding comment. He proposed to explain why *Tirpitz* and the rest of the German force were unlikely yet to have sailed. Denning had the authority to release such intelligence signals although, in a situation of this importance, he would probably have consulted Eccles. In the event, before he could finish, Eccles returned with Pound and Brind. Having studied these initial decrypts, Pound asked what Denning proposed to say. He then instructed him to stick to the facts and delete the comment. Oddly, the revised signal despatched at 1918 referred only to *Tirpitz*'s arrival and the shadowing U-boats the previous day but omitted the sixth decrypt suggesting that Hamilton's force included a battleship. It did clarify that *Scheer* was already present at Altafiord but did not mention *Lützow*.

Only now did Pound cross-examine Denning on what the decrypts meant. Denning advised that the *Tirpitz* group would take three hours to fuel and a realistic intercept speed to reach the convoy was about 25 knots although less if the pocket battleships were in company. Looking at the chart, Pound surmised that the Germans could therefore reach the convoy at midnight, now only four and a half hours away. Hamilton separately was making a similar calculation – hence his signal to Broome regarding the proximity of enemy forces.[4] Pound then asked Denning why he thought *Tirpitz* had not yet left Alta. Denning set out his arguments. First, there was no evidence that U-boats had been ordered to clear away from the convoy, as he would expect in advance of any surface attack to avoid the risk of friendly fire. Indeed, D/F intercepts of U-boat transmissions showed them still near the convoy. Secondly, despite intense air reconnaissance, the Germans had not relocated Tovey's force which they had lost at 0430 on 3 July. This must be a concern. Thirdly, they had made several sightings of Hamilton's force near the convoy with some suggesting the presence of a battleship or even a carrier. The Germans would want to clarify precisely what they were taking on. Fourthly, although Bletchley had not yet broken into the traffic beginning 1200 on 4 July, transmissions during the afternoon did not show the normal pattern when a major force was at sea. Finally, there had been no sighting report from the British and Russian submarine screen spread across the North Cape area. Although Brind and Eccles intervened regularly with questions and comments, Pound apparently said little. At about 1930, he got up to go to the adjacent U-boat tracking room, headed by Commander Rodger Winn. Before doing so, he asked Denning if he could assure him that *Tirpitz* was still in Altafiord. Denning responded that, although confident she was, he could not provide absolute certainty but hoped to get it once Bletchley broke the latest daily settings. It seems Denning's arguments convinced Brind and Eccles and he thought he had persuaded Pound too, but this soon proved not to be the case.[5]

Two things are missing from surviving informal accounts of this meeting. First, the arrival of the *Tirpitz* group in Altafiord must have been a shock to all present. Until now, the British command all apparently envisaged the Trondheim and Narvik groups operating separately, with the pocket battleships alone using the forward base at Altafiord. Hence the assessment earlier in the day that *Tirpitz* was not yet in the Barents Sea, with the implication that her aim was probably to keep the Home Fleet heavy covering force well to the west of Bear Island, and that Hamilton could therefore safely stay for longer with the convoy as a deterrent to the pocket battleships acting alone. It now seemed that the Germans had not only decided to deploy as an overwhelming concentrated force but that their intent had always been to strike well to the east of Bear Island. This intent was consistent with Denham's intelligence from the previous night although that had lacked detail and given no warning of concentration. Pound must have felt the threat to the convoy was now greater than any previous worst-case assessment but also, through his misjudgement that afternoon, that he had left Hamilton horribly exposed. He must also have considered that, if Denham's latest intelligence that the Germans intended to attack in the area between longitudes 15° and 30° East was correct, the convoy would soon reach the eastern limit of that bracket. Did that not imply that the German force would sail as soon as fuelling was complete?

The second omission from the accounts is any reference to challenges to Denning's arguments. Were none of the obvious counterpoints aired? The

German force at Altafiord might be communicating with Group North via landline which could not be intercepted and then have sailed under strict radio silence giving none of the usual clues. The British/Russian submarine screen had to cover a substantial distance and there was no guarantee they would sight the departing Germans, especially if visibility was poor. If intercept was planned for midnight or the early hours of 5 July, it was too soon to order U-boats clear of the convoy and every reason to keep them shadowing. If the Germans planned an intercept 150 miles east of Bear Island, would they really see much risk from the Home Fleet heavy covering force? Finally, radio communication in the Arctic region was notoriously variable. There was no guarantee every German message had been picked up. All these limitations in coverage would be demonstrated to some extent the following day. Pound must also have considered that a rather more elaborate alert system had completely failed to warn of the Cerberus breakout from Brest in February.[6]

Whatever the full scope of the debate with Denning and Pound's conclusions, almost nothing is known of the subsequent discussion with Winn in the U-boat tracking room. Twenty years later, by which time he was a senior judge, Winn claimed to have informed Pound that the U-boat situation was 'very serious indeed' and particularly 'dangerous' to Hamiton's cruiser force.[7] However, in making these comments, he carefully avoided any reference to Ultra. What is now clear is that Hinsley alerted Winn and Denning around 1930 that the Dolphin settings for the 24 hours from 1200 on 4 July had now been broken, so Pound would have learnt this on arrival in the U-boat tracking room or soon after. However, the first decrypt from the new period was not teleprinted through until 2000. Whether Pound was still there and stayed to see the four valuable decrypts which arrived by 2015 is unknown although he must have left by 2020 to attend a full staff meeting called for 10 minutes later in the First Sea Lord's room upstairs. Prior to the arrival of the new decrypts, Winn's picture of the U-boat threat depended on intercepted signals prior to 1200, now more than eight hours old, and D/F intercepts which by their nature were neither comprehensive nor accurate. However, his plot was probably good enough to suggest there were at least half a dozen U-boats in the vicinity of PQ 17 and Hamilton's cruisers. There were in fact eight at sea in the area at this time.[8]

The first decrypts from the post-1200 settings arriving between 2000 and 2015 now revealed that at 1500 two U-boats (*U-88* and *U-334*) were shadowing the convoy while *U-457* was in touch with Hamilton's force. Simultaneously, Schmundt, who as Admiral Arctic had control of the U-boats, ordered the respective shadowers to maintain contact but all other boats, exploiting *U-457*'s sighting reports, were to attack Hamilton's cruisers, described as a 'battleship formation'. It was clear therefore that, in mid-afternoon, elements of the German command still believed there was at least one battleship providing close cover to PQ 17 although an air sighting transmitted at 1455 got Hamilton's composition right apart from judging that three of the four heavy cruisers were American. A final decrypt received in this 15-minute period, originating at 1430, reported that seven Fw 200 aircraft conducting a reconnaissance sweep out to the west, clearly targeted at the Home Fleet heavy covering force, had sighted nothing.[9]

Denning received these decrypts in parallel to Winn and at 2031 a new one arrived, albeit from the previous day's Dolphin settings, giving the text of a signal from Schmundt to all U-boats sent at 1020 that morning. It stated that there were no friendly forces in the operational area and, although the position of the 'heavy enemy group' (clearly Hamilton's force) was not known at present, it was the main target when encountered. Meanwhile, U-boats shadowing the convoy should keep at it.[10] Denning claimed later that he attached great significance to this decrypt, arguing that it proved *Tirpitz* had not sailed that morning. He rushed to find Clayton who was on his way to Pound's meeting and hastily briefed him. It is not known how Clayton reacted to this specific item. In reality, it did not change the arguments already put to Pound and it predated the afternoon decrypts from the latest settings. It had been agreed that refuelling would take until 1200, so apparent confirmation that *Tirpitz* had not sailed at 1130 added nothing. In any case, Schmundt did not say *Tirpitz* was still in Altafiord, merely that there were no forces in the 'operational area' which could reasonably be interpreted as 200 miles away. *Tirpitz* could have left at 1200 and still permitted the U-boats a free hand until early evening.[11]

Having briefed Clayton, Denning drafted an Ultra signal to Tovey and Hamilton summarising all the latest intelligence, emphasising that arriving after 2000. He then added a comment which assessed that *Tirpitz* and the rest of the German force had not left Altafiord by 1200 and the balance of probability was that they had still not sailed. Furthermore, it was unlikely they would sail until they had located and established the strength of all forces supporting the convoy. Denning stated that normally he would have despatched an intelligence signal of this type on his own authority but, given the discussion with Pound, felt he should get Clayton's approval when he returned from Pound's meeting. Meanwhile, about 2045, Winn arrived to show Denning his own Ultra drafts concerning the U-boat situation. These were despatched to Hamilton, copied to Tovey, as two factual signals without comment at 2108 and 2110. He also confided the disturbing news that discussion during Pound's visit to his room suggested a belief that *Tirpitz* was already at sea and had been accompanied by talk of 'dispersing' the convoy. Separate later testimony from Moore appears to confirm such 'talk' but, if Pound was edging towards dispersal when he left Winn's room, it is unlikely he had reached a final decision.[12]

The staff meeting called by Pound in the First Sea Lord's room apparently began slightly later than 2030 and lasted at most 45 minutes.[13] Its main purpose was clearly to decide how to respond to the German concentration in Altafiord and their known intent to attack PQ 17 probably in the area 150 miles east of Bear Island. Apart from Pound, those present included Moore, Brind, Eccles, Clayton, the Assistant Chief of Staff Trade, Rear Admiral Edward King, and Captain Charles Lambe, Director of Plans. There was no formal contemporary record of the meeting and its content can only be gleaned from the sparse testimony of some participants 20 years later. Furthermore, there are few similar staff meetings on operational matters that provide a useful parallel. The meeting presumably opened with an update on the progress of the convoy and current whereabouts of the covering forces, followed by a summary of the latest intelligence and its implications. Pound probably delegated this to Eccles with supporting input from Clayton and Brind. How far these three had sufficiently absorbed all the Ultra material received in the last 90 minutes, the context provided by earlier intelligence including Denham's overnight report, and the assessments and arguments supplied by Denning and Winn, to provide a coherent picture is difficult to judge but, as highly competent officers, it is fair to assume they got the essentials across.[14]

The meeting would then have turned to the action now needed. The first decision was relatively easy. Hamilton's cruisers were about 50 miles east of the 25° East limit originally planned, they could not fight or deter *Tirpitz* as opposed to the pocket battleships, and they were under serious U-boat threat. They should therefore be withdrawn and at high speed to reduce their vulnerability to submarine attack. Churchill suggested after the war that the fact that half of Hamilton's force was American influenced this decision. While there is little evidence to support this, the American presence probably did make Pound even more uncomfortable that he had encouraged Hamilton east against Tovey's advice. If one or more American cruisers were sunk or seriously damaged nearly a thousand miles from a friendly base, awkward questions would be asked. At 2111, a signal was accordingly despatched – 'Cruiser force withdraw westward at high speed'. The urgency of the message, without explanation, was compounded by the highest precedence of 'Most Immediate'. It is inexplicable why no explanation to Hamilton was forthcoming. He might have inferred from Winn's two signals, sent almost simultaneously, that the reason was the U-boat threat but, by the time these were decrypted aboard *London*, he had other things on his mind. Nor could Pound and Moore use Winn's signals as an excuse for brevity because they had not yet seen them.[15]

The more difficult decision was what to do about the convoy. There were essentially three options. The first was to turn the convoy back either temporarily or permanently although it is not clear if this possibility was aired. It was not a realistic choice. The shadowing U-boats would report the turn and, by the time it was complete, the convoy would have retreated barely 20 miles by midnight when the German force could intercept. It was true that an untroubled run for a further eight hours would bring it to 50 miles north-east of Bear Island by 0800. It was also true that the Home Fleet, currently south-west of Spitzbergen and 360 miles from the convoy, could halve that distance in the same period if it moved rapidly east. An attacking German force would then be in comfortable range of *Victorious*'s torpedo bombers. But all this depended on convenient assumptions that the Germans had not yet sailed and would be willing to strike much further west. They were more likely either to let the convoy withdraw permanently in which case no supplies reached Russia or, if it reversed again, wait until it was vulnerable. In any case, the escorts had insufficient fuel to allow a round trip back to Bear Island which would probably also consume precious anti-aircraft ammunition. Pound would also inevitably have drawn lessons from Vigorous three weeks previously. That had surely demonstrated that reversal ended in permanent withdrawal and meant running the gauntlet of air and submarine attack to no benefit. The other choices were to disperse/scatter or to let the convoy continue as planned, hoping that the Germans had not sailed. Pound apparently insisted that the Admiralty must decide between these options. It alone had the full intelligence picture and, with the departure of Hamilton, it was not fair to place the burden of decision on Broome. In any case, it is hard to see how Broome could make any sensible decision without guidance until the enemy actually hove over the horizon. Apart from anything else he was not an Ultra recipient and had little of the previous intelligence picture available to Hamilton and Tovey. However, in reserving the decision to the Admiralty, it is striking that Tovey was seemingly left out of the equation and he, after all, was supposed to be the overall commander of the PQ 17 operation.

Pound now stated that he favoured dispersal but sought the view of each officer present. All were apparently against immediate dispersal except Moore who later claimed he was completely convinced *Tirpitz* was at sea.[16] He alone insisted it was essential, apparently arguing with chart and dividers that the Germans would be on the convoy in five hours at most and that, because of the proximity of the ice edge, dispersal could only be in a southerly direction. Unless the merchant ships split now, they would run directly into the guns of the approaching Germans. If this is an accurate reflection of Moore's argument, it was flawed. Whatever the merits of immediate dispersal, lack of sea room, as Hamilton or Broome could have confirmed, was not an issue. Ships could and subsequently did disperse nearly a hundred miles northward before hitting impenetrable ice. To the east there was about 400 miles of clear water to Novaya Zemlya. Nevertheless, as the most senior and experienced officer present after Pound, Moore's advice carried weight and was probably critical in reinforcing Pound's existing inclination.

According to Eccles, Pound now leaned back in his leather-backed chair and closed his eyes long enough for Charles Lambe to whisper irreverently – 'Look, Father's fallen asleep' – before reaching for a signal pad and announcing 'The convoy is to be dispersed'. He then made an 'eloquent gesture' conveying that this was his decision taken against the advice of most present. The signal that now issued at 2123, 12 minutes after the withdrawal message to Hamilton said little more – 'Owing to the threat from surface ships convoy is to disperse and proceed to Russian ports'. Moore now raised the distinction between 'disperse' and 'scatter' described in the previous chapter. It is uncertain whether this distinction had been addressed during the previous discussion but Moore pointed out that 'disperse' merely involved a break in formation that allowed ships to proceed in an extended line to Archangel, easy for the Germans to pick off. Surely Pound wanted them to 'scatter' in all directions? Pound confirmed this. A second signal therefore issued at 2136, 13 minutes after the first – 'My 2123/4 Convoy is to scatter.' To reduce the time delay, this second signal was given 'Most Immediate' precedence compared to the previous 'Immediate', either for greater emphasis or in the hope it would be decrypted first on receipt.[17]

How strongly Clayton pressed the OIC case that the Germans had not yet sailed during the meeting and what support he had from Eccles and Brind is unknown. When he returned to the OIC to announce the decision to scatter to an appalled Denning, the latter later described Clayton as 'clearly perturbed' and in 'full agreement' with the Ultra signal he had drafted. Denning persuaded him to take this to Pound and beg him to reconsider. However, Pound was adamant that he had made his decision and was not going to change it. Denning would always regret that, when Pound was in the OIC earlier, he had not made his case more forcefully. However, the hard truth was that Clayton and Denning could not provide Pound with the certainty that the Germans were still in Altafiord. Denning had hoped that decrypts of one or more German signals originated after 1200 would confirm his arguments of two hours ago but no such intelligence had yet arrived. Pound therefore had to balance the inevitable high losses to U-boat and air attack once the convoy scattered against the probability of complete destruction if the Germans were on their way. Two other factors probably exerted influence. If there had been no intelligence warning of *Tirpitz*'s arrival in Altafiord, what faith could he place in getting warning she had sailed? As Pound well knew, the OIC had advised Tovey six weeks previously in regard to Ultra that 'movements of German units are not certain to be detected by this source'. It is often forgotten that when a German cruiser force led by Kummetz sailed from Altafiord to attack a convoy nearly six months after PQ 17, neither Ultra decrypts nor any other source provided any warning. Furthermore, German intent to destroy PQ 17 with their surface fleet and to do so well east of Bear Island now seemed clear. Pound did not know that Hitler had imposed crippling limitations on *Tirpitz*'s deployment, nor could he know that German naval commanders were themselves increasingly risk averse. After all, the Germans had recently executed the extremely bold Cerberus operation. In their present position, Pound would have sailed and Force K in its action against the Beta convoy the previous November showed what a far weaker force than the Germans had now could achieve.[18]

Whether or not Pound was right to act now rather than to await more intelligence, the three signals, sent in such quick succession, have rightly been described 'as badly drafted as any in recent British naval history'.[19] They contained no context or explanation for Hamilton and Broome, allowed no discretion to exercise judgement on the spot, and gave no advice or guidance on how the orders might best be implemented. Taken together, they conveyed a sense of panic that could only imply that the arrival of *Tirpitz* was imminent. One of many mysteries in the PQ 17 story is why nobody spoke up at the staff meeting to make these points. Since Pound did the drafting, it is possible that nobody else saw exactly what was written but that surely did not prevent suggestions being offered. Even if explanation and guidance had followed the final 'scatter' signal that might have mitigated some of the damage that was to follow. However, after Pound confirmed that the scatter order must stand, it appears that Eccles, Brind and Clayton struggled to decide how to encapsulate Admiralty thinking for Tovey and the now fast-retreating Hamilton. No doubt they hoped a new decrypt would bring clarification. Not until 0238 on 5 July, five hours after the fateful scatter order, did they finally despatch a version of Denning's 2030 draft. This Ultra signal emphasised that it was not yet known if German forces had sailed from Altafiord but they were unlikely to have done so before 1200/4. It added that the Germans seemed uncertain whether Hamilton's force included a battleship and were still apparently unsighted on the whereabouts of the Home Fleet. A parallel signal for non-Ultra recipients merely stated that enemy ships were north of Tromsø but it was not known if they were at sea.[20]

## The Implementation of the 'Scatter' Order

Although the cumulative effect of the Admiralty's three signals on Hamilton and Broome was ultimately the same, the initial impact was different. Hamilton received the order withdrawing the cruisers at about 2200 and was then in sight of the convoy, about five miles ahead of it. *Norfolk* had just flown off her Walrus on ice patrol and Hamilton continued east for half an hour, possibly eight miles or so, in a vain attempt to recover it, and for the American *Tuscaloosa* to pick up her aircraft which had been on anti-submarine patrol. It was 2230 before he finally turned westward, first steering south of the now-scattering convoy to keep between it and any approaching enemy. Although, as a repeat addressee, he may not have had the 'disperse' and 'scatter' signals in hand until as late as 2215, his overall delay in turning is surprising, given that he knew somewhat more of the context than Broome. The latter states that, as action addressee, he received the 'disperse' signal at 2207 and the 'scatter' signal a few minutes later. He did not see the cruiser withdrawal signal, for which he was a repeat addressee, placing it at the back of the queue for decryption, until well after 2230. As Broome stated subsequently, the withdrawal signal was not technically related to the two that followed but a connection evolved once the series was complete and there was time for reflection. Neither Hamilton nor Broome read the 'scatter' signal as a correction to its predecessor. Although they received it just minutes after the 'disperse' order, they noted the 13-minute time difference in despatch from the Admiralty. Taken with its more urgent precedence, this surely meant that the Admiralty had new intelligence that attack was definite and imminent, rendering scattering the only prospect of saving any of the convoy. Broome expected to witness 'either the cruisers open fire, or to see enemy masts appearing over the horizon' at any moment.

By 2215, Broome had received two direct orders from the Admiralty. If context was lacking, they conveyed extreme urgency, bordering on panic, and they were consistent with Hamilton's earlier warning and *Pozarica*'s possible distant contact. He was in no position to question Admiralty judgement. They must know what they were doing. In accordance with Hamilton's 2040 order, the convoy was on a base course of 045, directly away from the likely threat direction. It was in nine columns, each four or five ships deep. The standard scatter pattern would disperse the ships over a semi-circular arc 90° either side of the base course which in the circumstances was the best option available.[21] Without more ado, Broome accordingly hoisted the flag signal to scatter and repeated the order by light and radio telephone. He also brought *Keppel* within hailing distance of the Convoy Commodore, John Dowding, in *River Afton* at the head of the central column to confirm the order and share what little else he knew. He now faced the difficult decision over what to do with his escorts. The role of his six destroyers was clear. They should initially provide a protective screen to the south-west in the likely path of the approaching enemy behind which the convoy could complete its semi-circular dispersal. The two submarines already had their orders which only required confirmation. That left the two anti-aircraft ships, four corvettes, three minesweepers and four anti-submarine trawlers which could contribute little useful to a surface engagement and 'could not be left mooning around the Barents Sea with no convoy to escort'. Broome therefore ordered them to proceed independently to Archangel. He later acknowledged to Hamilton that these orders were 'hurried and inadequate'.[22]

At 2230, as Broome began pulling away with his destroyers to the north-east with the intention then of reversing course to starboard through the southerly group of the dispersing ships, he saw Hamilton's cruisers 10 miles ahead beginning their own turn westward and evidently moving at high speed. Broome quite reasonably assumed that Hamilton too intended to position his force in the path of the approaching enemy and that it was surely logical to join forces. As yet he remained unaware of the Admiralty signal ordering Hamilton's withdrawal. He made his proposal by light to Hamilton who immediately agreed. Broome later presented this as a spur of the moment opportunistic decision. Had the cruisers 'been fifty miles away', well on the way to Bear Island as Tovey had wanted that afternoon, they would have been 'out of mind' and the linking up would never have happened. As it was the two forces joined up at around 2300 and proceeded west at high speed through the southerly group of merchant ships, close enough for a final exchange of good luck and best wishes with Dowding.[23]

Hamilton was acutely aware that, to the merchant ships he was passing which lacked access to the key signals and could only imagine looming disaster, it must inevitably seem that the most powerful escort ships were running away and at high speed. He later implied that, had he appreciated that the Admiralty's intelligence on the current whereabouts of the German fleet was no better than his own, he would have remained covering the convoy until it was widely dispersed. In practice, this presumably meant establishing a patrol line out to the south-west across the German line of approach and using his remaining aircraft for a reconnaissance sweep.[24] It is not clear why he did not do this anyway. By 2330 he was clearing the south-western edge of the scattering convoy, the sea was calm and visibility excellent with no sign of the Germans out to 15 miles and no radar contacts.[25] He subsequently told Tovey that he had no intention of engaging *Tirpitz* although he thought that might be unavoidable. This rather missed the point. Nobody expected him to get into an unequal battle with the Germans but he had sufficient speed to keep out of trouble, while shadowing the attackers and obliging them to proceed with caution, thereby losing them precious time. This was consistent with Tovey's standing orders to Arctic convoy escorts if encountering a superior surface force. It was true that the Admiralty had given Hamilton an unequivocal order to withdraw but, as a rear admiral, he surely had some discretion in balancing this against supporting the convoy until dispersal was complete. He would also have provided the Admiralty and Tovey with crucial intelligence even if it was negative.

In the event, Hamilton did not linger but proceeded west at 25 knots with Broome's destroyers in tow. This put him on a diverging course from the probable German line of approach and, at 0015, he ran into dense fog which persisted until morning. If any members of the force still harboured a belief that their role was to head off the Germans and potentially fight a battle, they now abandoned it. Hamilton's fear that his departure would be perceived as desertion applied to his own ships too. Feelings in *London* were apparently mutinous. Lieutenant William O'Brien, second-in-command of Broome's most modern destroyer *Offa* and a future admiral, vividly testified nearly 30 years later to the sense of shame that engulfed her bridge team. Leaving the convoy was something 'the navy just did not do'. He and his captain seriously contemplated reporting a fictitious machinery breakdown to permit their surreptitious return. For the rest of his life, he regretted not pushing this idea more strongly and he felt only shame when awarded a Distinguished Service Cross for his Arctic service at the end of the year.[26]

If the rapid departure of Hamilton and Broome poses questions, so does the minimal guidance given to the non-destroyer escorts and merchant vessels. Standard convoy instructions on scattering ordered ships to hold the course defined in the scatter plan for several hours after losing sight of any potential enemy. Thereafter, failing orders to the contrary, ships should proceed to their destination with the route chosen at the discretion of individual captains. However, the instructions also anticipated that the convoy escort commander and commodore might agree rendezvous points whereby the entire convoy could be reconstituted or several mini-convoys established. Scattering was not therefore envisaged as permanent and irrevocable in all circumstances. In the North Atlantic, where independent sailings remained widespread and the threat was largely confined to U-boats, it was unusual to designate any rendezvous arrangement. However, in the different geographic and threat conditions of the Barents Sea, there was a stronger case for restoring some protection for scattered ships. That said, there is no evidence of post-scatter planning for PQ convoys in general or PQ 17 in particular. The failure to contemplate any arrangement primarily lies with Tovey and the Admiralty. Pound's firm belief that scattering was an option did not apparently cause him to inquire into contingency planning apart from his question to Allen on communications at his morning meeting on 4 July. Nor was this issue raised at the crucial staff conference that evening. It was raised on 14 July, 10 days after the PQ 17 scattering, by Eccles who asked Tovey, Hamilton and Broome whether the merchant ships had received any additional guidance. This was not only a bit late, but if it implied criticism, blame surely lay as much with the Admiralty.[27]

If there was no prior planning, is it fair to criticise Hamilton and Broome, when faced with the unexpected Admiralty order, for not providing the scattering ships and light escorts with better guidance, and would this have reduced the casualty rate? To answer this question, it is useful to examine what happened in the absence of guidance. There was a general consensus that heading direct for the White Sea was too risky. Both merchant ships and residual escorts therefore made for the region of the Matochin Strait which divides Novaya Zemlya at its mid-point and lay 400 miles south-east of the scatter point. Those that scattered northward, half the convoy and escorts, skirted the ice edge and thence down to the Strait. The southerly ships took a more direct route. The residual escorts struggled to reconcile Broome's minimalist order to proceed independently to Archangel with, for many, a continuing sense of duty towards their charges, although for some their own survival came first. Many undoubtedly felt abandoned and bitter. The gravitation towards similar routes and support from more activist escorts resulted in several ad hoc mini convoys forming. The overall story of the PQ 17 ships after the scattering, the loss of nineteen merchant ships out of thirty-one remaining, one of the three rescue ships and the tanker *Aldersdale*, all to air and U-boat attack, and the terrible privations undergone by many merchant vessels and their crews has been well described elsewhere.[28]

Despite the time pressures, Hamilton and Broome could have brought clarity and structure to this process of somewhat chaotic individual initiative after the scattering, above all by emphasising a continuing role and responsibility for the escorts. These could, for example, have been divided into two groups, under designated commanders and ordered to holding points 100 miles to the north-east and south-east respectively by 1000 the following morning when new instructions would follow. This would have given the British command a more effective means of communication and the capability to conduct rescue work, to resume convoying for ships that could be rounded up if this became appropriate, and for cooperating with the Russians. It would also have made the return of Broome's destroyers a feasible proposition. By no means least it would have assuaged the sense of betrayal and desertion. Initial responsibility for implementing such arrangements rested with Broome but Hamilton as a flag officer should have identified the requirement and ensured it was addressed. As it was, in a message to his retreating force at 0115, repeated to Dowding for all PQ 17 ships, he merely registered distress at 'leaving that fine collection of ships to find their own way to harbour' and sorrow that 'the good work of the close escort could not be completed'.[29] It seems unlikely that offered much solace to those now fighting to survive on their own. Tovey and the Admiralty, neither of whom learnt Broome's destroyers were with Hamilton until the evening of 5 July,[30] too could have intervened or at least questioned what guidance had been given. Only on 6 July did the Admiralty attempt to direct the residual escorts exploiting a picture of the PQ 17 survivors drawn from Ultra decrypts of German U-boat and air reports.[31]

*The Picture on the German Side*

Throughout the evening of 4 July, the entire German force remained in Altafiord awaiting clarification of the composition of Hamilton's force, the possibility of a carrier in the vicinity, and the whereabouts of the Home Fleet heavy covering force which certainly did have a carrier. As late as 2130, a 5th Air Fleet report again claimed that Hamilton's force included a battleship. It inevitably took Group North some hours, based on U-boat and aerial sightings, to make sense of PQ 17's scattering and the withdrawal of the cruiser force. However, by 0600 on 5 July, they were confident that the convoy had broken up initially into a northern group of eighteen and southern group of twelve merchant ships which now seemed to be further dispersing with small groups or individual ships heading for Russian ports but keeping as far north-east as possible. Three destroyers and two corvettes were associated with the northern ships and a cruiser (clearly *Palomares*) with the southern group.[32] The dispersal was judged to be due to the air attacks the previous evening although as the full scale of the dispersal became apparent, the German leadership was increasingly bemused at the British action. Meanwhile, the cruiser force supporting the convoy had been sighted by a U-boat at 0110 steering west at high speed and it appeared it had permanently withdrawn from the operational area.

Given these developments, Admiral Carls sought approval to execute Rösselsprung, arguing that, despite the lack of a recent sighting, the Home Fleet and its carrier were too distant to intervene in an operation 200 miles east of Bear Island and would not risk attack from the 5th Air Fleet. Furthermore, the effective deadline for departure from Altafiord was now 1300 since otherwise engagement with the convoy would occur too near the Russian coast. However, Raeder again emphasised Hitler's order that the enemy carrier must be definitively located and refused approval.

The situation changed following a sighting of the 'carrier force' 200 miles almost due west of Bear Island at 0655, apparently withdrawing in a 'westerly direction' (in reality south-west). This allowed Carls to return to the charge, arguing that it confirmed British reluctance to expose their carrier to land-based air attack. In addition, since the Home Fleet had been at sea since at least 1 July, it was unlikely they now had the fuel to move east. Overall, the threat from this force was minimal and separate air reconnaissance sorties had confirmed no enemy presence over the sector from 75 miles west to 100 miles east of Bear Island from the Norwegian coast up to the ice edge. This time Raeder agreed to get Führer approval which was achieved by 1140. The codeword to commence Rösselsprung was transmitted to Schniewind, who had come to immediate readiness, one minute later. In fact, anticipating approval, he had begun moving up Altafiord at 1100. Schniewind was briefed on the dispersed state of the convoy, that there were only light British forces in the area, and that U-boats were being kept clear. Group North was also confident that the British had not yet detected his presence in Altafiord. He was also advised that the 'probable area of operations' for 1200 on 6 July was centred about 120 miles west of the Matochin Strait. Had Schniewind ever reached this point, he would have found few, if any, targets. Hardly any ships from the convoy had reached this far south and those that arrived over the coming days kept much closer to the coast of Novaya Zemlya.[33]

The German force cleared the head of Altafiord by 1300 and turned north-east at 22 knots. Although the German Naval Staff judged prospects for Rösselsprung to be 'decidedly favourable', a signal at 1610 from Group North dampened any expectations of achieving comprehensive destruction of the scattered convoy. Carls directed Schniewind that a 'short operation with partial success' was preferable to 'complete victory involving longer period of time'. He was immediately to report arrival of 'enemy planes' and break off if any serious threat developed. 'Under no circumstances' was the enemy to score success against the 'nucleus fleet'. The risk appetite of the German naval command was evidently minimal, and by early evening, they knew from B-Dienst intercepts that the force had been sighted at 1700 when it was approaching North Cape and again just over an hour later.[34] The first sighting was by the Russian submarine *K-21*, which claimed wrongly to have hit *Tirpitz* with two torpedoes, and the second by a Russian aircraft. *K-21*'s sighting of *Tirpitz*, *Scheer* and eight destroyers was passed to Rear Admiral Douglas Fisher, who had just relieved Richard Bevan as SBNO North Russia, who passed it to the Admiralty where it was received at 1937.[35]

In fact, the Admiralty had learnt five hours previously that the German force had left Altafiord heading east. At 1420, Bletchley forwarded the OIC a decrypted signal from Schniewind to Group North sent at 1014, stating that he expected to be south of Rolvsoy Island, 20 miles north-east of Hammerfest by 1430.[36] It was shared with Tovey by Ultra signal at 1517. The decrypt was acquired 15 minutes before the daily Dolphin settings changed at 1200 on 5 July and the new day was not broken until 1015 the following morning. However, fragmentary though it was, the message left no doubt that the German taskforce, presumably including *Tirpitz*, must have cleared Altafiord two hours before 1430 and intended to attack PQ 17. At 1625, the Admiralty advised all forces and stations that surface attack was now likely 'tonight' or early 6 July with the enemy striking north-east from North Cape.[37] With no prospect of further Ultra, the last news of the Germans' progress on 5 July was a sighting by the British submarine *P 54* (later renamed *Unshaken*) at 2030 which put them 60 miles north-east of North Cape and confirmed the presence of *Hipper*.[38]

B-Dienst's report of the two sightings of Schniewind provoked immediate concern shared between Group North and the Naval Staff.

They feared the British heavy covering force would now turn back and target the *Tirpitz* group during its return journey to Altafiord. Three options were considered: continuing with Rösselsprung and accepting the risk of interception; limiting time in the operational area thereby reducing scope for enemy intervention; or turning back at once and leaving PQ 17 to the 5th Air Fleet and U-boats which it was believed had already accounted for a dozen ships during the day. Carls favoured breaking off, arguing that, with the convoy scattered, there was now no success that justified the potential risk. He also felt that persisting after the force had been located required fresh Führer approval. Naval Staff Operations Division insisted the risks of British interception remained minimal. Raeder agreed with Carls and, at 2132, Group North cancelled the operation when Schniewind was just 100 miles beyond North Cape and still 200 miles from the assigned target area.[39]

Judged in cold terms of risk/benefit, the abandonment of Rösselsprung looked logical but it provoked lasting controversy and resentment within the German naval leadership. A 'chasm opened' between Operations Division and Fleet on the one hand and Raeder and Carls on the other. This was exacerbated when it was learnt that it was not Hitler but Raeder, the Navy's own commander, who had broken off an operation months in the making. Raeder justified his decision because of the 'responsibility' he owed to the Führer to avoid unnecessary risks with the 'few valuable units' left to the navy. However, it was not just Hitler's influence that drove Raeder here. He himself was risk averse, determined to preserve a 'fleet in being'. 'A defeat at sea', he stated, 'would in the present situation' be 'very burdensome'. Meanwhile, behind his back, many accused Carls of playing politics with an eye to succeeding Raeder rather than promoting the Navy's interest. If the battlefleet could not be used now for the complete destruction of a convoy with minimal protection, in pursuit of a clear policy defined by Hitler on 14 March, then when? What did this bode for the future of the battlefleet and those serving in it?[40]

German fears were exaggerated. When Schniewind turned back, Tovey, who had been tracking south-west all day, was 500 miles west of Altafiord. It was true that, had the Germans persisted with their attack plan, there was ample time to position *Victorious* in strike range 200 miles from the final section of their return route. However, the logistic challenges of fuelling her escorts were formidable, as some on the German side understood. Schniewind would be hugging the coast with several alternative routes available and in easy reach of fighter cover while *Victorious* would be in equally easy range of 5th Air Fleet bombers. Impeccable reconnaissance and much luck would be needed to get the timing and location of an intercept right. Altogether, this was a far more formidable proposition than the attack on 9 March. Meanwhile, although the Admiralty did not learn of Rösselsprung's cancellation until late morning on 6 July, by which time Schniewind was long back in Altafiord, during the night they pressed Tovey to consider an air strike in the hope *Tirpitz* had indeed been damaged by *K-21*'s attack and was limping back. Tovey did briefly reverse course to the north-east but he was not convinced by the damage report, given that *P 54* had observed *Tirpitz* steering east at 22 knots three and a half hours later, and weather was now unsuitable for air reconnaissance. He therefore soon judged an interception operation fruitless and turned for home. As he did so, the OIC notified him that Dolphin settings from 1200 on the previous day had been broken and they followed up with an Ultra signal at 1317 reporting the cancellation of Rösselsprung the evening before. The suffering of the merchant ships and their crews would continue for many days but otherwise the PQ 17 operation was over.[41]

Denning was proved right that *Tirpitz* and the rest of the German task force had not yet sailed when Pound gave the order to scatter PQ 17. However, it does not follow that a different decision would have saved the convoy. The problems in turning it around have been aired. If, as was more likely, Pound had conceded it should continue, then allowing for some further ground made north towards the ice, it would have been about 400 miles north-east of North Cape at 1430 when Bletchley reported the German sortie on 5 July. Hamilton's cruisers would definitely have left by then, Tovey was far out of reach and, at 22 knots, Schniewind could reach the convoy in 20 hours, so mid-forenoon on 6 July. A convoy reversal now would merely reduce the distance the Germans had to cover. As with Vian and Vigorous, it was unrealistic to expect Broome indefinitely to hold off a known force comprising *Tirpitz*, *Scheer*, *Hipper* and eight destroyers, nor could attrition by the Allied submarine force be assumed. Pound would therefore have been obliged to scatter later that afternoon or early evening. If the Germans then called off the sortie, the PQ 17 losses, despite the presence of Broome's destroyers, would probably have been little different, especially as there would have been some further attrition from air and U-boat attacks while the convoy was still intact on 5 July. If Schniewind was allowed to continue, losses might have been worse.[42]

Furthermore, while the events of 5 July validate some of Denning's arguments the previous evening, such as absence of submarine sightings, they also show the fragility of Ultra coverage. Apart from the crucial decrypt of Schniewind's 1145 departure signal, Ultra then contributed nothing for almost 24 hours, until late morning on 6 July. Schniewind might not have sent that signal if he had not pre-empted approval to sail while the onset of fog, all too frequent in July, might have prevented the crucial submarine sightings. Pound got the judgement wrong on 4 July, but he was wrestling with uncertainty and his decision to scatter, although not its communication, deserves more sympathy than it usually receives.

## Initial Reaction to PQ 17 Losses

The scattering of PQ 17 and the losses of men, ships and war material which followed damaged relations with Russia and to a lesser extent the United States, provoked anger within the Merchant Navy and for the Royal Navy brought controversy and shame that lingered more than 30 years until the last participants had retired. If hindsight and reflection permit more understanding of Pound's decisions, most of those involved in the Admiralty or in command positions at sea at the time felt that the order to scatter was at best premature and at worst disastrous. Their blame inevitably focused on the First Sea Lord who, during the remaining 15 months of his life, never shirked responsibility. In the midst of war, there was naturally no desire to criticise him publicly, especially when he retained the confidence of the prime minister, so doubts about his judgement and indeed health remained private. The preference for silence was underlined and extended well beyond the war because few others involved felt entirely comfortable with the parts they had played. The onset of the Cold War ensured that potential for political discomfort continued too.

Criticism of Pound, both contemporary and by many historians later, brought two aspects of his performance as First Sea Lord leadership into sharp focus. In the first place, the PQ 17 disaster is judged a consequence of his chronic tendency to 'centralise', to engage in 'back-seat driving', and unwillingness to delegate. There is also a widespread belief that his decision-making was compromised by fatigue and poor health, that he was not only in constant pain from arthritis but suffering symptoms from the brain tumour that brought his death the following year. There is certainly some truth in the first point. However, the charge of 'centralisation' over PQ 17, as with other operations, must be balanced against the underlying reality that only the Admiralty had the overall picture of the war at sea, and that requirements for radio silence allied with communication limitations sometimes rendered operational control from the centre inevitable. On this occasion, Pound's deputy, Moore, was equally insistent that PQ 17 must scatter. Had he counselled delay, Pound's decision too might have been different. Moore must also share responsibility for the appalling way the decision was transmitted. As regards delegation, Pound had already accepted the desirability of further support by creating the new post of

Deputy First Sea Lord which he announced formally on 10 July would be filled by Admiral Sir Charles Kennedy-Purvis. This proved a great success. Contemporary witnesses, and therefore later historians, differ on whether Pound's health influenced his performance at this time. His most recent biographer, after carefully reviewing all the research, doubts it was a factor before 1943.[43]

It was inevitably many weeks before the Admiralty could provide a final account of the PQ 17 losses but, on 11 August, these were confirmed as twenty-two merchant ships, comprising six British and one Dutch loaded in the United Kingdom and fourteen American and one Panamanian loaded in the United States. These had carried just under 100,000 tons of cargo, including 430 tanks, 210 aircraft and 3350 vehicles. This loss was somewhat less than initially feared but broadly that anticipated by Pound when he reported to the War Cabinet a fortnight earlier.[44] The impact was compounded by the Defence Committee decision on 13 July to cancel the sailing of PQ 18, scheduled to depart five days later. This followed bleak advice from Pound that, if the convoy sailed, ice, weather and constant daylight would be the same and no additional protective measures were possible. The Germans had steadily improved their tactics and the new combination of U-boats attacking west of Bear Island and heavy surface forces to the east was impossible to overcome. He could not therefore guarantee that a single ship would get through. Three days earlier, he had reiterated that deploying heavy ships in the Barents Sea would court disaster with any losses risking control of the North Atlantic and even compromising the Bolero build-up. Despite the outcome of PQ 17, the prime minister was loathe to suspend a convoy while the Russians were under intense pressure from the German southern offensive. However, reflecting a general consensus, he said that, while he had always judged that maintaining the convoys was justified even in the face of 50 per cent losses, it was pointless continuing if the risk was higher. Such losses in ships and material would not help Russia and would be disastrous to the wider Allied cause.

From the Russian perspective, when the gap after PQ 16, the losses to PQ 17 and now the cancellation of PQ 18 were taken together, they would receive only 11 per cent of the tanks and 7 per cent of the aircraft promised for the three months May to July with a comparable shortfall in other vital supplies. As Eden stressed, this supply failure would hit the Russians just when they were to be disappointed over a second front in 1942. Suspension of PQ 18 also meant the six Royal Air Force fighter squadrons which Stalin had accepted in June as a contribution to the defence of Murmansk could no longer be provided. This was unfortunate because Murmansk was suffering badly from air raids at this time. In September, Rear Admiral Miles reported that large areas of the city had been devastated and three quarters of the population evacuated. Although damage to port facilities was fortunately limited, he doubted it was possible to cope with a convoy of more than twenty-four ships. To add further insult to injury, Stalin had also just agreed with Roosevelt that forty American A-20 bombers could be diverted from Russia to Egypt to help forestall the imminent German offensive there. At a time when he was facing collapse on the southern front as Plan Blue gathered pace, there was reason for Stalin to feel aggrieved.[45]

The Russian naval leadership was appalled not just by the sudden scattering of PQ 17 but the complete lack of prior warning, let alone consultation. An equally uninformed Miles was called to an urgent meeting with the Deputy Chief of the Naval Staff, Admiral Vladimir Alafusov, at midday on 5 July where he was upbraided with demands for a full explanation as to why undefended merchant ships were now being decimated. Miles could only draw on a cursory Admiralty briefing received in the early hours of the morning. This referred to the threat posed by the heavy German ships at Altafiord as the reason behind the scattering but failed to state whether they had actually sailed. The presentation of the signal was perhaps also unfortunate in demanding the Russians undertake immediate strikes on German airfields and reconnaissance of Altafiord while stressing that the Royal Navy was withdrawing all its surface forces east of Bear Island.[46] Miles apparently received no further briefing before a meeting with Kuznetsov on 11 July. Kuznetsov, admittedly now reflecting hindsight, clearly regarded 'dispersal' as a mistake, arguing that the threat of surface attack was less than the known dangers from the air and U-boats. By causing the convoy to scatter, leaving it defenceless, *Tirpitz* had achieved her aim. Rather bravely, Miles told the Admiralty that, with only the 5 July briefing to go on, he agreed with Kuznetsov that dispersal seemed premature. Kuznetsov also asked some pointed questions about the guidance given to ships in the event of scattering. He assumed that, if this happened before reaching a certain longitude, ships would return to Iceland? If it occurred later in the passage, there were many temporary anchorages, such as Novaya Zemlya to aim for and, with prior warning, the Soviet Navy could help identify these and provide wider support.[47] Miles later described the formal part of this interview as 'chilly' but Kuznetsov subsequently took him aside with caviar and cognac and commiserated with his British colleague for being landed in an awkward position by his superiors.[48] Chilliness also entered relations in Murmansk and Archangel. Russian security paranoia and reluctance to admit limitations in support services at the ports and in naval capability, neither ever far away, strengthened and made cooperation more difficult in the coming months.

Meanwhile, in London on 14 July, Eden briefed Maisky on the latest PQ 17 news and the Defence Committee decision on PQ 18 taken the previous day although the latter still required American endorsement. In an effort to soften Russian attitudes, Churchill also invited Maisky and his wife to an informal dinner the following day at which Pound was present. The exchanges with the latter were tetchy. Maisky's questions were perceptive but sharp and aggressive while Pound was defensive and patronising. Maisky 'took the greatest exception' to the 'gouty 65-year-old, who has won not a single battle in his entire life' and felt the prime minister's support for his naval adviser lacked enthusiasm.[49]

Churchill recognised that he must brief Stalin personally on the decision to cancel PQ 18 and the day following the Defence Committee meeting shared his proposed message with Roosevelt along with the bleak British assessment of current prospects on the Arctic route. Roosevelt responded next day that, following consultation with King, he reluctantly accepted the decision on PQ 18 and thought the message for Stalin was a good one.[50] Acutely aware of the negative impact his message would have on Stalin, Churchill tinkered with it for two more days but without major changes. The long telegram contained some post facto rationalisation of the history of German countermeasures against the convoys but the core point was that the Royal Navy had no effective answer to a German battlefleet operating east of Bear Island. Deploying heavy ships of the Home Fleet in this area would expose them to loss or damage, compromising control of the vital North Atlantic lifeline. Running further convoys over the remaining summer period would incur similar loss to PQ 17 or worse and to no purpose. Churchill sought to soften the blow with promises of new effort on the Persian supply route, willingness to discuss joint operations in northern Norway and positive progress in the Middle East.[51]

Stalin's response received six days later was predictably short and sharp. He drew two conclusions. The British government was now refusing to send vital war supplies via the Arctic, when they were needed more than ever, and reneging on its promise of a 'second front' in 1942 which for Stalin meant a major landing in France. Churchill's single fleeting and rather unwise reference to the latter came at the end of his message which covered the release of three Polish divisions from Russia for service in Palestine. He suggested that, without these, forces would have to come from those being readied for the 'Anglo-American mass invasion of the Continent'. Although no date was mentioned here, there was a clear implication that this referred to 1943 and that, as Stalin already suspected, nothing would now happen in the current year. Given this context, implying that failure to release the Poles would noticeably weaken Allied strength was both tactless and absurd. Three divisions were useful but irrelevant to a full invasion of the Continent. On the naval arguments, Stalin was neither sympathetic nor convinced. War entailed losses and risks. With goodwill and collaboration, the convoys could surely be maintained. His own experts found the dispersal of PQ 17 'difficult to understand', a view that Kuznetsov no doubt told him had supporters within the British naval leadership.[52]

If the politics of cancelling PQ 18 were difficult, so were the logistic problems from a suspension likely to last until early autumn. There was now a backlog of more than fifty ships waiting in Iceland with more en route from the United States. Twenty-two vessels were brought to the United Kingdom where their cargo was unloaded, with some diverted to British and American use. Other ships, already loaded with cargo for PQ 19 which had been planned to depart Iceland at the end of August, were left waiting in Scottish ports until the future of the Arctic route was resolved. Not only was this probably the most flagrant waste of cargo shipping in 1942, but it made it impossible for the United States to recover the shortfall in its First Protocol commitments. By mid-August, six weeks after the expiry of the protocol, only two-thirds of the promised aircraft and half the trucks had been shipped and this did not account for losses.[53]

## Operation Torch and its Impact on Support for Russia

Churchill had good cause to be circumspect on the second front. The crisis over PQ 17 and its damage to relations with Russia coincided with a fraught debate between the two Western Allies over future strategy. This was probably their most difficult argument of the war and the primary focus was Sledgehammer to which the American military leadership remained committed at the beginning of July. On 11 June, in the wake of Molotov's visit, the British War Cabinet had set two conditions for Sledgehammer – no substantial landing unless the forces involved were going to stay and the Germans must be demoralised by failure against Russia. This ruled out the 'sacrificial' operation mentioned by Roosevelt.[54] At the third Anglo-American summit code-named Argonaut held in Washington on 18–25 June, the British and American Combined Chiefs of Staff initially reached agreement on three core points: reaffirmation of 'Germany first'; reaffirmation of Bolero, the movement of sufficient American forces to the United Kingdom to mount a full-scale invasion of the Continent (Roundup) in 1943; and rejection of Gymnast, the invasion of North-west Africa which had featured strongly at the previous Arcadia summit, as an effective use of Allied resources. The consensus against Gymnast reflected concern that it would undermine existing Middle East operations, cause unacceptable dilution of naval forces in all other theatres, slow up Bolero reinforcement, and be executed in a complex political environment where consequences were impossible to predict. Differences over Sledgehammer were papered over. The British chiefs did not believe it was feasible while their American counterparts remained committed to the concept of emergency intervention if a Soviet collapse seemed imminent. The compromise which suited both sides was to continue planning for Sledgehammer and to view the resources allocated to it as a strategic reserve to be used depending on events. For the American chiefs therefore, 'emergency intervention' remained in play. For the British, maintaining a rapid build-up of American forces provided security against a new German invasion attempt following Russian collapse and could potentially facilitate alternative options, if German strength in the West following defeat of Russia made a 1943 Roundup impossible. Such alternatives might include less ambitious attacks on France, a landing in Portugal or Spain, a variant of Gymnast in North Africa or conceivably an attack on Norway.[55]

In agreeing this preferred strategy, the joint chiefs underestimated the attractions of Gymnast for their political masters who, following the weekend of 20/21 June spent together at Roosevelt's Hyde Park home, insisted it remained firmly on the table as an option. Churchill's view, summarised in a note given to Roosevelt at the start of their private meeting, is usually judged decisive here, even attracting the claim that it would 'alter the whole course of the war'.[56] The note began by emphasising British commitment to Bolero and a 1943 Roundup but also the importance of reducing Atlantic shipping losses. It then undermined Sledgehammer by arguing that there was so far no credible plan giving a reasonable prospect of success. If Sledgehammer proved impossible, what should be done instead? Was it acceptable to remain idle in the Atlantic theatre through 1942? Did Gymnast offer an alternative prospect of strategic advantage and means of taking some weight off Russia?

Churchill's arguments over this weekend were undoubtedly influential and built on those deployed by Mountbatten at a dinner with Roosevelt and Hopkins earlier in the month. Roosevelt had always seen the strategic value of intervention in North-west Africa as far back as Stark's 'Plan Dog' exposition in November 1940 but, as he had told Mountbatten, he did not want to accumulate one million Americans as a home guard in the

United Kingdom relieving British forces to deploy in the Middle East and India to protect the British Empire.[57] On the other hand, he did not want to face the mid-term November elections on the back of a Sledgehammer disaster while a successful Gymnast would be politically positive and avoid accusations of inaction against Germany, encouraging those who wanted to focus on Japan as America's real foe. Desire to strengthen Britain's position in the Middle East and secure the Persian supply line to Russia was a further factor in Gymnast's favour and given added force by news of the fall of Tobruk on the afternoon of 21 June. This mix of political and strategic factors convinced Roosevelt to support Churchill in directing a far from convinced Brooke and deeply opposed Marshall that Gymnast must now be developed as an alternative project in parallel to Sledgehammer using American forces allocated to Bolero which had not yet left the United States. Roosevelt had not yet decided on Gymnast and knew he faced determined opposition from Marshall, King and Secretary of War Stimson but by the end of Argonaut he was undoubtedly inclining in its favour.[58]

The joint chiefs' compromise on Sledgehammer lasted barely two weeks. On 30 June, the British chiefs remained committed to the understanding, recognised Marshall's belief in the feasibility of Sledgehammer in the coming autumn and were content for planning and preparation for such an operation to continue even if they judged final execution unlikely.[59] The next day brought dramatic change when the chiefs were advised on the opportunity costs to shipping and the disruption of long-term Roundup training if Sledgehammer preparations continued. 'On purely military grounds, the disadvantages on "Roundup" of mounting "Sledgehammer" heavily outweighed the advantages.' However, halting Sledgehammer preparations presented obvious political difficulties with potentially serious damage to relations with the United States and Russia on which the War Cabinet must rule.[60] At a staff conference on 6 July, conducted simultaneously with the unfolding PQ 17 crisis, the prime minister and chiefs agreed that Sledgehammer had no prospect of success and that continuing preparations would 'ruin' Roundup in 1943. Perhaps disingenuously, the prime minister claimed certainty that the president would support Gymnast if Sledgehammer was impracticable although he himself favoured Jupiter to secure the Arctic convoys. It was agreed that the Americans must now be informed that Sledgehammer was effectively off the table and alternatives were being explored.[61] The War Cabinet endorsed this decision the following day.[62] Although it was an inevitable consequence of the decision taken almost a month earlier on 11 June, both Cabinet and chiefs should have recognised the logistic imperatives attached to Sledgehammer much sooner and therefore been honest about the implications with the Americans. As it was, the latter had good cause for complaint.

This withdrawal from Sledgehammer certainly had an impact in Washington, in the case of the American chiefs rather greater than their British counterparts perhaps anticipated. Marshall not only felt deceived over Sledgehammer at Argonaut but now doubted whether the British commitment to Roundup was genuine or merely a ploy to gain American forces for the defence of the United Kingdom. He remained bitterly opposed to Gymnast, viewing it as 'expensive and ineffectual'. When the American chiefs met on 10 July to consider the British decision, he accordingly proposed a momentous shift in strategy which would rule out Gymnast and put the British firmly in their place. This was to turn to the Pacific and concentrate the bulk of American effort on the early and decisive defeat of Japan, a view that naturally received enthusiastic backing from King.[63]

In parallel with communication between the respective chiefs of staff, Churchill lobbied Roosevelt direct on the evolving arguments against Sledgehammer and the case for Gymnast, casting the latter as 'the best chance for effective relief to the Russian front in 1942', a proposition certainly open to challenge, and, describing it even less accurately, as Roosevelt's 'commanding idea'.[64] Roosevelt was probably still more equally poised between Sledgehammer and Gymnast than Churchill wanted to believe. However, as the American chiefs rapidly learnt, he was clear on four things: 'Germany first' was sacrosanct; maintaining agreed supplies to Russia remained crucial; American ground forces must take the offensive in the Euro-Atlantic region before the end of the year; and the importance of the Middle East which must be held 'as strongly as possible whether Russia collapses or not'. If the British would not support Sledgehammer, then, for Roosevelt, Gymnast was a credible alternative and perhaps the best available. These principles meant that the 'Pacific first' option put to him by Marshall and King, with support from Stimson, on 10 July, and in more detail two days later, received short shrift. Nor was he prepared to use the Pacific option as a threat which could only undermine necessary and effective collaboration. He recognised a risk that the British would prove no more willing to undertake Roundup in 1943 than Sledgehammer but he was willing to trust next year's stated intent for the present. Roosevelt's 'principles' now framed his formal directive as 'Commander-in-Chief' to Marshall, King and Hopkins, instructing them to visit London immediately and reach agreement with the British on future joint operational plans. Partly to assuage his advisers, but probably from genuine conviction too, these instructions retained Sledgehammer as the preferred option. But, if British opposition remained solid, they must agree a suitable alternative consistent with his principles and the overall strategic situation. Given Marshall's determined resistance to Gymnast, Roosevelt avoided specific reference to this or any hint that it was the only alternative.[65]

Three days of talks over 20–22 July demonstrated that the British were immovable on Sledgehammer and it appears they were aware of Roosevelt's bottom line, probably through Hopkins who favoured Gymnast.[66] Marshal later claimed that, facing stalemate, unambiguous instructions from the president and two political leaders apparently fixed on Africa, he focused on a variant of Gymnast as the 'least harmful diversion'.[67] His more formal contemporary justification was his realisation that, without a collapse in German morale, of which there was no sign, a cross-Channel operation in 1943 did not look viable. For the next year therefore, the Western Allies must adopt a 'defensive, encircling line of action against Germany' for which an operation in North-west Africa made sense.[68] This thinking was of course consistent with the concepts of 'containment' and 'wear down' which the British had first disclosed at Riviera the previous year and promoted further at Arcadia in January. Marshall's language also has strong echoes of the strategic arguments for intervention in North-west Africa identified by the Joint Intelligence Committee when assessing 'German Strategy in 1942/43' on 16 July. In a prescient sentence, the committee stated that an operation here would insure against Russian collapse but possibly delay victory if Russia did not collapse. It seems these arguments were deployed to some effect by the British chiefs.[69]

The final result of this London Conference, promoted by the Americans and agreed with only minor changes by the British chiefs and the War Cabinet over the two days 24/25 July, was entitled 'Operations in 1942/43', later designated 'CCS 94' for 'Combined Chiefs of Staff', and incorporated three core points:

- No reduction in preparations for Roundup while there was a reasonable chance of its successful execution by July 1943.
- If, by 15 September, the situation in Russia rendered a 1943 Roundup impracticable, a 'combined operation', now code-named 'Torch', would be launched 'against the North and North-west coast of Africa at the earliest possible date before December 1942'.
- Commitment to this operation rendered Roundup 'in all probability impracticable' in 1943 and acceptance of a 'defensive, encircling

line' of the 'continental European theatre' except for air operations and blockade.[70]

The phrasing of the second point provoked some War Cabinet concern as it implied doubt that Torch would proceed and it was unclear how the impact of events in Russia on Roundup would be measured. In the event, a combination of political pressure and military necessity to conduct preparations caused the removal of the 15 September caveat in early August despite ongoing reluctance from Marshall.

Despite Churchill's claim that Gymnast would provide effective support for Russia and Roosevelt's stress on maintaining supplies, the crafting of CCS 94, whatever the merits of the wider strategic arguments noted by the Joint Intelligence Committee, did not address the practical impact on Russia's prospects over the next year. There was no attempt to assess whether countering Allied landings in North-west Africa over the winter of 1942/43 might ultimately absorb comparable German land and air power to meeting a putative Sledgehammer. Nor was the impact on supply lines to Russia of the substantial shipping requirements for the landings initially considered. Above all, less than two months after the promises made to Molotov in Washington and less than a week after Churchill had reaffirmed to Stalin his commitment to a full-scale landing on the Continent in 1943, it appeared there would now be no second front in Europe before 1944. Stalin's response to Churchill's PQ 17 message, which reached London the day before Marshall presented the first draft of CCS 94, had already expressed angry disappointment over the postponement of a second front until 1943. Perceived further backsliding would not only provoke fury in the Kremlin but could even resurrect the spectre of a separate Soviet–German peace. Equally, it fed Stalin's conviction that the Western Allies, especially Churchill, were content to fight 'to the last Russian'. Anger and disappointment over the lack of a second front and the perceived limitations of Western aid was not confined to the Soviet leadership but extended across the wider Russian population as described in a thoughtful report by the *News Chronicle*'s Moscow correspondent which Eden shared with the War Cabinet in early August.[71] It is striking that, although the War Cabinet discussed the cancellation of PQ 18 and Stalin's related response at the same meeting which approved CCS 94, they drew no obvious link between the two.

The failure to consider these issues in agreeing to CCS 94 is surprising because, through July and August, assessments of Russia's prospects in the face of Germany's summer offensive did not fundamentally change.

By mid-July, it was clear the Germans were advancing more rapidly than the Joint Intelligence Committee had expected six weeks earlier. However, a new appreciation at the beginning of August, shared with Dominion prime ministers, was confident that even the loss of Stalingrad and the Caucasus would not provoke Russian collapse although it would strain her economic resources.[72] It followed that, setting apart the respective costs and benefits of Sledgehammer versus Torch, there was no obvious change in the prospects of a 1943 Roundup during this period. Nor was there any reason to reassess the pace and quantity of Second Protocol supplies.

Just as the decision to execute Torch preceded consideration of the implications for Russia, the same was true of intelligence assessments of the various risks to the operation. The first comprehensive Joint Intelligence Committee study for the attack on North Africa was not issued until 7 August. It addressed three issues which preoccupied planners for the next six weeks: the reaction of Vichy French forces; the German threat to and through Spain, and that from Spain itself; and the scope of wider retaliation from the Axis powers. The committee correctly judged that the threat from French forces was limited and manageable and the risk of Spanish intervention minimal. However, its assessment of the scale and effectiveness of German intervention, which it confirmed two weeks later, proved a serious underestimate in every respect with the result that the operation took far longer and consumed far more resources to complete than originally anticipated.[73] On the plus side, as explained later, by absorbing substantial German forces, especially precious air power, Torch did bring benefit to Russia comparable to anything Sledgehammer would have delivered and at lower cost.

## The Scope for Resuming PQ Convoys

Stalin's harsh message of 23 July and the simultaneous decision to proceed with Torch, with its awkward implications for the second front, convinced Churchill, after consultation with Roosevelt, to seek an early meeting with the Soviet leader and propose resuming PQ convoys in September subject to provision of Russian air support. Stalin invited Churchill to proceed to Moscow after his early August trip to the Middle East and the Admiralty conceded that a new convoy of forty ships could be attempted in early September. The political desirability of renewing convoys was naturally shared by Eden who, as chair of the ASE, faced the additional task of reconciling Second Protocol commitments with the halting of what until now had been the primary supply route.[74] There was also concern about leaving ships idle in Iceland where some crews were already giving trouble. If convoys were not resumed, the ships should probably be withdrawn to the United Kingdom.⁷⁵ By 31 July, the ASE was planning not only for the early September convoy, now with the restored designation PQ 18, but at least two further convoys, PQ 19 at the end of September and PQ 20 in October. It was hoped these three convoys together would comprise 120 ships. If these all sailed with a maximum load, they would only meet two-thirds of the supply target set for the Arctic route in the first four months of the Second Protocol but catching up later with help from other routes seemed feasible.⁷⁶

The Admiralty soon dampened expectations. On 7 August, the First Lord, A V Alexander, advised the War Cabinet that, in addition to its standard commitments, the Royal Navy currently faced three major tasks: Torch; Malta convoys; and PQ convoys. It only had resources for one of these at a time and further time was needed to move forces from one operation to another. While planning for PQ 18 was now underway, its implementation depended on the outcome of the major Malta convoy, Operation Pedestal, the departure of which was imminent. If the escort here suffered heavy casualties, it might be impossible to provide sufficient escort vessels for PQ 18. The running of further convoys beyond PQ 18 depended on the timing of Torch. If, as currently hoped, Torch took place in early October, PQ 19 could not be run at the end of September and, until the outcome of Torch was clear, no guarantees made on the possibility and timing of subsequent convoys. Pound stressed that the minimum gap between PQ convoys was 26 days while the advance notice required for loading PQ ships was a further constraint. Eden rightly worried there was a risk of falling between two stools with Torch delayed and PQ 19 cancelled, causing further ructions with Russia. The Cabinet recognised that the timing of Torch and availability of PQ shipping also depended on American decisions.⁷⁷

*The Search for Alternative Supply Routes*

The PQ 17 losses, the subsequent suspension of July and August convoys, and the uncertainty over implementing a programme beyond the new PQ 18 in early September, inevitably brought renewed focus on alternative supply routes. As described earlier, two months before the July crisis on the Arctic route and the subsequent demands raised by Torch, the review initiated by Admiral King had demonstrated that the Second Protocol target of 4.4 million tons of aid over the year beginning 1 July 1942 was unrealistic given current shipping demands and availability. Roosevelt's subsequent proposal to Molotov that shipments be sharply reduced in order to facilitate the build-up of a second front had neither been formally agreed nor pursued and, by the end of July, revisiting this was clearly undesirable politically. When the Second Protocol was negotiated during May and June, the target of 3.4 million tons via the Arctic route was at least theoretically possible logistically with three convoys of thirty ships every two months. However, at the start of the protocol period, the goal of supplying a further million tons through the Persian Gulf was distinctly aspirational with little regard for realities on the ground.

In 1942, control of the Persian Gulf and the southern half of Iran was a British strategic responsibility. Their development of an effective supply route to Russia competed for limited resources with support for the build-up of forces in Iraq and Iran capable of meeting a putative German attack from the north, was constrained by limited and generally primitive port facilities and road and rail networks, and by a Russian attitude which until mid-year was unhelpful. The Russian view was that shipment via Iran took too long and was too distant from combat areas compared to the Arctic. Although the British still had ambitious plans to boost delivery capacity to Russia up to 100,000 tons per month, execution depended on American aid and in the early months of 1942 such practical assistance was limited and the flow of aid a trickle. That said, some of the Allied war material delivered on this route in the second quarter, notably tanks now surplus to British requirements in the Middle East, was still useful. The Russian army defending the Caucasus in August had virtually no T-34s and only about forty T-60s while limited rail links made delivery of tanks from the Urals extremely difficult. The arrival of forty-three British Valentines and sixty-three American Lees through Persia was therefore disproportionately valuable in helping stem the German advance at the Terek river before Grozny.[78] These were not the first tanks to reach Russia by this route. A batch of twenty British Tetrarch light airborne tanks arrived in Azerbaijan in January. They had limited military value and for the rest of 1942 were used for training and in border patrols.[79]

Given this background, when Hopkins, under pressure from Roosevelt, insisted on despatching twelve additional ships to the Gulf in each of the months May and June following the British imposed limits on the Arctic convoy cycle, neither ports nor railways could cope with the cargo. Although nearly 200,000 tons were shipped in the second quarter, including 91,000 tons in June alone, only 12,500 tons of Russia-bound supplies could be handled by Iranian State Railways in August and little more by the road network. Shipments from the United States therefore had to be reduced by a third in July and August and the June figure was not surpassed until October.[80]

In early July, even before the convoy suspension provoked by the PQ 17 crisis, Harriman, as Lend-Lease coordinator, suggested to Hopkins that the Americans should take over responsibility for Iranian State Railways, a proposal immediately adopted by Roosevelt. Over the next six weeks, with full British support, this translated into far more substantial American commitment and investment. By late August, after Churchill and Harriman, who had significant railway expertise, had discussed matters on the ground while in transit through Teheran to Moscow for the meeting with Stalin, it was agreed that the Americans would not only take over the railway but also several key port facilities and the operation of a substantial trucking fleet. The aim was to increase capacity to achieve 200,000 tons of aid to Russia per month without reducing supplies to British military forces which also retained control of Basra and Abadan, the latter a critical source of oil for the whole Eastern war theatre. As Churchill said to Roosevelt – 'Your people would thus undertake the great task of opening up the Persian corridor, which will carry primarily your supplies to Russia'. He readily acknowledged that Britain was 'unable to find the resources' for such an operation without American help.

In the event, achieving the planned capacity took much longer than anticipated and the route did not get close to the 200,000-ton monthly target until October 1943, more than a year later. Far more ships therefore arrived in the last half of 1942 than the ports and transport system could handle. In mid-October, the average turnaround time at Iranian ports was 55 days, qualifying therefore as another 'flagrant waste of shipping' in the Russia Lend-Lease story. Of 705,000 tons of supplies shipped to the Gulf in 1942, barely half had reached Russia by the end of the year. Only 18,800 tons of weapons were delivered, just over 11 per cent of weapon tonnage via the Arctic route. This meant that increases on the Persian Gulf route did not remotely compensate for the reductions on the Arctic route in the critical second half of 1942. In those six months, shipments actually reaching Russia, after allowing for losses, on the two routes combined were less than 60 per cent of those achieved in the first half of the year with serious implications for the credibility of Second Protocol commitments. On a more positive note, the American supplies that reached Russia on the Persian route between May, when Hopkins began to divert shipments from the Arctic, and the end of the year included 703 aircraft, almost all light and medium bombers and covering most of their commitment to this category under the first half of the Second Protocol, 800 tanks, mainly light Stuarts, about 25,000 trucks and 50,000 tons of food. These assets, especially the mobility and logistic support provided by the trucks, made a useful and timely contribution to the Soviet Stalingrad counter-offensive.[81]

The Persian Gulf route was not the only alternative. As noted earlier, the Pacific route from the United States west coast to Vladivostok made only a modest contribution to supplies in the first half of 1942. The 175,000 tons delivered by a shuttle service of thirty-seven mostly Soviet-flagged ships was 20 per cent less than shipments via the Persian Gulf and less than a quarter of arrivals on the Arctic route. The decision not to include weapons, to avoid provoking Japan, also meant the deliveries here were less valuable. Nevertheless, the July crisis made this route more important and, by transferring twenty-seven American merchant ships and seven tankers to the Soviet flag, accompanied by the transfer of some Soviet vessels from the Arctic convoy route, capacity was significantly increased with a tripling of shipments in the second half of the year, primarily food, raw materials, oil and trucks, but also, despite the risk of Japanese interference, 5,200 tons of weapons. From this point the Pacific became the leading route for tonnage shipped although it faced similar port handling and transport challenges to the Persian Gulf and, for the present, it could not contribute to the most pressing Soviet priorities.[82]

A further option, given the priority the Soviet leadership placed on supplies of aircraft to meet the German southern offensive, was flight delivery. There were two possible ferry routes. First, from Brazil across to the Gold Coast (modern Ghana) and thence using the British developed trans-Africa route to Sudan, and on to Iran. This was long and demanding over difficult, lonely terrain and suitable only for twin-engine light and medium bombers. There were also capacity issues since it was already heavily used for British aircraft deliveries to the Middle and Far East theatres. Nevertheless, 103 B-25 bombers and some A-20s took this route in 1942. The second option, which despite difficult climatic conditions looked more promising, was from Alaska into Siberia. The United States proposed this to the Russians as early as December 1941 but found the latter unreceptive and suspicious. In May 1942, the Russians reluctantly conceded they would take delivery of planes in Alaska and use their own pilots for onward shipment. However, they continued to make difficulties, insisting that the Americans provide forty-three transport planes to ferry their pilots to Alaska and then engaging in constant reversals of policy for no reason, causing the War Department to lose patience. Only in October was agreement on the operation of the route finally reached but it was another six months before supplies were significant. Up to the end of 1942, only eighty-five planes were delivered, significantly less than the 112 light and medium bombers per month agreed under the Second Protocol.[83]

As the Western Allies struggled to explore and develop these alternative routes through the autumn of 1942, it was clear they all had potential.

But it was equally clear that, in the present year as Russia struggled to contain Operation Blue, they could not compensate for the lost traffic on the Arctic route and reduce the growing backlog in Second Protocol commitments. Planning for the Second Protocol had assumed, however optimistically, that the Arctic route would carry 1.65 million tons of supplies between July and December, the first half of the protocol period. For reasons that will become clear, the final total delivered was not even one-tenth of this. By the end of November, five months into the protocol period, barely half the scheduled supplies for this period had been shipped, let alone delivered, across all the available routes.[84]

## PQ 17 in Royal Navy and National Memory

The PQ 17 disaster certainly scarred direct participants and heavily influenced future convoy planning. However, the reasons behind the disaster, above all Pound's decision to scatter, received little contemporary scrutiny or even comment from the wider political and military leadership. At the political level, it was overshadowed by the fall of Tobruk two weeks earlier and the prospect of wholesale collapse in the Middle East. The chiefs of staff, as already described, were focused on the strategic arguments with the Americans leading to the Torch decision. From mid-July, the naval leadership were preoccupied with the immensely complicated convoy operation Pedestal to relieve Malta to be mounted in the western Mediterranean in early August. Later the same month, the Dieppe raid provided a higher-profile disaster than PQ 17 and one, along with Tobruk, far more visible to the general public. Furthermore, despite the doubts over the cost/benefit of the Arctic convoys held by the naval leadership, there was no immediate expectation that PQ 17 would trigger a fundamental shift in policy. The suspension of the July PQ 18 was seen as a temporary measure pending improved cover from autumn darkness and weather.

No formal blame or censure was applied to the commanders at sea. Given the constraints of policy and resources faced by Tovey, there was little cause to question his dispositions or decisions. While he never enjoyed the favour of the prime minister, he had the confidence of everyone else and remained in post for a further 10 months. Despite some claims, there is no evidence that Hamilton's career suffered. He remained in command of 1st Cruiser Squadron for a further year, received good personal reports from Tovey and his successor, Admiral Sir Bruce Fraser, and both recommended him for promotion. In 1943, he became Flag Officer Malta as a vice admiral and ended his career as Chief of the Naval Staff Royal Australian Navy as a full admiral from 1945–8.[85] Although

Broome claimed that anyone associated with PQ 17 had a potential black mark on their record, he too suffered no apparent career setback. He was promoted captain at the end of 1942, received a Distinguished Service Cross, and commanded the new escort carrier *Begum* in the Indian Ocean with distinction in 1943–4 before retiring from the Royal Navy soon after the war to pursue a career as author and illustrator.

The lack of formal blame reflected widespread recognition among key naval participants that ultimate responsibility lay with Pound and the way his orders to scatter were communicated. Tovey emphasised that, in his opinion, scattering was premature and the results 'disastrous' but, officially, he was more circumspect on the role of Hamilton and Broome in withdrawing the destroyers. On 15 July, Churchill focused specifically on Hamilton's role. Now aware that it was apparently Hamilton who had 'ordered' the destroyers to quit the convoy, he sought Pound and Alexander's views on this decision. However, as he soon appreciated, it was not possible to censure anyone lower down the chain of command without exposing Pound and relevant members of the naval staff to critical scrutiny.[86] Within the Admiralty, the realisation of how the three successive orders transmitted from Pound's meeting had impacted on Hamilton and Broome now provoked embarrassment. Nor was there clear consensus over whether Broome's destroyers could have offered much practical help to the dispersing convoy. Brind doubted they would have 'saved many ships'. Moore thought that, with the benefit of hindsight, 'they might have dealt with the U-boats to some extent'. In a private message to the DNI John Godfrey, Douglas Fisher, the new SBNO North Russia, was highly critical of the attitude and performance of the non-destroyer escorts, with the notable exception of the trawler *Ayrshire*. Fisher felt the escorts should have scattered with the convoy but attached themselves to one or more merchant ships which would have given some protection and facilitated a more effective recovery operation once the danger of surface attack had passed. The young Lieutenant Leo Gradwell of *Ayrshire* brilliantly demonstrated what should have been done. He had accompanied one merchant ship northward, collected two more, and brought his little convoy safely to the Matochkin Strait with outstanding initiative. Sadly, most of his escort colleagues had looked only to themselves, had stuck in a group, and made little effort to search for survivors even when ordered to do so.[87]

The centrality of Ultra and its related security sensitivities was a further constraint. Two weeks after Churchill posed his questions, there was also fleeting Parliamentary interest. On 29 July, the Labour MP Emanuel Shinwell, currently one of Churchill's most persistent critics on the back benches but also a post-war Minister of Defence, asked George Hall, the Financial Secretary to the Admiralty, if he was aware that 'a recent convoy proceeding in a very important direction was denuded of protection almost at the last minute and that a large number of vessels were lost'. Hall stonewalled but Shinwell threatened to revert during a future naval debate and the government felt obliged to prepare a response. Even before this intervention, Alexander told the prime minister that 'unpleasant rumours' were circulating regarding PQ 17 with claims the Royal Navy had 'deserted' the merchant ships. He felt an early statement was desirable. Churchill initially thought this unwise. The Russians had announced the 'safe arrival' of the convoy and the Royal Navy had little to fear from 'slanders'.[88]

Pound reported on the events leading to the 'dispersal' of PQ 17 to the War Cabinet on 1 August. Whether the timing was influenced by Shinwell's intervention or Churchill's queries regarding Hamilton is unclear. The Admiralty had ordered the convoy to 'disperse' because of a perceived 'dangerous threat' of surface attack. In a less than honest rationalisation, Pound then claimed that the order to 'disperse' had been superseded with one to 'scatter' because of the slow speed of the convoy and limited time available for dispersal. He acknowledged that this gave the convoy the impression that it would be attacked at any moment. The close escort commander (Broome) believed the best means of dealing with imminent surface attack was to add his destroyers to Rear Admiral Hamilton's cruiser force, a proposal which Hamilton approved. Hamilton had acted 'correctly' until ordered by the Admiralty to retire westward when it would have been preferable to despatch the destroyers back to the vicinity of the convoy. His failure to do so 'could hardly be regarded as more than an error of judgement'. Even accounting for the brevity of the Cabinet record, this account of Hamilton's 'error', perhaps for Churchill's benefit, was distinctly misleading given that he had been ordered westward 12 minutes before the order to scatter![89]

Pound's report underpinned a draft statement for the First Lord to deploy in a secret session of Parliament which the War Cabinet approved on 4 August while Churchill was absent in the Middle East. It too was misleading. It implied the order to scatter had coincided with the sortie of the German fleet rather than anticipating it by 15 hours. It also claimed that 'cruisers and destroyers of the escort force' had immediately formed a 'striking force' to attack the enemy 'before he could reach the merchant ships' which was certainly not what either Pound, Tovey or Hamilton intended. Finally, while deliberately avoiding detail, it implied losses were lighter than they actually were. These points were reinforced in defensive lines for use if Shinwell asked supplementary questions. He would also be advised that effective rescue work had reduced merchant deaths to 5.6 per cent of all personnel sailing in the convoy.[90] The draft was never deployed in its original form, but it did underpin a statement on PQ 17 made to Parliament on 17 December 1946 in response to accusations directed at the Royal Navy's role in the Russian press. Some of that statement's careful ambiguities caused difficulty later.[91]

The Cabinet and Admiralty may have avoided awkward contemporary publicity and official scrutiny but the sense of shame felt by those at sea ensured that their absence did not prevent informal judgement and condemnation both at the time and in the decades that followed. Here a central issue was indeed whether the impact of Pound's orders could have been mitigated by those on the spot, above all Hamilton and Broome. Assessing the nature and validity of these informal judgements as they evolved over three decades is difficult because almost all key participants in the PQ 17 story, including Tovey, were inevitably defensive over their own roles and often subtly shifted their testimony over time. The views of later historians were not always consistent either.

Tovey's real views on the performance of Hamilton and Broome appeared in a personal letter to Percy Noble, who was Broome's ultimate commander, on 12 July just over a week after the fateful order to scatter. Tovey endorsed the original decision to concentrate Broome's destroyers with Hamilton's force as a reasonable response to Pound's three signals which surely implied that the arrival of a major German force including *Tirpitz* was imminent and action unavoidable. However, he then argued that, after two hours with no sign of the Germans, both commanders should have recognised that the situation was now entirely different and that the destroyers should return to the dispersing convoy to help defend it against inevitable air and U-boat attack. Tovey was categoric that responsibility for failing to return the destroyers lay with Hamilton who had badly misjudged the situation. He deeply regretted Hamilton's 'mistake' which denied important assistance to the convoy and might have saved many lives. Although reluctant to blame Broome, a commander in rank now under the orders of a rear admiral, he would have been happier if, after the two-hour gap, Broome had made clear representations to Hamilton that his duty lay with the convoy. He also felt Broome underestimated the difficulty his destroyer force could have posed to an attacking German force. Heavy ships did not like thrusting through smokescreens, knowing they faced torpedo-armed destroyers on the other side. In making these criticisms, Tovey stressed that primary blame for the disaster nevertheless lay with the premature action of the Admiralty and the confused nature of their signals. Tovey had himself assumed the signals implied new intelligence which would shortly be shared and was appalled to discover this was not the case.[92]

There were problems with Tovey's view here as Hamilton emphasised in a letter to the former on 6 July. It is not obvious why the situation facing Hamilton and Broome at 0100, two hours after commencing their withdrawal, was 'entirely different'. The Germans might be slower to arrive but, in any case, Hamilton had never been steering a reciprocal to the probable German intercept course. There was no new intelligence or guidance from the Admiralty. Only with receipt of the Admiralty's long-delayed 0238 Ultra which Hamilton would not have received before 0300 did the situation begin to look different. Even if the destroyers had turned around at about 0100, they would not have reached the position where the convoy scattered until five hours after the initial order. By this time the merchant ships had spread in all directions and, even travelling at only 8 knots, would be more than 30 miles away and far out of sight. So, what were the destroyers to do? Split up and each hope to find one or two merchant ships they could protect and perhaps, with the help of the non-destroyer escorts, create a series of mini-convoys? Tovey did not say. Nor did he address the fuel issue. A high-speed return, followed by equally high-speed searching, would have left the destroyers desperately short of fuel with at least 800 miles to go to Russian ports. Finding and refuelling from the tanker *Aldersdale* which had dispersed with the convoy would be difficult to reconcile with rounding up merchant vessels and *Aldersdale* was bombed and abandoned on the afternoon of 5 July. Whether any destroyer could have found her and prevented this can only be hypothetical. The reality is that Tovey could not have it both ways. He could not endorse the destroyers joining Hamilton and insist they could still have mitigated the subsequent German killing spree. Once the destroyers left, the die was cast. It is also hard not to detect regret and guilt on Tovey's part. He could and perhaps should have intervened, on receiving the Admiralty orders, with clear instructions to Hamilton and Broome on how they should manage the 'scattering'.

Tovey appears privately to have maintained his criticism of Hamilton until his death in 1971 and, but for Admiralty pressure, would have put it on public record when his despatch on the Arctic convoys was published in 1950. The case of the despatch reveals that, five years after the war ended, the PQ 17 story was perceived as retaining potential to embarrass both the Admiralty and wider government. The Admiralty concern was that parts of Tovey's coverage of PQ 17, not confined to the Hamilton issue, were inconsistent with the 1946 statement to Parliament, and, if combined with similar inconsistencies in Churchill's imminent fourth volume of his Second World War history, would create unwelcome publicity in the United States and offer a propaganda coup to the Soviet Union. The issue was viewed seriously enough to reach Prime Minister Clement Attlee. A neat irony was that the Minister of Defence also involved was none other than Emanuel Shinwell! The immensely loyal Tovey reluctantly accepted the changes and deleted adverse reference to Hamilton. Pressed by journalists on PQ 17 following publication, Tovey suggested there was more he could say but that he would maintain a discreet silence.[93]

Tovey did later confide his criticism of Hamilton to the official naval historian, Stephen Roskill, apparently in trenchant terms. Roskill's subsequent reference to this criticism in his official history was muted. He merely stated that Tovey 'condemned the failure [by Hamilton] to send Broome's flotilla back' once it was clear attack was not imminent. He also separately endorsed Pound's statement to the War Cabinet that Hamilton's withdrawal of the destroyers should not be viewed as more than an 'error of judgement'.[94] Roskill's restrained treatment here of the destroyer withdrawal may have reflected desire not to feed the 'lurid reports' of betrayal and abandonment by the Royal Navy which remained prevalent in merchant-ship circles on both sides of the Atlantic, but especially the United States, in the first post-war decade. At any rate, in a new history published just four years afterwards without any obvious new source, Roskill was harsher – 'If the Admiralty's intervention was untimely, and the wording of the signals misleading, Admiral Hamilton's removal of the destroyers was certainly an error of judgement of some magnitude'.[95] He underlined this tougher judgement in a newspaper article two years later, now stating that Tovey was 'astonished and dismayed' at the withdrawal of the destroyers and 'left his junior in no doubt of his views'.[96] For his part, despite the Admiralty's fears in 1950, Churchill was also relatively restrained in writing his history. He gave a brief but fair summary of Hamilton's arguments for withdrawing the destroyers before judging that it was nevertheless 'certainly a mistake' and that 'all risks should have been taken in defence of the merchant ships'.[97]

Despite Roskill's more forthright views on Hamilton, the story of PQ 17 rather faded from public consciousness through the 1960s. There was a consensus that it was a tragedy of war to which errors of judgement, most notably the Admiralty's order to scatter, had contributed but there had been other convoy disasters and as a set-piece naval tragedy, PQ 17 lacked the drama of the loss of the *Hood* or *Prince of Wales* and *Repulse*. However, matters changed at the end of the decade with the publication of David

Irving's book, *The Destruction of Convoy PQ 17*, and the subsequent decision of Jack Broome to sue Irving and his publisher Cassell for libel, leading to a 23-day trial at the Royal Courts of Justice in early 1970. Broome won his case and received £40,000 in damages, the highest award for libel in England up to that time. The intense drama, emotion and pain of the story painted vividly by the prosecution, drawing on a host of now-distinguished naval witnesses, ensured the trial attracted huge publicity in Britain and the United States and well beyond. The witnesses included Roskill as expert historian but also the holders of the current most senior sea and shore commands in the Royal Navy, respectively Admiral Sir William O'Brien, Commander-in-Chief Western Fleet, and Admiral Sir John Frewen, Commander-in-Chief Naval Home Command, who had both served as junior officers in the PQ 17 escort.

Viewed more than 50 years later, the trial poses fascinating issues and questions over the way it framed perceptions of the PQ 17 story, many of which persist. The then 33-year-old Irving was successfully portrayed by the prosecution as an arrogant, ambitious, unpleasant upstart, lacking the experience, maturity or discretion to unravel a complex naval operation, let alone pass judgement on individual participants – as described by Lord Denning in the subsequent Court of Appeal hearing, he was 'an author who knew nothing about the war, because he was a babe in arms at the time'. Irving's subsequent notoriety as a Holocaust denier, powerfully exposed in a later court case, not only destroyed his reputation but undermined any previous claim to be viewed as a serious historian. His earlier work is therefore tainted with presumptions of unreliability and bias with few comfortable recognising his PQ 17 research or disposed to debate the outcome of the 1970 trial. PQ 17 historians are nevertheless left in an uneasy position. Not only has most of Irving's baseline account of the operation stood the test of time but it includes a wealth of personal testimony from living witnesses that is unique and which subsequent histories have been obliged to exploit and acknowledge. Importantly, Irving has produced the only account of Pound's crucial staff meeting on the evening of 4 July based on interviews with participants. There was no formal record and all those present were dead by 1980.[98]

Several aspects of the context and conduct of the trial require emphasis. First, there was no reference to Ultra, whose existence was only acknowledged several years later. The way intelligence and its limitations influenced key decisions during the PQ 17 operation was thus not apparent to the court. Secondly, contrary to the impression deliberately promoted by the prosecution, Irving's book was not primarily about Broome. Although inevitably present as a key participant, he featured in only forty of 306 pages of text in the 1968 version. Many references were brief and he received less than half the index space allocated to Hamilton. Thirdly, a comparison between the 1968 book and the version published by William Kimber in 1980 demonstrates that excisions demanded after the trial were surprisingly few. One of the more damning judgements in the original book – 'In the Barents Sea, nobody had "taken charge"' (in giving clear direction to the scattering ships and non-destroyer escorts), clearly pointed at both Hamilton and Broome, appeared unchanged in the 1980 version.[99] Few would now disagree with Irving's claim here.

Finally, several members of the judiciary demonstrated sympathy for Broome and the Royal Navy to a point which might now be considered partisan. The summing up to the jury by the trial judge, Sir Frederick Lawton, was viewed this way by some contemporary observers and mercilessly lampooned in the satirical weekly *Private Eye*.[100] It is also ironic, given Irving's subsequent disgrace as a Holocaust denier, that while at Cambridge in the early 1930s, Lawton joined the British Union of Fascists, founded a university Fascist Association, and in 1936 was adopted as a BUF Parliamentary candidate.[101] When the exemplary damages awarded were reviewed by the Court of Appeal in early 1971, one of three judges was the Master of the Rolls, Lord Tom Denning, brother of 'Ned' who had been at the centre of the PQ 17 intelligence debate. By this time 'Ned' was retired Vice Admiral Sir Norman Denning and had served as the last Director of Naval Intelligence before the post was absorbed into a new tri-service organisation. It is impossible to know how far the Denning brothers discussed the trial and the wider history of PQ 17. It is also impossible now to verify whether, as Irving has claimed, 'Ned' described his book as 'magnificent' although it is intriguing that the prosecution did not call him as a witness. What is reasonable to argue is that Tom Denning had naval sympathies and potential 'insider' access sufficient to test his impartiality. Similarly, at the subsequent House of Lords appeal, the casting vote against the defendants came from the Lord Chancellor, Lord Hailsham, after the other six judges split equally. Hailsham had previously served as First Lord of the Admiralty in 1956–7 and was a devoted guardian of the Royal Navy's reputation.

It is striking how Denning began his summary of the libels with short excerpts from the dust jacket of the book – 'Many people were convinced' that the merchantmen 'had been shamefully deserted by a Navy which had lost only a fleet oiler in the convoy's passage' – and 'The massacre of PQ 17' was due to 'blunders, miscalculations and misunderstandings' which many wanted to 'remain hidden like so much dirty linen', and that 'elaborate deceptions have been practised to ensure this'. Denning's implication was that such claims, which research by his 'babe in arms' were supposed to validate, were ridiculous. Yet, allowing for 'colourful' sales promotion language, nothing here was factually inaccurate. There had been widespread accusations of desertion during and after the war and Admiral O'Brien, a star prosecution witness at the trial, described the shame felt on *Offa*'s bridge, even if he did not hold Broome directly responsible. Had Tovey testified, he would surely have confirmed the 'blunders' and subsequent Admiralty 'economy with the truth'.

Denning then upheld two specific areas of libel against Broome, the accusations of consistently disobeying orders from Hamilton to move the convoy northward, and of 'cowardly deserting the convoy'. He dismissed the first accusation on the basis that Irving had exaggerated and that anyway Broome was entitled to exercise his own judgement. While this was one interpretation given the ambiguity Tovey had left in the respective roles of Hamilton and Broome, there was also no question that Broome had disobeyed orders from a rear admiral and subsequently apologised for this to Tovey.[102] The balance of the argument surely lay with Irving rather than Denning. Denning's treatment of the second accusation was selective and misleading. Nowhere in the book did Irving accuse Broome of 'cowardice' or suggest 'he had lost his head' as Denning claimed. Irving did say that, on receiving the order to scatter, 'Broome needed no second bidding'. However, the book explained clearly, as Denning did not, that this was driven by Hamilton's warning of the proximity of enemy surface forces and *Pozarica*'s radar report of a possible enemy formation to the south-west. Denning also emphasised a final attack on Broome in the proofs of the book in the last sentence of the second appendix which stated that 'the point of error' determining the fate of the scattering merchant ships was Broome's withdrawal of his escorting destroyers and not Hamilton's refusal to send them back. However, in the book as published, 'point of error' became 'point of no return' as Denning reluctantly acknowledged while implying the change made no real difference. In reality, the change seems fundamental. The book does not accuse Broome of an error but observes that he took a decision on his own initiative which, however justifiable at the point of scattering, subsequently proved impossible to reverse. While the practical impact of withdrawing the destroyers and Hamilton's role in endorsing Broome's decision can all be debated, the judgement in the sentence as published does not now seem to carry the 'grave imputation' claimed by Denning.[103]

If Denning's sympathy for Broome and the wider Royal Navy is evident, he was also reflecting testimony at the trial where the defence, perhaps surprisingly, called no witnesses. Denning's summary also underlines that a trial of this type does not seek to establish ground truth, if such exists, but to convince the jury of an argument and narrative within the existing libel laws. The prosecution was hugely successful in presenting Broome as an elderly war hero, personifying all the best values of his wartime generation, service, sacrifice, courage, honour, and loyalty, which were being steadily trashed and threatened by the rebellious generation coming of age in the 1960s. The complexities of the PQ 17 operation and the factors that drove the actions of key players, hard for any jury to grasp, probably ultimately mattered less than the view that, not just Broome, but all those who had fought the war at great personal cost were being subjected to criticism and disrespect. The trial also came at a point where the writing of history was changing. Top-down history with its clear narrative, focus on the big picture and key events, judiciously balanced and eschewing criticism of individuals, was being challenged by a new generation determined to critique established opinion, sometimes harshly, freely criticise the actions of senior figures and to make greater use of first-hand testimony from those serving at lower level. Irving's book fell into the latter category and represented a fundamental shift in approach to Roskill's work. Roskill probably therefore felt doubly threatened by perceived disrespect to a service he loved and to the way he felt the recent history of the Royal Navy should be told. If Irving had written even 10 years later, his approach would have seemed standard and his questioning of individuals and their actions reasonable. As it was, he wrote when memories were still raw.[104]

## Chapter 9

# Recovery: PQ 18 and the Impact of Torch

The Admiralty agreement, however reluctant, that a new PQ convoy would be run in early September posed obvious operational challenges for Tovey. He accepted that, even in late summer, a convoy could always fight through U-boat and air attack if there was political will to accept heavy losses. A stronger close escort, and above all inclusion of one of the new escort carriers coming into service, could help contain these losses. The more difficult problem, as PQ 17 demonstrated, was finding a solution to a strike by German heavy surface units in the eastern sector of the Barents Sea. Here Tovey acknowledged that the cover provided by his battlefleet and carrier 'had always been more threatening than real' for he remained resolutely opposed to exposing his heavy ships to air and U-boat attack in the relatively confined waters east of Bear Island. Screening the battlefleet here would also absorb substantial numbers of destroyers better deployed in direct support of the convoys.[1]

*Planning and Preparation for PQ 18*
Operation 'EV' to protect PQ 18 and the parallel inbound QP 14 was accordingly the most elaborate plan yet, comprising several innovations. In preparing it, Tovey recognised correctly, possibly drawing on further intelligence from Denham, that the Germans would not necessarily leave the westbound convoy alone. For this reason, the option of running a westbound convoy on its own in early August to clear the backlog of ships in Murmansk was ruled out although lack of submarine cover was also an issue.[2] The most important innovation for PQ 18 was to rely on a large 'fighting escort' of sixteen fleet destroyers to protect against surface attack, under the Rear Admiral Commanding Home Fleet Destroyers, Robert Burnett, unusually for an officer of his rank a physical training specialist and flying his flag in the new anti-aircraft cruiser *Scylla*. Burnett was a magnificent sportsman but, by his own estimation as well as that

of his peers, a man of limited intellect. However, he was a born fighter, a fine seaman, and natural guile made him a shrewd tactician. He was also a destroyer man to his fingertips, including command of Broome's *Keppel* in the early 1930s, and he would play a major role in successive Arctic convoy operations over the next 18 months. He was a demanding leader, not universally loved but highly respected and trusted by all and generally known as 'Uncle Bob'. Another of his accomplishments and passions was amateur dramatics. When serving as second-in-command to Cunningham in the battleship *Rodney*, he famously dressed up as a female guest in place of someone who had fallen out, was duly received at the captain's table for lunch and got away with the impersonation although deceiving Cunningham was a high risk business![3]

Four of Burnett's destroyers were of the large 'Tribal' class completed just before the war and another eight were from the latest 'M' and 'O' classes, all completed in the last year and four only commissioned in the last three months. This fighting escort was additional to a standard 'close escort' accompanying each convoy throughout its journey. For PQ 18, the close escort was identical in strength to that for PQ 17 but with three less destroyers. To enable the fighting escort to support both outbound and inbound convoys, these were now timed sequentially rather than in parallel. The fighting escort would therefore transfer from PQ 18 to QP 14 off Novaya Zemlya, leaving PQ 18 to complete the final 300 miles with its close escort and whatever support the Russians could offer. All this posed major logistic challenges. Two tankers were therefore positioned in Lowe Sound, Spitzbergen, and two more accompanied PQ 18 but then moved over to QP 14 with the fighting escort. The concept of a fighting escort was clearly modelled on that developed for the abortive Vigorous convoy two months earlier, but Tovey evidently had greater confidence than Harwood that it would prove effective in holding off a major surface strike.[4]

A second important innovation was the inclusion of the escort carrier *Avenger* in direct support of the convoy. *Avenger* was one of the five *Archer* class escort carriers which, as described earlier, were ordered from the United States in mid-1941 as improved versions of the pilot carrier *Audacity*. The commissioning of the *Archer*s had been much delayed and PQ 18 marked both *Avenger*'s own debut and the first deployment of an escort carrier in action since *Audacity*'s loss the previous December. For this operation, *Avenger* carried twelve Sea Hurricanes, double the fighter complement of *Audacity*, and three Swordfish in the anti-submarine role. She also carried six crated spare Hurricanes in her hangar. As was customary in the Mediterranean, she was assigned two dedicated destroyer escorts, *Wheatland* and *Wilton*, so that she could manoeuvre independently to fly off and recover aircraft, with the entire force under the command of her captain, Commander Anthony Colthurst. The presence of *Avenger*, along with *Scylla* and the destroyer fighting escort, meant that for the first time a PQ convoy enjoyed an anti-aircraft screen comparable in quality and numbers to that available to Somerville with Halberd a year earlier. This protection was certainly needed because, during August, the German 5th Air Fleet attack force reached its zenith with 92 torpedo aircraft and 120 conventional bombers. Ultra decrypts enabled Tovey and his staff to monitor the status of the German air threat in considerable detail and the OIC also issued weekly reports on the 'Maximum Scale of Attack' from air, U-boat and surface forces in the Arctic theatre.[5] The overall threat picture was summarised in Tovey's EV operation orders issued on 24 August.[6]

PQ 18 also enjoyed other support not available to its predecessor. Eleven Royal Air Force Catalinas and thirty-two Hampden torpedo bombers were flown to North Russian airfields to provide reconnaissance, anti-submarine and surface-strike capability. Group Captain Frank Hopps was appointed to command this substantial force and coordinate its deployment with the Russians, and he was equipped with much enhanced communications to facilitate delivery of intelligence and advice on targeting. The Hampdens, which flew out initially to Afrikanda airfield near Kandalaksha on 4 September, were adapted versions of the obsolescent, and never very effective, bomber, compensating now for the shortage of the superior Beauforts. PQ 17 had clearly changed the Admiralty's June view on the release of Hampdens but there were now many more aircraft available. It was a daunting journey geographically and navigationally, at the extreme edge of their range, and nine aircraft were lost on passage. One of these came down in Norway, providing the Germans with a significant intelligence haul on PQ 18. Three days later, the twenty-three survivors flew to one of the Vaenga fields which became their operational base and where they were matched with their torpedoes and ground crew delivered by sea. As described later, the British crews flew just one abortive operation to the approaches of Altafiord on 14 September and the surviving aircraft with their equipment and weapons were then gifted to the Soviet Northern Fleet Air Force a month later. Despite the limitations of the Hampden, Russian crews had some success over the next six months in torpedo attacks against German transports and in night bombing raids on Kirkenes port and other targets. Three PR Spitfires were also flown to Vaenga in early September via Afrikanda to improve coverage of the north Norwegian fiords. When one aircraft was damaged in a German raid, a fourth was sent as a replacement. These were operated successfully by a Royal Air Force detachment until late October when the aircraft and their camera equipment were also gifted to the Russians who rated them highly.[7]

The fighting escort absorbed the majority of the Home Fleet's destroyers, leaving barely sufficient to support a cruiser covering force west of Bear Island and a substantial fuelling force at Spitzbergen. Indeed, the total commitment of nineteen fleet destroyers to all aspects of EV was perhaps one-third of the Royal Navy's current operationally available strength in this category. As a result, Western Approaches Command had to loan ships not only for the convoy close escort but also to escort the covering battlefleet, comprising *Duke of York* and her newly completed sister *Anson*. Inevitably the battlefleet escort, under Jack Broome, therefore comprised second-rate vessels, lacking the speed and range of their fleet counterparts which constrained the mobility of the heavy ship force. Tovey, drawing lessons from his isolation during PQ 17, delegated command of the battlefleet to his second-in-command, Vice Admiral Sir Bruce Fraser, and remained at Scapa Flow in the now-repaired *King George V*, to ensure that he, not the Admiralty, would control this highly complex operation.[8]

As planning for EV evolved through August, it was inevitably influenced by new intelligence on German dispositions and intentions and developments and requirements in other theatres, especially the Mediterranean. Dolphin decrypts in the second week of July revealed the damage to *Lützow* and to Schniewind's three destroyers, and the former's transfer to Trondheim pending return to Germany for repairs which took the rest of the year. They also showed that the light cruiser *Köln* would be deployed from the Baltic to Trondheim as a partial replacement for *Lützow*. Although subsequent decrypts provided valuable detail on their respective movements, they were not timely enough to enable successful British interception. Following a false U-boat report that the next PQ convoy was on its way, *Köln* was moved to Narvik, there to join *Tirpitz*, *Scheer* and *Hipper*, but the OIC only learnt this after her arrival.[9]

What Dolphin could not provide, and Denham's Swedish source did not either, was any insight into Hitler's strengthening reluctance to sanction any operations by heavy ships against the PQ convoys, a message conveyed informally to Raeder by Vice Admiral Krancke on 17 July. Krancke, drawing partly on comments from Lieutenant General Alfred Jodl, OKW Chief of Operations, thought the success of air and U-boat operations against PQ 17 would convince Hitler to abandon big-ship operations until German aircraft carriers were available. Although glad that *Köln* had arrived in Trondheim, Hitler evidently wanted to keep her confined to defensive use. Krancke saw that this passive stance would be hard on the ships' crews, but he doubted Hitler would shift his view which was heavily influenced by his fears of an Allied attack on the Petsamo nickel mines.[10]

Meanwhile Ultra decrypts provided some insight into the extensive German air and U-boat effort mounted over the first two weeks of August to find 'PQ 18' which they were convinced had departed Iceland at the beginning of the month. The conviction the convoy was imminent was supported by an agent report sent on 25 July which reported eighteen merchant ships loaded with tanks and planes as deck cargo entering Hvalfiord a week earlier.[11] On 6 August, following the false U-boat sighting of 'PQ 18' which triggered the move of *Köln*, Group North prepared to deploy the whole cruiser force from Narvik with the intention of attacking an anticipated parallel westbound QP convoy. The attack would ideally occur in the eastern part of the Barents Sea but would be subject to the same constraints as PQ 17 and Führer approval would be needed.[12] Thereafter, the search for both convoys was hampered by fog for five days.[13] A notable development in this period was the first use of airborne search radar in an Fw 200 on 7 August which detected a contact, not sighted visually, at a range of 20km.[14] Amidst mounting frustration, the weather cleared on 12 August and a massive aerial search, involving 140 sorties and 1603 hours of flying time, was mounted that day and the next, expending nearly one million litres of fuel. It found nothing.[15] By 14 August, Group North therefore had 'very grave doubts as to the facts concerning convoy PQ 18', with scrutiny inevitably focusing on the 6 August U-boat report. Two days later, there was a reluctant consensus, albeit without much conviction, that the convoy must have reached Russian ports, and that further search effort was pointless.[16]

Dolphin decrypts, complemented by intelligence from Denham's Swedish coverage, also illuminated Operation Wunderland, the deployment of *Admiral Scheer* from Narvik to the Kara Sea east of Novaya Zemlya, during the last fortnight of August, to attack Russian shipping using the north coast route which extended from Murmansk and Archangel as far as the Bering Strait and was open during the summer months. In planning the operation, the Germans had intelligence from Japanese[17] and Russian prisoner of war sources correctly reporting the presence of significant convoys in this period, although the preferred start date was put back because of the possible presence of PQ 18. In the event, the results of Wunderland, conducted with support from two U-boats, were meagre, the sinking of the small icebreaker *Alexander Sibiryakov* and limited damage to shipping and shore facilities following the bombardment of the important port of Dikson. For the British, Wunderland did, nevertheless, demonstrate German capability and will to operate out to Novaya Zemlya and beyond and, if *Scheer*'s cruise had been longer, or PQ 18 had sailed earlier, her presence would have been a complication.[18] Nor, unknown to the British, did the poor results deter the Germans from immediately contemplating further operations in the eastern Barents and Kara Seas.[19] However, Raeder had other plans for *Scheer*. On 26 August, before the results of Wunderland were known, he sought Hitler's permission to deploy her on a raiding cruise in the South Atlantic beginning in November. Hitler refused, insisting that all heavy units must remain in the Arctic to repel any Allied landing which he judged especially likely during the winter months. Raeder reluctantly acquiesced.[20]

As with *Lützow*, partly due to careful German route planning and radio silence, news of *Scheer*'s departure from Narvik on 16 August and her initial movements was not good enough to allow her to be targeted by the patrolling British submarines off northern Norway. To conceal her presence she also carefully avoided a 5000-ton Russian merchant ship she sighted 150 miles east of Bear Island and which was one of two sailing independently to Archangel.[21] However, by the last week of August, there was enough intelligence of her presence in the Kara Sea to persuade Tovey briefly to consider retaining the American cruiser *Tuscaloosa* and five assorted American and British destroyers in Murmansk where they had delivered ammunition and stores for returning ships and personnel and supplies for the Hampden torpedo bombers. He hoped that, if further intelligence pinpointed *Scheer*'s whereabouts, the Allied force could intercept her. However, the risk of air attack in Murmansk and in the Barents Sea ruled against this. There was a compensatory prize. Dolphin decrypts revealed the arrival of the minelayer *Ulm* in Narvik on 19 August and six days later the full plans for Operation Zar, her mission to lay 300 mines off the north-west coast of Novaya Zemlya. The intercepted signal summarising Zar, which originated from Admiral Arctic, not only provided coordinates of the proposed minefield but also *Ulm*'s approach route along with a description of her appearance and the likelihood she would fly an American or other merchant flag. This level of detail was necessary to avoid a 'friendly fire' incident with U-boats or with *Scheer* on her way back from Wunderland. Zar probably followed a suggestion by Jodl in mid-July, and seized on by Hitler, that mining offered a cheap means of disrupting the PQ convoys especially in winter.[22] On receipt of the Zar decrypt, and following consultation with the OIC and Naval Staff, Tovey ordered the three British destroyers escorting *Tuscaloosa* during her transit back to Iceland to detach temporarily and conduct a sweep to the southward before rejoining the cruiser near Bear Island. The sweep made no reference to *Ulm* but was designed to bring them across her path and they were also advised that there were no friendly vessels in the area. They duly intercepted *Ulm*, which was flying the Panamanian flag, and sank her, a textbook example of Ultra used to great operational effect with minimal risk to the source.[23] There were subsequent German claims that the destroyers had not only failed to pick up survivors but also fired on them, leading Hitler to demand reprisals.[24]

## Operation Pedestal and its Implications for the Arctic

While these developments were underway in the Arctic, as explained earlier the feasibility of running PQ 18 also depended on Pedestal, the August convoy through the Gibraltar Straits to Malta, being achieved without severe losses to escorting warships which would subsequently be needed in the North. The Home Fleet detached *Victorious*, four cruisers and eleven fleet and escort destroyers at the beginning of August to support Pedestal. Of these, the cruiser *Manchester* and fleet destroyer *Foresight* were sunk while *Victorious* and the cruisers *Nigeria* and *Kenya* were damaged. The damage to *Victorious*, although comparatively light, meant Tovey had no fleet carrier with its long-range strike capability to cover PQ 18. Eight of seventeen fleet destroyers deployed during Pedestal came from the Home Fleet with seven returning to support PQ 18. Three escort destroyers also covered both convoys and Broome in *Keppel* was not unusual in moving seamlessly from PQ 17 to Pedestal and then to PQ 18 – or as he put it 'from polar bears to pineapples and back again' – in less than three months.[25]

Pedestal, conducted between 10 and 15 August, provides many parallels with the forthcoming PQ 18 although only some of its lessons could be absorbed before the latter departed.[26] The overall threat facing the two convoys was remarkably similar, closer in composition and scale across the two theatres than it had been before or would be again. British knowledge of the potential threat it would face in the western Mediterranean in August, as in the Arctic, was drawn primarily from SIGINT, and was generally excellent although inevitably with some gaps. The air threat facing the Pedestal convoy comprised about 330 strike aircraft, divided almost equally between the German and Italian air forces, and including ninety torpedo bombers. This was 50 per cent greater than the force that would confront PQ 18 and double that facing Somerville during Halberd the previous year. The proximity of the convoy route to the enemy air bases in Sardinia and Sicily also meant that, unlike in the Arctic, the Axis commanders could deploy Stuka dive-bombers and draw on 300 fighters to protect their strike groups. Proximity also enabled a higher sortie rate and easier navigation than in the Arctic. It is notable that the combined strength of twin-engine bombers composing the long-range strike forces deployable against the convoys in the western Mediterranean and Arctic was 400 aircraft in early August. This was about the same as the then twin-engine bomber strength in the 4th Air Fleet supporting the southern offensive in Russia.[27]

The submarine threat in the western Mediterranean at this time, comprising twenty boats, two German and eighteen Italian, was identical to that in the Barents Sea. However, on paper, the surface threat was much greater with the Italians potentially able to call on four battleships, thirteen cruisers, twenty-one destroyers and substantial additional light forces. In practice, the heavy ships were immobilised due to lack of fuel, just as the Germans had been hampered in the Arctic, and Italian planners had to consider threats in the eastern Mediterranean and the Royal Air Force strike force in Malta including two squadrons of highly effective Beaufort torpedo bombers. All this meant they could only muster three heavy and three light cruisers and twelve destroyers against the Pedestal convoy, more comparable therefore to that now available to the Germans in the Arctic. As during Halberd, an important threat not present in the Arctic was the Italian and German torpedo boats operating in the Sicilian Narrows. These sank a cruiser and three merchant ships and damaged two more.

Pedestal and PQ 18 were the most complex convoy operations yet mounted by the Royal Navy or indeed any navy. Given the similarity of threat across three dimensions, the overall naval forces deployed in protection were remarkably similar, for battleships, cruisers, total fleet and escort destroyers, and submarines, almost identical. However, there were three key differences. First, the entire Pedestal escort group operated as a closely integrated unit as far as the Sicilian Narrows when, as with Halberd, the heavy units turned back. For PQ 18, Tovey maintained the distinction between close escort, now reinforced with *Avenger* and the fighting destroyers, all under the command of Burnett, and separate cruiser and distant heavy covering forces. Secondly, Pedestal enjoyed far greater fighter protection. An unprecedented seventy-two fighters (sixteen Fulmars, forty-six Hurricanes and ten Martlets) were embarked in three fleet carriers, *Victorious* (detached from the Home Fleet), her sister *Indomitable* (from the Eastern Fleet) and the older *Eagle*. They also carried twenty-eight Albacores for surface strike and anti-submarine support. This carrier-borne fighter group, supported by excellent radar direction, compared with the twelve Hurricanes with *Avenger* and the twenty-seven Fulmars embarked in *Ark Royal* for Halberd. Finally, Pedestal had the support of a substantial Royal Air Force group at Malta. When the convoy reached the Sicilian Narrows, its operational strength included, ninety Spitfires, twenty-two long-range Beaufighters and thirty-four strike aircraft. This offered considerable protection over the final 150-mile stretch to Malta, whereas Russian fighter cover in the approaches to Murmansk had so far proved erratic and the newly-arrived Hampdens had to struggle with primitive facilities.

The Pedestal carrier fighters were critical in containing the Axis air threat prior to the Sicilian Narrows. Two days of intense attacks on 11 and 12 August up to this point sank only one of the fourteen merchant ships which were their primary target although they achieved minor damage to *Victorious* and more serious damage to *Indomitable*. Indeed, on the morning of 12 August, 117 Italian aircraft and 58 German achieved just the one ineffective hit on *Victorious*. Never before had the Axis air forces used so many aircraft for so little result.[28] This begs the question as to why more carrier support was not allocated to PQ 18 which was to lose ten merchant ships, 25 per cent of the convoy, to air attack. Churchill had raised this issue with Alexander and Pound on 15 July, two days after the Defence Committee cancelled the PQ convoy planned for later that month. He proposed that, if Pedestal went well, its entire carrier group should be redeployed north and enhanced with five escort carriers. A convoy together with a battleship escort would then complete its entire journey to the Russian ports under a fighter umbrella capable of meeting anything the Germans could throw at it.[29]

This suggestion may have been designed to provoke fresh thinking by the Admiralty and Tovey rather than to be taken literally. It was never a starter because none of the three Pedestal carriers was available for PQ 18 in September. *Eagle* had been sunk by a U-boat, *Indomitable* was under repair until the end of the year and *Victorious* until the end of September. Although four more escort carriers were nearing operational readiness, none was available to support *Avenger* in September. Furthermore, despite their sterling achievements on 11/12 August, Pedestal underlined the risks carriers would face in the Barents Sea. They would not only be exposed to damage or worse from air or U-boat attack for longer than in the Mediterranean, but a crippled ship might have to travel up to 1500 miles to reach a friendly dockyard capable of repairing her. Not surprisingly, the naval leadership viewed the risk/benefit equation in the Arctic rather differently to Pedestal. Loss or damage to two or three major units in the Barents Sea would threaten control of Atlantic communications.[30] Churchill was also more sensitive to political risk in the wake of the censure debate in Parliament following the fall of Tobruk. The scale of the PQ 17 losses had been successfully hidden but the loss of high-value warships could not be concealed for long. This sensitivity was evident when, on 1 August, the War Cabinet was asked to rule on whether the Pedestal battleships (*Rodney* and *Nelson*) should turn back at the Sicilian Narrows or accompany the convoy through to Malta. The risk to the battleships in these waters from multiple threats was high and the loss of one or both would have serious consequences for the naval balance. On the other hand, if the Italian battlefleet intervened during the final approach to the Island, and it was not known at this point that they were effectively immobilised, they could decimate the convoy. As the prime minister stated, 'searching questions' would then be asked about the convoy's protection. The Cabinet accepted the Admiralty advice that the risks beyond the Straits were too high and the convoy must rely on light forces and air cover from Malta.[31] Although in the event the Italian battlefleet did not intervene, the convoy suffered badly in the final 24-hour passage from the Straits to Malta. Eight of the thirteen surviving merchant ships were lost together with the cruiser *Manchester* and anti-aircraft cruiser *Cairo* to a combination of air, submarine and motor torpedo boat attack. Overall, despite the massive Royal Navy investment in protecting the Pedestal convoy, two-thirds of the ships were sunk, a loss rate almost identical to PQ 17. The lesson was that, when an enemy could deliver substantial force simultaneously across three dimensions, effective defence was immensely difficult.

## Churchill's Visit to Moscow

The Pedestal operation coincided almost exactly with Churchill's visit to Moscow and his first meeting with Stalin. Churchill faced three challenges. The most difficult was informing Stalin that there would be no second front in the form of a cross-Channel operation in 1942. He then hoped to soften this unwelcome message by convincing Stalin of the value of Torch. He also had to persuade him that, despite the hiatus over the PQ convoys, the Western Allies remained committed to delivering the supplies agreed under the First and Second Protocols. Finally, he wanted to achieve a personal relationship sufficient to reduce future misunderstandings. At their first meeting, Stalin's reaction to the abandonment of Sledgehammer was bleak. He claimed not to find the prime minister's arguments convincing and felt promises made to Molotov in June were now being broken. He repeated his favourite maxim that wars could not be won without risk. However, he was positive towards Torch, shrewdly identifying the advantages and asking perceptive questions. A second meeting the following day was cooler. Stalin emphasised a sense of betrayal over the abandonment of the second front and, while still positive towards Torch, implied it was ultimately an Anglo-American initiative of little direct value to Russia. There were regular references to Russia, currently under extreme pressure, doing all the fighting and gratuitous insults implying British Army cowardice. There were also swipes at the Lend-Lease programme. Aid was welcome but deliveries were running well behind promises. Stalin felt the lag here was less the result of enemy action and more due to underestimation of the importance of the Russian front.[32]

Churchill found the change of tone hard to read and bridled at the insults, speaking back forcefully when he had enough. 'I have come round Europe in the midst of my troubles – yes Mr Stalin, I have my troubles as well as you – hoping to meet the hand of comradeship; and I am bitterly disappointed I have not met that hand.' This provoked a smiling Stalin to respond – 'I do not understand the words, but by God I like your spirit'. Churchill followed up with a succinct note, stating that Torch was the best 'second front' in 1942 and would do more for Russia than any other operation as Stalin appeared to have recognised at their first meeting. He fiercely refuted any charge of broken promises, pointing to the aide-memoire given to Molotov on his departure in June which had emphasised there was only a small chance of Sledgehammer being adopted. Such was Churchill's anger that the visit might have ended on cold terms if he had not been persuaded by his ambassador Clark Kerr to seek a third, ideally private meeting. Had Churchill considered the consequences if Russia went down for want of Allied support? How many young British and American lives would have to be sacrificed to make this good. He must not 'leave Russia in the lurch', just because Stalin had hurt his pride. This proved good advice and a meeting between the two leaders at Stalin's private residence over the night of 14/15 August, with much alcohol consumed and only Molotov and interpreters present, not only cleared the air but achieved a genuine personal connection and understanding. As Churchill subsequently told Maisky – 'On that evening, or rather night, I saw Stalin's soul'.[33]

It is doubtful whether Churchill's message that there would be no cross-Channel second front this year came as a surprise to the Kremlin. Maisky from London and Litvinov from Washington had already expressed pessimism. There were indications too from intelligence sources. Looking back more than 30 years later, Molotov claimed that neither he nor Stalin believed it would happen and that they had pressured the Anglo-Americans to gain moral advantage and win concessions on other issues. A more interesting question is whether Stalin believed there would be a major cross-Channel invasion in 1943 as Churchill still insisted. As Churchill well knew, barely three weeks previously, the War Cabinet and chiefs of staff had approved CCS 94 which stated that the implementation of Torch would render a 1943 Roundup impracticable. Had Stalin received no hint of this? And was Churchill not laying the ground for more accusations of betrayal in the future? There was also scope for trouble over the aid programme. Churchill confirmed the intent to run PQ 18 in September and warned that Torch might 'affect the convoy position' thereafter. What he did not say, and did not yet appreciate, was that after PQ 18 only fifteen more ships would reach Russia by the Arctic route before the end of the year. Harriman, who was also present in Moscow, added a further hostage to fortune by stating that in the United States supplies for Russia had 'overriding priority'. Given the American delivery record to date, Stalin was likely to treat that claim with scepticism. And, simultaneously in Washington, the Combined Chiefs of Staff gave the Arctic convoys the lowest priority in the allocation of merchant vessels and naval escorts.[34]

Harriman's statement correctly reflected Roosevelt's attitude. On 20 August, five days after Churchill's final meeting with Stalin, by which time the prime minister was back in Egypt, the president called King and Cunningham to a meeting at the White House which Hopkins also attended. Cunningham had arrived as head of the British Admiralty Delegation in Washington two months earlier but would soon be appointed Torch naval commander. Roosevelt emphasised the 'absolute necessity' of maintaining the PQ convoys. Cunningham agreed their importance but stressed the need to coordinate resources with Torch. Roosevelt insisted 'nothing must prevent PQ convoys' which had equal priority with Torch. A two-month suspension was 'not acceptable'. Shipping and escorts must be found by sacrifices elsewhere. This certainly demonstrated the president's commitment to supporting Russia but, as Pound informed the prime minister, showed scant understanding of the scale of naval commitment required to juggle Torch and the Arctic or the reductions that had already been made in the Atlantic to resource the imminent PQ 18 and prepare for the North African landings. Pound also rightly stressed that the Torch commitment was not limited to the landings. There would be ongoing 'maintenance' demands and the operation would no doubt generate momentum and further requirements. The only way of meeting the president's goal was to transfer American naval forces from the Pacific but that was improbable. For a fortnight following his return to the United Kingdom, the prime minister clearly hoped there would be some means of avoiding hard choices but, by 12 September, he reluctantly accepted that if Torch went ahead in early November, PQ 18 must be the last convoy until mid-December.[35]

*PQ 18: Execution*

To reduce the risk of early detection, most of PQ 18 left Loch Ewe in western Scotland on 2 September, rendezvousing with a smaller section of eight ships off Iceland six days later. After two early returns and three vessels detached to Reykjavik, it then comprised forty merchant ships (nineteen American, eleven British, seven Russian and three Panamanian), two tankers and one rescue ship, the largest Arctic convoy to date and only surpassed by JW 58 in March 1944. Its cargo included 835 tanks, 523 fighters, 43 bombers, 43 gun-laying radar sets, 4,400 vehicles, 11,300 tons of TNT explosive, 10,000 tons of fuel oil, and a further 157,500 tons of miscellaneous items.[36] The total warships involved in its support numbered more than eighty. Burnett joined the convoy on 9 September south-west of Jan Mayen with half the fighting escort. The other half and the *Avenger* group went ahead to Spitzbergen to refuel before relieving Burnett's half to refuel in their turn. The full escort was not therefore in place until the afternoon of 13 September when the convoy was 150 miles north-west of Bear Island and steering to pass 90 miles north of it.

The Germans assessed a convoy was imminent on 6 September, two days before PQ 18's convergence off Iceland, partly from the accumulation of warships spotted in air reconnaissance of Hvafiord and Reidar Fiord and partly from papers recovered from the crashed Hampden which included much detail on convoy communications and timings. The following day, intercepted orders from the Commander, Russian Northern Fleet Air Force, provided further detail on PQ 18's route. Drawing on this intelligence, Group North sought permission in principle from Raeder to move *Scheer*, *Hipper*, *Köln* and five destroyers to Altafiord ready to attack QP 14 which the Germans now knew would depart two days after PQ 18. Raeder agreed so long as any attack occurred outside the range of 'the probable escort forces of PQ 18'. This constraint clearly implied the standard heavy and cruiser covering forces evident with earlier convoys. The Germans had not yet identified the 'fighting destroyer' innovation. Raeder also ruled out commitment of *Tirpitz*. By 8 September, Group North had made an accurate assessment of the route and timings of both convoys. It correctly judged that QP 14 would depart on 12 or 13 September and pass the incoming PQ 18 off northern Novaya Zemlya two days later when its escort would transfer to the outbound convoy. Because both convoys would skirt the ice well to the north, it would be 'very difficult' for surface forces to close on either convoy. However, Group North thought a surface strike on QP 14 might be feasible using the shortest possible approach from North Cape during the night although it also conceded that submarine and air attack had 'the best prospects of success'.

Given a potentially excellent intelligence picture, the German thinking here appeared muddled. It was not clear why QP 14 was the preferred target when it was correctly assumed it would have the same protection as the inbound convoy including support from a heavy covering force which Group North feared might exploit the more distant ice edge to move east of the Spitzbergen/Bear Island line. The risks were therefore the same but the value in attacking QP 14 was much less. Given that the convoys on this occasion were sequential, if air and U-boat attack sufficed for PQ 18, then surely the same applied to its companion. The Germans again rightly judged that the escort of both convoys would be at its weakest between northern Novaya Zemlya and the entrance to the White Sea. Yet, despite planning a surface raid in exactly this area for early September before it was overtaken by news of the forthcoming convoys, a strike here in preference to north of Bear Island was not initially prioritised. The sense of muddle was compounded by some dissension over including *Tirpitz* in an operation against QP 14. Group North was opposed given the well-known Führer constraints on her deployment but Kummetz, Schniewind and the new Admiral Arctic Ocean, Rear Admiral Otto Klüber, who had just replaced Schmundt, were in favour. Group North anxiety over the risks in a surface attack were no doubt exacerbated by the first air sighting of the fully formed PQ 18 north of Iceland on 8 September which reported that the close escort included a battleship.[37]

Despite these unresolved issues, on 10 September, Group North nevertheless advised all Arctic theatre commands and Admiral Krancke at Führer headquarters that it was moving the cruiser force to Altafiord where it would arrive at 0500 next day. It accompanied this with an assessment of the PQ 18 escort strength which was hardly reassuring. The estimated thirty-five ships were accompanied by at least one battleship, up to four cruisers, fifteen destroyers and possibly an escort carrier. Nothing was yet known of the whereabouts of the heavy covering force which was expected to include at a minimum a fleet carrier and another battleship. The risks facing the German force were underlined when they were spotted near Anda Island, just north of the Lofotens, by the submarine *Tigris* which fired five torpedoes unsuccessfully against *Hipper*. *Tigris*' patrol area reflected considerable research by Bletchley into the transit routes between Narvik and Altafiord used by the Germans during

Rösselsprung. *Tirpitz* meanwhile came to three hours' notice and torpedo boats were allocated for her escort if it was decided she too would move north from Narvik.[38]

If deployment of the surface-strike group was marked by caution, that did not apply to the Norway U-boats. As was now customary, Klüber enjoyed delegated command of the force and could potentially call on fifteen boats, eventually allocating twelve to target PQ 18 and three to focus on QP 14 along the initial part of its route in the eastern Barents Sea. The PQ 18 group were told that their primary target was the escort carrier and they were thus designated 'Traegertod' (Carrier's death) but in addition they were to prioritise tankers. Dönitz also diverted another seven boats which were in transit to Atlantic patrol areas to positions near Iceland where they could intercept QP 14 in the final phase of its voyage. This was an unprecedented submarine attack force but the results against PQ 18 were modest and costly, partly reflecting timely Ultra intelligence provided to British commanders on U-boat dispositions. The first contact occurred on the evening of 12 September when a patrolling Swordfish spotted *U-88* six miles south of the convoy. The destroyer *Onslow* peeled off to investigate, got a good sonar contact and sank her. Three boats found the convoy the following day 130 miles south-west of the southern tip of Spitzbergen and sank two merchant ships, PQ 18's first losses. One of the attackers, *U-589*, did not last long. Next morning, she too was sighted by a Swordfish and hunted to destruction by the destroyer *Faulknor*. The same day, Traegertod achieved its last success, not the desired prize of *Avenger* but the British tanker *Atheltemplar*, so badly damaged by a torpedo from *U-457* that she had to be sunk by the escort. *U-457* also did not survive, being detected and sunk by the destroyer *Impulsive* early on 16 September, when PQ 18 was 400 miles east of Bear Island and about to turn south for the White Sea. Although the German Naval Staff believed the boats had achieved the slightly higher score of four merchant ships and two destroyers damaged, the loss of three boats and four more with heavy battle damage was 'a high price' for an 'unsatisfactory achievement'. They ascribed this outcome to strong convoy defences and the U-boat commanders' inexperience in dealing with escorts. Group North too emphasised that the U-boats had been 'handicapped' by strong air and destroyer escorts but also the 'disciplined' and 'efficient' handling of the convoy. As the Italians had found during Halberd the previous year, taking on a Royal Navy destroyer screen on the scale of that covering PQ 18, if a submarine had technical, tactical or training weaknesses, was a high-risk business.[39]

Poor weather shielded PQ 18 from the air for four days after the sighting on 8 September, but it was spotted again midway between Jan Mayen and Spitzbergen at 1320 on 12 September and surveillance became continuous early the following day. The Home Fleet heavy covering force was spotted almost simultaneously and correctly reported as comprising two battleships, a cruiser and five destroyers.[40] The PQ 18 shadowers worked in large teams and Commander Colthurst found that even four Hurricanes, armed solely with .303 machine guns, were insufficient to drive off the heavily-armed German aircraft. The first of four air attacks that day began at 1500 when the convoy was 75 miles west of the southern tip of Spitzbergen and 450 miles from the nearest German airfields. This attack from about a dozen Ju 88s bombing through cloud gaps from medium height did no harm. However, an attack by forty torpedo aircraft, most carrying two weapons, half an hour later was the most damaging that PQ 18 suffered in its whole passage. The Germans deployed a dedicated anti-shipping tactic christened *Goldene Zange* (Golden Comb), perfected over the last couple of months, whereby the entire attacking force approached in line abreast on the starboard bow of the convoy at a height as low as 60ft and with aircraft just 50 yards apart, before releasing their torpedoes at about 1000 yards. Despite intense anti-aircraft fire and an emergency turn by the convoy, the attackers pressed home with great determination and, with the best part of eighty weapons, they were bound to get multiple hits. Eight merchant ships totalling 46,099 tons were sunk for the loss of five aircraft.

Colthurst admitted that this attack taught a harsh lesson in managing *Avenger*'s small Hurricane force. When the initial bombing raid was picked up 60 miles out on radar, two sections of four fighters each were in the air pursuing shadowers. It proved difficult to recall them in time to meet the new threat, some were out of ammunition, and only two more Hurricanes could be launched. The fighter force could therefore do little to deter or engage successive groups of attackers. Colthurst accordingly decided to leave the shadowers alone in future and concentrate on maintaining a continuing cycle of sections airborne and on standby ready to meet incoming raids. This shift in fighter management proved effective in countering four German raids between 1235 and 1430 the following day, 14 September, although the defenders also benefitted from smaller numbers of attackers and the German decision to concentrate on warships, especially *Avenger*, rather than merchantmen. The order to focus on *Avenger* originated directly from Göring and was motivated as much by the prestige of destroying a carrier as compelling military rationale.[41] As a result, only one more merchant ship was sunk that day while the Germans lost more than twenty aircraft. For PQ 18, the worst was now over. On 15 September, when the convoy was into the eastern Barents Sea 300 miles beyond Spitzbergen, raids were confined to ineffective medium level bombing. Despite their earlier successes, the attrition to the Germans in destroyed and damaged aircraft, especially to their highly-trained torpedo force, was becoming unsustainable.

Overall, 5th Air Fleet conducted 330 sorties against PQ 18 and sank ten ships for the loss of forty-four aircraft, nearly a third of the serviceable strike strength in Northern Norway on 10 September. Within this total, the loss of thirty-eight precious torpedo aircraft, 40 per cent of the force, was especially serious. On 18 September, when the Germans achieved a final aerial success, with the torpedoing of a merchant ship at the entrance to the White Sea, the primary torpedo group, KG 26, could barely put a dozen of its original ninety-two aircraft into the air. British contemporary and post-war analyses concluded that Colthurst's change in tactics had contributed significantly to the protection of the convoy and made it much harder for the Germans to target *Avenger*, although they also recognised that more fighters were desirable and that Hurricane IIs were inadequately armed to deal with current German aircraft effectively. The substantial escort screen, deployed in the numbers and pattern pioneered by Somerville during Halberd, had also made launching torpedoes against the inner merchant ships an 'extremely hazardous undertaking'. The significant increase in attackers brought down by gunfire, compared to previous convoys, was ascribed to the better armament of modern fleet destroyers and improved control systems effectively integrated with radar.[42]

The air sighting of PQ 18 on 12 September brought to a head the issue of deploying the German cruiser force which had arrived in Altafiord early the previous day. It was now clear that *Scheer* had engine problems which ruled her out for any operation. She arrived in Germany for repairs at the beginning of November and never returned to Norway. On 13 September, Group North therefore proposed two options for deploying the smaller force of *Hipper* and six destroyers against QP 14. If QP 14 was successfully sighted and tracked, the force would make a fast run, aiming for interception in the area due north of North Cape. If the convoy was not sighted, the *Hipper* group would head for the Matochkin Strait area of Novaya Zemlya and then search south-west while maintaining sufficient distance from the Russian coast to minimise the risk of attack from the newly-deployed British torpedo bombers. The German Naval Staff thought the second alternative, which clearly reflected post-Wunderland ideas, would either meet complete failure through missing the convoy or inflict considerable damage since the escort would be weak during this phase of its journey.

On the same day, Raeder discussed these surface attack options by telephone with Hitler, who had been kept abreast of PQ 18's progress by Vice Admiral Krancke. Hitler once again emphasised the defensive value of the heavy ships in Norway and the need to avoid losses without adequate return. Raeder apparently admitted that the prospects of success for the *Hipper* operations was small and the risk from enemy submarines and planes (presumably the Hampden force) significant. Hitler therefore refused Group North permission to proceed. Raeder seems to have made little effort to win Hitler round. This no doubt reflected his awareness of Hitler's views transmitted by Krancke two months earlier in the wake of PQ 17. However, he must also have recognised that the latest proposals had a flavour of 'action for action's sake' and were difficult to sell with any conviction.[43]

For their part, the British had only partial insight into these developments. Dolphin decrypts confirmed the arrival of the cruisers in Altafiord and showed that they had come to one hour's notice on the afternoon of 13 September when PQ 18 was 100 miles from the longitude of Altafiord and set to pass at least 300 miles north of the entrance to the fiord. The same day a Mosquito reconnoitred Narvik and reported the German anchorages empty, suggesting *Tirpitz* had also moved north. A German surface attack during 14 September therefore seemed to the OIC eminently possible. The likelihood that the Germans would exit over the night of 13/14 September unfortunately coincided with unplanned gaps in the programme of Catalina sweeps of the area north of North Cape and Group Captain Hopps therefore initiated a reconnaissance in force by the whole Hampden group which found nothing. However, later in the day one of his PR Spitfires was able to cover Altafiord and confirm the Germans were still there. For the three days from late on 14 September, coverage of Altafiord by Spitfires and the Barents Sea by Catalinas was sufficient to give considerable assurance against a surprise sortie. The Catalinas flew fifteen sorties totalling 282 hours with seven of these reaching PQ 18. The one doubt was the status and whereabouts of *Tirpitz*. Denham, drawing on Swedish SIGINT, reported on 16 September that she had a defect and would not leave Narvik unless urgently required but it was only on 18 September that another Mosquito flight confirmed she was at her usual anchorage in Bogen Bay.[44]

Valuable though this intelligence was, it told the British nothing of the discussion between Raeder and Hitler and the latter's insistence on a no-risk policy. Tovey therefore subsequently concluded that the German failure to deploy from Altafiord must be ascribed to a combination of factors: the strength of the British destroyer escort; fear of submarine attack following *Tigris*' intervention; the known presence of a Royal Air Force torpedo strike group; awareness of constant air surveillance; and doubt about the precise whereabouts and intent of the Home Fleet heavy covering force.[45]

As the Germans had anticipated, QP 14 sailed from Archangel on 13 September, composed of fifteen merchant ships and two rescue ships, including four surviving vessels from PQ 17, and appropriately under the command of the doughty Commodore Dowding who after many vicissitudes following the scattering of PQ 17 had reached Archangel. Because warships had accumulated in the Russian ports over the last three months, the close escort was stronger than normal for a westbound convoy, comprising two destroyers, the returning anti-aircraft ships *Palomares* and *Pozarica*, and eleven corvettes, minesweepers and trawlers. Although the Germans spotted the convoy departing, thick weather over the first three days meant it was untroubled by air or U-boat attack and it rendezvoused early on 17 September as planned with Burnett's force about 75 miles west of Admiralty Peninsula on the northern coast of Novaya Zemlya. The next two days were also uneventful. Klüber rapidly recognised that QP 14 was now as well protected as PQ 18 and, judging the prospects of attack against what was a less valuable target to be poor, ordered his U-boats for the present to conduct shadowing only. Swordfish and Catalina patrols helped keep the U-boats at a distance and, apart from conducting their own shadowing, 5th Air Fleet left the convoy alone, no doubt reflecting their heavy losses suffered against PQ 18.[46]

Having reached the southern tip of Spitzbergen on the morning of 19 September without loss, Burnett turned the convoy north-west to hug the ice edge. He wanted to maximise his distance from the Norwegian airfields and any sortie by the Altafiord force which in his view remained a threat. He also knew from Ultra reports and his own reconnaissance that U-boats were tracking the convoy and their numbers increasing. He therefore used part of the escort to disguise the turn and also picked up one of the tankers from Lowe Sound so that his escorts could refuel within the convoy. The Germans were not fooled by the turn and five U-boats tracked the convoy through 19 September and began attacks early the following day, having positioned ahead of the convoy when it made its expected turn south-west. *U-435* sank the minesweeper *Leda* and later in the day, *U-703* hit the destroyer *Somali* and *U-255* sank a merchant ship. *Somali* was taken in tow by her sister *Ashanti* but, after 420 miles, sank in bad weather four days later, demonstrating the sheer difficulty of recovering damaged ships in Arctic waters. Klüber, who remained in command of the U-boat force and could now call on twenty-one boats, including some deployed in the North Atlantic and on transit, positioned seven boats ahead of the convoy ready to intercept the following day. They had no success on 21 September but, next morning, the best 'shooter' of the Norway boats, Siegfried Strelow in *U-435*, who had already accounted for *Leda*, sank two merchant ships and the tanker *Gray Ranger* within five minutes, earning him a Knight's Cross. Although the British responded aggressively during these three days of attacks, determinedly following up several air sightings by Swordfish and Catalina, this time they had no success against the U-boats. *U-606* shot down a Catalina and an attack by *P 614* on *U-408*, conducted by fleeting periscope sightings between snow squalls, failed.[47]

The U-boat record against QP 14 was thus much better than against PQ 18, although it should be emphasised that they only sank one extra supply ship and in better weather *Somali* might have survived. Their success reflected greater numbers deployed but also growing fatigue within the escort which had been operating continuously and under great strain for 10 days. The intensity of the anti-submarine effort was demonstrated by the surface and air escorts conducting a total of fifty-nine attacks in defence of the two convoys.[48] *Avenger*'s Swordfish had performed magnificently but, with only three aircraft and tired crews, by 20 September she was struggling to maintain a useful operational cycle. Burnett, recognising therefore that as a target for U-boats she risked becoming a liability more than an asset, decided to send her home independently with *Scylla*, transferring his flag to the destroyer *Milne*. For their part, the Germans also had some luck and Klüber was aware that 'most of the success' should be 'credited' to Strelow.[49] Sadly, *Avenger* survived less than two months. After supporting the Torch landings, she was torpedoed and sunk by *U-155* in the early hours of 15 November, shortly after leaving Gibraltar on her way home. More than 500 of her crew were lost.

The losses suffered by PQ 18 and QP 14 were substantial, close to one-third of the merchant ships in each convoy, and higher than those to PQ 16. The cargo lost from the thirteen ships sunk with PQ 18 included 221 tanks, 107 fighters, thirteen bombers, 1500 vehicles, 9000 tons of fuel and 65,500 tons of general stores.[50] Burnett argued that these losses could easily have been greater if one or both tankers had been sunk, making it impossible to maintain an adequate escort force, if further air attacks had exhausted anti-aircraft ammunition needed for the return journey, or the Germans had synchronised air and surface attacks. These points were valid but underestimated the costs and difficulties these convoy operations had posed for the Germans, even if they grossly exaggerated their success, initially assessing they had sunk twenty-five of forty-five supply ships.[51] 5th Air Fleet had lost at least half its torpedo strike fleet, destroyed or damaged beyond recovery, and had expended most of its available torpedo stock, with Bletchley decrypts revealing barely fifty functional weapons available at the beginning of October.[52] It could not regenerate before winter darkness rendered operations ineffective. The Arctic U-boat force, despite the notable successes against QP 14, had also seen its front-line force reduced by a third through loss or damage. Furthermore, leaving aside Hitler's risk aversion, the commitment of the German naval leadership to a surface strike was at best half-hearted. The combined risks posed by the presence of *Avenger*, the overall strength of the escort, and the presence of the Hampden torpedo strike force on which they were well-sighted, meant a surface attack on PQ 18 was never seriously contemplated.

The scale of merchant ship losses means Operation EV has been viewed as delivering at best a Pyrrhic victory[53] for the Royal Navy and the Allied supply effort, at worst confirmation of a strategic victory for the Germans by demonstrating that the effort in running convoys was unsustainable.[54] Such judgements seem too bleak but it is true that several underlying factors made the passage of these two convoys another watershed moment in both Western support for Russia and the associated Arctic war. First, EV demonstrated that, by deploying an escort carrier and fighting destroyer force, the Royal Navy now had a credible operational concept for getting convoys through in the face of a maximum German combined threat, although the concept was arguably an evolution of that pioneered by Somerville with Halberd a year earlier. Secondly, like Pedestal, this concept was very expensive, in this case absorbing the whole of an enhanced Home Fleet, and at least one-third of the Royal Navy's best fighting strength, for an entire month. At this point of the war, devoting these resources on a continuing basis would have severe opportunity costs for other operations and theatres. The Western Allies would have to reassess the priority given to Russian aid and make choices over how and when it was delivered. Thirdly, the Germans too faced hard choices. They had invested significant air and naval resources in stopping the convoys over the last six months. EV demonstrated that PQ 17 was perhaps an aberration and that inflicting the prohibitive losses they desired would require major reinforcement they would struggle to find. Finally, this autumn marked the point where the balance of war potential began shifting decisively towards the Allies. American merchant ship construction was overtaking Atlantic losses to win the tonnage war, new warships were reaching both Western navies in substantial numbers, and Western aircraft production was far outstripping the Axis.

This new watershed is further emphasised because PQ 18 marked the end of First Protocol deliveries and because there was now a two-and-a-half-month lull before the next convoy sailed. When the convoys resumed in December, they did so under new designations, JW for outbound and RA for inbound, and in many respects their pattern, composition and experience was different to what had gone before. The statistics here are striking. If Dervish is included, PQ 18 was the nineteenth Arctic convoy, spread over a 13-month period, and there would be a further twenty-one between December and the end of the war, a 30-month period. In convoy numbers therefore, PQ 18 almost marked the halfway point. However, as shown in Appendix 1, 80 per cent more ships sailed in the JW convoys than the PQs, 521 compared to 290, carrying just over twice the overall tonnage of cargo and more than twice as many reached the Russian ports, 503 compared to 217. This reflected fewer early returns but above all a dramatic shift in the loss rate. Only five ships were lost in the JW convoys compared to fifty-three in the PQs and nineteen convoys suffered no loss at all. Nevertheless, in so far as the overall figures imply broad consistency in cargo tonnage delivered across the PQ and JW periods, they are deceptive because there were eight months in summer 1943 and three months in summer 1944 when no convoys operated. These gaps, which influenced the value and impact of the aid as well as the shipping loss rate, reflected the complex interaction of the factors identified in the previous paragraph.

*First Protocol Performance and Impact*

The supplies delivered with PQ 18 were a mixture of outstanding items committed under the First Protocol and the first tranche of Second Protocol items to be delivered via the Arctic route. PQ 18 was therefore seen at the time as a formal closing of the First Protocol account although some items were still moving through the Persian route.[55] On the Arctic route, 200 ships (ninety-one British, forty-five American, thirty-three Russian and thirty-one other flags) had reached Russian ports in the protocol period from PQ 2 onward. These delivered about one million tons of cargo, out of 1,250,000 tons shipped, including 160,000 tons of weapons, with its origin split about one-third from the United Kingdom and two-thirds from the United States. Ninety per cent of weapons delivered under the First Protocol went via the Arctic. Out of a total of 459 merchant ship sailings (inbound and outbound) over the period, sixty-six ships were sunk, a rate of 14.4 per cent, with the vast majority in the last four convoy pairs. Five hundred and forty-three merchant seamen were lost, 70 per cent of them British. The naval effort protecting these First Protocol supplies represented a huge commitment, was almost entirely British, and concentrated over the seven months March to September. The total of Royal Navy warship passages is revealing: twelve battleships, two battlecruisers, six fleet carriers, fifty-four cruisers, 211 destroyers, fifty minesweepers, forty-three anti-submarine trawlers, twenty-four corvettes, sixty-four submarines, ten anti-aircraft ships and two escort carriers. The US Navy contributed just three battleship passages, five by cruisers and twelve by destroyers. This vividly demonstrates how, with the exception of loans to Pedestal and Vigorous, almost the entire Royal Navy Home Fleet, much of its home-based submarine flotillas and significant elements of Western Approaches forces were devoted to Arctic operations from March onward. Overall, the convoy operations to date had cost the Royal Navy two cruisers, three destroyers, three minesweepers and one submarine, with 766 personnel killed.[56]

Despite the slowing of the convoy schedule from May, the losses from PQ 17 and the delay in mounting PQ 18, the British could point to a strong First Protocol delivery record. The key military items promised, 2250 tanks and 1800 aircraft, had all been shipped. Of these, 77 per cent of the tanks had reached Russia, 1554 via the Arctic and a further 176 by the Persian Gulf. For aircraft, 1489 or 83 per cent had arrived, all via the Arctic.[57] Eighty-seven per cent of overall supplies from the United Kingdom were delivered in British ships even though the Western Allies had never committed to transporting supplies. The most important non-military item only partially met was machine tools with only 1210 delivered against the commitment of 3752. There were some reductions in agreed quotas of rubber and tin due to loss of Empire supplies in the Far East, but 85 per cent and 65 per cent of the substantial commitments here were still met as was most of the promised aluminium. Other raw materials, notably copper, were made available but shipments were delayed due to shortage of Soviet vessels for collection and Soviet decisions to give higher priority to military goods. A vast range of military supplies requested by the Russians but not listed under the protocol had also been provided, including generous provision of ammunition and spares at significant opportunity cost to British forces. Britain also supplied significant food additional to the protocol, including 77,000 tons of sugar and 56,000 tons of wheat. Perhaps 50,000 tons of raw materials and food and a handful of weapons reached Russia via Iran but at least 85 per cent of British supplies went via the Arctic. Two final British contributions require emphasis: the provision of radar and sonar equipment, both areas where Soviet capability was weak; and a vast range of naval supplies. The first improved military performance in the short term but also laid the basis of long-term Soviet capability in these areas. The second made the Northern Fleet more effective than it would otherwise have been.[58]

The American record after its slow start was more mixed but still impressive overall. American delivery was also spread across three routes and its total tonnage by the autumn just under four times that of Britain. Nearly 50 per cent of overall American supplies and more than 85 per cent of its weapons went via the Arctic, 25 per cent with 10 per cent of weapons via Iran, and the final 25 per cent, mainly food and raw materials but including 2.5 per cent of weapons, on the Pacific route. By the end of August, the United States had shipped all the promised tanks but only 71 per cent of aircraft. However, a significant proportion of both categories were held up in Iceland or Iran and the shipment figures ignore subsequent losses. Only 796 tanks (363 Lees and 420 Stuarts), one-third of the 2250 promised, had reached Russia by the end of June, 1352 or 60 per cent, divided evenly between Stuarts and Lees by the end of October and, following losses, only 1825 or just over 80 per cent by the end of the year. At the end of June, prior to PQ 17, only 284 American bombers and 244 fighters of the 900 of each promised had actually reached the Soviet Union, and 596 and 486 respectively, or 60 per cent, by the end of October. Because of its own urgent needs following Pearl Harbor, very few of the promised anti-aircraft and anti-tank weapons were made available and only 43 per cent of the 85,000 trucks, of which barely half had arrived. The deficit in agreed communications equipment (field telephones and cable) was similar. As with Britain, there was a significant shortfall in promised machine tools and, as noted earlier, a small shortfall in the promised supply of aluminium and duraluminum so prized by Stalin. On a more positive note, all the explosives and chemicals on the list and most of the armour plate had been despatched. American toluene and TNT were sufficient to underpin half of Soviet munitions production through the coming winter with two-thirds arriving via the Arctic. Like Britain, the United States had also provided many items not on the protocol list.[59]

The key question is what impact this First Protocol aid had on Russia's fighting capability, overall war potential and perhaps survival over the summer and autumn. Most accounts of Western aid to Russia, while accepting it was more important than the recipient later acknowledged, still imply that its primary value came in 1943 onward in providing the Red Army with mobility, communications and food, and the Soviet economy with raw materials and specialised equipment. Its contribution in 1942, especially the value of weapon supplies, remains downplayed, reflecting the post-war Soviet claim that quantities here were marginal and quality low. This tendency to undervalue the impact of the First Protocol compared to its successors overlooks crucial context in 1942. The first year of Russia's war saw its GDP decline by about one-third, taking it from parity to 70 per cent of its German enemy. Yet, extraordinarily, it outperformed Germany in weapons production in every category except warships, often by a considerable margin, turning out twice the combat aircraft and four times the tanks. This was because resources mobilised for defence increased 'both relatively and absolutely'. This was achieved by 'ferocious' squeezing of the civilian sector, reducing living standards to 40 per cent of pre-war levels with widespread malnutrition and excess mortality. With the important exception of Operation Uranus, the Stalingrad counter-offensive launched in late November, the year 1942 saw only limited improvement in Soviet military leadership or fighting effectiveness so that the impressive defence production was largely consumed for little benefit. Two major offensives launched almost simultaneously with Uranus that winter, Mars in the Moscow region and Pole Star to relieve Leningrad, were costly failures. For that reason, they have received little historical attention. Yet, on 19 November, the day Uranus launched, the Western Front where Mars took place, holding 17 per cent of the front line compared to 14 per cent for the South-Western Stalingrad/Don Front, absorbed 70 per cent more manpower, 50 per cent more artillery, over twice the tank strength, and 25 per cent more aircraft. The share of personnel, artillery and armour deployed that day on the North-Western Front around Leningrad was little different to that in the South-West. Meanwhile, German concentration on Blue inevitably reduced their strength on these northern and central fronts and the sheer scale of Soviet forces opposing them by November, to which Western tanks and aircraft contributed, made it quite impossible to send further reinforcements south to meet the threat around Stalingrad.[60]

Nevertheless, Soviet numerical advantage across the whole Eastern Front this autumn still rested on a fragile base. There is a compelling argument that, as the Blue offensive inflicted further military losses and seized new territory and resources, the Soviet economy came close to collapse. Against a falling GDP, further transfers to the defence sector risked becoming unsustainable when output of weapons already barely exceeded losses, while the growing privations suffered by the civilian sector must inevitably sharply reduce productivity. Western aid added about 5 per cent to GDP across the year, mainly from First Protocol deliveries since most supplies despatched after 1 July had insufficient time to have an impact. This contribution seems small, but its role was also 'psychological', a promise of future support, as well as physical assistance in the present. If the Soviet economy really was balanced on a 'knife edge' during the first months of Blue, then that 5 per cent perhaps prevented collapse.[61]

Furthermore, an overall percentage does not convey the impact of Western aid in specific areas. Throughout 1942, but especially in the first half, Soviet priorities remained those emphasised by Stalin at his first meeting with Hopkins: tanks, aircraft, aluminium and machine tools and other specialised industrial equipment. The first two helped buy time and save scarce domestic resources over the short term. The last two were important to longer-term war potential, making the military output from 1943 onward possible. While there were countless other items on the current Soviet wish list, they proved willing to sacrifice most of these during the year to release shipping space for these main priorities. The continuing emphasis on tank and aircraft supply reflected the Soviet belief that German production of both was at least equal to and probably greater than theirs. When Churchill, drawing on excellent Ultra coverage, informed Stalin on 23 September that German aircraft production was only 1300 per month, the latter refused to believe this accurate figure, insisting that Soviet information put it at nearly twice that.[62]

The Soviet Union built 11,000 tanks in the first half of 1942, its peak year for tank production, of which about 4100 comprised medium T-34s and 1300 heavy KV-1s. The remainder were T-60 and T-70 light tanks of limited military value, with the latter only reaching the front line from April onwards. The overall 1600 Western tanks arriving in this period, mainly by the Arctic route, therefore added 14.5 per cent to total Soviet production but the 1250 medium tanks added 23 per cent to Soviet medium/heavy output. This was a valuable margin, helping compensate for further Soviet losses of about 7000 tanks over these six months and a tank exchange rate at this time averaging 7:1 in the Germans' favour. It enabled the Soviet tank force to keep growing while their own production was still ramping up. As a result, at the start of the German Blue offensive, Red Army overall tank stock had risen to 12,700 compared with 7700 at the start of the year. About 1000 of this total, allowing for losses, comprised Western-supplied tanks, two-thirds British and one-third American, and almost all delivered under the First Protocol. On 1 July, 310 of these (fifty-five Matildas, fifty-three Valentines, 114 Lees and eighty-eight Stuarts), were at the Gorkiy tank centre where they equipped five new armoured brigades awaiting deployment. The Western tanks represented nearly 8 per cent of the total Soviet stock but about 10.5 per cent of medium/heavy tanks, the highest proportion at any point in the war. Another measure of their value is by comparison with the German tank force in the East at this time. At the start of Blue, the Germans had dramatically rebuilt their armoured strength after the losses of the winter, but they still only had 2276 tanks across the whole Eastern Front, of which 70 per cent were to be deployed in the south, and they had virtually no reserves. Numerically, Western tanks were therefore over 40 per cent of this German strength and for about the same proportion they were qualitatively competitive. The Western tanks were widely deployed across the whole Eastern Front, mainly in an infantry support role, but some, as noted earlier, in the new tank armies. Numbers engaged on the critical southern front are hard to estimate but probably 300 were deployed here over the first three months of the Blue offensive. By November, the Germans estimated that, out of about 190 Soviet tank brigades, twenty were fully equipped with Western tanks and thirty-three partially equipped.[63]

Soviet combat aircraft stock was 12,000 at the start of 1942 with about half this number lost in the first half of the year. Domestic production in this period added about 9750, taking numbers at the start of Blue to around 15,750. By this point the Western Allies had delivered 1868 combat aircraft, of which 70 per cent were British and all but 267 were single-seat fighters and predominantly Hurricanes. If Western losses by the end of June were half this figure, which seems reasonable, then at this time Western aircraft added 6 per cent to overall Soviet combat aircraft stock but about 15 per cent to fighter stock. As with tanks, this was a valuable margin while Soviet aircraft production was building up. This increased by 60 per cent between the first and second quarters of the year and would increase by a similar amount over the second half.[64]

As explained earlier, this dramatic rise in aircraft and tank production across 1942 relied heavily on Western supplies of aluminium with nearly 25,000 tons delivered by the end of June, 80 per cent of which was committed under the First Protocol with three-quarters of the total coming from Britain and Canada. It also relied on Western machine tools with at least half the reduced quantity delivered under the First Protocol destined for aircraft production. The importance of Western technology and expertise was well understood by Stalin who had drawn significantly on American know-how and, to an extent finance, in driving Soviet industrial development through the 1930s. This American input underpinned the creation of modern aluminium and aviation industries and introduced the Soviet Union to the latest mass production techniques which were applied in huge new state-of-the art-plants and had contributed to an eightfold increase in industrial output across the decade. This background and thus understanding of where the Western Allies could contribute informed many of the specialised requests made under the First Protocol.[65]

## Torch Triggers Suspension of the Arctic Convoys

At a meeting with the Torch commanders on 22 September, before QP 14 had arrived, Churchill faced the hard reality that the naval requirements for the operation, now set for 8 November, made it impossible to provide an adequate escort for the next PQ convoy scheduled for early October. Indeed, Torch demands meant no further PQ convoy until January. Furthermore, the meeting confirmed what was already explicit in CCS 94 – execution of Torch meant no cross-Channel invasion in 1943 – although the prime minister was still reluctant to acknowledge this. Churchill notified Roosevelt the same day, emphasising the potential double blow to Stalin at a critical time and that Western failure to meet previous promises risked 'grave consequences'. Managing the political and strategic challenges here was difficult enough but Churchill made matters worse by resurrecting the Jupiter attack on northern Norway. He presented this as an alternative to the 'danger, waste and effort' involved in resuming the PQ convoys in January. His logic here was obscure but he presumably intended Jupiter to remove the threat to future convoys. He also argued, rather implausibly, that it would help appease Stalin. Churchill got a holding reply from Hopkins, stating that Roosevelt was absent on a trip to the West Coast and that he should say nothing to Stalin pending full discussion since any new commitment made might be a 'turning point in the war'.[66]

It took two weeks to craft a message to Stalin during which Churchill was frustrated and anxious. To his intense annoyance, but predictably, Jupiter got no support from the Americans, the Canadians or his own chiefs of staff, nor would the Russians prove any more enthusiastic. The stakes with Stalin increased when he informed Churchill that the Stalingrad situation was deteriorating and that he desperately needed more Western fighter aircraft, ideally 800 per month, double the Second Protocol total.[67] The president insisted the Torch deadline was sacrosanct and that, while convoy suspension would be a 'tough blow' for the Russians, the decision was 'inevitable'. He evidently accepted it might last beyond January.[68] However, following advice from Admiral King, he subsequently floated a proposal for separating the forty ships of the proposed PQ 19 into small groups of two or three, each with a similar number of escorts, sailing at 24- to 48-hour intervals. The Admiralty flatly rejected this, pointing out that it required the same escorts overall as a single convoy, that current German air surveillance rendered successful evasion by such groups unlikely, and that they would be an easy and tempting target for even light German surface forces. They were, however, willing to support independent sailings after the successful transit of two Russian ships in August. It was therefore agreed that ten ships would depart in the dark period 28 October to 8 November at 200-mile intervals.[69] To further console Stalin, there was convoluted discussion over providing a British–American air group to the Caucasus although this was dependent on British success in the forthcoming Alamein offensive.[70]

Churchill's message to Stalin which finally issued on 8 October accordingly began with positives: the scale and imminence of Torch combined with the Alamein offensive in Egypt; a Caucasus air deployment, with nine British fighter squadrons, a similar-size bomber group, half British and half American, and an American transport group; and, to meet Stalin's latest plea for fighters, 150 Spitfires with spares delivered via Iran. The carefully-crafted negative news followed: suspension of the Arctic convoys until January to meet Torch escort requirements, softened marginally by the promise of at least ten independent sailings in the coming weeks.[71] The 1943 cross-Channel 'second front' was wisely not mentioned although Roosevelt and Hopkins recognised that this was indeed now ruled out by Torch.[72] Churchill implied that Roosevelt would make a similar commitment of additional fighters and clearly expected him to do so. However, Roosevelt's own messages to Stalin on 8 and 11 October were short on specifics and not convincing on promises either.[73] This underlined that, at this stage of the war, American resources remained limited with little to spare from the demands of Torch and the Pacific. In particular, Roosevelt had little to offer and thus little leverage over naval operations in the Arctic or indeed the Indian Ocean. Of Churchill's commitments, the Caucasus deployment, always contingent on success in North Africa, never happened, overtaken by sheer logistic difficulty and the changed strategic environment post Stalingrad. It was three months before the first Spitfires reached Basra and, although 143 eventually arrived in the Soviet Union, none flew operationally until late April.[74]

The independent sailings began from Iceland on 29 October, in theory drawing on specially-selected skippers and volunteer crews. Four trawlers and two submarines were positioned along the western half of the passage to provide a rudimentary rescue and protection service. Twelve British and American ships and one Soviet attempted the eastward voyage of which five reached Archangel, four were sunk by U-boats, one was wrecked on Spitzbergen, and the rest turned back. Bletchley decrypts showed that air and U-boat sightings had alerted the Germans to the 'independents' tactic and that *Hipper* and two destroyers had sortied on a sweep on 5 November. The OIC monitored this operation carefully and knew the Germans had sunk a Soviet anti-submarine vessel and the Soviet tanker *Donbass* but were otherwise unsuccessful. For crew members who survived the sinkings of these independents, prospects were grim and most faced an appalling ordeal with few escaping death to tell their tales. The Russians had more success, sailing twenty-two further independents west in November/December with only *Donbass* lost.[75]

Stalin responded to Churchill with a terse 'thank you' and was no more forthcoming with Roosevelt. However, in exchanges with Maisky, his disappointment over Western delivery and broken promises, at a time when Russia was under acute strain, was clear. As he had indicated to Churchill, the Stalingrad battle was reaching its climax. It seemed possible the city would fall before the counter-offensive was ready and there was no guarantee this would succeed. With the economy squeezed to the limit, Stalin and the rest of the leadership must have perceived the 'tipping point' described earlier. Stalin not only felt Russia was being left to bleed but paranoia over the prospect of British collusion with Germany and a separate peace also returned to the fore.[76]

This begs the question of how far Western leaders perceived the same 'tipping point' and whether the aid they were providing was sufficient to guard against Soviet collapse. The view of the British chiefs of staff was evident in their American–British strategy report produced at the end of October and shared with the War Cabinet and their American counterparts. It stated that the Red Army was currently the only force capable of defeating the German army or indeed containing it. Britain and the United States could not challenge the bulk of the Axis forces on land. If the Russians collapsed, future Western operations would be curtailed, and it would be difficult even maintaining existing commitments. Russia was the greatest single contributor to wearing down Germany, making it vital to support her resistance with an increasing flow of supplies. Reviewing Russian war potential, the report stated that, even if Russia was forced back to the Dvina–Volga line, she would retain just under half her defence industrial capacity, sufficient to sustain half the forces deployed at the start of the war. If she lost the Caucasus oil, she would still have reserves to last a year. There was no sign of a Russian collapse, but the present German offensive was draining her fighting power and depriving her of food and fuel, creating increasing hardship. The best Western contribution would be the diversion of German forces elsewhere and increased weapon supplies.[77]

This strategy report was discussed at a Staff Conference chaired by the prime minister at Chequers on 14 November at which South African premier Field Marshal Jan Smuts, always a trusted Churchill confidante, was also present.[78] It was then reviewed by the Defence Committee, rather than the War Cabinet, the following day.[79] Most of those present would also have seen a bleak paper on supplies to Russia circulated by Eden two days earlier.[80] He emphasised that PQ 18 had only carried part of the July supplies, comprising the first month of the Second Protocol. With the convoys suspended until January, nearly six months of British and American supplies earmarked for the Arctic route would not begin arriving in Russia before then. This was not only a 'serious loss' at a critical time but it would be difficult to make up arrears when convoys resumed. Following the sailing of the 'independents', there were twenty-seven loaded ships awaiting convoy in Iceland. If the convoy proposed for early January was limited to thirty vessels as the Admiralty currently intended, these waiting ships would absorb almost all available places, meaning no progress against the current backlog. Meanwhile a further twenty-five American ships with Russia supplies had been forced to unload in British ports alongside four months of cargo already awaiting shipment. Although much effort was going into expanding capacity on other routes, none of these options could make much impact on arrears until well into 1943.

*Pressure to Resume the Convoys*

The prime minister evidently found the chiefs of staff paper too long and, with its grand sweep, lacking focus on immediate goals. However, he absorbed the emphasis on Russia's contribution, scrawling on his own copy, next to the reference that only the Red Army could defeat Germany, 'I hope Stalin will not see this'.[81] He now criticised the paper's failure to address the impact on Russia of not opening a Western land front against Germany in 1943, sufficient to relieve the pressure on the Eastern Front. Together with Eden's update, it probably also caused him to chivvy the Admiralty on resuming the PQ convoys although Maisky had pressed him on this on 8 November after lobbying the First Lord A V Alexander and Rear Admiral Brind 10 days earlier.[82]

At any rate, by the time the Defence Committee met, Pound had agreed to sail twenty ships from Iceland on 20 December, two weeks earlier than the January target. Pound and Tovey had also already agreed to run a westbound convoy to reduce the accumulated shipping held up in Russian ports, with the risk many would soon become icebound in the White Sea over the winter, and QP 15 left Archangel with twenty-eight ships on

17 November. This cleared all waiting ships in Russian ports apart from the recently arrived 'independents'. The convoy met atrocious weather, becoming badly scattered by the time it passed Bear Island. However, the same weather hampered German reconnaissance and caused Admiral Arctic to abandon a planned sortie against the convoy by *Hipper* and two destroyers, on which Bletchley kept the OIC well informed.[83] It also caused problems for the three British submarines covering the approaches to Altafiord, making accurate navigation impossible. *P312* sighted *P216* and *Uredd* although they were supposedly positioned far apart and *Uredd* sighted a Russian boat, fortunately without fatal consequences.[84] Two of QP 15's ships were lost to U-boats but the rest arrived safely in Iceland.[85] Admiralty willingness to contemplate this earlier resumption of convoy traffic, potentially with more limited escort cover than previously, reflected the benefits of winter weather and reduced daylight, but also SIGINT revelations of substantial German air force withdrawals from northern Norway to meet the threat posed by Torch.[86]

German air reinforcement to the Mediterranean began in late October partly to meet the potential threat posed by Allied shipping and air activity detected in the Gibraltar area but also to strengthen defences against the gathering British offensive in Egypt. The scale and purpose of the Torch convoys was not foreseen. When first detected moving through the Straits, the Germans assumed their aim was to supply Malta, reinforce the Eighth Army, or possibly to execute a landing in Tunisia or even the south of France. They did not anticipate systematic occupation of the whole French North African coast which posed far-reaching consequences for the Axis position across the whole theatre requiring a major response. On the day of the Torch landings, 8 November, there were 400 German combat aircraft in the western Mediterranean. A month later this force had more than doubled to 850 aircraft. The bulk of these reinforcements came from northern Norway and southern Russia. At least 150 strike aircraft were transferred from the former, including almost all the torpedo aircraft. The demands of the Mediterranean over the next year meant this Norway force could never be reconstituted except on a very limited scale. Simultaneously, 120 strike aircraft were moved from south Russia just when they were most needed to meet the Soviet Stalingrad counter-offensive, Uranus. Both theatres lost a significant number of fighters to the Mediterranean too.[87] Bletchley followed these moves in detail and real time. On 9 November, the OIC informed Tovey that, when current re-deployment to the Mediterranean was complete, there would be only thirty Ju 88 bombers left in Norway. Two days later it confirmed that the remaining long-range strike force comprised just nine torpedo-capable

He 115s and twenty-four bomber/recce Ju 88s north of Trondheim and a further twelve Ju 88s in south-west Norway.[88]

The Torch campaign proved catastrophic for the German air force. It lost 2422 aircraft in the Mediterranean over the seven months November 1942 to May 1943. This was 40 per cent of its nominal overall front-line strength in all theatres at the beginning of November.[89] These Mediterranean losses broadly equalled those on the Russian front in the same period, although in some categories, notably fighters, they were much higher. The German response to Torch, although initially fast and effective and imposing significant cost and time on the Allies, also absorbed large numbers of transport aircraft to reinforce Tunisia. Three hundred and twenty Ju 52s were deployed in November and December with half lost by the end of January, 14 per cent of Germany's nominal overall transport fleet strength at the beginning of this period.[90] The despatch of these precious heavy transport aircraft significantly reduced German airlift capacity at Stalingrad. In reducing German air power, Torch made a direct and important contribution to the Stalingrad battle and then severely hampered any prospects of a lasting German recovery in the East. Stalin's dismissal of Torch as no substitute for a true second front and largely irrelevant to Soviet needs was therefore hardly fair. Torch certainly achieved more than was ever likely with Sledgehammer and at much less cost. These benefits were not yet visible to the Defence Committee on 15 November but the success of the Torch landings and the intelligence on far-reaching German redeployment undoubtedly helped assuage any concerns over Russia's survival through the winter, despite the interruption in Western supplies.

When first contemplating a late December convoy, the Admiralty planned to sail at least thirty ships with a similar fighting destroyer escort to PQ 18. This reflected both the September experience and the pressure from Eden to clear the backlog of supplies. However, Torch and other commitments meant the Royal Navy could only find seventeen of twenty-nine destroyers required for this escort and to screen covering forces. Churchill accordingly sought help from Roosevelt in meeting the deficit, reminding him that he had repeatedly pressed for early resumption of PQ convoys.[91] Despite agreeing that 'every effort' should be made to sail another convoy 'as soon as possible', Roosevelt regretted that none of the requested twelve destroyers could be sent. He quoted the strain posed by commitments to Torch, existing Atlantic escort, and recent losses in the Pacific.[92] These demands were valid but applied equally to the Royal Navy which was providing two-thirds of the Torch naval forces, the same proportion of Atlantic escorts and faced significant demands in the Indian

Ocean. If sending twelve destroyers was impossible, four would have been helpful and have acknowledged that the Arctic was a joint commitment. As the end of 1942 approached therefore, once again, presidential commitment to what was supposedly a critical American strategic goal to support Russia was not matched by practical delivery.

Roosevelt's acquiescence in PQ convoy suspension and willingness subsequently both to deny naval support and simultaneously to refuse any uplift in fighter supplies despite pressure from Stalin reflected a growing American/British consensus that the German offensive was culminating and that early Soviet collapse was now unlikely. This view was not grounded in any lack of realism about Russia's economy or war potential. American and British assessments agreed that industrial output was down by at least a third although both underestimated the scale of the shift from the civil to the defence sector. Estimates of the loss of raw materials and their processing were also accurate but they judged Russia had good reserves and that Western aid was covering key gaps. There was also realism about food shortages and the hardship faced by the civilian population but there was agreement that morale was high and there were no signs of internal unrest. In short, by late autumn neither London nor Washington believed the Russians had the capacity for a successful counter-offensive but neither feared an imminent 'tipping point'. Continuing aid was important to improve Soviet war potential and sustain its commitment, but it was not judged critical to immediate survival.[93]

At a meeting with the British chiefs of staff on 15 December, Clark Kerr, visiting from Moscow, argued that the situation in Russia was more nuanced. The discussion also offered important insights into how the chiefs saw Russia's contribution at this time and its impact on British strategy.[94] Clark Kerr's main message was that Stalin believed he had been guaranteed a second front in 1943 involving the landing of one million men in Western Europe. He did not view Torch as a substitute and would not be convinced by a wider Mediterranean offensive backed by raids on the French coast. He did not understand the maritime and logistic challenges facing the Western Allies or the shipping constraints. He probably already sensed a lack of serious preparation for a 1943 second front and, if he did not get it, he would turn 'very sour'. It was also questionable whether Russian morale would hold. Clark Kerr did not exclude the possibility of a separate peace. With Stalin nothing was ever off the table. Portal thought it was 'probably true' that 'we could only get on the continent if the Russians beat the Germans' and that the best way of helping them was through exploitation of Torch and knocking out Italy. Stalin should be made to understand that the Western Allies already contained 'two-thirds of German fighting strength', half their bomber force and all the Italian air force. Without the West, this Axis effort would be applied on the Russian front. Clark Kerr thought neither this line of argument nor the huge challenges involved in executing a major landing in Europe would cut much ice with Stalin. The issues were Russian morale and suspicion that they were deliberately being left to do all the fighting. Ways must be found to convince them they were not alone.

It is doubtful any of the British chiefs were convinced that a separate peace was a real threat and Brooke was privately dismissive.[95] They also knew by now from Ultra decrypts that the Russian counter-offensive at Stalingrad was enjoying considerable and unexpected success. Ten days earlier, the Joint Intelligence Committee had also judged that Stalin would firmly reject any German peace proposal and 'remain determined to eliminate for ever the German threat which has for years been Russia's principal anxiety'. Nevertheless, they had also applied a caveat not dissimilar to Clark Kerr's points. If, by next spring, the Western Mediterranean offensive had not established a convincing 'second front' and Soviet offensive operations had stalled, then it was conceivable Stalin might consider negotiations although it was difficult to see what conditions could possibly satisfy both sides.[96] In fact, during November and December, the idea of negotiating a second Brest-Litovsk peace settlement was raised three times with Hitler by the Italian leader Benito Mussolini. Hitler rejected the suggestion, along with similar soundings by Japan, out of hand, insisting that there was no prospect of reconciling conflicting German and Russian interests or living with a permanent threat from the Red Army.[97] Overall, if a separate peace seemed unlikely to the chiefs as 1942 drew to a close, Clark Kerr's arguments probably did convince them that a major continuing aid programme was a necessary price to preserve an effective 'United Nations' alliance even if the western and eastern wars ended up largely separate. Furthermore, the chiefs may have been too dismissive of peace talks. There is circumstantial but intriguing evidence that Stalin did put out feelers through intelligence channels shortly before the Stalingrad counter-offensive and again between April and June 1943. What really motivated these moves and how serious they were is difficult to gauge. Perhaps both sides saw any talks as a useful tactical ploy to create uncertainty in their opponent. Certainly, there were no substantive results.[98]

Despite Roosevelt's refusal to provide destroyers, the prime minister insisted, and Pound accepted, that the convoys must resume in December. However, in acquiescing, Pound stressed the burden this would impose on Royal Navy resources which meant carrying more risk not just to the resumed Arctic convoys but also with North Atlantic traffic than was desirable. He emphasised the growing loss rate in the Atlantic and stated that overall escort demands meant the agreement reached with the Americans and Russians back in the spring to run three Arctic convoys every two months was now 'out of the question'. The best schedule possible was one convoy every 33 days and even this would put severe strain on Home Fleet destroyers, with valuable cruisers having to be used instead.[99] The Defence Committee endorsed the decision to resume on 23 November and Churchill informed Stalin the following day that a thirty-ship convoy would sail on 22 December. Despite Pound's reservations, the committee, steered by the prime minister and Eden, also agreed that, after this sailing, there should be a maximum effort to continue the convoys which should only be interrupted if there was an opportunity for 'large-scale' offensive operations that could favourably affect Russia's position.[100] This policy was confirmed by the committee at the end of December when they approved the British future strategy position for the forthcoming Anglo-American summit at Casablanca. However, in what proved an unfortunate hostage to fortune, Churchill again followed this meeting with a letter to Stalin, expressing satisfaction with the progress of the December convoys, and promising a further thirty-ship convoy in January. In the event, only half this number sailed that month.[101]

While the Admiralty still favoured a minimum thirty-ship convoy if sufficient escorts could be found, Tovey's view differed. He believed that, in winter darkness from mid-November to mid-January when enemy air reconnaissance was almost impossible, a well-handled convoy had an excellent chance of evading U-boat and surface attack and even avoiding detection completely. However, this required the convoy keeping together and the experience of QP 15 showed that winter gales could rapidly disperse a large one. Ships spread out over a wide area were then more liable to detection by U-boat or an offensive surface sweep such as that planned by *Hipper* against QP 15. While British escorts were always hampered by the need positively to identify a radar contact which could be friendly, the Germans could generally safely treat any contact as hostile. On 25 November, two days after the Defence Committee met, Tovey therefore proposed sailing a succession of smaller more manageable convoys of ten ships with a proportionately smaller escort and starting as soon as possible to maximise the advantage of the dark period. Interestingly, Tovey's plan was remarkably similar to that suggested by Maisky in a meeting with the First Lord and Rear Admiral Brind almost a month earlier.

However, the Admiralty initially insisted that lightly escorted convoys were too risky given the present scale of U-boat and surface threat. In the end, a compromise was reached. The December thirty-ship convoy would be broken into two almost equal parts, each escorted by seven fleet destroyers and lighter escorts. A close covering force (Force R) of two 6in cruisers, *Sheffield* and *Jamaica*, and two destroyers, again under Burnett, would patrol to the south of the convoys as added insurance against surface attack, following the model of cruiser deployments the previous winter. *Sheffield* had been intensively worked for six months with little respite and no leave for her crew which had led to some disgruntlement. Burnett dealt with this superbly in an address to his new flagship when he came aboard: 'Last night in the starboard hangar, you were singing "I'm dreaming of a White Christmas". Well, in the words of a famous comedian, "you lucky people" because you're going to have one.' There was no more trouble![102]

Burnett's force was judged adequate to counter the present German group in Altafiord, known to comprise *Hipper*, *Köln* and four destroyers, given the additional insurance of British submarines patrolling of the entrance to the fiord.[103] Four of the latter were to cover the approaches to Altafiord during the passage of the three convoys, lying eight to ten miles off the coast. Because of the duration of the operation, two groups had to be deployed with a changeover on 29 December.[104] Tovey himself would provide the customary distant heavy cover well to the west of Bear Island with *King George V*, the heavy cruiser *Berwick* and three destroyers, as a deterrent to any sortie by *Tirpitz* now at Trondheim. There was no carrier available and constant darkness would anyway limit its usefulness. (*Victorious* had left to join the US Navy Pacific Fleet which faced a desperate carrier shortage over the next six months and, although *Furious* had been allocated to the Home Fleet, she was detached to the Mediterranean. Torch commitments meant no escort carrier was available until February.[105]) Mindful of the U-boat threat and the experience of *Edinburgh*, Tovey did not want Burnett's cruisers to go beyond the 25° East limit set for Hamilton with PQ 17. However, given the reduced destroyer force in the close escorts, the Admiralty insisted they must accompany the convoys along their whole route, refuelling in the Kola Inlet. Tovey later conceded that events fully justified this instruction.[106]

In making these dispositions, Tovey and the Admiralty would have been further reassured had they been aware of the decision of the German naval command on 9 December to release eleven of the twenty-three boats currently based in the Arctic theatre for Dönitz to use in the North Atlantic. This reflected Dönitz's long campaign to move boats from a task which he regarded as unsuitable and unproductive, especially in winter, but also the heavy U-boat losses and disruption caused by Torch. Dönitz calculated that the Arctic U-boat force had sunk 263,000 tons over the 11 months to 30 November although British records suggest it was 40 per cent less. An equivalent force in the Atlantic had sunk 910,000 tons in the same period, so for Dönitz his U-boats had sunk 650,000 tons less than 'we might have done'. It was even more galling that much of the Arctic traffic had to pass through the Atlantic first. The Arctic boats had to be overhauled for Atlantic duty so the transfers were slow, four in January, one in March and two in April, but it still meant fewer front-line boats immediately available in late December.[107]

However, by the time the first new convoy JW 51A sailed, the surface situation looked less comfortable. Ultra decrypts showed that *Lützow*, repaired after her grounding, had arrived in Bogen Bay on 13 December and had moved to join *Hipper* in Altafiord five days later.[108] On paper at least, this force now significantly outgunned *Sheffield* and *Jamaica*. Furthermore, Ultra had also confirmed the arrival of the light cruiser *Nürnberg* at Narvik on 2 December. Decrypts had previously revealed that she had been working up with *Scharnhorst* and *Prinz Eugen* in the Baltic and that all three had been specifically exercising convoy attacks. However, exploitation of subsequent decrypts to target her on her passage northward failed. Raeder had originally planned that *Prinz Eugen* should accompany *Lützow* to Norway with *Scharnhorst* to follow in January but, at his meeting with Hitler on 19 November, it was decided that shortage of fuel meant only *Lützow* could move at this time.[109] Meanwhile, the OIC also knew that *Tirpitz* had been refitting at Trondheim during the autumn but judged she could be operational again by late December.[110] The first news of *Tirpitz*'s refit, primarily overhaul of her engines, had been passed to Henry Denham in October by Norwegian resistance contacts. His relationship with Björnstjerna and thus access to Swedish SIGINT had been broken the previous month after it was detected by Björnstjerna's superiors. Dolphin decrypts offered little bar hints of *Tirpitz*'s forthcoming readiness for sea.[111]

The two December convoys duly sailed from Loch Ewe in north-west Scotland, one week apart, on 15 and 22 December respectively, under the new designations JW 51A and JW 51B. (Loch Ewe was now judged a more convenient and comfortable departure point than Iceland for the Arctic convoys in winter.) An inbound convoy, RA 51, sailed from Murmansk on 30 December, timed so that it could be escorted by the destroyers bringing in JW 51A. JW 51A, comprising fifteen merchant ships and an oiler, enjoyed fine weather and an uneventful passage. It was not sighted at all by the Germans and reached the Kola Inlet on Christmas Day. RA 51 too had a trouble-free trip, helped by OIC advice on steering clear of three patrolling U-boats.[112] The story of JW 51B would be different.

## Chapter 10

# The Battle of the Barents Sea and its Impact

During the three months following PQ 18, German policy for the deployment of its surface fleet in the Arctic theatre was the subject of debate and some division within their naval leadership, reflecting differing views over what operations could and should be sanctioned. Hitler's insistence, transmitted in regular meetings with Raeder and through Vice Admiral Krancke, that the primary role of the fleet was to be a defensive bulwark against an Allied attack on Norway, and that no offensive operation against the supply convoys must jeopardise this, was clear enough. Raeder never seriously challenged this view but it left open what level of risk was acceptable in deploying against the convoys. Here, as winter drew in, the risk/benefit equation changed. Darkness and severe weather sharply reduced the effectiveness of German air and U-boat operations, with the former now further constrained by Torch withdrawals. It also reduced the Royal Navy carrier threat. On the other hand, finding and fixing a convoy and its escort was more demanding, as experience with QP 15 and JW 51A demonstrated. Indeed, the German Naval Staff judged that, during the darkness period, no adequate picture of the enemy position – the 'most important pre-condition' for surface operations – might be achievable. In addition, it reduced the advantage of long-range guns while increasing the risk of dangerous short-range encounters with enemy destroyers.[1]

Risk management was further complicated by convoluted command arrangements which meant surface operations in the Arctic drew in four distinct authorities, Raeder and the Naval Staff, Group North still under Admiral Carls, Schniewind as Fleet Commander, and Klüber as Admiral Arctic Ocean. Each of these not only brought their own perspective but accountability was often distinctly blurred. Thus Klüber, reporting to Carls, would direct an operation by the Altafiord cruiser group under Vice Admiral Kummetz, but the latter was also accountable to Schniewind, who in theory reported direct to Raeder but whose northern operations were directed by Carls. Having Klüber as a rear admiral giving orders to Kummetz as a vice admiral was also likely to create problems.

## Operation Regenbogen and its Execution against Convoy JW 51B

Through November and December, Carls, partly through concern for morale and with strong support from Schniewind, was anxious to avoid leaving ships inactive in their bases and to seize every opportunity for an attack on the supply traffic. Raeder was apparently also sympathetic to this view but remained risk averse. On 19 November, he assured Hitler that operations would only be undertaken in the Arctic if the objectives were worthwhile. In early December, he reiterated in a formal directive that no operation would be approved unless 'as far as one can foresee' no heavy ships would be lost. Throughout the last quarter of 1942, he certainly failed to clarify how in practice offensive operations might be reconciled with Hitler's position. Despite this uncertainty, Kummetz was directed to prepare an operation designated Regenbogen (Rainbow) for when a suitable convoy target appeared. The arrival of *Lützow* somewhat complicated this planning since, by December, she was earmarked for two different tasks. In the short term she became part of the Altafiord strike force, but from January she would undertake a raiding cruise in the North Atlantic designated Operation Aurore. Obviously, if she suffered damage in an earlier Regenbogen, this might prevent Aurore and it was never clear which took priority.[2]

In planning Regenbogen, Kummetz identified two key problems: finding and fixing the convoy in the first place; and avoiding exposing his force to destroyer attack at night. The engagement must therefore be executed within the two hours of polar twilight and the dawn/dusk illumination which lasted at most for an hour either side. For the first he depended on aerial and/or U-boat sightings, possibly assisted by SIGINT, and he required assurance there was no danger from covering forces. Once the convoy was found, he intended to approach astern of its predicted position by night and, a few hours before dawn, extend his six destroyers, line abreast 15 miles apart, on a 75-mile moving reconnaissance front. Since the destroyers would not have sight of each other at this range, they would maintain contact by shortwave radio telephone. The two cruisers would be positioned just astern of the two wing destroyers, the faster *Hipper* to the north and *Lützow* to the south. If shadowing reports were accurate, even allowing for navigational error, this wide net should catch the convoy from behind, ideally as dawn was breaking. The first objective was destruction of the escort, followed then by the merchant ships, immobilising as many as possible in the shortest time. This would be achieved through a pincer attack with *Hipper* and three destroyers attacking from the north to drive the convoy on to the guns of *Lützow* and the other three destroyers to the south. All the German destroyers were expected to be superior in firepower to their British counterparts.[3]

JW 51B left Loch Ewe on 22 December. It numbered fourteen ships (four British including two tankers, nine American and one Panamanian) and carried 2046 vehicles, 202 tanks, 87 fighters, 33 bombers, 11,500 tons of fuel oil, 12,650 tons of high-quality aviation fuel and 54,321 tons of general cargo.[4] Although this was 60 per cent less ships than PQ 17 had on sailing, the tonnage carried, averaging nearly 6,500 tons per ship, was almost two-thirds that in the earlier convoy. If the Germans achieved its complete destruction therefore, the supply loss to Russia would equate to that suffered in July. The close escort, most of which joined off Iceland, comprised five modern 'O' class destroyers, all completed since mid-1941 and three only in September/October, and one older ship *Achates*, two corvettes, the minesweeper *Bramble* and two trawlers. It was led by Captain Robert Sherbrooke in *Onslow*, who had commanded destroyers almost continuously since 1936, during 1940–1 regularly exchanging ships with Philip Vian, his then flotilla commander. He had gained a DSO for getting his badly-damaged ship *Cossack* back home after the Second Battle of Narvik. He was now the newly appointed Captain (D) 17th Destroyer Flotilla but one of the Royal Navy's most experienced wartime destroyer commanders. Although austere and reserved in personality, he was highly professional, and few were better suited by experience to deal with the challenge he would shortly face in the Barents Sea.[5] His wife Rosemary was making her own contribution to the Arctic war, handling signals in the Admiralty Operations Division registry where she had personally dealt with Pound's notorious PQ 17 'scatter' signal. She would be there again for JW 51B.[6] The other covering forces in support were the same as for JW 51A, with Burnett's Force R heading west from Kola on 27 December but with *King George V*'s sister *Anson* and *Berwick*'s sister *Cumberland* now substituting as the heavy group.

The first six days of passage were uneventful apart from a fleeting German air sighting west of the Faeroes on Christmas Eve which would not have established whether the convoy was bound for Iceland or heading directly to Russia. However, on the night of 28/29 December, five merchant ships along with the destroyer *Oribi* and trawler *Vizalma* became separated in a violent gale when the convoy was 200 miles south-west of Bear Island. *Bramble* was detached the following day to look for the stragglers. *Oribi*, which had suffered a gyrocompass failure, neither found the convoy again nor any missing ships and reached Kola alone on 31 December. Three merchant ships found the convoy independently on 30 December and *Vizalma* re-joined with another two days later. The final missing ship made her own way to Kola. Burnett's cruiser force meanwhile passed 100 miles north of North Cape at midday on 28 December and, 24 hours later, when it was 30 miles south of the convoy and 120 miles south-west of Bear Island, turned back to the east after detaching its two destroyers to Iceland to refuel. As with JW 51A earlier, Burnett's intent was to keep between the convoy and Altafiord, maintaining sufficient distance from the former, ideally at least 50 miles, to avoid becoming a target for shadowing U-boats. The lesson of *Edinburgh* had been well learnt.[7] By early evening of 27 December, the Germans were aware from B-Dienst intercepts that a convoy, which they designated PQ 19 rather than JW 51A, had arrived in Kola and that Burnett's cruisers with two destroyers had sailed that day. Klüber expected them initially to move east along the coast – presumably assuming they would then turn north, skirting the ice edge before turning west. He also advised all units to watch for further traffic concerning enemy forces in Seydisfiord Iceland and to expect traffic through the Bear Island channel soon.[8] It is not clear the Germans saw the departure of the cruisers implying another inbound convoy was imminent. The cruisers might be preparing to escort an outbound convoy which the Germans surely expected. The reference to Seydisfiord would be more consistent with the belief that another convoy would leave Iceland at the end of the month on the fortnightly cycle of the previous winter.[9]

The first definitive sighting of JW 51B as a convoy clearly bound for Murmansk was made mid-morning on 30 December by *U-354*, newly arrived in Arctic waters and one of four boats currently out on patrol. She initially reported the convoy passing 50 miles south of Bear Island, comprising six to ten merchant ships and 'weakly escorted'. Klüber ordered her to shadow, to transmit beacon signals for *U-629*, and, in wishing her a 'successful hunt', gave permission to attack.[10] He also submitted to Group North and Raeder that this was a perfect opportunity to implement Regenbogen. They rapidly agreed and, at 1300, Klüber ordered Kummetz to bring *Hipper*, *Lützow* and six destroyers to immediate readiness for sea.[11] By then, Raeder had teleprinted details of the sighting to Krancke at Führer headquarters in Rastenburg, East Prussia, seeking approval for the Altafiord force to intercept 'subject to confirmation from available sources that no superior force was accompanying the convoy'.[12] Raeder's willingness to support an operation reflected his judgement that it was low risk but was probably also influenced by sensitivity to fleet morale and growing questioning both inside and outside the navy over the value of the heavy ships. Whether Hitler's approval was actually required for an operation that only involved cruisers and not battleships is doubtful. What is clear is that briefing Hitler and thus implicitly sharing responsibility increased the stakes for both Raeder and Hitler.[13]

According to Krancke's subsequent account, Hitler was in a foul mood and had earlier made disparaging remarks about the navy in the presence of Göring, describing it as a 'miserable copy' of the Royal Navy and the heavy ships in Norway as so much 'scrap iron'. Krancke accordingly tried to cast the recommended sortie as a chance to show what the navy could do against an important target. Hitler was gradually won over. Faced with increasingly grim news from Stalingrad, he clearly recognised the importance of doing all possible to disrupt Russian war supplies while a decisive naval victory would offer a welcome propaganda coup at that time.[14]

Klüber went aboard *Hipper* at 1430 to issue final orders for targeting the convoy and Kummetz briefed his captains on how he intended to execute a modified version of Regenbogen. Although he still intended to position *Hipper* and *Lützow* 75 miles apart, updated positions from the shadowing U-boats might allow a division into two forces for the pincer attack earlier than originally planned. The force sailed at 1745, 45 minutes later than intended due to delayed arrival of a tug and a minor defect in *Hipper*, and cleared the north-western Lopphavet exit channel from Altafiord four hours later. From there, the predicted intercept point with the convoy was 230 miles to the north-east. However, even as the force made its way through the fiord, debate over risk management again came to the fore with unfortunate consequences. The original operational directive to Kummetz was straightforward, if hardly expressed in decisive terms: avoid a superior force but otherwise destroy the convoy according to the tactical situation. However, in transmitting Hitler's assent, Admiral Kurt Fricke, Chief of Staff in the Naval War Staff, pointed out that, in line with standing directives, 'not too great a risk should be taken'. By the time this stipulation reached Klüber, via Group North, he felt obliged to radio Kummetz a revision to his orders barely an hour after his departure: 'Contrary to the operational rules of engagement: exercise restraint even with an opponent of equal strength, as the Führer does not wish any risks taken with the cruisers.' Given subsequent events, the precise origin of this caveat and whether it reflected any specific condition set by Hitler for this operation was the subject of considerable later controversy. Fricke claimed he was merely issuing a reminder of long-standing guidelines. Kummetz inevitably felt he had been ordered to play matters completely safe.[15] Oddly this risk debate apparently paid scant heed to the current status of any British covering forces. The two British cruisers leaving Kola on 27 December had not been relocated since. If they were covering the recent 'PQ 19', might they not now be covering the newly identified 'PQ 20'? Nor was any thought given to interception by a Home Fleet battle group during the return passage to Altafiord following a convoy action. Perhaps the threat was judged negligible in winter darkness. Events in exactly 12 months' time demonstrated it was entirely possible.

As Kummetz's force readied to depart, U-354 updated the convoy's position, confirmed that it comprised ten merchant vessels (although there were now twelve), with several destroyers and possibly a cruiser as escort. He had fired one three-torpedo spread which had failed due to zigzagging.[16] Two hours later, U-354 tried another attack, subsequently informing Klüber that she had been in the middle of the convoy at 1940 and had fired four more torpedoes, from which she wrongly claimed at least two hits. She was then forced down and depth-charged but was later able to surface and continue shadowing, joined soon by U-629. By this time, to avoid 'friendly fire' incidents, Klüber had ordered the boats to cease attacks against surface forces and vice versa.[17] At 2259, Klüber also ordered U-354 to transmit beacon signals for Kummetz every half an hour.[18]

Almost nothing of German knowledge of the progress of JW 51B and their plans for a strike by Kummetz's cruisers was visible to the British. When Burnett turned back to the east at midday on 29 December, he knew that Lützow had joined Hipper in Altafiord, that two U-boats were at sea in the area south of Bear Island and two more further north near the ice edge. However, the German report of his departure from Kola on 27 December was only decrypted by Bletchley as he was making his turn and therefore reached him that afternoon of 29 December. None of the German traffic relating to U-354's shadowing on 30 December or the dramatic events the following day reached the OIC until early on 1 January. On 30 December, the only Ultra signal Burnett received told him that 'strong indications' placed Kummetz still in Altafiord at 0045 that morning. That was true but, by the time Burnett received it, Kummetz was on his way.[19]

Lack of intelligence did not lull Burnett into any false sense of security. He judged German surface intervention entirely possible and most likely on 31 December when the convoy reached its furthest point east and began heading south for Kola. For 30 hours following his turn on 29 December, he steered east-south-east, keeping at least 60 miles south of JW 51B's predicted track. At 1800 next day, he then turned north-west, believing this kept him between the convoy and any approaching German force from Altafiord. At 0830 next morning, he planned to complete a zigzag by turning due east, intending thereafter to steer a parallel route a few miles north of the convoy's track but 40 to 50 miles astern from where any attack must surely develop. He would also here be outside the probable position of any shadowing U-boats. However, Burnett could only predict where the convoy should be based on the original planned route and sensible allowances for the impact of weather. He had no means of knowing where it really was and indeed would never sight it throughout the whole operation. In reality, at 0830 on 31 December, he was not 50 miles astern of the convoy as he believed but 30 miles due north of it. This situation illustrates how the challenges of navigation in the Arctic in this era, especially in winter darkness, are often underestimated. Convoys and their escorts were almost never in sight of land, so the only means of an accurate fix was through astro-navigation, a star sight or sun sight, which was weather dependent. It was not unusual for bad weather to prevent astro fixes for days at a time, forcing reliance on dead reckoning. When *Oribi* lost the convoy on the night of 28/29 December, she ended up so uncertain of her position that she was obliged to close the Norwegian coast to get a fix before making her way to Kola.[20]

Sherbrooke, leading the close escort, was not privy to Ultra and could be no more certain of Burnett's whereabouts than the latter was of his. He did know that a U-boat (*U-354*) had been close to the convoy at around 1930 on 30 December because the destroyer *Obdurate* sighted a boat on the surface which she tried to ram before it submerged. She and her sister ship *Obedient* then hunted the contact for two hours without success, the attack which *U-354* later notified to Klüber. Sherbrooke could assume therefore his position had been reported, thereby increasing the risk of a surface attack which he too had always judged the greatest threat facing JW 51B.[21] His plan for meeting such an attack required the five 'O' class destroyers of the 17th Flotilla (reduced to four with *Oribi*'s departure), without waiting for orders, to leave their normal screen positions and immediately gather in line ahead on the threatened side. The convoy would then turn away from the threat with the rearmost merchant ships dropping smoke floats. The remaining destroyer, *Achates*, would lay a further smokescreen behind the merchant ships as they retreated. The other remaining escorts would then reform around the convoy which would manoeuvre to keep the enemy astern while heading away at maximum speed. In most respects, this was an excellent, easily understood plan, admired by all its recipients as a model of clarity and brevity. But it had one potential flaw. It assumed the threat would come from a single sector.[22]

Dawn broke for JW 51B at around 0830 on New Year's Eve. The reduced convoy now comprised twelve merchant vessels with five destroyers, two corvettes and a trawler in company. It was still steering east, about 220 miles north-west of Kola with some 30 hours to run. *Bramble* was 15 miles to the north-east, returning after her vain search for the two stragglers. The trawler *Vizalma* had found the merchant ship *Chester Valley* and they were now 45 miles to the north, while Burnett's two cruisers were 30 miles to the north. None of these four groups knew where the others were or the whereabouts of *Oribi* or the remaining merchant straggler. The weather at dawn was generally clear but interrupted by snow squalls and twilight visibility seven miles to northward and ten southward. However, as the morning wore on, snow showers and mist increased, rendering visibility more intermittent especially in the south.

By contrast, it had been a dark night with poor visibility when Kummetz left Altafiord and this helped him evade the British submarine patrols. Although *P49* saw three dark shapes at 0142, she was unable to see what they were and therefore made no report. Twenty-four hours later, the submarine *Graph*, formerly *U-570* captured intact in August 1941, patrolling in almost the same spot, did identify the returning *Hipper* but was too far off to attack although she did fire unsuccessfully at one of the accompanying destroyers.[23] The British commanders thus had no warning of Kummetz's approach from the south-west. The latter had adopted his planned search formation at 0230 and, guided by *U-354*'s beacon signals, detected the faint shadow of ships to the eastward just before 0800. Cautious about torpedo attack, he took *Hipper* across the wake of the convoy to a holding position 20 miles north-west until the light improved, while his three destroyers moved in closer to shadow. *Lützow* with the other three destroyers was still 50 miles away but approaching fast south-south-west of the convoy. However, her captain, Rudolf Stange, had received a surprise signal from Klüber three hours earlier which injected new hesitancy into an already cautious man. He was informed that *Lützow* was to embark directly on the Aurore Atlantic raid once the present convoy action was complete without returning to Altafiord. He was also advised that execution of Aurore depended on the outcome of Regenbogen. He was to proceed only if he had at least half his ammunition left, could avoid detection by a superior enemy force and, by implication, had suffered no damage. Stange was evidently surprised by this order for which he felt ill-prepared. He was now confronted by conflicting goals and was not a man who coped well with ambiguity.[24]

At 0830, *Hipper*'s destroyers were sighted in the distance on the starboard quarter of the convoy by *Obdurate* and the corvette *Hyderabad*. The subsequent movements of British and German forces over the next two hours are shown on Map 5 overleaf. The Germans initially made no effort to close, obliging *Obdurate* to move out to investigate. The possibility that they were Russian disappeared when they briefly opened fire an hour later before heading off to the north-west to rejoin the cruiser although the British did not yet know of her presence. Meanwhile Kummetz reported to Klüber and other Naval Commands that he was north of the convoy in between four enemy destroyers.[25] The gunfire caused Sherbrooke to implement his plan, gathering his four 'O' class destroyers on the northern side of the convoy while it began turning south-east away from the threat under smoke from *Achates*. At 0939, Sherbrooke sighted *Hipper* to the north-west, and for the next half hour, there was an intermittent gunnery engagement between the cruiser and the British destroyers at a range of 11,000 yards. *Hipper* steered just north of east and made no effort to close the range with the British later describing her fire as 'aimless and erratic' in this period. A kind interpretation is that Kummetz was pursuing his plan to lure the British destroyers away from the convoy while it drove into the arms of *Lützow*. A harsher judgement is that the requirement to avoid risk compounded by a tactical picture increasingly confused by smoke and deteriorating visibility rendered him unable to act decisively. He was wasting a lot of time and, inexplicably, made no effort to use his destroyers which had circled north to join him. These were 40 per cent larger than their British counterparts and could potentially deliver twice the weight of fire, enabling them alone to inflict considerable damage on the escort if used aggressively and effectively.

Sherbrooke had not forgotten the three German destroyers which had clashed earlier with *Obdurate*. Although he himself had not yet spotted them, he worried they would now attack the convoy from the west while his flotilla was kept occupied by *Hipper*. He accordingly ordered *Obdurate* and *Obedient* back to the convoy, leaving him with just *Onslow* and *Orwell*. Perhaps because Kummetz now felt a reduced torpedo threat, at 1015 *Hipper* 'pulled herself together' and, for the first time, brought down accurate fire on Sherbrooke's remaining two ships. *Onslow* was hit four times and so badly damaged she was soon obliged to disengage with *Orwell* behind a new smokescreen. Sherbrooke was severely wounded, ultimately losing an eye, but refused to leave his wrecked bridge until he was sure he had achieved a successful, if temporary, retreat, and had passed command to the newly-promoted Commander David Kinloch in *Obedient*. For his outstanding leadership, continuing commitment and

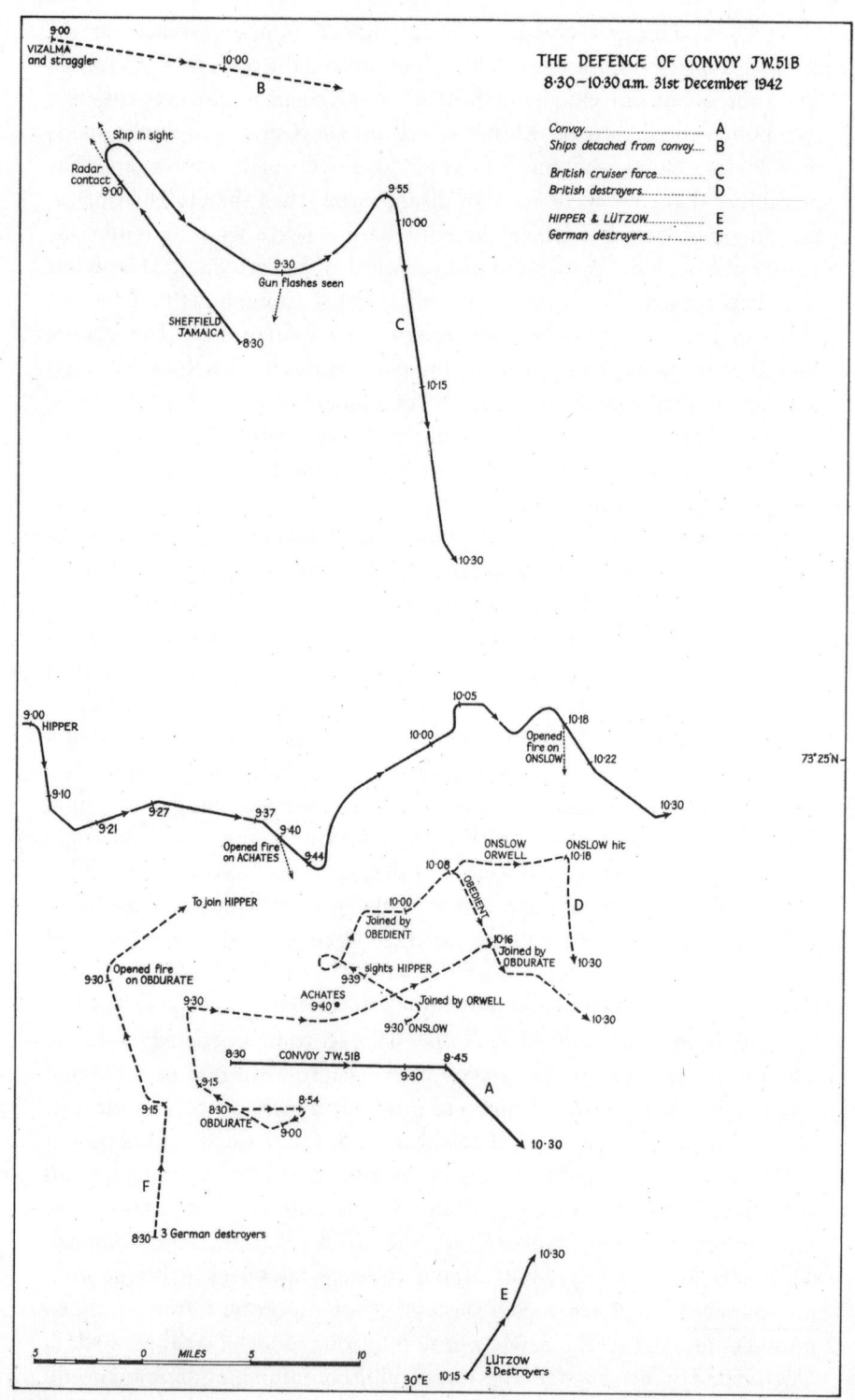

Map 5

presence of mind while in terrible pain, Sherbrooke subsequently received a VC. At 1035, Kinloch now faced an increasingly confused and complex situation. *Hipper* still seemed the most immediate threat and, with the convoy now heading directly south, he positioned his three undamaged destroyers on its port quarter while *Achates* continued weaving across its stern, laying smoke as she did so. The crippled *Onslow*, with fires still burning, made her way to the head of the convoy, receiving rousing cheers from *Obedient*'s crew as she did so, ready to home in Force R which Kinloch hoped would emerge from the south.

The relative British and German movements over the 90 minutes beginning 1030 are shown in Map 6 on p 385. In the event, *Hipper* did not pursue her advantage but turned north-east at high speed. Presumably, Kummetz thought he could lure away the remaining British destroyers but he was also reluctant to expose himself to torpedo attack amidst the smokescreens. Furthermore, he was now distracted by a new radar contact target ahead of him. This was the luckless minesweeper *Bramble*, choosing this moment to reappear, having relocated the convoy through the gunfire of the last two hours. Although the Germans made short work of despatching the almost defenceless *Bramble*, tragically lost with all hands after escorting no less than thirteen Arctic convoys, the detour cost Kummetz a further half hour before he turned southward then south-west in pursuit of the retreating JW 51B. At 1115, he sighted *Achates* emerging from her smokescreen and delivered several crippling hits which caused her to sink two hours later.

Meanwhile the *Lützow* force had finally appeared on the scene, albeit to little immediate effect. Just as Kinloch took command, he received somewhat garbled reports of a large ship crossing ahead of the convoy from west to east before the scene was blotted out in a heavy snow squall. Stange, constrained by *Lützow*'s maximum speed of 26 knots, had sighted gun flashes to the north-east at 0930 and steered towards them, recalling his three destroyers from their search line. At 1045, with his force now concentrated, he had several contacts ahead on his radar, at a range of three to seven miles, which he assumed were probably the convoy, but nothing was visible through the snow showers. In common with *Hipper*, *Lützow* also seems to have lacked a plotting organisation for translating radar contacts into a coherent picture for the command. He also failed to inform Kummetz of his latest position and intentions or the contacts detected. The risk-aversion which had underpinned the whole operation now combined with Stange's own cautious temperament. He opted to steer east across the front of the contacts, and then south-east, hoping the snow would clear and clarify the picture. By 1115, he could occasionally see the shadows of ships through the murk on his starboard quarter but still failed to act. At no point did he use one or more destroyers to investigate on the basis that, if these became mingled with enemy units, it would prevent *Lützow* gaining a clear field of fire later. As Raeder later stated, Stange had missed 'a favourable opportunity to score a success and possibly finish the appointed job in one blow', for Kummetz's pincer plan had worked almost perfectly.[26] When Stange crossed in front of the convoy, the merchant ships were oblivious to his presence, there were no escorts yet in the immediate vicinity and his force anyway possessed overwhelming firepower. As he now waited for a break in the snow and mist to the west, he was distracted by heavy firing to the north which he identified coming from *Hipper* and, apparently forgetting the pincer plan, decided his best move was to join her.[27]

As Stange turned, the balance of advantage still seemed to lie with the German attackers. It was true that Kummetz's caution combined with indecision by Stange had now used up half the polar twilight period without any damage to the JW 51B merchant ships whose destruction was the whole purpose of Regenbogen. Kummetz later acknowledged that the handling of the convoy and defensive tactics of the escort had so far been exemplary. On the other hand, two of five British destroyers had now been disabled and a minesweeper sunk without any damage to the German ships. Kummetz now had crushing superiority in numbers and, above all, firepower. The weather had so far helped the defenders, but nobody would bet on this holding off a determined attack for much longer and certainly not the remaining three hours of twilight. *U-354*, still in the vicinity, had signalled a partial running commentary, whetting the appetite of Klüber and fellow commanders ashore. At 0945 she reported sighting *Lützow* and gunnery action underway. Just before 1100, she then signalled that the battle had reached its 'culminating point' and 'I can only see red'.[28] But the Germans were about to receive a major surprise and within minutes of Stange's turn north-west towards *Hipper*, their chance to get at the convoy was gone for good.

Three hours earlier at 0830, as Kummetz's destroyers began probing the rear of the convoy, Burnett's two cruisers were positioned 30 miles to the north. He was steering north-west across what he believed was the wake of JW 51B located 50 miles east of him. Just before 0900, *Sheffield*'s radar picked up a radar contact seven miles ahead which, in the circumstances, was potentially hostile. By 0930, it was clear there were two ships steering east south-east at 10 knots, suggesting they might be stragglers. They were in fact *Chester Valley* and the trawler *Vizalma*, hoping to return to the convoy. At 0932, gunfire, initially thought to be

# THE BATTLE OF THE BARENTS SEA AND ITS IMPACT

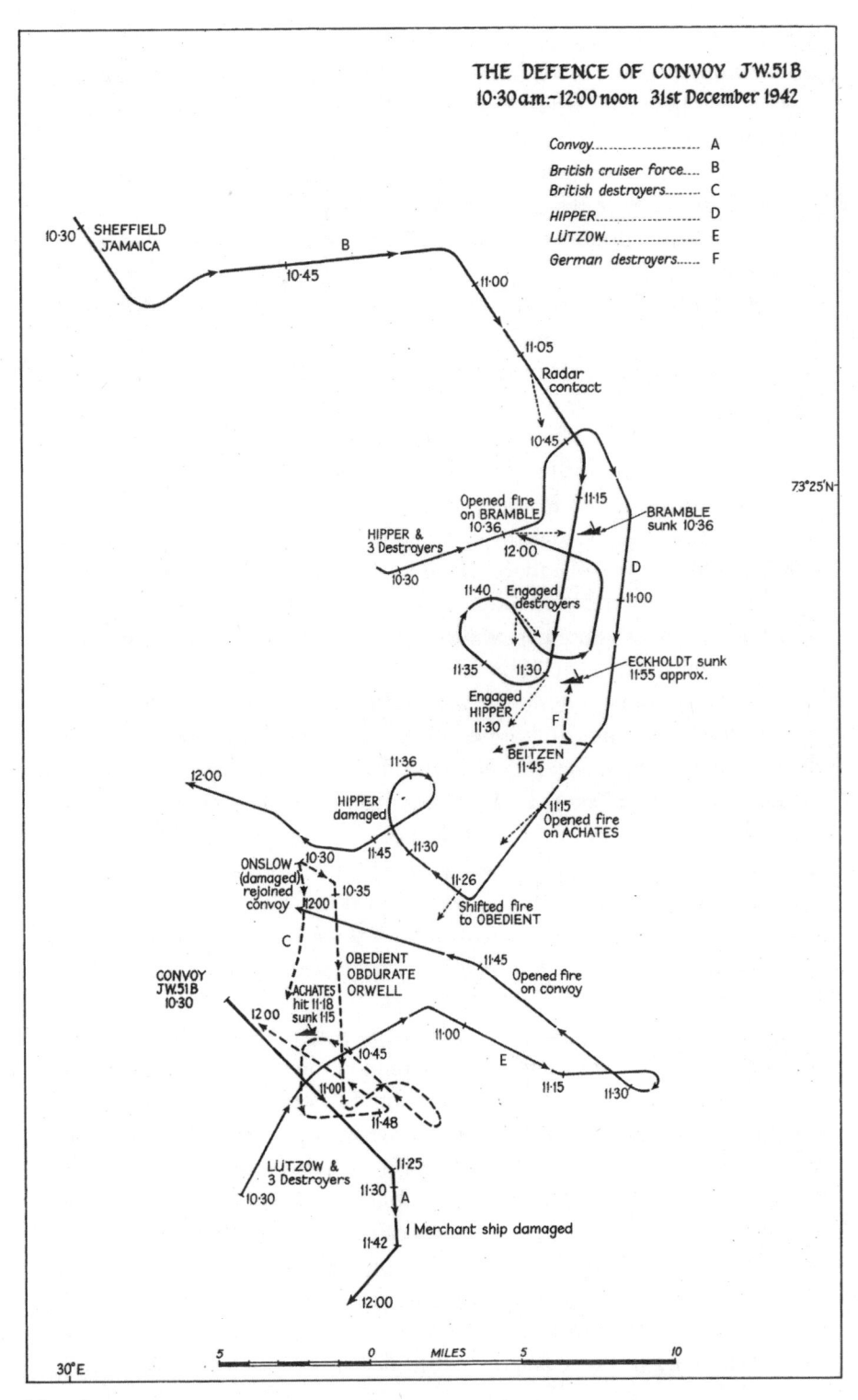

**THE DEFENCE OF CONVOY JW.51B**
**10·30 a.m.–12·00 noon 31st December 1942**

| | |
|---|---|
| Convoy | A |
| British cruiser force | B |
| British destroyers | C |
| HIPPER | D |
| LÜTZOW | E |
| German destroyers | F |

Map 6

anti-aircraft, was heard from the south as the German destroyers fired on *Obdurate*, followed 15 minutes later by the much heavier fire from *Hipper* and an enemy report from Sherbrooke. Burnett hesitated another 10 minutes, concerned that the firing was from detached escorts and the convoy was where he believed – out to the east. However, at 0955, he felt he must embrace the fundamental principle of Royal Navy fighting policy – 'When in doubt steer for the sound of the guns'. He turned south and soon wound up to 31 knots. Burnett received some later criticism for not adopting this maxim 20 minutes earlier, a period in which more decisive German action might have inflicted considerable damage. But Burnett also had an overriding duty to the 'safe and timely arrival of the convoy' and would have been harshly criticised if he had been drawn into a diversionary engagement while the convoy was attacked further east.[29]

The orchestration of Burnett's run to the south to achieve surprise and an optimum fighting position against what he anticipated might prove a stronger German force, and the subsequent successful engagement, owed much to superior use of radar. British naval radar had come a long way over the last 18 months. The radar superiority Burnett's cruisers enjoyed over their German opponents was not just technical, although the latest version of the centimetric Type 273, first fitted in *Prince of Wales* prior to Halberd and now in both *Sheffield* and *Jamaica*, gave an advantage in surface detection range and fire control of perhaps 50 per cent. It lay in the way radar data was exploited tactically through incorporation in the operational plot and presentation to the command. It also reflected the sheer extent of sea time and frequency of combat for most Royal Navy ships in this war. For senior officers, use of radar for searching, fighting and managing their own forces, its strengths and limitations, was now second nature in a way the German surface ships in Norway with limited time at sea could not match. Without radar, the results of the cruiser battle might have been very different.[30]

At 1030, *Sheffield* detected a large ship on her Type 273 at a range of 10 miles and a brief sighting some minutes later suggested an enemy cruiser which was of course *Hipper*. Burnett did not immediately close but for the next 45 minutes tracked her movements primarily by radar and built up his tactical picture while all the time manoeuvring to optimise his own position and light. He observed *Hipper* move south-west to engage a destroyer (*Achates*) and then alter westward as she engaged another target (*Obedient*). This placed the German broadside-on and now clearly identifiable fine on his starboard bow, a perfect target at 16,000 yards. It was now 1130. Kummetz had dealt with *Achates*, was clear now where the convoy was and was determined to deal with the other escorts and finish matters. He accordingly signalled *Lützow*: 'In action with escorting force. No cruiser with the convoy' and ordered Stange to reverse course. Seconds later cruiser shells began plunging around him.

Burnett had achieved complete surprise. *Hipper*'s turrets were all trained to port, firing at *Obedient*, and more than four salvoes had landed from the two British cruisers before they could be trained round to deal with the new threat to the north. Within five minutes, *Hipper* had received three hits, one severely damaging a boiler room and temporarily reducing her speed to 23 knots and another starting a fire in her aircraft hangar. Tovey subsequently assessed that these hits were entirely due to radar-directed fire with no useful results available from optical rangefinders. Both sides found the latter inoperable for extended periods due to icing.[31] Nevertheless, the British gunnery performance also validated the Admiralty judgement in the mid-1930s that, at typical cruiser engagement ranges, twelve 6in guns was a better armament on a 10,000-ton displacement than eight 8in because it delivered twice the weight of fire per minute.[32] Kummetz was evidently completely shocked by this attack from an enemy he could barely see in now-fading light. *Hipper* initially turned to point Burnett's force while his accompanying destroyer *Z 29* laid smoke. To the bemusement of the British, she then completed a full circle and headed west. Kummetz claimed later that, caught between British cruisers to the north and destroyers to the south, and unable to get a clear picture of the tactical situation because of gathering darkness, mist and snow flurries, he had to withdraw. Attacking the convoy was 'out of the question' given the uncertain condition of *Hipper*. At 1137, just seven minutes after Burnett had opened fire, he therefore signalled all ships: 'Break off action and retire to the west.'

This proved a wise decision because, half an hour later, flooding from *Hipper*'s damaged boiler room spread to a second, bringing her speed down to 15 knots for an extended period. Indeed, the extent of the damage to the machinery spaces strongly suggests more than one shell hit here. Extraordinarily, Kummetz's signal to withdraw coincided almost exactly with an order from Klüber implying he should do the same. Klüber's message, which originated at 1145 but was not received by Kummetz until more than an hour later, informed him that two British cruisers, including *Jamaica*, were in the 'Murmansk area' and that he should return at 'increased speed'. This signal clearly reflected B-Dienst intercepts of transmissions from Burnett as he headed south towards the action. The phrasing was ambiguous and not entirely helpful. If intended as an instruction not to get entangled with cruisers following assumed successful destruction of the convoy, it made sense. However, if action was still underway, it was less clear what Kummetz was meant to do, given that Murmansk was 200 miles away and the cruisers surely counted as an 'inferior force'. Nevertheless, it certainly underlined the earlier messages to take no risks.

Meanwhile, within minutes of Kummetz's withdrawal signal, further disaster hit the Germans. *Hipper*'s other two destroyers, *Friedrich Eckholdt* and *Richard Beitzen*, were returning from dealing with *Bramble* out to the east and mistook the British cruisers for *Hipper*. *Eckholdt* was blown apart by *Sheffield* at close range and, like *Bramble*, had no survivors. *Beitzen*, somewhat further away, was straddled by *Jamaica* but made a high-speed escape.[33]

Following *Eckholdt*'s destruction, there was a brief exchange of fire half an hour later between Force R and *Lützow* which with her destroyers was following *Hipper* west. Slightly earlier, as she began her withdrawal, *Lützow* had caught brief sight of the convoy and fired on one merchant ship, inflicting minor damage. Neither side now gained any hits and, although they continued to shadow for a further hour, it was soon clear to the British that the German withdrawal was final and the battle therefore over. The proximity of Burnett's cruisers also ruled out the detachment of *Lützow* to undertake Aurore.[34] Judged by ships lost and damaged, the result of the morning's engagement was about equal but it was the operational outcome that mattered. There was no dispute that Sherbrooke and Burnett had won a fine defensive victory, holding off a superior German battle group for three hours and then forcing its retreat while preserving the convoy intact. The British wasted no time in publicising this as soon as the bulk of JW 51B reached Kola the following day and the core facts were known. The Germans had been comprehensively outfought at every level as the German Naval War Staff later frankly admitted.[35]

## Aftermath and Impact

It suited most, although not all, the German naval leadership to blame the failure of Regenbogen, or the 'Battle of the Barents Sea' as the British named it, on the crippling 'no risk' restrictions imposed by Hitler. This explanation soon gained wider acceptance and remains dominant to this day. It received additional early credence in German quarters from the false claim that Kummetz received a signal, just as he was engaged by Burnett, containing the three words 'No Unnecessary Risk' which explained his decision to withdraw.[36] This traditional view requires challenge. First, although Klüber's parting order to Kummetz clearly stipulated minimal risk to the cruisers against a force of equal size, the evidence that this specific condition on this occasion stemmed from Hitler himself is tenuous. Indeed, in reviewing the lessons learnt from Regenbogen on 10 March, the Naval Staff stated categorically that Klüber's modification to the operational order was 'unnecessary', was 'not contemplated' by Fricke, and the specific reference to 'not desired by the Führer' 'most unfortunate'. It had emerged therefore from the successive and convoluted levels of naval command. It no doubt reflected impressions of what commanders judged the Führer wanted, fear of his wrath and, in Carls' case, losing preferment, but it also demonstrated cautious attitudes prevailing within the naval leadership itself and, above all, with Raeder. Hitler was not always against risk. He had after all insisted on Cerberus against naval advice.[37]

Furthermore, as the Naval Staff review also observed – 'there was no question of a superiority of enemy forces'. Only 'anticipated forces' appeared and it was to German advantage that the British cruisers 'from Kola' did not reach the battle 'until dusk had fallen'. The enemy 'achieved superiority' only when *Hipper*'s 'fighting strength' was reduced by a hit at the beginning of the engagement. The reality is that at no stage during the operation did Kummetz face an 'equal force', let alone a superior one. Even after the hit to *Hipper*, his heavy cruisers significantly outmatched Force R in displacement and firepower, as did his destroyers with their counterparts. And, as the German Naval Staff conceded, for three hours, he faced no cruiser opposition at all. Indeed, his six destroyers alone, if effectively used, could have overwhelmed Sherbrooke's force.[38]

Even allowing for Kummetz's desire to minimise the risk to his big ships following Klüber's unfortunate qualification, the harsh truth is that he dithered, failed to coordinate his two forces or to use his own northern group effectively from the start. In drawing out the lessons, the Naval Staff inevitably focused on Stange's failure to exploit a 'favourable situation' as he crossed ahead of the convoy. If his perception of Klüber's 'restrictions' made him reluctant to take *Lützow* into the 'snowstorm', they insisted he should still have used his destroyers and Kummetz should have encouraged him to do so.[39] However, Kummetz was equally tentative using his own three destroyers in the north. For example, he should have ordered them to knock out *Obdurate* in their initial clash. It is therefore an extraordinary feature of the entire battle that the six German destroyers tamely followed their respective heavy ships and hardly participated in the various actions, to the mystification of the British. Kummetz, echoing Stange, later claimed that a destroyer attack would have resulted in his ships being confused with those of the enemy and left him denuded of protection. These considerations never held the

British back and suggested Kummetz lacked confidence in his ships or his ability to control them. Perhaps most important of all, Kummetz forgot the fundamental precept that no plan survives contact with the enemy. His basic 'pincer' plan was a good one and, had Stange arrived earlier and the weather been better, Sherbrooke's defence plan might have further played into his hands. However, Sherbrooke quickly adjusted to circumstances, detaching *Obedient* and *Obdurate* to guard the convoy against a potential separate destroyer attack, while Kummetz continued his northward 'lure' long after it was clear that it was not working. He needed quickly to try something else.[40]

Contrasting German passivity with the performance of the British destroyers brings out a wider point. These acted entirely within the spirit of the 1939 Fighting Instructions discussed previously, always moving quickly and boldly, 'pressing the enemy' and keeping him off balance, and not influenced by 'possible damage their ships may receive'. Sherbrooke also adapted rapidly to 'unforeseen circumstances' that 'always arise'. When Sherbrooke was wounded Kinloch seamlessly took over, showing the same resolve and initiative, as did Lieutenant Commander Claude Sclater of *Obdurate* when *Obedient*'s wireless aerials were demolished. None of them hesitated to act as 'judgement dictates' but they never forgot that their primary goal was the safety of the convoy. This willingness to act offensively and to take the initiative while exercising judgement had been inculcated in Royal Navy destroyers by successive commanders in the Mediterranean during the inter-war period and especially by Cunningham and Somerville. The Barents Sea engagement was typical of what they had trained for and expected.

Comparing German performance here with Force K's clinical destruction of the Beta convoy off Malta 13 months earlier is equally striking. Both engagements centred on eliminating a convoy and the respective attackers each had a clear and credible plan to achieve this. Both actions involved cruisers and destroyers pitted against each other without air or submarine intervention, and both were conditioned by darkness or low visibility. In one case, an inferior attacking force comprehensively achieved its goal while, in the other, a superior force achieved little before humiliating withdrawal. The obvious difference lay not only in appetite for risk but leadership and fighting effectiveness. William Agnew executed his plan rapidly and decisively, confident that his captains and their crews knew his intent, had defined roles, and that determination and training would cope with the unexpected. Kummetz claimed to want swift action but in practice he and Stange lacked the will to match aspiration with execution and the ability to cope comfortably with the inevitable uncertainties of battle.

The failure of Regenbogen and the consequences that followed for Raeder and the future of the German heavy ships, described below, caused the Naval Staff to examine the origins, consequences and contradictions of the 'no risk' policy, and whether blame for restrictions lay solely with Hitler or was shared with the naval leadership. This investigation reviewed terms such as 'equal strength' and 'superior' when applied to enemy forces. Even before this study concluded, Raeder recognised that, in prioritising preservation of a 'fleet in being', he had allowed a policy of minimising risk at the strategic level to extend to the tactical. This was evident in a directive issued on 28 January 1943, one of his last acts as Commander-in-Chief. He acknowledged that desire to prevent losses on strategic grounds had encouraged commanders at sea to believe they must avoid any risks at all. The Führer had now ruled that such a restrictive culture could never deliver success. Senior commands must judge the overall risks and benefits of an operation. However, once an operation was underway, commanders at sea must put aside thoughts of damage or loss and focus on striking the enemy with maximum power drawing solely on proven tactical guidelines.[41]

In suggesting the drive for change had come from the Führer, the directive rather implied that the previous 'no risk' culture also stemmed from Hitler. The Naval Staff investigation completed in February concluded that responsibility should be shared more widely. It was especially critical of Raeder who it noted had repeatedly ascribed views to Hitler on 'restrictions' although they were apparently only ever expressed orally to Raeder in person. If objections were raised by others in the leadership or staff, Raeder would claim that changing the Führer's mind was impossible although it was never clear how far he had tried. When Dönitz, as Raeder's successor, suggested to Hitler that restrictions on avoiding losses had severely limited the heavy ships, Hitler emphatically denied he had ever issued an order restricting commanding officers from fighting effectively. If in contact with the enemy, 'ships must go into action'. A fair judgement is that the 'no risk' culture had many authors. Hitler and Raeder, but also other senior leaders, had all encouraged it for a variety of motives and with varying intensity over time.[42]

The British only learnt after the war that their fine defensive victory had triggered wider strategic consequences. Having been persuaded to authorise Regenbogen, Hitler clearly harboured expectations of dramatic success which Krancke did little to discourage. Pressed for news by Hitler at the Führer situation conference on the afternoon of 31 December,

Krancke described the fragmentary signals so far received from the Barents Sea, including *U-354*'s report stating that she could only see 'red', allowing Hitler and others present to believe that this confirmed destruction of the convoy. Although *U-354*'s signal was to be greeted with hilarity in the OIC in London when Bletchley decrypted it next day, that reflected hindsight.[43] It was certainly an odd signal, which the German Naval Staff later insisted should not have been sent 'in this form', and should therefore have been treated with extreme caution.[44] But, taken with the earlier signals showing that both *Hipper* and *Lützow* had successfully intercepted the convoy, Krancke's optimism was understandable. Kummetz had after all reported he was engaging the convoy as early as 0844.[45] Hitler accordingly anticipated a celebratory announcement on New Year's Day to offset the grim news from Stalingrad. For the rest of the day, he pressed Krancke for further updates which the latter stalled by emphasising Kummetz's need for radio silence. Raeder later accused Krancke of handling Hitler in a 'clumsy way' during this long wait that could only make matters worse. But that was easy to say and again drew on hindsight.[46]

There would never be a good time to confront Hitler with the reality of the Barents Sea engagement. However, managing potential fallout from his expectations was made infinitely worse by stunning prevarication, economy with the truth and sheer political naivety on the part of Kummetz, as a vice admiral serving in the atmosphere of Nazi Germany. Once within the shelter of Altafiord at around 0400 on 1 January, Kummetz transmitted a short report which described sighting the convoy followed by a series of clashes with British cruisers and destroyers in which he implied the Germans came off best. The merchant ships were not mentioned. When *Hipper* finally berthed in Kaafiord in the extreme south-west corner of Altafiord at 0600, Kummetz saw no need for haste in expanding his account. Despite being chased twice by Klüber[47] for more detail, he did not produce a second report until shortly after 1200 following consultation with Stange and others. Not only was this too late for the midday Führer conference, but it added only minimally to his first message, still made no mention of the actual convoy, and with remarkable complacency suggested everything possible had been done within the framework set by his directives. Later that afternoon, Kummetz adopted a distinctly patronising tone in a radio telephone call to Klüber in Narvik. Given the constraints posed by winter darkness and weather, decisive results in this type of operation were always unlikely as everyone ought to know. It was hardly his fault if a random U-boat signal had been misinterpreted. He dismissed criticism that he had been slow to report.

Significant successes and casualties were always speedily communicated. Otherwise, silence, as in this case, indicated nothing urgent worth passing on. That was surely standard practice!

If Klüber harboured criticisms of Kummetz's performance, he made no headway. Schniewind and Group North emphasised that they endorsed all key decisions taken by Kummetz and Stange. Only in March, as already noted, did the Naval Staff venture criticisms in the guise of lessons learnt. One of these was the need for a clear early report from the commander at sea, summarising 'performance of the task assigned, i.e. on the successes achieved and those not achieved'. However, none of the implicit criticisms of Kummetz harmed his career. He was promoted full admiral on 1 March and remained in command of the Northern Task Force, the premier seagoing command, until February 1944. His excellent relations with Dönitz no doubt helped. Kummetz had been appointed Inspector of the Torpedo Department at the end of 1939 and, in Dönitz's view, had played a critical role in identifying and solving the notorious problems with U-boat torpedo reliability.[48]

At the midday conference, Krancke was in a hopeless position. He now knew from Naval Staff Operations Division that matters had not gone well but had no definitive report and had been told by Raeder not to expect one until the evening. Meanwhile, over the last 12 hours, there had been several triumphant but essentially accurate announcements from British sources. Inevitably, Hitler now flew into a rage. The prejudices he had aired against the useless big ships 48 hours earlier returned with a vengeance. According to Krancke's record for Raeder, Hitler ranted that German naval commanders were only prepared to act 'against merchant ships that don't shoot back' while the continuing failure to report on the operation was a 'colossal insolence'.

> Such conduct and the entire action showed that ships were completely useless, and served only as a bulwark of revolution because the crews spent time lying round and were lacking in zeal; it meant the death of the High Seas Fleet, it was now his unalterable decision to get rid of these useless ships at last, to make more productive use of the good personnel, the good weapons, the armoured material.

These references to only fighting defenceless merchant ships and an inglorious record in the First World War were deeply insulting to a naval leadership sensitive to matters of honour. Krancke, who sensibly made no response, was ordered to pass this decision to scrap the heavy ships to Raeder, who was to report to the Führer immediately. Hitler also ordered the decision on the ships and reasons for it formally recorded by Field Marshal Wilhelm Keitel, the Chief of OKW.[49]

Krancke rapidly summarised Hitler's comments for Raeder but did not complete a detailed record until 5 January and it is unclear whether Raeder saw this before he had his last known meeting, as Commander-in-Chief Navy and Chief of the Naval Staff, with the Führer the following day. It hardly mattered for, in the presence of Keitel, Hitler repeated his case for scrapping the navy's heavy ships at length. Nor did he spare Raeder his other criticisms even if the language was moderated. He was again scathing about the navy's contribution in the previous war and the 1918 'revolution'. Presumably taking a swipe at the latest Barents Sea action, he implied that the navy was too ready to measure its numbers against the enemy before engaging. By contrast, the army, once committed, always fought to a decision. This led him to the view that, with the critical situation facing Germany and the need to mobilise all its fighting power, large ships could not 'ride idly at anchor for months'. Protection of this fleet was absorbing major resources while light naval forces did most of the fighting at sea. It was not large ships which protected the small but the reverse. He then tasked Raeder with questions. Should aircraft carriers be retained and could some of the heavy ships be converted as carriers? Where should the heavy guns released by scrapping be mounted on land? In what order should ships be decommissioned? Could the submarine programme be expanded and accelerated if the big ships were eliminated?[50]

Hitler had expressed scepticism regarding the heavy ships before, notably during the run-up to Cerberus, and it is unclear whether Raeder thought he was now immovable. Raeder did win two concessions which suggested possible scope for negotiation. He asked whether *Scharnhorst* and *Prinz Eugen*, both now operational after spending most of 1942 under repair, should still deploy to Norway. Hitler answered – yes – since, for the present, Norway was to be defended as strongly as possible, a decision hardly consistent with the scrapping policy. Hitler also agreed that Raeder could have one final chance to make his case for retaining the heavy ships in a written justification. Despite these concessions, Raeder found the attitude Hitler had expressed towards the navy both at this meeting and earlier with Krancke deeply insulting but beneath his dignity to challenge in detail. He accordingly felt obliged to resign, a decision he communicated in private after Keitel withdrew, insisting that his authority had been fatally undermined. Hitler initially tried to dissuade him, conscious that the impression of a high-profile clash with the navy could be damaging given looming catastrophe at Stalingrad. However, he eventually agreed when Raeder proposed linking his retirement with the symbolic date of 31 January, 10 years after Hitler had become chancellor.[51]

Hitler invited Raeder to nominate two potential successors and he proposed Carls and Dönitz. Although it is often suggested that Raeder's preferred candidate was Carls, partly because of his notoriously difficult relationship with Dönitz, his assessment of their relative merits seems remarkably balanced. Raeder had recently endorsed a glowing report on Dönitz from Schniewind and the only disadvantage he saw in appointing him his successor would be that he could no longer give the U-boat war exclusive attention. At any rate, Hitler chose Dönitz. He may have seen an all-out focus on the U-boat war as the sole remaining route to German victory and he certainly expected Dönitz enthusiastically to support his policy for scrapping the heavy ships, although here he was soon disappointed. Dönitz was also much more compatible ideologically and offered youth and vigour.[52]

Raeder delivered his memorandum justifying retention of the heavy ships on 15 January. He argued that the German fleet in northern waters presented a serious threat to Britain, forcing her to deploy several modern battleships, carriers and cruisers to protect the North Atlantic shipping routes. Dismantling this fleet would give Britain and her allies a 'bloodless victory'. British naval forces could then operate in German coastal waters where they chose with little threat from a much-depleted German air force and Britain would be free to deploy major resources to other theatres with unforeseeable adverse consequences for Germany and her allies. Meanwhile the personnel and steel released from scrapping would make only a marginal contribution to Germany's resource needs elsewhere and realising the small benefit would itself require considerable time and effort. Oddly, the memorandum made no reference to deployment of the heavy ships against the Arctic convoys, the one issue that might have given Hitler pause.[53] This is especially surprising because the Naval Staff must have been aware of contemporary assessments produced by Gehlen's Foreign Armies East and OKW's war economy department on the growing importance of Western supplies to Russia and their anticipated rapid expansion during 1943. At the turn of the year, these assessments overestimated total 1942 deliveries across all three routes by about 17.5 per cent but they somewhat underestimated supplies via the Persian Gulf and Pacific while massively overstating those through the Arctic, assessing deliveries here to be 85 per cent higher than they actually were. Their understanding of what the shipments actually comprised also remained poor. They exaggerated the scale of Western deliveries of aircraft, tanks and guns, which they judged equated to 20 to 30 per cent of Soviet domestic production, and continued to underplay the importance of raw materials, transport supplies, communications equipment and specialist goods such as machine tools. The figures for the Arctic might be too high but they certainly made a powerful case for intervention and this was the only route Germany could attack.[54]

Hitler was not swayed by the memorandum, if indeed he read it. His determination to proceed with decommissioning the heavy ships was conveyed first to Krancke and then Dönitz at a meeting on 25 January. His message to the former was that all effort must now be concentrated on tackling the critical situation in the East. That meant diverting all available steel and labour to tank production. When Krancke ventured that the resources released from scrapping the big ships might in practice be limited, Hitler responded that even small quantities helped. Two days after the meeting with Dönitz, the Naval Staff transmitted a formal order to all commands. Work on construction or conversion of big ships, including aircraft carriers, was to cease immediately. Unless required for training, battleships and heavy and light cruisers were to be paid off and naval resources released used to speed up construction and support of U-boats. On 8 February, at his first conference as the new Commander-in-Chief with Hitler, Dönitz produced a schedule which was approved. The badly-damaged *Gneisenau* on which little work had been done over the last year would be scrapped forthwith, *Hipper* and the light cruisers *Leipzig* and *Köln* would be paid off in March, *Scharnhorst* in July and *Tirpitz* in the autumn. The remaining vessels would be allocated to training and no longer available for operations. By the time this conference took place, *Scharnhorst* and *Prinz Eugen* had already made two attempts to reach Norway, on 11 and 25 January, but on each occasion turned back following sightings by British aircraft in the Skagerrak. In both cases, British intelligence drawn from SIGINT and air reconnaissance was good enough to justify mounting air strikes but these failed due to indifferent weather and the German withdrawals. These attempted breakouts were consistent with Hitler's authorisation to Raeder on 6 January. It is not clear whether the decision to decommission *Scharnhorst* in July meant the transfer was now cancelled.[55]

By his own account, Dönitz initially acquiesced in, rather than supported, decommissioning the heavy ships in his first meetings with Hitler. He claimed he lacked the background information to question the decision but he probably also believed it would bring added focus and resources to the U-boat war.[56] However, within a fortnight, he had changed his mind, having absorbed and endorsed the arguments in Raeder's 15 January memorandum almost in their entirety. He quickly grasped the value of retaining a 'fleet in being' to tie down British forces and accepted that few resources would in practice be released.[57] In an essay written for British Naval Intelligence Division in 1945, Dönitz underlined the goal of containing the maximum possible British fleet in home waters, thereby preventing resources being deployed to the Mediterranean and Far East theatres.[58]

Remarkably therefore, at his next meeting with Hitler held at Vinnitsa in the Ukraine on 26 February, Dönitz then talked the Führer into largely reversing the planned scrapping policy after softening him up first with confirmation that *Hipper*, *Leipzig* and *Köln* had already decommissioned. His key argument here was the one that Raeder failed to deploy – that the Arctic convoys made excellent targets for the heavy ships and given the present difficult position on the Eastern Front, Dönitz considered it vital to exploit their maximum potential. *Scharnhorst* should therefore deploy to Norway to join *Tirpitz* and *Lützow* which with six destroyers would make a powerful task force. When Hitler reiterated his lack of faith in the effectiveness of the heavy ships, contrasting their feeble performance with soldiers fighting in Russia, Dönitz emphasised the stifling impact of the 'no risk' restrictions already described. If these were lifted, he guaranteed to get the ships into action whenever suitable targets were found. Asked how long it would take to find targets, Dönitz ventured three months. Hitler doubted anything would happen in six but gave Dönitz reluctant approval although the latter's son-in-law, Commander Günther Hessler, later claimed the discussion was 'more stormy' than official records implied. In the event it would be nine months before further worthwhile targets appeared. *Scharnhorst* now finally achieved a successful exit from the Baltic on 7 March and reached Bogen Bay at Narvik two days later, although without *Prinz Eugen*. Alerted by SIGINT, the British made strenuous attempts to intercept her but were defeated by bad weather. *Prinz Eugen* was held back partly due to fuel shortage but probably also because Dönitz did not want to press his luck with Hitler. In arguing the case for retaining the heavy ships in the Arctic, Dönitz no doubt recalled his long-standing conviction that the theatre was inappropriate for U-boats, a judgement certainly borne out by poor productivity. They had difficulty finding targets in the winter darkness and were too vulnerable in summertime. If the U-boats were to be redeployed, with the Arctic force down to twelve by the summer, and strike aircraft numbers permanently curtailed, then heavy ships became the only means of tackling the convoys successfully.[59]

In addition to achieving the reprieve of the heavy ships, during March Dönitz began to refresh and streamline the German navy's senior command positions. The most important change was the retirement of Carls and his replacement by Schniewind who took over Group North but retained his role as fleet commander, creating a combined command and staff at Kiel and thus bringing more coherence to the surface fleet's primary operational theatre. Kummetz, who as previously noted, enjoyed Dönitz's full confidence, remained commander of the now enhanced Northern Task Force. Krancke took over Group West and Fricke Group South covering the eastern Mediterranean and Black Sea. The appointment of Admiral Wilhelm Meisel as Chief of the Naval Staff, in place of Kurt Fricke, has been judged less happy. He was conscientious and hard working but too compliant, lacking the imagination, critical intellect and, above all, strength of personality to challenge Dönitz who certainly needed this.[60]

Dönitz was equally quick to endorse the revised approach on managing risk established in Raeder's parting directive of 28 January. His own directive issued on 19 February confirmed that it was up to shore commands to address the relative risk/benefit in any surface fleet operation but then to permit those at sea freedom of action in meeting a defined operational goal. Sceptics felt this merely shifted risk responsibility around without changing fundamentals and Dönitz admitted that conditions for successful operations in the Arctic would occur 'very seldom' given the superior forces the enemy could deploy. Nevertheless, he emphasised that he favoured 'action' over 'threat' and, when an opportunity did arise, it must be seized with 'determination'. It might also be necessary to attack even a heavily-defended convoy if its destruction was of critical strategic importance. Schniewind in his new combined command also injected more offensive spirit, suggesting large-scale operations must not be hampered by traditional 'orthodoxy'. In parallel, the Naval Staff clarified that destruction of Arctic convoys was now a 'primary objective' not to be overshadowed by the requirement to protect Norway from invasion.[61] Dönitz's commitment to action was evident in the Naval Staff order sent to Group North on 10 March following *Scharnhorst*'s arrival in Bogen Bay. Possibilities for deploying the enhanced fleet against enemy traffic in northern waters were now to be 'resolutely exploited' in accordance with the 19 February directive. To avoid warning the enemy of this intent, it would be advisable to conduct the first operation direct from the Narvik area.[62]

However, less than a week later, on 16 March, both Group North and Klüber lobbied strongly for an early move of the task force to Altafiord. This was much closer to the preferred attack area against convoys, which was east of the North Cape–Bear Island line, increasing the prospect of surprise. Operating out of Narvik also brought greater risk of interception by heavy covering forces of the Home Fleet which normally kept well west of Bear Island. There was little difference in the respective vulnerability of Narvik and Altafiord to air reconnaissance but the threat of agent reporting was less from the latter.[63] Dönitz supported these arguments and agreed the move on 19 March which went ahead four days later.[64] Naval Staff Operations Division reiterated that, with the arrival of *Scharnhorst*, the Northern Task Force was now well placed to meet its primary role 'the attack and destruction of convoys'.[65]

*British Awareness of German Changes in Command and Policy*

The British achieved only a gradual and partial perspective on the German reaction to the Barents Sea engagement and gained no direct intelligence insight into the subsequent high-level debates over the future of the heavy ships which had triggered Raeder's resignation. They did see potential significance in Klüber's signal to Kummetz sent at 1145 on 31 December ordering him to expedite his withdrawal because of the presence of British cruisers. On 14 January, at the Casablanca Conference, Pound told the joint chiefs of staff that this suggested the Germans were following a policy of avoiding damage to their ships. That could possibly indicate desire to keep them intact prior to a breakout into the Atlantic.[66] Given the intent to deploy *Lützow* on Aurore, that assessment was partly right. Meanwhile, Dolphin decrypts in early January showed that *Lützow* was undamaged, but nothing was known about *Hipper* until 18 January when Denham learnt from Swedish sources that she had been hit. A few days later, an 'officer only' signal decrypted by Bletchley after three weeks' delay confirmed her No 3 boiler room had been flooded by a hit from a British cruiser. Subsequent decrypts and reports from SIS coast watchers enabled the OIC to track the withdrawal of *Hipper* and *Köln*, via Narvik and Trondheim, to the Baltic which they reached on 6 February. This intelligence was not rapid enough to allow the ships to be targeted and nor was there any insight into their subsequent decommissioning. *Hipper* received rudimentary repairs in Wilhelmshaven before being moved to Pillau in East Prussia. She was briefly recommissioned as a training ship in 1944 but never restored as an effective fighting unit.[67]

The possibility of new German operations with their heavy ships in the Atlantic, emphasised by Pound at Casablanca, was a constant Admiralty preoccupation through the first quarter of 1943 and preventing this was the first priority of the Home Fleet. This had inevitable implications for its second priority, protecting the resumed Arctic convoys.[68] Although major Atlantic operations were now far from the current reality of German intent, this British fear certainly validated the argument Raeder had tried to make to Hitler for retaining a fleet in being. The appointment of Dönitz gave added force to British concerns. On 5 February, less than a week after his accession, a meeting of the British Naval Staff chaired by Pound concluded that, while it was possible Dönitz would maximise resources on the U-boat war to the detriment of the surface fleet, it was more likely he would use the latter more aggressively to target Allied convoys, working in conjunction with U-boats. The Director of Plans, Captain Charles Lambe, himself a future First Sea Lord, thought the Germans might feel that their large U-boat force was not performing as effectively as hoped and that this created scope for unconventional surface fleet operations. A probable scenario therefore was to use *Tirpitz* and cruisers against the Russian convoys while deploying the two pocket battleships to the South Atlantic and/or Indian Ocean. This campaign might be preceded by redeploying a significant U-boat force specifically to target the major units of the Home Fleet in the vicinity of Scapa Flow and its Iceland bases to reduce its margin of superiority.[69]

Although accumulating evidence by late February pointed to increased emphasis on U-boat building and development, and to pressures from fuel and manpower shortages, Norman Denning emphasised the OIC view that Germany's heavy ships remained an important asset. In the present state of the war, Dönitz would surely use them offensively despite obvious risks. The Joint Intelligence Committee agreed.[70] Denning pointed to Dolphin decrypts showing *Scharnhorst* and *Prinz Eugen*, both now repaired, conducting intensive exercises in the Baltic with particular emphasis on convoy attacks. By the end of January, decrypts had also revealed their two attempts to exit the Baltic undetected. Denning therefore agreed that Dönitz might deploy these into the North Atlantic to support a more intense U-boat campaign, while simultaneously sending a pocket battleship on a raiding cruise further south. Meanwhile, *Tirpitz*, following her refit at Trondheim, together with other available units, potentially including the carrier *Graf Zeppelin*, which PR suggested could be operational by June, would act as a 'containing force' in Norway and a continuing threat to the Arctic convoys. Denning nevertheless stressed the challenges the Germans would face in mounting Atlantic raiding operations after a long gap, notably in successfully evading the Home Fleet, coping with the extensive air surveillance now in place, and providing logistic support. He also noted that, during the last months of 1942, the German surface fleet had shown signs of 'lethargy and cautiousness' strikingly different to their previous 'enthusiasm and zeal'. Operations also appeared to have been subject to restrictive and rigid directives, as illustrated by the withdrawal order sent to *Hipper* on 31 December.[71]

## The Casablanca Conference and its Impact on Aid to Russia

The Casablanca Conference (code name Symbol) which took place between 14 and 23 January 1943 was the third wartime conference bringing together the entire British and American political and military leaderships following the two Washington meetings, Arcadia the previous January and Argonaut in June. Casablanca marked a shift in attitudes to Russia and its support in several important respects. The conference coincided with the final stages of the Stalingrad battle and there was sufficient intelligence to show that the Germans had suffered a catastrophic defeat, not only in the destruction of their Sixth Army but in being pushed back across the whole southern front towards the starting point of the Blue offensive. This did not yet guarantee Russian victory – stalemate, even a separate peace, remained possible – but it did ensure Russia's survival. It accordingly meant that the purpose of future aid to Russia would not be to prevent her defeat but to boost her military effectiveness and war potential. From now on, the focus would steadily shift from weaponry to facilitating military mobility through transport, communications and logistic support, building industrial capacity, and meeting shortages of food and raw materials. The decline in the importance of weaponry rendered the Arctic route less critical and it was clear to planners at Casablanca that all the other routes now had considerable potential for expansion. For geographic reasons, given its ready access to the Pacific routes, the sheer scale of its resources but also the shifting composition of aid, Casablanca marked the point where the United States became the dominant provider of aid not just in promises but practical delivery. Nevertheless, it is important to stress that the shift in the composition of aid was gradual. Claims that 'hundreds of thousands of American cargo trucks and half-tracks motorised the Red Army's logistical train', enabling a 'relentless pace of advance throughout 1943 and 1944' are wide of the mark.[72] Only 75,000 trucks had reached Russia by the end of June 1943, well short of the First Protocol promise, and only 175,000 a year later.[73] Leaving the pace of shift aside, Roosevelt's commitment to continuing aid was still unambiguous. A week before the conference, he emphasised to Stimson, his Secretary for War, that the Army and Navy had both confirmed that sustaining Russia in the war was of 'cardinal importance'. Providing her with 'maximum' supplies was accordingly 'a basic factor in our strategy' and successfully meeting her needs still therefore of 'paramount importance'.[74]

Casablanca also obliged the Western Allies to accept the logical consequences of committing to Torch and CCS 94. They were now inexorably bound in to exploiting further opportunities in the

Mediterranean, specifically the invasion of Sicily (Operation Husky) in late summer, and resources were inadequate to support a cross-Channel attack in parallel. It would be sometime before Churchill and Roosevelt formally admitted this to Stalin and, in the meantime, his pressure for a 'second front' was stalled by reference to Mediterranean progress, an ever-heavier bombing offensive, promises of cross-Channel action in early autumn (although in reality this could only be large raids or a 'Sledgehead' type 'bridgehead' operation), and, above all, the major continuing aid programme. For Stalin, as the year progressed, desire for a true 'second front' was no longer driven by vital need to release German pressure but to save Soviet time and blood.

Against this background, the Casablanca conference agreed that the first charge against British–American shipping was defeat of the submarine menace and aid to Russia came next. However, there were qualifications built into to this second priority which ultimately dictated the pattern of Arctic convoy operations across the year and beyond. The first point was that 1943 started with a substantial backlog in deliveries promised under the Second Protocol. Only 50 per cent of those due for its first six months had been met. Three-quarters of overall protocol commitments were therefore due in the first half of the present year and, if commitments under a new protocol beginning 1 July were similar, then a further two-thirds of first-half supplies must be delivered by the end of the year. This was assessed to require 834 sailings (722 from the United States and 112 from the United Kingdom), 45 per cent via the Pacific route and 27.5 per cent each via the Persian Gulf and Arctic routes (the latter including all the British sailings). Meeting this target was possible but would require some reduction in troop movements from the United States to the United Kingdom (perhaps 100,000 men) and also assumed that United Nations monthly shipping losses would not exceed 2.6 per cent. Any new military or civil commitments would involve trade-offs against the protocols – hence the need to retain the clause in the present protocol that 'supply to Russia will not be continued at prohibitive cost to the United Nations effort'.[75]

In addition, Pound emphasised two problems with the Arctic route. First, from February onward, increasing daylight meant convoys were only possible in the face of a combined German threat, air, surface and U-boat, with a powerful destroyer force on the lines of PQ 18. This normally implied sixteen destroyers and eight lighter escorts. The Royal Navy could only find sufficient destroyers to support thirty-ship convoys at this level on a six to seven-week cycle. Secondly, the escort demands for Husky would require a two- to three-month suspension as with

Torch, beginning six weeks before the Husky start date. It followed that, if Husky took place on 1 August, then with Royal Navy resources alone, it would be possible to run four convoys of thirty ships between mid-February and mid-June on a 40-day cycle. Allowing for 20 per cent losses, ninety-six ships would reach Russia and, at an average of 7000 tons per ship, deliver 672,000 tons of supplies. This would be only 40 per cent of required deliveries, meaning the rest must be made up in the final quarter of the year. If sixteen American destroyers were also provided in this period, the cycle could be reduced to 27 days, allowing a fifth convoy and delivery of an extra 168,000 tons of supplies. King insisted that this remained impossible. There was already a shortage of Atlantic escorts and Husky demands would make this worse. New construction would only produce a small net gain towards the end of the year. This debate certainly underlined the resource costs in protecting the Arctic convoys. However, it also demonstrates that any claim that Pound now judged running summer convoys to be impossible is wrong. The issue was rather where scarce Royal Navy effort was best applied.

The prime minister and president, while recognising the pressures imposed by Husky, were reluctant to see further suspension on the Arctic route. By contrast. Hopkins, perhaps playing devil's advocate, argued for stopping traffic on this route completely. He saw scope to increase supplies substantially through Persia and Alaska, including weapons and munitions, a shift which Lieutenant General Brehon Somervell, responsible for delivering all American war supplies, thought possible. Hopkins also proposed negotiating increased quantities of aircraft, which would be attractive to the Russians and could be delivered through Alaska, while reducing other items previously passed via the Arctic. Cutting the Arctic route would save around 500,000 tons of shipping for use elsewhere and avoid significant cargo loss due to enemy action. This view undoubtedly had some support across the combined chiefs of staff. At the beginning of the conference, Marshall had already expressed concern about the cost/benefit of the Arctic convoys. It was within German power to make shipping losses here unacceptable and it was unnecessary to take 'excessive punishment' just to 'placate Stalin'. In the end, the desire of Churchill and Roosevelt to avoid damaging relations with Stalin and to underline the genuine importance they attached to Russia's contribution drove acceptance that the Arctic convoys would continue on Pound's schedule for the present. The Hopkins option was too radical at this stage and the Arctic passage remained the fastest for delivery. However, the increasing possibilities for substitution on other routes had been recognised and Pound and King probably left Casablanca convinced they would eventually win the argument that the Arctic route was too costly.[76]

## The Early 1943 Convoys and Second Suspension of the Arctic Route

Following the successful defence of JW 51B, the next convoy, JW 52, left Loch Ewe on 17 January, just under a month after its predecessor. It comprised fourteen ships, ten British and four American, and the British share of the cargo included 250 Hurricanes, 235 tanks, including 65 Churchills, 300 lorries and 55,000 tons of miscellaneous supplies.[77] It seems the Admiralty had been willing to sail up to twenty-eight ships in JW 52, either as a single convoy or, if Tovey insisted, once again in two halves. However, a week before departure the Ministry of War Transport could find only eighteen ships, subsequently reduced further to fourteen.[78] The escort and cover arrangements were therefore similar to JW 51B but the close escort was strengthened with an extra destroyer and the cruiser force increased to three, comprising the 8in *Berwick* and the 6in *Glasgow* and *Bermuda*. The cruisers this time were commanded by Rear Admiral Hamilton, making his first appearance back in the Arctic since PQ 17. Vice Admiral Fraser with the battleship *Anson* and cruiser *Sheffield* provided heavy support south-west of Bear Island against any sortie by *Tirpitz*, suspected to be potentially operational again following her refit at Trondheim, or indeed *Scharnhorst* which made her second attempt to exit the Baltic a week into the convoy's passage.

The damage to *Hipper* and wider turmoil around the future of the German heavy ships meant a surface strike against this convoy was never likely, although the British did not know that. In the event therefore, JW 52 had an easy and trouble-free journey. The weather was benign and the close escort was strong enough to beat off attempted U-boat and air attacks on 23 January by the now-weakened German forces without loss. By this time, most destroyers were being fitted with HF/DF, including the superior FH4 variant, and this now proved a crucial asset in the Arctic, as elsewhere, in both evading U-boats and forcing them down to permit an Asdic-directed attack. The one problem, highlighted by Hamilton, was the difficulty the convoy and cruiser force had keeping track of their relative positions which risked the latter being too far away to protect the convoy from an attacking surface force. Tovey thought this difficulty could in future be somewhat mitigated if each party reported their position when they knew they had been sighted by the enemy and would therefore give nothing away. Thirteen ships reached Kola on 27 January following one early return (the British *Empire Baffin*) due to mechanical difficulties. Two days later the westbound RA 52 with eleven ships sailed, timed to use the same close escort as had brought in JW 52. This convoy was also little troubled although it lost one ship to a U-boat.[79]

JW 53 was the first of Pound's thirty-ship convoys but was five short of this total due to loading delays when it left Loch Ewe on 15 February. Three ships followed next day but were forced to turn back temporarily by appalling weather. The same weather played havoc with the main convoy and its planned escort. Given the size of the convoy and the lengthening daylight, the close escort, under Captain Ian MacIntyre in the cruiser *Scylla*, was similar to that accompanying PQ 18. It comprised thirteen destroyers, the escort carrier *Dasher* with two more dedicated destroyers in attendance, three corvettes and two trawlers. *Dasher* was one of the five additional ships procured and converted by the Americans for the Royal Navy at the same time as *Avenger*, of which four were now operational. This escort compared with an ideal scale for Arctic convoys agreed at Casablanca of fifteen destroyers and two escort carriers. To guarantee two carriers for each convoy, six would have to be permanently allocated to the Home Fleet but the Royal Navy had only four at this time, projected to rise to eight by the end of April and eleven by the end of June.[80] The covering forces also equated to those for PQ 18, three cruisers under Burnett, and a heavy force under Tovey in *King George V* with another battleship, a cruiser and six more destroyers. Although it had been hoped to loan Tovey the fleet carrier *Formidable* from the Mediterranean to strengthen distant cover for this convoy, she could not be released.[81] By the time the convoy reached the vicinity of north-east Iceland, serious weather damage had forced the withdrawal of *Dasher*, the cruiser *Sheffield* and six merchantmen. However, from 20 February, the weather moderated allowing the partially-scattered convoy, now comprising twenty-two ships, to reform. This reconstitution owed much to skilful exploitation of *King George V*'s radar, another demonstration of how the British were steadily enhancing its operational value. Thereafter, although tracked by German reconnaissance, the convoy, like its predecessor, was never subject to serious attack. The substantial escort, again using HF/DF to great effect, kept the U-boats at bay and two weak bombing attacks were beaten off. For the reasons addressed earlier, German surface forces were not yet disposed to intervene either. The return convoy RA 53 with thirty ships was again timed sequentially, sailing from Kola two days after the arrival of JW 53 so that it could use the incoming escort. It was less fortunate. One ship was lost to U-boat attack while in convoy and two more after they became stragglers in a severe gale in which another ship foundered. Two of the U-boat victims, including *Executive* sunk in convoy, were achieved by Reinhart Reche's *U-255*. Reche had now sunk ten ships for 53,519 tons in the Arctic, including four from PQ 17, making him the highest scorer in the theatre.[82] Although nobody yet knew it, JW 53 and RA 53 were the last Arctic convoys for nine months.

The passage of the first four JW convoys and preparations for the fifth in the second half of March coincided with a period of growing warmth in the political relationship between the Western Allies and the Soviet Union. This was especially true of the personal exchanges between Churchill and Stalin. The victory at Stalingrad, promising a fundamental turn on the Eastern Front, the success of Torch, the potential of the bombing offensive, and the resumption of the convoys all had a positive impact which, for the present, overcame Soviet doubts over Western commitment to a true 'second front'. By mid-April, Clark Kerr reported that he had never seen Stalin in a 'sunnier temper' while, in London, Churchill confided to Maisky that 'we are much closer to one another than a year ago'.[83] This cordiality was less well-grounded than Churchill wanted to believe and did not survive the month. Furthermore, it coincided with a serious downswing in the operational and intelligence relationships, caused by a new bout of Soviet obstruction and security paranoia, which brought the always-tenuous goodwill of the British chiefs of staff to breaking point.

The two specific issues that came to a head in late February followed a series of disputes and arguments over arrangements for supporting the Arctic convoys, stretching back over six months. The primary source of tension lay in how many British personnel were required in North Russia to support the convoys. For security reasons, the Russians wanted numbers kept to a minimum, but they were also inevitably sensitive to any implication that British personnel and equipment were there to compensate for Soviet shortcomings. They therefore restricted the granting of visas, refused to allow personnel from visiting British ships to go ashore or sometimes even to transfer between ships, and obstructed delivery of vital stores and equipment for Royal Navy warships operating from the Northern ports, including that needed to repair damage. They even refused permission to land a hospital unit to treat convoy casualties. On 23 February, the Defence Committee asked the Foreign Secretary to raise these problems with Maisky. The British could justifiably claim that complex convoy operations were seriously hampered but their complaints were sometimes unnecessarily confrontational, thereby exacerbating rather than easing friction.[84]

The first new problem to arise in February was triggered by a British request to send two further Hampden torpedo squadrons to North Russia to help meet the increasing risk of German surface attack as the days lengthened (Operation Grenadine). On the British side this was viewed as a natural and non-controversial extension of the arrangements for PQ 18. The Russians initially accepted this deployment and several hundred personnel to support the force were en route when, on 20 February, they announced that no accommodation for them was available. They proposed that the Soviet air force take over responsibility for protecting the convoys with the Hampdens transferred for them to operate. This stipulation was unacceptable to the British chiefs of staff who had no confidence the aircraft would be prioritised to carefully orchestrated attacks on German heavy units. Nor would it be possible to implement the air/sea coordination and communication, essential for effective targeting, without months of training. British frustration turned to fury when the Russians further announced that two of four British radio transmitters at Polyarnoe and all those at Archangel must be closed down as should the 'meaconing' equipment used to mislead German aircraft through redirecting, rebroadcasting, or perverting radio navigation signals. The radio transmitters were used primarily to forward intercepts of German traffic to the United Kingdom for processing at Bletchley. Without these transmitters, intercepts would have to be routed via 30 Mission at Moscow creating unacceptable delay. As Admiral Miles stated, with this action the Russians had moved beyond 'mere irritation' to compromise the 'safety and operational control' of the convoys. After six months as head of 30 Mission, Miles had also complained forcefully to the chiefs of staff over the one-sidedness in the intelligence relationship. He did not advocate holding back essential information but argued that Britain should stop gifting material that was not directly relevant to the war effort. He also wanted more reciprocity in access between 30 Mission and the Soviet mission in London. On 25 February, the War Cabinet therefore instructed Eden to inform Maisky that, unless the Royal Air Force received the necessary facilities to operate the Hampden force, the continued running of the convoys would be reviewed.[85] Churchill was certainly ready to cancel the March convoy, while giving the Russians ten ships without crews but with escorts only as far as Bear Island, in order to make a point.

Eden saw Maisky the following day. He addressed not only the Hampden issue but also, reflecting the earlier discussion at the Defence Committee, the closure of the radio transmitters, which he argued posed an even greater threat to convoy operations, and the obstructive attitude which the British felt was undermining operations at the Russian ports. He emphasised that the new Hampden force differed from that deployed for PQ 18 in that it was intended to operate for six months throughout the summer season. He also underlined the costs the British had incurred to date in delivering the convoys: two cruisers, ten destroyers, six other warships and seventy-two merchant ships lost, along with 1000 Royal Navy and 500 Merchant Navy personnel killed.[86] Clark Kerr delivered a parallel message to Molotov. In response, the Russians gave some ground, agreeing to concede on the radio and meaconing issues but not the Hampdens. It is unlikely the demand to close the transmitters was approved by or even known to the Soviet naval authorities who had consistently emphasised that they valued SIGINT cooperation and evidently now quietly lobbied for it to continue. The demand probably originated within the Soviet security apparatus without awareness of the political and operational consequences and Molotov no doubt convinced Stalin that it was not worth disrupting the convoys on this issue. Nevertheless, the Soviet concessions were grudging and their whole response couched in litigious language totally inconsistent with effective operational cooperation in wartime.[87]

On the Hampdens there was no backing down, but during the first week of March some confusion emerged in the British position. It became apparent that the Admiralty and Air Ministry had never seen the Hampdens as essential to the March convoy since weather in this month would probably limit their operational effectiveness. Indeed, Air Marshal John Slessor, the Assistant Chief of the Air Staff and from early February Commander-in-Chief Coastal Command, was sceptical the deployment made any sense at all. He did not rate the Hampden an effective daytime torpedo bomber, they were ill-suited to Arctic conditions and would be difficult to support. He anticipated high casualties for negligible benefit. Given these doubts and questions, threatening immediate suspension of the convoys was premature. The War Cabinet therefore agreed that the March convoy, JW 54, should sail as planned, leaving time to negotiate a face-saving agreement before the next convoy in May. In fact, the Russians had a point about numbers. The Air Ministry originally sought approval for 400–500 personnel but then upped the requirement to 750 which seemed excessive to support a maximum of thirty-five aircraft.[88]

In early March therefore, despite this 'February crisis' and its wider reservations over the challenges posed by the Arctic route, the Admiralty remained committed to the 40-day convoy schedule agreed at Casablanca.[89] JW 54 would leave the United Kingdom with thirty ships on 23 March and a further thirty ships would follow on 3 May. However, the further convoy planned for 11 June had now been deferred until the autumn after the launch of Husky was brought forward to early July although nothing had been said to the Russians on this. Ismay confirmed to the prime minister on 10 March that the chiefs of staff endorsed this programme. Their only caveats were insistence that the Hampden force must be in place under British control for the May convoy and that the deployment of 'really strong' German forces to 'North Cape' (i.e. Altafiord) would alter the risk equation.[90] The prime minister responded that he was not yet ready to abandon a June convoy. The Hampden case would be strengthened with the Russians if the aircraft were clearly covering more than one convoy and he was willing to press the president again for destroyers.[91]

On the afternoon of 16 March, three days after this exchange, the prime minister received a minute from First Lord A V Alexander which radically changed the Admiralty position. This drew on Enigma decrypts received over the last two days.[92] Alexander reported that *Tirpitz*, *Scharnhorst*, *Lützow*, one 6in cruiser (*Nürnberg*) and eight destroyers were now concentrated at Narvik. There were also fifteen U-boats in Arctic waters and significant air strike units remained in northern Norway even if reduced from the previous summer. The ice edge was now at its furthest south, meaning the Bear Island channel was only 200 miles wide, rendering the option of a PQ 17 type dispersal impossible. By the time JW 54 sailed, there would be no period of complete darkness. It was wise to assume that Dönitz as new Commander-in-Chief was prepared to use his surface units aggressively. In these circumstances, similar escort arrangements to those provided for the four previous JW convoys were inadequate. To provide sufficient protection, it would be necessary to send the Home Fleet battle group and a carrier into the Barents Sea and possibly a battleship escort all the way to Murmansk. In the Admiralty view, potential U-boat and air attack rendered this option unacceptably risky. Leaving aside loss or damage to Royal Navy heavy ships, deployment into the Barents Sea would take the Home Fleet 'out of position' for an extended period giving the Germans scope to mount Atlantic raids. Significant destroyer attrition was also probable, prejudicing escort forces needed for Husky. In these circumstances, the Admiralty judged the March convoy must be cancelled.[93]

Alexander's submission was addressed in detail at the Defence Committee meeting the same night. The prime minister reluctantly bowed to Admiralty advice and accepted that suspension of JW 54 was probably inevitable. However, he advocated, and the committee agreed, that the convoy should sail to a point 150 miles short of Bear Island in the hope of luring the Germans out to be engaged by the Home Fleet or targeted with submarines and minelaying. If the Germans suffered attrition or reacted cautiously, it might be safe for the convoy to continue. Otherwise, it would return to Iceland. Stalin and the Americans would be briefed on these lines.[94] The extensive discussion left an odd omission. If a 'fighting destroyer escort' had been judged adequate to deter a similar German surface strike force from attacking PQ 18, it was not clear why the JW 54 position was fundamentally different. A PQ 18 scale of escort had, after all, just been provided for JW 53. It was true that ice conditions in March were less favourable than September but the air threat was now less. Meanwhile, it is unlikely either Pound or Tovey found the 'luring' plan credible. Since the prospect of the Germans buying it was low, it implied expending considerable escort resources for no benefit. Pound revealed his real opinion by saying 'we had run twenty-three convoys through to Russia in circumstances which had never justified their sailing'. 'We could not in the present state of the U-boat war' deploy the Home Fleet to escort the convoy and risk an enemy breakout causing 'havoc' in the Atlantic.

Indeed, the deteriorating position in the Atlantic U-boat war now influenced the JW 54 decision as much as the threat from the German heavy ships. In briefing the War Cabinet on 18 March on the outcome of the Defence Committee, the prime minister stated that the decision to cancel JW 54 was now reinforced by the 'severe losses' in the Atlantic with twenty ships sunk in two days. Royal Navy resources were 'stretched to the uttermost' with the Atlantic escort force inadequate to meet the current U-boat threat. The Cabinet therefore endorsed the prime minister's view that the Arctic convoys should now be suspended, probably until the autumn after Husky, to concentrate forces on the Atlantic lifeline. It was later estimated that the cancellation of JW 54 enabled the release of one escort carrier and twenty-seven assorted escorts to form Atlantic support groups.[95] Although the 'luring' plan lingered for some days, the need to transfer the maximum possible escorts from the Home Fleet to Western Approaches, formally approved by the prime minister by 22 March, rendered its abandonment inevitable.[96] As Churchill said three days later to Eden, currently visiting Washington, persisting with the 'lure' achieved 'the worst of both worlds', Stalin's displeasure and no relief in the Battle of the Atlantic.[97] Furthermore, by 24 March, Enigma decrypts revealed that the German heavy ships had moved to Altafiord and that intensive reconnaissance patrols were being flown in the belief that a JW convoy was imminent.[98]

On 18 March, in parallel with the War Cabinet meeting, Churchill briefed Roosevelt on the implications of the German concentration at Narvik. The issue now, which provoked intense debate both within Whitehall and across the Atlantic over the next 10 days, was how to inform Stalin not only that JW 54 was cancelled but that there would probably be no more convoys before September. This 'double blow' would follow the latest message from Stalin received three days earlier which criticised slow

Anglo-American progress in North Africa, emphasised the strain imposed by the German post-Stalingrad counter-offensive leading to their recapture of Kharkov on 14 March, and reiterated 'how dangerous' would be any further delay in opening a second front in France.[99] Roosevelt agreed there was 'no military justification' for proceeding with JW 54 but he initially argued that conveying the bad news to Stalin should be phased by delaying 'three or four weeks' before notifying him of the longer Husky-related suspension.[100] Cadogan counselled strongly against this phasing. He convinced the prime minister that it would be more disruptive to Russian planning if they continued counting on future convoy deliveries for a further month, thereby increasing Stalin's annoyance when he was eventually let down. Furthermore, apparently only discovering Husky disruption at the last minute would look either incompetent or deceitful. And sudden silence on the Hampden issue after Eden's forceful representations would look like a climbdown which was undesirable. Finally, there was no reason why Stalin would take suspension better later on. A clean breast now might be a shock but prevarication would imply dishonesty and foster suspicion. This was good advice which the prime minister found compelling. In telling Eden to lobby Roosevelt accordingly, he agreed 'we might just as well be hanged for a sheep as a lamb'.[101]

Churchill nevertheless despatched the final message to Stalin on 30 March with considerable nervousness. As finally drafted, the primary focus was the cancellation of JW 54 and the revelation that there would be no more convoys until the autumn was buried in the third paragraph. Against Roosevelt's advice, this was softened slightly with an ambiguous sentence implying the possibility of an early May convoy was still open. It was also softened with a paragraph emphasising a maximum effort on the Persian route with a promise to raise monthly capacity to 240,000 tons by August. In the event, the autumn rate was 25 per cent short of this figure. Churchill asked Roosevelt to send a supporting message in parallel but the president demurred, not for the first or last time content to let Churchill take the flak. To Churchill's huge relief, and the surprise of Maisky who anticipated something sharper, Stalin's response on 2 April was resigned rather than angry. According to Maisky's account, Churchill was almost euphoric in his relief, describing the response as 'magnanimous' and 'courageous'. This was probably complacent. The reply was short and certainly devoid of obvious emotion but it still described 'this unexpected action' as a 'catastrophic diminution of supplies of arms and military raw materials' which 'cannot fail to affect the position of the Soviet troops'.

He was equally clear that he did not expect the Pacific and Persian routes to deliver adequate compensation.[102]

Although, several times in the coming days Churchill proposed resurrecting a May convoy, the logistic complexities and continuing escort demands in the Atlantic meant this was never likely.[103] The demands posed by Husky and successor operations in the Mediterranean also inevitably delayed the resumption of the JW convoys. It would be seven and a half months before the next one sailed and for most of the interregnum quiet descended on the Arctic theatre. However, it was not entirely forgotten by the Admiralty. The problem of the German heavy ships remained and this was now their primary focus.

*The Overall Impact of the Winter 1942–3 Deliveries via the Arctic Route*

The decision to suspend the Arctic convoys coincided with two Joint Intelligence Committee assessments published in mid-March which reviewed military prospects on the Eastern Front and Soviet capabilities. There is no evidence that these directly influenced the decision to suspend the convoys. Their preparation was not driven by any perceived urgent need to reassess Russia's prospects, still less the impact of Western aid. They contributed to a review by the Joint Planning Staff into the likely evolution of German strength in France through the rest of the year. However, the assessments undoubtedly shaped the underlying attitude of British political and military leaders and reassured them that the costs of suspension were manageable. They probably also fed a perception within the chiefs of staff, and certainly Pound, that aid to Russia was discretionary rather than essential, especially the major weapon items going via the Arctic. The committee judged that current German counter-attacks had stabilised their position in the south. However, the Germans would struggle to make good their manpower and material losses over the winter, were chronically short of oil and faced acute transport difficulties. The Russians had also suffered heavy losses but they had numerical advantage and now superior air power. Little was known of their overall war resources but they appeared adequate. Looking ahead, the least favourable outcome for the Allies was for the Germans to stem further Russian advances and improve their position in the summer with a limited offensive. However, this was unlikely to repeat the early gains of Blue and the prospect of Germany defeating Russia 'had receded to vanishing point'.[104]

Assessing Russia's wider situation, the committee judged that industrial output was still one-third below pre-war output and inadequacies of the transport system limited economic recovery as did shortages of certain key raw materials and commodities. In fact, this was too pessimistic. Industrial output was now rising fast and over the full year would end nearly 5 per cent above the immediate pre-war level.[105] The committee did recognise that the oil and steel situation had improved, helped by improved communication with the Caucasus, and Western aid shipments would further sustain the war effort and ensure food was sufficient until the next harvest. Civilian morale was high, spurred by recent victories, the impact of German atrocities and a relatively mild winter. Unless there was an unexpected deterioration in the military situation, this should maintain production and services behind the front. The committee was close to reality on key areas of weapons production. Overall munitions production was put at 100 to 110 per cent of pre-war output but was qualitatively and quantitatively much higher for certain weapons. Output of tanks and combat aircraft was correctly estimated at about 2000 per month with a growing proportion of medium tanks and fighters and light bombers.[106]

The Americans judged this Joint Intelligence Committee picture too optimistic, as initially did the British chiefs of staff. As the Americans saw it, the British now viewed Soviet military strength as 'markedly superior' to German, with numerical superiority in the field and economic potential still growing while Germany's was declining. United States military intelligence believed Germany could easily replace its losses and launch extensive renewed offensives against the Red Army. It thought the British overestimated Soviet strength and underestimated German. The Americans accepted that Soviet military strength would probably 'at least equal' German in the summer but Soviet economic 'staying power' was deteriorating faster than German.[107] German intelligence, represented by Foreign Armies East, was not so sanguine. On 1 April, it estimated that the Red Army had almost twice as many men as Germany's eastern army and three to four times as much artillery and tanks. By any standard, this was a grim picture and, as regards tanks, it still seriously underestimated Soviet superiority. At this time actual Soviet front-line tank strength was 4882 compared to a German figure of 2755. Although Hitler tended to ignore Gehlen and not everyone in the German military leadership accepted his figures, Colonel General Kurt Zeitzler, who had replaced Halder as Chief of Army Staff the previous September, certainly did. He also understood that Germany's comparative strength must deteriorate and this would be exacerbated by the impact of Western supplies.[108]

Stalin's low-key soundings regarding a separate peace which apparently began primarily in Sweden at this time and lasted until June seem inconsistent with this growing advantage in Soviet fighting power.[109]

However, the Russians, like the Americans, overestimated German strength and powers of recovery after their winter setbacks. German ability to create a powerful counter-offensive, seemingly out of nowhere, to retake Kharkov and inflict devastating losses amply demonstrated this resilience. Stalin probably now had guarded confidence that he could certainly win but that the road to victory would be long and bloody, all the more so if, as he feared, the Western Allies let him down and there was no proper second front. A victory which sapped Russia's strength, leaving her exhausted, could only benefit the West. There were thus motives here to explore possibilities, leaving aside the opportunity to exert pressure on the Western Powers and win political and military concessions. Churchill was right therefore to worry about the impact of suspending the convoys.[110]

Given this background, the four outbound convoys over the period December–February had comprised seventy-two ships, of which sixty-five reached the Russian ports with seven turning back following weather damage or mechanical failure. The three return convoys comprised fifty-five ships of which five were lost, four to U-boats and one sunk in a storm. The sixty-five arrivals equated exactly to the combined total arrivals of the three previous convoys PQs 16–18. The four new convoys delivered a maximum of 300,000 tons of cargo, about the same as the three preceding ones, and one-quarter of this load comprised weapons. Although Britain provided less than half the merchant ships, about 90 per cent of the overall cargo was loaded in the United Kingdom although much originated from the United States. This reflected the backlog built up in the United Kingdom following the suspension and the unloading of some American ships transferred from Iceland. But, in addition, only 57,178 tons of supplies destined for the Arctic ports were shipped from North America in the four months September to December. The headline military items in the latest convoys included approximately 450 British Hurricanes and 500 American fighters, mainly Airacobras, 50 American bombers, about 1000 tanks, 800 British/Canadian, the rest American split between Lees and M4A2 Shermans, 15,000 lorries and 5000 jeeps, mainly American. At the beginning of April 1943, following these winter convoys and 18 months from the beginning of the First Protocol, Britain and Canada had delivered 5 per cent less aircraft but 10 per cent more tanks to Russia than had the United States. Admittedly half the American aircraft deliveries were bombers while those from Britain were almost entirely fighters but nearly half the American tanks were Stuarts of little military value. Seventy-eight per cent of British aircraft deliveries and 86 per cent of British/Canadian tank deliveries had been via the Arctic while American deliveries had been split almost evenly between the Arctic and Iran.

Judged against the overall PQ record, as shown in Appendix 2, these initial JW convoys were a respectable contribution although the nil loss rate to enemy action was clearly influenced by mid-winter conditions and reduced German air and U-boat forces. However, set against the original schedule for Second Protocol deliveries on the Arctic route, the outcome was less positive. The Arctic route was supposed to contribute 3.3 million tons over the year from 1 July 1942, or 275,000 tons per month. The four JW convoys had therefore delivered just over one month's planned deliveries over the three months December to February. Furthermore, the arrival of JW 53 marked the effective end of Second Protocol deliveries via the Arctic. When the contributions of PQ 18 and the independent sailings are added, it seems total Second Protocol deliveries on this route did not exceed 300,000 tons, just over 9 per cent of its original target. These Arctic deliveries were therefore only about 10.3 per cent of the overall Second Protocol outcome of 2.9 million tons, in turn two-thirds of the original target of 4.4 million tons, with the Pacific and Persian routes eventually making up the rest in a ratio of 1.5:1.[111]

It is therefore easy to argue that the Arctic supplies delivered over the six months September 1942 to February 1943 contributed little to Russia's fighting capability or war potential and did not justify the Royal Navy resources expended. The argument increasingly put by Pound and his colleagues that this was essentially a political rather than military operation seems justified. The reality is more complex. Although shipments to the Persian Gulf expanded significantly in the second half of 1942 and were at least 60 per cent greater than via the Arctic in the six months from September, port handling and onward land transport could not cope with the rate of arrivals. At the end of January 1943, there was a backlog of 175,000 tons awaiting discharge and this only started to reduce a month later. It follows that overall quantities, including aircraft and tanks, actually reaching Russian users via the two routes over the six months to the end of March were not much different.[112]

If the Arctic remained important for weapons, their quality and therefore value can still be questioned. Over half the fighters shipped via the Arctic under the Second Protocol were Hurricanes, nearly 60 per cent of the tanks were still Valentines and Matildas, and the remaining 40 per cent were mainly Churchills and Lees, both poorly regarded by the Russians. The approximately 200 Churchills which arrived via the Arctic by the end of February 1943 were predominantly early models and this accounts for a long list of shortcomings and 'unfinished' quality identified by the Russians. However, they commended the Churchill's armour, judged its 6-pounder gun adequate and accepted that its average speed was comparable to a KV-1. Importantly, they still judged it capable of fighting any current German tank.[113] For all their criticisms, the Russians relied on Western weapons for specific tasks and in particular theatres. They also appreciated consistent construction quality, engine reliability, and internal fittings like radios. Thus, although the 600 Hurricanes reaching the Russian air forces over the six months to the end of February represented 3.5 per cent of the combined receipts of fighter aircraft from domestic production and Western supplies during 1943, over 800 Hurricanes were on average deployed in the PVO fighter defence force in the first half of the year. This was more than any other aircraft type and comprised 25 per cent of its strength. They were also still the primary fighter used by the Northern Fleet Air Force. Furthermore, fighter attrition this year remained huge with the equivalent of the total stock at the beginning of the year (11,600 aircraft) lost by its end. Western deliveries across all supply routes in 1943 represented nearly 24 per cent of the total new fighter supplies, their peak share in the war. Furthermore, the Western share of medium bombers was twice this proportion. Western aircraft aid therefore still mattered hugely. Even in June 1944, Western aircraft comprised half of the PVO inventory of 2790 fighters in Russia's Western theatres.[114]

Russian tank production in 1943 averaged 1660 per month, with two-thirds the excellent T-34. Western supplies added 3000 over the full year with about half delivered via the Arctic. Their share of combined total Red Army receipts was therefore just over 13 per cent, the highest proportion reached in the war, although the share of medium tank receipts was nearly 18 per cent. Despite the prolific Soviet output, with domestic production alone twice that of Germany, attrition of the Soviet army tank force remained high. Total losses over the year of 22,400 almost matched combined domestic and Western receipts of 22,900 and were four times that of their German opponent. Within this figure, 14,700 medium tanks were lost out of 16,300 received.[115] The 1000 tanks delivered in the first four JW convoys equated to just about 10 per cent of total heavy/medium tank stock in the middle of the year. The quality shortfall in firepower compared to T-34s and KV-1s, albeit compensated by greater reliability, meant their contribution was not critical. Nevertheless, they could be expended in defence to conserve more valuable T-34s, while the Valentines were rated above the T-70 for reconnaissance as well as infantry support and training. Not least, Western tanks helped the Soviet tank force to keep slowly growing despite its enormous losses.

The continuing importance of Western tanks is evident in a report from Gehlen's Foreign Armies East at the beginning of June. Ninety-six identified Red Army tank brigades were composed solely of Soviet-produced tanks, twenty-one had only Western tanks, while thirty-one were mixed. A month later, at the start of the Battle of Kursk, there were 375 Western tanks assigned to the Central and Voronezh Fronts, about 12 per cent of the total tank force there. Many of the Western heavy/medium tanks present had arrived in the JW convoys over the winter. They included forty-two Churchills, fifty Valentines, eighteen Matilda IIs, some 150 American Lees, thirty-eight of the newer M4A2 Sherman medium tanks, and seventy-seven Stuarts. The Churchills provided the sole unit of 'heavy tanks' in the 5th Guards Tank Army. The SS Panzer Corps met these and destroyed many on 12 July at the famous battle of Prokhorovka. Lees, some from earlier 1942 convoys, were also deployed and destroyed in large numbers on the southern front at Kursk, making up possibly 20 per cent of Soviet tank casualties in the opening days of Fourth Panzer Army's assault. This rather justified the pejorative term 'a grave for seven brothers' given to them but it also illustrated the deliberate tendency to expend less valuable Western tanks to wear the Germans down. The first M4 Shermans had arrived with PQ 18 but with the Torch convoy suspension it took a while for stocks to build up and they were not initially popular because of their height and perceived poor-quality armour. Views changed at Kursk where the Sherman won praise for its ease of operation, manoeuvrability, reliability and the penetration power of its high-velocity 75mm gun. The latter outranged the guns of the German Panzer IV and Panther. Above all it was durable and low maintenance at a time when there were growing quality-control problems with the T-34. Even after improvements to T-34 production, the Sherman was rated several times more durable which was important in the long offensives of 1944–5, and a total of 3664 was delivered between PQ 18 and the end of the war, almost all via the Arctic.[116]

## Chapter 11
# The Destruction of the German Battlefleet

With the JW convoys suspended until the autumn, the main threat posed by the German northern task force through the summer months was an Atlantic breakout by some or all of its elements. This was the dominant preoccupation of the Home Fleet under its new commander Admiral Sir Bruce Fraser who relieved Tovey in May. Fraser had served nearly a year as Tovey's deputy, enjoyed his full confidence and was the logical successor. He was equally well regarded by Pound, having served as the latter's chief of staff in the Mediterranean 1938–9 before becoming Controller and Third Sea Lord six months before the outbreak of war. Fraser shared many qualities with Somerville, notably a mastery of new technology and how to use it to best effect, and an attractive, unflappable leadership style that inspired the trust and enthusiastic commitment of all who worked for him. He perhaps lacked the hard driving ruthlessness of Cunningham which contributed to some clashes when the latter became First Sea Lord from September 1943, but his intelligence and innate understanding of people enabled him to get the best out of difficult and aggressive subordinates such as Vian.[1]

Through the summer, Fraser's margin over the German force, had they been deployed into the Atlantic with creativity and skill, was small. The commitments to Husky, the requirement to begin rebuilding an Eastern Fleet, and the loan of *Victorious* to the Americans in the Pacific, meant there were rarely more than two of the Royal Navy's modern battleships available and hardly ever a fleet carrier. The continuing pressures of Atlantic escort also meant he remained chronically short of destroyers. Fortunately, as in the previous summer, the US Navy provided valuable additional support, two battleships between May and July, replaced in August by the old light carrier *Ranger* and two heavy cruisers. These force limitations did not prevent Fraser attempting to lure the Germans out. He sortied with a substantial Anglo-American force in late May to cover delivery of supplies to the weather station in Spitzbergen and mounted two deliberately provocative feints off the north Norwegian coast in early July to focus German attention on the threat to Norway while Husky got underway. These forays enjoyed the rare presence of a fleet carrier, first *Furious* and then *Illustrious*. The Germans made no response either with their surface units or by air beyond reconnaissance. The operations did demonstrate that, with reduced German fighter strength, the carriers now fully equipped with Martlet fighters and Coastal Command long-range Beaufighters also available in strength, Home Fleet units could operate off Norway with considerable confidence.[2]

Meanwhile definitive intelligence on the future state and intentions of the German surface fleet remained lacking. Rumours of decommissioning garnered from prisoners of war had some support from Enigma decrypts which confirmed there was a drastic comb-out of personnel to crew the U-boat fleet including the requirement for extra numbers to man the additional anti-aircraft armament being introduced to combat the Coastal Command offensive in the Bay of Biscay. With only occasional short breaks, Enigma decrypts also kept the OIC well-informed on the specific activities of the heavy ships in Altafiord from their arrival in late March to the end of the year. All the evidence here suggested they were maintaining their readiness for action. Meanwhile, in the Baltic, although *Prinz Eugen*, *Scheer* and the remaining light cruisers were mainly occupied in training U-boats, they still appeared capable of operational deployment. NID therefore concluded that Dönitz wanted to keep the surface fleet in 'a high state of battle efficiency'.[3] Nevertheless, by mid-May, Pound doubted the Germans would contemplate an Atlantic breakout during the short nights of summer. They knew it would be difficult to avoid detection by Allied air surveillance and there was no sign of necessary pre-positioning of tankers and supply ships. He thought they would be content to sit in the North threatening the convoy route and tying down Home Fleet resources from there at least until the autumn.[4]

At the end of June, Fraser therefore reviewed the prospects for resuming the JW convoys in September, the earliest time that he felt light and ice conditions would be suitable. He did not believe the present overall threat had changed since the decision to suspend the convoys in March. German air strength was less but their reconnaissance capability remained as good as ever. U-boat strength was also down but still sufficient for effective action in the restricted waters of the Barents Sea. However, German surface strength was greater than at any previous time and cruiser reinforcements were available in the Baltic. In Fraser's view, unless the surface threat could be reduced, further convoys were only justified if supplies by the Arctic route were judged vital to Russia's prosecution of the war, or they enabled the Germans successfully to be brought to action. From the information available to him, he did not believe the convoys were vital and he did not believe the Germans would put to sea unless they were confident there was no risk of Home Fleet interception, or a heavy covering force had been sufficiently damaged by submarine or air attack to permit an engagement on favourable terms. It followed that, for Fraser, the naval effort required to mount each convoy was not justified by the benefit. If the decision was nevertheless to resume, then the scale of forces deployed in protection must at a minimum match that for PQ 18, including equivalent Royal Air Force reconnaissance and strike support.[5]

## *Evolving Anglo-American Strategy in Spring 1943*

Fraser's scepticism over the benefits from a renewed series of Arctic convoys reflected Tovey's long-standing position and was consistent with Pound's remark to the Defence Committee on 16 March. However, it contrasted sharply with the importance the British chiefs of staff attached to supporting Russia during the latest Anglo-American summit (Trident) held in Washington the previous month. In the run-up to the summit, the Joint Intelligence Committee had hardened its assessment that Germany's overall strength in Russia had declined markedly compared to the previous two summers and that they could only contemplate a limited offensive in one sector of the front. The most probable option now was an attack at the end of May or in June to bite off the Soviet salient around Kursk where they were gathering twenty armoured divisions. This would significantly shorten their line and restore the position held at the end of 1941.[6] Brooke concurred with this view. German strategy on the Eastern Front in 1943 would be an 'offensive-defensive' with limited aims but could still be damaging. He and Churchill therefore argued that the Western Allies must help Russia by stretching Germany's resources further through action in the Mediterranean, Husky and subsequent operations, threatening the collapse of Italy, and forcing withdrawal of troops from the East. Churchill noted that, despite the suspension of the Arctic convoys, Stalin had for the first time publicly acknowledged Western efforts and support. Nevertheless, Russia's contribution was 'prodigious' and the Western Allies remained firmly in her debt. It was therefore important not to remain inactive on land between the successful capture of Sicily and a spring 1944 Roundup. Meanwhile Brooke also stressed that the success of Roundup next spring required further prior weakening of German strength which in turn depended heavily on Russian progress. A cross-

Channel attack was inevitably initially confined to a narrow frontage where the Germans on interior lines could reinforce more quickly – hence reducing their power was essential. In sum, Roundup was only one part of a wider continental war and supporting Russia through Mediterranean wear-down and through aid was essential to make it possible.[7]

The American chiefs were not convinced that further offensive operations against Italy after taking Sicily would deliver sufficient benefit to justify the investment. They judged the collapse of Italy less important to Germany than the defeat of Russia and that nothing the Western Allies could achieve in the Mediterranean would sway her actions in the East. Nor did they accept the elimination of Italy was a prerequisite for Roundup. On the contrary, further operations against Italy would suck in critical resources at the expense of the main effort in the West.[8] In the end, there was compromise. Some forces would be withdrawn from the Mediterranean but General Dwight Eisenhower, the Allied Commander-in-Chief, could plan and propose new operations following a successful Husky aimed at eliminating Italy and containing the maximum number of German forces. The forces left in the Mediterranean for such operations and for garrison commitments were substantial – about 27 divisions, over 1000 bombers, 2000 fighters and 400 transport aircraft. This continuing Mediterranean commitment over the next year was consistent with one of the Trident summit's overarching goals – to take all necessary and practicable measures to aid Russia's war effort. This in turn included supplying and transporting the greatest volume of munitions possible without compromising overall Western objectives.[9]

Brooke's reading of Germany's position and intentions in Russia for summer 1943 was certainly right. Their offensive in the south, Citadel, which the Joint Intelligence Committee had correctly identified would focus on the Kursk salient, was essentially a giant spoiling operation to disrupt and destroy a significant part of Russia's anticipated offensive strategy in 1943. Brooke was also right in seeing a link with Italy. Hitler fully recognised Italy's vulnerability to collapse and hoped Citadel could exploit a narrow window before this happened. The success of Citadel would then permit withdrawals of key forces to shore up Italy. In the event, the operation failed and Husky made those withdrawals necessary at the worst possible time, leaving the Germans vulnerable to the Russian counter-offensives. However, American fears that Italy might become a quagmire, drawing in too many resources for too little additional gain, were also correct.

In addition to the Husky withdrawals, Western support made two other important contributions to the defeat of Citadel. British intelligence, primarily SIGINT decrypts of German traffic, delivered officially in sanitised summaries and unofficially in raw form by the Russian agent Captain John Cairncross who worked at Bletchley, gave the Russians valuable insights into German plans and their knowledge of Soviet defences. The value of Cairncross's contribution was later acknowledged in internal Soviet assessments and he was awarded a high-level decoration.[10] Secondly, as already noted, Western tanks were expended to conserve superior Soviet T-34s for counter-offensive operations. Neither of these contributions was decisive to the defeat of Citadel and the Husky withdrawals took place after the German effort had culminated. However, the defeat of Citadel and the subsequent counter-offensives were very costly. During the German attack phase between 5–17 July, the Soviets lost perhaps six times more tanks and three times more personnel than their opponent. Over the whole of July and August, Soviet tank losses may have exceeded 6000, 50 per cent more than production in those months. Western support undoubtedly made this price less than it would otherwise have been.[11]

*Operations to Target Tirpitz*

At the time he wrote his June review, Fraser could hardly be expected to have much insight into Citadel whose launch was anyway still a week away. However, Pound could have done more to summarise the Trident debates and conclusions and, above all, the rationale for a continuing effort to maximise aid to Russia. What Fraser did know was that a major operation to reduce, or even eliminate, the threat from the heavy ships in Altafiord was in advanced preparation. This was Operation Source which aimed to use innovative new midget submarines to target primarily *Tirpitz* but also *Scharnhorst* and *Lützow*. At this point, proposals for targeting *Tirpitz*, using various forms of attack, stretched back almost 18 months. Indeed, the prime minister began pressing for action against her with the chiefs of staff on 25 January 1942, just 10 days after her initial arrival in Trondheim. With characteristic hyperbole, he insisted that a successful attack would 'alter the entire naval situation throughout the world'.[12] Before the end of the month, John Godfrey, the DNI, was also pressing for ideas no matter how far-fetched. On 4 March, five weeks after his first intervention, the prime minister demanded to know why no attempt had yet been made to bomb her. Portal explained the difficulties. She was berthed under the shadow of cliffs and well camouflaged on the northern side of Faettenfiord, a small arm off Aasfiord, 20 miles northeast of Trondheim city, with anti-aircraft protection on the same scale as that provided for the battlecruisers at Brest, and fighters available nearby at Vaernes. Despite extensive PR sorties flown over the Trondheim area from 18 January after SIGINT and agent reports of her arrival, it had taken five days to spot her well-concealed berth. The German defences made daylight air attack suicidal while the problems of night navigation and target spotting exacerbated by German use of smokescreens were formidable. The geography of the berth and protective nets also ruled out airborne torpedo attack. *Tirpitz* would therefore have to be tackled by bombing but could only be reached by Halifax and Stirling bombers operating from Lossiemouth in north-east Scotland. These conducted an initial raid on the night of 29/30 January, a round trip of some 2500 miles, but only one aircraft found the battleship and there were no hits.[13]

A more sophisticated bombing operation was mounted on 30 March two weeks after *Tirpitz*'s return from the PQ 12 sortie. This comprised thirty-four of the latest Halifax aircraft with some armed with innovative aerial mines designed to be dropped just short of the target so that they rolled underneath. Bad weather obscured the target, there was again no damage and six aircraft were lost. An even more complex operation involving more than forty aircraft from five squadrons, including twelve of the new Lancasters, was executed a month later on the night of 27 April. The core tactic, dropping Mark XIX spherical aerial bombs in the narrow space between the cliff and battleship, was almost impossible to achieve. As Pound told the prime minister, it was the maritime equivalent of bombing a slit trench and, by this time, the Germans had added smoke generators to obscure *Tirpitz*. Furthermore, the explosive charge in the mines was too small to inflict serious underwater damage while the heavy 4000lb blast bombs had unsuitable fuses for penetrating her heavy armoured deck. They could only do superficial damage to the superstructure. Thus, despite heroic efforts, once again nothing was achieved and six aircraft lost. A repeat raid the following night did no better.[14]

With bombing seemingly ineffective, the Admiralty looked to alternative methods. Distance and technology posed two linked challenges here. First, in choosing berths for their heavy ships in Norway, the Germans exploited the navigable length of the fiords to make hostile access as difficult as possible. Secondly, as the Royal Air Force emphasis on aerial mines already demonstrated, the only sure means of inflicting crippling damage on a heavily-protected battleship like *Tirpitz* was through underwater attack on the lower hull below the armoured belt, which was immensely difficult to achieve in a well-defended anchorage. There was an obvious recent precedent for such an attack in the operation by the Italian two-man submersibles which had disabled the battleships *Valiant* and *Queen Elizabeth* in Alexandria harbour the previous December.[15] Although Churchill is often credited with pushing for a similar British capability a month after this attack, the British were already well aware of this weapon, which the Italians called Siluro a Lenta Corsa (SLC), prior to Alexandria.[16] They had captured one intact following an abortive attack at Gibraltar two months earlier, although it was the Army rather than the Admiralty that initially commissioned work on creating a replica with the intention of using it during commando raids on the West European coast. However, by the end of the year, Admiral Sir Max Horton, Admiral Submarines, had recognised the potential of the 'Chariot' or 'human torpedo', as the British preferred to call it, for targeting Axis naval targets and an order for six Chariots had been placed by the end of January. By late March, he had also established a team to oversee their development and operational exploitation. Six months later two Chariot versions and four trained crews were available for operations. The Mark I, 20ft long, weighing 1.5 tons and capable of diving to 90ft, could convey a 600lb charge 12.5 miles at 2.5 knots. The Mark II at 30ft long was 50 per cent larger, twice as fast and carried a 1000lb warhead nearly 25 miles.[17]

In parallel with the Chariot project, another initiative got underway to address the *Tirpitz* problem, stimulated by Godfrey's call for ideas and continuing prime-ministerial pressure. Initially sponsored by SOE, this was a variant of the Chariot concept. It was essentially a one-man mini-submarine capable of delivering a similar 500lb detachable charge but with the operator inside rather than astride, thus avoiding the need to wear diving gear. SOE envisaged that the craft might be taken into Trondheim fiord by a fishing vessel before being clandestinely released for its final run to the target. The operation, soon designated Frodesley, would also draw on the sabotage group (Lark) which SOE was establishing in the Trondheim area. It was soon clear that development of the Frodesley vehicle was beyond SOE's capability and the concept therefore again passed to Horton. Although development proceeded, and a prototype was under trial by the end of the year leading to a production run in 1943, the Welman as it became was never operationally satisfactory. It lacked a periscope, making covert navigation problematic, and it had no means of cutting through torpedo nets.[18]

Meanwhile, in mid-1941, Horton had already sponsored a more ambitious and ultimately far more important project, the X-Craft midget submarine. Displacing around 30 tons submerged and 50ft long, with a planned crew of three, eventually four, this was a far larger and more capable boat than the Welman and promised to solve most of the latter's shortcomings. Indeed, the planned X-Craft was in all respects a miniature submarine, diesel-electric powered, with a surface range of at least 500 miles and 80 miles dived, compared to the Chariot's realistic limit of 20 miles. It had an expected test depth of 300ft, was capable of 5.5 knots submerged and, not least, possessed the all-important periscope. It also delivered a formidable punch comprising side charges, each containing two tons of amatol, carried either side and designed to be released on the bottom underneath the target with timed fuses. A final innovation was a 'wet/dry' compartment based on a submarine escape chamber from which a diver could exit and re-enter to cut anti-submarine or anti-torpedo nets or undertake other tasks. If it could be made to work, this promised to be a powerful weapon system with the potential to solve the *Tirpitz* problem.

The designer of the X-Craft was a First World War submariner, Commander Cromwell Varley DSO who had retired from the navy in 1920 following the 'Geddes Axe' and started a boat-building business on the Hamble in Hampshire. He had served alongside Horton, they remained close friends and regularly discussed the concept of a midget submarine. By the outbreak of war, Varley felt he had a viable design, which with Horton's encouragement, he put to the Admiralty, only to meet rejection despite Horton lobbying Churchill as First Lord. Varley nevertheless persevered, creating a much-improved design, and in mid-1941, the Admiralty agreed to commission him to produce a prototype designated *X3*. The role envisaged at this time was not primarily attack on heavy ships either in Norwegian anchorages where the Germans had yet to deploy or at bases elsewhere. As with the Welman, the midget was intended for use in covert operations in mainland Europe such as placing charges on the base of bridges over inland waterways. *X3* was launched in mid-March 1942 by which time the prospect of *Tirpitz* as a target was certainly on the agenda and commenced five months of extensive trials. By May these had progressed well enough to justify construction of a second prototype, *X4*, by Portsmouth dockyard. In July, it was agreed the midget concept was viable and six operational boats, *X5* to *X10*, incorporating significant improvements, were ordered from Vickers Armstrong in Barrow for completion between December and February. The following month, *X3* moved to the Isle of Bute in Scotland where she was soon joined by *X4* to begin training operational crews.[19]

Clearly the midgets could not be available for operations before spring 1943 at the earliest and the Welman was showing limited potential. If *Tirpitz* was to be attacked in 1942, it must be done with Chariots. However, getting Chariots to Faettenfiord was a much tougher proposition than the Italians faced at Alexandria. They had 10 miles to cover from their launching submarine whereas *Tirpitz*'s berth was over 60 miles from the entrance to Trondheim fiord and the maximum range of the British Mark I was 15 miles. Recalling the early discussions on Frodesley and the idea of using a fishing vessel to approach the target area, Horton turned again to SOE for help. Various options were then examined for 'Operation Title' from June onwards. Use of an offshore island as a forward base with the Chariots delivered by submarine, surface warship or even aircraft and onward delivery by SOE-procured local fishing boat was considered but had to be discarded. In the end the solution was to use a Norwegian fishing vessel, the *Arthur*, stolen by the Norwegian naval officer Leif Larsen the previous year and sailed to Scotland. Larsen had escaped from Norway in early 1941, trained with the Linge Company and then become a key member of the 'Shetland Bus' operation which maintained a link between the Shetlands and Norway under SOE supervision. He made an outstanding contribution to numerous Norway special operations through the war, ending it with a string of decorations. He now volunteered to lead Title which has rightly been described as 'one of the most imaginative, enterprising and daring operations mounted by SOE during the war'. *Arthur*, carrying a plausible cargo and equipped with false papers, would carry two Chariots and their operators (four crew and two assistants in support) direct from Shetland through the fiord to a nighttime launching point off Faettenfiord.

The planning and initial execution of Title was meticulous. It had to cope with shifts in the target site to Bogenfiord off Narvik following *Tirpitz*'s move there for Rösselsprung in late June and then, at very short notice, her return to Trondheim in late October when Title was finally launched. However, all operations require some luck and it ran out for Title in its final phase. Having overcome numerous difficulties on passage and successfully passed through German checkpoints at the entrance to Trondheim fiord, *Arthur* was hit by a vicious autumn squall. Large waves sheered the deep wires which now secured the Chariots underneath the fishing vessel and both were lost just 10 miles from *Tirpitz*'s berth. Larsen had no option but to scuttle *Arthur* and implement the plan for the team to escape to Sweden. All made it successfully apart from one of the Chariot crew, Able Seaman Bob Evans, who was captured after being wounded in a gunfight with German security police. Despite wearing naval uniform guaranteeing prisoner of war status, he was harshly interrogated and then tragically executed two months later, a victim of Hitler's notorious 18 October Commando Order. Title therefore came tantalisingly close to success. The team had reached their launching point and a full-scale rehearsal earlier in the month against the battleship *Howe* had demonstrated their ability to get through anti-torpedo nets and secure their charges without detection. It is not clear how much intelligence the Germans gleaned from Evans but it was sufficient to trigger a significant upgrading of defences.[20]

## Operation Source

While Title was underway, trials and training with the midget prototypes, *X3* and *X4*, continued in Loch Striven east of the Isle of Bute off the Clyde. Much was learnt but it was a hazardous business. *X3* was lost in November following a valve failure although fortunately the three crew achieved a dramatic underwater escape. There were other accidents and fatalities, not least to the divers who had to master underwater exit and re-entry and net-cutting at the limits of contemporary equipment. For all the crew, operating and living conditions on board were to say the least primitive. It was originally hoped to mount an attack on *Tirpitz* in Faettenfiord in March 1943 while the nights remained long enough to provide the boats with protection during their long transit up Trondheim fiord. However, this date was always ambitious given that the last operational boats did not arrive from Vickers until mid-January. It was also clear many issues still had to be resolved. The attack, soon designated Operation Source, was therefore rescheduled for September when there was again adequate darkness. By the end of April, it was also clear that the probable location of a September attack was Altafiord but it could never be ruled out that *Tirpitz* would shift to Narvik or back to Trondheim and separate plans for these were prepared and kept ready. Altafiord posed special challenges in gathering necessary targeting intelligence, arranging adequate aerial reconnaissance and, not least, transporting the midgets 1350 miles from north-west Scotland to near North Cape. On the positive side, it offered additional attractive targets, given the presence of *Scharnhorst* and *Lützow*, and thus scope for a more ambitious operation.

There were only two possible options for getting the midgets to North Cape, towing by fishing vessel as with Title, or by conventional submarine. After extensive trials with the submarine *Thrasher* in June, it was decided to opt for the latter. Achieving covert transit with one or two fishing boats, drawing on SOE and Shetland Bus resources, was potentially feasible but not for the six attackers planned and trials showed that suitable fishing craft struggled with the weight of an X-boat in all but the calmest seas. By contrast, submarines had more power, could potentially tow either surfaced or submerged, had better communications, had more resilience to cope with the unexpected and were better equipped to recover boats following the attack. It was also recognised that midget crews would be in no condition to cope with the rigours of an attack if they had already been cooped up for 10 days in their tiny tube during transit. Separate passage and attack crews were therefore required and submarines could accommodate the latter in greater security and relative comfort. Nevertheless, the operation would be very demanding of submarine resources. By summer 1943, new boats were completing in substantial numbers and in September the strength of the Home flotillas was expected to rise to thirteen. But, with six boats required and two reserves, Source would absorb virtually all immediately available Home submarines for a month.[21]

The requirement for a long-range tow proved the biggest weakness in the operation. Title had already shown that operational success depended on the fastening between 'weapon' and towing vessel. The towing lines provided were 600ft lengths of manila hemp and training exercises demonstrated that these ropes were inadequate with too many breaks that did not bode well for autumn weather in the North Atlantic and Arctic. The submarines carried a spare but that was limited comfort. Better nylon ropes existed, developed by the Royal Air Force for gliders, but only three towing submarines received these at the last minute. A telephone line was woven around the tow ropes to enable communication between midget and mother submarine but this arrangement too enjoyed less than perfect reliability.[22]

In April, the entire midget force was incorporated in a new 12th Submarine Flotilla and moved from Loch Striven north to Loch Cairnbawn, 15 miles south of Cape Wrath together with the 10,000-ton support vessel *Bonaventure*. Loch Cairnbawn was chosen partly for its isolation and partly because the mountain surroundings were a reasonable match for Altafiord. It was also much closer to Scapa Flow, facilitating the occasional detachment of a battleship to act as target. There was still much to be done over the four summer months, improving the reliability of the boats, perfecting attack tactics, and incorporating the divers most of whom arrived in this period. At the end of August, the towing submarines arrived and exercised with their matching X-Craft. It had also been decided that all three heavy ships in Altafiord would be targeted. *X5, 6* and *7* would attack *Tirpitz, X9* and *10 Scharnhorst*, and *X8 Lützow*. *Tirpitz* and *Scharnhorst* were believed to be berthed in Kaafiord located at the south-west end of Altafiord. *Lützow* was in Langfiord, a separate 20-mile long arm of Altafiord, which opened 15 miles north of Kaafiord. The attack was set for 22 September when conditions of weather, seasonal darkness, moon and tides were judged optimum.[23]

Meanwhile, the Admiralty mounted a huge intelligence effort on the precise location of the Altafiord berths and their defences. SIGINT provided some important insights as did Denham's Norwegian sources reporting to him in Stockholm although there was later some dispute as to whether his information on the status of anti-torpedo nets had been correctly interpreted.[24] Despite considerable effort, SIS had nobody based in or close to Altafiord during the preparations for Source although they managed to land the agent Torstein Raaby by submarine in early September. He then established himself with a job in the area the following month. Meanwhile, they did contribute some important intelligence on the defences around *Tirpitz* as well as the topography and water conditions in the fiord through an agent visiting from Tromsø, Torbjøhn Johansen. Nevertheless, regular real-time intelligence on the status of the ships in Altafiord and any changes in defences was clearly crucial and this required aerial reconnaissance. The risk was therefore taken to brief the Soviet Northern Fleet commander, Admiral Golovko, and he agreed to a shuttle service of Royal Air Force PR Mosquitoes between the United Kingdom and Vaenga and the deployment of a new detachment of three PR IV Spitfires together with a photographic interpretation unit sent by fast destroyers. Catalina flying boats were also laid on to get photographs speedily back to the United Kingdom. This intelligence collaboration was in marked contrast to the difficulties experienced at the beginning of the year. However, Golovko no doubt recognised it was strongly in the Soviet interest to agree and the promise to transfer the Spitfires once the operation was over helped too. In the event, the Mosquito flights were frustrated by poor weather and, while the Spitfires arrived on 3 September, they could not achieve the first overflight of Altafiord until four days later. This delivered alarming news. *Tirpitz* and *Scharnhorst* were gone and the Source convoy must leave no later than 12 September to meet the ideal attack date 10 days later.[25]

## *Operation Zitronella – German raid on Spitzbergen*

The absence of the German ships was due to Operation Zitronella, a raid on the British/Norwegian facilities in Spitzbergen conducted between 6 and 9 September by a force comprising *Tirpitz*, *Scharnhorst* and nine destroyers with an embarked Grenadier regiment. This was the most powerful single force the German navy deployed in the war. Zitronella was partly a reprisal for the discovery and elimination of a small German meteorological station on the island by a Norwegian patrol in mid-June, one of a series of incidents between rival weather-reporting parties over the last two years. Although the operation would consume 27 per cent of available fuel supplies in northern waters and Dönitz admitted destruction of the Allied base would have limited impact, he apparently hoped the loss of meteorological reporting and perhaps SIGINT services would hamper the JW convoys expected over the winter months. It would also be a useful demonstration of continuing German capability in defence of Norway. Above all, Dönitz and his front-line commanders were increasingly anxious that long months of idleness in Altafiord were steadily eroding the efficiency and morale of the Northern task force. Even within the safety of the fiord, lack of fuel meant exercises were increasingly infrequent.[26]

Given the scale of force deployed, the raid under the command of Kummetz could hardly fail to achieve the destruction of the bases in Advent Bay and Barentsburg and their equipment although some personnel from both escaped into the surrounding hinterland. The bombardment was the only time *Tirpitz* fired her main armament against an enemy during her three-year career. Although the defenders had minimal weapons capable of engaging the ships, they still managed to damage two destroyers, one seriously.[27] The achievements of the raid were inevitably temporary. There was no realistic possibility of reinstituting a permanent German base in the face of British naval dominance while the British were able to begin rebuilding before the end of the month. The submarine *Tantalus* on patrol off Bear Island when the Germans attacked tried to intercept them before they left Spitzbergen. Although she failed, she confirmed destruction of the Barentsburg base which she reconnoitred on 15 September, narrowly avoiding *U-277*, which she had briefly spotted three days earlier and was still hunting for her.[28] *Seadog*, one of the reserve submarines for Source, then loaded 12 tons of stores to re-establish the base and landed these along with eight men on 25 September. More substantial supplies followed in October. None of this stopped Dönitz offering effusive congratulations when the force returned and singling out the 'courageous action' of the destroyers. He added that the 'relatively small strategic success' was less important than 'at long last' getting the heavy ships into action. This was a great boost to morale and the reminder of the continuing power of the northern fleet must make the enemy uneasy. To boost morale further, he allowed the award of 400 Iron Crosses.[29] By contrast, in an essay written for British Naval Intelligence Division in 1945, Schniewind was dismissive of Zitronella, claiming the limited and temporary results could just as easily have been achieved by a couple of destroyers. That said, he also appeared to acknowledge it was a useful 'work-up' cruise in preparation for attacking PQ convoys over the coming winter.[30]

The departure of the Zitronella force was accompanied by a German air force reconnaissance effort on a scale unprecedented in recent months to cover the risk of Home Fleet intervention. However, Bletchley and the OIC were slow to spot its significance, initially judging it was associated with a possible deployment by *Lützow* into the Kara Sea. The Home Fleet was therefore caught by surprise when the Spitzbergen base reported the German force early on 8 September and soon after Bletchley provided a decrypt showing that the Germans were closely monitoring the weather between North Cape and Spitzbergen. This was followed by the report from the PR Spitfire which, as described above, had overflown Altafiord the previous day and found the fiord empty of heavy ships. Even then, Fraser was slow to react and did not put to sea with two battleships and five destroyers until early evening. By then it was far too late to intercept. This may have been fortunate. Had the various intelligence indicators been correctly interpreted in time for the fleet to sail in the early hours of 8 September, it might have been possible to close with the returning Germans but, with no carrier, the two sides were evenly matched and the British vulnerable to U-boat and air attack in coastal waters. The episode did demonstrate that Ultra and PR could still not guarantee adequate warning of a German sortie.[31]

## Source Execution

Rear Admiral Claude Barry, now Admiral Submarines having succeeded Horton at the end of 1942, arrived in Loch Cairnbawn on 10 September to supervise the departure of the Source force from the depot ship *Titania*. By this time, two Enigma decrypts had confirmed that the Germans were due back in Altafiord at 1500 the previous day but photographic confirmation was anxiously awaited. Bad weather prevented flying on 8 and 9 September but it cleared next day, enabling a Spitfire to photograph all the German ships in their usual berths. Source could now proceed. Five of the six X-Craft departed behind their respective towing submarines at two-hour intervals from 1600 on 11 September and *X10* followed at 1300 next day. The towing submarines were allocated parallel routes, 20 miles apart and 100–200 miles off the Norwegian coast. To minimise the strain on the X-Craft passage crews, the submarines proceeded on the surface for most of the journey north allowing a speed of advance of 8–10 knots. The X-Craft were generally towed submerged but had to surface to ventilate periodically, a process agreed with the towing submarine by telephone and requiring the latter to slow down. The towing submarines could dive in the event of air or U-boat threat. The latter posed a serious risk, partly mitigated by SIGINT coverage of U-boat dispositions but ultimately by keeping sharp lookout. There were three sightings of U-boats during the whole operation but the Germans were avoided successfully and apparently themselves saw nothing. Further good aerial photographs were obtained on 14 September, which enabled a detailed study of the latest net defences, and the results were passed by signal to the submarines the following day along with confirmation of the targeting plan.[32]

For the first three days, the passage north was trouble free in relatively good weather. However, from 15 September, the three submarines using hemp ropes all suffered problems with broken tows. *Stubborn* quickly secured *X7* with her spare tow and helped *X8* who had lost contact with *Seanymph* but it took nearly 36 hours to get these two together again. Unfortunately, within 24 hours of resuming her tow behind *Seanymph*, *X8* had trouble with her side charges which both began to flood. They eventually had to be released but then exploded, seriously damaging the X-Craft. Early on 18 September, her crew was taken off and *X8* scuttled. Tragically, the crew of *X9* were less fortunate. Two days earlier, she parted her tow from *Syrtis* and was never seen again. The four surviving craft reached the planned release point north-west of the island of Sørøya on 20 September and transferred the operational crews after dark. From here they had 50 miles to run to reach the northern end of Altafiord, starting with a surface transit of the known German minefield west of Sørøya. Further tragedy was only narrowly averted during the release when, as *Stubborn* was about to part with *X7*, the tow rope became entangled with a drifting mine, easily capable of destroying both X-Craft and mother submarine. With extraordinary coolness, Lieutenant Godfrey Place, *X7*'s operational commander, managed to disentangle it and push it away.[33]

All four X-Craft successfully crossed Sørøya Sound on the surface during the night of 20/21 September to reach the channel south of Stjernøya Island leading into Altafiord where they dived at first light. The three craft designated to attack *Tirpitz* then completed a 25-mile dived transit during the day which by dark took them to the Brattholm Islands in the southern part of Altafiord five miles from the entrance to Kaafiord where their target was berthed. Meanwhile *X10*, the only surviving non-*Tirpitz* boat which was to attack *Scharnhorst*, had developed serious defects to her periscope and compass while negotiating the Stjernøya channel and was forced to lie up in a position north of this island to attempt repairs. Unfortunately, this effort was unsuccessful and, with the boat completely blind once submerged, she was forced to withdraw seaward where she was eventually picked up by the faithful *Stubborn* a week later. (*Stubborn* won high praise from Admiral Submarines for her part in Source. Her captain, Lieutenant Anthony Duff, aged only 23 at this time, had a remarkable post-war career. Transferring to the Diplomatic Service in 1946, he became High Commissioner to Kenya in the mid-1970s, played a crucial role justifying the renewal of the British nuclear deterrent, chaired the Joint Intelligence Committee in the Falklands War, and ended his career as Director General of the Security Service.) In fact, *X10* could never have found *Scharnhorst* because the latter was absent from her usual berth conducting gunnery exercises at the northern end of Altafiord between 21–23 September. The Admiralty discovered this forthcoming exercise from an Enigma message originating on 19 September and decrypted mid-morning the following day but for security reasons could not pass this intelligence on. Admiral Submarines perhaps also calculated that *X10* would switch to *Tirpitz* on her own initiative since both ships were berthed in Kaafiord.[34]

The arrival of the three *Tirpitz* attackers at the Brattholm Islands coincided with SIGINT decrypts reaching the Admiralty suggesting the southward departure of a heavy unit from Altafiord was imminent. It became apparent two days later that this was *Lützow* returning to Germany for a much-needed refit. Subsequent sightings by air reconnaissance should have facilitated her successful interception off southern Norway but, unfortunately, a combination of miscommunication between Fraser, Admiralty and Coastal Command and insufficient available land-based strike aircraft conspired against this.[35] However, on the evening of 21 September, Fraser feared this imminent move presaged the long-anticipated German breakout into the Atlantic and that *Tirpitz* was involved. He accordingly asked the Admiralty to cancel Source. Fraser's action here is puzzling and it is telling there is no reference to his intervention in the official despatch on Source. The intelligence was non-specific, providing neither direct evidence suggesting an Atlantic operation nor referring to *Tirpitz*. If such an operation was contemplated, it was more likely to involve *Scharnhorst* since her known firing exercise, now underway, could be linked with a new decrypt suggesting a ship of the northern battle group would shortly take on ammunition at Narvik or Tromsø.[36] With the X-Craft now presumably on the threshold of Kaafiord, it was also difficult to see what a cancellation order at this stage could possibly achieve, assuming the attackers could be reached at all. If they found Kaafiord empty next morning, there was every chance they could retreat without compromising the operation. Fortunately, Admiral Submarines injected common sense and convinced the Admiralty that the operation should proceed as planned.[37]

The subsequent attack has been described in detail elsewhere.[38] It was planned as a coordinated operation in which the three boats would strike simultaneously with three hours allocated for laying charges followed by a one-hour explosion period when all boats should keep clear. *X6* and *X7* accordingly left Brattholm in the early hours of 22 September and entered Kaafiord from 0400. *X6*, under Lieutenant Donald Cameron, was hampered by problems with her periscope and compass similar to those suffered by *X10*. However, she followed a supply tender through the gate in the net defences and, despite becoming virtually blind and unmanoeuvrable, managed to drop both her charges under the forward section of *Tirpitz* about 0700. This success came at the price of two involuntary surface excursions which thoroughly alerted *Tirpitz*. With escape clearly impossible, the crew scuttled their boat and all four were picked up and taken prisoner. Meanwhile *X7* initially got trapped in the net defences but eventually wriggled through as much by luck as good judgement and then executed a textbook attack dropping one charge forward under 'B' turret and one aft under the engine room at around 0710. She was again caught trying to exit the nets and, with persistent depth-charging now underway, her commander Godfrey Place was also obliged to surrender although two of his crew failed to get out before *X7* sank. There had been no sign of *X5* since transiting Sørøya Sound but there is wide agreement that a third X-Craft was sighted 500 yards outside *Tirpitz*'s nets at 0843 and sunk by gunfire and depth charges. There were no survivors. This was clearly *X5* and it is judged unlikely she had yet managed to lay her charges.

All four of the charges laid by *X6* and *X7* apparently detonated at 0812. Their impact was mitigated by the rapid reaction of *Tirpitz*'s commanding officer, Captain Hans Meyer. Recognising that charges had been laid following the capture of *X6*'s crew, he used the ship's cables to move the bows away from those laid forward. Nevertheless, the damage, especially from *X7*'s charge below the engine rooms, was serious. All three main engines were out of action, propeller shafts badly distorted, steering compartments flooded and one rudder inoperable. Two main-battery turrets were lifted clear of their mountings and there was widespread shock damage especially to sensitive equipment such as fire control. The overall impact was exacerbated by Dönitz's decision three days later, following consultation with Hitler, that the damage could only be repaired in situ. Moving *Tirpitz* to Germany, even under the heaviest escort, was judged too risky and no German dockyard could safely accommodate her. Gdynia was fully occupied with U-boat work which had higher priority. It was at the extreme limit of bombing range but the arrival of *Tirpitz* would bring attention and air attacks would 'deal a decisive blow against the expansion of the submarine arm'. Wilhelmshaven and Bremerhaven were too vulnerable. In addition to these risks, a round trip to Germany would consume precious fuel that could not easily be spared. If conducting repairs in Kaafiord made it impossible to restore *Tirpitz* to her 'full fighting strength', that would have to be accepted.[39] By 18 October, a survey by German Naval Construction Division concluded that repairs could be carried out on *Tirpitz* in Kaafiord 'despite rather serious damage' but these were expected to take four months once the necessary workers and support vessels were in place. A realistic completion date was mid-March and the project was now 'Operation Paul'.[40]

The first intelligence to reach the OIC and Admiral Submarines on the results of the attack came from Enigma decrypts. By 15 October, these provided a good overview of the damage and news that repairs would definitely be carried out in Altafiord, posing obvious difficulties for the Germans in providing specialist equipment and personnel.[41] Valuable complementary reporting also came from the two SIS sources, Torbjøhn Johansen and Torstein Raaby. The latter's job enabled him to pass *Tirpitz*'s berth regularly and he reported on activity around the battleship from his covert radio station, code name Ida, established near the village of Alta. Both agents also collected useful gossip from *Tirpitz* crew members. At the end of October, the Germans apparently attempted a deception operation using a double agent to suggest to the British that damage to *Tirpitz* was less than it actually was. The identity of this agent is unclear and there is no evidence that the British were ever misled.[42] By November, it was known that extensive leave was being granted to the crew but a precise completion date for the repairs remained elusive until an Enigma decrypt acquired on 2 January indicated that work on the hull, engines and electrics was expected to finish by 15 March, although NID was doubtful that gunnery repairs could meet that target. A meeting of all interested parties chaired by the British Naval Construction Department at the end of February appears as well informed on the damage as the Germans. It concluded that *Tirpitz* should be fully mobile with a working armament within a month. However, even leaving aside the current damage, she had not been docked for two and a half years. A docking and associated refit lasting at least three months was judged essential to make her fully effective.[43]

Source had not destroyed *Tirpitz*, and the British constructors' postwar analysis questioned whether this was ever achievable with the midget charges because of the depth of water in which they had to be laid.[44] However, by any standard, the crippling damage meant the operation had still been a remarkable success. An innovative weapon had been created in two years and successfully projected nearly 1500 miles in the face of difficult weather and geographical conditions and formidable German defences. It was a masterpiece of assiduous intelligence collection and meticulous planning and, above all, sheer determination and courage by the crews to execute one of the finest feats of arms of the war. Cameron and Place richly deserved their Victoria Crosses.

## The Resumption of the Convoys in Winter 1943

Reaching agreement on resuming the JW convoys following their suspension through the spring and summer of 1943 provoked almost unprecedented acrimony in British–Soviet relations. In announcing the suspension to Stalin back in March, Churchill stated that it was hoped to resume the convoys in September although this aspiration was carefully caveated. However, what Churchill regarded as a statement of intent was viewed by Stalin as an obligation which the signing of the Third Protocol covering Western aid over the year from 1 July 1943 had made a contractual commitment. Furthermore, the positive and cordial relationship over which Churchill enthused in mid-April had proved a false dawn. Relations soured rapidly from the end of that month triggered first by tensions in relations with the Poles following exposure of the Katyn massacre and then Soviet suspicion and unhappiness over the outcome of the Trident Conference and confirmation there would be no 'real' second front in 1943. For Stalin, this was a betrayal of clear commitments made by Churchill and Roosevelt and confirmation that Russia was being deliberately left to do the fighting and dying.[45] For Britain specifically, there were also recriminations over the type of aircraft and tanks it was offering. The Russians no longer wanted Hurricanes but it was difficult to provide Spitfires in the numbers required let alone Mosquitoes and Typhoons. Meanwhile, they rejected Churchill and Centaur heavy tanks but wanted more Valentines which required maintaining a production line which could be better used. The Director of Armoured Fighting Vehicles was mystified by the popularity of the Valentine which was now 'definitely obsolete'. Every modern gun went through its armour while its own 2-pounder was no longer effective for anti-tank or anti-personnel work. A further souring element in the British–Russian relationship was the unfortunate choice of Lieutenant General Giffard Martel to replace Miles as Head of 30 Mission in March. Martel's arrogant and patronising style and peremptory demands were deeply resented by his Soviet interlocutors.[46]

Against this context, Soviet pressure to resume the convoys began building up in August backed by claims that the Persian Gulf route was running well below promised capacity while Japan was causing problems with the Pacific route. To Russian fury, the British insisted that operational considerations made a September start date impossible.[47] On 21 September, Molotov intervened with Clark Kerr. He quoted Western information showing that the U-boat threat in the North Atlantic was declining and highlighted the growing naval strength of Britain and America as well as the resources released by the opening of the

Mediterranean. All this should free escorts and merchant shipping for the Arctic route and further postponement of the convoys was 'unjustifiable'. Their contribution was crucial to the wide-ranging Soviet offensives currently underway.[48] Molotov's demand was not mere political point scoring. It undoubtedly reflected a genuine requirement for help in meeting the huge losses suffered by the Red Army over the three months since the beginning of the Kursk battle – perhaps two million casualties and 9000 tanks, 40 per cent of overall 1943 armoured vehicle receipts.[49] Nor is it fair to see Churchill's reaction as 'largely politically motivated'.[50] While it is unlikely Churchill knew the scale of Soviet casualties, he did recognise how their huge offensive effort was wearing down German capability to Western benefit. Molotov's message therefore spurred him to inform the chiefs of staff that it was 'our duty if humanly possible' to resume the convoys as soon as feasible. He proposed running at least five, one per month, between November and March.[51]

Prior to this prime-ministerial edict, Lyttleton, as Minister for Production, together with the Admiralty had already done some preparatory planning. Lyttleton partially endorsed Molotov's claims, explaining that, while the Persian Gulf and Pacific routes could now in theory meet all Third Protocol requirements, inland transport constraints to the former and the potential Japanese threat to the latter did make a compelling case for reopening the Arctic route as insurance.[52] The Admiralty meanwhile recognised the pressures to reopen but stressed that the viability of a new convoy programme remained conditional on Operation Source first reducing the German surface threat.[53] Vice Admiral Neville Syfret, the Vice Chief of the Naval Staff standing in for Pound who was dying from a brain tumour, now replied to the prime minister that, subject to escort availability, Commander-in-Chief Home Fleet hoped to bring out about half the twenty-three ships currently stuck in Russian ports at the end of October, and then run three sixteen-ship convoys to Russia over the dark period November to January. Further convoys must depend on circumstances nearer the time. This relatively positive Admiralty response reflected the new intelligence that the surface threat had indeed significantly reduced. The early Enigma decrypts suggested *Tirpitz* had suffered some damage from the X-Craft attacks four days earlier and it was clear that *Lützow* was on her way back to Germany although she managed to dodge all efforts to intercept her.[54]

On 28 September, under pressure from the prime minister, the Defence Committee significantly expanded on these initial Admiralty proposals. The first convoy to Russia would run in November but would now comprise thirty-five ships. Three more of similar size would then sail between December and February. It was estimated that forty-seven shiploads over this period, one-third of the planned total, would meet Britain's Third Protocol commitments. Given the speed advantage in delivery on the Arctic route, there would be no difficulty finding American and Russian ships to make up numbers and filled with United States origin cargo. Fraser, who was present, pitched his escort demands at a high level, closer to PQ 18 standard than that allocated to JW 53 the previous February. This no doubt reflected continuing scepticism over the benefit versus risks in running the convoys. He seemed to take limited account of declining German power in the North and the growing likelihood that surface strike was now reduced to *Scharnhorst* and a flotilla of destroyers. However, the prime minister was determined to push this schedule through, emphasising the 'great results' the Russians were achieving and hinting at the need to compensate for lack of a second front. Syfret also had to acknowledge that an estimated twenty-nine new escorts would join the fleet over the next four months.[55]

The Defence Committee view that there would be no difficulty finding American ships and cargo for a resumed Arctic convoy programme was not entirely accurate. By September, despite the Russian claims to the contrary, monthly shipments on the Pacific route had reached 345,000 tons and over 200,000 tons on the Persian route with a further 20 per cent boost in capacity for the latter achievable. This was comfortably meeting Third Protocol commitments. The Arctic route might be faster and more convenient but switching would involve considerable shipping dislocation. However, two factors made a switch desirable that autumn. First, much Third Protocol cargo comprised heavy and bulky equipment such as railway locomotives, power and construction equipment and industrial machinery that were not easily handled in the Gulf and for which there were insufficient suitable ships in the Pacific. Secondly, the prospect of Japanese interference forced Pacific shipping to take a more northerly route from the autumn where winter navigation posed considerable difficulty. Monthly shipping fell sharply to barely 100,000 tons in January. Arctic availability therefore came just when it was needed.[56]

Given this background, the fact that two-thirds of the cargo in the four planned convoys would be American yet again underlines a key point regarding the Arctic route. Despite the capacity improvements on the other routes, with the notable exception of aircraft delivery via Alaska, in late 1943, the Arctic route remained valued by all three Allied powers for its speed of delivery to Soviet ports, ready onward access to the front line and key production centres, and its ability to carry weapons and specialised heavy goods. Yet Britain as a minority and declining shareholder in cargo conveyed was almost entirely responsible for its management and protection and consequently bore the full weight of Russian ire for any perceived failings while usually receiving minimal American help.

Not for the first time therefore, Britain now bore the brunt of a major row with Stalin. The trigger was Churchill's determination to use the resumption of the convoys as an opportunity to address what he described to Roosevelt as the 'ill-usage' of 'our people' (some of whom were American) based in North Russia.[57] The grievances here were largely those which caused trouble at the beginning of the year and had festered further over the summer – Russian refusal to grant visas to support staff the British judged essential, including replacement of existing personnel, petty security restrictions making a difficult environment more miserable, the refusal to allow a British-run medical facility, and arrest and imprisonment of merchant seamen for trivial offences. They formed the second half of a letter to Stalin on 1 October announcing the new convoy schedule. Rather unwisely, given the emphasis on complaints, Churchill insisted the convoys should be viewed as a goodwill gesture rather than a 'contract or bargain', as he revealingly put it to Roosevelt, 'a great strain to us' but 'valuable boon to them'. This rather overlooked the obligation created by the Third Protocol and was hardly tactful given the intensity of the fighting in the East over the last three months. It took Stalin two weeks to respond, partly perhaps because this period overlapped with complex negotiations over the forthcoming 'Big Three' meeting in Teheran due in November and a preparatory meeting of foreign ministers in Moscow. The reply, when it came, was brutal in tone. If Churchill expected gratitude, there was none. Instead, Stalin emphasised that the convoys were an essential part of a contractual commitment critical to maintaining Russian war potential at a time of extreme stress. He responded almost contemptuously to the complaints, making no concessions.[58]

Churchill told the War Cabinet that his initial reaction to this 'unhelpful and grudging' message was that, if the Russians would not address the ill treatment of Allied personnel, then the convoys should be stopped. However, the war effort required them to continue if this could be managed. To avoid escalation, Eden now in Moscow would seek an outcome both sides could accept. Meanwhile, to signal his displeasure, he had refused to accept the formal version of Stalin's letter from the new Russian ambassador Fedor Gusev, a man dismissed by Clark Kerr as 'like a sea-calf and apparently no more articulate'.[59] He also halted the sailing of the destroyers being despatched to bring out an initial convoy of merchant ships trapped in Russian ports over the summer. Churchill's willingness to hold his ground here was partially influenced by the latest

Joint Intelligence Committee assessment of the Eastern Front which he saw on 5 October. This painted a picture of continuing Soviet advances with the Germans under severe pressure. Significantly, it also suggested the Russians were doing better than expected in repairing transport networks while food supplies were holding up well. Overall, it did not make a case for more aid delivered more quickly.[60]

Eden's subsequent meeting with Stalin and Molotov on the evening of 21 October substantially defused the crisis. He explained the continuing pressures on naval resources in terms the Russians evidently found convincing and insisted that Britain was genuinely committed to running four convoys while *Tirpitz* was out of action that should deliver 860,000 tons from 130 to 140 cargoes. For his part, Stalin explained that he took exception to the prime minister's implication that even one convoy was a gift. In his view, Britain had made a commitment to deliver these goods. He and Eden agreed respective positions had been misunderstood. However, Stalin still initially held out on the personnel issues before softening. If only his people in North Russia had been treated 'as equals', problems would not have arisen. He left Eden and Molotov to reach an agreement in which British complaints were substantially met. It seemed to some on the British side that a mixture of 'stick and carrot' had worked, with Cadogan applauding the need occasionally 'to treat Stalin rough', although the British had also learnt lessons about Soviet sensitivity to perceived broken promises and being patronised. However, for the Russians, the real driver of rapprochement was confirmation from the Western foreign ministers of convincing British and American commitment to a cross-Channel invasion the following May. Ismay, who had accompanied Eden, won plaudits from them for the quality of his presentation on the invasion plan to be designated Overlord.[61]

Arguably the convoy row was ultimately driven by fundamentally different viewpoints. Stalin was acutely aware that the horrendous Soviet losses of the last three months, equal to the entire British casualties in the previous war, had barely restored the pre-Typhoon front line of October 1941. Defeating Germany was confirmed as a long and bloody business. Roosevelt had promised him a second front in 1942 and Churchill one in 1943. What faith could he now have in 1944? The British and Americans could legitimately argue that, leaving Overlord aside, the combined Mediterranean, Bombing and Atlantic fronts were already doing easily as much damage to Germany's war potential as the Russians, but Stalin primarily saw the disparity in blood. Perceived British litigation over the convoys seemed petty. And it no doubt rankled even more that Russia needed the aid. Tanks now mattered less, but lorries, communications equipment, raw materials, food and machine tools all remained important.

## The Death of the Scharnhorst

Following Eden's meeting with Stalin on 21 October, Churchill agreed to release the destroyer force waiting in Iceland to bring out thirteen of the ships stuck in Kola since the spring. Eight of the destroyers were of the latest fleet design and completed in the last two years, a testament to the way new build was steadily boosting Royal Navy capability at this stage of the war. The force was sighted by German air reconnaissance 250 miles east of North Cape on 28 October and the Germans correctly assessed it was probably collecting a convoy.[62] Nevertheless, the subsequent convoy, RA 54A, which sailed from Archangel on 1 November, reached the United Kingdom two weeks later without loss and undetected. The Defence Committee meeting on 28 September and Churchill's subsequent letter to Stalin left open the possibility that the planned outgoing monthly convoys might be split into two parts as in the previous winter. Fraser decided on this policy, judging, like Tovey, that smaller convoys would be easier to keep together during the dark period and somewhat harder for a reduced German air and U-boat force to find. The November convoy therefore sailed from Loch Ewe as JW 54A with eighteen ships on 15 November and JW 54B with fourteen ships a week later. Each of these convoys also had a tanker in addition.

The risk of air and U-boat attack was assessed low in these winter months, and by November Fraser knew that *Tirpitz* and *Lützow* were out of the picture. The surface threat therefore comprised *Scharnhorst* and a handful of destroyers. However, the view formed earlier in the year that Dönitz would use whatever forces he had aggressively persisted, and Enigma decrypts showed that *Scharnhorst* was at full readiness and exercising regularly in Altafiord.[63] Although now on her own, she was a more powerful opponent than *Hipper* and *Scheer* the previous year. Fraser therefore strengthened the covering forces of the new convoys, partly to maximise their protection but also in the hope of bringing *Scharnhorst* to action. The cruiser force gained an extra 8in ship and he planned to bring his battleships further forward than in the past. As had been customary during previous convoy periods, submarines were also positioned in the approaches to Altafiord.[64] One of these was the newly completed *Storm*, whose captain, Lieutenant Commander Edward Young, a publisher in civilian life and inventor of the Penguin brand, wrote a vivid post-war account of life on one of these Arctic patrols.[65] Otherwise, the close escort, drawn from the Home Fleet and Western Approaches, broadly mirrored the pattern for smaller convoys established by Tovey at the end of 1942. In the event, neither November outgoing convoy detected any enemy attention. However, the parallel return convoy RA 54B, which used the escorts of JW 54A, was sighted on 1 December by *U-307* which was detected and driven off after being depth-charged for four hours.[66]

In fact, the Germans also knew of the existence of JW 54A from 'radio intelligence' and an agent report and, on 22 November, when they assessed it was still west of Bear Island, deployed seven U-boats in a patrol line 150 miles further east to intercept it. They probably also identified JW 54B from radio monitoring the same day. However, there were no subsequent sightings of either outbound convoy.[67] Meanwhile, a month earlier, Dönitz had ordered Naval Staff Operations Division to consider how *Scharnhorst* and available destroyers might be deployed if enemy Arctic convoys were resumed.[68] No conclusions had been reached prior to the detection of JW 54A. Until then, the Naval Staff were doubtful whether convoys would resume and their Directive for 'Fleet Operations' in 'Winter 1943/44' approved by Dönitz on 20 November reiterated that the primary role of the residual Northern Task Force, now confined to *Scharnhorst* and five destroyers, was to counter invasion. This was consistent with Führer Directive 51, issued at the beginning of the month, which required a reorientation of German strategy towards defence in the West. Given the scale of naval force the enemy could now deploy against Norway, the Naval Staff recognised the difficulty of successful intervention against invasion but Altafiord remained the best possible base. It was agreed that any decision to deploy *Scharnhorst* was reserved to Dönitz and Schniewind, as commander Group North/Fleet, had been so informed.[69]

By 2 December, with growing evidence that 'PQ convoys' as the Germans still called them had resumed, the Naval Staff proposed that, despite the Regenbogen experience, deployment of *Scharnhorst* in the dark months was practicable and had good prospects of success. Deployment of destroyers alone would be high risk with minimal chance of results. The destroyer force was now reduced to the five ships of the 4th Flotilla under Captain Rolf Johannesson, following withdrawal of the 6th to the South. Johannesson had previously served with distinction in Mediterranean destroyer operations and was a future commander-in-chief of the postwar German navy.[70] Effective use of *Scharnhorst* required good air reconnaissance but the situation on the Eastern Front made it undesirable to hold back a valuable offensive weapon. Dönitz agreed and wondered whether Kummetz, currently on extended sick leave in Germany, should return to command such an operation. He was persuaded that Rear

Admiral Erich Bey, the commander of destroyers, could cope.[71] However, on 5 December, in his own guidance on 'winter operations', Schniewind was more sceptical that *Scharnhorst* on her own could achieve much. Accurate information on both convoys and covering forces and weather conditions was a prerequisite for success and he insisted that current air surveillance, especially during the winter months, was inadequate. He and Bey were also acutely conscious of the superiority of British radar and the seakeeping of Royal Navy destroyers.[72] The need for appropriate air support for action against the convoys was raised again 10 days later by the Naval Staff but it was decided that a single convoy operation would not justify withdrawing reconnaissance aircraft from the Atlantic theatre where 'combined operations' were much improved.[73]

On the British side, the December convoy pattern followed that established the previous month with similar cover arrangements. JW 55A with nineteen ships sailed from Loch Ewe on 12 December and reached the Russian ports without interference 10 days later. On this occasion, Fraser decided to bring his 'heavy cover' group, comprising the battleship *Duke of York*, cruiser *Jamaica* and four destroyers, ahead of the convoy into the Barents Sea. He anchored in Kola between 16 and 18 December to view local conditions for himself and have talks with Admiral Golovko. Golovko got on well with Fraser as he did with the jovial Burnett. He gave the latter another reindeer and offered Fraser his huge writing desk which was politely declined. As Fraser said later – 'What might he have done if I had admired his wife?'.[74] Fraser then returned to Iceland, passing JW 55A on the final phase of its journey. His decision to take his battle group through the Barents Sea, which marked a fundamental change in all previous policy, underlines how much had altered with the damage to *Tirpitz* and departure of *Lützow* since his review at the end of June. Not only was *Duke of York* comfortably superior to *Scharnhorst*, Germany's sole remaining heavy ship, in one-on-one combat, but there was no longer any serious prospect of an Atlantic breakout on the lines postulated by Denning at the beginning of the year. It remained possible that, despite winter darkness, *Duke of York* could suffer crippling damage from a lucky U-boat attack as with *Edinburgh* 18 months earlier, but the chance was low and the Royal Navy now had sufficient superiority with Royal Air Force assistance to be reasonably confident of recovering a damaged ship. More important, even the total loss of *Duke of York* would no longer have any real influence on the overall balance of naval power. The visit to Kola was thus a risk worth taking.

However, it did not reflect intelligence that JW 55A had been sighted by the Germans as sometimes suggested.[75] Fraser did receive Ultra signals late on 19 December and early next day after he had left, drawing on decrypts which suggested the Germans were expecting a convoy to enter the Barents Sea by 18 December, had requested air reconnaissance, assigned new U-boat attack areas, and ordered *Scharnhorst* to three hours' notice.[76] This Ultra intelligence presented a more coherent picture of German knowledge and intent than existed in reality, where it was also complicated by differences between Klüber, as Admiral Arctic, and other parts of the German command. U-boats were indeed given new attack areas on 17 and 19 December, the latter establishing a 90-mile north/south patrol line just south-east of Bear Island,[77] and Dönitz simultaneously decided to reinforce the Arctic with four extra boats but these decisions did not reflect specific intelligence of an imminent convoy. Two U-boats also reported enemy activity 140 miles east-south-east of Bear Island on 18 December, but they too had never sighted a convoy.[78] Two days later, the Germans did conclude that the combination of 'radio intelligence' and the U-boat reports suggested a convoy 'on the way' but they remained uncertain whether it was still at sea or had reached port. Furthermore, the U-boat reports were not viewed as definite proof. Air searches had been requested but weather conditions were difficult.[79]

German understanding of the convoy pattern at this time was subsequently drawn together by their Naval Staff on 22 December. They assessed correctly that traffic had resumed in mid-November after a gap of nine months and that currently convoys were running at about fortnightly intervals. Intelligence had not yet established whether convoys were starting at Iceland or from British ports. Nor could the overall strength of the traffic be estimated although the first convoy in the present series (presumably meaning JW 54A) had comprised nineteen ships. It was possible the new traffic reflected decisions taken at the Moscow meeting of Foreign Ministers at the end of October. The Naval Staff shared this assessment with OKW and Army and Air Force operational staffs.[80]

Although the Admiralty and Fraser perhaps overestimated German knowledge of JW 55A, the decrypts showing that *Scharnhorst* had come to increased readiness convinced Fraser that she would sortie once a future convoy was firmly located. In his later report of proceedings, he was more specific, claiming he was convinced she would target JW 55B which left Loch Ewe on 20 December, again with nineteen ships.[81] The new convoy was timed to coincide with the westbound RA 55A with twenty-two ships, sailing from Kola on 22 December. This meant the two convoys would cross in the vicinity of Bear Island around Christmas Day, giving *Scharnhorst* two potential targets. RA 55A would be covered by three cruisers, *Norfolk*, *Belfast* and *Sheffield*, once again commanded by

Bob Burnett, who had been promoted to vice admiral earlier in the month. Burnett had accompanied JW 55A into Kola and, after covering RA 55A safely into the Atlantic, would turn back to support JW 55B. Fraser's claimed conviction that *Scharnhorst* would attack JW 55B possibly owed something to hindsight but also reflected genuine belief that JW 55A had been a near miss and the long-standing assessment of Dönitz's aggression. Some post-war British accounts of the *Scharnhorst* story with access to German records noted the German belief that their failure to attack JW 55A or previous convoys in the series would lead to British complacency and a lowering of defences. It is unclear how widely this view was shared by German commanders prior to the operation. However, Dönitz certainly seized on it after *Scharnhorst*'s loss as part justification for a risky operation. It therefore further fostered a British narrative that an attack on JW 55B was always inevitable.[82]

Fraser's reading of Dönitz's aggressive attitude was certainly correct. Despite Schniewind's considerable reservations over the viability of a *Scharnhorst* sortie, at a conference of flag officers on 16 December, Dönitz underlined his intent 'should the opportunity arise for the battlegroup to strike'. He would 'under all circumstances go at the enemy'.[83] This was consistent with the decision taken with the Naval Staff a fortnight earlier but the determination to override Schniewind's caution is striking. Whether this reflected Dönitz's personality, ideological commitment, determination to fulfil the bargain on the heavy ships reached with Hitler back in February, or a conviction the navy must support the army in the East, is hard to say. Probably all these factors played a part. Foreign Armies East continued grossly to exaggerate the flow of Western aid through the Arctic, assessing it at 1.7 million tons in 1943, nearly four times the real figure for that year. Dönitz certainly saw these estimates and, given how closely he tracked the 'tonnage war' in the Atlantic, they no doubt exerted influence.[84]

Bey, who would have to execute a sortie, fully shared Schniewind's reservations. He had also originally been appointed to stand in for Kummetz on the understanding that, with *Tirpitz* immobilised and *Lützow* gone, no operations would happen. His career had been spent almost entirely in destroyers with little big-ship experience and he arrived to find that Kummetz's key staff officers, including the highly able and experienced Chief Operations Officer, Captain Hansjürgen Reinicke, had been posted away. He had also lost half his destroyer force in November. In addition, his Flag Captain in *Scharnhorst*, Fritz Julius Hintze, was new, having taken command in mid-October. In winter conditions, as a destroyer officer, Bey would prefer to attack with these alone but the five left were not enough. Nor, in his view, could the shortage be made good by *Scharnhorst* who would need protection. He developed a plan whereby three destroyers would scout for the convoy, leaving two in her defence. *Scharnhorst* would then attack during the brief Arctic twilight period since at night she could not exploit her potential and was vulnerable to British radar and destroyers. Bey apparently felt bitter about the predicament he faced and resorted to fatalism – hoping that this time 'luck may be on our side'. Johannesson, commanding the destroyers, who knew Bey well, was gloomy too, noting that success 'cannot be rated all that highly'.[85] Dönitz, however, was resolute. On 19 December, three days after the meeting with flag officers and while the Germans were still struggling to make sense of JW 55A, he informed Hitler that *Scharnhorst* and the destroyers of the task force would attack the next Allied convoy if a successful operation seemed assured. No doubt reflecting his inherent trust in Dönitz, Hitler did not demur.[86]

German air reconnaissance first detected JW 55B mid-morning on 22 December, two days into its passage, and about 120 miles north northeast of the Faeroes. Forty merchant ships, possibly accompanied by a carrier, were reported steering north-east at 10 knots. The Naval Staff assessed this was probably a 'PQ' convoy, Dönitz allocated three additional U-boats to Northern waters and Group North brought *Scharnhorst* again to three hours' notice.[87] The convoy was then lost for 24 hours until 1125 on 23 December when a rather more accurate report recorded seventeen merchant ships, three tankers, three to four cruisers, and nine destroyers 280 miles west of the Lofotens. Although the sighting aircraft correctly counted thirteen warship escorts, the 'cruisers' were actually destroyers. Group North agreed this was probably a PQ convoy since its composition did not fit with a raid on the Norwegian coast, although an operation to lure out the Northern Task Force was possible. It was essential therefore to establish if there was a heavy covering force which would probably be out to the north of the convoy. Meanwhile Group North intended to deploy eight U-boats initially in the Bear Island gap and then in a patrol line further south-west. Schniewind also sought delegated authority to deploy *Scharnhorst* to attack east of the Bear Strait by which time the U-boats should be shadowing the convoy. However, he stressed that operational success depended on 'extensive and continuous' air reconnaissance both to track the convoy and identify possible covering forces. It was soon clear that 5th Air Fleet would struggle to provide this and requests from Dönitz to the Air Force General Staff for reinforcements were refused.[88]

JW 55B was spotted again midday on 24 December when it was 300 miles west of the entrance to Altafiord and tracked for the rest of that afternoon. Meanwhile, the U-boat patrol line was repositioned 75 miles west of the Bear Island gap and Miesel, as Chief of Staff, Naval Staff, briefed Dönitz on Bey's proposed tactics for deploying the *Scharnhorst* task force which he supported. In its own assessment shared at midnight with the Naval Staff and Arctic theatre commanders, Group North expected the U-boats to contact the convoy in the forenoon of Christmas Day and judged that the optimum place for the *Scharnhorst* force to intercept was north of North Cape 24 hours later. However, the viability of a surface attack depended on assurance that there were no additional British covering forces in range and weather and visibility. Group North stressed that, despite valiant efforts, 5th Air Fleet reconnaissance was not comprehensive. And, at best, *Scharnhorst* would have a bare two hours of twilight in which to use her guns effectively. It was doubtful if she could break through the escort screen to get at the convoy in this time, given the dangers of torpedo attack. For Schniewind, in line with his earlier caution, the prospects of 'major success' were 'slight' and the risk 'great'. He evidently preferred use of the destroyers alone but recognised they would probably be forced to withdraw by superior enemy forces. Nevertheless, Group North would bring the task force to one hour's notice at 1300 on Christmas Day and awaited Dönitz's final decision.[89]

Given Schniewind's reservations, an odd feature of the *Scharnhorst* story is his failure to emphasise the potential significance of a B-Dienst intercept he received at 1830 which appeared to suggest another British force 180 miles astern of the 'PQ convoy'. Although the position fix was poor, Captain Rudolf Peters, commanding Arctic U-boats from Arctic headquarters at Narvik, and currently standing in for Klüber who was now on Christmas leave, believed this was the distant cover force. So did Fliegerführer Lofoten who made it a priority for investigation next day by BV 138 flying boats which were fitted with radar, albeit far less effective than the British centimetric ASV III now widely fitted across Royal Air Force Coastal Command. Schniewind apparently accepted the intercept might derive from a heavy force but judged that a transmission from the convoy itself or a straggler were also possibilities. Only an air sighting could give a definitive answer.[90]

While the Germans watched JW 55B and considered intervention, Enigma decrypts gave the British a partial but valuable view of their knowledge and intentions. As already noted, the British had two convoys to worry about. The westbound RA 55A left Kola on 22 December with its strong destroyer escort drawn from the incoming JW 55A. Burnett's cruisers, now designated 'Force 1', followed in its wake 24 hours later. The convoy was routed as close to the ice as possible, passed 30 miles south of Bear Island in the early hours of Christmas Day and was never detected by the Germans. Burnett broke off to stay well east of the Bear Gap ready to protect the incoming JW 55B. Meanwhile, Fraser with *Duke of York*, *Jamaica* and four destroyers, now designated Force 2, had also sailed late on 23 December, after refuelling in Iceland, to provide heavy support for both convoys. By early afternoon the following day, as Force 2 headed north-east, the OIC had briefed Fraser and Burnett that the Germans had identified JW 55B as a 'PQ convoy' as opposed to an invasion operation, were probably continuing to track it, were positioning U-boats to intercept, and apparently preparing to deploy *Scharnhorst* although she had not yet sailed. The OIC added that the Germans recognised the possible presence of a covering British battlegroup and it summarised air searches planned that day by the radar-equipped BV 138s sweeping the area 250 miles south-west of the line between Bear Island and Tromsø, which were therefore unlikely yet to find Force 2. Fraser now had to balance the primary goal of ensuring the safety of two convoys with the prospect of trapping *Scharnhorst* if she sortied. There was a risk that, if she acted boldly, she could get at JW 55B while he was too far away to intervene. He accordingly broke radio silence to order JW 55B to reverse course for three hours to slow its progress east and for RA 55B to keep as far north as possible and ideally to detach four of its destroyers to reinforce the eastbound convoy. This was the signal picked up by B-Dienst.[91]

At 0900 on Christmas Day, *U-601* sighted JW 55B 150 miles south-west of Bear Island, heading north-east at 8 knots, and successfully tracked it until early evening when she was driven off by destroyers in deteriorating weather. There was also one definitive air sighting in the early afternoon. During the forenoon it became clear to Bey that he would be ordered to attack with *Scharnhorst* and he protested vigorously that present reconnaissance over the convoy was 'completely inadequate' and it was 'absolutely necessary' to extend it to identify covering forces. He also insisted that light and weather conditions made it impossible to use *Scharnhorst*'s guns effectively. However, at 1412, the Naval Staff issued the formal order to Group North that Bey was to sail in good time to intercept the 'PQ convoy'. In Dönitz's absence in Paris, where he was preparing to spend Christmas with his U-boat crews in the French bases, the order was issued by Meisel as his chief of staff. Meisel justified proceeding with the operation, now designated 'Ostfront', because: no covering group had been detected by either air reconnaissance or other means; since two previous PQ convoys had got through unmolested, there was a good chance of catching the enemy by surprise; and, while bad weather might hinder the German destroyers, the same was true for their British counterparts. The Naval Staff added that, if the destroyers could not ride the sea, *Scharnhorst* must conduct the operation alone in 'cruiser style'. In a heavy sea, she would not be in much danger from cruisers or destroyers. This throwaway reference to 'cruiser style', undoubtedly stemming from Meisel, took scant account of the known close escort strength. Single German raiders had attacked convoys but not against the minimum dozen destroyers reported two days earlier and in semi-darkness at best.[92]

Meisel had kept his Commander-in-Chief closely briefed on the proposed *Scharnhorst* sortie and Dönitz had been copied on Schniewind's reservations. However, given the stakes involved in Ostfront, he decided he must return to 'Koralle', his new naval headquarters 20 miles north of Berlin, opened a month earlier and located to avoid bombing. He arrived at 1430, learnt there was no fundamental change in the situation other than the weather, on which Meisel was apparently dismissive, and approved the Ostfront order just issued.[93] Bey had based himself aboard *Tirpitz* in Kaafiord until this time since she enjoyed secure landline communications with all the naval commands. Accepting the die was cast, he set off for *Scharnhorst*, berthed 40 miles away in Langfiord. By the time he arrived, the weather prospects for next day had worsened, predicting gale-force winds from the south-west, sea state 6 to 8 and poor visibility with snow showers. The prospects of Ostfront achieving any worthwhile results were clearly now bleak. Air reconnaissance would be impossible and Johannesson's destroyers would struggle, making finding the convoy a matter of luck. *Scharnhorst* would have little chance of using her gunpower even in the brief twilight period. Bey had no choice but to obey his orders but his attitude must have been grimly fatalistic as *Scharnhorst* sailed at 1900, rendezvoused with Johannesson's 4th Flotilla, and made her way through the fiords into the wild Barents Sea. It was the first time Fritz Hintze, her new captain, had left the shelter of Altafiord. The morale of her crew was, by all accounts, high. Despite the interruption of Christmas festivities, most looked forward to real action after endless dreary waiting. However, in view of what was to come, it is hard not to view this as one of the most poignant moments of the war. Of nearly 2000 men who sailed with her that night, only thirty-six survived the next 24 hours.

Bey had been somewhat reassured that morning when Meisel confirmed that, in accordance with Dönitz's February directive on fleet operations, he would retain discretion to execute the operation as he saw fit. However, the subsequent order that *Scharnhorst* must if necessary 'go it alone' rather constrained his freedom and Dönitz now took this further with a five-point attack directive issued at 1925 as Bey was exiting Langfiord. This stressed the importance of stopping arms for Russia – 'we must help' – and emphasised both *Scharnhorst* and destroyers were to attack, thereby closing off the option of the former holding back in a support role. Dönitz then emphasised that 'partial success' was not enough – the battle must be 'fought out', making full use of *Scharnhorst*'s firepower. Bey was given discretion to withdraw but implicitly only if 'heavy forces' appeared. After insisting his message be conveyed to all personnel, Dönitz expressed confidence in Bey's 'initiative' and 'fighting spirit'.[94] The sense of Dönitz's message was clear – 'Come back with your shield or on it' – and made a striking contrast with Klüber's parting message to Kummetz almost exactly a year previously. What Bey thought will never be known but, having kept his counsel all day, Schniewind, on seeing the message and with strong urging from Peters in Narvik, now pressed for Ostfront to be cancelled. He argued that the rapidly deteriorating weather ruled out any chance of the 'sweeping success' Dönitz sought. The reply came around midnight. The operation must proceed. If the destroyers could not cope with the seas, Bey must consider using *Scharnhorst* alone as a 'raider'.[95]

During Christmas Day, the British obtained no insight into the high-level German debates around the *Scharnhorst* deployment or sight of Dönitz's message. The relevant traffic either went by landline or in ciphers which Bletchley could not read. Enigma decrypts did keep Fraser and Burnett informed of U-boat dispositions, including *U-601*'s sighting, and proposed air searches aimed at locating any heavy covering force. They also confirmed *Scharnhorst* was still in Langfiord at midday. The decisive break came early on Boxing Day morning when Bletchley decrypted Admiral Arctic's order to *Scharnhorst* to sail accompanied by other messages indicating her departure from Altafiord. This was conveyed succinctly by the OIC at 0217 – 'Emergency. *Scharnhorst* probably sailed 1800A/25 December'. Almost simultaneously the OIC reported that all but one German search aircraft had landed and Force 2 had not yet been sighted. This was also the conclusion of the 'Headache' monitoring team in *Duke of York*. An hour later, for the benefit of non-Ultra recipients, the Admiralty sent a brief signal to all forces – 'Admiralty appreciates *Scharnhorst* at sea'.[96] The report on *Scharnhorst*'s sailing was Bletchley's last operational contribution before the end of Ostfront. It was now up to those at sea.[97]

At 0400, following receipt of this latest intelligence, the British dispositions were as follows. The homeward-bound RA 55A was now

200 miles west of Bear Island, well out of *Scharnhorst*'s way, clear also of the U-boat patrol line and still undetected by the Germans. The outbound JW 55B, *Scharnhorst*'s target, was now 50 miles south of Bear Island steering east-north-east at 8 knots to keep close to the ice. Burnett's Force 1 was 150 miles east of the convoy, steering south-west to intercept the probable German track from Altafiord. Fraser's Force 2 was 200 miles south-west of the convoy, currently steering slightly north of east at 24 knots. The *Scharnhorst* force reached the open sea north-west of Sørøya Island at 2300. From there Bey judged it was a 10-hour run to intercept JW 55B approximately due north of North Cape if he could maintain 20 knots. It followed that, with Force 1 and the convoy closing each other at 25–30 knots, Burnett should encounter *Scharnhorst* about the same time, around 0900. Fraser's plot therefore revealed a complex picture with multiple moving parts. He was potentially well placed to cut *Scharnhorst* off on the direct route back to Altafiord, although if she was alerted and fled south-east, his task would be more difficult. She also had a reasonable chance of avoiding Burnett and getting at the convoy. Furthermore, Fraser could not be certain where everybody was and the fuel state of the destroyers across all the forces was a constant concern.[98] He therefore again broke radio silence at 0401 to request positions from all British forces while sharing his own. Two hours later, having assessed the latest picture, he ordered the convoy to steer further north to maximise her distance from the approaching Germans, and for Burnett to close as fast as possible. It is not clear whether B-Dienst intercepted these transmissions and/or obtained useful D/F bearings. If they did, they had no impact on the German command and did not reach Bey.[99]

At 0730, Bey judged he had crossed ahead of the convoy on its predicted track and turned west-south-west at 12 knots with Johannesson's five destroyers spread in a search line 10 miles ahead. It is not clear why he dispensed with the two destroyers originally earmarked to protect *Scharnhorst*. JW 55B was probably only 30 miles away at this time and with luck the northernmost destroyer might have sighted outlying ships of the convoy before 1000. In theory, Bey might also have benefitted from air and U-boat sightings reported at around 0945 but in winter darkness and atrocious weather, navigational accuracy was a challenge for both sides and quoted positions were invariably out by many miles. Whatever the possibilities, shortly after 0830, for unknown reasons, *Scharnhorst* turned north and due to oversight or miscommunication Johannesson was not informed. The forces rapidly diverged and in the high seas and darkness never regained contact. To compound this disaster, Johannesson's most northerly destroyer suddenly emerged in the centre of his search line, meaning she was far out of position just when she might have seen the convoy. *Scharnhorst* would now operate 'cruiser style' but not by choice.[100]

Meanwhile Burnett was fast approaching and, soon after *Scharnhorst*'s turn north, picked her up on *Norfolk*'s radar at 0840 at 16 miles. The relative movements of British and German forces over the next six hours are shown in Map 7 below. For 45 minutes from 0840 Force 1 tracked *Scharnhorst* by radar and Burnett manoeuvred skilfully to position between the German and the convoy before opening fire and taking *Scharnhorst* by surprise at 0930. *Scharnhorst* suffered two 8in hits from *Norfolk*, losing her own forward radar, but did not respond and broke away to the south-east. Burnett did not attempt to pursue since in the prevailing conditions *Scharnhorst* had a considerable speed advantage and his first duty was protection of the convoy. He therefore turned north-west to join it but, before losing radar contact, observed *Scharnhorst* also turning northward evidently set on another attempt to intercept. An hour later Force 1 was in contact with JW 55B and successfully positioned 10 miles ahead of it, reinforced on Fraser's orders with four destroyers released from the close escort.

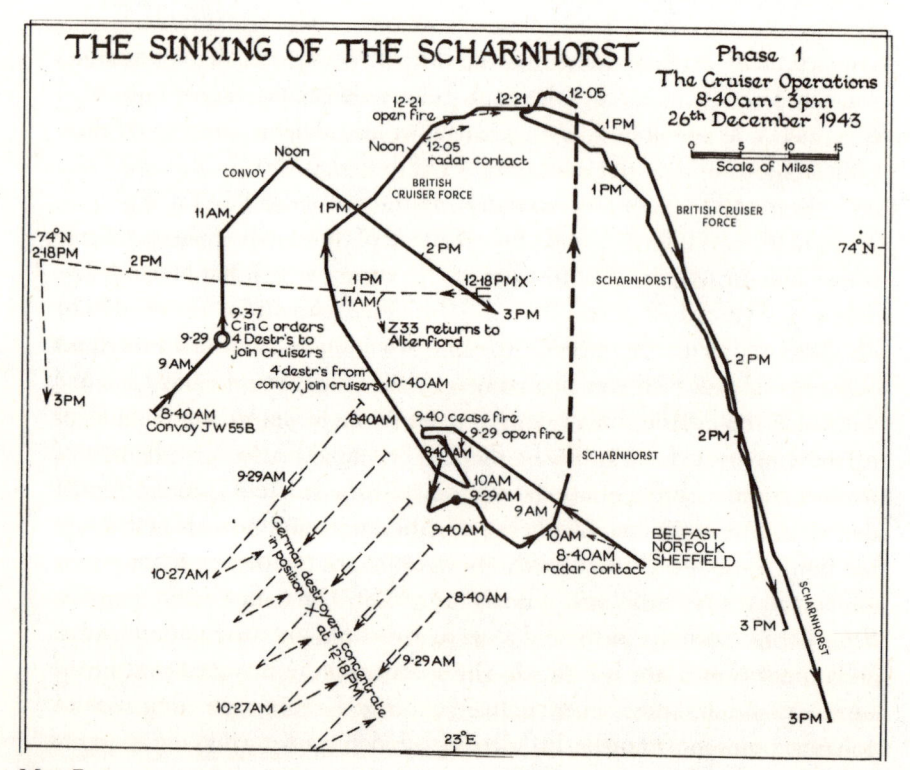

Map 7

The Germans now received two vital pieces of intelligence which, had they been correctly interpreted and speedily communicated to Bey, could have produced a different outcome to the day. Although there is doubt whether B-Dienst D/F-ed Force 2 from Fraser's earlier signals, Burnett's enemy reports from 0930 convinced them that a second British command authority was in the theatre. By 1100, Group North/Fleet accepted that, while it was conceivable the two authorities were the cruiser force and convoy, it was also possible the evidence pointed to the long-anticipated 'heavy covering force'. However, they did not inform Bey who also, unusually for an operation such as Ostfront, had no B-Dienst party of his own aboard. More definitive intelligence came from a radar-equipped BV 138, one of three launched by Fliegerführer Lofoten despite the atrocious weather. Shortly after 1000, the aircraft detected and reported 'five warships, one apparently a big one' by radar 85 miles north-west of North Cape which were apparently steering south at high speed. Although this was certainly Force 2, the position given was nearly 50 miles further east north-east of where Fraser actually was. The quoted course was also wrong.

The reports from this aircraft which stayed in the area for an hour were later subject to intense German scrutiny and controversy over who received them when, in what form and what action was taken. What is clear is that Fliegerführer Lofoten did not rebroadcast the report to the key naval commanders ashore and afloat until after 1300, three hours after the initial detection, and that he removed the reference to a heavy ship on the basis that radar evidence here was too tenuous. Allowing for reception and decryption time it probably did not reach those who could recognise its importance much before 1400 and, even then, a key part was missing. Dönitz subsequently described this as a 'tragedy'. Peters, as Acting Admiral Arctic, certainly judged that it could only refer to an enemy force intent on cutting off *Scharnhorst* on her way back. With growing foreboding, he and others now linked this sighting with B-Dienst's earlier warning of the presence of a second British commander and the intercept acquired out to the west the previous day. Bey also received Fliegerführer Lofoten's report early afternoon and a *Scharnhorst* survivor recalls lookouts being told, as the ship raced homeward, to keep a sharp eye to the west following an 'air sighting' of enemy ships. It remains possible that *Scharnhorst* picked up the original sighting report at 1000, as did *Duke of York*'s Headache team, but Bey's subsequent actions suggest this is unlikely. Certainly, there is no sign he perceived an existential threat.[101]

Burnett's decision to prioritise protecting the convoy at the cost of losing radar contact with *Scharnhorst* was undoubtedly correct. Not only might *Scharnhorst* evade him with her superior speed to hit the convoy from a new direction exploiting air and U-boat reports but there was the threat posed by five powerful German destroyers he assumed were in the area. However, the two British admirals faced an anxious couple of hours. Fraser knew that, if *Scharnhorst* now judged an attack too risky and headed home, there was scant chance of finding and intercepting her. His destroyers were too short of fuel to linger in the Barents Sea. He must either head for Murmansk or return to Iceland. Burnett was guardedly confident that *Scharnhorst*'s observed northward turn just before losing contact suggested intent to have another go at the convoy, but he worried he had made a critical misjudgement and should have tried to shadow her.

In the event, his hunch that *Scharnhorst* would return was correct. Drawing on U-boat reports, including a sighting sent by *U-277* at 1000, Bey believed he had fixed JW 55B's location and could work around the British cruiser force to attack from the north-east. He would also direct Johannesson to attack simultaneously on a north-east heading from the south, helping to keep the escort occupied. Unfortunately, the convoy was further north than *U-277* believed, partly due to dead reckoning errors and partly Fraser's earlier order to steer further north. It followed that, when Bey turned south-west to intercept, he would inevitably again run into Force 1, while Johannesson was also too far south of the convoy and found nothing. Shortly after 1200 therefore, as Burnett steered north-east with the convoy now about 10 miles west-north-west of him, *Belfast* acquired a radar contact 13 miles to the east which could only be *Scharnhorst*. Burnett turned towards, revealing that *Scharnhorst* was on a reciprocal course with the range closing rapidly. Beginning 1220 with the range just under six miles, there was another short sharp twilight engagement with added illumination from star shells. *Scharnhorst* was again taken by surprise by radar-directed fire but was skilfully manoeuvred by Hintze and had the best of the exchange, badly damaging *Norfolk* while taking one inconsequential hit. Five minutes into this battle with the range down to two miles she turned sharply to port to head away south-east at high speed.[102]

At 1240, as he broke away, Bey signalled Narvik that he had again been engaged by several opponents, including 'radar directed fire from heavy units'. The reference to 'heavy units' which rather implied battleships was puzzling. Even in semi-darkness there was a profound difference between 8in and 14in shell splashes. It is hard to believe Bey and his staff thought they faced more than cruisers and destroyers. He turned briefly further eastward, possibly to review his options, perhaps also in an attempt to throw off pursuers. By 1300 at the latest he had decided to return to Altafiord and came round to a course of south-south-east still at 28 knots. His intentions for Johannesson at this stage were somewhat confused. At 1218, just prior to running into Burnett, Bey ordered Johannesson, who was still searching north-east, to sweep to the west instead and prepare to conduct an independent flotilla attack on the convoy exploiting a further, albeit dated, shadowing report from *U-277*. In fact, Johannesson now passed very close south of the convoy at 1300 when it was steering south-east after its detour northward. If Bey had ordered his turn ten minutes later, he might have found it. As it was, Johannesson continued west without sighting anything until 1340 when Bey ordered him also to withdraw. It is not clear why Bey delayed this order for at least 40 minutes after his own departure. If he felt it was still worth a final check westward, why leave Johannesson without heavy support? A surprised Johannesson sought confirmation of the order but reported on his return that destroyer success at this stage could only have been achieved under 'exceptionally favourable conditions' which did not exist. His destroyers had clearly struggled with the weather all morning and *Z 33* now completely lost contact and returned alone to Altafiord. Naval Staff Operations Division also struggled to understand Bey's intentions at this time but correctly speculated that he was planning for his destroyers to attack without *Scharnhorst*.[103]

The lack of survivors from Bey's command team mean the factors that drove withdrawal cannot be known with certainty. He had twice found his way to the convoy barred by the British cruiser force and was evidently disturbed by their demonstrable radar advantage. Twilight was now over and, with his own less-effective forward radar out of action, the British tactical advantage must increase. They could see him while he could not see them. The British destroyer threat would have weighed heavily too and he was no longer certain where the convoy was. He may also have worried about the toll the awful weather was taking on an inexperienced crew. Bey's underlying doubts about the operation must also have exerted influence. His fatalistic hope for 'luck' had not been met. Schniewind, equally impressed by British radar, later endorsed the decision to withdraw. By contrast, Dönitz clearly felt Bey lacked aggressive spirit and that 'the correct thing' was to have finished off the already 'hard hit' British cruisers, creating the means for a successful attack on the convoy. This was easy to say from a distance as Dönitz grudgingly later acknowledged.[104]

Where Dönitz was on somewhat firmer ground was in criticising Bey for choosing a course of south-south-east which allowed Burnett to keep up rather than turning south-west directly into the gale-force sea where *Scharnhorst*'s superior seakeeping at speed would have quickly shaken off her shadowers. When Bey broke off the engagement, he was 55 miles due east of Bear Island and his chosen heading aligned with North Cape 215 miles away and about seven and a half hours run at 28 knots. Approaching North Cape he would turn south-west to enter Altafiord via the eastern end of Sørøya Island. As Dönitz suggested, the south-south-east course was one of very few on which Burnett's cruisers and destroyers could keep up, which they did successfully, keeping outside visibility distance at a range of about eight miles and transmitting regular position reports to Fraser. The latter subsequently described this as a model of successful shadowing although the speed and conditions still subjected Force 1 to considerable pounding and two of the cruisers were forced by mechanical difficulties to drop back. Bey knew he was being followed which begs the question why he did not adopt the south-west option. He could have taken this as far as the latitude of Sørøya before turning east. It would have doubled the journey time but, with a speed advantage which Burnett thought was at least 8 knots, he would have shaken Force 1 off in under two hours. The rest of the journey would have been in total darkness with low chance of rediscovery. However, Bey probably initially adopted the North Cape course as the quickest route back. By the time he established Force 1 was firmly in pursuit, he had received the air sighting report of Force 2 and therefore perhaps calculated that a south-west course might take him straight into this apparent second British group with the risk of long-range radar detection. In fact, at 1330, Force 2 was about 120 miles south-west of *Scharnhorst*. Heading further east for Kirkenes was also possible and, early that evening, *Scharnhorst* would make a desperate run for Tanafiord, 65 miles south-east of North Cape. But for now, Bey probably judged that offered little advantage and North Cape was the least bad option although at 1430 he altered to just east of south to take him direct to Sørøya.[105]

In the event, Burnett's shadowing reports made interception by Fraser, coming up from west south-west at 25 knots, relatively straightforward. In another tribute to British radar, *Duke of York*'s Type 273Q detected Scharnhorst at 1617 at the extraordinary range of 23 miles, only two minutes more than Fraser had predicted an hour earlier. Just over half an hour later, after closing the range to 12,000 yards, *Duke of York* illuminated *Scharnhorst* with star shells, and then opened fire, straddling her with the first salvo. The subsequent engagement leading to *Scharnhorst*'s sinking at about 1920 has been comprehensively and vividly described elsewhere.[106] Although caught by surprise, and with the odds hugely stacked against her, Hintze came remarkably close to extricating his ship and enabling her escape, as Fraser freely acknowledged. Her end was the result of one lucky hit from *Duke of York* at extreme range, creating the opportunity for a brilliant and dangerous close-quarters British destroyer attack conducted at a closing speed of more than 50 knots.[107]

For the British, the 'Battle of North Cape' as it became known eliminated the German surface threat to the JW convoys for at least three months and, if *Tirpitz* could not be made operational, perhaps indefinitely. The residual threat from Johannesson's destroyers was unlikely to take effect and easily dealt with. The action fought in Arctic winter storm and darkness proved to be the last in which a Royal Navy battleship fought a peer adversary. It was also the penultimate time Royal Navy destroyers executed a torpedo attack on an enemy heavy ship using the tactics developed so assiduously in the interwar period.[108] The conditions also meant that air power which was fast becoming the dominant element in naval warfare played little part. In some respects, for the British, the engagement therefore marked the end of an era, a throwback to warfare closer to Jutland than that being pioneered in the Pacific theatre. But in other ways, the exploitation of radar and intelligence and the combined arms manoeuvre of multiple forces, it was very modern. The Action Information Organisation (AIO as it became known) had come of age. A year on from the Barents Sea battle, Fraser and Burnett hardly ever visited the bridge of their respective flagships. They fought the battle from the plot below with radar the dominant sensor. As Fraser said afterwards, British radar was 'far superior' to anything in German ships and it enabled the Home Fleet 'to find, fix, fight, and finish off the *Scharnhorst*'. Indeed, *Duke of York* may have had the finest overall radar fit in the world at that time.[109] There were also again two more enduring factors behind British success – the seamanship that only comes from long exposure to the sea and willingness to 'engage the enemy more closely' whatever the odds.

On the German side, Naval Staff Operations Division concluded that British radar had effectively enabled them to turn night into day, eliminating any prospect of the German force achieving surprise.[110] Schniewind was equally clear that 'the enemy enjoyed unequivocal superiority owing to his ability to direct his fire by radar' although he also stressed the inadequacy of German air reconnaissance. In neither the morning nor noon actions had it been possible for *Scharnhorst* to exploit her fighting qualities. 'To have carried out the appointed task successfully would only have been possible with a lot of luck.'[111] This scarcely veiled criticism of Dönitz was probably widely shared by those involved in planning and executing Ostfront with the notable exception of Meisel. Dönitz endorsed the assessment of British radar superiority. In a message on *Scharnhorst*'s loss to be shared with all naval personnel, which can hardly have boosted morale, he stated that the enemy had detected her at 30 miles and fired accurately beyond visual range out to 18,000m.[112]

Dönitz also emphasised the radar factor when he reported to Hitler at the beginning of January. However, no doubt anxious to protect his own position and reputation, he encouraged Hitler to believe that the primary blame lay with Bey for failing to finish off the cruisers and press on to the convoy during the 1220 engagement. Interestingly, in his previous message circulated to naval personnel, Dönitz claimed that a 'heavy enemy unit' had been present with the cruisers which was hardly consistent with this criticism of Bey. He then followed up with the muddled argument that, while superior enemy radar prevented use of the fleet in an anti-invasion role, he intended to continue targeting the convoys and hoped to deploy the heavy cruiser *Prinz Eugen* to the North.[113] This apparently drew on equally confused Naval Staff ideas a few days earlier for a much expanded fleet equipped with 'highly efficient radar' to carry the fight to the convoys although there was no clue as to how these resources would be acquired.[114] While his scapegoating of Bey was unattractive, Dönitz perhaps had a point in highlighting the failure to go aggressively for Burnett's cruisers and ideally destroy them. Despite the British radar advantage, *Scharnhorst* had enough visibility to exploit her superior speed, gunpower and armour to do this. Even if this never opened a path to the convoy, destroying the cruisers as an effective force would have been a significant victory, severely damaged British morale and, not least, have enabled *Scharnhorst* to then retreat to Altafiord unscathed. Such a victory and escape would then have significantly complicated the protection of future convoys.

Dönitz was more circumspect about scapegoating Bey within the navy given that the latter had died a hero's death and Dönitz had insisted on persevering with Ostfront against the clear advice of Schniewind and Peters. His solution was to regret his own failure to recall Kummetz from leave and to endorse arguments put by Schniewind and Johannesson that crew inexperience and lack of sea training had contributed to the disaster. Dönitz was deluding himself if he really thought Kummetz would have acted differently but the other points were true enough.[115]

## Chapter 12

# Last Convoys and the Final Stand of the Kriegsmarine

Churchill learnt of the sinking of the *Scharnhorst* in Morocco where he was recovering from pneumonia. Already a firm fan of Fraser, whom he would have preferred as First Sea Lord in place of Cunningham, he was naturally delighted.[1] He lost no time in exploiting the success with Stalin and in pressing the Admiralty to plan a fifth monthly convoy in the present winter series to be programmed for March. He confided to Attlee, acting for him in his absence, that he wanted this as a 'sweetener' to deploy with Stalin if Overlord, the invasion of France currently set for early May, was delayed by a month.[2] After chairing the Defence Committee on 4 January 1944, Attlee informed the prime minister that there were no naval objections to running a further convoy but there were two complications. First, the rate of unloading in Russian ports, especially Murmansk, had not kept pace with arriving ships. British and American crews had been forced to unload some of the November ships themselves due to lack of skilled Soviet personnel. With the arrival of JW 56A at the end of the month, there would probably be sixty-five merchant ships accumulated in the Kola Inlet. Unless the backlog could be speedily addressed, an extra homeward convoy in April would be required when light and ice conditions were unfavourable and there would still be a significant number of ships left idle in Kola over the summer. In the event, a carefully veiled threat from Rear Admiral Fisher that the second January convoy might have to be postponed brought a marked improvement in Soviet performance. Secondly, with the planned February convoys, Britain would have completed its commitments under the Third Protocol with the exception of 150 fighters due between April and June to be delivered via Persia. Britain could fill two ships with extra non-military supplies but that meant the Americans must make up the remainder of a convoy of thirty ships with the risk that many of the vessels would then be trapped in

Russia. They would probably only consider trucks and food and the latter was not a high-priority item.[3] In the event, within 10 days the Americans did promise seventeen ships and with three British, a convoy of twenty was programmed for mid-March. The prime minister duly informed Stalin on 18 January who responded rapidly expressing appreciation.[4]

While the British planned to exploit the elimination of *Scharnhorst* by boosting convoy traffic, Dönitz implemented a major increase in the Arctic U-boat force. He ordered the transfer of six additional boats on 26 December, taking numbers in the theatre to twenty-four, and on 10 January a further nine boats were assigned to bring the planned force to thirty-three. Allowing for losses and replacements in the next six months, the maximum strength briefly achieved was thirty-two boats in July. The force was split mainly between Trondheim and Narvik and divided into the 11th and 13th Combat Flotillas. Peters, as Captain Arctic U-boats at Narvik, had overall command. All these additional U-boats were Type VIICs and all had arrived by the end of February. None were fitted with 'schnorchels' or snort masts, a modification which enabled diesel engines to charge batteries at periscope depth and was being steadily rolled out across the fleet.[5] Snorts did not arrive in the Arctic until the autumn. However, most of the newcomers had the Naxos radar-warning system, the latest sonar, improved anti-aircraft armament, and were armed with G7es (T5) *Zaunkönig* acoustic homing torpedoes which the British called 'Gnats' (for 'German navy acoustic torpedo') and had been used in the Atlantic, primarily to target escorts, albeit with only modest success, since the previous autumn. The Allies had advance intelligence warning of the T5's arrival and therefore rapidly introduced countermeasures, both tactical and technical. The latter was a towed noisemaker, with the Royal Navy version 'Foxer' fitted to most of its escorts by the spring of 1944. American and Canadian escorts were similarly equipped but with slightly different models. At the beginning of April, the British Admiralty assessed that about 13 per cent of T5 attacks to date had achieved either a sinking or damage but the proportion was falling as countermeasures improved. In the first quarter of 1944, a limited reserve stock of T5s began arriving at the northern U-boat bases.[6]

This U-boat reinforcement was only partly linked to the loss of *Scharnhorst*. Although, until mid-1943, Dönitz consistently judged the Arctic a poor operating environment for U-boats and hence a waste of resources, Hessler, as First Staff Officer at U-boat Headquarters, claimed that by the end this year the picture had changed. The growing strength of Allied anti-submarine forces made North Atlantic operations increasingly difficult and unproductive. That was certainly true. In the last four months of 1943, 101 U-boat patrols in the North Atlantic sank six escorts and eight merchant ships at the cost of forty-nine U-boats, an appalling rate of return. Operational prospects were therefore now viewed as better in the Arctic where the U-boats could benefit from still-strong German air reconnaissance and interdiction of the revived 'PQ convoys' was judged 'supremely important' to holding Germany's position in the East. The new emphasis on anti-invasion measures triggered by Führer Directive 51 was also a factor. There were no heavy surface forces available and few light forces to cover the huge Norwegian coastline. Enhanced U-boat strength was accordingly the best available countermeasure.[7]

Against this background, the January convoy of thirty-six ships in total again sailed in two parts, with the first twenty leaving Loch Ewe as JW 56A on 12 January. A heavy battleship covering force was now unnecessary but Fraser took no chances with a possible German destroyer sortie and therefore deployed the customary cruiser cover. Enigma decrypts kept the OIC well sighted on the enhanced U-boat threat and the close escort was as strong as that for the December convoys. JW 56A ran into dreadful weather, forcing five ships to return, and was then attacked by U-boats in the vicinity of Bear Island. Fifteen boats were deployed, over half current strength and predominantly new arrivals, mainly in the approaches to the Bear Island Gap. The OIC recognised this concentration and diverted the convoy northward to evade the bulk of the pack. However, the convoy was spotted by the most northerly positioned boat, *U-956*, and a total of eight boats closed to conduct attacks over the two days 25/26 January, with most firing T5s. They sank three of the remaining fifteen merchant vessels and damaged the destroyer *Obdurate*, one of the heroes of the Battle of the Barents Sea 13 months earlier. This was the first U-boat success against an outbound convoy since PQ 18 and it would be the last for more than a year.

Fraser ordered immediate countermeasures. He postponed sailing the linked westbound RA 56A so that the incoming JW 56A escorts could be sent instead to reinforce the approaching JW 56B which had left Loch Ewe on 22 January as it transited the U-boat danger area. Intelligence that Johannesson's destroyers had come to two hours' notice was also a factor in this decision. Although the Germans attacked this second January convoy of sixteen ships with as many U-boats as its predecessor, firing a similar number of T5s, the mass escort ensured no merchant ship was lost, although the destroyer *Hardy* was sunk by a T5 from *U-278*. In compensation, the British escorts sank the newly arrived *U-314* 100 miles south-east of Bear Island on 30 January, the first U-boat sunk in the Arctic theatre since PQ 18. The combined escorts from JW 56A and B, twenty-six in total, then took out a single return convoy RA 56, comprising thirty-seven merchant ships. Due to clever evasion at the start of its journey, it was not detected until it reached the vicinity of Bear Island when a German air sighting reported it heading east. It therefore received no serious German attention. The British were aware from an Enigma decrypt that the Germans grossly exaggerated their success against the two eastbound convoys. Peters encouraged his crews from Narvik by claiming seven destroyers and four merchant ships sunk, three destroyers and six merchant ships probably sunk, and others damaged, in all a total of twenty-seven hits. This suggested 100 per cent success for T5 firings, an implausible result apparently not questioned by Arctic U-boat command.[8]

The success of RA 56 persuaded Fraser to run single large convoys, inward and outward, during February. With the winter ice now extending further south, there was little prospect of evading the substantial U-boat forces now positioned in the Bear Island Gap. Single convoys permitted a much larger escort to fight them through and take a more aggressive approach in prosecuting U-boat contacts. Fraser's decision was made easier by the availability of the escort carrier *Chaser*. She became the first carrier to complete a full Arctic convoy cycle since *Avenger* with PQ 18. As one of the next class of escort carriers completed for the Royal Navy in the United States, she incorporated important improvements. The hangar was lengthened to accommodate twenty aircraft with lifts at each end of the flight deck. As a specialist anti-submarine carrier, she was also fitted with state-of-the-art radar, HF/DF and communications suites and the latest model of operations room. For February's JW 57, she carried eleven Swordfish and eleven Martlet fighters.[9] The Swordfish, equipped with the latest ASV XI radar and armed with rockets as well as depth charges, remained a useful ASW aircraft. However, it was much inferior to the Avenger (or Tarpon as the British sometimes called it) strike aircraft with which American escort carriers in the Atlantic operated. This was one important factor underpinning the strikingly higher rate of U-boat sinkings achieved by American carriers in the ASW role across 1943 – seven times that of their Royal Navy counterparts.[10] The Fleet Air Arm was gradually acquiring Avengers but in early 1944 they remained in short supply. Nevertheless, despite its shortcomings and deficiencies, Royal Navy escort carrier practice was improving fast. Every future Arctic convoy would include at least one escort carrier but often two. To say that their record measured in U-boats sunk and aircraft shot down proved respectable belies the appalling weather in which Arctic flying often took place. Cunningham, who rarely indulged in compliments, described the work of the aircrews, operating in 'indescribable' conditions, as 'beyond praise'.[11] In addition to *Chaser*, the close escort of the present convoy comprised seventeen destroyers, including a Western Approaches support group, under the overall command of Rear Admiral Irvine Glennie, who had relieved Burnett and flew his flag in the new cruiser *Black Prince*, making her operational debut. Glennie, as an Ultra recipient, could also be constantly updated on U-boat dispositions by the OIC.

With this escort, JW 57, originally programmed to be the last winter convoy, sailed from Loch Ewe on 20 February with forty-two merchant ships and an additional tanker. With two more ships than PQ 18 it was the largest Arctic convoy to date. Enigma decrypts showed that at least fourteen U-boats had been deployed against it and the first attack by six of these commenced four days after departure about 150 miles due west of North Cape. The destroyer *Mahratta* was sunk with all but seventeen of her crew lost by a T5 from *U-990* on her first war patrol. However, in some compensation, the same day the destroyer *Keppel*, Broome's former command during PQ 17 and now back with the Western Approaches B1 Support Group, sank *U-713* on her fourth Arctic war patrol. The following day, a Catalina flying from the Shetlands which had been in the air 12 hours found the very experienced *U-601* 150 miles north-west of Tromsø nine days into her tenth patrol in northern waters and sank her with two depth charges. *Chaser*'s Swordfish frustrated all subsequent U-boat attacks and with her Martlets keeping shadowers at bay there were no more losses.

The U-boats maintained a maximum effort against the homeward-bound RA 57 of thirty-one ships which left Kola on 2 March, two days after JW 57's arrival, and supported by the incoming escort. Five U-boats attacked on 4 March, sinking one merchant ship, the convoy's single casualty, but then suffered badly from *Chaser*'s Swordfish, losing *U-472* later that day and *U-366* and *U-973* over the next two days, as the convoy transited the Bear Island Gap. All three U-boats had arrived in Norway in the last five weeks. Overall, with an average of fifteen boats at sea for these two convoys, the U-boat return was one destroyer and one merchant ship for five of their own sunk and several others damaged. The German Naval Staff had stressed at the beginning of the month that every ship reaching Russia unloaded material that then had to be destroyed in hard fighting on the Eastern Front. Yet, there had been no impact at all on these incoming supplies to Russia. A campaign imposing these costs for negligible benefit did not look sustainable.[12]

When he originally lobbied for an additional March convoy, Churchill hoped it would comprise twenty ships, a figure he confirmed to Stalin on 8 February.[13] However, the problems on the Pacific route over the winter and effective pressure on the Russians to improve cargo handling at Murmansk encouraged the Americans to seize the opportunity to despatch the maximum possible cargo. When it sailed from Loch Ewe on 27 March, JW 58 therefore contained forty-nine ships, making it by far the largest Arctic convoy of the war. Close escort arrangements followed the model established for the February pair but with the important addition of a second escort carrier. The British-built *Activity* had seven Martlets and three Swordfish while the American-built *Tracker*, the first British-operated escort carrier to have a catapult, had seven Martlets and twelve Avengers. The provision of air cover was thus more flexible and the Avengers made it more capable. The entire close escort under Vice Admiral Frederick Dalrymple-Hamilton in the cruiser *Diadem*, *Black Prince*'s new sister, numbered thirty-three warships, including twenty destroyers. Importantly, it also included the five sloops of Western Approaches Support Group 2 under the vastly experienced and now famous U-boat destroyer, Captain Johnny Walker. The secondment of Walker demonstrated Max Horton's belief that the Arctic was now an important theatre in which to kill U-boats. Walker was quick to get a result. Two days into the passage, his own ship *Starling* detected and sank the new *U-961* which had left Bergen six days earlier to join the Atlantic U-boat force and probably ran into JW 58 by chance about 100 miles north-east of the Faeroes.

Enigma decrypts revealed that at least sixteen boats were deployed to meet the next convoy and these conducted at least eighteen identified attacks, mainly with T5s, in the Bear Island Gap over the period 1–3 April. None of these succeeded but three more U-boats were sunk, two succumbing to air attack from the carriers and the other a further success for *Keppel*. U-boat T5 claims again bordered on the absurd, with nine destroyers 'confirmed' sunk and a further four 'probably'. In reality, no U-boat sank anything and JW 58 reached Kola unscathed on 6 April although one ship was forced to return due to ice damage. The carrier fighters also destroyed six German air force shadowers, leading to high praise for both pilots and fighter direction teams from Horton. The westbound RA 58 with thirty-six ships left Kola next day under the care of the incoming escort, was left alone by the Germans, and therefore reached Loch Ewe without loss a week later.[14]

The March convoys reinforced the conclusion that Fraser had already reached from experience the previous month regarding the value of carrier support. Their aircraft could pursue HF/DF contacts and force U-boats down more rapidly and economically than could destroyers and without exposing them to T5 attack or compromising the integrity of the anti-submarine screen.[15] Post-operation analysis conducted on these 1944 convoys clearly underlined how important HF/DF now was in monitoring U-boat movements and establishing their whereabouts.[16] At the tactical level, with support from ASV radar, its contribution was far more significant than Enigma decrypts although the latter remained essential in assessing the wider operational and strategic picture of the U-boat war.[17] Horton strongly endorsed Fraser's views and hoped two escort carriers would be available for future convoys. He saw the Arctic as now the only remaining area where there were 'prolific' opportunities to inflict heavy losses on both U-boats and German long-range maritime aircraft. This goal should not be 'secondary' to the 'safe and timely arrival of the convoy', an aspiration gently disputed by Fraser.[18] It is not clear Horton's claim that the Arctic offered especially rich pickings was justified. Over the five months January to May, seventy-eight U-boat patrols in the North Atlantic resulted in thirty-seven losses, a rate of 47 per cent. A similar number of admittedly much shorter Arctic patrols in these months produced twelve losses, a third of those in the Atlantic. However, it is true that average monthly losses compared to average monthly strength in the Arctic in this period slightly exceeded average loss against strength for the whole U-boat force.[19]

Although Fraser also commended the contribution of the Western Approaches support groups, the February and March convoys nevertheless posed questions as to why sonar conditions in the Arctic were so poor. Indeed JW 58 convinced Walker that only aircraft could kill U-boats effectively in this area. Under American influence, the Admiralty was already taking an interest in bathythermograph readings which showed the existence of pronounced temperature layers below the surface which then affected sound propagation. Bathythermograph trials undertaken by the destroyer *Saumarez* in the autumn revealed sharp drops in temperature in the Arctic at 150–200ft which rendered U-boats virtually immune from detection below that depth.[20]

It is unlikely that Dönitz believed the exaggerated claims of escort sinkings. When he met Hitler on 12 April, he emphasised the problems posed by carrier aircraft which prevented his U-boats closing the 'PQ' convoys. He argued that the German air force could easily locate the carriers and neutralise them with torpedo strikes. Göring, who was present, was sceptical that the carriers were the only problem facing the U-boats and shrewd enough to recognise the practical and resource constraints in meeting Dönitz's demand. Nevertheless, Hitler insisted on air force action and Göring went through the motions of complying. Since the next inbound convoy did not run until August, the issue was for the present anyway academic.[21]

## Operation Tungsten

During the month leading up to the departure of JW 58, intelligence monitoring of *Tirpitz* through SIGINT, SIS agents and PR Spitfires flying from Vaenga reported her conducting trials consistent with regaining operational status by the end of March. The earlier assessment emphasising the need for a docking initially persuaded the OIC that she would move south to Germany but by 21 March there was no evidence to support this. The OIC therefore judged that, given the importance the Germans placed on disrupting supplies to Russia, they might take the risk of sailing her against a convoy if they were convinced it had no heavy covering force. The Admiralty accordingly ordered Fraser to provide battleship cover for JW 58 but added that there was compelling intelligence that *Tirpitz* would be at her normal berth in Kaafiord until at least 2 April. This persuaded Fraser to combine support for the convoy with a Fleet Air Arm strike on the battleship.[22] In fact, while it was true she would remain based in Kaafiord, she was to undertake intensive daily sea trials in Altafiord during the first half of April.[23]

Knowing that *Tirpitz* would probably complete repairs by late March, Fraser had two months earlier ordered his deputy, Vice Admiral Henry Moore, to prepare a plan for a carrier strike, designated Operation Tungsten. This was an immensely challenging operation requiring meticulous intelligence. The terrain at Kaafiord ruled out torpedo attack and was demanding for dive-bombing. The approach to the target had to ensure surprise to minimise the chance of the Germans obscuring *Tirpitz* with their smoke generators. Enemy fighters had to be countered and the layered anti-aircraft defences identified and suppressed. Up-to-date weather reports were essential, and so was final confirmation that *Tirpitz* was still in her anchorage. Torstein Raaby, reporting through Station Ida, was the intelligence star, providing most of the detail on flak locations, radar, and high tension cables. At considerable risk, he also provided two-hourly weather reports. The Inter-Service Topographical Department, drawing on PR coverage as well as Raaby's reports, provided detailed topographical models of the target area. The quality of this target picture, painstakingly constructed from multiple sources, far surpassed what had been available for the Taranto attack three and a half years previously, let alone Wake-Walker's operation against Petsamo. It demonstrated how far the Royal Navy had evolved in applying intelligence to operational planning. Training of the strike crews was equally meticulous and included construction of an exercise range at Loch Eriboll in Northern Scotland, chosen because it most nearly resembled Kaafiord, thereby giving the attackers on the day the feeling they had done it before. A final rehearsal was conducted at Loch Eriboll on 28 March from the carriers operating off Scapa Flow.[24]

The Tungsten carrier force comprised the fleet carriers *Victorious* and *Furious*, which had together conducted the Petsamo strike nearly three years earlier, and four escort carriers, *Emperor*, *Pursuer*, *Searcher* and *Fencer*. With *Activity* and *Tracker* covering JW 58, there were therefore six escort carriers simultaneously in the Arctic. *Victorious* had only just returned from her loan to the US Navy in the Pacific and this required Tungsten to be postponed for two weeks to ensure her participation. The carriers were grouped in two forces. Force 7 had Moore's flagship, the battleship *Anson*, together with the two fleet carriers, supported by the cruisers *Belfast* and *Jamaica* and six destroyers. Force 8, under Rear Admiral Arthur Bisset in the cruiser *Royalist*, had the four escort carriers, the cruiser *Sheffield* and a further six destroyers. Fraser was also at sea providing additional distant cover with *Duke of York* and her destroyer escort. The Tungsten strike force comprised forty-two Barracudas embarked in the fleet carriers and they were supported by 110 fighters, split across all six carriers. Nearly half of these were Corsairs and Hellcats, the latest American naval fighters, and the rest Martlets and Seafires. The Barracuda had been designed to replace the Swordfish and Albacore but had a long and troubled development history and had only entered service in the last half of 1943. Tungsten was its first major operation. The Barracudas were to attack in two equal waves, one hour apart, each supported by forty fighters. They were armed with a mix of 1600lb heavy armour-piercing bombs designed to penetrate *Tirpitz*'s main armoured deck if dropped above 2000ft and two types of 500lb bomb designed to cause damage to upper works and target gun crews. Thirty fighters remained to conduct defensive combat air patrols around the two task forces.[25]

The forces reached their flying-off position 150 miles north-west of Kaafiord undetected in the early hours of 3 April and the first wave arrived over *Tirpitz* at 0530. The battleship was caught unmooring in preparation for exercises in Altafiord and taken completely by surprise. Had the attack arrived even half an hour later, she would have been underway in Altafiord and a far more difficult target. While half the fighters maintained top cover, the other half strafed the anti-aircraft batteries in the positions that had been identified ashore along with those aboard *Tirpitz*. This enabled the Barracudas to conduct their diving runs relatively untroubled by flak. They achieved nine hits and one 'profitable near miss' with only one aircraft lost. The second wave arrived an hour later and conducted a repeat performance with five further hits and again just a single Barracuda lost. By 0800 all aircraft had landed and the two task forces moved rapidly away from the coast. Moore had retained the option of a further strike the following day but assessed sufficient damage had been achieved and therefore returned to Scapa Flow.[26]

Tungsten was the largest strike operation conducted by the Fleet Air Arm in any theatre to date and arguably its most complex of the whole war in Europe. The prior research and subsequent planning and coordination of two strikes conducted across six carriers had been almost faultless. Unfortunately, although the Barracudas had performed superbly to achieve fourteen hits from forty attacking aircraft, only two bombs reached the main armoured deck and none penetrated it. This was because most aircraft had released their weapons from too low a height. On 15 April, the Director of Naval Construction concluded that 'little damage of a vital nature affecting seagoing or fighting efficiency was inflicted'. If it was essential for *Tirpitz* to put to sea, sufficient repairs could be completed in three weeks.[27] This assessment may have been too pessimistic. The shock damage from hits and near misses must have been considerable, inflicting harm to sensitive equipment even if not immediately apparent, and possible compromise of repairs to the earlier Source damage. Seven months later, Cunningham, as First Sea Lord, confided that he had written off *Tirpitz* as a fighting unit after Tungsten and the only requirement was to prevent her returning to Germany.[28] When he reported to Hitler in mid-April, Dönitz too apparently doubted *Tirpitz* would see further action but was determined to have her repaired so that she continued to tie down British forces.[29]

With only limited intelligence on *Tirpitz*'s precise operational status following Tungsten, the Admiralty had to assume she would become a potential threat again by July at the latest and that further strikes were necessary. If Cunningham really did doubt her fighting value, this did not stop him goading a sometimes reluctant Fraser into mounting more strikes. Three planned operations in late April and May had to be abandoned due to adverse weather. An operation in mid-July was foiled because the Germans had enough warning to obscure the battleship with smoke. This provoked the idea of flying long-range Mosquitoes off a carrier to attack from an unexpected direction. Before this idea could be implemented, a series of more traditional Barracuda attacks the following month came closer to success when a 1600lb bomb finally penetrated *Tirpitz*'s armoured deck but unfortunately failed to explode. After this, Royal Air

Force Lancasters, carrying 12,000lb 'Tallboy' bombs, were deployed from North Russia. A raid on Kaafiord on 15 September inflicted crippling damage which it was estimated would take nine months to repair.[30] Two months later, after *Tirpitz* had been towed to Tromsø, Lancasters operating from Scotland finally sank her. The problem *Tirpitz* posed for the British in this summer of 1944 was different to that in the previous two summers. There were ample naval resources available to deal with a specific threat to a convoy or any other attempted sortie but the Admiralty was anxious to transfer all its modern battleships and fleet carriers to the East. Dönitz was correct therefore that she only had to be theoretically operational to oblige the British to hold some forces back. There was also a political angle. A successful move back to Germany would have been militarily pointless at this stage of the war but still deeply embarrassing for Churchill and the Royal Navy leadership.[31]

*The Impact of the 1943/1944 Winter/Spring Convoys*
The successful arrival of March convoy JW 58 and its westbound counterpart RA 58 completed the winter/spring programme initiated at the Defence Committee at the end of the previous September. However, a considerable body of merchant ships that could not be unloaded in time for RA 58 remained in Kola. In a sign of the dominance the Royal Navy had now established over the route, Fraser ran a further westbound convoy at the end of April to bring these out even though its passage was in almost perpetual daylight. This also enabled more than 2000 Russian personnel to travel to the United Kingdom to take over the battleship *Royal Sovereign* and other ships being loaned to the Russian navy. Rear Admiral Rhoderick McGrigor took out a substantial escort, including the carriers *Activity* and *Fencer*, to collect a total of forty-five ships. Although the escort arrived in Kola undetected, RA 59 was attacked in the Bear Island Gap, losing one merchant ship to *U-711* on 30 April. However, *Fencer's* Swordfish countered by sinking three U-boats over the next two days, taking the Arctic theatre score to thirteen since 30 January.

Following the passage of RA 59, Fraser reported that the 'convoy season' had achieved a successful close. Supplies carried over five convoy months had reached Russia virtually intact and the Germans had suffered far greater losses than they had inflicted.[32] It is striking how the concept of a 'convoy season' had taken hold within the British political and naval leadership and their American counterparts. It has also been perpetuated by many later historians. In the winter of 1943/44, it is exemplified in the attitude of the Defence Committee. In September, it assumed there would be four to five months of convoys over the winter while, in early January, it was concerned that adding a March convoy would mean ships trapped in Kola over the summer. It was clearly true that continuous summer daylight had previously made the Arctic air and surface threats difficult to handle and therefore resource intensive for the defence. However, the only period when seasonal factors alone caused convoy suspension was the two months after PQ 17 in July 1942 and even here the demands of Pedestal in the Mediterranean somewhat delayed the start of PQ 18. That convoy demonstrated that the Royal Navy had potential solutions to fight its way through against the toughest opposition. Thereafter, periods of suspension were dictated more by the resource demands of other theatres than seasonal factors alone. In the summer of 1943, the Arctic air threat was a pale shadow of that the previous year. The surface threat was greater but would have been manageable if one or more fleet and escort carriers were available. In the spring of 1944, the outlook was very different. It was clear that two escort carriers and the destroyer numbers now available could deal comfortably with the residual surface and air threats and the enhanced U-boat numbers. The latter would anyway find summer daylight operations more difficult.

Since January, Churchill had kept Stalin closely informed on the progress of the convoy programme and on 3 May he summarised the overall results: 191 ships had reached Russian ports compared to the 140 projected by Eden in October. The original target of one million tons of cargo had been exceeded by 25 per cent with three-quarters deriving from the United States. Only three outbound ships had been lost and two on return. Major damage had been inflicted on the German navy while British losses were light. Churchill concluded that supplies would resume as soon as Overlord commitments permitted though he was careful to give no date. He clearly made an impact because Stalin responded with seemingly genuine appreciation underlined by his wish to give Oliver Lyttleton 'who has done so much' a Soviet decoration.[33] This positive exchange followed a difficult few months. The relative cordiality of the first 'Big Three' summit between Roosevelt, Churchill and Stalin in Teheran at the end of November was strained by subsequent profound and ill-tempered disagreements over Poland's future and arguments over Russia's entitlement to part of the surrendered Italian fleet.[34]

It was originally assumed the escort requirements of Overlord dictated a minimum two-month pause after RA 59, an impression Churchill initially conveyed to Stalin. However, by the beginning of June, he was pressing Roosevelt to support the earliest possible resumption so long as Overlord did not cause major destroyer losses.[35] He was pushing at an open door because American doubts about the value of the Arctic route had by now evaporated and the American chiefs of staff were already lobbying their British colleagues to restart the convoys as soon as the Overlord landings were secure. They emphasised that the cargo-handling problems at the northern ports had been resolved. The ports could now cope comfortably with 20,000 tons a day, more than double the rate in December. Given the significant savings in Western shipping time in using this route, it was vital not to let this new capacity lapse. Reopening the northern route was also a crucial hedge against a growing risk of Japanese disruption to Pacific traffic. Finally, it was clear the Russians preferred the northern route because delivery was faster and it imposed less demand on their internal transport capacity.[36] By 15 June, one week after D-Day, Lord Frederick Leathers, the Minister of War Transport, advised the ASE that planning for JW 59 and subsequent convoys was well underway. He expected JW 59 to comprise ten ships loaded in British ports and twenty loaded in the United States.[37] A month later Admiral Land emphasised to Roosevelt the value of the Arctic route. It was important in meeting urgent Soviet requirements for large railway locomotives and heavy factory machinery. Anticipating that JW 59 would sail mid-August, he planned to allocate 170,000 tons for despatch on this route in both July and August, temporarily overtaking shipments to the Persian Gulf.[38]

The supplies arriving in the Soviet northern ports between late November 1943 and early April 1944 represented 45 per cent of all those delivered via the Arctic route since Dervish nearly three years earlier. They were also nearly 50 per cent more than deliveries actually reaching the Soviet Union on either the Persian Gulf or Pacific routes in these five months as Stalin's own sources no doubt revealed.[39] The American component was not only easily three times the British tonnage but more relevant and important to Soviet needs at this stage of the war. The main focus was on transport, including 20,000 lorries, 100 heavy steam locomotives with the first 20 sailing on JW 55A, 500 assorted rail cars and a vast amount of railway building materials, battlefield communications, heavy industrial machinery, and specialised raw materials. Soviet domestic production of railway track during the war years was barely 10 per cent of 1940 output while output of locomotives, rail cars and wagons virtually ceased.[40] Most convoys also included two tankers bringing refined oil products such as high-quality aviation fuel. There were still significant weapon shipments, notably 300 P-40 fighters and about 1000 Sherman M4A2 medium tanks but these were a minor part of the cargo. The vast majority of aircraft were now flown in via Alaska.[41] By contrast, the smaller British component was focused on weapons and raw materials, including nearly 550 fighters, still predominantly Hurricanes, and 1050 Valentines.[42] Overall, this latest

Arctic contribution, provided entirely under the protection of the Royal Navy, was an outstanding success but it poses two questions. What were the real motives driving this substantial continuing aid effort at this point in the war and what difference did it make on arrival?

The last half of 1943 saw surprisingly little debate between Western political and military leaders over the purpose, composition and overall quantity of aid to Russia. It was not a major agenda item at the Anglo-American Quebec and Cairo conferences held in September and November respectively. Perhaps more surprisingly, it hardly featured at the subsequent Teheran summit where the primary focus was the Western commitment to proceed with Overlord the following spring.[43] By Quebec, with the failure of Citadel, it seemed clear that Germany would be steadily pushed back in Russia and that there was now no prospect of a separate peace. However, this provoked no reassessment of whether present levels of aid were necessary or the opportunity costs of providing it. The Third Protocol which had commenced on 1 July, although only formally signed in October, was negotiated in the same way as its predecessors. The Soviets made ambitious demands and the Western Allies offered a maximum response subject to the constraints of production, their own operational needs, and the capacity and feasibility of the transport routes. Only rarely were items held back for security reasons. There was a continuing underlying political assumption by Churchill and Roosevelt that the Soviet military contribution was vital to the success of Overlord which it was noted at Teheran rested on a 'narrow margin'. Furthermore, as Roosevelt's Soviet Protocol Committee told the War Department, the aid protocols did not just serve an immediate military purpose. They were intended to encourage Russia to 'assist in the defeat of Japan and in the negotiation of a sound peace'.[44] For Roosevelt, the latter included constructive Soviet participation in the proposed 'United Nations' organisation first raised with Molotov in June 1942.[45]

While Western military leaders sometimes resented the diversion of military equipment, were frustrated at the lack of information from the Soviets on their own production and plans, and often found them maddening to deal with, they did not question the core political assumptions. Their report to their political principals at Teheran therefore merely endorsed measures 'necessary and practicable' to 'aid the war effort of Russia'. There was minimal political or military inclination to use aid as a bargaining tool nor until perhaps early 1945 was much thought given to whether aid would advance Soviet post-war interests to Western detriment. There were a few prominent dissenters such as Averell Harriman and General John Deane who became respectively American ambassador and head of the United States Military Mission in Moscow in late 1943. Both recommended using aid for leverage and adopting a more questioning attitude to Soviet demands. They also opposed supplies that could be used to rebuild Russia after the war. But they had little success and Harriman was not entirely consistent. He later admitted his core role was 'to keep Russia in the war and save American lives'.[46] Nor was he yet much concerned with the Red Army going too far – 'The further they go, the more I like it'.[47] Saving lives was much on Churchill's mind if perhaps mixed with gathering worry about the fate of Eastern Europe, especially Poland. He acquiesced in Overlord with deep reluctance, sought to hedge it with conditions, and, almost to the end, harboured hopes that it might somehow be avoided. Even a month before its launch, he confided to Harriman that he retained oppressive doubts. If increasing aid to Russia reduced the risks, it had his firm support. Churchill's view that Overlord could fail was widely shared, not least by Ismay who enjoyed a more authoritative view than most on its prospects.[48]

The Western political position was therefore neatly encapsulated by one of Roosevelt's periodic directives on Soviet supply on 14 February 1944. He emphasised that Russia remained a 'major factor in the defeat of Germany'. It was therefore still 'of paramount importance' to provide 'maximum' supplies to her ports.[49] By contrast, Stalin now seemed more relaxed about continuing Western support. Following his return from Teheran, he told senior colleagues that Roosevelt had promised large-scale action in France in 1944. He conspicuously did not mention Churchill, rightly spotting that he was far more ambivalent. Stalin believed Roosevelt would keep this commitment but, even if he did not, 'we have enough forces of our own to complete the rout of Germany'. Of course, this comment referred to Western invasion and he would no doubt be less sanguine about losing Western supplies.[50] At Teheran, he had apparently also confided to his advisers that the war would have been lost without American aid which he referred to as an 'absolute necessity'.[51] It is also striking that, despite Stalin's confidence in routing Germany on his own, and whatever designs he harboured in Eastern Europe, he clearly preferred Overlord to happen and succeed. Reducing the cost to Russia in blood and treasure mattered.

Meanwhile, reflecting his reservations about Overlord, Churchill wanted to share Stalin's confidence in Soviet potential. On 11 January, still in Morocco, he asked for an urgent Joint Intelligence Committee review of prospects on the Russian front. Specifically, he wanted to know if a German collapse in the southern sector could trigger widespread German breakdown allowing Western armies to move into France largely unopposed (a scenario code-named Rankin).[52] The committee responded with an interim assessment on 14 January followed by an expanded piece approved by the chiefs of staff a week later.[53] The committee judged that the Germans were heavily outnumbered in personnel, armour and air power and consequently under severe pressure along the whole front. They therefore expected the Germans to lose considerably more territory by the end of the winter taking them at least back to the June 1941 Russian frontier. However, they expected them to avoid major encirclements and there were no signs of any general breakdown in command or morale across the German army. Nor did they expect any early collapse across Germany's East European allies. Overall, the thrust of the assessment was firmly to dampen any expectation of imminent Russian success on a scale sufficient radically to change prospects in the West and render Overlord unnecessary.

A further assessment three months later, specifically examining the implications of military developments in Russia for Overlord, broadly confirmed the January prediction. The front line had reached the 1941 Russian frontier, slightly further west of it in the south but still east of it in the centre north of the Pripet marshes and Germany still held the Baltic states and the Crimea. Germany could still afford to concede territory in the centre and, although nothing was known of Russia's intentions, this was their most likely area for a summer offensive since the Carpathians in the south were a strong natural barrier. Importantly, the Joint Intelligence Committee saw no evidence that events in the East were compelling Germany to transfer major forces from the West. Their strategy appeared to be to keep Western forces at their present level and accept risk in the East.[54]

These assessments, although they carried weight with the British leadership, were only a tiny sample of a vast range of reporting on both sides of the Atlantic bearing not just on Russia's military intentions and prospects but her overall war potential. By early 1944, there was general recognition in both British and American reporting that the Soviet economy had proved remarkably resilient although there was also growing appreciation of the scale of damage encountered in territory recovered from German occupation. There was also awareness of particular pressure points, notably food and transport and perhaps manpower. Some American reports at the turn of the year feared that, by the summer, Soviet food and manpower would be so strained that military capabilities would be reduced.[55]

Despite all the analysis of Soviet prospects through the winter of 1943/44 and subsequent spring, the are no British or American assessments that directly link this with justification of the ongoing aid programme. It triggered no critical examination of whether the commitments agreed under the Third Protocol or those being sought under the Fourth commencing 1 July 1944 were necessary. Within the American and British political and military leadership there remained minimal desire to curtail aid. Indeed, far from slowing, it accelerated through the first half of 1944 to the extent that Third Protocol commitments were exceeded by 130 per cent, easily wiping out the deficit on the Second Protocol.[56] It is understandable why this was so. The Germans were being pushed back in the East but were apparently still fighting doggedly and resisting withdrawals from the West. If Overlord was 'finely balanced' as Roosevelt and Churchill believed, then a maximum aid programme remained sacrosanct. The American economy could support it and the Royal Navy now had ample resources to protect the Arctic route. Marshall too is on record telling Roosevelt in early March that Lend-Lease remained crucial to the Soviet war effort and that the Germans might still defeat the Soviet Union if it ended.[57]

With the benefit of hindsight, it is easy to dismiss Marshall's comment as an absurd exaggeration even if it does reveal contemporary attitudes. However, if a German victory was virtually impossible, especially given the pressures they faced elsewhere, the continuing fragility of the Soviet war economy must not be underestimated. Soviet GDP at the end of 1944 was still 13 per cent below that of 1940. Western aid in 1944 added 10.4 per cent to GDP, not quite covering the gap. That enabled 1944 domestic defence expenditure to keep growing, 3.5 per cent above the previous year and 15.6 per cent above 1942. However, the civilian output remained 40 per cent below 1940. Even with Western aid running at 1944 levels, that deficit was not sustainable for long. Had Western aid stopped with the Third Protocol, Russia would have faced hard choices and some reduction in defence outlays seems inevitable. That would not have given the Germans victory. But it might have significantly prolonged the war with unknowable consequences. Marshall therefore had a point as did the American reporting anticipating Russia coming under strain in the autumn. Here too is ample explanation for Stalin's enthusiasm for Overlord.[58]

If the delivery of accelerating Western aid was denied any rigorous cost/benefit analysis, its value is evident in the major Soviet summer offensive 'Bagration' which, over two months from 22 June, achieved the destruction of German Army Group Centre. This has been aptly described as the heaviest defeat in German military history with personnel losses of at least 400,000. Bagration partly reflected overwhelming Soviet firepower with a 23:1 advantage in tanks, and 10:1 in artillery and aircraft.[59] The vast majority of this was domestically produced. Western tanks still comprised about 10 per cent of Soviet stock but their operational contribution was marginal although, as previously noted, the Shermans were valued for their reliability and firepower. Western fighters, now being delivered in great numbers through Alaska, made up about 12 per cent of deliveries to the Soviet air force in the first half of 1944 but lack of German opposition made them a useful supplement rather than essential. American twin-engine bombers which comprised almost 50 per cent of the Soviet inventory were more important. However, the real value of Western aid, including that recently delivered through the Arctic, to Bagration lay in enabling mobility. Bagration demonstrated that the Red Army had now mastered manoeuvre at the operational level, repeating the penetrating armoured thrusts of the Germans in 1941 and 1942 but on a vastly greater scale. This would not have been possible without Western vehicles and communications equipment. The Red Army had lost at least half its 272,000 pre-war trucks and light vehicles by the end of 1941 with much of the rest suffering extreme wear. Domestic production over the three years 1942–4 barely covered subsequent losses in those years. By the end of May 1944, just before the start of Bagration, the United States had successfully delivered 190,000 trucks and 36,000 jeeps (65,000 and 11,000 in the last six months, about one-third via the Arctic) and both of superior capability to their Soviet counterparts. Britain had added a further 4000 lorries, all via the Arctic. It was a similar story with military communications. The Red Army had lost half its pre-war capacity in 1941 and struggled to replace this. By mid-1944, the United States had provided 25,000 field radio stations and 260,000 field telephones, over half of these in the last 12 months. The impact of Western vehicles was also enhanced by vast support given to railway reconstruction and re-equipment. The United States provided twice as many heavy steam locomotives, primarily via the Arctic, as came from Soviet domestic production across the entire five years 1941–5.[60]

These mobility elements, of which about one-third of the November 1943 to May 1944 deliveries came through the Arctic, enabled deep armoured thrusts to be supported by infantry and technical units, and supplied on a continuing basis with ammunition, fuel and food. Without this Western support, Bagration and all other offensive operations would have become bogged down after achieving only shallow inlets into the German lines allowing the Germans time to rebuild their defences. As it was, in summer 1944, it was normal to see German troops on foot supported by horse-drawn wagons pursued by Red Army units on tanks and trucks.[61] As the future Soviet leader Nikita Khrushchev acknowledged in his memoirs,

'Just imagine how we would have advanced from Stalingrad to Berlin without them [American trucks and jeeps]. Our losses would have been colossal because we would have had no manoeuvrability.'[62]

### The Final Convoys – August 1944–May 1945

The combination of political pressure from Churchill and Roosevelt, the preference of the American chiefs of staff and Admiral Land's War Shipping Administration, and lower than expected escort losses during Overlord ensured that Arctic convoys resumed with JW 59 which left Loch Ewe with thirty-three ships on 15 August. Eight more convoys followed, at approximately monthly intervals with the last leaving the Clyde on 12 May, four days after Germany's formal surrender. These final nine convoys comprised 252 ships and only two were lost. Nine parallel westbound convoys brought back 236 ships with four lost. Two more designated westbound ships were lost off Kola immediately before joining RA 64 in February 1945. The outbound convoys delivered almost two million tons of cargo, nearly twice traditional estimates, 60 per cent more than the previous 1943/44 winter series and just over 40 per cent of total deliveries on the Arctic route across the whole war.[63]

These final Arctic deliveries comprised part of the Fourth Protocol signed in April 1944 which promised Russia a further 6.6 million tons of aid over the year beginning 1 July. 5.7 million tons was American with Canada adding just under 500,000 tons and Britain about 400,000 tons, of which all but 50,000 tons was oil products from the Abadan refinery delivered through Iran. By the end of May, deliveries had slightly exceeded this commitment with a month still to run. The Arctic contributed about one-third of the total across all routes over the 10 months August 1944 to May 1945, more than three times those via the Persian Gulf which, from January 1945, was largely replaced by delivery through Black Sea ports. Given that more than half the Canadian aid went via the Pacific, 87 per cent of the cargo in this final convoy series was American and, as with the previous series, weapons were a minor element, comprising about 100,000 tons or 5 per cent of the total, although the small British contribution included 1050 Spitfires. Nevertheless, it is worth emphasising that weapon tonnage delivered via the Arctic in 1944–5 was approximately the same as that in 1941–3 and the five months of 1945 were 17 per cent of the total.[64] Hindsight reveals that the aid arriving after the end of 1944 had little practical impact on the European war, again posing the question why the need for the convoys was not reassessed. One answer is that, in December 1944, it was not obvious that the European war would end in four months. The Red Army had not yet entered East Prussia or advanced beyond the Warsaw–Budapest line. That month, Field Marshal Erich von Manstein, widely regarded as Hitler's most outstanding commander in the East, was sufficiently deluded over Germany's prospects to contemplate buying an estate in Pomerania.[65] More realistically, at the end of November, the Joint Intelligence Committee anticipated a renewed Soviet offensive once the ground hardened but was not sure it would have early decisive results.[66] In the West, the Germans would soon launch their own surprise 'Ardennes Offensive'. Meanwhile, the two other justifications for maintaining the momentum of the aid effort, ensuring Russian participation in the war against Japan and encouraging her constructive engagement in a durable post-war settlement, remained extant. Stalin gave Churchill a firm promise when the latter visited Moscow in October 1944 to attack Japan three months after operations in Europe ended, although typically he bracketed this with demands for yet more aid. In early 1945, the two Western Allies expected the war with Japan to last well into 1946 with potentially high casualties. Soviet intervention was judged critical to reduce these. If continuing aid helped achieve it, the consensus was that the price was worth paying.[67]

These motives for continuing aid meant there was no greater enthusiasm to use it as a bargaining tool. At the end of March 1945, the Admiralty wanted to lay an anti-U-boat minefield off Kola to reduce the growing threat to convoys in its approaches but found the Russians obstructive. They were equally obstructive over allowing Western access to the captured German naval base at the Polish port of Gdynia (also Gotenhafen) despite earlier assurances. First Lord Alexander accordingly suggested cancelling the May convoy JW 67. The prime minister refused, judging that this would be provocative given many other quarrels with the Russians currently extant.[68] In his final days, Roosevelt was even less willing to antagonise Stalin.[69] Churchill's reluctance to use the convoys as a pressure point is intriguing given that, a month later, he asked the chiefs of staff to assess, in deepest secrecy, whether it would be possible to use Western military force to 'impose upon Russia the will of the United States and British Empire', a project known as 'Operation Unthinkable'. There were no specific examples of Western 'will' offered although the Joint Planning Staff assumed one might be 'a square deal for Poland'. The planners reported that Soviet superiority of three to one in land forces rendered 'quick and limited' success 'doubtful'. Defeating Russia would require 'total war' and take 'a very long time'.[70] Brooke thought the whole idea 'fantastic' and the chances of success 'quite impossible'. From now on, Russia would be 'all powerful in Europe.[71] Although the prime minister apparently accepted the planners' conclusion, he asked the chiefs for advice on the consequences for the United Kingdom if the Russians pushed west to the Atlantic coast following withdrawal of American forces from Europe. The chiefs responded that the only threat to British territory would come from novel weapons such as 'rockets'. It would take 'years' to mount an invasion or threaten sea communications.[72]

The loss of only two ships in the nine outbound convoys belies the effort the Germans maintained in targeting the Arctic route until a week before the war ended. Twenty-seven new or replacement U-boats deployed for service in the Arctic theatre in the final year of the war after the sailing of RA 59 at the end of April 1944. These comfortably covered the loss of twelve boats there over the year and ensured front-line strength for Arctic operations remained close to thirty boats through the autumn before declining to twenty by the end of January 1945. This strength was sufficient to allow regular deployment of twelve to eighteen boats against individual JW and RA convoys during this final cycle. The first schnorchel-equipped boats designated for the Arctic arrived in September and retrofitting of the existing force began at their Arctic bases the same month. However, only half those operating in the Arctic were ever schnorchel fitted.[73] In October, two groups of Ju 88 torpedo bombers, comprising nearly seventy aircraft, arrived, the first to be stationed in the Arctic for nearly two years. There was a simultaneous reinforcement of both fighters and reconnaissance aircraft. Fighter strength in Norway was now larger than at any time since 1940.[74]

These air additions, which were accompanied by significant land reinforcements taking troop levels to half a million by October, were not solely directed at the Arctic convoys. They reflected the wider strategic importance Germany placed on Norway in the final 10 months of the war. With the loss of the U-boat bases in France, it became the primary location from which to continue Atlantic operations and there were high hopes that the new Type XXI electro-boats could yet inflict heavy damage on Allied shipping.[75] By mid-January, the British Naval Staff were well informed on this threat, expected the Type XXIs to start operating the following month, and to undertake pack attacks in mid-Atlantic. They were also concerned about the growing threat in British inshore waters which had implications for Arctic convoy frequency given expanded demand for escorts. Nevertheless, while there was potential for severe shipping losses, German progress would be constrained by Allied land and air attacks on the German homeland and the effectiveness of new anti-submarine countermeasures.[76] Meanwhile, the Germans faced other challenges in Norway. Iron ore supplies from Narvik were increasingly critical to Germany's remaining war industry. Both U-boat bases and coastal supply traffic therefore had to be defended against increasing Allied air and naval attack and the threat of major raids or invasion. By September, the withdrawal of Finland from the war and a Soviet offensive across the Litza imperilled Germany's position in the far North. Petsamo was given up on 14 October and the Kolosjoki nickel mines were evacuated a week later after thorough destruction. This allowed withdrawal to a defensive line based on the narrow 25-mile corridor connecting Lyngenfiord, 75 miles south-west of Alta, with the Swedish border. This in turn dictated the final move of *Tirpitz* to Tromsø fiord where she would act as a coastal defence battery helping protect the north-west approaches to the new defensive line.[77]

Thirty-seven schnorchel-fitted U-boats moved from France to Norway between July and September, where they joined the 11th Flotilla at Bergen and 13th at Trondheim. These had been designed to support a thirty-boat Arctic force and struggled to cope with the new additions. Most of the boats operating in the Arctic now came under the 14th Flotilla at Narvik but facilities there were limited and boats had to go to the other bases to repair battle damage or resolve major defects. Between July 1944 and May 1945, the Norway-based boats conducted 199 North Atlantic patrols, sinking seventy-eight ships for seventy-two U-boats lost.[78] This demonstrated that schnorchel boats were neither improving productivity nor alleviating a dreadful loss rate. On 13 October, Dönitz told Hitler that he planned to have forty Type XXIs in action by February.[79] In practice, although several Type XXIs moved to Bergen from Kiel from March onward, only one boat ever deployed operationally. *U-2511* arrived to join 11th Flotilla at Bergen on 23 March but continuing defects meant she did not commence a first war patrol until 30 April. Her commander, Adalbert Schnee, claimed to have conducted a successful mock attack on the cruiser *Norfolk* on 4 May after receiving the order to cease hostilities.[80]

British intelligence coverage of German U-boat and air dispositions and intentions in the Arctic during this final phase of the war remained excellent. Although in September, the Arctic U-boat force at last received a new four-wheel Enigma key to replace Dolphin which GC&CS called Narwhal, its decryption posed 'few difficulties' given the long experience with the Atlantic U-boat Shark key.[81] Given knowledge of continuing German strength, the new convoy cycle followed the pattern established the previous spring. The convoys ran on a 30-day cycle, initially comprising thirty to thirty-five ships although numbers dropped by a third in the final three months. The standard escort allocated was two escort carriers, on several occasions three, one cruiser, ten fleet destroyers and eight specialist anti-submarine vessels from Western Approaches. Although inbound and outbound convoys were again arranged sequentially with the same escort covering both, a 30-day cycle was too tight to allow a single escort force to cover successive convoy pairs. Two escort forces were therefore required and this final convoy cycle was accordingly expensive in resources.[82] However, the escort power deployed did allow an aggressive approach towards U-boats, with aircraft and surface support groups often sent ahead to target known concentrations.[83] Growing winter darkness also hampered German reconnaissance so that their contact with convoys was often fleeting.

Of the eight convoy passages completed between August and December, four outward and four returns, only the second outgoing convoy, JW 60, successfully avoided all enemy attention. Of the remaining seven, which did come under varying degrees of attack, only RA 60, the second return, suffered merchant losses with two ships sunk when it overran *U-310* which successfully escaped. U-boats also had some success against escorts. The frigate *Kite*, which had been part of Walker's Second Support Group, was sunk by a pattern-running torpedo fired by *U-344* while escorting the first outbound convoy JW 59. Two others were damaged by T5s, the frigate *Mounsey* with RA 61 and the destroyer *Cassandra* with RA 62. Both these were hit in the approaches to Kola and were able to get back there for temporary repair. These limited results cost six U-boats with three sunk in the first convoy pair and two with RA 62. The sixth, *U-921*, initially believed to have succumbed to Swordfish operating with RA 60, is now ascribed to accident. The Martlet fighters lacked radar, reducing their capability as winter darkness increased, but they still shot down at least three radar-equipped BV 138 shadowers in this period. Ju 88 torpedo bombers executed half-hearted attacks on the last convoy pair but were beaten off without achieving any damage. Although the U-boats again grossly overclaimed, the reality was that they had a hopeless rate of return. The tactic briefly promoted by the new commander of Arctic U-boats, Captain Reinhard Suhren, of using massed night surface attacks to overwhelm escorts proved futile in the face of British radar. Switching to a massed ambush in the approaches to Kola where convoys had to pass ultimately proved no more effective as the British had ample strength to clear the area.[84]

The first convoy pair of 1945, JW 63/RA 63, was untroubled in either direction, helped by winter darkness. JW 63 had the distinction of being the last convoy to leave Loch Ewe. Future convoys came and went from the Clyde. By contrast, the February convoy JW 64, under the command of Rear Admiral Rhoderick McGrigor, received significant German attention although it was largely abortive. For the first time, McGrigor chose one of the two escort carriers, *Campania*, as his flagship instead of a cruiser. This provided better access to the overall air picture and, as an Ultra reader, he could more easily apply its insights to air operations. The convoy was first detected by a German reconnaissance flight on 6 February, three days into its passage when 100 miles north-east of the Faeroes. A subsequent Ju 88 shadower was soon shot down by Martlets from *Campania*, but the Germans maintained sufficient intermittent contact to attempt a substantial torpedo strike with over forty aircraft the following morning, their largest air effort since PQ 18. However, the combination of radar failure in another German shadower and further fighter disruption prevented most attackers finding the convoy and the dozen that did proved reluctant to engage. Three days later, as the convoy passed south of Bear Island and at its closest point to the airfield at Bardufoss, there was a more determined and skilful attack comprising about thirty aircraft. It was no more successful, broken up by fighters from the two carriers and murderous anti-aircraft fire from the powerful and well-constructed escort screen. The attackers lost a third of their number with another third damaged. No ships were hit.[85]

The Germans combined these air attacks with a maximum U-boat effort. Eight boats were deployed against JW 64 in a patrol line in the Bear Island Gap but, warned by Ultra and exploiting constant air patrols from the carriers, the convoy eluded these. The U-boats then raced ahead to join a separate group positioned in the Kola approaches bringing total strength in the area to fourteen. One of these torpedoed the frigate *Denbigh Castle* off the entrance with a T5. She was towed in but damaged beyond repair. Other U-boats sank four ships from an incoming Soviet convoy including two destined to join the imminent return convoy RA 64. Drawing on Ultra and HF/DF reports, McGrigor knew this would now have to run the gauntlet of U-boats along the first 40 miles of its route with little scope for evasion. He therefore deployed an advance hunting group to sweep the area the night before RA 64 sailed on 17 February. This caught and sank the schnorchel-fitted *U-425*, a veteran of nine Arctic patrols. However, the U-boats hit back as the convoy began its journey, sinking one merchant vessel and the corvette *Bluebell*, and damaging the sloop *Lark*, which had contributed to sinking *U-425*, again beyond repair. The convoy now sailed into possibly the worst storm of the Arctic campaign which, with brief lulls, lasted nine days until it was past the Faeroes. The weather prevented the U-boats following the convoy which at times became badly scattered but there was another air attack when the weather briefly moderated on 20 February. This was beaten off with at least three aircraft downed and no casualties to the convoy, but a merchant straggler, the Liberty ship *Henry Bacon*, was found and sunk by a torpedo strike group three days later, the last Allied ship to be sunk by air attack in the European war. Following arrival in the Clyde, many of the escorts required docking to repair storm damage.[86]

The February convoys were the last to encounter serious and consistent air and U-boat attacks. *Henry Bacon* was not only the last ship sunk by aircraft but the last attacked from the air in the Arctic. The recently-deployed torpedo strike force had suffered badly in the engagements with JW 64 and RA 64. For a single merchant straggler, it had lost fourteen aircraft destroyed and perhaps another ten damaged beyond repair, one-third of its strength. This poor return partly reflected declining skill levels and fighting commitment although, in early April, the German air force demonstrated it could still hurt the Royal Air Force badly when it destroyed a substantial part of a Beaufighter force sent to attack the destroyer *Z 33* in southern Norway.[87] However, the main factors were the availability of a significant defensive fighter force, with fourteen Martlets divided between the two carriers, and the combined firepower of nearly twenty escorts including the anti-aircraft cruiser *Bellona* and eight of the most modern fleet destroyers. Overall, it is striking how little the Royal Navy tactics and capabilities deployed in defending JW 64 and RA 64 from air attack, the last such assault on a convoy in the European war, differed from those used for Halberd three and a half years previously. Radar, Action Information Organisation and fighter control had all improved, and the Martlet was a better fighter than the Fulmar. But the deployment of the escorts in an anti-aircraft screen and use of barrage fire was little changed. There had been limited evolution in anti-aircraft fire control or the capability of heavy anti-aircraft guns for most ship classes although there were many more light weapons. Proximity fuzes for anti-aircraft shells had arrived from the United States but for the Royal Navy these were in short supply and almost all destined for the new Pacific Fleet.[88] The air side of the Arctic war, just as in the Mediterranean, was ultimately more about numbers of defensive fighters and guns than principles or technology.

If the air war was over, Ultra decrypts in early March revealed German intent to maintain a maximum U-boat effort but focused in the approaches to Kola. On 6 March, Suhren as Captain Arctic U-boats emphasised that attacks on the Arctic convoys remained 'an important relief to the Eastern Front in its important struggle' and that the fitting of schnorchels allowed 'effective convoy attacks' from 'unobserved' positions 'close to the shore', 'even when daylight is continuous'.[89] Five days later, JW 65 left the Clyde with twenty-four merchant ships and a similar scale of escort to the February convoys. Two days later, the Germans suspected from intercepted radio transmissions that the next convoy was on its way and Suhren began deploying U-boats to the Kola area although without ruling out earlier interception if the convoy was precisely located. In the event, the convoy was not sighted before it was well into the Barents Sea and Suhren therefore positioned twelve boats off Kola. The British were aware the entrance to Murmansk would be contested and had agreed with the Russians to create a new swept channel to the east of the normal route. JW 65 did not take the new route to avoid compromising its use by the departing RA 65 and, although the escort took extensive countermeasures with air patrols and deterrent depth-charging, the Germans had some success with the five boats which attacked. These were helped by a snowstorm which briefly interrupted the flying of anti-submarine air patrols. The experienced *U-968*, one of the most successful Arctic boats on her seventh patrol, sank one merchant ship and the sloop *Lapwing* while *U-995* badly damaged another merchant vessel which subsequently had to be beached although her cargo was saved. *U-995*, after allotment to Norway after the war, was returned to Germany to become a museum outside Kiel, the only surviving Type VIIC. Suhren was determined to ambush the outgoing RA 65 and inflict maximum damage. However, although he correctly anticipated the departure date of 23 March, the deception of the new route worked, helped by the distraction of four destroyers making a high-speed dash up the old route dropping depth charges and firing star shells. Despite Suhren trying to rush his U-boats ahead of the convoy to the Bear Island Gap, RA 65 avoided all enemy attention.[90]

The Germans maintained their U-boat effort against the last wartime convoy pair. The outbound JW 66, which sailed from the Clyde with the usual escort on 17 April, successfully avoided a cordon of six boats placed just west of the Bear Island Gap and eight further boats positioned off Kola by using the same new eastern channel as RA 65. However, the Germans had now identified this route and were not fooled by diversionary tactics when the return convoy RA 66 left on 29 April. *U-968* fired two T5s at the frigate *Alnwick Castle* which exploded in her wake but then blew apart the frigate *Goodall* with a further T5. British counter-attacks detected and sank *U-307*. Two U-boats attempted further attacks as the convoy made its way westward that night but neither was successful. *U-427* survived a hunt of several hours in which nearly 700 depth charges were dropped but *U-286* was sunk. The sinking of *U-286* early on 30 April was not only the last convoy engagement in the Arctic but the last of the war in all theatres.[91]

Overall, in this final wartime convoy series since August, the average Arctic U-boat strength of twenty-five boats had sunk six merchant vessels in convoy, another two 'pre-joiners', and four escorts. Two more escorts were damaged beyond repair. It is notable that half the merchant losses and all but one of the escort casualties occurred in the Kola approaches. Suhren's tactic of exploiting schnorchel to position boats in an area where they would previously have been too vulnerable, and where the convoys had limited scope for evasion, therefore had some success. As with the parallel 'inshore campaign' underway in British waters, it potentially signalled a new chapter in the history of submarine warfare. However, in doing so it also demonstrated a limitation of schnorchel use. Boats deployed in this way lost mobility and had a very narrow time window in which an attack was possible. A strong escort could keep them away from the convoy even if it took some casualties in doing so.[92] As a result, the overall loss rate for merchant ships in convoy, the primary focus of the U-boats, remained very low, 1.35 per cent, and for outbound convoys a mere 0.87 per cent. If the six escorts sunk and damaged beyond repair are added to the merchant casualties, a total score of fourteen, then for about 100 Arctic patrols over the nine months August to May, U-boat productivity per patrol was 0.14. This was about one-third of that achieved by Norway-based boats operating in the North Atlantic in the same period. It was a pitiful return for the price of nine U-boats sunk and, with only one incoming cargo lost, the impact on supplies to delivered to Russia was negligible, while the destruction of six escorts had no practical effect on the now overwhelming British anti-submarine resources. The Germans had fought to the end in the Arctic but the loss of lives on all sides in the final months of conflict for German goals that were unachievable was tragic.[93]

# Reflections

The story in this book requires awareness of how perceptions of the Western Allies' relationship with the Soviet Union in the Second World War, the impact of Western aid, and the more specific contribution of the Arctic convoys, have evolved over the 80 years since 1945. Two themes are widespread and persistent. With some notable exceptions, the conflicts in the Western theatres and on the Russian Front are generally seen as distinct with limited emphasis on the influence or overlaps between them. This separation has inevitably coloured attitudes to Western aid which, outside specialist works, invariably attracts surprisingly little attention. That lack of coverage is evident, albeit for different reasons, in British, American, Russian and German accounts of the war. Whether at political/economic, strategic or campaign level, references to this aid have usually been partial and selective and too often misleading.

For the Soviet Union, admitting any critical military or economic dependence on the capitalist West or acknowledging any Western technical advantage was ideologically awkward since it potentially challenged the superiority of the communist system. It posed equally difficult questions over the competence and credibility of the Soviet leadership, especially in their initial response to the German onslaught in the first 18 months of the war. Soviet leaders therefore had a powerful motive to downplay the significance of Western aid. Marginalisation of the Western contribution was evident during the war itself where public recognition and gratitude were minimised. Occasional high-level acknowledgements of its value from Stalin and other leaders were quickly balanced with emphasis that it was useful rather than essential. The downplaying of aid was pursued more determinedly during the Cold War that followed with the persistent claim that it contributed at most 4 per cent to Soviet war production. There was grudging acknowledgement that the West contributed a higher proportion of tank and aircraft supplies (quoting 7 and 13 per cent respectively) although this combined with criticisms of their quality. The prevailing Soviet view to the end of the 1980s was therefore that Western aid was too small to impact significantly on the war. It emphasised that most supplies were received after Stalingrad when they were no longer needed, while during the period of most acute strain, the first six months of the war, quantities were derisory, just 0.1 per cent of Soviet production. Along with the claims of poor quality, there stress on broken Western promises with frequent delayed and cancelled shipments further diminishing the value of aid. There was some important qualifying testimony. In private, Khrushchev and, to a lesser extent, Zhukov, both central figures in the conduct of the war, admitted that, in certain areas, the Western contribution had been crucial. Khrushchev indeed reported that on several occasions Stalin had confided to his close circle that, without aid, Russia could not have coped.[1]

Perhaps more surprisingly, until the end of the Cold War when Soviet records became accessible, there was limited Western challenge to the Soviet narrative. This was partly because, although the quantity of Western deliveries was known, it was difficult to relate them to a largely undisclosed Soviet domestic output. The perceived magnitude of the Soviet achievement in confronting and then breaking the bulk of German land power and the subsequent apparent consolidation of its 'superpower' status also lent credibility to Soviet claims. Meanwhile, in post-war testimony it suited some British and American military leaders to blame Western defeats on a diversion of resources to Russia that was certainly 'thankless' and perhaps unnecessary.[2] As knowledge of the scale of Soviet losses became more widely known, with associated guilt over the blood price they had paid, that too discouraged critical examination of the Soviet war record. The view expressed by the popular historian and future politician Alan Clark in 1964 in one of the first books on the Eastern Front to reach a broad audience became quite widely shared:

> It does seem that the Russians could have won the war on their own, or at least fought the Germans to a standstill, without any help from the West. Such relief as they derived from our participation – the distraction of a few enemy units, the supply of a large quantity of material – was marginal, not critical. That is to say, it affected the duration but not the outcome of the struggle.[3]

If this view seems eccentric today, given the proportion of Germany's war effort now known to have been focused in the Western theatres,[4] Clark could have called on the support of Admiral King who, in November

1942 when Russia's prospects remained finely balanced, observed that, 'in the last analysis', 'Russia will do nine-tenths of the job of defeating Hitler'.[5] Admittedly, King's attitude was coloured by his particular and persistent desire to get on with the 'real war' in the Pacific. However, influential histories written a generation later than Clark still insisted that the Soviet contribution on the Eastern Front 'effectively determined the outcome of the war'.[6] Attitudes such as Clark's therefore undoubtedly shaped a popular, even standard, narrative of Western aid which took root during the remaining Cold War decades and, despite releases of Soviet records in the 1990s, lingers well into the twenty-first century. Influenced by the Soviet perspective, this portrayal downplays the significance of Western supplied weapons while acknowledging the value of transport, communication and food supplies. It confirms a contribution heavily weighted towards the period 1943–5, with an impact useful rather than decisive and thus, largely discretionary.[7] This narrative of limited impact fits comfortably with the wider picture of the Second World War now projected by Vladimir Putin's Russia. This promotes Russia as the innocent victim of German aggression, ignoring its Western expansion in 1939–40, and therefore encouraging a neat parallel with perceived NATO expansion today. It also inevitably emphasises the centrality of the Eastern Front and the appalling death toll suffered by Russia to reinforce a contemporary message that Russia can and will bear any sacrifice to meet its perceived just national goals. Given this context, outside specialist works specifically assessing the Soviet wartime economy or describing the Western aid programmes, it still remains rare to see much critical assessment of the impact of Western aid on overall Soviet war potential in the Second World War. Nor has there been much recognition of a strategic rationale underpinning Western supplies or the opportunity costs in providing them.[8]

The central proposition of this book is that Western aid to Russia, in concept and delivery, is best understood as a means of weaving Russia into the Anglo-American grand strategy for defeating Germany comprised of 'containment' and 'wear down'. The genesis of this strategy lay in ideas first articulated by the British chiefs of staff in September 1940 and which evolved through successive Anglo-American summits over the next two and a half years, notably at Riviera (Placentia Bay) in August 1941 shortly after Germany attacked the Soviet Union, then at Arcadia in Washington in January 1942 and Symbol at Casablanca a year later. At Riviera, Churchill and Roosevelt recognised that the survival of Russia was key to containing German power. Supporting her with aid therefore moved from 'hesitant aspiration' to 'determined commitment' through the Moscow supply conference which led to the First Protocol. By Arcadia, the British chiefs saw the British Empire and Russia containing Germany within an 'iron ring'. Meanwhile, in their Joint Board estimate produced shortly after Riviera, the American chiefs stressed that an active front in Russia created potential for a land offensive against Germany, and that arming Russia was therefore an important opportunity for the Western Powers. If Russia held going into 1942, then with America's entry into the war, the three new Allies had a land front from which eventually to assault the frontiers of Germany. The original means which Britain had identified of 'wearing down' Germany, bombing, blockade and subversion, were thus now joined by 'assistance to Russia' 'by all available means'. Symbol at Casablanca a year later signalled a shift in the purpose of aid. With success at Stalingrad imminent, it was no longer focused on 'containment', preventing Russian defeat or a separate peace, but would now boost her military effectiveness and war potential so that she played a central role in the 'wear down' of Germany alongside the evolving Atlantic, Mediterranean and bombing offensives. Hence aid to Russia became the 'second charge' on Anglo-American shipping after defeat of the U-boat menace. Symbol also marked the shift from weaponry to transport, communications, industrial capacity building, and food supplies.

Although this concept of a strategic journey is important in understanding Allied prosecution of the war in the three years 1941–3, its execution in practice was far from seamless. The often bitter Anglo-American debates over Sledgehammer, 1943 Roundup, Torch and Husky, and the subsequent British stalling on Overlord, allowed scope for alternative pathways as well as fostering misunderstanding and distrust with Russia. The two Western Allies often had to make decisions with limited knowledge of Russian intentions or developments on the ground in the East. Operations had critical consequences that were not foreseen. Torch provoked the withdrawal of German air strike forces from northern Norway and had a substantial impact on German air transport at Stalingrad. Husky heavily influenced the German decision to terminate the Citadel Kursk offensive on what proved unfavourable terms. However, the key point is that the delivery of aid to Russia always had a compelling strategic rationale. Initially it aimed to keep Russia fighting, later to fight more effectively. Viewing the aid programme as essentially 'political', if that means discretionary, is therefore wrong. Military leaders on both sides of the Atlantic certainly regularly questioned whether Soviet demands were excessive or whether aid was being deployed effectively. They also highlighted opportunity costs and the comparative advantages of different routes, although not always in a way that was timely and constructive. However, it is hard to find examples where British or American chiefs of staff, acting nationally or jointly, questioned the principle of providing aid. At successive summits they consistently advised their political leaders that Russia's contribution to the war was crucial and should receive maximum possible support.

Political leadership was of course critical in promoting this Western strategy, articulating it, and then driving it through. Military leaders often emphasised the importance of supporting Russia when conferring in Whitehall or Washington or at summits yet found multiple reasons for delaying or suspending delivery in practice. Left to decide themselves, Pound and Tovey would have halted Arctic convoys through the entire summer of 1942 and reduced their frequency at other times. Their perspective is understandable. They had to manage the risks and meet other essential commitments. Given a free hand, the combined chiefs might also have embraced Hopkins' suggestion at Casablanca that the Arctic route be abandoned entirely. It required consistent political insistence from Churchill and Roosevelt that aid to Russia was prioritised and, when delivered through the Arctic, at a higher level of risk than their military advisers judged comfortable. It is also true, as Churchill and Roosevelt well understood, that aid, especially via the Arctic, did have political and symbolic impact going beyond its practical contribution to Russia's war potential. Nevertheless, their political motives, compensation for the delayed second front, reassuring Stalin that Russia was not being left to bleed, and countering the spectre of a separate peace, cannot be detached from the overall strategic goals identified above. There is an argument that aid became more political in the final 18 months of the war with huge volumes delivered with too little scrutiny. Roosevelt has been charged with naivety along with accusations that key American decisionmakers, including Hopkins, had fallen under Soviet influence.[9] This view owes too much to hindsight. It was not obvious in the spring of 1944 when the Fourth Protocol was negotiated that Germany would necessarily be defeated in a year. The success of Overlord was not guaranteed, Soviet participation against Japan was judged important, and her participation in a constructive post-war international framework both desirable and feasible.[10] The factors and decisions that broke the wartime alliance between the Western Powers and Russia and provoked the descent into Cold War confrontation lie outside the scope of this book. Hindsight again reveals ample warning of coming tensions at the Yalta summit and that at Potsdam in late July 1945, nearly three months after the European war ended. However, respective leaders did not at this time judge hostile confrontation inevitable and different choices over the next three years could have brought different outcomes.[11]

A related question is how far Western leaders perceived Russia's role through the war not only as vital to wearing down German military power but, more specifically, to save Western lives. Put bluntly, was greater Western wealth used consciously 'to help the Russians to kill and be killed' so that Western soldiers did not have to. Although there are some direct quotes to this effect from senior Western figures, notably from Harriman and Roosevelt's successor, President Harry S Truman, these mainly originate in the post-war period when they inevitably influenced the evolving Soviet Cold War aid narrative.[12] It is harder to pinpoint contemporary comments suggesting such a trade-off beyond the generalities of 'wear down' while the war was underway. As leaders subject to democratic accountability, both Roosevelt and Churchill always had the human cost to their own people in mind – hence the attraction of bombing and, in Churchill's case, the enduring fears for Overlord. Both recognised the blood sacrifice paid by the Russians even if they did not know just how great it was. It also appears that, in his blacker moods, Churchill apparently doubted whether his own country could again endure the bloodletting of the previous war. Senior army leaders, notably Brooke, Wavell and Kennedy, certainly felt Britain had become 'softer' than its enemies, 'not as tough as we were in the last war'.[13] However, there is no evidence such prejudices drove opposition to Sledgehammer or the postponement of Roundup which were decided by compelling military argument. Furthermore. such views were seemingly not shared in the leadership of the other services and the appalling British casualty rates in Bomber Command certainly belied theories of generational 'softness'. In sum, there was recognition of and gratitude for the human cost suffered by Russia in its contribution to wearing down Germany but, just as there were no formal British or American assessments of the overall benefits versus costs of Western aid, so there were no formal attempts to quantify Western lives saved.

If aid to Russia was a key component of Western grand strategy, what was the specific contribution of the Arctic deliveries and did they justify the resources expended and losses incurred? About 4.5 million tons reached the northern ports between 1941–5, slightly higher than usually stated and just under 25 per cent of supplies by all routes.[14] The most crucial supplies were those over the 18 months from September 1941 to February 1943, from the arrival of Dervish to that of JW 53, the last convoy before the summer 1943 suspension. 1.45 million tons of cargo arrived at the Arctic ports in this period, just over half the total supplies under the First and Second Protocols that reached Russia in these months.[15] There was never a realistic option of transferring these Arctic supplies to other routes at this time. This Arctic cargo included 240,000 tons of weapons, 85 per cent of all those delivered during this period.[16] The headline weapons included 3100 fighters, 200 bombers, 3800 tanks and nearly 1700 Bren Gun Carriers, along with considerable quantities of small arms, ammunition, explosives, radar and Asdic equipment. While 60 per cent of overall cargo in the period was American, over two-thirds of the fighters and tanks and all the Bren Carriers were British.[17] The tanks supplied represented 10.4 per cent of total Red Army tank receipts in this period but 21 per cent of medium tank receipts if Valentines are included in this category. The fighters delivered, of which 60 per cent were Hurricanes and most of the rest Airacobras, comprised 18.8 per cent of Red Air Force fighter receipts. No fighters or medium tanks reached Russia by other supply routes in this period. Although military supplies comprised only about 10 per cent of tonnage delivered across all routes in this period, the Soviets estimated their financial share of all cargo at 57 per cent, a useful indication of their value. Even in 1944, the financial share of military supplies was still 45 per cent, more than three times that of industrial and technical imports.[18]

Apart from weapons, the Arctic route contributed importantly in this period to transport, communications, and raw materials essential to support the war industries. Of 50,000 trucks reaching Russia from the United States by the end of February 1943, about equal to Soviet domestic output over the previous 18 months, at least 20,000 came via the Arctic along with 5000 jeeps and 5000 motorcycles. Half of the 90,000 American-supplied field telephones and 450,000 miles of telephone wire arriving by this time also came through the Arctic. Britain, Canada and the United States delivered two-thirds of the 70,000 tons of aluminium and duraluminum arriving in this period by this route. Total aluminium supplies matched Soviet domestic output in these months. They were accompanied by over 32,000 tons of hot rolled aircraft steel of which two-thirds again went via the Arctic. Although impossible directly to translate these metal tonnages into aircraft output, an assessment that Western-supplied aluminium and special aircraft steel shipped via the Arctic enabled about 25 to 30 per cent of the Soviet output of 25,000 combat aircraft over the 12 months from 1 July 1942 seems reasonable. Western aluminium was equally important to sustaining T-34 tank output. Indeed, the prodigious Russian aircraft and tank output achieved throughout the war not only often overlooks the contribution of Western materials and machine tools but also their pervasive problems of quality control and reliability with consequent high levels of wastage. Apart from aircraft steel, the Americans supplied 450,000 tons of other specialised steel products, at least half through the Arctic, in this period, which saw domestic steel output drop by 55 per cent. Zhukov later acknowledged that this steel contribution was critical. So was copper for production of communications equipment and ammunition with 60,000 tons delivered, two-thirds from the United States and one-third from Britain, adding 50 per cent to Soviet 1942 output. Britain supplied over 50,000 tons of rubber, about half its own 1942 consumption, 12,000 tons of tin, and large quantities of naval equipment including 100 Asdic sets.[19] Finally, 19,250 tons of American toluene and a similar quantity of TNT reached Russia in this period, which together equated to 50 per cent of the TNT used in Soviet munitions production in 1942. About two-thirds of this American contribution came via the Arctic, so the convoys effectively provided one third of Red Army firepower from the middle of that year, releasing valuable domestic resources for use elsewhere. Key indicators drawn from this paragraph and the preceding one are shown in Appendix 2.[20]

Weapons provided through the Arctic in this 18-month period were more significant to Russia than later acknowledged. They contributed a valuable margin to the Moscow counter-offensive from late December 1941, on the southern front in the subsequent summer and autumn, and even at Kursk the following year. The margin was important in bolstering other fronts too. Without it, generating adequate forces for the Stalingrad counter-offensive would have been more difficult. The claim that Western aid in this period added little to wider Russian war potential is also dubious. The 4.7 per cent it added to GDP in 1942, rising to 10.2 per cent in 1943, was well targeted at aircraft production, at underpinning the industrial relocation to the Urals, and filling major gaps in transport and communications. The aid delivered via the Arctic to the end of February 1943 equated to about 3.4 per cent of 1942 GDP.[21] Arctic-delivered weapons represented a significant opportunity cost to the Western Powers. Taking account of items destroyed on route or still in transit, Britain exported one-third of its 1942 fighter production to Russia in this period and the United States 13.6 per cent of its output. Britain exported one-third of its 1942 medium tank output (including Valentines) along with all of Canada's while the United States sent a quarter of all the M3 Lees it ever produced.

Arctic deliveries had their maximum impact during this crucial period when Russia's fate was in the balance and Western aid perhaps tipped the balance in ensuring her survival through 1942. Without the addition of

Western weapons and, equally important, the critical supplies to underpin domestic defence production along with significant quantities of food, the Red Army might have been pushed beyond the Volga. GDP would have then continued falling in the first months of 1943, starving the civilian sector further of essential resources and raising the possibility a Brest-Litovsk peace.[22]

Although the United States provided two-thirds of the cargo during this period until February 1943, delivery of these Arctic supplies fell almost entirely on the Royal Navy, as was true of the further 18 months from the following November. The convoy programme was planned and managed by the British Admiralty in concert with the Ministry of War Transport, Commander-in-Chief Home Fleet was responsible for the operation of the convoys and, apart from the brief contribution of Task Force 99, the Royal Navy provided all the escorts. Despite Roosevelt's enduring emphasis on the importance of the Arctic route, British pleas for more American naval support were never met. It was British sea power therefore that facilitated and sustained not just the quarter of Western aid delivered via the Arctic through the war, but the further quarter sent through the Persian Gulf. Arctic delivery up to JW 53 cost fifty-three merchant vessels in the outbound convoys with five additional independents and twenty-two in the returns with one independent. The losses comprised thirty-six American ships, twenty-seven British, nine Russian and the remaining eight Panamanian/Dutch, and 390,000 tons of cargo, 22.4 per cent of the total despatched, was lost including 620 fighters, 1000 tanks, 6000 tons of aluminium and 45,000 tons of steel, adding considerably to the opportunity costs of the programme. These tank losses alone equalled nearly 40 per cent of German tank losses in all theatres in 1942.[23]

The overall loss rate for the 362 ships in the outbound convoys was 15 per cent. By comparison, the rate for the six Malta convoys over the 18 months from July 1941 was nearly twice as high, with successful arrivals there only two-thirds of the nearly 85 per cent achieved in the Arctic. However, 81 per cent of Arctic losses came in the three successive convoys PQ 16 to PQ 18 with 43 per cent in PQ 17 alone. Only in these three, facing the peak German threat in high summer, did Arctic losses match the worst Mediterranean experience. Without these three, the loss rate for the remaining outbound convoys was 4.8 per cent. Although this was still two and a half times the rate for eastbound ships in the North Atlantic convoys over the nine months September 1942 to May 1943, the latter faced no significant air and surface threat. The cost to the Royal Navy for this 18-month Arctic record was two cruisers, four fleet destroyers, four minesweepers and a submarine, about half the warship losses on the

Malta run. The Germans lost three fleet destroyers, six U-boats and at least seventy-five aircraft.[24]

It follows that, despite the privations of climate, geographical constraints, and duration of exposure to enemy attack, losses on the Arctic run were not disproportionate compared to convoys in other theatres. At the height of their Arctic strength over the nine months from March 1942, the Germans could only rarely combine their considerable capabilities to deliver decisive effect. They fell well short of the destruction rate of Axis supplies achieved by the British with far fewer forces in the central Mediterranean in the second half of 1941, a result which contributed as much to the air balance on the Eastern Front that winter as the 484 Hurricanes delivered to Russia by the end of that December. This lack of decisive German impact in the Arctic demonstrates that British measures to protect the convoys, shaped not least by excellent intelligence, were generally effective.

There is a compelling argument that the destruction rate achieved by the Germans against convoys which sailed was only part of the story. That the threat they posed to the route was equally important, effectively closing it over three successive summers, preventing sailings in 12 of 16 months between July 1942 and November 1943, and then the further four months April to July 1944. The true German victory therefore lay in confining convoys to only eight months out of twenty-five across these two years. German success should thus be measured less by cargo losses than cargo undelivered in those seventeen lost months, a minimum of two and a half million tons using Pound's Casablanca calculations.[25] The problem here is twofold. First, while the German threat, especially when it coincided with summer weather, was undoubtedly one factor in periods of suspension, the requirement for escorts to meet other commitments, notably Torch, the early 1943 Atlantic U-boat offensive, Husky and D-Day was the dominant driver. Secondly, periods of Arctic suspension provoked displacement to other routes which would not have happened otherwise, so calculating cargo denied is complicated. The only months when adequate escorts were available, but convoys were still suspended due to the perceived German threat, were July 1942, March and April 1943, and arguably September and October 1943. This reduces German-driven cargo denied to about 750,000 tons but much of the deficit after mid-1943 still reached Russia by other routes, if more slowly. A fair judgement is to accept that the eight lost months, July/August and October/November in 1942, and March to June inclusive in 1943, cost Russia about one and a quarter million tons of aid, matching the Second Protocol deficit, but at least half of this must be set against the benefits of

Torch and Husky. Leaving aside the long term strategic gains from these operations, they made direct and important contributions to Russia at Stalingrad and Kursk respectively. 600,000 tons was a minor price for the overall benefit they delivered.

The four key convoys conducted in the Mediterranean and Arctic between June and September 1942 further illuminate these trade-offs. Vigorous, the Malta convoy mounted from Alexandria in mid-June, and PQ 17 two weeks later demonstrated the sheer difficulty of running convoys in relatively confined waters, against an enemy operating substantial forces in three dimensions, without the air and gun power enjoyed by Somerville during Halberd. Both demonstrated that good intelligence was not enough unless backed by adequate force. PQ 17 faced the additional challenges of longer exposure and continuous daylight. Vigorous led to retreat and PQ 17 to disastrous scattering. The only solution to this level of threat was substantially to increase the power of the escort. Pedestal, the August Malta convoy, resumed Halberd levels of cover but with a much-expanded fleet carrier force. PQ 18 substituted an escort carrier and a large force of the latest fleet destroyers for the fleet carriers and battleships used with Pedestal. Both concepts demonstrated that convoys could get through under the toughest opposition but only at the cost of huge warship resources and severe merchant losses. Refinements and experience might reduce future losses and, in both cases the enemy also suffered heavy attrition. But without American help, the Royal Navy could not mount this effort in two theatres simultaneously before autumn 1943. The 12 months following PQ 18 inevitably therefore meant Arctic trade-offs with the Mediterranean and other theatres until new ships, especially escort carriers, were available in substantial numbers. It is often forgotten that trade-offs extended as far as the Pacific with the loan of *Victorious* to the US Navy for the whole of 1943 to cover their carrier losses in that theatre. This left the Home Fleet without a regular fleet carrier that year. Had she stayed, the summer 1943 suspension might have been shorter.

This need for trade-offs has contributed to a wider critique of the Arctic convoys. That the fate of convoys PQ 16 to PQ 18 confirms Pound's May 1942 claim to King that the Arctic convoys were a 'millstone' and 'most unsound' operation of war, requiring a commitment of naval and merchant resources over four years disproportionate to any benefit. Leaving aside the loss of warships and merchant vessels and the wider wear and tear on ships and men of the 'worst journey in the world', this Arctic effort expended on a 'Verdun' of maritime war would therefore have been better spent elsewhere. Once initial aid requirements were met, effort should have focused on building up the other routes.[26] This argument underestimates the benefit to the Allied cause of the first 18 months of Arctic deliveries and overlooks the negligible scope for further diversion to other routes before mid-1943. It is true that the benefit to Russia is easier to calculate with the advantage of hindsight than at the time. However, contemporary intelligence was good enough to show how finely balanced prospects were on the Eastern Front through 1942. Hence why the principle of maximising assistance to Russia was never seriously questioned by military leaders in London or Washington during this period. Whatever Pound's reservations, he neither pushed for a formal cost/benefit study nor proposed a credible alternative to Arctic deliveries.

Furthermore, Pound's comments to King came when daylight and ice conditions were at their worst and Royal Navy resources at their nadir and must be seen in this perspective. There are also dangers in over generalising from the experience of PQs 16–18. Each case was different with PQ 18 piloting an effective protection system that set the desired escort standard from JW 53 the following February onward. The periods of Arctic suspension can also be interpreted positively, reflecting not only the inevitable trade-offs but sensible balancing of benefit against risk and increasing capacity of alternative routes. Finally, in weighing the burden on the Home Fleet, it is essential to recognise that its core strength was ultimately dictated by the presence of the German heavy ships in northern waters and the threat of an Atlantic sortie rather than cover for the convoys, as emphasised by Denning in early 1943. Here the balance worked both ways. The Germans could claim to hold down valuable British assets which could be used to advantage elsewhere – the fleet-in-being concept well understood by both Raeder and Dönitz – as well as protecting Norway. But, for a rather modest investment set against overall Royal Navy strength, the British kept the German ships locked up in the fiords where their efficiency and value steadily declined.

When convoys resumed in November 1943, the European war had 18 months to run, identical in length therefore to the earlier period analysed above. There were again four months with no convoy, this time due to Overlord. This second convoy phase saw 3.25 million tons of cargo delivered under the Third and Fourth Protocols, two and a half times that of the first period, arriving in 395 ships compared to 282. This Arctic cargo, of which well over 80 per cent derived from the United States, was almost exactly one-quarter of that delivered across all routes in this period, and it equated to about 5 per cent of Soviet 1944 GDP. The proportion of weapons carried was down by nearly half, reflecting the general shift to transport and industrial goods and the availability of the

Iran and Alaska routes as alternatives, but, perhaps surprisingly, weapon tonnage was still up 50 per cent in absolute terms.

By the start of this second period, there was enough capacity on the other routes to have dispensed with the Arctic, as Hopkins suggested at Casablanca, and in late 1944 the opening of Black Sea ports created another option. Furthermore, at the start of this period in November 1943, Western aid by whatever route had become a 'multiplier'. It made Soviet offensive operations more effective and efficient and aided the recovery of the Soviet economy. Its absence was unlikely to stop the Red Army ejecting the Germans from Russian territory although it would have taken longer and incurred more cost, perhaps then rendering further advances into Eastern Europe less attractive. To that extent it became discretionary but stopping it posed costs and risks for the Western Allies too. It compensated for the delay in the 'second front', potentially weakened the German opposition this would face, and was a downpayment for help in the Far East. Against that background, the Arctic retained three important advantages: it was by far the fastest route both by sea and then inside Russia; it saved the Western Allies significant shipping; and it was best suited to handling large items such as railway locomotives. Partly for the first and third reasons, it was the route the Russians preferred, hence the pressure to reopen it from late summer 1943. Stalin undoubtedly also saw it as a symbol of Western commitment to promises made at Teheran, giving Churchill and Roosevelt therefore a strong political motive to prioritise this route.

These advantages would have been less compelling without the reduction in risk, resulting from German air force withdrawals and then the successful attack on *Tirpitz*, combined with growing Royal Navy resources helped by a declining Mediterranean commitment. The reduced risk is underlined by the loss of only five ships in the sixteen outgoing convoys between November 1943 and the end of the war, a rate of only 1.25 per cent. If two ships sunk off Kola outside convoy are deducted, the return loss rate was similar. As regards, the naval balance, the Royal Navy victory in this period was overwhelming. In return for losing two destroyers and five light escorts, it eliminated *Tirpitz* as a fighting unit and sank *Scharnhorst* and twenty-five U-boats, the equivalent of the average Arctic U-boat front-line force through most of this period.

Overall, the Arctic convoys and the operations they provoked had a significant impact on the outcome of the war. They were not primarily a political project. They were important to Russia's survival through 1942, her subsequent evolution as an effective fighting power and thus to the wearing down and defeat of Germany. By providing aid, the Western

Allies ensured ultimate Soviet victory in the East and it enabled them to fight their war more efficiently and at less cost than would otherwise have been the case.[27]

The Royal Navy made mistakes in the Arctic naval war, notably with the attack on Petsamo and, above all, convoy PQ 17. But the former was redeemed with the 1944 Fleet Air Arm attack on *Tirpitz* and the latter by successfully fighting through the next convoy against considerable odds. The mistakes were far outweighed by fine achievements, often in stormy seas and winter darkness, the defensive Battle of the Barents Sea, the destruction of *Scharnhorst* culminating in one of the outstanding destroyer attacks of the war, and the bravery and triumph of the 'X men' against *Tirpitz*. The Germans were consistently outmatched, tactically, technically, in seamanship, in exploitation of intelligence, and, not least, in sheer fighting spirit. The conduct of the convoys exemplified all the values instilled in the 1939 Royal Navy Fighting Instructions. As they anticipated, 'superior fighting qualities and stamina' and the will to 'engage the enemy more closely' proved decisive, as they had 'so often in the past'.[28]

# Appendix 1
# Arctic Convoys Summary

**Convoy Overview**

| Number of convoys | 1941 | 1942 | 1943 | 1944 | 1945 | Total | Tonnage Shipped/ Arrived |
|---|---|---|---|---|---|---|---|
| To North Russia | 8 | 13 | 6 | 9 | 4 | 40 | 5,200,000/ 4,500,000 |
| Ships | 64 | 256 | 112 | 284 | 95 | 811 | |
| From North Russia | 4 | 13 | 6 | 9 | 5 | 37 | |
| Ships | 49 | 188 | 93 | 249 | 136 | 715 | |

**Merchant Ship Losses**

| | UK | USA | Panama | Russia | Holland | Norway | Total | Tonnage |
|---|---|---|---|---|---|---|---|---|
| Convoys to Russia | 21 | 29 | 5 | 2 | 1 | 0 | 58 | 353,366 |
| Convoys from Russia | 6 | 15 | 2 | 5 | 0 | 1 | 29 | 178,317 |
| Independents | 3 | 1 | 0 | 2 | 0 | 0 | 6 | 42,004 |
| In Russian ports | 3 | 2 | 0 | 0 | 0 | 0 | 5 | 27,278 |
| Other | 2 | 0 | 0 | 0 | 0 | 0 | 2 | 4872 |
| Total | 35 | 47 | 7 | 9 | 1 | 1 | 100 | 604,837 |

## Analysis of Losses

|  | Ships in convoy ||| Independents |||
|---|---|---|---|---|---|---|
|  | Eastbound | Westbound | Escorted | Straggling | Eastbound | Westbound |
| Surface attack | 1 | 2 | 0 | 3 | 0 | 1 |
| Submarine | 23 | 18 | 24 | 17 | 4 | 0 |
| Air bombs | 17 | 2 | 9 | 10 | 0 | 0 |
| Air torpedo | 17 | 1 | 17 | 1 | 0 | 0 |
| Mined | 0 | 5 | 5 | 0 | 0 | 0 |
| Foundered | 0 | 1 | 1 | 0 | 0 | 0 |
| Wrecked | 0 | 0 | 0 | 0 | 1 | 0 |
| Total | 58 | 29 | 56 | 31 | 5 | 1 |

**Notes:**
1. Convoy Overview, courtesy Schofield, *Russian Convoys*, Appendix 1. Estimate of total tonnage shipped/lost drawn from earlier calculations in this book.
2. Merchant losses and analysis, Naval Staff History, *The Royal Navy and the Arctic Convoys*, Appendix A, V. Its seven appendices in total provide further details of every convoy with numerous tables of analysis.

# Appendix 2
# Arctic Aid Deliveries

**Cumulative Key Indicators – August 1941–February 1943**

| Category | 31 March 1942 | 30 September 1942 | 28 February 1943 |
|---|---|---|---|
| US tonnage shipped | 452,365 | 1,074,306 | 1,350,252 |
| US tonnage arrived | 148,000 | 820,000e | 1,080,200 |
| UK tonnage shipped | 191,500e | 310,000e | 475,000e |
| UK tonnage arrived | 171,500 | 250,000e | 370,000e |
| US Fighters | 189 (2200a) | 456 (6600a) | 942 (11,033a) |
| UK Fighters | 1373 (9910b) | 1594 (11,300b) | 2047 (12,900b) |
| US Medium Tanks | 215 (2750a) | 785 (8250a) | 1087 (13,300a) |
| UK Medium Tanks | 1089 (2700b) | 1864 (6250b) | 2751 (8550b) |
| US Vehicles | 6886 (7750a) | 10,000e (23,250a) | 25,000e (38,500a) |
| UK Vehicles | 3249 | 4000e} | 4000e} |
| Aluminium | 17,000e (10,000a,e) | 25,000e (35,000a,e) | 45,000e (62,000a) |
| Aircraft Steel | Nil | 8000e | 21,000e |
| Standard Steel | Nil | 100,000e (6.1m) | 225,000e (9.5m) |
| Toluene | 3000 (8000a) | 6000e (16,000a) | 13,000e (37,325a) |
| TNT | 500 (22,750a) | 6500e (68,250a) | 13,000e (106,150a) |
| Field Telephones | 4000e | 12,000e | 45,000e |
| Telephone Wire (miles) | N/A | 125,000e | 225,000e |

**Notes:**

Sources are those already referenced in the text.

Figures to 30 September (prior to the pause that autumn) include deliveries by Dervish and PQ 1, those under the First Protocol and initial Second Protocol deliveries included in PQ 18.

Figures to 28 February 1943 include all of those up to JW 53 prior to the eight month summer pause.

All British tanks here (Matilda, Valentine, and Churchill) have been classified 'medium' and Soviet comparative figures are for this category only.

e = estimated from available figures which often fail sufficiently to specify how shipments in a given period split between the different aid routes. Any errors are unlikely to exceed 10 per cent.

a = cumulative Soviet domestic production from 1 January 1942.

b = cumulative total Soviet stock available, including Western supplies, from 1 January 1942.

m = million

# Notes

**Introduction**

1 The best early general history of the Arctic convoys is that by Vice Admiral B B Schofield, *The Russian Convoys* (UK: B T Batsford, 1964, and Pan Books edition 1984) who was Director of Trade in the Admiralty 1941–2. A more modern overview is Richard Woodman's *Arctic Convoys, 1941–1945* (London: John Murray, 1994). 2 Malcolm Llewellyn-Jones, *The Royal Navy and the Arctic Convoys: Naval Staff History* (Abingdon: Routledge, 2007). 3 S W Roskill, *The War at Sea*, three volumes (London: HMSO, 1954–1961); Samuel Eliot Morison, *The Two Ocean War* (USA: Little, Brown & Co, 1963); T H Vail Motter, *US Army in World War II, The Persian Corridor and Aid to Russia* (Washington USA: US Government Printing Office, 1952); Richard M Leighton and Robert W Coakley, *United States Army in World War II, Global Logistics and Strategy 1940–1943* (Washington USA, US Government Printing Office, 1955); Earl F Ziemke, *United States Army in World War II, German Northern Theater of Operations 1940–1945* (Washington USA: US Government Printing Office, 1959). 4 The first comprehensive account, but also most notorious, was David Irving's *The Destruction of Convoy PQ 17*, first published by Cassell & Co in 1968 and the subject of a famous libel action in 1970. Successive editions up to 2005 incorporated intelligence material, especially Ultra, not previously accessible. Despite issues of reliability, Irving interviewed many key participants, so his book contains much information not available elsewhere. Other important accounts include: Patrick Beesly, 'Convoy PQ 17: A study of intelligence and decision-making', *Intelligence and National Security*, 5:2, 1990, pp 292–322; and Milan Vego, 'The Destruction of Convoy PQ 17, 27 June–10 July 1942', *US Naval War College Review*, 69:3, Summer 2016. 5 Patrick Bishop, *Target Tirpitz: X-craft, Agents and Dambusters – The Epic Quest to destroy Hitler's Mightiest Warship* (London: Harper Press, 2012). 6 Angus Konstam, *The Battle of North Cape: The Death Ride of the Scharnhorst, 1943* (Barnsley: Pen & Sword, 2009). 7 The most comprehensive history of the German navy in the Second World War remains Michael Salewski's *Die Deutsche Seekriegsleitung*, 1935–1945, Volume I, 1935–1941 (Munich, Bernard und Graefe, 1970) and Volume II, 1942–1945 (Frankfurt: Bernard und Graefe, 1970). Although there is no English translation, it is widely referenced in the multi-volume semi-official history *Germany and the Second World War*, Volumes IV, VI and VIII. The latest version of the English translation of the *Fuehrer Conferences on Naval Affairs 1939–1945*, edited by Jak Mallman Showell (Stroud: History Press, 2015) is also a valuable source. 8 James Levy, 'Holding the Line: The Royal Navy's Home Fleet in the Second World War' (unpublished doctoral thesis, University of Wales, 2001), pp 186–7, has a good summary of these views, also reflected in his subsequent article 'The Needs of Political Policy versus the Reality of Military Operations: Royal Navy Opposition to the Arctic Convoys, 1942', *Journal of Strategic Studies*, 26:1, 2003, pp 36–52. 9 A partial exception here is Joan Beaumont's *Comrades in Arms: British Aid to Russia 1941–1945* (London: Davis–Poynter, 1980). However, this is primarily focused on British aid, it is not limited to the Arctic route which makes it difficult to disentangle the specific contribution here, and much relevant

primary source material was still closed when it was written. **10** Alexander G Lovelace, 'Amnesia: how Russian History has viewed Lend-Lease', *The Journal of Slavic Military Studies*, 27:4, 2014, pp 591–605. **11** Important here is the extensive and influential work done by Alexander Hill and Mark Harrison along with Russian historians such as Mikhail Suprun and Boris Sokolov. **12** For example, David Kenyon's *Arctic Convoys: Bletchley Park and the War for the Seas* (Yale University Press, 2023).

**Prelude: August 1941: Churchill and Roosevelt at Placentia Bay**
**1** H V Morton, *Atlantic Meeting* (London: Methuen & Co, 1943), pp 84–6. **2** Ibid. **3** Daniel Todman, *Britain's War: Into Battle, 1937–1941* (London: Allen Lane, 2016), Chapter 25; and David Reynolds, *In Command of History: Churchill Fighting and Writing the Second World War* (London: Allen Lane, 2004), Chapter 16. **4** Warren E Kimball, *Churchill & Roosevelt: The Complete Correspondence*, Volume 1, *Alliance Emerging* (London: Collins, 1983), pp xxxiii–xliii. **5** Ibid, Introduction. For additional background on Roosevelt's motives for corresponding and his assessment of Churchill in this period: James Leutze, 'The Secret of the Churchill–Roosevelt Correspondence: September 1939–May 1940', *Journal of Contemporary History*, 10:3, July 1975, pp 465–91. **6** Andrew Boyd, *British Naval Intelligence through the Twentieth Century* (Barnsley: Seaforth, 2020), pp 432–3 and 436. **7** Theodore A Wilson, *The First Summit: Roosevelt and Churchill at Placentia Bay, 1941* (USA: University Press of Kansas, 1991), pp 8–11. **8** Ibid. **9** Roy Jenkins, *Churchill* (London: Pan Macmillan Ltd, 2002), pp 647–8. **10** Ibid **11** Quoted by Martin Gilbert, *Finest Hour: Winston S Churchill 1939–1941* (London: Heinemann, 1983), p 991. **12** Alan Allport, *Britain at Bay: The Epic Story of the Second World War: 1938–1941* (London: Profile Books, 2020), Chapter 22. **13** Todman, *Britain's War: Into Battle*, Chapter 25; Reynolds, *In Command of History*, Chapter 16. **14** War Cabinet Memorandum, WP (41) 202 of 20 August 1941, Annex III, British–American Chiefs of Staff Discussions, CAB 66/18/25. **15** Quoted in Gilbert, *Finest Hour*, p 1159. **16** Theodore A Wilson, *The First Summit*, p 98. **17** Winston S Churchill, *The Second World War*, Volume III, *The Grand Alliance* (London: Cassell & Co, 1950), p 384. The 'half soon to die' referred primarily to casualties from the sinking of *Prince of Wales* by the Japanese in the South China Sea four months later. Twenty per cent of her crew were lost with the ship including Captain John Leach. However, many survivors of the sinking subsequently became prisoners of war of the Japanese and died in captivity over the next three and a half years. **18** Quoted in Theodore A Wilson, *The First Summit*, p 99. **19** Mark Skinner Watson, *United States Army in World War II: Chief of Staff: Pre-war Plans and Preparations* (Washington: US Army Center of Military History, 1991), p 401; WM (41) 84th Conclusions, 19 August 1941, CAB 65/19/20. **20** First Lord minute to Prime Minister on Defence Plan No 4, 15 July 1941; 'Notes on Plan 5 (BAD Washington's 1039R/1st October)'; and 'Escort Forces: Benefits of Plans IV and V', paper for First Sea Lord, undated but probably early October 1941. All in ADM 205/10. **21** Theodore A Wilson, *The First Summit*, pp 126–7. **22** WM (41) 84th Conclusions, Annex, Secretary's File Only, CAB 65/19/20, and letter from Rear Admiral Robert Ghormley, Special Naval Observer London, to First Sea Lord, 26 August 1941, ADM 116/4877. **23** WM (41) 84th Conclusions, Annex, Secretary's File Only; Kimball, *Churchill & Roosevelt: The Complete Correspondence*, Volume 1, pp 229–30; Gilbert, *Finest Hour*, p 1168. **24** Ghormley letter to First Sea Lord, 26 August 1941, ADM 116/4877. **25** Ian Kershaw, *Fateful Choices: Ten Decisions that Changed the World* (London: Penguin Group, 2007), p 301 and 316–17. **26** Ibid, pp 319–23. **27** Ibid, pp 300 and 326. **28** Jak Mallmann Showell, *Fuehrer Conferences on Naval Affairs 1939–1945* (Stroud, Gloucestershire: History Press edition, 2015), pp 231–3. **29** Ibid, p 239. **30** Adam Tooze, *The Wages of Destruction: The Making and Breaking of the Nazi Economy* (London: Penguin Books edition, 2007), pp 501–3 and 664. **31** For valuable background on this paragraph: Kershaw, *Fateful Choices*, Chapter 9; and Horst Boog, Werner Rahn, and Bernd Wegner, *Germany and the Second World War*, Vol. VI, The Global War (OUP, 2001), pp 112–16. **32** Kimball, *Churchill & Roosevelt: The Complete Correspondence*, Volume 1, p 227. **33** Theodore A Wilson, *The First Summit*, Chapter 2; Gilbert, *Finest Hour*, pp 1130–6; Kershaw, *Fateful Choices*, pp 302–11;

Paula G Thornhill, 'Catalyst for Coalition: The Anglo-American Supply Relationship, 1939–1941' (unpublished doctoral thesis, University of Oxford, 1991), pp 264–5; Watson, *Pre-war Plans and Preparations*, pp 329–30; Roosevelt memorandum to Wayne Coy, 2 August 1941, President's Secretary's File, FDR Library. For the attitudes of military leaders, Gabriel Gorodetsky, 'An Alliance of Sorts: Allied Strategy in the Wake of Barbarossa', in John Erickson and David Dilks, *Barbarossa: The Axis and the Allies* (Edinburgh University Press, 1994), especially pp 102–3 and 110. 34 Ibid. Also: Thornhill, 'Catalyst for Coalition', p 263. 35 Gorodetsky, 'An Alliance of Sorts: Allied Strategy in the Wake of Barbarossa', p 113. 36 Churchill, *Grand Alliance*, p 383; Theodore A Wilson, *The First Summit*, pp 72–3. 37 There are numerous biographies of Beaverbrook. The most modern is Charles Williams' *Max Beaverbrook: Not Quite a Gentleman* (London: Biteback Publishing, 2019) which has a comprehensive list of earlier studies. Williams is generally critical and unsympathetic but also has surprising gaps which mean genuine achievements are overlooked. A J P Taylor's much older *Beaverbrook* (London: Hamish Hamilton, 1972 and Penguin, 1974) is a 'semi-official' study exploiting his close friendship with Beaverbrook, first-hand testimony and extensive access to his papers. It is therefore essential reading although it is often judged to border on hagiography. Roy Jenkins, *Portraits and Miniatures* (London: Macmillan, 1993), has a fine short essay, 'Beaverbrook', pp 249–52. 38 Theodore A Wilson, *The First Summit*, pp 45–50; Kershaw, *Fateful Choices*, pp 306–9; Sean McMeekin, *Stalin's War: A New History of the Second World War* (London: Allen Lane, 2021), Chapter 21. 39 WM (41) 84th Conclusions, Annex, Secretary's File Only, CAB 65/19/20. 40 Beaumont, *Comrades in Arms*, p 42. 41 Schofield, *Russian Convoys*, pp 15–16; Vladimir Kotelnikov, *Lend-Lease and Soviet Aviation in the Second World War* (Warwick: Helion & Co., 2017), pp 45 and 166. 42 Watson, *Pre-war Plans and Preparations*, pp 321–6; Richard M Leighton and Robert W Coakley, *United States Army in World War II: Global Logistics and Strategy 1940–1943* (Washington: US Government Printing Office, 1955), pp 89–96. 43 President's letter, 9 July 1941, included in Directive, p 1 of Joint Board Estimate of Overall United States Production Requirements, 11 September, PSF, FDR Library; Watson, *Pre-war Plans and Preparations*, pp 338–9. 44 Thornhill, 'Catalyst for Coalition', pp 271–6: Churchill to Roosevelt, C-107x, 25 July 1941, Kimball, *Churchill & Roosevelt: The Complete Correspondence*, Volume 1, p 224; Churchill, *Grand Alliance*, pp 396–7 and Appendix I; Wilson, *First Summit*, pp 179–83. 45 Thornhill, 'Catalyst for Coalition', p 276. 46 Watson, *Pre-war Plans and Preparations*, pp 346–9. 47 Sir Alexander Cadogan, OM, *Diaries 1938–1945*, edited by David Dilks (London: Faber & Faber, 2010), p 401; Peter Ricketts, 'Sir Alexander Cadogan – Churchill's indispensable man', portrait in *Englesberg Ideas*, March 2022. 48 Theodore A Wilson, *The First Summit*, p 59, quoting Robert Sherwood. 49 Ibid, p 60, quoting Arnold. 50 Joint Board Estimate of Overall United States Production Requirements. For the way the two teams prepared for Riviera, Wilson, Chapter 4. 51 Quoted by Clay Blair, *Hitler's U-boat War: The Hunters 1939–1942* (London: Weidenfeld & Nicolson, 1997), p 444. 52 Captain Tracy B Kittredge, USN, Notes 95N, September 1956, p 2, George C Marshall Foundation. 53 Theodore A Wilson, *The First Summit*, p 112. 54 The 'General Strategy' paper is at Annex I of the Riviera Summit records, COS (41) 504, 20 August 1941, in CAB 99/18. 55 'Future Strategy', W.P. 362, 4 September 1940, CAB 66/11/42. 56 Annexes II–V of Riviera records, CAB 99/18. 57 Watson, *Pre-war Plans and Preparations*, p 401. 58 Thornhill, 'Catalyst for Coalition', pp 261–2. 59 War Cabinet Memorandum, WP (41) 202, Annex III, British–American Chiefs of Staff Discussions, CAB 66/18/25; Riviera Annexes I–IV, CAB 99/18. 60 Watson, *Pre-war Plans and Preparations*, pp 400–8. 61 Ibid, pp 352–7 and 375–82; Thornhill, 'Catalyst for Coalition', pp 279–86. 62 For background and references on Philippines air reinforcement, Andrew Boyd, *The Royal Navy in Eastern Waters* (Barnsley: Seaforth, 2017), pp 278 and 287–9. 63 Riviera records, Annexes I–V, CAB 99/18; Beaumont, *Comrades in Arms*, pp 40–1. 64 Thornhill, 'Catalyst for Coalition', pp 279–86; Joint Board Estimate of Overall United States Production Requirements. 65 COS (41) 215 (O), 'Victory Requirements', 22 September, CAB 80/59. 66 For a useful comparison of British and American strategy development in the second half of 1941 and the consensus achieved: Grant Golub, 'The Eagle and the Lion: Reassessing Anglo-American strategic planning and the foundations of US grand strategy for World War II', *Journal of Strategic Studies*, July 2022. **67** Walter S Dunn, *The Soviet Economy and the Red Army1930–1945* (Westport, CT, USA: Praeger, 1995), pp 126–7. **68** For these shipping calculations: John Ellis, *The World War II Data Book* (London: BCA and Aurum Press, 1993), Tables 72 and 96; and W K Hancock and M M Gowing, *The British War Economy* (British Official History Civil Series) (London: HMSO, 1949), Table (d) p 205 and Table (e) pp 354–5. **69** Beaumont, *Comrades in Arms*, pp 44–6; Cadogan, *Diaries*, entries for 4 and 5 September, pp 404–5. **70** WM (41) 90 Conclusions, Minute 1, 5 September 1941, CAB 65/23/14; Beaumont, *Comrades in Arms*, pp 44–6. **71** Llewellyn-Jones, *Naval Staff History*, Appendix A; Woodman, *Arctic Convoys*, Chapter 4; Kotelnikov, *Lend-Lease and Soviet Aviation*, p 45. **72** Boog et al, *Germany and the Second World War*, Vol. VI, pp 45–6. **73** Woodman, *Arctic Convoys*, Chapter 4.

### Chapter 1: The Royal Navy in Autumn 1941: Brightening Prospects?
**1** Malcom Llewellyn-Jones, *The Royal Navy and the Mediterranean Convoys: A Naval Staff History* (Abingdon: Routledge, 2007), p 23; David Hobbs, *Taranto and Naval Air Warfare in the Mediterranean, 1940–1945* (Barnsley: Seaforth, 2020), Chapter 7. For Somerville's London discussions: Somerville letter to Cunningham, 7 September 1941, Item 182, NRS Volume 134, *The Somerville Papers*, edited by Michael Simpson (Scolar Press, 1995). **2** Llewellyn-Jones, *Royal Navy and the Mediterranean Convoys*, pp 98–9. **3** Nicholas Rodger, *The Command of the Ocean: A Naval History of Britain, 1649–1815* (London: Allen Lane, 2004), p 526. **4** Derek Howse, *Radar at Sea: The Royal Navy in World War II* (Basingstoke: Macmillan, 1993), pp 32–3. **5** Ibid, pp 15–22. **6** Boyd, *British Naval Intelligence*, pp 440–3. **7** COS 304th and 307th meetings, 30 August and 2 September, CAB 79/14. **8** 'Report of Proceedings, 5–14 August 1941', paragraph 4, Item 176, NRS Volume 134, *The Somerville Papers*. **9** Boyd, *British Naval Intelligence*, p 445. **10** F H Hinsley and others, *British Intelligence in the Second World War*. Volume 2 (London: HMSO, 1981) p 325. **11** Llewellyn-Jones, *Royal Navy and the Mediterranean Convoys*, p 27. **12** Ibid, Appendix G, p 120. **13** Richard J Hammond, 'An Enduring Influence on Imperial Defence and Grand Strategy: British Perceptions of the Italian Navy, 1935–1943', *International History Review*, 39:5, 2017, pp 810–35. **14** Jack Greene and Alessandro Massignani, *The Naval War in the Mediterranean 1940–1943* (UK: Chatham Publishing, 2002), pp 184–5. For German air strength in Northern Norway in mid-1942, Llewellyn-Jones, *Royal Navy and the Arctic Convoys*, Appendix F, p 172. **15** Llewellyn-Jones, *Royal Navy and the Mediterranean Convoys*, p 22; Somerville letter to Admiral Sir Dudley North, 30 July 1941, Item 173, NRS Volume 134; Greene & Massignani, *The Naval War in the Mediterranean*, pp 178–9; Hobbs, *Taranto and Naval Air Warfare in the Mediterranean*, Chapter 7; Boyd, *The Royal Navy in Eastern Waters*, pp 252–3. For evidence that the Royal Navy was less impressed with Italian air capability: Hammond, 'An Enduring Influence on Imperial Defence and Grand Strategy'. **16** Greene and Massignani, *The Naval War in the Mediterranean*, p 178. **17** Llewellyn-Jones, *Royal Navy and the Mediterranean Convoys*, pp 19–22; Somerville 'Report of Proceedings, 27 July–4 August 1941', Item 174, paragraph 60, NRS Volume 134. **18** Boyd, *British Naval Intelligence*, pp 440–1; Hammond, 'An Enduring Influence on Imperial Defence and Grand Strategy'. **19** Howse, *Radar at Sea*, p 112. **20** Showell, *Fuehrer Conferences*, pp 225–30 and 240–1; Hobbs, *Taranto and Naval Air Warfare in the Mediterranean*, Chapter 7. **21** Llewellyn-Jones, *Royal Navy and Mediterranean Convoys*, pp 24–5; Greene and Massignani, *The Naval War in the Mediterranean*, pp 185–6. **22** Howse, *Radar at Sea*, pp 61 and 65. **23** For insight into Hermione's RDF role: 'Report of Proceedings from Commanding Officer, HMS Ark Royal to Flag Officer Commanding, Force H', 27 August 1941, pp 488–94, esp. p 493, Item 150, NRS Volume 159, *The Fleet Air Arm in the Second World War 1939–1941*, edited by Ben Jones (London: Ashgate, 2012). Howse, *Radar at Sea*, pp 61–2, for *Sheffield*'s role. **24** Llewellyn-Jones, *Royal Navy and Mediterranean Convoys*, pp 25–7, Plans 5 and 7; Greene and Massignani, *The Naval War in the Mediterranean*, pp 187–8; Hobbs, *Taranto and Naval Air Warfare in the Mediterranean*, Chapter 7. **25** Llewellyn-Jones, *Royal Navy and Mediterranean*

*Convoys*, pp 27–8; Greene and Massignani, *The Naval War in the Mediterranean*, pp 188–9; Hobbs, *Taranto and Naval Air Warfare in the Mediterranean*, Chapter 7; Somerville, 'Report on Operation Halberd, 24–30 September 1941', paragraphs 190–1, Item 185, NRS Volume 134. **26** Llewellyn-Jones, *Royal Navy and Mediterranean Convoys*, pp 29–32 and Plans 5 and 8; Greene and Massignani, *The Naval War in the Mediterranean*, pp 191–2. **27** Howse, *Radar at Sea*, pp 137–8. **28** Somerville, 'Report on Operation Halberd', paragraphs 60–2, NRS Volume 134; Norman Friedman, *Naval Anti-Aircraft Guns and Gunnery* (Barnsley: Seaforth, 2013), Chapters 4 and 8. **29** Quoted in Vincent O'Hara, *Six Victories: North Africa, Malta and the Mediterranean Convoy War November 1941–March 1942* (Annapolis: Naval Institute Press, 2019), p 65 drawing on ADM 239/138. **30** H T Lenton, *British and Empire Warships of the Second World War* (London: Greenhill Books, 1998), pp 85–6. **31** Douglas Austin, 'The Place of Malta in British Strategic Policy 1925–1943' (unpublished doctoral thesis, University of London, November 2001), Table 6, pp 181–2. **32** Howse, *Radar at Sea*, Appendix F. **33** Richard Hammond, *Strangling the Axis: The Fight for Control of the Mediterranean in the Second World War* (Cambridge University Press, 2020), p 85. **34** John Wingate, *The Fighting Tenth: The Tenth Submarine Flotilla and the Siege of Malta* (UK: Sapere Books, 2021), Chapter 11. **35** Fabio De Ninno, 'The Mediterranean Battle of the Convoys: some revaluations', paper published 2021 on www.academia.edu, p 11. **36** Hammond, *Strangling the Axis*, pp 70 and 94. **37** First Sea Lord to Prime Minister, 24 August 1941, ADM 178/322; Austin, pp 183–5; O'Hara, *Six Victories*, Chapter 3. **38** Greene and Massignani, *The Naval War in the Mediterranean*, p 193; David Brown, *Atlantic Escorts: Ships, Weapons & Tactics in World War II* (Barnsley: Seaforth, 2022), p 74. **39** O'Hara, *Six Victories*, pp 39–41. **40** Ibid, pp 41–53; Greene and Massignani, *The Naval War in the Mediterranean*, pp 193–6. **41** German Naval Staff Operations Division (NSOD) War Diaries, Part A, Volume 28, December 1941, 6 December, p 58, ONI translation, US Naval War College Archives. **42** Showell, *Fuehrer Conferences*, pp 243–4. **43** David Stahel, *The Battle for Moscow* (Cambridge University Press, 2015), pp 241–2. **44** Phillips Payson O'Brien, *How the War Was Won: Air-Sea Power and Allied Victory in World War II* (Cambridge University Press, 2015), Chapter 5, Table 21. **45** For the above two paragraphs, see also: O'Hara, *Six Victories*, pp 53–78; Hammond, *Strangling the Axis*, Table 4.1, p 94 and Table 4.3, p 100; 1948 Air Ministry publication, *The Rise and Fall of the German Air Force (1933–1945)*, pp 133–4 and 172; Williamson Murray, *The Luftwaffe 1933–45: Strategy for Defeat* (London: Brassey's, 1983), pp 86–8; Boog et al, *Germany and the Second World War*, Volume IV, pp 763 and 814–15; First Sea Lord to Prime Minister, 30 November 1941, ADM 205/10. **46** The Fighting Instructions are in ADM 239/261. For further context and commentary, including comparison with contemporary US Navy and IJN thinking, James Levy, 'Royal Navy Fleet Tactics on the Eve of the Second World War', *War in History*, 19:3, 2012, pp 379–95. **47** CB 04234 (2), Atlantic Convoy Instructions, Operations Section, September 1942, ADM 239/344, and Admiralty Convoy Instructions to Escorts, North Russian Section, December 1944, ADM 239/348. **48** NRS Volume 137, The Defeat of the Enemy Attack on Shipping, 1939–1945, edited by Eric Grove, Plan 10; Blair, *The Hunters*, Appendix 9; Marc Milner, *The Battle of the Atlantic* (Stroud: The History Press, 2011), Chapter 3; David K Brown, *Atlantic Escorts: Ships, Weapons & Tactics in World War II* (Barnsley: Seaforth, 2022), Chapters 1 and 2 and pp 67–8. **49** COS (41) 277 (O), 14 December 1941, 'Future British Naval Strategy', CAB 80/60. **50** First Sea Lord note to Prime Minister, 10 October 1941, ADM 205/10. **51** First Sea Lord papers, late August 1941, ADM 178/322. **52** Blair, *The Hunters*, Appendix 9; Lenton, *British and Empire Warships*, pp 163–72. **53** First Sea Lord draft letters to Admirals Stark and Little, November 1941, ADM 205/9. **54** Hammond, *Strangling the Axis*, pp 45–8. **55** Ibid, tables 3.3 and 4.1, pp 70 and 94. **56** Benjamin Jones, 'Ashore, Afloat and Airborne: The Logistics of Naval Airpower, 1914–1945' (unpublished doctoral thesis, King's College, University of London, 2007), pp 16 and 81; Naval Aviation 1919–1945, Vol 1, Appendix VII, ADM 234/374; Admiralty Board memorandum, ADM 167/112. **57** www.armouredcarriers.com, Fairey Fulmar, service history. **58** Vice Admiral Sir Louis Le Bailly, *From Fisher to the Falklands* (London: Marine Management (Holdings) Ltd, 1991), p 63. **59** Notes by Fifth Sea Lord of Fleet Air Arm

Meeting held on 4 January 1940, 22 January, ADM 1/10752. 60 For more detail: Boyd, *Royal Navy in Eastern Waters*, pp 44–6 and 257–65; Jones, Logistics of Naval Airpower, pp 136–58. 61 See article 'Were the Armoured Carriers Worthwhile' at website www.armouredcarriers.com. 62 Boyd, *Royal Navy in Eastern Waters*, pp 44–6. 63 1948 Air Ministry publication, *Rise and Fall of the German Air Force*, pp 104–08; NRS Volume 137, *The Defeat of the Enemy Attack on Shipping, 1939–1945*, edited by Eric Grove (London: Ashgate Publishing, 1997), pp 157–64; Richard Overy, *The Bombing War: Europe 1939–1945* (London: Allen Lane, 2013), Chapter 2. 64 NRS Volume 159, *The Fleet Air Arm in the Second World War, 1939–1941*, Item 93, 'Minutes by Director of Naval Air Division of meeting held at Admiralty on 12 December 1940', 'Provision of shipborne fighters with convoys', 14 December 1940; Jones, 'Ashore, Afloat and Airborne', pp 46–8. 65 Lenton, *British and Empire Warships*, pp 113–15. 66 www.royalnavyresearcharchive.org.uk/Escort; Lenton, pp 114–21 and 127–9. 67 'History of HMS Audacity', www.royalnavyresearcharchive.org.uk/Escort; Corelli Barnett, *Engage the Enemy More Closely: The Royal Navy in the Second World War* (London: Hodder and Stoughton, 1991), pp 275–6; Howse, *Radar at Sea*, pp 119–20; *Rise and Fall of the German Air Force*, p 106; Adam R Claasen, *Hitler's Northern War: The Luftwaffe's Ill-Fated Campaign, 1940–1945* (University Press of Kansas, 2001), p 181. 68 NRS Volume 159, *The Fleet Air Arm in the Second World War, 1939–1941*, Items 160 and 161, 'Aircraft requirements for Auxiliary Aircraft Carriers', 29 and 30 November 1941, pp 514–15; Lenton, *British and Empire Warships*, p 129. 69 NRS 159, Item 165, 'Extract from minutes of War Cabinet Defence Committee (Supply) (41) 15th Meeting on 9 December 1941, p 524. 70 WP (41) 308, 29 December 1941, Memorandum by First Lord, 'Auxiliary Aircraft Carriers', CAB 66/20/31. 71 NRS Volume 165, *The Fleet Air Arm in the Second World War, Volume II 1942–1943*, edited by Ben Jones (London: Routledge, 2018), Item 5, 'Minute by Fifth Sea Lord', 5 February 1942, 'Requirements for Aircraft Carriers'. 72 Jones, 'Ashore, Afloat and Airborne', pp 206–12. 73 John Buckley, 'Coastal Command in the Second World War', *Air Power Review*, 21:1. 2018. 74 Ibid. 75 NRS Volume 159, *The Fleet Air Arm in the Second World War, 1939–1941*, pp 308–10; Jones, 'Ashore, Afloat and Airborne', p 177; Hobbs, *Taranto and Naval Air Warfare in the Mediterranean*, Chapter 6. 76 Jones, 'Ashore, Afloat and Airborne', p 177; Hobbs, *Taranto and Naval Air Warfare in the Mediterranean* Chapter 5. 77 Hammond, *Strangling the Axis*, pp 70 and 94. 78 Buckley, 'Coastal Command in the Second World War'. 79 Boyd, *British Naval Intelligence*, pp 487–9. 80 Howse, *Radar at Sea*, Chapter 2. 81 Ibid, pp 30–1. 82 Ibid, pp 99–101 and Appendix F. 83 Ibid, pp 66–71 and 109–15. 84 Ibid, pp 54–7, 64–5, 97–8, quoting Ellis' unpublished autobiography. 85 Ibid, pp 62 and 112–13. 86 For more detail: Boyd, *British Naval Intelligence*, Chapters 23 and 24. 87 Ralph Erskine, unpublished paper 'Allied Shipborne High Frequency Direction Finding in WWII', February 2021; Boyd, *British Naval Intelligence*, p 414. 88 *Tirpitz*, Volume 1, Section 2 – The Ship, p 4, ADM 234/349. 89 For more, Boyd, *The Royal Navy in Eastern Waters*, pp 36–54 and references. 90 Le Bailly, *From Fisher to the Falklands*, pp 55–6, 69–73. 91 Ibid, p 64. 92 George Wilton, 'The Royal Fleet Auxiliary and Post-War Change', *British Journal of Military History*, 8:3, November 2022. 93 Hammond, *Strangling the Axis*, Tables 4.1 and 4.3. 94 De Ninno, 'The Mediterranean Battle of the Convoys', p 14; O'Hara, *Six Victories*, pp 90–4. 95 NSOD War Diaries, Volume 28, December 1941, 1 and 2 December, pp 6 and 15–16. 96 Blair, *The Hunters*, pp 410–17 and Appendix 18. 97 COS (41) 277 (O), 14 December 1941, 'Future British Naval Strategy', CAB 80/60.

**Chapter 2: Barbarossa and the Reluctant Opening of an Arctic Theatre**
1 For a full discussion: Boog *et al*, *Germany and the Second World War*, Volume IV, *The Attack on the Soviet Union* (OUP, 1996), Introduction. Also, Kershaw, *Fateful Choices*, pp 56–65. 2 Boog *et al*, *Germany and the Second World War*, Volume IV, pp 25–6; War Journal of Colonel General Franz Halder, Volume IV, Part 2, entry for 31 July 1940, pp 141–5, US Army Historical Division, Fort Leavenworth, Kansas, USA. 3 Halder War Journal, Volume IV, Part 2, diary entry for 30 July, pp 138–41. 4 Halder, Volume IV, pp 144–5. 5 Ibid, p 145. 6 Ibid, p 141. 7 Boog *et al*, *Germany and the Second World War*, Volume IV,

pp 26–38; Kershaw, *Fateful Choices*, pp 65–71. **8** Halder, Volume IV, Part 2, entry for 30 July, pp 138–41; Kershaw, *Fateful Choices*, pp 68–9. **9** Boog et al, *Germany and the Second World War*, Volume IV, pp 38–9; Boyd, *The Royal Navy in Eastern Waters*, pp 127–9. **10** The August survey had the title 'Brief strategic survey of the continuation of the war after the campaign in Russia', EDS Appreciation 8, 'The War in the Mediterranean February to November 1941', pp 61–4, CAB 146/9. See also Halder diary for 13 September 1941 which contains a summary, Volume VII, Part 2. **11** Boog et al, *Germany and the Second World War*, Volume III, p 639. **12** Note 10; Boyd, *Royal Navy in Eastern Waters*, pp 136–8. **13** Boog et al, *Germany and the Second World War*, Volume IV, pp 42–3. **14** Kershaw, *Fateful Choices*, pp 263–70. **15** Boog et al, *Germany and the Second World War*, Volume IV, pp 43–6 and 438–40; Kershaw, *Fateful Choices*, pp 262–3; Sean McMeekin, *Stalin's War*, Chapters 11 and 12. **16** Boog et al, *Germany and the Second World War*, Volume IV, pp 46–8. **17** Kershaw, *Fateful Choices*, pp 263–70; Geoffrey T Waddington, 'Ribbentrop and the Soviet Union 1937–1941', in *Barbarossa: The Axis and the Allies*, edited by John Erickson and David Dilks (Edinburgh University Press, 1994); Evan Mawdsley, *Thunder in the East: The Nazi–Soviet War 1941–1945* (London: Bloomsbury, 2015), pp 32–7. **18** Boog et al, *Germany and the Second World War*, Volume IV, pp 275–85; Tooze, *The Wages of Destruction*, pp 456–9. **19** F H Hinsley, 'British Intelligence and Barbarossa', in Erickson and Dilks, *Barbarossa: The Axis and the Allies*. **20** Michael S Goodman, *The Official History of the Joint Intelligence Committee: Volume I, From the Approach of the Second World War to the Suez Crisis* (Abingdon, Oxon: Routledge, 2014), p 95. **21** Defence Committee DO (40) 39th meeting, 'Review of Situation', CAB 69/8. **22** Hinsley, 'British Intelligence and Barbarossa', pp 48–56; Goodman, *Official History of the Joint Intelligence Committee*, pp 95–7. **23** Churchill minute to Eden and Beaverbrook, 14 October 1941, CAB 120/681. **24** Hinsley, 'British Intelligence and Barbarossa', pp 56–65. **25** JIC (41) 218 of 23 May, CAB 81/102. **26** Hinsley, *British Intelligence*, Volume 2, pp 470–3; Goodman, *Official History of the Joint Intelligence Committee: Volume I*, pp 96–7. **27** JIC (41) 229, 30 May, 'Germany's Next Move', COS (41) 196th Meeting, CAB 79/11/56. **28** 'Germany's Next Move', extract from COS (41) 197th Meeting, 31 May 1941, Secretary's Standing File, CAB 79/86. **29** Hinsley, *British Intelligence*, Volume 2, pp 472–9. **30** Ibid, p 478. **31** Eden to Prime Minister, 9 June 1941, FO 954/24B/315. **32** JIC (41) 252, 'German Soviet Relations', 12 June 1941, COS (41) 210th Meeting, 13 June, CAB 79/12. **33** JIC (41) 234, 'The Possible Effect of a German–Soviet War', 14 June 1941, COS (41) 208th Meeting, 11 June, CAB 79/12. **34** COS 210th Meeting, Item 2. **35** 'GAF Intentions', GC&CS Intelligence Summary, 31 May, HW 13/2. **36** JIC (41) 234. Details of Russian order of battle in Annex A. Modern figures drawing on Russian archives from: Mawdsley, *Thunder in the East*, Chapter 2, Table 2; and David M Glantz and Jonathan M House, *When Titans Clashed: How the Red Army Stopped Hitler* (USA; University of Kansas Press, 2015), Chapter 3 and Appendix, Tables A and B. Also: McMeekin, *Stalin's War*, Chapter 13 although some of his numbers for Russian tanks and aircraft look high. **37** JIC (41) 234: Joseph Ryan, 'The Royal Navy and Soviet Seapower, 1930–1950: Intelligence, Naval Cooperation and Antagonism' (unpublished doctoral thesis, University of Hull, 1996), pp 37–9. **38** Martin Kahn, *The Western Allies and Soviet Potential in World War II* (Abingdon, Oxon: Routledge, 2017), pp 95–6. **39** Bradley F Smith, *Sharing Secrets with Stalin: How the Allies Traded Intelligence, 1941–1945* (USA: University Press of Kansas, 1996), pp 33–4, 73, 87, 116 and 144: McMeekin, Chapter 21. **40** Mawdsley, *Thunder in the East*, p 42; Boog et al, *Germany and the Second World War*, Volume IV, pp 320–5 and 350–3. **41** WM (41) 58th Conclusions, 9 June; WM (41) 59th Conclusions, 12 June; and WM (41) 60th Conclusions, 16 June. All CAB 65/22. **42** WM (41) 60th Conclusions, 16 June, CAB 65/22. **43** Ibid. **44** Ivan M Maisky, *The Maisky Diaries: Red Ambassador to the Court of St James 1932–1943*, edited by Gabriel Gorodetsky (Yale University Press, 2015), entry for 18 June 1941. **45** Gorodetsky, 'An Alliance of Sorts', pp 102–3. **46** Maisky diary entry for 13 June; War Cabinet WM (41) 59th Meeting Conclusions, 12 June, CAB 65/18/38. **47** Kimball, *Churchill & Roosevelt: The Complete Correspondence*, Volume 1, C-100x, 14 June, p 209. **48** Defence Committee Operations, DO (41), 42nd Meeting, 17 June, CAB 69/2/2. **49** DO (41) 43rd Meeting,

19 June, and DO (41), 44th Meeting, 25 June, CAB 69/2/2. **50** For the origin, composition and role of the Joint Planning Staff, see: Boyd, *The Royal Navy in Eastern Waters*, p 51–2. **51** COS (41) 218th Meeting, 20 June, Item 9, CAB 79/12. **52** JP (41) 465, 19 June, CAB 79/12. **53** JP (41) 444, 14 June, CAB 79/12. Russia was addressed in paragraphs 132–134. **54** COS (41) 115 (O), Future Strategy, CAB 80/58. **55** COS (41) 221st Meeting, 23 June, CAB 79/12. **56** COS (41) 116 (O), 'Raid on Northern France', 23 June, CAB 80/58. **57** JP (41) 478, Action Arising out of German–Russian Conflict, 23 June, CAB 79/12. **58** COS (41) 224th Meeting, 25 June, Item 2, CAB 79/12. **59** For Churchill's speech, Churchill, *Grand Alliance*, pp 332–3. For Maisky's reaction, diary entries for 22 and 27 June. For Churchill's expectation of Russian defeat, Gilbert, *Finest Hour*, pp 1118–19. **60** Quoted by Avram Lytton, 'In the House of Rimmon: British Aid to the Soviet Union, June – September 1941', *Journal of Slavic Military Studies*, 26:4, 2013, pp 677–8. **61** Quoted in Beaumont, *Comrades in Arms*, p 26. **62** Keith Neilson, '"Pursued by a Bear": British Estimates of Soviet Military Strength and Anglo-Soviet Relations, 1922–1939', *Canadian Journal of History*, XXVIII:2, August 1993, p 215. **63** Major General Sir John Kennedy, *The Business of War: The War Narrative of Major General Sir John Kennedy* (London: Hutchinson, 1957), p 147. **64** COS (41) 223rd Meeting, 24 June, item 1, and JP (41) 482, Mission to Russia, 24 June, CAB 79/12. **65** Bradley Smith, *Sharing Secrets with Stalin*, pp 21–2. **66** Ibid, pp 23–4; Gorodetsky, 'An Alliance of Sorts', p 106; Ryan thesis, p 74. **67** Bradley Smith, *Sharing Secrets with Stalin*, pp 37–8. **68** Admiral Miles, farewell 30 Mission report, 31 December 1942, paragraph 17, ADM 223/252. **69** WP (41) 145, 'Russia: Denial of Oil to the Enemy', 30 June, CAB 66/17/18. **70** Alexander Hill, 'British Lend-Lease Aid and the Soviet War Effort, June 1941–June 1942', *Journal of Military History*, 71:3, July 2007, p 779. **71** COS (41), 231st Meeting, Item 1, 2 July, CAB 79/12; DO (41) 45th Meeting, Item 2, 3 July, CAB 69/2/2; for concern over Northern Fleet falling into German hands, Gorodetsky, 'An Alliance of Sorts', pp 108–9; for Admiralty knowledge of Northern Fleet strength, JIC (41) 234, 14 June 1941, 'The Possible Effect of a German–Soviet War', Appendix A, and Ryan thesis, pp 37–9. **72** Pound note to First Lord, 7 July, ADM 205/10. **73** DO (41) 45th Meeting, 3 July; COS (41) 234th Meeting, Item 6, 5 July. **74** DO (41) 46th Meeting, Item 1, 4 July. **75** Eden to Cripps, 7 July 1941, FO 954/24B/337. **76** JP (41) 523, 'Russian Mission to England', 6 July, CAB 79/12. **77** Gorodetsky, 'An Alliance of Sorts', p 112, drawing on Russian memoirs. **78** For example, Maisky, diary entry of 5 September. **79** WP (41) 156, 'Record of an Interview between the Foreign Secretary and the Members of the Soviet Military Mission', 9 July, CAB 66/17/29. **80** Boog *et al*, *Germany and the Second World War*, Volume IV, Table I.iv.5, p 364; Claasen, *Hitler's Northern War*, p 188. **81** COS (41) 133 (O), 'Liaison with the USSR', 9 July, CAB 80/58. **82** COS (41) 239th Meeting, Item 6, 10 July, CAB 79/12. The questionnaire is in COS (41) 134 (O), 11 July, CAB 80/58. Also, Gorodetsky, 'An Alliance of Sorts', p 112. **83** Quoted by Gorodetsky, 'An Alliance of Sorts', p 110 and Bradley Smith, *Sharing Secrets with Stalin*, pp 30–1. The original message, of 10 July, drafted by a colonel in MO1 is in WO 193/666. **84** COS (41) 244th Meeting, Item 1, 14 July, CAB 78/12. **85** Quoted in Churchill, *Grand Alliance*, p 341. **86** DO (41) 50th Meeting, Item 2, 10 July, CAB 69/2/3. **87** Gorodetsky, 'An Alliance of Sorts', pp 112–3; Beaumont, *Comrades in Arms*, pp 34–6.

### Chapter 3: The Case for Helping Russia: Ends, Ways and Means
**1** Hinsley, *British Intelligence*, Volume 2, pp 69–70. **2** Bradley Smith, *Sharing Secrets with Stalin*, p 42. **3** Ibid, pp 59–61; Keith Jeffery, *MI6: The History of the Secret Intelligence Service 1909–1949* (London: Bloomsbury, 2010), p 563; Ryan thesis, p 94; Lytton, 'British Aid to the Soviet Union', pp 682–3. **4** COS (41) 441, Weekly résumé No 98, 17 July, paragraphs 22 and 69, CAB 80/29. **5** Cadogan, *Diaries*, entry for 14 July 1941; Lytton, 'British Aid to the Soviet Union', p 689. **6** Kennedy, *Business of War*, p 152. **7** Bradley Smith, *Sharing Secrets with Stalin*, pp 32–3. **8** Jeffery, *MI6*, pp 564–5. **9** Telegrams, Sir Miles Lampson, Cairo, to Foreign Office, 29 September 1941, and Cripps (Moscow) to Foreign Office, 6 October, AIR 8/565; Kahn, *Western Allies and Soviet Potential*, pp 119–20. **10** JPS (41) 557, 'Operations in the North', 17 July, and COS (41) 249th Meeting, 17 July, CAB

79/12. **11** Barnett, *Engage the Enemy More Closely*, p 498. **12** Martin Stephen, *The Fighting Admirals: British Admirals of the Second World War* (London: Leo Cooper, 1991), pp 150–7. **13** Admiral Arseni G Golovko, *With the Red Fleet: The War Memoirs of the Late Admiral Arseni G Golovko*, edited by Sir Aubrey Mansergh (London: Putnam, 1965), pp 83–4. **14** Rear Admiral Burrough report 145/773, Appendix VI, 5 December 1941, ADM 199/72; Woodman, *Arctic Convoys*, Chapter 2. **15** The translated memoirs edited by Mansergh were originally published in the Soviet Union in 1960. **16** Rear Admiral 10th Cruiser Squadron's Report of Proceedings, 5 December 1941, Appendix III, ADM 199/72; Ryan thesis, pp 108–9. **17** COS (41) 253rd Meeting, Item 1, 20 July, CAB 79/13; Admiral of the Fleet Sir Philip Vian, *Action this Day: A War Memoir* (London: Frederick Muller, 1960), p 65. **18** Churchill, *The Grand Alliance*, pp 342–3. **19** COS (41) 145 (O), 'Aid to Russia', 21 July, CAB 80/58; Woodman, *Arctic Convoys*, Chapter 2; Schofield, *Russian Convoys*, pp 16–17; Lytton, 'British Aid to the Soviet Union', p 686; Ryan thesis pp 64–5. **20** Jeffery, *MI6*, p 562. **21** For more on this paragraph, Ryan thesis, pp 76 and 83–4; Martin H Folly, '"They treat us with scant respect": prejudice and pride in British Military Liaison with the Soviet Union in the Second World War', *The International History Review*, November 2021, p 3; Admiral Miles, farewell 30 Mission report, 31 December 1942, paragraphs 27–30, and 62–3, ADM 223/252. **22** Bradley Smith, *Sharing Secrets with Stalin*, pp 44–5 and 54–5. **23** Martin H Folly, 'From Sevastopol to Sukhumi – and back again: British naval liaison in action with the Red Navy in the Black Sea, 1941–1945', *War in History*, 28:4, 2021, pp 873–8. **24** Ryan thesis, pp 80, 83, 88 and 107–8; Golovko, *With the Red Fleet*, pp 67 and 85. **25** Ibid. **26** COS 253rd Meeting. **27** Churchill letter to Stalin of 20 July, Churchill, *The Grand Alliance*, pp 343–5. **28** COS (41) 255th Meeting, Item 1, 23 July, CAB 79/13. **29** Website: www.uboat.net. **30** COS (41) Meeting on 23 July at 9.45pm, CAB 79/86/9; COS (41) 260th Meeting, Item 1, 24 July; COS (41) 262nd Meeting, Item 2, 25 July; COS 263rd Meeting, Item 5, 26 July; COS 264th Meeting, 28 July, Item 8; COS (41) 272nd Meeting, Item 1, 2 August, COS (41) 275th Meeting, Item 2 and Annex, 4 August, all CAB 79/13. Also: Schofield, *Russian Convoys*, p 15. **31** DO (41) Defence Committee Operations, 57th Meeting, Item 2, 11 August, CAB 69/2/3; Kotelnikov, *Lend-Lease and Soviet Aviation*, pp 45 and 166. **32** Lytton, 'British Aid to the Soviet Union', p 694. **33** Ibid, p 697. **34** Ibid, pp 695–6. **35** Earl F Ziemke, *United States Army in World War II, German Northern Theater of Operations 1940–1945* (Washington USA: US Government Printing Office, 1959), pp 121–39. **36** Ibid, pp 114–5 and 185. For background on Kolosjoki: Peter Stadius, 'Petsamo: Bringing Modernity to Finland's Arctic Ocean Shore 1920–1939', *Acta Borealis*, 2016; and Jari Eloranta and Ilkka Nummela, 'Finnish Nickel as a Strategic Metal, 1920–1944', *Scandinavian Journal of History*, 32:4, 2007, pp 322–45. **37** Hinsley, *British Intelligence*, Volume 2, pp 131–2. **38** Christopher Mann and Christer Jörgensen, *Hitler's Arctic War: The German Campaigns in Norway, Finland, and the USSR 1940–1945* (Barnsley: Pen & Sword, 2016), Chapter 3; Alf Jacobsen, *Miracle at the Litza: Hitler's First Defeat on the Eastern Front* (Oxford, UK: Casemate Publishers, 2017), Chapter 1 and Appendix 1. **39** Boog *et al*, *Germany and the Second World War*, Volume IV, pp 381–2 and 956; Blair, *The Hunters*, pp 324–5. **40** Showell, *Fuehrer Conferences*, pp 176–7, 193; Halder diaries, Volume VI, entries for 17 March 1941, p 29, and 5 July, pp 202–3. **41** Showell, *Fuehrer Conferences*, p 224; Blair, *The Hunters*, pp 324–5. **42** Jacobsen, *Miracle at the Litza*, for a comprehensive account of the northern operation; Ziemke, *German Northern Theater of Operations*, pp 140–56; Boog *et al*, *Germany and the Second World War*, Volume IV, pp 941–5; Mann and Jörgensen, *Hitler's Arctic War*, Chapter 3. **43** Ziemke, *German Northern Theater of Operations*, pp 157–84; Boog *et al*, *Germany and the Second World War*, Volume IV, pp 940–53; Mann and Jörgensen, *Hitler's Arctic War*, Chapter 3; Halder diary, Volume VII, entries for 1 August 1941, p 5, 12 September, p 92, and 23 September, p 119. **44** Churchill, *Grand Alliance*, pp 474–5. **45** Boog *et al*, *Germany and the Second World War*, Volume IV, Diagram II.i.8, Luftwaffe Operations in the East in 1941, pp 806–8; Claasen, *Hitler's Northern War*, p 189; *Rise and Fall of the German Air Force*, pp 113–14; Generalleutnant Hermann Plocher, *The German Air Force versus Russia, 1942*, US Air Force Historical Studies: No 154 (USAF Historical Division, Aerospace Studies Institute, Air University, June 1966), pp 19–20;

Department of the Army Pamphlet, No 20-292, *Warfare in the Far North* (Department of the US Army, October 1951), pp 10–12; 'Report on Fulfilment of the Moscow Protocol, October 1941–June 1942, WP (42), 17 September 1942, Part II, paragraph 16, CAB 66/28/47. **46** Generalleutnant Hermann Plocher, *The German Air Force versus Russia, 1941*, US Air Force Historical Studies: No 153 (USAF Historical Division, Aerospace Studies Institute, Air University, July 1965), Chapter 8. **47** Jacobsen, *Miracle at the Litsa*, Appendix 1; Ziemke, *German Northern Theater of Operations*, pp 184–7; Mann and Jörgensen, *Hitler's Arctic War*, Chapter 3; Claasen, *Hitler's Northern War*, pp 188–9. **48** Department of the Army Pamphlet, No 20-292, *Warfare in the Far North*, p 11. **49** Golovko, *With the Red Fleet*, p 82. **50** Showell, *Fuehrer Conferences*, pp 233–4. **51** Alf Jacobsen, *Miracle at the Litsa*, p 90. **52** David Hobbs, *The Fleet Air Arm and the War in Europe 1939–1945* (Barnsley: Seaforth, 2022), Chapter 5; NRS, Volume 159, *The Fleet Air Arm in the Second World War, Volume 1, 1939–1941*, edited by Ben Jones (UK: Ashgate Publishing, 2012), Items 158 and 166. **53** Ibid. **54** Claasen, *Hitler's Northern War*, p 188. **55** Hobbs, *Fleet Air Arm and War in Europe*, Chapter 5. **56** Matthew Christopher Mann, 'British Policy and Strategy towards Norway, 1941–1944' (unpublished doctoral thesis, King's College, University of London, 1998), p 53, quoting Tovey to Admiralty, 12 September 1941, CAB 106/341. **57** Vice Admiral Sir Arthur Hezlet, *British and Allied Submarine Operations in World War II, Volume 1* (Royal Navy Submarine Museum, 2001), Chapter X; Jurgen Rohwer, *Allied Submarine Attacks of World War Two: European Theatre of Operations, 1939–1945* (London: Greenhill Books, 1997), pp 16–20. For 30 August attacks by *Trident*, Jacobsen, *Miracle at the Litsa*, pp 114–17. **58** NSOD War Diaries, Volume 28, December 1941, 2 December, p 10. **59** Rohwer, *Allied Submarine Attacks of World War Two: European Theatre of Operations*, pp 16–21. **60** U-boat.net; Alastair Mars, *Submarines at War 1939–1945* (London: William Kimber, 1971), pp 123–4; Schofield, *Russian Convoys*, p 16; Golovko, *With the Red Fleet*, pp 67, 82, 91. For intelligence: ZIP/ZG/101, 26 September, 'Notes on German Shipping and Air Activity in North Norway since mid-August', ADM 223/3. **61** Captain Dan Conley, 'Animals in Submarines', *Naval Review*, Volume 107, February 2019, p 70. **62** Hobbs, *Fleet Air Arm and War in Europe*, Chapter 5. **63** Prime Minister's minute D.244/1, 27 August, attached to COS (41) 299th Meeting, CAB 79/13. **64** Showell, *Fuehrer Conferences*, pp 233–4. **65** Halder diary, Volume VI, entry for 17 March 1941, pp 26–7; Showell, *Fuehrer Conferences*, pp 248 and 260. **66** COS (41) 23rd Meeting (O), 29 July, and associated papers, CAB 79/55. **67** COS (41) 158 (O), 'Occupation of Spitzbergen', 5 August, CAB 80/59 and DO (41) Defence Committee 54th Meeting, Item 1, 5 August, CAB 69/2/3. **68** DO (41) 55th Meeting, Item 2, 7 August, CAB 69/2/3. **69** DO (41) Defence Committee 57th Meeting, Item 1, 11 August, CAB 69/2/3; COS (41) 282nd Meeting, Item 3, 9 August; COS (41) 283rd Meeting, Item 5, 11 August, CAB 79/13, and COS (41) 158 (O), 'Occupation of Spitzbergen', 5 August, CAB 80/59. **70** COS (41) 285th Meeting, 12 August, and COS (41) 287th Meeting, Item 8, 14 August, CAB 79/13. **71** Mann thesis, p 101. **72** Vian, *Action this Day*, p 69. **73** Ibid, p 72; Woodman, *Arctic Convoys*, Chapter 4. **74** Ziemke, *German Northern Theater of Operations*, p 237; Boog et al, *Germany and the Second World War*, Volume 4, p 969. **75** Boyd, *Royal Navy in Eastern Waters*, pp 134–5 and 359–62. **76** DO (41) 44th Meeting, Item 5, 25 June, CAB 69/2/2. **77** COS (41) 226th Meeting, Item 3, 27 June, CAB 79/12. **78** Hinsley, *British Intelligence*, Volume 2, pp 82–3. **79** JP (41) 532, 'Eastward Extension of the War in the Middle East', 9 July, and COS (41) 246th Meeting, Item 8, 15 July, both CAB 79/12. **80** WM (41) War Cabinet 67th Conclusions, 9 July, CAB 65/19/3, and WM (41) War Cabinet 68th Conclusions, Item 2, 10 July, CAB 65/19/4. **81** Joan Beaumont, 'Great Britain and the Rights of Neutral Countries: The Case of Iran, 1941', *Journal of Contemporary History*, 16:1, January 1981, p 216. **82** COS (41) 435, 'Operations in Iran (Persia)', 18 July, CAB 80/29. **83** JP (41) 580, 'Situation in the Middle East', 23 July, CAB 79/13. **84** COS (41) 246th and 249th Meetings, 15 and 17 July, CAB 79/12. **85** JP (41) 580, 'Situation in the Middle East', 23 July, paragraph 14(iv), CAB 79/13. **86** JP (41) 594, 'Operations in Iran (Persia)', 26 July, CAB 79/13. **87** DO (41) Defence Committee 53rd Meeting, Item 1, 1 August, CAB 69/2/3. **88** DO (41) Defence Committee 59th Meeting, Item 1, 20 August,

CAB 69/2/3. **89** WM (41) War Cabinet 86th Meeting Conclusions, Minute 2, 25 August, CAB 65/23/12. **90** Kimball, *Churchill & Roosevelt: The Complete Correspondence*, Volume 1, C-113x, 1 September, pp 235–6. **91** DO (41) Defence Committee 60th Meeting, Item 1, 3 September, CAB 69/2/3. **92** WM (41), War Cabinet 89th Conclusions, Minute 2, 4 September, CAB 65/23/13. **93** COS (41) 274th Meeting, Item 2, 2 August, and JIC (41) 307 (O), 'The Effect of the Russian Campaign on the Prospects of Invasion', 1 August, both CAB 79/13. **94** Kahn, *Western Allies and Soviet Potential*, p 114; Bradley Smith, *Sharing Secrets with Stalin*, p 58; WP (41) 204, 'Visit of General Macfarlane to the Russian Front', 24 August, CAB/66/18/27. **95** JIC (41) 311, 'German Intentions up to the end of 1941', 8 August, CAB 79/13. **96** Kahn, *Western Allies and Soviet Potential*, p 114. **97** Jacob to Prime Minister, 29 August 1941, CAB 120/681. For German losses, Williamson Murray, *Strategy for Defeat*, Table XIII, p 89. For Russian losses, Glantz and House, *When Titans Clashed*, Table R. **98** JP (41) 691, 'Assistance to Russia', 23 August, CAB 79/13. **99** Ibid. **100** JP (41) 733, 'Operations to Divert Enemy Forces from the Eastern Front', 7 September, CAB 79/14. **101** COS (41) 314th Meeting, Item 4, 8 September, CAB 79/14. **102** JP (41) 735, 'Operations in the North', 7 September, CAB 79/14. **103** COS (41) 316th Meeting, Item 2, 9 September, CAB 79/14. **104** COS (41) 337th Meeting, Item 7, 30 September, CAB 79/14: COS (41) 222 (O), 'Operation AJAX, 2 October, CAB 80/59; DO (41) Defence Committee 63rd Meeting, Item 1, 2 October, and DO (41) Defence Committee 64th Meeting, 15 October, both CAB 69/2/3; Mann thesis, pp 133–40. For more background on the Swedish dimension: COS (41) 217 (O), 23 September 1941, 'Sweden: Draft Report', CAB 80/59. **105** Maisky, diary entry for 5 September. **106** Beaumont, *Comrades in Arms*, pp 45–6. **107** Relevant statistics from: DO (41) 11, 'Conference on British – United States Assistance to Russia', 22 September 1941, paragraph 12, CAB 69/3/1; DO (41) 33, 1 December 1941, 'Production and Allocation of Tanks between Different Theatres', CAB 69/3/2; and Ellis, *World War II Data Book*, pp 277–8. **108** Thornhill, 'Catalyst for Coalition', pp 277–9. **109** Beaumont, *Comrades in Arms*, pp 46–7; Thornhill, 'Catalyst for Coalition', p 267; DO (41) 11, paragraphs 13 and 19. **110** Beaumont, *Comrades in Arms*, pp 50–1; COS (41) 207 (O), 'Allocations of Aircraft to Russia from American Production and the effect on RAF Expansion', 17 September, CAB 80/59. **111** DO (41) Defence Committee 62nd Meeting, 19 September, CAB 69/2/3. **112** Text attached to WM (41) War Cabinet 90th Conclusions, Minute 1, 5 September, CAB 65/23/14. **113** Kimball, *Churchill & Roosevelt: The Complete Correspondence*, Volume 1, R-57x, 17 September, p 241, and C-116x, 22 September, p 242. **114** Ibid, Volume 1, C-119x, 5 October, pp 244–5. **115** Ellis, , *World War II Data Book*, Table 17, p 231. **116** WM (41) War Cabinet 90th Conclusions; Kimball, *Churchill & Roosevelt: The Complete Correspondence*, Volume 1, C-114x, 5 September, p 238. **117** Beaumont, *Comrades in Arms*, p 52. **118** Kimball, *Churchill & Roosevelt: The Complete Correspondence*, Volume 1, C-115x, 7 September, pp 238–9. **119** JIC (41) 357, 'The Effect on Russian War Potential of Successive Withdrawals', 13 September, CAB 79/14; Kahn, *Western Allies and Soviet Potential*, pp 121–3. **120** *The Great Patriotic War: The Anniversary Statistical Handbook* (Federal State Statistical Service, 2020), p 69. The *Anniversary Handbook* has been through many editions since 1956 when the first secret version was produced for internal use. However, most of its statistics through to 2020 were those originally collated in wartime and immediately after and have never been revised. **121** Boog et al, *Germany and the Second World War*, Volume IV, pp 136–42. **122** Ibid, Volume VI, pp 889–903. **123** JIC (41) 357. **124** Kahn, *Western Allies and Soviet Potential*, pp 123–4. **125** DO (41) 12, 'Anglo–American–Russian Conference', 22 September, CAB 69/3/1 and DO (41) Defence Committee 62nd Meeting. Churchill, *Grand Alliance*, also has a copy of the Directive at Appendix J. **126** A J P Taylor, *Beaverbrook* (London: Penguin Books, 1974), pp 624–32. **127** For the above two paragraphs, Beaumont, *Comrades in Arms,* pp 52–60; Hill, 'British Lend-Lease Aid and the Soviet War Effort, June 1941–June 1942', p 782. **128** For a fine new biography of Ismay, describing his role and contribution throughout the war, John Kiszely, *General Hastings 'Pug' Ismay: Soldier, Statesman, Diplomat: A New Biography* (London: Hurst & Co, 2024). **129** Beaumont, *Comrades in Arms*, pp 54–8; Taylor, *Beaverbrook*, pp 631–4; General the Lord Ismay, *Memoirs* (London: Heinemann, 1960), pp 230–1; Kiszely, *Ismay*, Chapter 6; Cadogan, Diary entry for 13 October 1941; Williams, *Beaverbrook*, pp 420–6. **130** Beaumont, p 58; David Reynolds and Vladimir Pechnatov, *The Kremlin Letters: Stalin's Wartime Correspondence with Churchill and Roosevelt* (New Haven and London: Yale University Press, 2018), Chapter 2.

## Chapter 4: The First Arctic Convoys and Their Impact

**1** Soviet Supply Protocols, US Department of State Publication 2759, US Government Printing Office, First Protocol, pp 1–10. **2** For a detailed discussion of the issues raised in these two paragraphs, Mark Harrison, *Accounting for War: Soviet Production, Employment, and the Defence Burden, 1940–1945* (Cambridge University Press, 1996), Chapter 6. For a colourful picture of Soviet leadership decision-making in the last months of 1941, Simon Sebag Montefiore, *Stalin: The Court of the Red Tsar* (Phoenix Paperback edition, 2004), Chapters 33–35. **3** 'Report on Fulfilment of the Moscow Protocol, October 1941–June 1942', WP (42) 417, 17 September 1942, CAB 66/28/47; Harriman report to Roosevelt, 29 October, PSF, Russia, FDR papers; Leighton and Coakley, *Global Logistics and Strategy 1940–1943*, p 113. **4** Foreign Office to Moscow, 18 December 1941, FO 954/24B/533. **5** COS (41) 710, 30 November 1941, 'The Situation in North Russian Ports', CAB 80/32. **6** JIC (41) 404, 20 October 1941, 'The Northern Supply Route to Russia', and supplement of 23 October, CAB 79/15. **7** For the above two paragraphs: WP (42) 417; Harriman's 29 October report: Leighton and Coakley, *Global Logistics and Strategy*, pp 113–15; T H Vail Motter, *The Persian Corridor and Aid to Russia*, United States Army in World War II, US Army Center of Military History (Washington, 1952), Appendix A, Table 1; Jan Drent, 'The Trans–Pacific Lend-Lease Shuttle to the Russian Far East, 1941–46', *The Northern Mariner*, XXVII:1, 2017, pp 31–58; Harriman to Roosevelt, 29 October 1941, US Department of State, Office of the Historian, Diplomatic Papers, and PSF, Russia, FDR papers; Roosevelt to Stalin, 10 February 1942, PSF, Russia 1942–43, FDR papers. **8** Gilbert, *Finest Hour*, p 1213. **9** Motter, *The Persian Corridor and Aid to Russia*, Appendix A, Table 1; Llewellyn-Jones, *Royal Navy and the Arctic Convoys*, Appendix A; 'Post Protocol Supplies to Russia', WP (42) 178, 26 April 1942, Annex II, paragraph 5, CAB 66/24/8. **10** Llewellyn-Jones, *Royal Navy and the Arctic Convoys*, Introduction, p 3. **11** Ibid, Chapter 1, p 5 and Appendix A. For *Waziristan*, uboat.net. **12** Boog *et al*, *Germany and the Second World War*, Volume IV, pp 956–7, and quoting Directive No 37. **13** Ibid, pp 953–5 and 817–18. **14** NSOD War Diaries, December 1941, entries for 15 and 27 December 1941, pp 148 and 274, and January 1942, entries for 5, 15, 16 and 19 January, pp 36, 133 and 178; Boog *et al*, *Germany and the Second World War*, Volume IV, p 958; Blair, *The Hunters*, pp 443–4 and Appendix 5, p 733. **15** Captain G E Colpoys, Admiralty Use of Special Intelligence in Naval Operations, Chapter X, p 122, HW 8/47. There is a parallel copy in ADM 223/88. **16** Llewellyn-Jones, *Royal Navy and the Arctic Convoys*, p 5. **17** 'Post Protocol Supplies to Russia', WP (42) 178, Annex II. **18** Ibid; 'Supplies of Aluminium to Russia', WP (42) 199, 12 May 1942, CAB 66/24/29; Ellis, *World War II Data Book*, Tables 87 and 93. **19** Beaumont, *Comrades in Arms*, pp 62–3. **20** Ibid, Chapter III; Churchill, *Grand Alliance*, Chapter XXVIII. **21** Field Marshal Lord Alanbrooke, *War Diaries, 1939–1945*, edited by Alex Danchev and Daniel Todman (London: Phoenix Press, 2002), diary entries for 10 and 17 August 1940, pp 98 and 100, 3 December 1941, p 206, 30 January 1942, p 225, 23 February 1942, p 233, and 13 August 1942, pp 299–300. **22** Beaumont, *Comrades in Arms*, pp 72–7. **23** Lieutenant General Sir Henry Pownall, *Chief of Staff: The Diaries of Lieutenant General Sir Henry Pownall*, Volume 2, 1940–1944, edited by Brian Bond (London: Leo Cooper, 1974), p 48. **24** Quoted by Beaumont, *Comrades in Arms*, p 73. **25** Jenkins, *Portraits and Miniatures*, 'Beaverbrook', p 249; Taylor, *Beaverbrook*, pp 632–49; Williams, *Max Beaverbrook*, pp 432–7 and 443. **26** Hinsley, *British Intelligence*, Volume 2, pp 69 and 73–4; Gilbert, *Finest Hour*, p 1209. **27** Mawdsley, *Thunder in the East*, p 96; Erickson, *Road to Stalingrad*, pp 297–8 and 694–6. **28** Rodric Braithwaite, *Moscow 1941: A City and its People at War* (London: Profile Books, 2010), Chapter 12. **29** Bradley Smith, *Sharing Secrets with Stalin*, p 84; Kahn, *Western Allies and Soviet Potential*, p 120; Ismay, *Memoirs*, pp 234–5; Kiszely, *Ismay*, Chapter 6. **30** Gilbert, *Finest Hour*, footnote 2, p 896 has a list of the thirty-one Ultra recipients authorised by Churchill on 8 November 1940. **31** DO (41) 22, 19 October

1941, 'Assistance to Russia', memorandum by Lord Beaverbrook, CAB 69/3/1, and DO (41) 67th Meeting, 20 October 1941, Item 2, CAB 69/2/3. **32** Secretary's Standard File, DO (41) 67th, 'Assistance to Russia' full record of discussion, CAB 69/8. **33** JIC (41) 433, 8 November 1941, 'Germany's Future Intentions', CAB 79/15. **34** Hinsley, *British Intelligence*, Volume 2, p 74. **35** JIC (42), 452, 2 December 1941, 'The Russian Campaign', CAB 79/16. **36** WM (41) War Cabinet 126th Conclusions, Minute 2, 10 December 1941, CAB 65/24/12. **37** JIC (41) 469, 11 December 1941, 'Enemy Withdrawals from the Russian Front', CAB 79/16. **38** Chiefs of Staff Weekly Résumé, No 120, 18 December 1941, paragraphs 19–23, CAB 80/32. **39** Hinsley, *British Intelligence*, Volume 2, p 87. **40** Ibid, p 86; Eden meeting with Stalin, 16 December 1941, FO 954/25A/3; Kahn, *Western Allies and Soviet Potential*, pp 159–60. **41** Kahn, *Western Allies and Soviet Potential*, pp 126–9. **42** Ellis, *World War II Data Book*, Tables 87 and 92. **43** Boog et al, *Germany and the Second World War*, Volume IV, pp 897–8 and footnote 268. **44** COS (41) 269 (O), 5 December 1941, 'Combined Strategy with Russia', CAB 80/60. **45** Annex IV, 'The Basis of Anglo-American Strategy', Note by Joint Planning Staff, 16 December 1941, CAB 99/17/1. **46** JIC (42) 34, 25 January 1942, 'Germany's Intentions', CAB 79/17. For German air strength, Luftwaffe Strength and Serviceability Tables, pp 19 and 24, Translation VII/107, Air Historical Branch. **47** Kimball, *Churchill & Roosevelt: The Complete Correspondence*, Volume 1, C-145x, 16 December 1941, p 294. There are several versions of Churchill's four-part grand strategy overview but this is the one shared with Roosevelt. **48** 'American and British Strategy', Annex 1 to 'Washington War Conference (Military Subjects)', 20 January 1942, CAB 99/17/3. **49** 'Washington War Conference', 2nd Meeting, 23 December 1941, CAB 99/17/3. **50** Approved report by United States–British Joint Planning Committee, 'Assistance to China', WW 10, 10 January 1942, CAB 99/17/3; records of Combined Chiefs of Staff meetings, beginning 24 December 1941, CAB 99/17/2. **51** Meeting of United States and British Chiefs of Staff, 12 January 1942, CAB 99/17/2; COS (42) 55, 26 January 1942, 'Tank Allocation', CAB 80/33; DO (42) 5th Meeting, 30 January 1942, Item 1, CAB 69/4/1; Beaumont, *Comrades in Arms*, pp 91–3. For Marshall's intelligence, Kahn, *Western Allies and Soviet Potential*, p 141. **52** 'Washington War Conference', 9th Meeting, 12 January 1942, CAB 99/17/3; Leighton and Coakley, *Global Logistics and Strategy*, p 556. **53** Leighton and Coakley, *Global Logistics and Strategy*, pp 102–7. **54** 'Washington War Conference', 2nd Meeting, opening remarks. **55** Leighton and Coakley, *Global Logistics and Strategy*, pp 114–15; USSR Embassy memorandum, 25 November 1941, PSF, Russia, FDR papers. **56** Quoted in Reynolds and Pechnatov, *Kremlin Letters*, Chapter 3. For Stuart M3 deliveries, Steven Zaloga, *Soviet Lend-Lease Tanks of World War II* (Osprey Publishing, 2017), 'Initial US Tank Deliveries: M3 Light Tank'. **57** Alexander Hill, *The Great Patriotic War of the Soviet Union, 1941–45: A Documentary Reader* (London: Routledge, 2009), Chapter 8, quoting Document 118, 9 January 1942, from G N Sevost'ianov, *Sovetsko-amerikanskie ot-nosheniia. 1939–1945*, 2004, p 192; 'Post Protocol Supplies to Russia' Annex II, CAB 66/24/8. For M3 tank deliveries with PQ 15, Zaloga, *Soviet Lend-Lease Tanks of World War II*, 'Initial US Tank Deliveries'. **58** Quoted in Reynolds and Pechnatov, *Kremlin Letters*, Chapters 3 and 11. **59** Sebag Montefiore, *Stalin: The Court of the Red Tsar*, footnote, p 398. **60** Leighton and Coakley, *Global Logistics and Strategy*, pp 552–3. **61** Henry Morgenthau, Presidential Diaries, Volume 5, Part 1, entry for 11 March 1942, FDR Library. Also, Beaumont, *Comrades in Arms*, p 105. **62** Ibid. Handwritten note from Roosevelt, dated 11 March, following the diary entry. **63** Henry Morgenthau Diaries, Volume 507, 11–14 March 1942, Part 1, entry for 11 March, FDR Library. **64** Beaumont, *Comrades in Arms*, p 105; Leighton and Coakley, *Global Logistics and Strategy*, p 556. For intelligence reaching Roosevelt at this time, Kahn, *Western Allies and Soviet Potential*, pp 143–6. **65** For tonnage and proportion of weapons delivered, Hill, *Great Patriotic War: A Documentary Reader*, Table 8.5. **66** Leo Mckinstry, *Hurricane: Victor of the Battle of Britain* (London: John Murray, 2010), Chapter 9. **67** Rear Admiral Miles 30 Mission report, 31 December 1942, paragraphs 38–44, ADM 223/252; Kotelnikov, *Lend-Lease and Soviet Aviation*, pp 90, 102 and 166. **68** Ibid, pp 103–5. Hill, 'British Lend-Lease Aid and the Soviet War Effort', p 806. For the report to Churchill, Gilbert, *Finest Hour*, p 1208. **69** Figures calculated from:

'Post Protocol Supplies to Russia', Annex II, CAB 66/24/8; Alexander Hill and David Stahel, 'British "Lend-Lease" Aid to the USSR and the Battle of Moscow in the Light of Soviet and German Sources', *Journal of Slavic Military Studies*, 34:4, 2021, p 553; and Alexander Hill, 'The Allocation of "Lend-Lease" Aid to the Soviet Union arriving with Convoy PQ 12, March 1942 – A State Defence Committee Decree', *Journal of Slavic Military Studies*, 19:4, 2006, p 732. 70 Colonel General G F Krivosheev, *Soviet Casualties and Combat Losses in the Twentieth Century* (London: Greenhill Books, 1997), Table IV, p 254. 71 Ellis, *World War II Data Book*, Table 93, p 278. 72 Hill, '*Great Patriotic War*', '*Documentary Reader*', Chapter 8, quoting Document 119, 'Order of the Commander of the VVS of the Leningrad Front to Air Forces, 8 December 1941'. Also, E R Hooton, *War over the Steppes: The Air Campaigns on the Eastern Front 1941–45* (Oxford: Osprey Publishing, 2016), pp 78–9 and 156–7. 73 Stahel, *The Battle for Moscow*, p 177. 74 Overy, *The Bombing War*, Chapter 4. 75 For above three paragraphs: Hill and Stahel, 'British "Lend-Lease" Aid to the USSR', pp 552–4; Hill, 'British Lend-Lease Aid and the Soviet War Effort', p 793; Dmitry Degtev and Dmitry Zubov, *Air Battle for Moscow 1941–1942* (Barnsley: Air World, 2021), Chapters 6 and 8; and Kotelnikov, *Lend-Lease and Soviet Aviation*, pp 106–9. For PVO support for the Moscow counter-offensive, John Erickson, *The Road to Stalingrad* (London: Panther Books edition, 1985), p 375. For claims in the last two sentences, Braithwaite, *Moscow 1941*, Chapter 10. 76 Hill, 'British Lend-Lease Aid and the Soviet War Effort', pp 795–6; Degtev and Zubov, *Air Battle for Moscow*, Chapter 8; Kotelnikov, *Lend-Lease and Soviet Aviation*, p 109. For Stalin's interest, Braithwaite, *Moscow 1941*, Chapter 8. For Soviet fighter troubles, Hooton, *War over the Steppes*, pp 22–3 and 168–9. For composition of the PVO on 1 May, Stanislas Gribanov, 'The role of US Lend-Lease aircraft in Russia in World War II', *Journal of Slavic Military Studies*, 11:1, 1998, p 100. 77 Kotelnikov, *Lend-Lease and Soviet Aviation*, pp 106–12 and 168–9; Hill, 'British Lend-Lease Aid and the Soviet War Effort', pp 792–5. 78 Degtev and Zubov, *Air Battle for Moscow*, Chapter 6–8; Hill and Stahel, 'British "Lend-Lease" aid to the USSR and the Battle of Moscow', pp 554–5. 79 Ismay to Prime Minister, 5 December 1941, FO 954/24B/528. 80 'Post Protocol Supplies to Russia', Annex II, CAB 66/24/8; ASE (42) 166, 1 August 1942, 'Supplies to Russia from USA', CAB 92/4; Hill, 'British Lend-Lease Aid and the Soviet War Effort'. For delivery numbers in 1942 and 1943, Zaloga, *Soviet Lend-Lease Tanks of World War II*, Final Assessment, 'Lend-Lease Tank and AFV Deliveries to the Soviet Union 1941–45'. 81 Krivosheev, *Soviet Casualties and Combat Losses*, Table III, p 252. 82 Hill, 'British Lend-Lease Aid and the Soviet War Effort', pp 788–90; Hill, *Great Patriotic War: A Documentary Reader*, Chapter 4. 83 Alexander Hill, 'British Lend-Lease Tanks and the Battle of Moscow, November–December, 1941 – Revisited', *The Journal of Slavic Military Studies*, 22:4, 2009, pp 575 and 580–1; Mawdsley, *Thunder in the East*, p 110; Erickson, *Road to Stalingrad*, pp 376–7; Zaloga, *Soviet Lend-Lease Tanks of World War II*, 'Initial British Shipments'. 84 Hill, 'British Lend-Lease Tanks and the Battle of Moscow', pp 581–7; Walter S Dunn, *Hitler's Nemesis: The Red Army 1930–1945* (Westport, CT, USA: Praeger, 1994), pp 158–61; Bruce Oliver Newsome, *Valentine Infantry Tank 1938 – 45* (Oxford: Osprey Books, 2016), pp 18–20; Mark Healy, *Zitadelle: The German Offensive against the Kursk Salient 4–17 July 1943* (Stroud: History Press, 2008), Chapter 18; and Dunn, *Soviet Economy and the Red Army*, pp 72–3. For T-34 quality control, Zaloga, *Soviet Lend-Lease Tanks of World War II*, pp 31–2. For Valentine preference, Beaumont, *Comrades in Arms*, pp 152–3, although Newsome claims the Matilda II was rated higher. For cross-country comparison with T-34, McMeekin, *Stalin's War*, Chapter 24, quoting 'secret' test report from 14th Soviet Tank Division to Stavka, 17 September 1942. 85 Hill, 'British Lend-Lease Tanks and the Battle of Moscow', pp 581–7. For Gorkiy visit, 30 Mission report of 31 May 1942 forwarded by General Ismay to the Prime Minister, CAB 120/680. 86 Glantz and House, *When Titans Clashed*, Chapter 6 and Tables F and G; Stalin and Zhukov quoted by Mawdsley, *Thunder in the East*, p 113. Last sentence, Erickson, *Road to Stalingrad*, p 377. 87 Hill and Stahel, 'British "Lend-Lease" Aid to the USSR', pp 543–4; Halder diaries, Volume VII, entry for 4 December. 88 O'Brien, *How the War was Won*, Chapter I; 'Comparison of Aluminium Alloys from Aircraft of Four Nations involved in the WWII Conflict using Multiscale Analyses and Archival Study' (MDPA: November 2019); Daniel

Petch, 'The Role of Scrap Aluminium in the United Kingdom's War Effort, 1940–1945' (Dissertation submitted for the degree of Batchelor of Arts, University of Hull). **89** Boris Sokolov, 'The role of Lend-Lease in Soviet military efforts, 1941–45', *Journal of Slavic Military Studies*, 7:3, 1994, pp 574–5; Kotelnikov, *Lend-Lease and Soviet Aviation*, p 498; CIA Report released 1999, 'Aluminium Production, Raw Materials and Trade, USSR, 1956', Section II, production estimates 1937–1960, CIA Digital Library. This put 1941 production at 35,000 tons. For Maisky's assessment in August 1942, Beaumont, *Comrades in Arms*, p 122. **90** O'Brien, *How the War was Won*, Chapter 1 for the quality differential between Soviet and Japanese aircraft. Also, Hooton, *War over the Steppes*, pp 168–9. **91** Mark Harrison, 'The Soviet Defence Industry Complex in World War II', in *World War II and the Transformation of Business Systems*, pp 237–62, edited by Jun Sakudo and Takao Shiba (Tokyo: University of Tokyo Press, 1994) Table 3, p 22. **92** Kahn, *Western Allies and Soviet Potential*, pp 159–60. **93** The most definitive figures are given in the exchange between Mavrogordato (Ministry of Aircraft Production), 6 October 1942, and the Allied Supplies Executive, reply of 7 October, CAB 111/431. See also WP (42) 199, 12 May 1942, 'Supplies of Aluminium to Russia', paragraph 1, CAB 66/24/29, stating the entire 18,000 tons pledged under the protocol 'has now been shipped'. This is confirmed in WP (42) 417, 17 September 1942, 'Report on Fulfilment of the Moscow Protocol, October 1941–June 1942, Part II, Section D, paragraph 43, p 11, CAB 66/28/47. **94** ASE (42) 166, 1 August 1942, 'Supplies to Russia from USA', and ASE (42) 206, 15 December, 'Supplies to Russia from USA', both CAB 92/4, and October 1942 correspondence between MAP and ASE, CAB 111/431. **95** Soviet Supply Protocols, Second Protocol, pp 23, 33, 37 and 47, Department of State, Wartime International Agreements, Publication 2759. **96** WP (42) 602, 23 December 1942, 'Supplies to Russia during January–March 1943', attached report by the Allied Supplies Executive, p 4, paragraph 14, CAB 66/32/32. **97** Production figures here from Ellis, *World War II Data Book*, Tables 87 and 92. **98** Ibid; Donaldson to Foreign Secretary, 16 December 1942, 'Aluminium for Russia', FO 954/3A/237; Eden to Maisky, 24 December 1942, FO 954/3A/247. **99** For example: Sokolov, 'Role of Lend-Lease', p 575; O'Brien, *How the War was Won*, Chapter 1; Nikolai Ryzhkov and Georgiy Kumanev, 'Food and other strategic deliveries to the Soviet Union under the Lend-Lease Act, 1941–1945', p 116. **100** 'Status of the Soviet Aid Program' 30 September 1943, 31 May 1944 and 30 June 1944, PSF, Boxes 15, 16 and 17, FDR Papers. Kotelnikov, *Lend-Lease and Soviet Aviation*, p 498, quotes a figure of 99,000 tons shipped by the United States by the end of the war which is far too low though it seems reasonably consistent with Mark Harrison, 'The Soviet Economy and Relations with the United States and Britain, 1941–1945', University of Warwick, 1993, Table 3, p 40. His figures suggest deliveries of about 12,000 tons in 1942, 24,000 tons in 1943, 41,000 tons in 1944, and 30,000 tons in 1945, again too low. For the American rolling mill, 'Status of the Soviet Aid Program', 30 June 1943, 'Progress of Industrial Projects for the USSR', PSF, Box 15, July 1943, FDR Papers. **101** ASE (43) 26, 1 April 1943, 'Supplies to Russia from USA', CAB 92/6; 'Status of the Soviet Aid Program', 30 June 1943 and 31 May 1944, PSF, Box 15 July 1943 and Box 16 July 1944, FDR Papers. **102** H G W Davie, 'Managing Shortfall: The Role of Centre Bases of the NKO in overcoming supply constraints in the Red Army, 1941–1945', *Journal of Slavic Military Studies*, 37:1, 2024, pp 57–8. **103** A N Balysh, 'Development of Explosives Production in the USSR in the 1930s and delivery under Lend-Lease in the Great Patriotic War', *RUDN University Bulletin*, Russian History, No 4, 2012, pp 9–11; Davie, 'Managing Shortfall', pp 57–60. **104** For American deliveries, Status of the Soviet Aid Program, 31 July 1942, PSF, Box 13, FDR papers. For British, 'Report on Fulfilment of the Moscow Protocol, October 1941–June 1942', p 19, CAB 66/28/47. **105** Status of the Soviet Aid Program, 30 June 1943, PSF Box 15, FDR papers. **106** Balysh, 'Development of Explosives Production in the USSR', p 13. **107** Erickson, *Road to Stalingrad*, p 737, gives 615 aircraft supporting Army Group Centre at the beginning of December. However, it is doubtful more than half these were normally available for operations. This compares with a strength of 1387 supporting Typhoon at the beginning of October, quoted by Williamson Murray, *Luftwaffe*, p 86. **108** 'Mr Eden's Visit to Moscow', 5 January 1942, FO 954/25A/3. **109** Boyd, *Royal Navy in Eastern Waters*, pp 170–3.

**Chapter 5: German Countermeasures**
1 Boog *et al*, *Germany and the Second World War*, Volume VI, pp 443–4. 2 NSOD, Volume 28, December 1941, 25 December, III.2, pp 251–2. 3 Mann thesis, pp 103–7. 4 COS (41) 42nd Meeting (O), 4 December 1941, 'Operation Anklet', CAB 79/55. 5 Mann thesis, pp 107–13. 6 Ibid, pp 113–16. 7 Ibid, p 120; Tony Insall, *Secret Alliances: Special Operations and Intelligence in Norway 1940–1945* (London: Biteback Publishing, 2019), pp 154–6. 8 Pound minute to Prime Minister, 9 January 1942, ADM 205/13. 9 Hugh Sebag-Montefiore, *Enigma: The Battle for the Code* (London: Phoenix, 2001), pp 219–28. 10 NSOD, Volume 28, 19 December, item III.2, pp 194–5, 26 December, III.2, p 263, 27 December, III.2, pp 272–3, and 28 December, III.2, pp 280–1. 11 Ibid, 28 December 1941, item V.2, pp 282–3. 12 Admiral Karl Dönitz, *Memoirs: Ten Years and Twenty Days* (Frontline Books edition, 2012), Chapter 10. 13 Showell, *Fuehrer Conferences*, 'Report of the C-in-C Navy to the Fuehrer in the evening of December 29, 1941, at Wolfsschanze', paragraph 1. 14 Ibid, paragraph 4. 15 'Mr Eden's Visit to Moscow', 5 January 1942, p 3 and record of 18 December meeting, FO 954/25A/3. 16 Mann thesis, p 140. 17 NSOD, Volume 28, 30 December 1941, III.2, p 300; Volume 29, January 1942, 2 January, III.2, p 11, 3 January, III.2, p 21, and 6 January, III.2, p 46. 18 For this paragraph also Mann thesis, pp 141–2. 19 The Channel transfer had at least six different codewords through January and early February. At this point it was designated 'Mandarine' or sometimes 'Torero'. 20 NSOD, Volume 29, 8 January, Special Items, II, pp 65–7; John Deane Potter, *Fiasco: The Breakout of the German Battleships* (London: Pan Books edition, 1974), pp 15–19. 21 NSOD, Volume 30, 4 February, Special Items, I, pp 33–4. 22 Showell, *Fuehrer Conferences*, Memorandum of 12 January 1942, pp 256–9; Potter, *Fiasco*, pp 21–5. 23 Showell, *Fuehrer Conferences*, Conference on 22 January, pp 259–60; NSOD, Volume 29, 22 January, Special Items, pp 207–8, 23 January, Special Items, p 217, and 24 January, 'Conference on the Situation with the Chief, Naval Staff', p 228. 24 Ciliax quoted by Potter, *Fiasco*, p 57. 25 'Vice Admiral Otto Ciliax', NID LC 57, 14 February 1942, ADM 223/835; Potter, *Fiasco*, p 15. 26 A good modern account of Cerberus is that by Milan Vego, 'Redeployment of the German Brest Group through the English Channel, 11–13 February 1942 (Operation Cerberus)', *US Naval War College Review*, 74:3, Summer 2021, Article 7. Potter's account in *Fiasco* is much older but still has valuable detail drawing on contemporary witnesses. For the intelligence aspects, Boyd, *British Naval Intelligence*, pp 425–6. 27 NSOD, Volume 30, 20 February, III.1, 'Operation Sportpalast', pp 210–13. 28 NSOD, Volume 29, 2 January, III.2, p 12, 6 January, III.2, p 47, 14 January, III.2, pp 126–7, 16 January, III.1, p 145, and 26 January, III.2, pp 251–2. 29 Showell, *Fuehrer Conferences*, Meeting on 11 July 1940, pp 113–14 and conference on 14 May 1942, p 280; Claasen, *Hitler's Northern War*, pp 142–3; NSOD, Volume 33, 12 May, Conference on the Situation with the Chief Naval Staff, IVe, p 152. 30 'Submarine Shelters', NID LC 2, 15 June 1942, ADM 223/835. 31 Boog *et al*, *Germany and the Second World War*, Volume VI, p 444; Boyd, *British Naval Intelligence*, pp 426, 495 and 500; OIC/NI 104, 'Operation Sportpalast', 25 February 1942, ADM 223/93; Hezlet, *British and Allied Submarine Operations in World War II*, Volume 1, Chapter XIII. 32 NSOD, Volume 29, 16 January, Special Items, p 143. 33 NSOD, Volume 29, 14 January, III.2, pp 126–7, 16 January, Special Item, p 143, 19 January, III.2, p 178, 26 January, III.2, p 251. 34 NSOD, Volume 30, 23 February, III.2, p 245, and 24 February, III.2, p 257. 35 NSOD, Volume 31, 21 March, III.2, p 211, 25 March, III.2, p 249, and 26 March, III.2, p 261. 36 Showell, *Fuehrer Conferences*, Report to the Fuehrer 13 November 1941, p 242, and p 274; NSOD, Volume 30, 26 February, 'Conference on the Situation with the Chief, Naval Staff, pp 274–5; and Volume 31, 27 March, V., 'Fuel Oil Situation', p 269; Cajus Bekker, *Hitler's Naval War* (London: Macdonald and Jane's, 1974), p 265. 37 ZIP/ZG/133, 11 January 1942, 'Fuel Restrictions in the German Navy', ADM 223/3. 38 Blair, *Hunters*, Appendix 5, pp 733–4. For estimated percentage of the front-line force, NSOD, Volume 30, 10 February 1942, V.2, p 105. 39 NSOD, Volume 29, 24 January, 'Conference on the Situation with the Chief, Naval Staff', p 228, and 25 January, V.2, p 243. 40 Blair, *Hunters*, pp 639–40; Bob Carruthers, *The U-boat War in the Atlantic*, Admiralty History by Günther Hessler, Volume 2 (Barnsley, Pen & Sword, 2013), Chapter 4,

January to July 1942. 41 Blair, *Hunters*, pp 638–9; www.uboat.net. 42 DOR Memorandum 158, 'Aircraft Attacks on Shipping on Russian Convoy Routes', February 1954, p 15, ADM 219/518; *Rise and Fall of the German Air Force*, p 113; Claasen, *Hitler's Northern War*, pp 193–4 and 201. 43 Claasen, *Hitler's Northern War*, p 194; NSOD, Volume 29, 24 January, 'Conference on the Situation with the Chief, Naval Staff', pp 229–30. 44 Showell, *Fuehrer Conferences*, Conference on 22 January, p 260. 45 *Rise and Fall of the German Air Force*, pp 108–10 and 112–13. 46 Michael Salewski, *Die Deutsche Seekriegsleitung 1935–1945* (Munich: Bernard & Graefe, 1971–78), Volume 2 1942–1945 (1975), pp 24–7. 47 NSOD, Volume 30, 11 February, III.2, p 113, 24 February, III.1, pp 255–6, and Volume 31, 2 March, III.2, pp 12–13, 6 March, 'Conference on the Situation with the Chief, Naval Staff, pp 52–3 and III.2, p 56, 7 March, III.1, p 64; Llewellyn-Jones, *Royal Navy and the Arctic Convoys*, pp 10 and 11. 48 A Hill, 'The Allocation of Allied "Lend-Lease" Aid to the Soviet Union arriving with Convoy PQ 12, March 1942 – A State Defense Committee Decree', *Journal of Slavic Military Studies*: 19:4, 2006, pp 732–7. 49 Note for First Sea Lord, 23 February 1942, ADM 205/19. For Ciliax's assessment, Salewski, *Die Deutsche Seekriegsleitung*, Volume 2, p 28. 50 For aircraft and U-boats, OIC/SI 112, 7 March 1942, and OIC/SI 114, 9 March, both ADM 223/93. Also, ZIP/ZG/144, 5 March 1942, 'German Preparations for Activity against the Northern Convoy Routes (U-boats and Focke Wulf Aircraft)', ADM 223/3. For agent coverage, Insall, *Secret Alliances*, Chapter 6. 51 OIC/SI 110, 3 March 1942, 'German Intentions in Norway', ADM 223/93; Director of Plans draft for VCNS, 17 February 1942, ADM 205/19. 52 Llewellyn-Jones, *Royal Navy and the Arctic Convoys*, pp 6–7; Colpoys, pp 123–4, HW 8/47. 53 'Battleship *Tirpitz* War Diary 1–15 March 1942', 6 March, p 7, www.kbismarck.com. 54 Ibid, pp 8–15; Hinsley, *British Intelligence in the Second World War*, Volume 2, pp 206–9. 55 Tovey's report to the Admiralty on operations in support of PQ 12, 13 March 1942, paragraphs 8–11, ADM 199/347. 56 Llewellyn-Jones, *Royal Navy and the Arctic Convoys*, pp 15–16 and Plans 2 and 3; Hinsley, *British Intelligence in the Second World War*, Volume 2, pp 206–9; *Tirpitz* War Diary, pp 21–2. 57 *Tirpitz* War Diary, pp 18–25. 58 Colpoys, pp 127–8, HW 8/47; Hinsley, *British Intelligence in the Second World War*, Volume 2, pp 209–10. 59 NRS, Volume 165, 'The Fleet Air Arm in the Second World War, Volume II, 1942–1943, edited by Ben Jones (London: Routledge, 2018), Item 29a, 'Report from Commanding Officer, HMS *Victorious*, to Commander-in-Chief Home Fleet, Air Attack on *Tirpitz*: 9 March 1942', 15 March 1942, pp 72–5; Hobbs, *Fleet Air Arm and War in Europe*, Chapter 6; *Tirpitz* War Diary, 9 March 1942, pp 27–9; Llewellyn-Jones, *Royal Navy and the Arctic Convoys*, pp 17–18. 60 NRS Volume 165, Item 15, Prime Minister to First Sea Lord, 13 March, and Item 16, Pound's reply, 15 March. 61 NRS Volume 165, Item 29a and Item 29, Tovey letter to the Admiralty, 11 April 1942, pp 71–2; Hobbs, *Fleet Air Arm and War in Europe*, Chapter 6; *Tirpitz* War Diary, p 28. 62 Boyd, *British Naval Intelligence*, p 499. 63 NSOD, Volume 31, 12 March, Special Items – Survey of the Situation in Norway by the Naval Staff, pp 116–17, and Group North report, pp 119–21; Salewski, *Die Deutsche Seekriegsleitung*, Volume 2, p 28. 64 Showell, *Fuehrer Conferences*, Conference on 12 March, pp 265–7; Salewski, *Die Deutsche Seekriegsleitung*, Volume 2, p 29. 65 Boog et al, *Germany and the Second World War*, pp 449–50; Salewski, *Die Deutsche Seekriegsleitung*, Volume 2, p 31; NSOD, Volume 31, 14 March, Special Items, pp 143–4 and III.2, p 146; Claasen, *Hitler's Northern War*, p 200. 66 Boog et al, *Germany and the Second World War*, Volume VI, pp 896–900; Ziemke, *German Northern Theater of Operations*, p 237; Glantz and House, *When Titans Clashed*, Chapter 8; General Reinhard Gehlen, Memoirs, *The Service (Der Dienst)*, English translation, Internet Archive, pp 52–4. 67 Report on Russian War Potential, probably early 1944, ADM 223/51. 68 OIC/SI 170, 26 April 1942, 'Appreciation of Present GAF Dispositions in Norway and Finland', ADM 223/93; Boog et al, *Germany and the Second World War*, Volume IV, pp 968–9, and Volume VI, p 450; Claasen, *Hitler's Northern War*, pp 200–1. For 5th Air Fleet percentage of GAF strength, 'Luftwaffe Strength and Serviceability Tables 1938–1945', Air Historical Branch. 69 Claasen, *Hitler's Northern War*, pp 200–1. 70 Ibid, p 200. 71 Ibid, pp 198 and 201–2. 72 NSOD, Volume 33, 12 May, Conference on the Situation with the Chief Naval Staff, IVg, p 152; Showell, *Fuehrer Conferences*, Conference 14 May 1942, p 280. 73 COS

(42) 92nd Meeting, 23 March, Item 10, COS (42) 99th Meeting, 30 March, Item 11 and JP (42) 330, 27 March, 'Spitzbergen and Bear Island', all CAB 79/13.

Chapter 6: The Beginning of German Combined Arms Attacks
1 OIC/SI 116, 12 March 1942, and OIC/SI 129, 21 March, ADM 223/93. 2 Llewellyn-Jones, *Royal Navy and the Arctic Convoys*, pp 23–7. 3 Hinsley, *British Intelligence in the Second World War*, Volume 2, pp 210–11. 4 NSOD, Volume 31, 25 March, III.2, p 249, 26 March, III.2, p 260, and 27 March, III.2, p 273. 5 Llewellyn-Jones, *Royal Navy and the Arctic Convoys*, pp 26–33; Howse, *Radar at Sea*, pp 139–41. 6 Llewellyn-Jones, *Royal Navy and the Arctic Convoys*, pp 31–2; Blair, *The Hunters*, p 549; www.uboat.net. 7 ZIP/ZG/153, 5 April 1942, 'German Effort against North Russian Convoy Routes', ADM 223/3. 8 Llewellyn-Jones, *Royal Navy and the Arctic Convoys*, pp 32–4; NSOD, Volume 31, 30 March, III.2, pp 303–4; Howse, *Radar at Sea*, pp 140–1. 9 Llewellyn-Jones, *Royal Navy and the Arctic Convoys*, p 34. 10 COS (42) 102nd Meeting, 1 April 1942, Item 3, 106th Meeting, 4 April, Item 1, and 114th Meeting, 10 April, Item 1, all CAB 79/20. Mason Macfarlane's comments were made to the captain of the cruiser *Kenya*, Captain Michael Denny, and forwarded by Tovey to the Admiralty on 9 April, ADM 199/72. 11 Cadogan Diaries, entry for 9 April. 12 For more background and references, Boyd, *Royal Navy in Eastern Waters*, pp 268–70. Pound's opening argument, including 'If we lose the war at sea …', is attached to DO (42) 23, 6 March 1942, 'Air Requirements for the Successful Prosecution of the War at Sea', CAB 69/4/3. 13 DO (42) 37, 8 April 1942, 'Supplies to Russia', Memorandum by First Sea Lord, CAB 69/4/4; WM (42) 47th Conclusions, 13 April, Item 2, CAB 65/26/8. 14 Kahn, *Western Allies and Soviet Potential*, pp 143–8; Hinsley, *British Intelligence in the Second World War*, Volume 2, pp 90–5. 15 Kimball, *Churchill & Roosevelt: The Complete Correspondence*, Volume 1, C-62, 1 April, p 438. 16 COS (42) 78th Meeting, 10 March 1942, Item 6, and attached JP (42) 243, 7 March, 'Offensive Operations'; COS (42) 91st Meeting, 21 March, Item 7, and attached JP (42) 298, 19 March, 'Operation Sledgehammer – Aide Memoire and Directive'; COS (42) 98th Meeting, 28 March, Item 11; all in CAB 79/19. For detailed discussion by the chiefs of staff: COS 9th Meeting (O), CAB 79/56/9; COS (42) 12th Meeting (O), CAB 79/56/12; and COS (42) 15th Meeting (O), CAB 79/56/15. For JIC: JIC (42) 75 (Final), 14 March 1942, 'Enemy Intentions', CAB 79/19. 17 COS (42) 77(O), 27 March 1942, and COS (42) 92 (O), 7 April, both titled 'Operation Sledgehammer', both CAB 80/62; COS (42) 15th Meeting (O), 28 March 1942, and COS (42) 21st Meeting, 8 April, both CAB 79/56. 18 Figures extrapolated from Williamson Murray, *Luftwaffe, Strategy for Defeat*, Table XXVIII, p 117, and Table XXIX, p 140. 19 Key records covering Marshall's April 1942 visit: COS (42) 23rd Meeting (O), 9 April, COS (42) 24th Meeting, 10 April, and COS (42) 25 the Meeting, 14 April, all CAB 79/56. Also: COS (42) 97 (O), 13 April, 'Comments on General Marshall's Memorandum', CAB 80/62, and Defence Committee DO (42) 10th Meeting, 14 April, CAB 69/4/1. For the Pacific theatre risks to Bolero: Marshall's Memorandum for the President, The 'Pacific Theatre' versus Bolero, 6 May 1942, PSF, FDR Papers; and Leighton and Coakley, *Global Logistics and Strategy*, p 383. 20 Ismay, *Memoirs*, pp 249–50. 21 COS (42) 97 (O), 13 April 1942, 'Comments on General Marshall's Memorandum'; CAB 80/62; COS (42) 103 (O), 18 April, 'Operations on the Continent', CAB 80/62; WM (42) 54th Conclusions, 29 April, 'Future Operations', CAB 65/30/7; COS (42), 46th Meeting (O), 27 May 1942, Minutes of Staff Conference, CAB 79/56/46; COS (42), 48th Meeting (O), 1 June, Item 1, 'Operation Sledgehammer', CAB 79/56/48; WM (42) 73rd Conclusions, 8 June, Item 1, 'Continental Operations', CAB 65/30/20. Also, Leighton and Coakley, *Global Logistics and Strategy*, pp 384–5. 22 The best account of the Marshall visit, addressing the motives of the two sides and the resulting misunderstandings and tensions is: Andrew Roberts, *Masters and Commanders: The Military Geniuses who led the West to Victory in WWII* (London: Penguin Books, 2009), Chapter 6. For Roosevelt's comments to Litvinov, Reynolds and Petchnatov, *Kremlin Letters*, Chapter 3. 23 NSOD, Volume 32, 6 April, V.2, p 56, 9 April, III.2, p 83, 11 April, III.2, p 107, and 13 April, III.2, p 127; Llewellyn-Jones, *Royal Navy and the Arctic Convoys*, pp 34–5; Blair, *Hunters*, pp 549–50. For cargo lost in *Empire Howard*: Note of conversations

with ACNS (Home) and First Sea Lord, 8 May 1942, FO 954/3A/56. **24** WP (42) 178, 26 April 1942, 'Post-Protocol Supplies to Russia', Annex III, 'Supplies to Russia', 17 April, p 12, CAB 66/24/8. **25** Quoted by James Levy, 'The Needs of Political Policy versus the Reality of Military Operations: Royal Navy Opposition to the Arctic Convoys, 1942', *Journal of Strategic Studies*, 26:1, 2003, pp 36–52, pp 43–4. **26** Showell, *Fuehrer Conferences*, Conference 13 April 1942, p 273. **27** Reynolds and Pechnatov, *Kremlin Letters*, Chapters 3 and 4. **28** Kimball, *Churchill & Roosevelt: The Complete Correspondence*, Volume 1, R-140/1, 24 April, p 471, C-79/1, 26 April, p 472, R-141, 26 April, p 473, and C-80, 28 April, p 474. For Admiralty willingness to trial thirty-five ships, 'Supplies to Russia – Convoy Arrangements', note for Foreign Secretary on President Roosevelt's telegram 141 of 27th April, ADM 205/13. Also, Leighton and Coakley, *Global Logistics and Strategy*, pp 557–8. **29** Reynolds and Pechnatov, *Kremlin Letters*, Chapter 4; Roberts, *Masters and Commanders*, pp 175–7. **30** Kimball, *Churchill & Roosevelt: The Complete Correspondence*, Volume 1, R-145, 2 May 1942, p 483. **31** Llewellyn-Jones, *Royal Navy and the Arctic Convoys*, pp 35–6, and 43. For details of *Ulster Queen*, Lenton, pp 85–6. **32** Hezlet, *British and Allied Submarine Operations in World War II, Volume 1*, Chapter XIII. **33** Kimball, *Churchill & Roosevelt: The Complete Correspondence*, Volume 1, C-44, 14 March 1942, R-119 and R-120, 16 March, and C-48, 17 March, R-123, 18 March, pp 404–8, 416, 419. **34** Vice Admiral Robert Ghormley to Pound, 14 February 1942, and draft replies from Director of Plans, ADM 205/19. **35** Llewellyn-Jones, *Royal Navy and the Arctic Convoys*, pp 43–5. For lost cargo: Note of conversations with ACNS (Home) and First Sea Lord, 8 May 1942, FO 954/3A/56. **36** Ibid, pp 36–8; NSOD, Volume 32, 30 April, VII, pp 314–15; Bekker, *Hitler's Naval War*, pp 266–8. **37** Llewellyn-Jones, *Royal Navy and the Arctic Convoys*, pp 39–45; NSOD, Volume 33, 1 May, III.3, pp 9–10, 2 May, III.3, pp 20–1, 3 May, III.4, pp 31–4, and 4 May, III.3, pp 47–8; Bekker, *Hitler's Naval War*, pp 268–72. **38** Blair, *Hunters*, Plate 11, p 425; Llewellyn-Jones, *Royal Navy and the Mediterranean Convoys*, Appendices M and N. **39** WP (42) 178, 26 April 1942, 'Post Protocol Supplies to Russia', CAB 66/24/8, and DO (42) 13th Meeting, 29 April, Item 2, 'Post Protocol Supplies to Russia', CAB 69/4/2. **40** Note of conversations with ACNS (Home) and First Sea Lord, 8 May 1942, FO 954/3A/56. **41** NID SI/933, 17 May, ADM 223/322; Llewellyn-Jones, *Royal Navy and the Arctic Convoys*, pp 45–6. **42** Ibid. **43** Stephen Roskill, *Churchill and the Admirals* (London: William Collins, 1977), pp 129–31 and 141–3; Martin Stephen, *The Fighting Admirals*, pp 102–12. **44** Ryan thesis, pp 93 and 141–2. **45** Churchill to Stalin, 9 May 1942, Stalin reply to Churchill of 12 May, and Stalin to Roosevelt of 15 May, Reynolds and Pechnatov, *Kremlin Letters*, Chapter 4. **46** Golovko, *With the Red Fleet*, pp 94–5. **47** Rohwer, *Allied Submarine Attacks of World War Two*, pp 16–26. **48** Figures drawn from: Llewellyn-Jones, *Royal Navy and the Arctic Convoys*, Appendix E; Blair, *Hunters*, Appendix 5; Clay Blair, *Hitler's U-boat War, The Hunted* (London: Weidenfeld and Nicolson, 1999), Appendix 6; and www.uboat.net. **49** Golovko, *With the Red Fleet*, p 95; Llewellyn-Jones, *Royal Navy and the Arctic Convoys*, pp 39 and 43. For Miles' comments, Ryan thesis, p 97. **50** Bradley Smith, *Sharing Secrets with Stalin*, p 99. **51** Ibid; Folly, 'From Sevastopol to Sukhumi', pp 878–9. **52** Bradley Smith, *Sharing Secrets with Stalin*, pp 99–100. **53** COS (42) 151st Meeting, 15 May 1942, and 152nd Meeting, 16 May, both CAB 79/21; Pound letter to Secretary, Chiefs of Staff Committee, 15 May 1942, CAB 121/461. **54** COS (42) 162 (O), 4 June 1942, 'Operation Jackpot', Memorandum by First Sea Lord, CAB 80/63, and COS (42) 170th Meeting, 5 June, Item 8, CAB 79/21. **55** Macfarlane comments to captain of cruiser *Kenya*, Captain Michael Denny, forwarded by Tovey to the Admiralty on 9 April – see ADM 199/77. **56** Pound to King, 18 May 1942, and King response, 21 May, ADM 205/19. **57** WM (42) 64th Conclusions, Minute 2, Confidential Annex, 18 May 1942, CAB 65/30/12; COS (42), 153rd Meeting, 18 May, CAB 79/21. **58** Exchange quoted in Reynolds and Pechnatov, *Kremlin Letters*, Chapter 4. **59** NSOD, Volume 33, 3 May, Special Item II, pp 27–8, 10 May, III.2 and III.3, pp 126–7; 12 May, Conference on the Situation with Chief Naval Staff I, pp 149–50, and 18 May, Conference on the Situation with the Chief Naval Staff, I, p 227. For Reinicke comments, Bekker, *Hitler's Naval War*, pp 273–4. **60** NSOD, Volume 33, 5 May, III.3, pp 62–3. **61** Dönitz, *Memoirs*, Chapter 12. **62** Figures from Llewellyn-Jones,

*Royal Navy and the Arctic Convoys*, Appendix A, and Blair, *Hunters*, Plate 12, p 695, and Appendix 5, p 753. **63** Boog et al, *Germany and the Second World War*, Volume VI, p 451. **64** Hinsley, British Intelligence in the Second World War, Volume 2, pp 212–13. **65** Llewellyn-Jones, *Royal Navy and the Arctic Convoys*, pp 47–8; 'Convoys to North Russia, 1942', Supplement to the London Gazette, 17 October 1950, p 5143; Woodman, *Arctic Convoys*, Chapter 10; Hezlet, *British and Allied Submarine Operations in World War II, Volume 1*, Chapter XIII; Lenton, *British and Empire Warships*, pp 85–6. **66** Kenyon, *Arctic Convoys*, pp 48 and 133; Woodman, *Arctic Convoys*, Chapter 10; Boyd, *British Naval Intelligence*, pp 449 and 498. **67** Llewellyn-Jones, *Royal Navy and the Arctic Convoys*, pp 50–1. **68** NID SI/905, 4 May 1942, ADM 223/322; NSOD, Volume 33, 4 May, II.1, pp 44–5, 9 May, III.3, pp 116–17, 13 May, iii.3, pp 172–3, 18 May, III.3, pp 232–3, and 25 May, III.2 and III.3, pp 310–11. **69** Llewellyn-Jones, *Royal Navy and the Arctic Convoys*, pp 27–9; OIC/SI 236, 15 June 1942, 'GAF Operations against Convoy PQ 16', ADM 223/94. NSOD, Volume 33, 25 May, III.3, pp 310–11, 26 May, III.3, p 321, and 27 May, III.2 and III.3, pp 331–3; 'German Air Attacks on PQ Convoys', entry for 29 May, Translation VII/60, Air Historical Branch; Boog et al, *Germany and the Second World War*, Volume VI, p 451. For breakdown of PQ 16 cargo lost, Roberts, *Masters and Commanders*, p 178. **70** Llewellyn-Jones, *Royal Navy and the Arctic Convoys*, p 51. **71** NSOD, Volume 33, 27 May, III.3, pp 332–3, and 28 May, III.3, p 344; 'German Air Attacks on PQ Convoys', entries for 25–29 May, Translation VII/60, Air Historical Branch. **72** NSOD, Volume 33, 26 May, V.2, p 323, and 27 May, III.2 and III.3, pp 331–3. **73** Ibid, 29 May, Special Items, pp 351–2, and 30 May, III.2, p 366. **74** Bekker, *Hitler's Naval War*, i, pp 272–3. **75** Mann thesis, pp 217–20: COS (42) 67th Meeting, 28 February, Item 11, CAB 79/18; C R Price Note to Stanley, 28 February, CAB 121/105; EPS (42) 49 (M), 15 February, 'Operation Hardboiled', and 'Operation "Hardboiled", Draft Administrative Appreciation', WO 106/1987. **76** Mann thesis, pp 217–20; Michael Howard, *British Intelligence in the Second World War*, Volume 5 (London: HMSO, 1990), pp 23–4 and Appendix 1. For the Double-Cross System, the 'W Board' to which it reported, the beginning of strategic deception, and Abwehr monitoring by GC&CS, Howard, Chapter 1, and Hinsley, *British Intelligence in the Second World War*, Volume IV, Chapters 6 and 7. **77** JP (42) 619, 18 June 1942, 'Strategic Deception – Machinery', paragraph 8, CAB 121/105. **78** For this Finnish source in Stockholm, Bekker, *Hitler's Naval War*, pp 259–60, and Howard, *British Intelligence in the Second World War*, Volume 5, pp 23–4. **79** Salewski, *Die Deutsche Seekriegsleitung*, Volume 2, p 30. **80** Blair, *Hunters*, pp 552–3. **81** *Arctic* interrogation reports, 19 April 1942, 'Plan Spider' notes, 21 and 22 April, and Commander-in-Chief Home Fleet to Admiral Commanding Iceland, 'Ruse de Guerre', 25 April, all KV2/1147. **82** MI5 B1A note 'Plan Tarantula', 29 May 1942, KV2/1137. **83** 'German Air Attacks on PQ Convoys', entries for 25–30 May; Llewellyn-Jones, *Royal Navy and the Arctic Convoys*, p 52. **84** Llewellyn-Jones, *Royal Navy and the Arctic Convoys*, pp 51–2. **85** NSOD, Volume 33, 29 May, Special Items, pp 351–2, and V.2, p 357. **86** Ibid, 4 March, III.2, pp 36–7. **87** Ibid, 27–28 April, Conference on the Situation with Chief Naval Staff, pp 272–4 and 284–5. **88** Ibid, 22 May, II, Operations in the Arctic Ocean, pp 270–1; Boog et al, *Germany and the Second World War*, Volume VI, pp 452–3, referencing German naval records. **89** Boog et al, *Germany and the Second World War*, Volume VI, p 949; Mawdsley, *Thunder in the East*, pp 138–9. **90** Forczyk, *Tank Warfare on the Eastern Front 1941-1942*, Chapter 3, Armoured Operations in 1942, 'Decision at Kharkov, 12–28 May'; Zaloga, *Soviet Lend-Lease Tanks of World War II*, 'The M3 Medium Tank'. **91** Forczyk, *Tank Warfare on the Eastern Front 1941-1942*, Chapter 3, 'Clearing up Loose Ends, 2 June–4 July', and 'Case Blau: Hoth's Advance to Voronezh, 28 June–15 July'.

### Chapter 7: Convoy PQ 17: The Germans Seek Decisive Victory
**1** Reynolds and Pechnatov, *Kremlin Letters*, Chapter 4; Dilks, Cadogan Diaries, entries 20 to 26 May, pp 453–5; Maisky Diaries, Gorodetsky commentary for May/June 1942. **2** Kahn, *Western Allies and Soviet Potential*, pp 191 and 195. **3** Reynolds and Pechnatov, *Kremlin Letters*, Chapter 4. **4** Quoted by Kahn, *Western Allies and Soviet Potential*, p 195. **5** Leighton

and Coakley, *Global Logistics and Strategy*, p 562. **6** Ibid, pp 562– 3. **7** Hubert Van Tuyll, *Feeding the Bear: American Aid to the Soviet Union, 1941–1945* (Connecticut, USA: Greenwood Press, 1989), p 32. **8** Reynolds and Pechnatov, *Kremlin Letters*, Chapter 4. **9** Ismay to Prime Minister, 10 June 1942, Aide Memoire, CAB 121/459, and COS (42) 51st Meeting (O), 8 June, Item 7, CAB 79/56. **10** Williamson Murray, *Strategy for Defeat*, Table XXV, p 114. **11** Mark Harrison, 'Economic Warfare and the Battlefield on the Eastern Front, 1941–45', draft chapter for a Festschrift in honour of Hein Klemann (Economics Department, University of Warwick, 2024), p 4. For the anti-air/anti-tank statistic, Andrew Corbett, 'The British Government, the Public, and Nuclear Deterrence', unpublished doctoral thesis, King's College, London, 2017, p 40, quoting T D Biddle, *Rhetoric and Reality in Air Warfare: The Evolution of British and American Ideas about Strategic Bombing 1914–1945* (Princeton University Press, 2002). **12** Forczyk, *Tank Warfare on the Eastern Front 1941-1942*, Chapter 3, 'Deep Battle, 16–30 December'. **13** Kotelnikov, *Lend-Lease and Soviet Aviation*, pp 109 and 112; Joel Hayward, *Stopped at Stalingrad: The Luftwaffe and Hitler's Defeat in the East 1942–1943* (University of Kansas Press, 1998), p 146; Hooton, *War over the Steppes*, pp 122–3; Overy, *The Bombing War*, Chapter 4. **14** Figures in this paragraph extrapolated from WP (42) 417, 17 September 1942, 'Report on Fulfilment of Moscow Protocol October 1941 – June 1942, CAB 66/28/47, Ellis, *World War II Data Book*, Tables 87 and 93; Glantz and House, *When Titans Clashed*, Appendices, Table R; Mark Harrison, 'Soviet Defence Industry Complex', Table 3; Mawdsley, *Thunder in the East*, Table 7.3, p 191; and I C B Dear and M R D Foot, *The Oxford Companion to World War II* (OUP, paperback edition, 2001), USSR, Table 2, p 951. **15** JIC (42) 200, 1 June 1942, 'The Possible Course of the Russian Campaign and its Implications', and Prime Minister minute to Ismay, 7 June, both CAB 120/681. Also CAB 66/25/26. **16** Boog et al, *Germany and the Second World War*, Volume VI, Tables VI.iv.1, p 962, and VI.iv.2, p 965. **17** Brigadier Hollis to Prime Minister, 5 June, CAB 120/681. **18** Kahn, *Western Allies and Soviet Potential*, p 148. **19** Post-war analysis figures from: *The Great Patriotic War: The Anniversary Statistical Handbook* (Federal State Statistical Service, 2020), pp 57 and 59; and Mark Harrison, *Accounting for War*, Table 5.1, p 92, and 'The USSR and Total War: Why didn't the Soviet Economy collapse in 1942?', in *A World at Total War: Global Conflict and the Politics of Total Destruction, 1939–1945*, pp 137–56, edited by Roger Chickering, Stig Forster and Bernd Greiner. For Molotov aircraft figures, Kahn, *Western Allies and Soviet Potential*, p 162. **20** Kimball, *Churchill & Roosevelt: The Complete Correspondence*, Volume 1, C-91, 28 May 1942, p 494. **21** COS (42) 155 (O), 2 June 1942, 'Operation "Jupiter"', Memorandum by the Prime Minister, D 106/2, CAB 80/63. Also Mann thesis, p 163. **22** COS (42) 50th Meeting (O), 5 June 1942, Item 1, 'Operation Jupiter', CAB 79/56; JP (42) 574, 5 June, 'Operation Jupiter', CAB 79/21. **23** JIC (42) 214 (O), 7 June 1942, 'Germany's Next Move in Russia', CAB 79/21; Prime Minister to Ismay for Chiefs of Staff, 15 June, CAB 120/656; Hinsley, *British Intelligence*, Volume 2, p 95. **24** COS (42) 51st Meeting (O), 8 June, Item 6, 'Operation Jupiter', CAB 79/56; JP (42), 583, 7 June, 'Operation Jupiter', CAB 79/21; COS (42) 168 (O), 13 June, 'Operation Jupiter', Memorandum by the Prime Minister, CAB 80/63; Mann thesis, pp 143–55. **25** WM (42) 70th Conclusions, Minute 2, 1 June 1942, CAB 65/26/31. **26** JP (42) 622, 7 May 1942, 'Supplies for Malta', paragraph 3, CAB 79/20. **27** Austin thesis, p 218. **28** For a modern revisionist account of Sirte, O'Hara, *Six Victories*, Chapters 10 and 11. **29** Llewellyn-Jones, *Royal Navy and the Mediterranean Convoys*, pp 55–7, 68–71 and Appendix J. **30** Ibid, pp 58–62. **31** Ibid, pp 62–7. **32** DO (42) 13th Meeting, 29 April 1942, Item 1, CAB 69/4/1. **33** COS (42) 145th Meeting, 9 May 1942, Item 6, and JP (42) 622, 7 May 1942, 'Supplies for Malta', both CAB 79/20. **34** 'Naval Appreciation', Annex 1 to JP (42) 622. **35** Llewellyn-Jones, *Royal Navy and the Mediterranean Convoys*, pp 68–71. **36** Ibid, pp 71–5. **37** Ibid, pp 75–9 and Appendix N. Barnett, *Engage the Enemy More Closely*, pp 509–15, is convincing on Harwood's 'dithering'. Harwood's biographer, Peter Hore, is more sympathetic to his subject in *Henry Harwood: Hero of the River Plate* (Barnsley: Seaforth, 2018), Chapter 14, and offers important qualifications to the Barnett view, especially regarding Vian's attitude. **38** Llewellyn-Jones, *Royal Navy and the Mediterranean Convoys*, p 79, quoting Harwood's report. COS (42) 182nd Meeting, 18 June

1942, Item 1, 184th Meeting, 20 June, Item 3, and 187th Meeting, 23 June, Item 6, all CAB 79/21. Also: COS (42) 54th Meeting (O), 21 June, Item 3, CAB 79/56/54, and 56th Meeting (O), 23 June, CAB 79/56/56. **39** NSOD, Volume 33, 29 May, Special Items 1, 'Command Organisation in the Arctic Ocean', pp 351–2; Milan Vego, 'The Destruction of Convoy PQ 17: 27 June–10 July 1942', *US Naval War College Review*, 69:3, Summer 2016, pp 94–6. **40** NSOD, Volume 34, 1 June, 'Special Items', p 2. **41** David Irving, *The Destruction of Convoy PQ 17* (London: William Kimber, revised 1980 edition), pp 33–4, quoting Schniewind's appreciation entitled *Operative Verwendung der Flottenstreite-krafte im Nordraum*, 30 May 1942, US Naval Archives, File PG/32586 (Film T-41-B). Also, Salewski, *Die Deutsche Seekriegsleitung*, Volume 2, p 43. **42** Salewski, *Die Deutsche Seekriegsleitung*, Volume 2, pp 43–6. **43** NSOD, Volume 34, 1 June, 'Special Items', pp 2–3, 6 June, 'Conference on the Situation with the Chief Naval Staff', 1., Operations in the Arctic Area, p 68, and 7 June, V.2, 'Supplies to Russia via the Northern Route', p 91–2. Comparative British figures on supplies delivered up to PQ 16, from Llewellyn-Jones, *Royal Navy and the Arctic Convoys*, Appendix A, and Ministry of Transport to Historical Section, Admiralty, 6 September 1950, ADM 1/20021. **44** NSOD, Volume 34, 8 June, 'In a very restricted circle', 3, a–f, pp 103–06, 9 June, 'Conference on the Situation with Chief Naval Staff, IV, 'Operation Roesselsprung', pp 119–20, and 10 June, Special Items I, 'Concerning Operation Roesselsprung', p 134. **45** NSOD, Volume 34, 10 June, Special Items I, p 134; Vego, 'The Destruction of Convoy PQ17', pp 94–8. **46** Showell, *Fuehrer Conferences*, 'Report on a Conference between C-in-C Navy and the Fuehrer at the Berghof on the afternoon of 15 June 1942', paragraph 2 and Appendix 'Operation Roesselsprung'; Boog *et al*, *Germany and the Second World War*, Volume VI, p 453. For Raeder's failure to press his case, Salewski, *Die Deutsche Seekriegsleitung*, Volume 2, p 45. **47** OIC/SI 219, 2 June 1942, 'Admiral Raeder and C-in-C Fleet visiting Trondheim', ADM 223/94. For a good diagram of German naval command arrangements at this time – Vego, 'The Destruction of Convoy PQ17', Figure 1, p 95. **48** Hinsley, *British Intelligence*, Volume 2, p 213. **49** David Kahn, *The Codebreakers, The Comprehensive History of Secret Communication from Ancient Times to the Internet* (New York: Scribner, 1997), p 482. **50** Lars Ulfving and Frode Weierud, 'The Geheimschreiber Secret: Arne Beurling and the Success of Swedish Signals Intelligence', originally published as 'Geheimschreiberns hemlighet, Arne Beurling och den Svenska signalspaningens framgangar', in '*I Orkanens Oga, 1941 - Osaker neutralitet*', edited by Bo Hugemark (Stockholm: Probus Forlag, 1992). **51** Henry Denham, *Inside the Nazi Ring: A Naval Attaché in Sweden, 1940–1945* (Sapere Books edition, 2021), Chapter 7; Charles Morgan, NID History, pp 77–9 and 81, ADM 223/464; C G McKay, *From Information to Intrigue: Studies in Secret Service based on the Swedish Experience, 1939–1945* (London: Frank Cass, 1993), p 109. **52** Denham, *Inside the Nazi Ring*, Chapter 7; Morgan, NID History, pp 80–1. **53** NID LC Report no 245, 14 June 1942, ADM 223/835. **54** Vego, 'The Destruction of Convoy PQ 17', pp 110–12. **55** *Aldersdale* and *Gray Ranger* swapped places after the latter was damaged by ice. **56** Llewellyn-Jones, *Royal Navy and the Arctic Convoys*, p 57. Captain Jack Broome, *Convoy is to Scatter: The Story of PQ 17* (London: Futura Publications, 1974), Part 1. **57** Ibid, pp 55; Vego, 'The Destruction of Convoy PQ 17', pp 104–6; Broome, *Convoy is to Scatter*, p 103. **58** Hezlet, *British and Allied Submarine Operations in World War II, Volume 1*, Chapter XIII. **59** Air Historical Branch, The RAF in Maritime War, Volume III, pp 326–7. **60** Roskill, *The War at Sea*, Volume II, Chapter V; Broome, *Convoy is to Scatter*, p 109. **61** Llewellyn-Jones, *Royal Navy and the Arctic Convoys*, p 59, footnote 5. **62** Hinsley, *British Intelligence*, Volume 2, p 214; Salewski, *Die Deutsche Seekriegsleitung*, Volume 2, p 47. **63** Llewellyn-Jones, *Royal Navy and the Arctic Convoys*, pp 54–5; C-in-C Home Fleet despatch, 'Convoys to North Russia, 1942', *London Gazette*, 17 October 1950, pp 5144–5. **64** Tovey letter to Admiralty, 30 June 1948, responding to Admiralty (Nigel J Abercrombie) M/TSD 204/46 of 18 May, ADM 1/20021. **65** For the text of this Admiralty signal, Broome, *Convoy is to Scatter*, pp 110–12. **66** For 1942 'Atlantic Convoy Instructions' used in the Arctic at this time, ADM 239/344 and for later 1944 'Admiralty Convoy Instructions to Escorts', 'North Russia Section', ADM 239/348. Also, Barnett, *Engage the Enemy More Closely*, p 711; for *Scheer* and HX84 and *Hipper* and SLS64, Blair, *Hunters*, pp 207 and 235; for MG1 'dispersal' and Harwood and 'sacrifice', Llewellyn-Jones, *Royal Navy and Mediterranean Convoys*, pp 52 and 75. **67** PQ 17 Cargo Analysis, ADM 237/168. British monthly production figures from Ellis, *World War II Data Book*, Tables 87 and 93, pp 277–8. Canada produced 943 Valentines in 1942, or roughly 79 per month, all of which were exported to Russia, Newsome, *Valentine Infantry Tank*, p 17. **68** Quoted by Irving, *The Destruction of Convoy PQ17* (1980), p 62. A better, if rough, approximation is to take the official declared overall value of Lend-Lease of USD 12.97 billion, assume the share delivered via the Arctic was 22.7 per cent and that PQ 17's percentage share of this by tonnage was 3.53 per cent. This gives USD 104 million. **69** Dear and Foot, *Oxford Companion to World War II*, USSR, Table 2, p 951, sourced from Mark Harrison, *Soviet Planning in Peace and War, 1938–1945*. Glantz and House, *When Titans Clashed*, Appendix R, figures are consistent and include the losses for the first month of Blue. **70** Note to Foreign Secretary, 'Convoys to North Russia', 4 July 1942, FO 954/3A/78, and First Sea Lord to Foreign Secretary, 24 June, FO 954/3A/74. For deliveries on Persian route, Motter, *The Persian Corridor and Aid to Russia*, Tables 1 and 2, pp 481–4. **71** AHB, RAF in Maritime War, Volume III, p 327. **72** For above two paragraphs, Hinsley, *British Intelligence*, Volume 2, pp 214–18 and footnotes pp 216 and 218; Patrick Beesly, 'Convoy PQ 17: A Study of Intelligence and Decision-making', *Intelligence and National Security*, 5:2, 1990, p 295; Denham, *Inside the Nazi Ring*, Chapter 7; Insall, *Secret Alliances*, pp 228–9 and 232–3. For references to an agent at Altafiord, Donald McLachlan, *Room 39: Naval Intelligence in Action 1939–45* (London: Weidenfeld and Nicolson, 1968), pp 40–1, 285 and 288; Irving's original 1968 version of *The Destruction of Convoy PQ 17* refers to an intelligence unit in the Altafiord area at p 115 but this disappears in later versions which include the Ultra dimension. Beesly persists with reference to an agent even in the 2005 version of *Very Special Intelligence*, at p 136, suggesting he was based at Porsa, a village on the north-eastern channel exiting from Altafiord. It is not clear where this reference to Porsa originates. It possibly dates from gossip Beesly picked up directly while serving in NID during the war. The choice of Porsa is odd since an agent there could not have observed 'all comings and goings' of German ships as Beesly claims since they usually took the more navigable channel to the west. Beesly, who had worked in the OIC, was always aware of Ultra and the first edition of *Very Special Intelligence* in 1977 was one of the first wave of books stressing its significance. He had no reason therefore to use the device of an agent to explain intelligence which again makes the Porsa claim odd. Hinsley also refers to an agent near Altafiord 'at the time of PQ 17' based 'between the mouth of the fiord and North Cape' but only able to report 'intermittently'. Volume 2, p 218 footnote. This seems identical to Beesly's Porsa agent. **73** Beesly, 'Convoy PQ17', pp 296–8; Hinsley, *British Intelligence*, Volume 2, Appendix 11; Boyd, *British Naval Intelligence*, pp 395–7, 429–31 and 475–6. **74** For these claims, Kenyon, *Arctic Convoys*, pp 74–6 and 139. German Naval Staff war diaries show that B-Dienst coverage of Arctic convoy movements was limited. **75** Hinsley, *British Intelligence*, Volume 2, Appendix I, Part (i), pp 634–40; Frank Birch, *The Official History of British Sigint 1914–1945*, Volume 1 (Part II) and Volume 2 (Milton Keynes: Military Press, 2007), Diagram No 47, pp 251–3. For B-Dienst decrypts in April/May, NSOD, Volume 34, 26 June, III.2, p 325. **76** NSOD, Volume 34, 16 June, III.3, p 209, 26 June, III.2, p 325, 28 June, III.2, p 345, and 30 June, III.2, p 365. **77** NSOD, Volume 35, 1 July, III.3, pp 6–7, and 2 July, III.2, pp 24–6. **78** ZTPG 59950, Fliegerführer Nord 0636/4, DEFE 3/110/6. **79** ZTPG 59922, Brandenburg (*U-457*) 1457/3 and ZTPG 59951, Fliegerführer Lofoten 2247/3, DEFE 3/110/6. **80** ZTPG 59915, To Eisteufel 2226/3, DEFE 3/110/6. **81** For above two paragraphs, see also NSOD, Volume 35, 3 July, 'In a very restricted circle', pp 36–7, and III.3, pp 41–4. **82** Ibid. **83** Llewellyn-Jones, *Royal Navy and the Arctic Convoys*, pp 56–8. **84** Hinsley, *British Intelligence*, Volume 2, p 215 and Appendix 11. **85** Llewellyn-Jones, *Royal Navy and the Arctic Convoys*, pp 57–8; AT 1708B, 3 July, ADM 237/168. **86** ATs 1659B and 1947B, 3 July, ADM 237/168. **87** Vego, 'The Destruction of Convoy PQ17', p 118. **88** ZTPG 59946, Bohmann (*U-88*) 1607/3, ZTPG 59972, Teichert (*U-456*) 1614/3, ZTPG 59969, Reche (*U-255*) 1737/3 and ZTPG 59944, 2030/3, all DEFE 3/110/6. **89** Beesly, 'Convoy PQ17', p 305; Hinsley, *British Intelligence*, Volume 2, Appendix 11; AT 2222B, 3 July, ADM 237/168. **90** Message to Admiralty of 1642, 3 July, received

2325, and ATs 0238B and 0758B, 4 July, all ADM 237/168. For passing to US Navy office, Map Room Papers 1941–1945, Box 121, MR442 (I) Sec 1, Russian Convoys 1942, FDR Library. Interestingly, this report from Denham is not mentioned by Hinsley. **91** Broome, *Convoy is to Scatter*, pp 146–51. **92** For evidence of this staff meeting and the question to Allen, Irving, *The Destruction of Convoy PQ17* (1980) p 101, based on interviews with participants. Allen's personal naval record is in ADM 196/53/63. **93** Reynolds, *In Command of History*, Chapters 6 and 21. **94** AT 1230B, 4 July, ADM 237/168. **95** Llewellyn-Jones, *Royal Navy and the Arctic Convoys*, p 59; Robin Brodhurst, *Churchill's Anchor: Admiral of the Fleet Sir Dudley Pound* (Barnsley: Leo Cooper), p 243. **96** ZTPG 59941, To Eisteufel 1239/4, ZTPG 59917, Fliegerführer Lofoten 1251/4, ZTPG 59963, Brandenburg (U-457) 1315/4, and ZTPG 59892 Fliegerführer Lofoten 1410/4, all DEFE 3/110/6. **97** ZTPG 59966, Fliegerführer Lofoten 1835/4, DEFE 3/110/6. **98** ZTPG 59910,To Eisteufel, 1020/4, DEFE 3/110/6. **99** NSOD, Volume 25, 4 July, III, Special Item, pp 56–7. **100** Broome, *Convoy is to Scatter*, Signals 34 and 35, pp 156–7; Hinsley, *British Intelligence*, Volume 2, pp 216–17. **101** 'German Air Attacks on PQ Convoys', PQ 17, 4 July entry, Translation VII/60, Air Historical Branch; ZTPG 59986, Fliegerführer Lofoten 1525/4, DEFE 3/110/6. **102** Llewellyn-Jones, *Royal Navy and the Arctic Convoys*, pp 59–60; Claasen, *Hitler's Northern War*, pp 212–13; Broome, *Convoy is to Scatter*, pp 165–6. **103** Ibid, Signal 39 quoted p 164 and p 166. **104** Llewellyn-Jones, *Royal Navy and the Arctic Convoys*, p 60; Broome, *Convoy is to Scatter*, p 167. **105** Broome, Report of Proceedings, *Keppel* letter 6 July, paragraph 48, ADM 205/22A; Broome, *Convoy is to Scatter*, Signals 41–45, pp 168–71, and p 179; Hinsley, *British Intelligence*, Volume 2, 1918 signal, Appendix 11, p 688. For *Pozarica*'s report, Irving, *The Destruction of Convoy PQ17* (1980), p 127.

### Chapter 8: PQ 17: Catastrophe and Aftermath

**1** Hinsley, *British Intelligence*, Volume 2, p 216–17. For more on Hinsley's GC&CS career and achievements, Boyd, *British Naval Intelligence*. **2** Hinsley, *British Intelligence*, Volume 2, footnote p 216. **3** Beesly, *Very Special Intelligence*, p 136, and 'Convoy PQ 17: Intelligence and Decision-making', p 309. The decrypts are in DEFE 3/110/6. The decrypt covering *Tirpitz*'s arrival is ZTPG 59870, 0612/4. **4** Broome, *Convoy is to Scatter*, p 183, quoting Hamilton's report of proceedings. **5** For above two paragraphs, Beesly, 'Convoy PQ 17: Intelligence and Decision-making', pp 310–11. Beesly's primary source here was an account by Denning which Beesly persuaded the latter to write in 1978. Beesly judged it to be authoritative and accurate but noted some caveats. Denning was recalling events that had happened 36 years previously and he was still working on a final draft when he died the following year. A copy of what Beesly judged was a 'penultimate' draft is in Roskill's papers at ROSK 5/72, CCA. This draft formed the basis of Hinsley's account in *British Intelligence*, Volume 2, pp 217–18. For Denning's belief that he had convinced Pound, Irving, *The Destruction of Convoy PQ17* (1968), p 122, based on an interview with Denning in April 1963. However, it is important to note that Irving's account of Pound's discussion with Denning is much less comprehensive and he also gets the timing wrong, stating that it took place at 2030 whereas in reality it was 90 minutes earlier. Donald McLachlan provides a slightly different slant from speaking to Vice Admiral Henry Moore probably in the mid-1960s in *Room 39*, note pp 410–11. He thought Denning was right in so far as Pound had not decided to disperse the convoy when he left his room. But that did not mean he definitely accepted that *Tirpitz* was still in Alta. **6** Boyd, *British Naval Intelligence*, pp 425–6. **7** Irving, *The Destruction of Convoy PQ17* (1968), p 116, and (1980), p 122. These passages drew on an interview with Winn in April 1963. As with the Denning meeting, Irving gets the timing wrong, implying the session with Winn occurred at perhaps 2045 and immediately triggered the order to withdraw the cruisers issued at 2111. **8** Blair, *Hunters*, pp 642–3. **9** Decrypts in DEFE 3/110/6. **10** ZTPG 59910, 1020/4, DEFE 3/110/6. **11** Beesly, 'Convoy PQ 17', p 312, quoting Denning's 1978 account. 2031 decrypt is in DEFE 3/110/6. **12** Beesly, 'Convoy PQ 17', pp 313–14. For Moore's testimony to McLachlan, probably mid-1960s, *Room 39*, Note pp 410–11. For Winn's Ultra signals, Hinsley, *British Intelligence*, Volume 2, Appendix 11, p 688. **13** A later claim by Moore, quoted in a *Daily Mail* article in February 1970 written during the PQ 17 libel trial, that 'we talked for over an hour' at this meeting is not credible. See Woodman, *Arctic Convoys*, Chapter 13. **14** The only account of the staff meeting which draws directly on the testimony of participants is that provided by Irving, *The Destruction of Convoy PQ17* (1968), pp 116–21, and (1980), pp 123–27. Irving interviewed Moore, Brind, Eccles and King who were all at the meeting, as well as Denning and Winn, in March/April 1963. Beesly, 'Convoy PQ 17', p 322, with his firsthand experience of the wartime OIC and Naval Staff, states that Irving's account 'rings true' but adds the caveat that he also knew that some of Irving's claimed sources were unwilling or unable to talk to him. Certainly, in 1963, none would have been willing to refer to Ultra which would have engendered caution and careful selection in what they said. **15** For Churchill's claim regarding the Americans, *Second World War*, Volume IV, pp 235–6. For withdrawal signal, AT 2111B, 4 July, ADM 237/168. **16** Interview for *Daily Mail* February 1970, quoted by Woodman, *Arctic Convoys*, Chapter 13. **17** For the above three paragraphs, Irving, *The Destruction of Convoy PQ17* (1968), pp 116–21, and (1980), pp 123–7. The 2123 and 2136 signals are in ADM 237/168. **18** Beesly, 'Convoy PQ 17', pp 316–17; Hinsley, *British Intelligence*, Volume 2, pp 213 and 219–20. **19** Beesly, 'Convoy PQ 17', p 315. **20** Ibid, pp 316–17, and Hinsley, *British Intelligence*, Volume 2, Appendix 11, p 689. For non-Ultra, 0236B 4 July, ADM 237/168. **21** Broome, *Convoy is to Scatter*, pp 184–5, and Irving (1980), p 94. **22** Broome signal to Hamilton, 0725B 5 July, Signal 61, *Convoy is to Scatter*, p 206. **23** For above three paragraphs, Broome, Report of Proceedings, *Keppel* letter 6 July, paragraphs 49 and 50, ADM 205/22A; Broome, *Convoy is to Scatter*, pp 172–96; Llewellyn-Jones, *Royal Navy and the Arctic Convoys*, pp 62–3. **24** Llewellyn-Jones, *Royal Navy and the Arctic Convoys*, p 63. **25** Broome, *Convoy is to Scatter*, p 200. **26** Ibid, pp 201–3; for *London*, Woodman, *Arctic Convoys*, Chapter 13 and Irving, *The Destruction of Convoy PQ17* (1980), p 139; for O'Brien, Woodman, *Arctic Convoys*, Chapter 13 and proceedings of 1970 PQ 17 libel trial. **27** AT 1222B, 14 July, DOD (H) to C-in-C Home Fleet and others, ADM 237/168. **28** The most comprehensive accounts are by Irving, *The Destruction of Convoy PQ17* (1980), and Woodman, *Arctic Convoys*, Chapter 13. Llewellyn-Jones, *Royal Navy and the Arctic Convoys* has a useful overview in Section 38, pp 66–9, as does Vego, 'The Destruction of Convoy PQ 17', pp 129–31. **29** Signal quoted by Vego, 'The Destruction of Convoy PQ 17', p 124, with sources at note 248; Irving, *The Destruction of Convoy PQ17* (1980), p 139. **30** CS1 1830B 5 July, ADM 237/168. **31** AT 0230B, 1946B and 1947B, all 6 July, ADM 237/168. Relevant Ultra decrypts in DEFE 3/111/1 and 3/111/2. **32** ZTPG 60140, Fliegerführer Lofoten 0214/5, decrypted by Bletchley and passed to OIC 0851, DEFE 3/111/1. **33** For the above three paragraphs, NSOD, Volume 35, 5 July, III.3 and 'Own Situation', 'Operation Rösselsprung', pp 69–74. **34** Ibid. **35** Hinsley, *British Intelligence*, Volume 2, p 221; SBNO North Russia to Admiralty, 1904B 5 July, ADM 237/168. **36** ZTPG 60237, C-in-C Fleet, 1014/5, DEFE 3/111/2. **37** AT to SBNO North Russia and AIG 47, 1625B 5 July, ADM 237/168. **38** *P 54* to Admiralty, 2029B 5 July, ADM 237/168. **39** NSOD, Volume 35, 5 July, pp 72–3. **40** Salewski, *Die Deutsche Seekriegsleitung*, Volume 2, pp 49–52; Keith W Bird, *Erich Raeder: Admiral of the Third Reich* (Oxford: Casemate Publishers, 2018), Chapter 9. **41** Llewellyn-Jones, *Royal Navy and the Arctic Convoys*, p 66; Hinsley, *British Intelligence*, Volume 2, Appendix 11, p 689. Relevant decrypts are in DEFE 3/111/3. **42** Hinsley, *British Intelligence*, Volume 2, p 222; Beesly, 'Convoy PQ 17', pp 317–20. **43** See Brodhurst, *Churchill's Anchor*, especially Chapter 14. For further discussion of Pound's performance as First Sea Lord, Boyd, *Royal Navy in Eastern Waters*, pp 112–13 and references. A medical assessment, Bengt Ljunggren, 'The Sleepy First Sea Lord who was Churchill's Friend', *Surgical Neurology*, 18:5, November 198), is now dated and somewhat compromised by statements on naval operations that are factually inaccurate or reflect partisan judgement. **44** PQ 17 Cargo Analysis, ADM 237/168; WM (42) 96th Conclusions, Item 4, 27 July, CAB 65/31/8. **45** For above two paragraphs, DO (42) 14th Meeting, 10 July, and 15th Meeting, 13 July 1942, CAB 69/4/2; Reynolds and Pechnatov, *Kremlin Letters*, Chapter 4. For Murmansk damage, COS (42) 275th Meeting, 29 September 1942, 'Meeting with Admiral Miles', CAB 121/464. **46** AT 0322B to Miles, 5 July, ADM 237/168; Irving (1980), pp 142–3. **47** Miles 1916C to

Admiralty, 11 July, ADM 237/168. 48 Irving, *The Destruction of Convoy PQ17* (1980), p 257. 49 Maisky diaries, entries for 14 and 15 July 1942. 50 Kimball, *Churchill & Roosevelt: The Complete Correspondence*, Volume 1, C-113, 14 July, p 528, C-115, 14 July, pp 529–32, and R-166, 15 July, p 533. 51 Ibid, C-118, 16 July, p 536, and C-120, 17 July, pp 537–8; Reynolds and Pechnatov, *Kremlin Letters*, Chapter 4. 52 Reynolds and Pechnatov, *Kremlin Letters*, Chapter 4. 53 Donaldson to Foreign Secretary, 4 July, 'Convoys to North Russia', FO 954/3A/78; Leighton and Coakley, *Global Logistics and Strategy*, pp 558–9, including Table 15. 54 WM (42) 73rd Conclusions, 11 June 1942, 'Continental Operations', CAB 65/30/20. 55 Combined Chiefs of Staff, 'Memorandum for Information', 19 June 1942, and 'Offensive Operations in 1942 and 1943, Memorandum', 20 June 1942, both CAB 99/20; Maurice Matloff and Edwin Snell, *US Army in World War II, Strategic Planning for Coalition Warfare 1941–1942* (Washington, USA: US Government Printing Office, 1953), pp 237–9. For alternative British options to Roundup, COS (42) 61st (O) Meeting, 30 June, CAB 79/56/61. 56 Churchill's 20 June note to Roosevelt is in CAB 99/20. For the claim that it altered the war, Roberts, *Masters and Commanders*, p 196. 57 Roberts, *Masters and Commanders*, pp 180–1. 58 CCS 83/1, 24 June 1942, 'Offensive Operations in 1942 and 1943', Note by the Secretaries, CAB 99/20; Roberts, *Masters and Commanders*, pp 197–201. 59 COS (42) 61st (O) Meeting, 30 June, CAB 79/56/61. 60 COS (42) 62nd (O) Meeting, 1 July, CAB 79/56/62, and COS (42) 63rd (O) Meeting, 2 July, CAB 79/56/63. 61 COS (42) 65th Meeting (O), 6 July, CAB 79/56/65. 62 WM (42) 87th Conclusions, 7 July, CAB 65/31/2. 63 Matloff and Snell, *United States Army in World War II, Strategic Planning for Coalition Warfare 1941–1942*, p 268. 64 Kimball, *Churchill & Roosevelt: The Complete Correspondence*, Volume 1, C-107, 8 July, pp 520–1. 65 Roosevelt memorandum to Marshall, King and Hopkins, 15 July 1942, various drafts, Marshall and Hopkins folders, PSF, FDR Library; Matloff and Snell, *United States Army in World War II, Strategic Planning for Coalition Warfare 1941–1942*, pp 273–8. 66 Roberts, *Masters and Commanders*, pp 237–8, 243–3, 247–8, and 251–2. 67 Ibid, p 253. 68 Quoted in Matloff and Snell, *United States Army in World War II, Strategic Planning for Coalition Warfare 1941–1942*, pp 279–80; Also, CCS 32nd Meeting, 24 July 1942, CAB 99/21. 69 JIC (42) 265 (Final), 16 July 1942, copy attached to COS (42) 210th Meeting, 18 July, CAB 79/22. 70 CCS 33rd Meeting, 25 July 1942, with copy of CCS 94 attached, CAB 99/21. For War Cabinet approval, WM (42) 95th Conclusions, Minute 3, CAB 65/31/7. 71 WP (42) 339, 5 August 1942, 'Russian Views about a Second Front', CAB 66/27/19. 72 JIC (42) 298 (O), 2 August 1942, copy attached to COS (42) 226th Meeting, 3 August, CAB 79/22; Hinsley, *British Intelligence*, Volume 2, pp 101–2. For version of JIC (42) 298 sent to Dominion premiers on 6 August, D No 362, CAB 121/464. 73 Hinsley, *British Intelligence*, Volume 2, pp 464–7; JIC (42) 316 (O), 19 August, 'German Strategy this Winter consequent on Operation Torch', CAB 79/57. 74 Kimball, *Churchill & Roosevelt: The Complete Correspondence*, Volume 1, C-124 and R-171, both 29 July, pp 544–6, and C-125A, 31 July, p 551; WP (42) 317, 27 July, 'Supplies to Russia', CAB 66/26/47: WM (42) 96th Conclusions, 27 July, CAB 65/31/8; and A V Alexander letter to Eden, 28 July, FO 954/3A/102. 75 WM (42) 96th Conclusions, Minute 4, 27 July, CAB 65/31/8. 76 Combined Shipping Adjustment Board tel to Washington, 31 July, FO 954/3A/106. 77 WM (42) 107th Conclusions, 7 August, CAB 65/31/12; WP (42) 344, 6 August, 'Convoys to Russia', memorandum by the First Lord, CAB 66/27/24. 78 Forczyk, *Tank Warfare on the Eastern Front 1941-1942*, Chapter 3, 'Von Kleist's Panzers Head for the Oil, 9 July–6 September'. 79 Zaloga, *Soviet Lend-Lease Tanks of World War II*, 'The Tetrarch Light Tank'. 80 Leighton and Coakley, *Global Logistics and Strategy*, pp 564–73; Motter, *The Persian Corridor and Aid to Russia*, Table 1, pp 481–2. 81 Leighton and Coakley, *Global Logistics and Strategy*, pp 574–83; Motter, *The Persian Corridor and Aid to Russia*, Tables 1, 2, 4, 10 and 11, pp 481–98; Hill, *Great Patriotic War*, Chapter 8, Table 8.5; Kimball, *Churchill & Roosevelt: The Complete Correspondence*, Volume 1, R-166, 15 July, p 533 and C-135, 23 August, pp 572–4. 82 Leighton and Coakley, *Global Logistics and Strategy*, pp 564 and 584; Drent, 'The Trans–Pacific Lend-Lease Shuttle to the Russian Far East' pp 45–6 and 48–9. 83 Leighton and Coakley, *Global Logistics and Strategy*, pp 565–6; Motter, *The Persian Corridor and Aid to Russia*, Tables 10 and 11, p 498; Hill, *Read Army and the Second World War*, Table 8.5. **84** Leighton and Coakley, *Global Logistics and Strategy*, p 586. **85** Hamilton's personal report for this period is in ADM 196/92/138. For the suggestion that his career suffered and he never went to sea again, Irving, *The Destruction of Convoy PQ 17* (1980), pp 285–6. **86** Prime Minister to First Lord and First Sea Lord, 15 July 1942, PREM 3/393/14; Churchill, *Second World War*, Volume IV, pp 237–8. **87** Brind to VCNS, 'PQ 17: Withdrawal of the Destroyer Escort', and VCNS to First Sea Lord, both 16 July 1942, ADM 205/14. For Fisher's remarks, 'Private Letter to DNI', NID LC 323, 6 August, ADM 223/835. **88** Hansard, House of Commons Debates, Volume 382, 29 July 1942, column 489; First Lord to Prime Minister, 24 July 1942, and Prime Minister response, 26 July, both PREM 3/393/14. **89** WM (42) 101st Conclusions, Minute 1, Confidential Annex, 'PQ Convoy No 17', 1 August 1942, CAB 65/31/9. **90** WM (42) 103rd Conclusions, Item 5, 4 August, CAB 65/27/19; WP (42) 337, 3 August 1942, 'The Russian Convoy: Proposed Statement in Parliament', PREM 3/393/14. **91** Hansard, House of Commons Debates, Volume 431, Columns 1777–81. **92** Tovey to Noble, 12 July 1942, ADM 237/168. **93** Relevant papers are in ADM 1/20021. **94** Roskill, *War at Sea*, Volume II, Chapter V. **95** Stephen Roskill, *The Navy at War 1939–1945* (London: Collins, 1960), p 207. **96** *Sunday Telegraph*, 11 February 1962. **97** Churchill, *Second World War*, Volume IV, p 238. **98** For a fair assessment of Irving's value and reliability on PQ 17, including Pound's staff meeting, Beesly, 'Convoy PQ 17: Intelligence and Decision-making', pp 321–2. **99** Irving, *The Destruction of Convoy PQ17* (1968), p 136, and (1980), pp 140–1. **100** *Private Eye*, Issue no 214, 27 February 1970. **101** Obituaries, *Guardian* 5 February 2001, and *Telegraph*, 6 February 2001. **102** Broome, Report of Proceedings, *Keppel* letter 8 July, paragraphs 34 and 35, ADM 205/22A. **103** Broome v Cassell & Co and another, All England Law Reports (1971) 2, pp 192–3, British Library. **104** Frances Houghton, 'The Trial of Convoy PQ 17 and the Royal Navy in Post-War British Cultural Memory', *Twentieth Century British History*, 31:2, June 2020, pp 197–219.

**Chapter 9: Recovery: PQ 18 and the Impact of Torch**
**1** C-in-C Home Fleet Despatch, 'Convoys to North Russia, 1942', pp 5147–8. **2** Llewellyn-Jones, *Royal Navy and the Arctic Convoys*, p 72. **3** Stephen, *The Fighting Admirals: British Admirals of the Second World War*, pp 174–9. **4** C-in-C Home Fleet Despatch, 'Convoys to North Russia, 1942', pp 5147–8. **5** These OIC weekly reports are in ADM 223/95. **6** Memorandum HF 01325/5/107, 24 August, ADM 199/758. **7** Ibid; Hinsley, *British Intelligence*, Volume 2, pp 222 and 224; AHB, RAF in Maritime War, Volume III, pp 331–3. For Hampdens, Kotelnikov, *Lend-Lease and Soviet Aviation*, pp 362–7, and for Spitfires, pp 143–5. For intelligence haul from crashed aircraft, NSOD War Diaries, Volume 37, 6 September, III.2, p 68, and 7 September, III.3, p 70. **8** Memorandum HF 01325/5/107, 24 August, ADM 199/758; Peter Smith, *Convoy PQ 18: Arctic Victory* (London: William Kimber, 1975), Appendix Two, pp 221–4. **9** Hinsley, *British Intelligence*, Volume 2, p 224. **10** NSOD, Volume 35, 20 July, 'In a Very Restricted Circle', pp 270–1. **11** NSOD, Volume 36, 2 August, III.2 and V.2, pp 13 and 15, 3 August, III.2, p 24, 4 August, III.2, p 35. **12** Ibid, 6 August, II.2, p 54. **13** Ibid, 6 August, III.2, p 57, V.2, p 58, 8 August, III.2, pp 80–1, 10 August, 'In a Very Restricted Circle' VII, p 101. **14** Ibid, 7 August, III.2, p 70. **15** Llewellyn-Jones, *Royal Navy and the Arctic Convoys*, p 75. **16** NSOD, Volume 36, 14 August, VI.6, p 155, and 16 August, III.3, pp 187–8. **17** Ibid, 2 August, III.2, p 13, and 6 August, II.3, p 54. **18** OIC/SI 317, 23 August, 'Operations off Novaya Zemlya', and OIC/SI 330, 30 August, 'Operations in the Kara Sea', both ADM 223/95; Decrypt 'Zeus' to Admiral Northern Waters, 0339 30 August 1942, DEFE 3/190/6; Hinsley, *British Intelligence*, Volume 2, p 223; Golovko, *With the Red Fleet*, Chapter VIII; William Barr, 'Operation Wunderland: Admiral Scheer in the Kara Sea, August 1942', *Polar Record*, 17:110, May 1975, pp 461–72. **19** NSOD, Volume 37, 1 September, 'Conference on the Situation with the Chief, Naval Staff', I, p 2, and Admiral Arctic Ocean, Wunderland report and recommendations, pp 8–9. **20** Showell, *Fuehrer Conferences*, Conference 26 August 1942, pp 291–2. **21** Ibid, Wunderland report. **22** For the German perspective, NSOD, Volume 35, 20 July, 'In a Very Restricted Circle', pp 270–1; Volume 36, 20 August, 'Mine Operations in the Arctic Region',

p 246. For British SIGINT, Colpoys, Admiralty Use of Special Intelligence in Naval Operations, pp 205–8, ADM 223/88, and Hinsley, *British Intelligence*, Volume 2, pp 223–4. The relevant decrypts are in DEFE 3/189. **23** C-in-C Home Fleet Despatch, 'Convoys to North Russia', p 5147; Colpoys, Admiralty Use of Special Intelligence in Naval Operations, pp 19–20 and 207–08. **24** C-in-C Home Fleet Despatch, 'Convoys to North Russia', p 5147; NSOD, Volume 37, 4 September, III.3, p 49, 6 September, III.3, p 69, 11 September, 'Conference on the Situation with the Chief, Naval Staff', p 127. **25** Compare Pedestal order of battle in Llewellyn-Jones, *Royal Navy and the Mediterranean Convoys*, Appendix K, pp 129–131, and Smith, *PQ 18*, Appendix Two. **26** For good summaries of Pedestal: Llewellyn-Jones, *Royal Navy and the Mediterranean Convoys*, Chapter VII and Plan 14; Greene and Massignani, *Naval War in the Mediterranean*, Chapter 19; and Milan Vego, 'Major Convoy Operation to Malta, 10–15 August 1942, Operation Pedestal', *Naval War College Review*, 63:1, Winter 2010, pp 107–53. **27** For western Mediterranean air strength, *Rise and Fall of the German Air Force*, paragraphs 15–23, pp 134–7; For 4th Air Fleet, Joel Hayward, *Stopped at Stalingrad*, p 195. **28** Greene and Massignani, *Naval War in the Mediterranean*, p 249. **29** Churchill, *Second World War*, Volume IV, *Hinge of Fate*, pp 238–9. **30** First Lord to Prime Minister, 15 July 1942, ADM 205/14. **31** WM (42) 101st Conclusions, 'Operation Pedestal', pp 2–3, CAB 65/31/9. **32** WP (42) 373, 23 August 1942, 'USSR: Prime Minister's Visit to Moscow', Items (a) to (c). **33** Reynolds and Pechnatov, *Kremlin Letters*, Chapter 5; Dilks, Cadogan Diaries, pp 471–2. For a more colourful account of this meeting, Sebag Montefiore, *Stalin: At the Court of the Red Tsar*, Chapter 37. **34** WP (42) 373, Item (c); Reynolds and Pechnatov, *Kremlin Letters*, Chapter 5; for last sentence, Matloff and Snell, *United States Army in World War II, Strategic Planning for Coalition Warfare 1941–1942*, pp 308–09. **35** BAD Washington for First Sea Lord, and Prime Minister from First Sea Lord, both 21 August 1942, First Sea Lord from Prime Minister, 26 August, VCNS to Prime Minister, 6 September, and Notes of Torch Staff Conference, 12 September, all PREM 3/393/5. **36** Note to First Sea Lord shared with Prime Minister, 'PQ 18', PREM 3/393/14. **37** NSOD, Volume 37, 6 September, III.3, p 68, 7 September, III.3, pp 78–9, 8 September, III.3, pp 91–3, 9 September, III.3, p 106. **38** Ibid, 10 September, III.3, p 119; www.uboat.net, *Tigris*, entry for 10 September; Hinsley, *British Intelligence*, Volume 2, p 225. **39** Blair, *The Hunted*, pp 19–22; NSOD War Diaries, Volume 37, 17 September, III.3, pp 199–200, 21 September, III.3, p 249; Hinsley, *British Intelligence*, Volume 2, p 225. **40** NSOD, Volume 37, 12 September, III.3, p 143. **41** Claasen, *Hitler's Northern War*, p 219; Smith, *Convoy PQ 18*, pp 66–8. **42** For above three paragraphs, comments on EV by Director Naval Air Division, 28 October, and Director Gunnery and Anti-Aircraft Warfare, 13 November, ADM 199/758; Llewellyn-Jones, *Royal Navy and the Arctic Convoys*, pp 77–81; Claasen, *Hitler's Northern War*, pp 219–20. For 'hazardous undertaking', *Rise and Fall of the German Air Force*, p 115. For serviceable strike strength on 10 September, DOR Memorandum 158, Section 3 (a), p 16, ADM 219/518. **43** For above two paragraphs, NSOD, 13 September, III.3, pp 152–4. **44** Hinsley, *British Intelligence*, Volume 2, pp 225–6; AHD, RAF in Maritime War, Volume III, pp 334–5. **45** C-in-C Home Fleet report on Operation EV, 8 October, ADM 199/758. **46** Llewellyn-Jones, *Royal Navy and the Arctic Convoys*, pp 81–2; NSOD, 15 September, III.3, p 185, and 18 September, III.3 (a), p 212. **47** Llewellyn-Jones, *Royal Navy and the Arctic Convoys*, pp 82–3; NSOD, 20 September, III.3, pp 238–9, VI.2, p 241; Blair, *The Hunted*, pp 21–2. **48** Comments by Director of Anti-Submarine Warfare, 28 November, ADM 199/758. **49** Llewellyn-Jones, *Royal Navy and the Arctic Convoys*, p 83; Woodman, *Arctic Convoys*, Chapter 15; NSOD, 24 September, III.3, pp 280–1. **50** 'Ships PQ 18', 21 September 1942, PREM 3/393/14. **51** NSOD, 19 September, III.3, pp 224–5, 23 September, III.3 (b), p 271, 24 September, III.3 (b), p 281. **52** SI 1244, 5 October, ADM 223/323. **53** Woodman, *Arctic Convoys*, Chapter 14. **54** Evan Mawdsley, *The War for the Seas: A Maritime History of World War II* (Yale University Press, 2020), Chapter 12; Malcom Murfett, *Naval Warfare 1919–1945* (London: Routledge, paperback 2013), pp 225–6. For a more positive view of PQ 18 and its consequences, Barnett, *Engage the Enemy More Closely*, pp 728–9. **55** WP (42) 525, 13 November 1942, 'Supplies to Russia', paragraph 6. **56** Warship contribution from WP (42) 470, 15 October 1942, 'The Russian Convoys', CAB 66/29/50. This is also a useful source for merchant ship passages and arrivals at Russian ports. Assessing tonnage delivered and its origin is difficult because there is no single definitive source. British, American and Russian records inevitably differ, cover different time periods, and do not always distinguish between initial shipment and delivery or differentiate between the Arctic and other routes. Many military supplies, notably tanks and planes, tended only to be recorded by number and not weight. The most definitive Ministry of Transport estimate for overall supply tonnages delivered each year is their letter to the Admiralty Historical Section of 6 September 1950 in ADM 1/20021 but they concede it is still an estimate. These are the annual figures quoted in Llewellyn-Jones, *Royal Navy and the Arctic Convoys*, Chapter VIII, p 129. WP (42) 178, 26 April 1942, 'Post-Protocol Supplies to Russia', Annex II, paragraph 4, p 11, CAB 66/24/8, is valuable for the first six months of the Protocol period and Donaldson's note to Eden's private secretary, 10 November 1942, FO 954/3A/198 for the remaining period up to the arrival of PQ 18. In September 1943, Molotov told Clark Kerr that Russia had received 764,337 tons of Western aid by the Arctic route in calendar year 1942 – Tel Moscow to FO, 23 September 1943, FO 954/3B/485. That figure looks low but agrees with that quoted in *The Great Patriotic War: The Anniversary Statistical Handbook* (Federal State Statistics Service, 2020), p 195. Motter, *The Persian Corridor and Aid to Russia*, Appendix A, Leighton and Coakley, *Global Logistics and Strategy*, Appendix D, 'Memorandum on Shipments to Russia', 17 November 1942, Russia 1942–43, and 'Statement of Cargo Shipped to USSR as of 30 June 1943', Box 15 Lend-Lease July 1943, both PSF, FDR Papers, are useful collateral on American deliveries. The one million ton estimate for the First Protocol period given in this paragraph averages out all these sources after accounting for deliveries in the last quarter of 1941 (the first quarter of the protocol) and deducting half the deliveries from PQ 18 which fall under the Second Protocol. For weapons shipments on the Arctic route in 1942, Hill, *Great Patriotic War*, Chapter 8, Table 8.5. **57** ASE (43) 6, 16 January 1943, 'Shipments of Tanks and Aircraft to USSR', CAB 92/6. **58** WP (42) 417, 17 September 1942, 'Report on Fulfilment of the Moscow Protocol, October 1941–June 1942', CAB 66/28/47; Hill, *Great Patriotic War*, Chapter 8. **59** For numbers of tanks and aircraft arriving by end June and end October, 'Status of the Soviet Aid Program', as of June 30 and 31 October 1942, both PSF, Box 13, FDR Papers. Also: ASE (42) 166, 1 August, 'Supplies to Russia from USA', and ASE (42) 192, 16 November 'Supplies to Russia from USA', both CAB 92/4. Other useful sources: Leighton and Coakley, *Global Logistics and Strategy*, Table 15, p 559, and Appendix D, p 731; Zaloga, *Soviet Lend-Lease Tanks of World War II*, 'Initial US Tank Deliveries' and 'Final Assessment' with table 'Lend-Lease Tank and AFV Deliveries to the Soviet Union 1941–45'; and Kotelnikov, *Lend-Lease and Soviet Aviation*, p 77. For geographical distribution of weapons shipments, Hill, *Great Patriotic War*, Table 8.5. **60** Mark Harrison, 'The USSR and Total War: Why Didn't the Soviet Economy Collapse in 1942', in *A World at Total War: Global Conflict and the Politics of Destruction, 1939–1945*, pp 137–56, edited by Roger Chickering, Stig Förster, and Bernd Greiner (Cambridge University Press, 2005). For comparative force strengths on 19 November 1942, H G W Davie, 'Patterns of War: A Re-interpretation of the Chronology of the German–Soviet War 1941–1945', *Journal of Slavic Military Studies*, 36:2, 2023, p 160 and Table 3. **61** Ibid. Also: Mark Harrison, 'Economic Warfare and the battlefield on the Eastern Front, 1941–45', pp 6–8 and Table 1; and Chris Bellamy, *Absolute War: Soviet Russia in the Second World War* (London: Pan Books, 2009), Chapter 15. **62** Mikhail Suprun, 'Lend-Lease and the Northern Convoys in the Allied Strategy during the Second World War', *Journal of Slavic Military Studies*, 32:4, 2019, pp 576–7. For Stalin's emphasis on fighters in preference to all other supplies, letter to Churchill of 3 October, quoted by Reynolds and Pechnatov, *Kremlin Letters*, Chapter 5. For Stalin on German aircraft production, Kimball, *Churchill & Roosevelt: The Complete Correspondence*, Volume 1, C-158, 6 October, pp 618–19. **63** Krivosheev, *Soviet Casualties and Combat Losses*, Table III, p 252; Zaloga, *Soviet Lend-Lease Tanks of World War II*, 'Clearing up Loose Ends, 2 June–4 July'; Forczyk, *Tank Warfare on the Eastern Front 1941-1942*, 'Combat in 1942: Operation Blau'; Glantz and House, *When Titans Clashed*, Table R. For Gorkiy, McMeekin, *Stalin's War*, Chapter 24. For German figures in November, Dunn, *Hitler's Nemesis*, p 132. **64** For Soviet air strength and losses, Krivosheev, *Soviet Casualties and Combat Losses,* Table IV, p 254, and Glantz and House, *When Titans Clashed,* Appendix R. For Soviet aircraft production, Mark Harrison, 'Soviet Defence Industry', Table 3, p 22. For Western numbers, 'Fulfilment of First Protocol', Table A, CAB 66/28/47, and Kotelnikov, *Lend-Lease and Soviet Aviation,* pp 77 and 499–500. **65** Dunn, *Hitler's Nemesis,* p 5; McMeekin, *Stalin's War,* Chapter 2; Mikhail Suprun, 'Strength and Weakness of Totalitarianism in Wartime Soviet Union', *Septentrio Conference Series,* 2015 (4), pp 8–12; Kotelnikov, *Lend-Lease and Soviet Aviation,* pp 499–500. **66** Kimball, *Churchill & Roosevelt: The Complete Correspondence,* Volume 1, C-151-4, all 22 September, and Hopkins reply, pp 602–7. **67** Ibid, C-158, 6 October, pp 618–19. **68** Ibid, R-187, 26 September, pp 612–13. **69** Ibid, R-189, 5 October, pp 616–17, and C-159, 7 October, pp 621–2. **70** Ibid, C-148, 14 September, pp 594–5, R-186/2 (not sent), 24 September, pp 607–8, R-189, 5 October, p 616, and R-191, 6 October, p 620. **71** Kimball, *Churchill & Roosevelt: The Complete Correspondence,* Volume 1, C-167, 8 October, pp 628–9. **72** Ibid, R-186/3 not sent, p 610. **73** Ibid, R-193, 8 October, p 630, and 11 October message provided in Reynolds and Pechnatov, *Kremlin Letters,* Chapter 5. **74** Kotelnikov, *Lend-Lease and Soviet Aviation,* pp 145–7. **75** For a detailed list of the 'Independents', William Smith, *Churchill's Arctic Convoys: Strength Triumphs over Adversity* (Barnsley: Pen & Sword, 2022), Appendices, Tables 17 and 18. Also:' Convoys to North Russia, 1942' pp 5150–1; 'The Trickle Movement', George C Dyer, 9 November, and Room 3612, 18 December, Russian Convoys, Map Room papers, FDR Library. Also, Woodman, *Arctic Convoys,* Chapter 16. For intelligence on *Hipper* sortie, DDIC Ultras 1301, 6 November, 1308 and 1312, 7 November, and 1355, 14 November, ADM 223/113. **76** Reynolds and Pechnatov, *Kremlin Letters,* Chapter 5. **77** COS (42) 345 (O), 30 October 1942, 'American–British Strategy Report, CAB 80/65/2. **78** COS (42) 181st (O), 15 November, CAB 79/58/31. **79** DO (42) 17th Meeting, 16 November, CAB 69/4/2. **80** WP (42) 525, 13 November 1942, 'Supplies to Russia'. **81** Kimball, *Churchill & Roosevelt: The Complete Correspondence,* Volume 1, p 622. **82** 'Meeting between First Lord and Mr Maisky', FO 954/3A/190. **83** DDIC AT to C-in-C HF, 2020 14 November, ADM 223/113. **84** Hezlet, *British and Allied Submarine Operations in World War II, Volume 1,* Chapter XVII. **85** Llewellyn-Jones, *Royal Navy and the Arctic Convoys,* pp 86–7. **86** C-in-C Home Fleet Despatch, 'Convoys to North Russia, 1942', p 5151. **87** *Rise and Fall of the German Air Force,* pp 144–9. **88** DDIC ATs 1828, 9 November, and 1557, 11 November, both ADM 223/113. **89** AHB VII/107, Luftwaffe Strength and Serviceability Tables August 1938–April 1945, p 30. **90** Williamson Murray, *Strategy for Defeat,* Tables XXX and XXXI, pp 148–9. **91** Churchill to Roosevelt, 18 November, Map Room, FDR Library. **92** Roosevelt to Churchill, 19 November, and King memorandum to Leahy of previous day, Map Room, FDR Library. **93** Kahn, *Western Allies and Soviet Potential,* Chapter 16. **94** COS (42) 346th Meeting, 15 December 1942, 'Record of a Meeting with Sir Archibald Clark Kerr', CAB 79/87. **95** Danchev and Todman, *Brooke War Diaries,* Entry for 15 December 1942. **96** JIC (42) 462 (Final), 3 December 1942, 'German Strategy in 1943', paragraph 22, CAB 79/24. **97** Boog et al, *Germany and the Second World War,* Volume VIII, pp 53–7. **98** The best account of these peace 'feelers' from the Soviet viewpoint, although dated, is Vojtech Mastny, 'Stalin and the Prospects of a Separate Peace in World War II', *The American Historical Review,* 77:5, December 1972, pp 1365–88. Boog et al, *Germany and the Second World War,* VIII, pp 57–61, is also perceptive. Also: James Reagan Fancher, 'The Arsenal of the Red Warriors: US Perceptions of Stalin's Red Army and the Impact of Lend-Lease Aid on the Eastern Front in the Second World War, unpublished doctoral thesis, University of North Texas, May 2023, pp 234–5 and references; McMeekin, *Stalin's War,* Chapter 25, and Healy, *Zitadelle,* Chapters 4 and 7. **99** First Sea Lord to Prime Minister, 22 November, PREM 3/393. **100** DO (42) 18th Meeting, 23 November 1942, Item 3, CAB 69/4/2. For text of 24 November letter to Stalin, Reynolds and Pechnatov, *Kremlin Letters,* Chapter 6. **101** DO (42) 20th Meeting, 29 December, Item 5, CAB 69/4/2; For 29 December letter to Stalin, Reynolds and Pechnatov, *Kremlin Letters,* Chapter 6. **102** Stephen, *The Fighting Admirals,* pp 175–6. **103** AT to C-in-C HF, Ultra 1304, 20 November, ADM 223/113. **104** Hezlet, *British and Allied Submarine Operations in World War*

*II*, *Volume 1*, Chapter XVII. **105** Hobbs, *Fleet Air Arm and War in Europe*, Chapter 6 and 7. **106** C-in-C HF Despatch, 'Convoys to North Russia, 1942', pp 5151–2; Llewellyn-Jones, *Royal Navy and the Arctic Convoys*, pp 88–90. For Maisky's meeting with the First Lord on 28 October, 'Meeting between First Lord and Mr Maisky', FO 954/3A/190. **107** Dönitz, *Memoirs*, Chapter 18; Blair, *Hunted*, p 123 and footnote; Boog *et al*, *Germany and the Second World War*, Volume VI, p 457. For British figures for 1942 shipping losses in the Arctic, Llewellyn-Jones, *Royal Navy and the Arctic Convoys*, Appendix A. **108** Ultra 1472, 13 December, and DDIC to C-in-C HF, 2140A 19 December, both ADM 223/113. **109** Showell, *Fuehrer Conferences*, Conference of 19 November, p 299. **110** Hinsley, *British Intelligence*, Volume 2, pp 526–8. **111** Denham memoir, Chapter 7; Hinsley, *British Intelligence*, Volume 2, p 526. **112** Llewellyn-Jones, *Royal Navy and the Arctic Convoys*, pp 89–90 and 102.

**Chapter 10: The Battle of the Barents Sea and its Impact**
**1** Boog *et al*, *Germany and the Second World War*, Volume VI, pp 456–7. **2** Ibid; Bird, *Raeder*, Chapter 9; Showell, *Fuehrer Conferences*, Conference of 19 November, pp 298–301. **3** Bekker, *Hitler's Naval War*, pp 282–3. **4** www.navweaps.com. Entry for Battle of the Barents Sea, Merchantmen. **5** Personal record, ADM 196/124/55; Dudley Pope, *73 North: The Battle of the Barents Sea* (London: Alison Press/Martin Secker and Warburg, 1988), pp 82–4. **6** Woodman, *Arctic Convoys*, Chapter 13; Pope, *73 North*, Chapter 22. **7** Llewellyn-Jones, *Royal Navy and the Arctic Convoys*, p 90 and Plan 14. **8** ZTPG 96334, Admiral Northern Waters 1918/27, DEFE 3/215/2. **9** Kenyon, *Arctic Convoys*, p 191. **10** ZTPG 96742 and 96693, Admiral Northern Waters to *U-354* 1054/30 and 1201/30, DEFE 3/215/5 and 3/215/4. **11** ZTPG 96682, Admiral Northern Waters to Admiral Cruisers, 1302/30, DEFE 3/215/4. **12** Bekker, *Hitler's Naval War*, p 280. **13** Bird, *Raeder*, Chapter 9, quoting Salewski, *Die Deutsche Seekriegsleitung*, Volume 2, footnote 79. **14** Boog *et al*, *Germany and the Second World War*, Volume VI, p 464, quoting Krancke's minute of 4/5 January 1943 (footnote 59); Pope, *73 North*, pp 131–5. **15** Boog *et al*, *Germany and the Second World War*, Volume VI, pp 458–60; Pope, *73 North*, pp 139–45; Kenyon, *Arctic Convoys*, p 192. **16** ZTPG 96720, *U-354* to Admiral Northern Waters, 1704/30, DEFE 3/215/5. **17** ZTPG 96704, Admiral Northern Waters, 1900/30, DEFE 3/215/5. **18** ZTPG 96723 and 96730, *U-354* to Admiral Northern Waters, 0250/31 and 0945/31, and ZTPG 96719, Admiral Northern Waters to *U-354*, 2259/30, all in DEFE 3/215/5. **19** Hinsley, *British Intelligence*, Volume 2, p 529. **20** Llewellyn-Jones, *Royal Navy and the Arctic Convoys*, pp 90–1 and Figure 7. **21** Woodman, *Arctic Convoys*, Chapter 17; Michael Pearson, *Red Sky in the Morning: The Battle of the Barents Sea 1942* (Barnsley, Pen & Sword Maritime, 2007), pp 50–1; Pope, *73 North*, pp 127–8. There is some dispute over how far this U-boat contact was judged credible. **22** Pope, *73 North*, pp 87–90. **23** Hezlet, *British and Allied Submarine Operations in World War II*, *Volume 1*, Chapter XVII; Schofield, *Russian Convoys*, p 146. **24** Pearson, *Red Sky in the Morning*, pp 55–6. **25** ZTPG 96701, Admiral Commanding Cruisers, 0928/31, DEFE 3/215/5. **26** Bekker, *Hitler's Naval War*, p 286. **27** For above four paragraphs, Llewellyn-Jones, *Royal Navy and the Arctic Convoys*, pp 93–8; Pearson, *Red Sky in the Morning*, Chapter 5; Pope, *73 North*, Chapters 15–17; Kenyon, *Arctic Convoys*, pp 195–7. **28** ZTPG 96730 and 96732, *U-354* to Admiral Northern Waters, 0945/31 and 1056/31, DEFE 3/215/5. **29** Minute Director of Staff Duties and Training, paragraphs 4–6, 2 April 1943, ADM 199/73. **30** Howse, *Radar at Sea*, pp 158–9. **31** C-in-C Home Fleet Report of Proceedings, paragraph 13, 9 February 1943, ADM 199/73. **32** Lenton, *British and Empire Warships*, table, p 60. **33** For above four paragraphs: Pope, *73 North*, Chapter 18 and Pearson, *Red Sky in the Morning*, Chapter 6. **34** ZTPG 96788, Admiral Commanding Cruisers, 1202/31, DEFE 3/215/5. **35** Boog *et al*, *Germany and the Second World War*, Volume VI, pp 461–2. **36** Ibid. See footnote 58 for the origin of this claim. **37** NSOD, Volume 43, 10 March, Special Item, pp 120–1, drawing on 'Final Report on the Engagement in Northern Waters on 31 December', compiled 23 January for the Fuehrer; Boog *et al*, *Germany and the Second World War*, Volume VI, p 465. **38** Ibid. **39** Ibid. **40** Llewellyn-Jones, *Royal Navy and the Arctic Convoys*, pp 103–4. **41** Bekker in *Hitler's Naval War* provides a copy of this directive, 'Policy Statement issued

after Operation 'Regenbogen' and the Arctic Engagement of 31st December 1942', as Appendix 8. **42** For above two paragraphs, Bird, *Raeder*, Chapter 9, quoting widely from German naval records. **43** Beesly, *Very Special Intelligence*, p 205. **44** NSOD, 10 March, p 121. **45** ZTPG 96691, Admiral Commanding Cruisers, 0844/31, DEFE 3/215/4. **46** Bird, *Raeder*, Chapter 9. **47** ZTPG 96789, Admiral Northern Waters to Admiral Cruisers, 0122/01, DEFE 3/215/5, and ZTPG 96872, 0901/01, DEFE 3/215/6. **48** Pope, *73 North*, pp 267–71 and 273–8; Vice Admiral Eberhard Weichold, *German Surface Ships – Policy and Operations in World War II* (GHS/4, US Naval Archives, c 1955), pp 119–20; NSOD, 10 March, p 121. For Dönitz's view of Kummetz's role with U-boat torpedoes, Dönitz, *Memoirs*, Chapter 7. **49** Boog et al, *Germany and the Second World War*, Volume VI, pp 464–5, quoting Krancke's minute of 4/5 January 1943 (footnote 59); Pope, *73 North*, pp 271–3; Bird, *Raeder*, Chapter 9. **50** Showell, *Fuehrer Conferences*, Conference on 6 January 1943, pp 306–8. **51** Ibid; Boog et al, *Germany and the Second World War*, Volume VI, pp 465–6; Pope, *73 North*, p 293; Bekker, *Hitler's Naval War*, pp 293–4. **52** Peter Padfield, *Dönitz: The Last Fuehrer: Portrait of a Nazi War Leader* (London: Lime Books edition, 2021), end of Chapter 5. For Carls as preferred candidate, Boog et al, *Germany and the Second World War*, Volume VI, p 466. **53** Pope, *73 North*, pp 295–9; Bekker, *Hitler's Naval War*, pp 298–9. **54** Walter S Dunn, *Soviet Economy and the Red Army*, p 80. Also, Boog et al, *Germany and the Second World War*, Volume VIII, pp 28–9 and footnotes, but some figures quoted here seem incorrect. **55** Pope, *73 North*, pp 299–304; Showell, *Fuehrer Conferences*, Conference of 8 February, pp 308–10; Bekker, *Hitler's Naval War*, p 299. For attempted breakouts by *Scharnhorst* and *Prinz Eugen*, Hinsley, *British Intelligence*, Volume 2, pp 531–2; and *The RAF in Maritime War*, Volume IV, pp 338–43. **56** Dönitz, *Memoirs*, Chapter 17. **57** Ibid, Chapter 19:4. **58** G H and R Bennett, *Hitler's Admirals* (Annapolis: Naval Institute Press, 2004), p 143. **59** Showell, Conference of 26 February, pp 311–12; Padfield, *Dönitz*, Chapter 6. For *Scharnhorst* transfer, NSOD, 8 March, III.2, p 97, and 9 March, III.2, p 109; Hinsley, *British Intelligence*, Volume 2, pp 534–5, Weichold, *German Surface Ships*, pp 127–8; and *The RAF in Maritime War*, Volume IV, pp 343–5. For Hessler, Bob Carruthers, *The U-Boat War in the Atlantic*, Volume III, 1944–1945 (Henley in Arden, Warwickshire: Coda Books, 2011), Chapter 7, 336, 'Question of the Big Ships'. **60** Dönitz, *Memoirs*, Chapter 19:3; NSOD, 20 March, 'Conference on the Situation with the Chief, Naval Staff', IV, pp 251–2; Weichold, *German Surface Ships*, p 122; Padfield, *Dönitz*, Chapter 6. **61** Dönitz, *Memoirs*, Chapter 19:4; Weichold, *German Surface Ships*, pp 124–5. **62** NSOD, 10 March, Conference on the Situation, with Chief, Naval Staff, III, p 117. **63** NSOD, 16 March, 'Special Item', II, pp 191–3. **64** NSOD, 19 March, 'Conference on the Situation with the Chief, Naval Staff', IV, p 234, 22 March, IIIf, p 281, 23 March, III.2, p 303, and 24 March, III.2, p 319. **65** NSOD, 24 March, 'Report by Chief, Operations Branch, Operations Division, pp 312–13. **66** Record of CCS 55th Meeting, 14 January 1943, p 4, CAB 99/24/1. **67** Hinsley, *British Intelligence*, Volume 2, pp 529–30; NSOD, 29 March, II (b), p 387. **68** CCS 55th, p 4. **69** Meeting in the First Sea Lord's Room, 'The Situation resulting from the accession of Admiral Donitz to the command of the German Navy', and Director of Plans minute to First Sea Lord, both 5 February, ADM 205/32. **70** JIC (43) 63, 10 March 1943, 'Future Action by the German Surface Fleet', CAB 79/26/10. **71** Denning, 'The Future Use of German Heavy Surface Craft', 22 February 1943, Denning papers, DENN 8/2, NMM; and reply to prime minister's M 141/3, 'Significance of recent German naval changes in high personnel', ADM 205/27. **72** Tooze, *Wages of Destruction*, p 601. **73** Status of Soviet Aid Program, 30 June 1943 and 31 May 1944, PSF, July 1943, Box 15, and July 1944, Box 16, FDR Papers. **74** Roosevelt Memorandum for the Secretary of War, 9 January 1943, CAB 122/935. **75** CCS 162/1, 20 January 1943, 'United States Aid to Russia', CAB 99/24/3. **76** For above two paragraphs, ANFA 2nd Meeting, 18 January, record p 4, 3rd Meeting, 23 January 1943, both CAB 99/24/1, and CCS 170/2, 23 January 1943, CAB 99/24/3. Also: First Sea Lord to Prime Minister, 'Supplies to Russia', undated but probably 14 January, ADM 205/27. **77** WP (42) 602, 23 December 1942, 'Supplies to Russia during January–March 1943', paragraph 3 and Annex, CAB 66/32/32. **78** First Sea Lord to First Lord, 11 January, and First Lord to Prime Minister, 12 January 1943, ADM 205/27. **79** Llewellyn-Jones, *Royal*

*Navy and the Arctic Convoys*, pp 104–5. **80** CCS/160, 18 January 1943, 'Minimum Escort Requirements to maintain the Sea Communications of the United Nations', paragraph 5 and Appendix 4, CAB 99/24/3. **81** Note to First Sea Lord, 10 January 1943, ADM 205/27. **82** Llewellyn-Jones, *Royal Navy and the Arctic Convoys*, pp 106–7. For Reche, Blair, *Hunted*, pp 235–6. **83** Reynolds and Pechnatov, *Kremlin Letters*, Chapter 7. **84** Beaumont, *Comrades in Arms*, pp 133–6; Folly, 'They treat us with scant respect', p 12; DO (43) 1st Meeting, 23 February 1943, Item 4, CAB 69/5/1. **85** WM (43) 35th Conclusions, Item 2, 'Supplies to Russia', CAB 65/33/35; Beaumont, *Comrades in Arms*, pp 134–6; Bradley Smith, *Sharing Secrets*, pp 125–7; Morgan NID History, pp 111–12, ADM 223/464. **86** Memorandum by Secretary of State for Foreign Affairs, 26 February 1943, FO 954/3B/331. **87** For the text of the Soviet memorandum of 10 March, 'Russian Convoys', Map Room, FDR Papers. **88** Beaumont, *Comrades in Arms*, pp 135–6; Ismay to Prime Minister, 6 March 1943, FO 954/3B/347; COS (43) 108 (O), 7 March, 'Operation Grenadine', minute by the Prime Minister, CAB 80/68; Foreign Secretary to Prime Minister, 10 March, FO 954/3B/352. For Slessor, ACAS(P) to Chief of the Air Staff, 7 January 1943, AIR 20/4987. **89** First Sea Lord to Prime Minister, 'Supplies to Russia', circa 14 January, ADM 205/27. **90** Ismay to Prime Minister, 10 March 1943, FO 954/3B/354. **91** Prime Minister to Ismay for chiefs of staff, 13 March, FO 954/3B/356. **92** Hinsley, *British Intelligence*, Volume 2, pp 534–5. **93** 'Copy of minute to the Prime Minister from First Lord of the Admiralty', 16 March 1943, Annex I to DO (43) 3rd Meeting, CAB 69/5/1. **94** DO (43) 3rd Meeting, 16 March 1943, 'Russian Convoys', CAB 69/5/1. **95** WM (43) 42nd Conclusions, 18 March 1943, CAB 65/37/12; COS (43) 47th Meeting (O), 17 March, Item 1, CAB 79/59/47. **96** WM (43) 44th Conclusions, 22 March, CAB 65/37/13; COS (43) 51st (O), 22 March, CAB 79/60/1; Roskill, *War at Sea*, Volume II, Chapter XVI; Llewellyn-Jones, *Royal Navy and the Arctic Convoys*, p 107. **97** Churchill to Eden, 25 March, copy in Churchill correspondence, Map Room, FDR papers. **98** Hinsley, *British Intelligence*, Volume 2, p 535. **99** Churchill to Roosevelt, 18 March, copying Defence Committee papers and Stalin's message of 15 March, Churchill correspondence, Map Room, FDR papers. **100** Roosevelt to Churchill, 20 March, Churchill correspondence, Map Room, FDR papers. **101** Churchill to Eden, 25 March; Cadogan diaries, entry for 23 March; WM (43) 46th Conclusions, Minute 3, 29 March, CAB 65/37/14. **102** Reynolds and Pechnatov, *Kremlin Letters*, Chapter 7; Maisky diaries, entry for 2 April 1943. **103** Donaldson to Cadogan covering 'Draft Minute from the Minister of Production to the Prime Minister', 6 April, FO 954/3B/404. **104** JIC (43) 99, 9 March 1943, 'Effect on German Strategy of the Recent Fighting on the Russian Front', CAB 79/26; Hinsley, *British Intelligence*, Volume 3, Part 1, pp 3–5. **105** Anniversary Statistical Handbook, p 58. **106** Kahn, *Western Allies and Soviet Potential*, Chapter 17, and quoting JIC (43) 102. **107** Ibid; Hinsley, *British Intelligence*, Volume 3, Part 1, pp 3–5. **108** Boog et al, *Germany and the Second World War*, Table I.iii.I, 'German estimate of relative strength on the Eastern Front (status: 1 April 1943), p 66; Healy, *Zitadelle*, Chapters 2, 5, and 18. **109** See earlier reference at page 369 and associated endnote 98. **110** Boog et al, *Germany and the Second World War*, p 57. **111** For general background on Second Protocol deliveries, WP (43) 475, 25 October 1943, 'Report on the Implementation of the Second Soviet Protocol, with comparisons between the Second and Third Protocols', CAB 66/42/25. For detailed delivery records: ASE (43) 6; ASE (43) 26, 'Supplies to Russia from USA', 1 April 1943, and ASE (43) 41, 'Shipments to USSR of Tanks and Aircraft to 30 April 1943', all CAB 92/6. For more specific British cargo background on JW 52 and 53 convoys, WP (42) 602, 23 December 1942, 'Supplies to Russia during January–March 1943', CAB 66/32/32. For details of American cargo, 'Status of the Soviet Aid Program', 31 January, 28 February and 31 March, PSF, Box 14, January–February, March and April, FDR Papers. For American shipments in this period via Iran, Motter, *The Persian Corridor and Aid to Russia*, Tables 1, p 482, 2 p 484, and 11, p 498. For estimate of overall weapon tonnage delivered, Hill, *Great Patriotic War*, Table 8.5. **112** For Persia, Motter, *The Persian Corridor and Aid to Russia*, Table 1, p 482, Table 3, p 486, Table 5, p 490, Table 10, p 498, Appendix A, pp 495–6, and Leighton and Coakley, *Global Logistics and Strategy*, p 589. **113** 'Lend-Lease Impressions: Churchill', 8 May 2013, www.tankarchives.ca. **114** Krivosheev, *Soviet Casualties and Combat Losses*,

Table IV, p 254; Hooton, *War over the Steppes*, pp 168–9 and 240; Hill, *Great Patriotic War*, Table 8.4. **115** These figures derive from Krivosheev, *Soviet Casualties and Combat Losses*, Table 3 p 252, and Zaloga, *Soviet Lend-Lease Tanks of World War II*, 'Final Assessment', table showing Lend-Lease tank deliveries in 1943. The domestic tank production figures are lower than those often quoted because they exclude self-propelled guns which were 4100 in 1943 with a further 300 from the United States. **116** Zaloga, *Soviet Lend-Lease Tanks of World War II*, 'The 1943 Campaign', 'Scorned but Redeemed: The M4', and 'Final Assessment Tables'; Healy, *Zitadelle*, Chapters 5 and 18. For Soviet views on the Sherman, Dunn, *Soviet Economy and Red Army*, p 85.

**Chapter 11: The Destruction of the German Battlefleet**
**1** Stephen, *The Fighting Admirals*, pp 179–83. **2** Roskill, *War at Sea*, Volume III, Part I, Chapter IV; Levy, 'Holding the Line', pp 228–9. **3** Hinsley, *British Intelligence*, Volume 3, Part 1, p 252. For specific coverage of Altafiord, Colpoys, Admiralty Use of Special Intelligence in Naval Operations, Chapter VIII, p 97, HW 8/47. **4** Trident Conference, CCS 83rd Meeting, 13 May 1943, p 6, CAB 99/22/2. **5** C-in-C Home Fleet to First Sea Lord, 30 June 1943, ADM 178/323. **6** COS (T) 16, 14 May 1943, 'The Russian Front', CAB 99/22/5. **7** Trident, First Meeting, 12 May, p 4, CCS 83rd Meeting, 13 May 1943, p 6, and 84th Meeting, 14 May, p 15, all CAB 99/22/2; CCS 88th Meeting, 19 May, pp 46–7, CAB 99/22/3; CCS 234, 'Defeat of the Axis Powers in Europe', 17 May, pp 138–47, CAB 99/22/4. **8** CCS 235, 18 May, 'Defeat of Axis Powers in Europe', CAB 99/22/4. **9** CCS 242/6, 25 May, 'Final Report to the President and Prime Minister', and CCS 242/1, 25 May, 'Implementation of Assumed Basic Undertakings and Specific Operations for the Conduct of the War, 1943–44', Annex 1, p 190, both CAB 99/22/4. **10** Christopher Andrew and Vasili Mitrokhin, *The Mitrokhin Archive: The KGB in Europe and the West* (London: Penguin Books edition, 2000), pp 159 and 166. **11** For above two paragraphs: Boog *et al*, *Germany and the Second World War*, Volume VIII, pp 62–4, 77, 138–42, 145–6, and 1101–3; Healy, *Zitadelle*, Introduction, Chapters 2 and 8, and Conclusion, Costs and Consequences. **12** COS (42) 28 (O), 27 January 1942, CAB 80/61; Prime Minister to Ismay, 25 January 1942, quoted in Churchill, *Second World War*, Volume IV, p 98. **13** DO (42) 7th Meeting, 4 March 1942, Item 4, CAB 69/4/1; The RAF in Maritime War, Volume III, pp 293–5. **14** *Tirpitz*, Volume 1, Section III, paragraph 2, p 6, ADM 234/349; Patrick Bishop, *Target Tirpitz: X-Craft, Agents and Dambusters – The Epic Quest to destroy Hitler's Mightiest Warship* (London, Harper Press, 2012), Chapter 8. **15** For details: Vincent P O'Hara and Enrico Cernuschi, 'Frogmen against a Fleet: The Italian Attack on Alexandria 18/19 December 1941', *US Naval War College Review*, 68:3, Summer 2015). **16** COS (42) 20th Meeting, 19 January 1942, Item 4, CAB 79/17; Boyd, *British Naval Intelligence*, p 441. **17** The British Submersible, Chariots, Underwater Heritage Trust; Keith Hall, *X3 to X54: The History of the British Midget Submarine* (Cheltenham: History Press, 2023), Chapter 2. **18** Ian Herrington, 'The Special Operations Executive in Norway 1940–1945: Policy and Operations in the Strategic and Political Context' (unpublished doctoral thesis, De Montfort University, Leicester, June 2004), pp 206–7; Insall, *Secret Alliances*, pp 308–9. **19** Paul Watkins, *Midget Submarine Commander: The Life of Rear Admiral Godfrey Place VC, CB, CVO, DSC* (Barnsley: Pen & Sword Maritime, 2012), Chapter 5; Hall, *X3 to X54*, Chapters 2 and 3; Lenton, *British and Empire Warships*, pp 236–8. **20** For above two paragraphs, Bishop, *Target Tirpitz*, Chapter 11, Insall, *Secret Alliances*, pp 311–15, and Herrington, 'The Special Operations Executive in Norway 1940–1945', p 207. **21** Hezlet, *British and Allied Submarine Operations in World War II*, *Volume I*, Chapter XXI. **22** For above two paragraphs, Bishop, *Target Tirpitz*, Chapter 13. **23** Ibid; Watkins, *Midget Submarine Commander*, Chapter 5. **24** Hinsley, *British Intelligence*, Volume 3, Part 1, Appendix 13, pp 529–30. **25** Hezlet, *British and Allied Submarine Operations in World War II*, *Volume I*, Chapter XXI; Hinsley, *British Intelligence*, Volume 3, Part 1, pp 258– 9; Bishop, *Target Tirpitz*, Chapter 13; Insall, *Secret Alliances*, p 321; Kotelnikov, *Lend-Lease and Soviet Aviation*, p 144. The above five paragraphs also draw on Admiral Submarines' Despatch on Operation Source published in the *Supplement to The London Gazette*, 10 February 1948, 'The Attack on the *Tirpitz* by

Midget Submarines on 22nd September 1943'. **26** NSOD, Volume 49, September 1943: 3 September, Special Items, pp 34–5; 4 September, Conference on the Situation with the Chief, Naval Staff, II, pp 49–50; 6 September, Special Items, I, pp 77–8; and 8 September, In a highly restricted circle, IIIc, pp 106–7. **27** Bishop, *Target Tirpitz*, Chapter 12. **28** ZTPG/165033, 1417 18 September, DEFE 3/341/01. **29** NSOD, 9 September, III.2, pp 128–9; Bishop, *Target Tirpitz*, Chapter 14; Hezlet, *British and Allied Submarine Operations in World War II, Volume 1*, Chapter XXI. **30** G H & R Bennett, *Hitler's Admirals*, pp 187–8. **31** Hinsley, *British Intelligence*, Volume 3, Part 1, pp 253–5; Colpoys, Admiralty Use of Special Intelligence in Naval Operations, Chapter IX, pp 112–14, ADM 223/88. **32** Hinsley, *British Intelligence*, Volume 3, Part 1, pp 259–60; Hezlet, *British and Allied Submarine Operations in World War II, Volume 1*, Chapter XXI. **33** Hezlet, *British and Allied Submarine Operations in World War II, Volume 1*, Chapter XXI. **34** ZTPG/165545, 1043 20 September, DEFE 3/341/02. **35** NRS Volume 165, Despatch from C-in-C Home Fleet, 25 November 1943, 'Passage of Lutzow from Altenfiord to Baltic, 26–27 September', pp 574–5. **36** ZTPG/166018, 1637 21 September, DEFE 3/342/01. **37** For a first-hand account of this episode, Alastair Mars, *Submarines at War 1939–1945* (London: Corgi Books edition, 1974), pp 197–9. Mars was on duty at Submarine headquarters in Northways and consulted by Barry. Also: Hezlet, *British and Allied Submarine Operations in World War II, Volume 1*, Chapter XXI. The above four paragraphs also draw on Admiral Submarines' Despatch on Operation Source published in the *Supplement to The London Gazette*, 10 February 1948, 'The Attack on the *Tirpitz* by Midget Submarines on 22nd September 1943'. **38** The most authoritative contemporary account is the series of updated despatches by Admiral Submarines, published in *The London Gazette*. In addition to his original despatch of 8 November, there were supplements dated 2 February 1944 and 26 July 1945, the latter incorporating the testimony of those taken prisoner, notably Cameron and Place. There are also excellent accounts in: Bishop, *Target Tirpitz*, Chapter 15; and Watkins, *Midget Submarine Commander*, Chapter 6. **39** NSOD, Volume 49, September 1943, 25 September, Chief, Operations Division, pp 358–60. **40** NSOD, Volume 50, October 1943, 15 October, 'Report by Naval (Ship) Construction Division on the condition of the *Tirpitz*', p 211, and 18 October, 'Operation Paul', pp 248–9. **41** For example: ZTPG 173612 and ZTPG 173637, both 15 October, DEFE 3/349/02. **42** NSOD, Volume 50, 26 October, III.2, pp 372–3. **43** *Tirpitz* Volume 2, Evidence for Detailed Accounts of Damage, pp 13–16, Minutes of DNC Meeting at Bath, 28 February 1944, ADM 234/350; Hinsley, *British Intelligence*, Volume 3, Part 1, pp 261–2 and Appendix 13; Insall, *Secret Alliances*, pp 227, 236, and 321–3; Kenyon, *Arctic Convoys*, p 238. **44** *Tirpitz*, Volume 1, Section 4, paragraph 6, p 12, ADM 234/349. **45** Reynolds and Pechnatov, *Kremlin Letters*, Chapters 8–10. **46** Beaumont, *Comrades in Arms*, pp 152–3, 156–7, and 159–60. **47** Ibid, pp 157–8. **48** Clark Kerr Tel 1005, 23 September, FO 954/3B/485. **49** Krivosheev, *Soviet Casualties and Combat Losses*, pp 132–8 and 262. **50** Beaumont, *Comrades in Arms*, p 166. **51** Prime Minister to Ismay, 25 September, FO 954/3B/486. **52** Minister of Production memorandum 'Delivery of Supplies to Russia', undated but probably c 20 September, AIR 20/4987. **53** COS (43) 584 (O), 26 September, covering 'Admiralty Note on Resumption of Convoys for North Russia', 20 September, AIR 20/4987. **54** VCNS to Prime Minister, 26 September, FO 954/3B/487. **55** DO (43) 9th Meeting, 28 September 1943, Item 1, CAB 69/5/1. **56** Leighton and Coakley, *Global Logistics and Strategy 1943–1945*, pp 676–8; Beaumont, *Comrades in Arms*, pp 166–8. **57** Churchill to Roosevelt, 1 October 1943, FO 954/3B/495. **58** Reynolds and Pechnatov, *Kremlin Letters*, Chapter 10, with text of Churchill's letter of 1 October and Stalin's reply of 13 October. **59** WM (43) 142nd Conclusions, 18 October 1943, CAB 65/40/5. For Clark Kerr on Gusev, Reynolds and Pechnatov, *Kremlin Letters*, Chapter 9. **60** JIC (43) 409 (O), 2 October 1943, 'Situation on the Russian Front', CAB 121/464. **61** For Churchill's meeting with Gusev and Eden's account of the 21 October meeting, Churchill, *Second World War*, Volume V, pp 241–4. For Cadogan, Diary entry of 18 October. Also, Reynolds and Pechnatov, *Kremlin Letters*, Chapter 10. For the Molotov/Eden agreement, Beaumont, *Comrades in Arms*, pp 163–5. For Ismay, Kiszely, *Ismay*, Chapter 8. **62** NSOD, Volume 50, October 1943, 28 October, 'Norway, Enemy Situation', pp 412–13. **63** Hinsley, *British Intelligence*, Volume 3, Part 1, p 262. 64 Hezlet, *British and Allied Submarine Operations in World War II, Volume 1*, Chapter XXI. 65 Edward Young, *One of Our Submarines* (London: Rupert Hart-Davis, 1953), Chapter XII. 66 NSOD, Volume 52, December 1943, 1 December, III.2, p 7. For above two paragraphs, Llewellyn-Jones, *Royal Navy and the Arctic Convoys*, pp 108–9. 67 NSOD, Volume 51, November 1943, 22 November, III, p 340, 23 November, III, p 349, and 24 November, I.A.1, p 353; Hinsley, *British Intelligence*, Volume 3, Part 1, p 263. 68 NSOD, Volume 50, 29 October, IIIa, p 425. 69 NSOD, Volume 51, 20 November, II.1, 'Instructions for Operations', pp 312–13. 70 Bekker, *Hitler's Naval War*, p 343. 71 NSOD, Volume 52, 2 December, VII, 'Report from Operations Branch', pp 15–17. 72 Bekker, *Hitler's Naval War*, pp 342–3. 73 NSOD, Volume 52, 12 December, 'Conference on the Situation', I, p 140. 74 A G F Ditcham, *A Home on the Rolling Main: A Naval Memoir 1940–1946* (Bodmin & Kings Lynn: MPG Books, 2012), p 162; Golovko, *With the Red Fleet*, pp 180–1. 75 Llewellyn-Jones, *Royal Navy and the Arctic Convoys*, p 110. 76 Hinsley, Volume 3, Part 1, p 263. ZTPG 192816, 1946 18 December and for *Scharnhorst* specifically, ZTPG 192806, 1747 18 December, both DEFE 3/368/4. 77 ZTPG 192952, 1426 19 December, DEFE 3/368/4. 78 ZTPG 192814, 1657 18 December, and ZTPG 192864, 2343 18 December, both DEFE 3/368/4. 79 NSOD, Volume 52, 18 December, 'Conference on the Situation', p 204, 18 December, III.2, p 210, 19 December, III.2, p 218, and 20 December, III.2, p 233. 80 NSOD, Volume 52, 22 December, III.2, p 254. 81 C-in-C Home Fleet Despatch, 25 January 1944, ADM 199/1440. 82 Referred to prior to *Scharnhorst* sortie in NSOD, Volume 52, 25 December, p 296, paragraph 4b. For Dönitz's post operation justification, NSOD, Volume 52, 27 September, C-in-C Order to Navy, p 322. For postwar British references, Roskill, *War at Sea*, Volume 3, Part 1, Chapter IV, and Beesly, *Very Special Intelligence*, pp 209–10. 83 Padfield, *Dönitz*, Chapter 6. 84 Dunn, *Soviet Economy and Red Army*, p 80. Dunn quotes an 'actual' figure of 680,000 tons for Arctic deliveries in 1943. It was more like 450,000. 85 NSOD, Volume 52, 24 December, 'Operations against the PQ Convoy', pp 279–80; Bekker, *Hitler's Naval War*, pp 343–5. 86 Showell, *Fuehrer Conferences*, Minutes of Conference on 19 and 20 December, 8 January 1944, p 374. For the evolution of German decisions on employing *Scharnhorst*, see also Roskill, *War at Sea*, Volume III, Part I, Chapter IV. 87 NSOD, Volume 52, 22 December, III.2, pp 254–5. 88 Ibid, 23 December, III.2, pp 264–7. 89 Ibid, 24 December, III.2, pp 278–82. 90 Kenyon, *Arctic Convoys*, p 220 and Bekker, *Hitler's Naval War*, p 345. 91 Hinsley, *British Intelligence*, Volume 3, Part 1, pp 264–5 and Appendix 14; Kenyon, *Arctic Convoys*, pp 219–20. 92 NSOD, Volume 52, 25 December, III.2, pp 293–6. 93 Padfield, *Dönitz*, Chapter 6. 94 Ibid; NSOD, Volume 52, 25 December, III.2, pp 294–5. 95 Padfield, *Dönitz*, Chapter 6; Bekker, *Hitler's Naval War*, pp 349–51. 96 Hinsley, *British Intelligence*, Volume 3, Part 1, pp 265–6, and Appendix 14; Kenyon, *Arctic Convoys*, pp 221–2; Beesly, *Very Special Intelligence*, pp 215–16. 97 Beesly, *Very Special Intelligence*, p 216. 98 Roskill, *War at Sea*, Volume 3, Part 1, Chapter IV; Colpoys, Chapter VIII, HW 8/47; Konstam, *Battle of North Cape*, Day 6. 99 Roskill, *War at Sea*, Volume 3, Part 1, Chapter IV. 100 Konstam, *Battle of North Cape*, Day 7, Forenoon Watch; NSOD, Volume 52, 26 December, III.2, p 309. 101 Bekker, *Hitler's Naval War*, pp 355–8; Hinsley, Volume 3, Part 1, p 267; Kenyon, *Arctic Convoys*, p 223; Schofield, *Russian Convoys*, p 182; Dönitz *Memoirs*, Chapter 19:4; Padfield, Chapter 6; John Winton, *Death of the Scharnhorst* (Ilkley: Sapere Books edition, 2022), Chapter 6; NSOD, Volume 52, 26 December, III.2, p 310. 102 Konstam, *Battle of North Cape*, Day 7, Afternoon Watch; Roskill, *War at Sea*, Volume 3, Part 1, Chapter IV; Llewellyn-Jones, *Royal Navy and the Arctic Convoys*, pp 112–13. 103 NSOD, Volume 52, 27 December, 'Special Item Scharnhorst', pp 318–20, and 28 December, 'Special Items', pp 333–4; Llewellyn-Jones, *Royal Navy and the Arctic Convoys*, p 113. 104 Konstam, *Battle of North Cape*, Day 7, Afternoon Watch; Dönitz, *Memoirs*, Chapter 19:4. 105 Ibid. 106 The two best accounts are those by Konstam, *Battle of North Cape*, Day 7, 'The Dog Watches', and Winton, *Death of the Scharnhorst*, Chapters 8 and 9. 107 The best and first-hand account of the destroyer attack is by Ditcham, *Home on the Rolling Main*, Chapter 11, including charts pp 178–9. 108 The final such attack was that on the Japanese heavy cruiser *Haguro* by the 26th Destroyer Flotilla off Penang, Malaya, on

16 May 1945. **109** Howse, *Radar at Sea*, pp 187–90. For *Duke of York*'s fit, Konstam, *Battle of North Cape*, Day 7, 'The Dog Watches'. **110** NSOD, Volume 52, 27 December, Special Items, 'Operation Scharnhorst', pp 320–1. **111** Quotations by Bekker, *Hitler's Naval War*, p 361. Also, NSOD, 28 December, Special Item, p 333. **112** NSOD, 27 December, p 322. **113** Showell, *Fuehrer Conferences*, 'Minutes of the Visit of the C-in-C Navy at Headquarters, Wolfsschanze, on January 1 to 3, 1944', pp 379–80. **114** NSOD, 27 December, p 321. **115** Padfield, *Dönitz*, Chapter 6, including input from Salewski, *Die Deutsche Seekriegsleitung*, Volume II, p 343; Weichold, *German Surface Ships*, pp 142–3.

## Chapter 12: Last Convoys and the Final Stand of the Kriegsmarine

**1** Stephen Roskill, *Churchill and the Admirals* (Barnsley: Pen & Sword, 1977, pp 236–7. **2** Frozen 1015, 31 December 1943, FO/954/3B/519; Frozen 1138, 6 January, FO 954/3B/532. **3** DO (44) 1st Meeting, 4 January 1944, CAB 69/6/1; Grand 1179, Prime Minister from Deputy, 5 January, FO 954/3B/530; Beaumont, *Comrades in Arms*, p 166. **4** Grand 1373, Prime Minister from Deputy, 15 January, FO 954/3B/533; Prime Minister to Stalin, 18 January, FO 954/3B/534; Stalin to Prime Minister, 20 January, FO 954/3B/535. **5** For a summary of 'snort' development and its introduction, Blair, *Hunted*, pp 313–15. **6** First Lord to Prime Minister, 6 April 1944, ADM 205/35. **7** NSOD, Volume 52, 27 December, Special Items II, p 323; Carruthers/Hessler, *The U-boat War in the Atlantic*, Volume III, Chapter 7, 415: U-boat losses strengthen need for containment, and 416: Anti-invasion planning; Blair, *Hunted*, pp 444 and 513 and Appendix 6, p 786; For July strength, Llewellyn-Jones, *Royal Navy and the Arctic Convoys*, p 171. **8** ZTPG 206042, 1 February 1944, DEFE 3/382; Llewellyn-Jones, *Royal Navy and the Arctic Convoys*, p 115; Blair, *Hunted*, pp 513–14; Uboat.net. **9** Lenton, *British and Empire Warships*, pp 115–16, and 128. **10** NRS Volume 165, Item 227, C-in-C Western Approaches to Admiralty Secretary, 7 November 1943, 'Employment of British and American Escort Carriers in Anti-U-Boat Warfare', pp 564–7, and Item 236, Report 9/44 by Directorate Naval Operational Studies, 12 February 1944, 'Achievements of British and American Escort Carriers in Anti-submarine Operations in 1943', pp 580–5. **11** Viscount Lord Cunningham, *A Sailor's Odyssey* (London: Hutchinson, 1957), p 617. **12** Llewellyn-Jones, *Royal Navy and the Arctic Convoys*, pp 115–16; Blair *Hunted*, pp 514–16; Uboat.net; Weichold, *German Surface Ships*, p 145. **13** Prime Minister to Stalin, 8 February, FO 954/3B/536. **14** Blair, *Hunted*, pp 516–17. **15** C-in-C Home Fleet to Admiralty, 17 April 1944, ADM 199/327. **16** 'Analysis of Operations in Vicinity of Convoys JW 56A, JW 56B, and RA 56, January–February 1944', 15 May 1944, ADM 199/2027. **17** Kenyon, *Arctic Convoys*, pp 248–50. **18** C-in-C Western Approaches W.A.00770/180, 31 May 1944, and Fraser's 912/H.F.01325/180, 9 June, both ADM 199/327. **19** Figures extrapolated from Blair, *Hunted*, pp 513, 518, and Appendices 2 and 6. For this issue, see also Andrew Lambert, 'Seizing the Initiative: The Arctic Convoys, 1944–45', in *Naval Power in the Twentieth Century*, edited by N A M Rodger (Palgrave Macmillan, 1996). **20** Marc Milner, *Battle of the Atlantic* (Stroud: History Press, 2011), Chapter 9. **21** Showell, *Fuehrer Conferences*, Conference 12 and 13 April 1944, p 390. **22** Hinsley, *British Intelligence*, Volume 3, Part 1, pp 272–3. **23** *Tirpitz*, Volume 1, Section III, paragraph 4.1, p 8, ADM 234/349. **24** Boyd, *British Naval Intelligence*, p 528; Hinsley, *British Intelligence*, Volume 3, Part 1, pp 273–4; Insall, *Secret Alliances*, pp 321–6 and Appendix. **25** Hobbs, *Fleet Air Arm and War in Europe*, Chapter 8. **26** Ibid. **27** 'Operation Tungsten', paragraphs 4.3 to 4.5, *Tirpitz*, Volume 1, ADM 234/349; 'Preliminary assessment by DNC of bomb damage', 14 April 1944, *Tirpitz*, Volume 2, pp 40–1, ADM 234/350. **28** NRS Volume 150, The Cunningham Papers, Volume II (Ashgate, 2006), Item 304, Diary entry 12 November 1944, p 244. **29** Showell, *Fuehrer Conferences*, Conference 12 and 13 April, pp 388–9. **30** NID report on 'The Sinking of the *Tirpitz*', 17 August 1945, ADM 223/51. **31** NRS 150, Cunningham Papers, Items 287 and 288, Diary entries, 13 and 14 April, Item 290, Diary entry 17 May, Items 293, 294, and 295, Diary entries, 17, 20, and 24 July, and Item 296, 'Meeting held by First Sea Lord', 24 July, and Items 301 and 302, exchanges with Prime Minister, 26 and 27 October, all between pp 234–40. Also: Hobbs, *Fleet Air Arm and War in Europe*, Chapter 8; Kenyon, *Arctic Convoys*, 241–3; and Hinsley,

*British Intelligence*, Volume 3, Part 1, pp 275–8. **32** Llewellyn-Jones, *Royal Navy and the Arctic Convoys*, p 117. **33** Churchill to Stalin, 3 May 1944, FO 954/3B/545, and Stalin response, 8 May, FO 954/3B/548. **34** Reynolds and Pechnatov, *Kremlin Letters*, Chapters 11 and 12. **35** Prime Minister to President, 3 June 1944, FO 954/3B/551, and Prime Minister to Field Marshal Dill, 29 May, CAB 122/935. **36** JSM Washington to A.M.S.S.O., 28 May 1944, AIR 20/4987. **37** ASE (44) 2nd Meeting, 15 June 1944, Item II, 'Oral Statement by Minister of War Transport', CAB 92/8. **38** Admiral Land, Memorandum for President, 10 July 1944, PSF, Box 16 July, FDR Papers. **39** Vail Motter, *Persian Corridor and Aid to Russia*, Appendix A, Table 1, pp 482–3, and Tables 5 and 6, pp 490–2. **40** Sokolov, 'Role of Lend-Lease', pp 573–4. **41** Interpolated from 'Status of the Soviet Aid Program' monthly reports, November 1943 to July 1944, PSF, Boxes 15 and 16, FDR Papers. **42** ASE (44) 41, 20 July 1944, 'Military and Civil Supplies to USSR', CAB 92/8; Beaumont, *Comrades in Arms*, Table 6, p 169. **43** For 'Collaboration with USSR' agenda at Teheran, CCS 407 (Revised), 26 November 1943, CAB 99/25/4, and CCS 426/1, 6 December, 'Report to the President and Prime Minister', paragraphs 6(g), 9, 10, and 16, CAB 99/25/5. **44** Beaumont, *Comrades in Arms*, p 147. **45** John Lukacs, *The Legacy of the Second World War* (Yale University Press, 2010), p 167. **46** Quoted by Richard Overy, *Why the Allies Won* (London: Pimlico, 2006), p 310. **47** Van Tuyll, *Feeding the Bear*, p 142. **48** For a good account of Churchill's reservations and how he was out-manoeuvred by the Americans at Teheran, Overy, *Why the Allies Won*, pp 172–6 and 192. For Ismay, Kiszely, *Ismay*, Chapter 9. **49** Leighton and Coakley, *Global Logistics and Strategy 1943–1945*, pp 671 and 678; Beaumont, *Comrades in Arms*, pp 185–6. **50** Bellamy, *Absolute War*, p 601, quoting Zhukov's memoirs. **51** Van Tuyll, *Feeding the Bear*, p 73. **52** Frozen 1225, 11 January 1944, Ismay from Hollis, PREM 3/396/10. **53** Grand 1336, 14 January, Hollis from Ismay, and JIC (44) 21 (Final), 20 January, 'Situation on Russian Front', both PREM 3/396/10. **54** JIC (44) 138 (O) Final, 13 April 1944, 'Developments on the Eastern Front and their Implications for 'Overlord'', CAB 81/21. **55** Kahn, *Western Allies and Soviet Potential*, Chapters 19 and 22. **56** Memorandum for the President, 10 July 1944, PSF, Box 16, July 1944, FDR Papers. **57** Kahn, *Western Allies and Soviet Potential*, Chapter 22 with Marshall reference, p 314. **58** Harrison, 'Economic Warfare and the battlefield on the Eastern Front', p 7 and Table 1. **59** Boog *et al*, *Germany and the Second World War*, Volume VIII, Part V.II, pp 522–4, and 589–92. **60** 'Status of the Soviet Aid Program', 30 June 1944, PSF, Box 17 September 1944 Part 1, FDR Papers; Krivosheev, *Soviet Casualties and Combat Losses*, pp 'Summary of Availability', Sections VI and VII, pp 257–8; Anniversary Statistical Handbook, p 61. Last sentence, Hill, *Great Patriotic War*, Table 8.9. **61** Boog *et al*, *Germany and the Second World War*, Volume VIII, pp 592–3. **62** Beaumont, *Comrades in Arms*, p 212, quoting *Khrushchev Remembers*, p 199. **63** Llewellyn-Jones, *Royal Navy and the Arctic Convoys*, Appendix A. For aid deliveries, Admiral Land, Memorandum for President, 11 April 1945, PSF, Box 17, Lend-Lease, March–April 1945, FDR Papers. **64** Hill, *Great Patriotic War*, Table 8.5. **65** Mungo Melvin, *Manstein: Hitler's Greatest General* (London: Phoenix Paperback, 2010), p 424. **66** JIC (44) 479 (O), 27 November 1944, 'The Russian Front', CAB 121/464. **67** Soviet Supply Protocols, Fourth Protocol, pp 87–91, 147–8, and 155–6; Vail Motter, *Persian Corridor and Aid to Russia*, Appendix A, Table 1, p 483; Beaumont, *Comrades in Arms*, pp 184–92. **68** First Lord to Prime Minister, 'Protection of Northern Convoys', 10 April 1945, and PM to Foreign Secretary, 6 April, PREM 3/393/14. **69** Lukacs, *The Legacy of the Second World War*, p 168. **70** Operation 'Unthinkable', Joint Planning Staff report, 22 May 1945, CAB 120/691. **71** Brooke War Diaries, entry for 24 May, p 693. **72** Prime Minister to Ismay, 8 June 1945, and Ismay response 10 June, CAB 120/691. **73** Blair, *Hunted*, Appendix 6, pp 786–7; V E Tarrant, *The Last Year of the Kriegsmarine May 1944–May 1945* (London: Arms & Armour Press, 1994), pp 145–7. **74** Claasen, *Hitler's Northern War*, p 244. **75** Carruthers/Hessler, *The U-boat War in the Atlantic*, Volume III, Chapter 11, Section 458. **76** From Admiralty, 'Brief Appreciation of the Anti-U-boat War', 17 January 1945, ADM 116/5456; COS (45) 59 (O), 20 January 1945, 'Northern Convoys to Russia', CAB 122/935. **77** Boog *et al*, *Germany and the Second World War*, Volume VIII, pp 997–9; Ziemke, *German Northern Theater of*

Operations, Chapter 14. 78 Blair, *Hunted*, Appendix 2, pp 756–61. 79 Showell, *Fuehrer Conferences*, Conference 12 October 1944, paragraph 2d, p 414. 80 Blair, *Hunted*, pp 676–7; uboat.net. 81 Hinsley, *British Intelligence*, Volume 3, Part 2, pp 490–3. 82 Cosu/45/2, 18 March 1945, AU (45) 1st Meeting – Conclusion (c), Report by the Admiralty, paragraph 4, FO 954/3B/563. 83 Lambert, 'Seizing the Initiative'. 84 WP (45) 119, 19 February 1945, 'Summary of Naval Air Operations – 1st November 1944, to 1st February 1945', Section I.3, CAB 66/62/24; Blair, *Hunted*, pp 599–600, and 677: Llewellyn-Jones, *Royal Navy and the Arctic Convoys*, pp 117–19; Kenyon, *Arctic Convoys*, p 253. 85 Llewellyn-Jones, *Royal Navy and the Arctic Convoys*, pp 120–1; Claasen, *Hitler's Northern War*, p 248. 86 Llewellyn-Jones, *Royal Navy and the Arctic Convoys*, pp 122–5; Blair, *Hunted*, pp 678–9; Tarrant, *Last Year of the Kriegsmarine*, pp 152–3. 87 Claasen, *Hitler's Northern War*, pp 245–7. 88 First Lord to Prime Minister, 29 November 1944, ADM 205/35. 89 David Syrett, 'The Last Murmansk Convoys, 11 March–30 May 1945', *Northern Mariner*, IV:1, January 1994, pp 55–63. 90 Blair, *Hunted*, pp 679–80; Llewellyn-Jones, *Royal Navy and the Arctic Convoys*, pp 127–8; Tarrant, *Last Year of the Kriegsmarine*, p 153. 91 Tarrant, *Last Year of the Kriegsmarine*, pp 153–4; Blair, *Hunted*, pp 680–1. 92 Syrett, 'Last Murmansk Convoys', pp 60–1. 93 Statistics drawn from Blair, *Hunted*, Appendix 2, pp 757–61.

**Reflections**

1 Sokolov, 'Role of Lend-Lease' pp 567–8; Van Tuyll, *Feeding the Bear*, Chapter 3, including notes on Soviet sources; Lovelace, 'Amnesia: How Russian History viewed Lend-Lease'; Harrison, *Accounting for War*, Chapter 6. 2 For examples, Schofield, *Russian Convoys*, pp 218–19. 3 Alan Clark, *Barbarossa: The Russian–German Conflict 1941–1945* (London: Phoenix paperback edition, 1996), Preface xxi. 4 For the distribution of German war effort, O'Brien, *How the War was Won*, is a good starting point. 5 Quoted in Richard Overy, *Why the Allies Won*, p 310. 6 Ibid, Chapter 3, especially p 120. 7 For example, Tooze, *Wages of Destruction*, pp 588–9, states that Western aid had no impact on the Eastern Front until 1943. He also emphasises the impressive Soviet aircraft output without reference to Western aluminium etc. It is striking that none of three acclaimed English language single volume histories of the Second World War published in the period 2009–12 devoted more than three pages to Western aid to Russia and its impact. They evidently did not feel it required any fresh appraisal. See: Andrew Roberts, *Storm of War: A New History of the Second World War* (London: Allen Lane, 2009); Max Hastings, *All Hell Let Loose: The World at War 1939–1945* (London: Harper Press, 2011); and Anthony Beevor, *The Second World War* (London: Weidenfeld & Nicolson, 2012). 8 Van Tuyll, *Feeding the Bear*, especially his introduction, for a good discussion and overview of the historiography of Western aid up to the end of the Cold War. It would also be invidious not to stress the work of Mark Harrison and Walter S Dunn and O'Brien's *How the War was Won* in presenting a more insightful and balanced view of Western aid and its impact. 9 For an authoritative view of Hopkins 'back channel' links to the Russian leadership and his underlying attitude to the Soviet system, Andrew and Mitrokhin, *The Mitrokhin Archive*, p 147. 10 For a powerful expression of this view, McMeekin, *Stalin's War*. 11 Reynolds and Pechnatov, *Kremlin Letters*, Epilogue, makes useful points here. 12 Harrison, *Accounting for War*, p 151. 13 For comments and sources here, William James, *British Grand Strategy in the Age of American Hegemony* (OUP 2024), Chapter 3. 14 For Arctic deliveries, see earlier calculations. For Russian figures on the breakdown of overall aid received 1941–5, see Anniversary Statistical Handbook, p 193. 15 Figures extrapolated from: 'Status of the Soviet Aid Program', 28 February and 30 June 1943, PSF, March 1943, Box 14, and July 1943, Box 15, FDR papers; *Royal Navy and the Arctic Convoys*, p 129, and Vail Motter, *Persian Corridor and Aid to Russia*, Appendix A, Tables 1 and 4, pp 481–2 and 488. 16 Hill, *Great Patriotic War*, Table 8.5. 17 Figures extrapolated from: WP (42) 417, 17 September 1942, CAB 66/28/47; ASE (43) 23, 27 March 1943, CAB 92/6; WP (43) 475, 25 October 1943, CAB 66/42/25; and Status of Soviet Aid Program, 28 February 1943, PSF Box 14, March 1943, FDR Papers. 18 Anniversary Statistical Handbook, p 187. 19 For American deliveries in this period, 'Status of the Soviet Aid Program', 28 February 1943, PSF, Box 14 March 1943,

FDR papers. This does not break down deliveries by route at item level but, by looking at losses against each item, it is possible to estimate what went via the Arctic. For Zhukov on American steel, Sokolov, 'Role of Lend-Lease', p 568. **20** For American quantities delivered, Status of the Soviet Aid Program, 28 February 1943, President's Secretary's File, Box 14, FDR papers. For overall Soviet TNT output, Balysh, 'Development of Explosives Production', p 13. **21** Figures from: ASE (43) 23, 27 March 1943, 'Military Supplies to the USSR'; 'Status of the Soviet Aid Program', 28 February; and Ellis, *World War II Data Book*, Tables 87 and 93, pp 277–8. **22** Harrison, 'Economic Warfare and the battlefield on the Eastern Front, 1941–1945', pp 7–8. **23** Dunn, *Soviet Economy and the Red Army*, p 70. **24** Llewellyn-Jones, *Royal Navy and the Arctic Convoys*, Appendices A I, II and IV, D and E; Llewellyn-Jones, *Royal Navy and the Mediterranean Convoys*, Chapter VIII, pp 99–100; Blair, *Hunted*, Appendix 3. **25** Dunn, *Soviet Economy and the Red Army*, p 87; Mawdsley, *The War for the Seas*, Chapter 12. **26** Schofield, *Russian Convoys*, p 222. **27** Harrison, 'Economic Warfare and the battlefield on the Eastern Front', p 8. **28** Levy, 'Royal Navy Fleet Tactics', p 383.

# Bibliography

**Primary Sources**

*National Archives*
Cabinet Office Papers
CAB 1: Miscellaneous Records 1866–1949.
CAB 65: War Cabinet and Cabinet Minutes (WM and CM Series) 1939–1945.
CAB 66: War Cabinet and Cabinet Memoranda (WP and CP Series) 1939–1945.
CAB 69: Defence Committee Operations Minutes and Papers 1940–1945.
CAB 70: Defence Committee Supply 1941–1946.
CAB 79: Chiefs of Staff Minutes 1939–1946.
CAB 80: Chiefs of Staff Memoranda (O) 1937–1947.
CAB 81: JIC Minutes and Reports 1939–1947.
CAB 84: Joint Planning Committee Papers 1942–1949.
CAB 88: Combined Chiefs of Staff Meetings 1945.
CAB 92: Committees on Supply, Production, Priority and Manpower.
CAB 99: US and UK Summit Conferences 1941–1945.
CAB 105: War Cabinet and Cabinet Office Telegrams.
CAB 106: Historical Section: Archivist and Librarian Files.
CAB 119: Joint Planning Staff: Correspondence and Papers.
CAB 120: Minister of Defence Secretariat Records.
CAB 121: Special Secret Information Centre: Files.
CAB 122: Records of British Joint Staff and Joint Services Missions Washington.
CAB 146: Historical Section, Enemy Documents Section: Files and Papers.
CAB 158: Ministry of Defence and Cabinet Office: Central Intelligence
CAB 159: Ministry of Defence and Cabinet Office: Central Intelligence Machinery: Joint Intelligence Sub-Committee, later Committee: Minutes.
CAB 186: Central Intelligence Machinery: Joint Intelligence Committee Memoranda.

Premier Files
PREM 3: Prime Minister's Office: Operational correspondence 1937–1946.
PREM 4: Prime Minister's Office: Confidential correspondence 1934–1946.

Foreign Office Records
FO 371: Political Developments: General correspondence from 1906–1966.
FO 954: Private Office Papers of Sir Anthony Eden, Secretary of State.

Intelligence Records
HW 1: Government Code and Cipher School: Signals Intelligence passed to the Prime Minister, messages and correspondence.

HW 3: Government Code and Cipher School and predecessors: Personal Papers, Unofficial Histories, Foreign Office X Files and Miscellaneous Records.
HW 5: Government Code and Cipher School: German Section: Reports of German Army and Air Force High Grade Machine Decrypts.
HW 8: Government Code and Cipher School: Naval Section: Reports, Working Aids and Correspondence.
HW 43: Government Code and Cipher School: Histories of British Sigint.
HW 50: Government Code and Cipher School: Records relating to the writing of the history of British signals intelligence in the Second World War.
KV 2: The Security Service: Personal (PF Series) Files 1913–1983.
KV 3: The Security Service: Subject (SF Series) Files 1905–1978.
KV 4: The Security Service: Policy (Pol F Series) Files.

Records of the Fighting Services
Admiralty
ADM 1: Admiralty: Correspondence and Papers.
ADM 116: Admiralty: Record Office: Cases.
ADM 167: Board of Admiralty: Minutes and Memoranda.
ADM 173: Admiralty: Submarine Logs.
ADM 178: Admiralty: Naval Courts Martial Cases, Boards of Enquiry Reports, and other papers.
ADM 196: Officers' Service Records.
ADM 199: Admiralty: War History Cases and Papers, Second World War.
ADM 205: Admiralty: Office of the First Sea Lord, correspondence and papers.
ADM 219: Directorate of Operational Research.
ADM 223: Admiralty: Naval Intelligence Division and Operational Intelligence Centre: Intelligence Reports and Papers.
ADM 234: Admiralty: Reference Books (BR Series).
ADM 237: Naval Staff: Operations Division: Convoy Records Second World War.
ADM 331: Admiralty and Ministry of Defence: Organisation and Methods Department.

War Office
WO 106: Directorate of Military Operations and Intelligence.
WO 193: Directorate of Military Operations and Plans: Planning and Intelligence.
WO 208: Records of Directorate of Military Intelligence 1939–1945.
WO 216: Office of the Chief of the Imperial General Staff: Papers.

Air Ministry
AIR 2: Air Ministry records comprising policy, case and committee reports.
AIR 8: Records of the Chief of the Air Staff.
AIR 14: Bomber Command operational and technical matters.
AIR 19: Air Ministry and Ministry of Defence, Air Department, Private Office Papers.
AIR 20: Papers accumulated by the Air Historical Branch.
AIR 22: Air Intelligence Summaries.
AIR 23: Royal Air Force Overseas Commands.
AIR 40: Air Ministry: Directorate of Intelligence: reports and papers.
AIR 41: Air Ministry and Ministry of Defence: Air Historical Branch: Narratives and Monographs.

Ministry of Defence
DEFE 3: Admiralty: Operational Intelligence Centre: Intelligence from Intercepted German, Italian and Japanese Radio Communications, WWII.

*Published official records*

*United Kingdom*
Navy Records Society
Volume 131, *British Naval Documents 1204–1960*, edited by John B Hattendorf, R J B Knight, A W H Pearsall, N A M Rodger and Geoffrey Till (Scolar Press, 1993).
Volume 134, *The Somerville Papers*, edited by Michael Simpson (Scolar Press, 1995).
Volume 137, *The Defeat of the Enemy Attack on Shipping, 1939–1945*, edited by Eric J Grove (UK: Ashgate Publishing, 1997).
Volume 139, *The Battle of the Atlantic and Signals Intelligence: U-boat Situations and Trends, 1941–1945*, edited by David Syrett (UK: Ashgate Publishing, 1998).
Volume 140, *The Cunningham Papers, Selections from the Private and Official Correspondence*, Volume 1, The Mediterranean Fleet, 1939–1942, edited by Michael Simpson (Ashgate Publishing, 1999).
Volume 144, *The Battle of the Atlantic and Signals Intelligence: U-boat Tracking Papers, 1941–1947*, edited by David Syrett (UK: Ashgate Publishing, 2002).
Volume 150, *The Cunningham Papers, Selections from the Private and Official Correspondence*, Volume 2, The Triumph of Allied Sea Power, 1942–1946, edited by Michael Simpson (Ashgate Publishing, 2006).
Volume 159, *The Fleet Air Arm in the Second World War, Volume 1, 1939–1941*, edited by Ben Jones (UK: Ashgate Publishing, 2012).
Volume 164, *The Naval Miscellany Volume VIII*, edited by Brian Vale (UK: Routledge, 2017).
Volume 165, *The Fleet Air Arm in the Second World War, Volume II, 1942–1943*, edited by Ben Jones (London: Routledge, 2018).
Air Ministry
*The Rise and Fall of the German Air Force (1933–1945)*, Pamphlet No 248, first published 1948.
Air Historical Branch
The RAF in Maritime War
Volume III: The Atlantic and Home Waters: The Preparative Phase: July 1941–February 1943.
Volume IV: The Atlantic and Home Waters: The Offensive Phase: February 1943–May 1944.

*United States*
Franklin D Roosevelt Presidential Library.
Department of State, Office of the Historian, Diplomatic Papers.
Department of State, Wartime International Agreements, Soviet Supply Protocols, Publication 2759.

*Russia and Union of Soviet Socialist Republics*
The Great Patriotic War: The Anniversary Statistical Handbook (Federal State Statistical Service, 2020).

*Private papers*
Alexander, Viscount A.V, Churchill College, Cambridge.
Beesly, Patrick, Churchill College, Cambridge.
Cunningham, Admiral of the Fleet Viscount of Hyndhope, British Library.
Davis, Admiral Sir William, Churchill College, Cambridge.
Denning, Vice Admiral Sir Norman, National Maritime Museum.
Denniston, Alistair G, Churchill College, Cambridge.
Godfrey, Vice Admiral J H, National Maritime Museum.
Halder, Generaloberst Franz, War Journal, US Army Historical Division, Fort Leavenworth, Kansas.
Roskill, Captain S.W, Churchill College, Cambridge.
Somerville, Admiral of the Fleet Sir James, Churchill College, Cambridge.
*Published memoirs*

Alanbrooke, Field Marshal Lord, edited by Danchev, Alex and Todman, Daniel, *War Diaries 1939–1945* (London: Phoenix Press, 2002).
Churchill, Winston S, *The Second World War* (London: Cassell, 1948–1954).
   *The Gathering Storm* (1948)
   *Their Finest Hour* (1949)
   *The Grand Alliance* (1950)
   *The Hinge of Fate* (1951)
Cadogan, Sir Alexander, OM, *Diaries, 1938–1945*, edited by David Dilks (London: Faber and Faber, 2010).
Cunningham, Admiral of the Fleet Viscount of Hyndhope, *A Sailor's Odyssey* (London: Hutchinson, 1957).
Denham, Henry, *Inside the Nazi Ring: A Naval Attaché in Sweden, 1940–1945* (Sapere Books edition, 2021).
Dönitz, Admiral Karl, *Memoirs: Ten Years and Twenty Days* (Frontline Books edition, 2012).
Gehlen, General Reinhard, *The Service, The Memoirs of General Reinhard Gehlen*, translated David Irving (London: Collins, 1972).
Golovko, Admiral Arseni G, *With the Red Fleet: The War Memoirs of the Late Admiral Arseni G Golovko*, edited by Sir Aubrey Mansergh (London: Putnam, 1965).
Goodall, Sir Stanley, *Diary of a Wartime Naval Constructor*, edited by Ian Buxton (Barnsley: Seaforth, 2022).
Ismay, General the Lord, *Memoirs* (London: William Heinemann, 1960).
Kennedy, Major General Sir John, *The Business of War: The War Narrative of Major General Sir John Kennedy* (London: Hutchinson, 1957).
Le Bailly, Vice Admiral Sir Louis, *The man around the engine* (Emsworth, Hampshire: Kenneth Mason, 1990).
Maisky, Ivan M, *The Maisky Diaries: Red Ambassador to the Court of St James 1932–1943*, edited by Gabriel Gorodetsky (Yale University Press, 2015).
Pownall, Lieutenant General Sir Henry, *Chief of Staff: The Diaries of Lieutenant General Sir Henry Pownall*, Vol 2 1940–44, edited by Brian Bond (London: Leo Cooper, 1974).
Slessor, Marshal of the Royal Air Force Sir John, *The Central Blue: Recollections and Reflections by Marshal of the Royal Air Force Sir John Slessor* (London: Cassell & Co, 1956).
Vian, Admiral of the Fleet Sir Philip, *Action this Day: A War Memoir* (London: Frederick Muller, 1960).

*Published official books and pamphlets*
Department of the Army Pamphlet, No 20-261a, *The German Campaign in Russia: Planning and Operations, 1940–1942* (Department of the US Army, March 1955).
Department of the Army Pamphlet, No 20-292, *Warfare in the Far North* (Department of the US Army, October 1951).
Hoeffding, Oleg, *German Air Attacks against Industry and Railroads in Russia, 1941–1945*, Memorandum RM-6206-PR (United States Air Force Project Rand, the Rand Corporation, 1970).
Leighton, Richard M, and Coakley, Robert W, *United States Army in World War II, Global Logistics and Strategy 1940–1943* (Washington USA, US Government Printing Office, 1955).
Leighton, Richard M, and Coakley, Robert W, *United States Army in World War II, Global Logistics and Strategy 1943–1945* (Washington USA, US Government Printing Office, 1968).
Matloff, Maurice, and Snell, Edwin, *United States Army in World War II, Strategic Planning for Coalition Warfare 1941–1942* (Washington, USA: US Government Printing Office, 1953).
Plocher, Generalleutnant Hermann, *The German Air Force Versus Russia, 1941*, US Air Force Historical Studies: No 153 (USAF Historical Division, Aerospace Studies Institute, Air University, July 1965).
Plocher, Generalleutnant Hermann, *The German Air Force Versus Russia, 1942*, US Air Force

Historical Studies: No 154 (USAF Historical Division, Aerospace Studies Institute, Air University, June 1966).

Plocher, Generalleutnant Hermann, *The German Air Force Versus Russia, 1943*, US Air Force Historical Studies: No 155 (USAF Historical Division, Aerospace Studies Institute, Air University, June 1967).

Vail Motter, T H, *United States Army in World War II, The Persian Corridor and Aid to Russia* (Washington USA: US Government Printing Office, 1952).

Watson, Mark Skinner, *United States Army in World War II: Chief of Staff: Pre-war Plans and Preparations* (Washington USA: Center of Military History, 1991).

Weichold, Vice Admiral Eberhard, *German Surface Ships: Policy and Operations in World War II* (GHS/4, US Naval War College, c1955).

Ziemke, Earl F, *United States Army in World War II, German Northern Theater of Operations 1940–1945*, Washington USA: US Government Printing Office, 1959).

**Secondary Works**

*Books*
Allport, Alan, *Britain at Bay: The Epic Story of the Second World War: 1938–1941* (London: Profile Books, 2020).

Andrew, Christopher, and Mitrokhin, Vasili, *The Mitrokhin Archive: The KGB in Europe and the West* (London: Penguin Books edition, 2000).

Barnett, Corelli, *Engage the Enemy More Closely* (London: Hodder and Stoughton, 1991).

Bath, Alan Harris, *Tracking the Axis Enemy: The Triumph of Anglo-American Naval Intelligence* (USA: Kansas University Press, 1998).

Beaumont, Joan, *Comrades in Arms: British Aid to Russia 1941–1945* (London: Davis-Poynter, 1980).

Beesly, Patrick, *Very Special Admiral: The Life of Admiral J H Godfrey* (London: Hamish Hamilton, 1980).

Beesly, Patrick, *Very Special Intelligence: The Story of the Admiralty's Operational Intelligence Centre 1939–1945* (Chatham Publishing edition, 2006).

Beevor, Anthony, *The Second World War* (London: Weidenfeld and Nicolson, 2012).

Bekker, Cajus, *Hitler's Naval War* (London: Macdonald & Jane's, 1974).

Bell, Christopher, *Churchill and Seapower* (Oxford University Press, 2012).

Bellamy, Chris, *Absolute War: Soviet Russia in the Second World War* (London: Pan Books, 2009).

Bennett, G H, and Bennett, R, *Hitler's Admirals* (Annapolis: Naval Institute Press, 2004).

Bennett, Ralph, *Behind the Battle: Intelligence in the War with Germany, 1939–1945* (Pimlico, 1999).

Birch, Frank, *The Official History of British Sigint 1914–1945*, Volume 1, Part 1, edited by John Jackson (Military Press, 2004).

Birch, Frank, *The Official History of British Sigint 1914–1945*, Volume 1, Part 2 and Volume 2, edited by John Jackson (Military Press, 2007).

Bird, Keith W, *Erich Raeder: Admiral of the Third Reich* (Oxford: Casemate Publishers, 2018).

Bishop, Patrick, *Target Tirpitz: X-craft, Agents and Dambusters – The Epic Quest to destroy Hitler's Mightiest Warship* (London: Harper Press, 2012).

Blair, Clay, *Hitler's U-boat War, The Hunters 1939–1942* (London: Weidenfeld & Nicolson, 1997).

Blair, Clay, *Hitler's U-boat War, The Hunted 1942–1945* (London: Weidenfeld & Nicolson, 1999).

Boog, Horst; Rahn, Werner; Wegner, Bernd; Maier, Klaus; Stegemann, Bernd; and others, *Germany and the Second World War* (OUP. 1990–2017).
Volume I, *The Build-Up of German Aggression* (1990)
Volume II, *Germany's Initial Conquests in Europe* (1991)
Volume III, *The Mediterranean, South-East Europe and North Africa 1939–1941* (1998)

Volume IV, *The Attack on the Soviet Union* (1996)
Volume VI, *The Global War* (2001)
Volume VII, *The Strategic Air War in Europe and the War in the West and East Asia, 1943–1944/45* (2006)
Volume VIII, *The Eastern Front 1943–1944: The War in the East and on the Neighbouring Fronts* (2017)
Boyd, Andrew, *The Royal Navy in Eastern Waters: Linchpin of Victory 1935–1942* (Barnsley: Seaforth, 2017).
Boyd, Andrew, *British Naval Intelligence through the Twentieth Century* (Barnsley: Seaforth, 2020).
Boyd, Carl, *Hitler's Japanese Confidant: General Ōshima Hiroshi and Magic Intelligence 1941–1945* (USA: University of Kansas, 1993).
Braithwaite, Rodric, *Moscow 1941: A City and its People at War* (London: Profile Books, 2006).
Broadberry, Stephen, and Harrison, Mark, *The Economics of the Second World War: Seventy-Five Years On* (London: Centre for Economic Policy Research, 2020).
Brodhurst, Robin, *Churchill's Anchor: The Biography of Admiral of the Fleet Sir Dudley Pound OM, GCB, GCVO* (UK: Leo Cooper, 2000).
Broome, Captain Jack, *Convoy is to Scatter: The Story of PQ 17* (London: Futura Publications, 1974).
Brown, David K, *Nelson to Vanguard: Warship Design and Development 1923–1945* (Seaforth Publishing, 2012 edition).
Brown, David K, *Atlantic Escorts: Ships, Weapons & Tactics in World War II* (Barnsley: Seaforth, 2022).
Budiansky, Stephen, *Battle of Wits: The Complete Story of Codebreaking in World War II* (London: Viking, 2000).
Burt, R A, *British Battleships 1919–1945* (Barnsley: Seaforth Publishing, 2014).
Butler, Professor J R M, *Grand Strategy Volume II: September 1939–June 1941* (London: HMSO, 1957).
Butler, Professor J R M, *Grand Strategy Volume III: June 1941–August 1942, Part II* (London: HMSO, 1964).
Carruthers, Bob, *The U-Boat War in the Atlantic*, edited version of three-volume official Admiralty history by Günther Hessler (Barnsley: Pen & Sword, 2013).
Claasen, Adam R, *Hitler's Northern War: The Luftwaffe's Ill-Fated Campaign, 1940–1945* (University Press of Kansas, 2001).
Clark, Alan, *Barbarossa: The Russian–German Conflict 1941–1945* (London: Pheonix Paperback edition, 1996).
Clayton, Tim, *Sea Wolves: The Extraordinary Story of Britain's WWII Submarines* (Little Brown, 2011).
Cradock, Percy, *Know Your Enemy: How the Joint Intelligence Committee saw the World* (London: John Murray, 2002).
Dear, I C B; and Foot, M R D, *The Oxford Companion to World War II* (Oxford University Press paperback edition, 2001).
Degtev, Dmitry, and Zubov, Dmitry, *Air Battle for Moscow 1941–1942* (Barnsley: Air World, 2021).
Dimbleby, Jonathan, *The Battle of the Atlantic: How the Allies Won the War* (Penguin, 2015).
Dimbleby, Jonathan, *Barbarossa: How Hitler lost the War* (Penguin, 2021).
Ditcham, A G F, *A Home on the Rolling Main: A Naval Memoir 1940–1946* (Bodmin & Kings Lynn, MPG Books, 2012).
Downing, Taylor, *Spies in the Sky: The Secret Battle for Aerial Intelligence in World War II* (London: Little Brown, 2011).
Dunn, Walter S, *Hitler's Nemesis: The Red Army 1930–1945* (Westport CT, USA: Praeger, 1994).
Dunn, Walter S, *The Soviet Economy and the Red Army 1930–1945* (Westport, CT, USA: Praeger, 1995).
Edgerton, David, *Britain's War Machine: Weapons, Resources and Experts in the Second*

*World War* (London: Allen Lane, 2011).
Ellis, John, *The World War II Data Book* (London: BCA and Aurum Press, 1993).
Erickson, John, *The Road to Stalingrad* (London: Panther Books edition, 1985).
Erickson, John, *The Road to Berlin* (London: Weidenfeld and Nicolson, 1983).
Erickson, John, and Dilks, David, *Barbarossa: The Axis and the Allies* (Edinburgh University Press, 1994).
Erskine, Ralph and Smith, Michael, *The Bletchley Park Codebreakers: How Ultra shortened the War and led to the birth of the computer* (Biteback Publishing, 2011).
Evans, Richard J, *The Third Reich at War* (London: Penguin, 2009).
Farrell, Brian, *The Basis and Making of Grand Strategy – Was there a Plan?* (UK: Edwin Mellen Press, 1998).
Faulkner, Marcus and Bell, Christopher, *Decision in the Atlantic: The Allies and the Longest Campaign of the Second World War* (Andarta Books, University of Kentucky, 2019).
Ferris, John R, and Mawdsley, Evan, *The Cambridge History of the Second World War*, Volume 1, *Fighting the War* (Cambridge University Press, 2015).
Forczyk, Robert, *Tank Warfare on the Eastern Front, 1941–1942 Schwerpunkt* (Barnsley: Pen & Sword Military, 2013).
Franklin, George, *Britain's Anti-Submarine Capability 1919–1939* (London: Routledge, 2003).
Friedman, Norman, *Network-Centric Warfare: How Navies Learned to Fight Smarter through Three World Wars* (Naval Institute Press, 2009).
Friedman, Norman, *British Cruisers: Two World Wars and After* (Barnsley: Seaforth, 2012).
Friedman, Norman, *Naval Anti-Aircraft Guns and Gunnery* (Barnsley: Seaforth, 2013).
Friedman, Norman, *The British Battleship 1906–1946* (Barnsley: Seaforth, 2015).
Gardner, W J R, *Decoding History: The Battle of the Atlantic and Ultra* (Annapolis: Naval Institute Press, 2000).
Gibbs, Professor N H, *Grand Strategy*, Volume I (HMSO, 1976).
Gilbert, Martin, *Winston S Churchill, Vol. VI, Finest Hour 1939–1941* and *Vol. VII, Road to Victory 1941–1945* (London: William Heinemann, 1983 and 1986).
Gilbert, Martin, *The Churchill War Papers, Vol. 3, The ever-widening war* (London: William Heinemann, 2000).
Glantz, David M, and House, Jonathan M, *When Titans Clashed: How the Red Army Stopped Hitler* (USA; University of Kansas Press, 2015).
Goodman, Michael S, *The Official History of the Joint Intelligence Committee: Volume I, From the Approach of the Second World War to the Suez Crisis* (Abingdon, Oxon: Routledge, 2014).
Gordon, Andrew, *The Rules of the Game: Jutland and British Naval Command* (London: John Murray, 1996).
Greene, Jack, and Massignani, Alessandro, *The Naval War in the Mediterranean 1940–1943* (UK: Chatham Publishing, 2002).
Grove, Eric, *The Royal Navy* (Basingstoke, UK, Palgrave Macmillan, 2005).
Gwyer, J M A, *Grand Strategy Volume III: June 1941–August 1942, Part I* (London: HMSO, 1964).
Haarr, Geirr H, *The Battle for Norway, April – June 1940* (Barnsley, Seaforth Publishing, 2010).
Hall, Keith, *X3 to X54: The History of the British Midget Submarine* (Cheltenham: History Press, 2023).
Hammond, Richard, *Strangling the Axis: The Fight for Control of the Mediterranean in the Second World War* (Cambridge University Press, 2020).
Hancock, W K, and Gowing, M M, *The British War Economy* (British Official History Civil Series) (London: HMSO, 1949).
Harding, Leighton, *Tirpitz Nemesis: A Short History of the X-Craft Midget Submarines* (Self-published, 2014).
Harding, Richard, *The Royal Navy, 1930–2000, Innovation and Defence* (London and New

York: Frank Cass, 2004).
Harrison, Mark, *Accounting for War: Soviet Production, Employment and the Defence Burden 1940–1945* (Cambridge University Press, 1996).
Hastings, Max, *All Hell Let Loose: The World at War 1939–45* (London: Harper Press, 2011).
Hayward, Joel S A, *Stopped at Stalingrad: The Luftwaffe and Hitler's Defeat in the East 1942–1943* (University of Kansas Press, 1998).
Healy, Mark, *Zitadelle: The German Offensive against the Kursk Salient 4–17 July 1943* (Stroud: The History Press, 2008).
Hezlet, Vice Admiral Sir Arthur, *British and Allied Submarine Operations in World War II, Volume 1* (Royal Navy Submarine Museum, 2001).
Hill, Alexander, *The Great Patriotic War of the Soviet Union, 1941–1945: A Documentary Reader* (London: Routledge, 2009).
Hill, Alexander, *The Red Army and the Second World War* (Cambridge University Press, 2016).
Hinsley, F.H., with Thomas, E.E; Ransom, C.F.G; and Knight, R.C, *British Intelligence in the Second World War. Its Influence on Strategy and Operations*, 4 Vols. (London: HMSO, 1977–1990).
Hinsley, F H, and Stripp, Alan, *Code Breakers: The Inside Story of Bletchley Park* (Oxford University Press, 1993).
Hobbs, David, *Taranto: And Naval Air Warfare in the Mediterranean, 1940–1945* (Barnsley: Seaforth, 2020).
Hobbs, David, *The Fleet Air Arm and the War in Europe 1939–1945* (Barnsley: Seaforth, 2022).
Hooton, E R, *War over the Steppes: The Air Campaigns on the Eastern Front 1941–45* (Oxford: Osprey Publishing, 2016).
Hore, Peter, *Dreadnought to Daring: 100 Years of Comment, Controversy and Debate in The Naval Review* (Barnsley: Seaforth Publishing, 2012).
Hore, Peter, *Henry Harwood: Hero of the River Plate* (Barnsley: Seaforth, 2018).
Howard, Michael, *British Intelligence in the Second World War*, Volume 5 (London: HMSO, 1990).
Howard, Michael, *The Mediterranean Strategy in the Second World War* (London: Greenhill Books, 1993).
Howse, Derek, *Radar at Sea: The Royal Navy in World War II* (Palgrave Macmillan, 1993).
Insall, Tony, *Secret Alliances: Special Operations and Intelligence in Norway 1940–1945 – The British Perspective* (London: Biteback Publishing, 2019).
Irving, David, *The Destruction of Convoy PQ 17* (London: Cassell & Co, 1968).
Irving, David, *The Destruction of Convoy PQ 17* (London: William Kimber, 1980).
Jackson, John, *Ultra's Arctic War* (Milton Keynes: Military Press, 2003).
Jacobsen, Alf R, *Miracle at the Litza: Hitler's First Defeat on the Eastern Front* (Oxford, UK: Casemate Publishers, 2017).
James, William, *British Grand Strategy in the Age of American Hegemony* (OUP, 2024).
Jeffery, Keith, *MI6: The History of the Secret Intelligence Service 1909–1949* (London: Bloomsbury, 2010).
Jenkins, Roy, *Portraits and Miniatures* (London: Macmillan, 1993).
Jenkins, Roy, *Churchill* (London: Pan Macmillan Ltd, 2002).
Kahn, David, *Seizing the Enigma: The Race to Break the German U-boat Codes* (Frontline Books version, 2012).
Kahn, Martin, *The Western Allies and Soviet Potential in World War II* (Abingdon, Oxon: Routledge, 2017).
Kennedy, Major General Sir John, *The Business of War: The War Narrative of Major General Sir John Kennedy* (London: Hutchinson, 1957).
Kennedy, Paul M, *The Rise and Fall of British Naval Mastery* (London: Allen Lane, 1976).
Kennedy, Paul M, *The Rise and Fall of the Great Powers* (London: Unwin Hyman, 1988).
Kennedy, Paul, *Engineers of Victory: The Problem Solvers Who Turned the Tide in the Second

*World War* (London: Allen Lane, 2013).

Kennedy, Paul, *Victory at Sea: Naval Power and the Transformation of the Global Order in World War II* (Yale University Press, 2022).

Kenyon, David, *Arctic Convoys: Bletchley Park and the War for the Seas* (Yale University Press, 2023).

Kershaw, Ian, *Fateful Choices: Ten Decisions That Changed The World* (London: Penguin Group, 2007).

Kimball, Warren E, *Churchill & Roosevelt: The Complete Correspondence*, Volume 1, *Alliance Emerging* (London: Collins, 1983)

Kingsley, F A, *Radar: The Development of Equipments for the Royal Navy 1939–45* (Macmillan, 1995).

Kirby, M W, *Operational Research in War and Peace: The British Experience from the 1930s to the 1970s* (London: Imperial College Press, 2003).

Kiszely, John, *General Hastings (Pug) Ismay: Soldier, Statesman, Diplomat: A New Biography* (London: Hurst & Co, 2024).

Konstam, Angus, *The Battle of North Cape: The Death Ride of the Scharnhorst, 1943* (Barnsley: Pen & Sword, 2009).

Kotelnikov, Vladimir, *Lend-Lease and Soviet Aviation in the Second World War* (Warwick: Helion & Co., 2017).

Krivosheev, Colonel General G F, *Soviet Casualties and Combat Losses in the Twentieth Century* (London: Greenhill Books, 1997).

Lenton, H T, *British and Empire Warships of the Second World War* (London: Greenhill Books, 1998).

Leutze, James R, *Bargaining for Supremacy: Anglo-American Naval Collaboration, 1937–1941* (USA: University of North Carolina Press, 1977).

Le Bailly, Vice Admiral Sir Louis, *From Fisher to the Falklands* (London: Marine Management (Holdings) Ltd., 1991).

Llewellyn-Jones, Malcolm, *The Royal Navy and the Arctic Convoys: A Naval Staff History* (Abingdon: Routledge, 2007).

Llewellyn-Jones, Malcolm, *The Royal Navy and the Mediterranean Convoys: A Naval Staff History* (Abingdon: Routledge, 2007).

Lukacs, John, *The Legacy of the Second World War* (New Haven, USA and London: Yale University Press, 2010).

MacIntyre, Captain Donald, *Fighting Admiral: The Life of Admiral of the Fleet Sir James Somerville* (London: Evans brothers, 1961).

Maiolo, Joe, *Cry Havoc: The Arms Race and the Second World War 1931–1941* (London: John Murray, 2011).

Mann, Christopher, and Jörgensen, Christer, *Hitler's Arctic War: The German Campaigns in Norway, Finland, and the USSR 1940–1945* (Barnsley: Pen & Sword, 2016).

Marder, Arthur J, *From the Dardanelles to Oran: Studies of the Royal Navy in War and Peace, 1915–1940* (London: Oxford University Press, 1974).

Mars, Alastair, *Submarines at War 1939–1945* (UK: William Kimber, 1971).

Mawdsley, Evan, *Thunder in the East: The Nazi–Soviet War 1941–1945* (London: Bloomsbury, 2015).

Mawdsley, Evan, *The War for the Seas: A Maritime History of World War II* (Yale University Press, 2020).

McMeekin, Sean, *Stalin's War: A New History of the Second World War* (London: Allen Lane, 2021).

McKay, C G, *From Information to Intrigue: Studies in Secret Service based on the Swedish Experience, 1939–1945* (London: Frank Cass, 1993).

McKay, C G, and Beckman, Bengt, *Swedish Signal Intelligence 1900–1945* (London: Routledge, 2014).

Mckinstry, Leo, *Hurricane: Victor of the Battle of Britain* (London: John Murray, 2010).

McLachlan, Donald, *Room 39, Naval Intelligence in Action 1939–45* (London: Weidenfeld and Nicolson, 1968).

Melvin, Mungo, *Manstein: Hitler's Greatest General* (London: Phoenix Paperback, 2010).
Millett, Allan R, and Murray, Williamson, *Military Effectiveness, Volume 2, The Interwar Period* (Cambridge University Press, 2010).
Millett, Allan R, and Murray, Williamson, *A War To Be Won: Fighting the Second World War* (USA: Harvard University Press, 2000).
Millett, Allan, and Murray, Williamson R, *Military Innovation in the Interwar Period* (Cambridge University Press, 1996).
Milner, Marc, *Battle of the Atlantic* (Stroud: The History Press, 2011).
Montefiore, Simon Sebag, *Stalin: The Court of the Red Tsar* (London: Phoenix, 2004).
Morison, Samuel Eliot, *The Two Ocean War* (USA: Little, Brown & Co, 1963).
Morton, H V, *Atlantic Meeting* (London: Methuen & Co, 1943).
Murfett, Malcolm H, *The First Sea Lords: From Fisher to Mountbatten* (Westport CT USA: Praeger, 1995).
Murfett, Malcolm H, *Naval Warfare 1919–1945: An operational history of the volatile war at sea* (Oxford: Routledge, 2009).
Murray, Williamson, *The Luftwaffe 1933–45: Strategy for Defeat* (London: Brassey's, 1983).
Newsome, Bruce Oliver, *Valentine Infantry Tank 1938–45* (Oxford: Osprey Publishing, 2016).
O'Brien, Phillips Payson, *How the War was Won: Air-Sea Power and Allied Victory in World War II* (Cambridge University Press: 2015).
O'Hara, Vincent P, *Six Victories: North Africa, Malta, and the Mediterranean Convoy War, November 1941–March 1942* (Annapolis: Naval Institute Press, 2019).
O'Keefe, David, *One Day in August: The Untold Story Behind Canada's Tragedy at Dieppe* (Knopf Canada, 2013).
Overy, Richard, *Russia's War* (London: Penguin Books, 1999).
Overy, Richard, *Why the Allies Won* (London: Pimlico, 2006).
Overy, Richard, *The Bombing War: Europe 1939–1945* (London: Allen Lane, 2013).
Overy, Richard, *Blood and Ruins: The Great Imperial War, 1931–1945* (London: Penguin, 2023).
Padfield, Peter, *Dönitz: The Last Führer: Portrait of a Nazi War Leader* (London: Lume Books edition, 2021).
Pearson, Michael, *Red Sky in the Morning: The Battle of the Barents Sea 1942* (Barnsley: Pen & Sword Maritime, 2007).
Peden, G C, *Arms, Economics and British Strategy: From Dreadnoughts to Hydrogen Bombs* (Cambridge University Press, 2007).
Playfair, Major General I S O, *The Mediterranean and Middle East* (HMSO, 1954).
  Volume 1, *The Early Successes against Italy* (1954)
  Volume 2, *The Germans Come to the Help of their Ally* (1956)
Pope, Dudley, *73 North: The Battle of the Barents Sea* (London: Alison Press/Martin Secker & Warburg, 1988).
Porch, Douglas, *The Path to Victory; The Mediterranean Theatre in World War II* (New York: Farrar, Straus and Giroux, 2004).
Potter, John Deane, *Fiasco: The Break-out of the German Battleships* (London: Pan books edition, 1974).
Redford, Duncan, *A History of the Royal Navy, World War II* (London: I B Tauris, 2014).
Reynolds, David, *From Munich to Pearl Harbour: Roosevelt's America and the Origins of the Second World War* (Chicago: Ivan Dee, 2001).
Reynolds, David, *In Command of History: Churchill Fighting and Writing the Second World War* (London: Allen Lane, 2004).
Reynolds, David, *The Creation of the Anglo-American Alliance 1937–41: A Study in Competitive Cooperation* (Europe Publications, 1981).
Reynolds, David, and Pechnatov, Vladimir, *The Kremlin Letters: Stalin's Wartime Correspondence with Churchill and Roosevelt* (New Haven and London: Yale University Press, 2018).
Roberts, Andrew, *The Holy Fox: A Life of Lord Halifax* (London: Weidenfeld and Nicolson,

1991).
Roberts, Andrew, *The Storm of War: A New History of the Second World War* (London: Allen Lane, 2009).
Roberts, Andrew, *Masters and Commanders: The Military Geniuses who led the West to Victory in World War II* (London: Allen Lane, 2008).
Rohwer, Jurgen, *Allied Submarine Attacks of World War Two: European Theatre of Operations, 1939–1945* (London: Greenhill Books, 1997).
Rohwer, Jurgen, *Critical Convoy Battles of WWII: Crisis in the North Atlantic, March 1943* (Stackpole edition, 2015).
Roskill, S. W, *The War at Sea* (London: HMSO, 1954–1961)
 Volume 1 *The Defensive* (1954)
 Volume 2 *The Period of Balance* (1956)
 Volume 3 *The Offensive* (1961)
Roskill, S. W, *The Navy At War 1939–1945* (London: Collins, 1960).
Roskill, S.W, *Naval Policy Between the Wars* (London: Collins, 1968–1976).
 Volume 1 *The Period of Anglo-American Antagonism, 1919–1929* (1968)
 Volume 2 *The Period of Reluctant Rearmament, 1930–1939* (1976)
Roskill, S. W, *Churchill and the Admirals* (London: Collins, 1977).
Roskill, S.W, *Naval Policy between the Wars* (National Maritime Museum, Maritime Monograph 29, 1978).
Rössler, Eberhard, *The U-Boat: The evolution and technical history of German submarines* (Cassell & Co., 2001 edition).
Salewski, Michael, *Die Deutsche Seekriegsleitung, 1935–1945* (Munich: Bernard & Graefe, 1971–1978).
 Band 1 – 1935–1941 (1970)
 Band 2 – 1942–1945 (1975)
 Band 3 – Denkschriften und Lagebetrachtungen 1938–1944 (1973)
Schofield, B, *The Russian Convoys* (UK: B T Batsford, 1964, and Pan Books edition 1984).
Sebag-Montefiore, Hugh, *Enigma: The Battle for the Code* (London: Weidenfeld and Nicolson, 2000).
Showell, Jak Mallmann, *Führer Conferences on Naval Affairs 1939–1945* (Stroud, Gloucestershire: History Press edition, 2015).
Smith, Bradley F, *The Ultra-Magic Deals and the Most Secret Special Relationship 1940–1946* (UK: Airlife Publishing, 1993).
Smith, Bradley F, *Sharing Secrets with Stalin: How the Allies Traded Intelligence, 1941–1945* (USA: University Press of Kansas, 1996).
Smith, Peter, *Convoy PQ18: Arctic Victory* (London: William Kimber, 1975).
Smith, William, *Churchill's Arctic Convoys: Strength triumphs over Adversity* (Barnsley: Pen & Sword, 2022).
Smith, William, *Allied Convoys to Northern Russia 1941–1945* (Barnsley: Pen & Sword, 2024).
Stafford, David, *Churchill and Secret Service* (UK: Overlook Press, 1997).
Stahel, David, *The Battle for Moscow* (Cambridge University Press, 2015).
Stephen, Martin, *The Fighting Admirals: British Admirals of the Second World War* (London: Leo Cooper, 1991).
Stoler, Mark, *Allies in War: Britain and America Against the Axis Powers 1940–1945* (London: Hodder Education, 2005).
Suprun, Mikhail, *Lend-Liz i severniye konvoi 1941–1945* (Lend-Lease and the Northern Convoys 1941 - 1945) (Moscow: Andreyesvkii Flag, 1997).
Tarrant, V E, *The Last Year of the Kriegsmarine, May 1944 – May 1945* (London: Arms and Armour Press, 1994).
Taylor, A J P, *Beaverbrook* (London: Penguin Books, 1974).
Terraine, John, *Business in Great Waters: The U-Boat Wars 1916–1945* (Barnsley Yorkshire: Pen & Sword, 2009).
Todman, Daniel, *Britain's War: Into Battle, 1937–1941* (London: Allen Lane, 2016).
Todman, Daniel, *Britain's War: A New World, 1942–1947* (London: Allen Lane, 2020).

Tooze, Adam, *The Wages of Destruction: The Making and Breaking of the Nazi Economy* (London: Penguin Books edition, 2007).
Van Tuyll, Hubert, *Feeding the Bear: American Aid to the Soviet Union, 1941–1945* (Westport, CT, USA: Greenwood Press, 1989).
Walling, Michael G, *Forgotten Sacrifice: The Arctic Convoys of World War II* (Oxford: Osprey publishing, 2012).
Watkins, Paul, *Midget Submarine Commander: The Life of Rear Admiral Godfrey Place VC, CB, CVO, DSC* (Barnsley: Pen & Sword Maritime, 2012).
Weeks, Albert L, *Russia's Lifesaver: Lend-Lease Aid to the USSR in World War II* (Plymouth: Lexington Books, 2010).
Williams, Charles, *Harold Macmillan* (London: Phoenix Paperback, 2010).
Williams, Charles, *Max Beaverbrook: Not Quite a Gentleman* (London: Biteback Publishing, 2019).
Wilson, Ben, *Empire of the Deep: The Rise and Fall of the British Navy* (London: Weidenfeld & Nicolson, 2013).
Wilson, Theodore A, *The First Summit: Roosevelt and Churchill at Placentia Bay, 1941* (USA: University Press of Kansas, 1991).
Wingate, John, *The Fighting Tenth: The Tenth Submarine Flotilla and the Siege of Malta* (UK: Sapere Books, 2021).
Winn, Godfrey, *PQ 17* (London: Arrow Press, 1966 edition).
Winton, John, *Cunningham: The Greatest Admiral since Nelson* (London: John Murray, 1998).
Winton, John, *The Death of the Scharnhorst* (Ilkley: Sapere Books edition, 2022).
Woodman, Richard, *Arctic Convoys 1941–1945* (London: John Murray, 1994).
Young, Edward, *One of Our Submarines* (London: Rupert Hart-Davis, 1953).
Zaloga, Steven J, *Soviet Lend-Lease Tanks of World War II* (Osprey Publishing, 2017).

*Articles and monographs*
Alvarez, David, 'Left in the Dust: Italian Signals Intelligence, 1915–1943', *International Journal of Intelligence and CounterIntelligence*, 14:3, pp 388–408, 2001.
Balysh, A N, 'Development of Explosives Production in the USSR in the 1930s and Delivery under Lend-Lease in the Great Patriotic War', *RUDN University Bulletin*, Russian History, No 4, 2012, pp 5–15.
Barnett, Corelli, 'The Influence of History upon Sea Power: The Royal Navy in the Second World War', in *Naval Power in the Twentieth Century*, edited by N A M Rodger (Basingstoke: Macmillan, 1996).
Barr, William, 'Operation Wunderland: Admiral Scheer in the Kara Sea, August 1942', *Polar Record*, 17:110, May 1975, pp 461–72.
Beaumont, Joan, 'Great Britain and the Rights of Neutral Countries: The Case of Iran, 1941', *Journal of Contemporary History*, 16:1, the Second World War: Part 1, January 1981, pp 213–28.
Beesly, Patrick, 'Convoy PQ17: A study of intelligence and decision-making', *Intelligence and National Security*, 5:2, 1990, pp 292–322.
Beesly, Patrick, 'Godfrey, Vice Admiral John Henry (1888–1971)', *Dictionary of National Biography*, OUP, 2004.
Bennett, George H, Introduction to *Fire and Ice: Arctic Convoys 1941–45*, new publication of Naval Staff History, Battle Summary 22 (Britannia Museum Trust Press, 2022).
Breemer, Jan S, 'Defeating the U-boat: Inventing Anti-submarine Warfare', *US Naval War College Newport Papers*, No 36, August 2010.
Buckley, John, 'Coastal command in the Second World War', *Air Power Review*, 21:1, 2018.
Davie, H G W, 'Patterns of War: A Re-interpretation of the Chronology of the German–Soviet War 1941–1945', *Journal of Slavic Military Studies*, 36:2, 2023, pp 139–63.
Davie, H G W, 'Managing Shortage: The Role of Centre Bases of the NKO in overcoming supply constraints in the Red Army, 1941–1945', *Journal of Slavic Military Studies*, 37:1, 2024, pp 53–79.

Drent, Jan, 'The Trans–Pacific Lend–Lease Shuttle to the Russian Far East 1941–46', *The Northern Mariner*, XXVII:1, 2017, pp 31–58.

Eloranta, Jari, and Nummela, Ilkka, 'Finnish Nickel as a Strategic Metal, 1920–1944', *Scandinavian Journal of History*, 32:4, 2007, pp 322–45.

Eshraghi, F, 'Anglo-Soviet Occupation of Iran in August 1941', *Middle Eastern Studies*, 20:1, January 1984, pp 27–52.

Faulkner, Marcus, 'The *Kriegsmarine*, Signals Intelligence and the Development of *B-Dienst* before the Second World War', *Intelligence and National Security*, 25:4, pp 521–46, 2010.

Ferris, John, 'The road to Bletchley Park: The British experience with Signals Intelligence, 1892–1945', *Intelligence and National Security*, 17:1, pp 53–84, March 2002.

Folly, Martin H, 'From Sevastopol to Sukhumi – and back again: British naval liaison in action with the Red Navy in the Black Sea, 1941–1945', *War in History*, 28:4, 2021, pp 870–88.

Folly, Martin H, '"They treat us with scant respect": prejudice and pride in British Military Liaison with the Soviet Union in the Second World War', *The International History Review*, November 2021.

Franklin, G D, 'A Breakdown in Communication: Britain's Over Estimation of ASDIC's Capabilities in the 1930s', *The Mariner's Mirror*, 84:2, pp 204–14, 1998.

Franklin, G D, 'The origins of the Royal Navy's vulnerability to surfaced night U-boat attack 1939–40', *The Mariner's Mirror*, 90:1, February 2004, pp 73–84.

Golub, Grant, 'The Eagle and the Lion: Reassessing Anglo-American strategic planning and the foundations of US grand strategy for World War II', *Journal of Strategic Studies*, July 2022.

Goodman, Michael S, 'Learning to Walk: The Origins of the UK's Joint Intelligence Committee', *International Journal of Intelligence and CounterIntelligence*, 21:1, pp 40–56, 2008.

Goodman, Michael S, 'The Foundations of Anglo-American Intelligence Sharing', *Studies in Intelligence*, 59:2, June 2015.

Gorodetsky, Gabriel, 'An Alliance of Sorts: Allied Strategy in the Wake of Barbarossa', in John Erickson and David Dilks, *Barbarossa: The Axis and the Allies* (Edinburgh University Press, 1994).

Gribanov, Stanislas, 'The role of US Lend-Lease aircraft in Russia in World War II', *Journal of Slavic Military Studies*, 11:1, 1998, pp 96–115.

Grove, Eric, 'A War Fleet built for Peace: British Naval Rearmament in the 1930s and the dilemma of Deterrence versus Defence', *US Naval War College Review*, Spring 1991, Vol 44, No 2.

Grove, Eric, "The Battle of the Atlantic': A Legend Deconstructed', *Mariner's Mirror*, 105:3, August 2019, pp 336–9.

Hamilton, Charles Iain, 'The Character and Organisation of the Admiralty Operational Intelligence Centre during the Second World War', *War in History*, Vol 7, No 3, 2000, pp 295–324.

Hammond, Richard J, 'Air Power and the British Anti-shipping Campaign in the Mediterranean during the Second World War', *Air Power Review*, 16:1, 2013, pp 50–69.

Hammond, Richard J, 'An Enduring Influence on Imperial Defence and Grand Strategy: British Perceptions of the Italian Navy, 1935–1943', *International History Review*, 39:5, 2017, pp 810–835.

Harrison, E D R, 'British Radio Security and Intelligence, 1939–43', *The English Historical Review*, Vol 124, No 506, February 2009, pp 53–93.

Harrison, Mark, 'The Soviet Economy and Relations with the USA and Britain', in *The Rise and Fall of the Grand Alliance, 1941–1945*, edited by Howard Temperley and Ann Lane, London and Basingstoke, Macmillan, 1995.

Harrison, Mark, 'The Soviet Defence Industry Complex in World War II', in *World War II and the Transformation of Business Systems*, pp 237–62, edited by Jun Sakudo and Takao Shiba (Tokyo: University of Tokyo Press, 1994).

Harrison, Mark, 'The USSR and Total War: Why Didn't the Soviet Economy Collapse in 1942', in *A World at Total War: Global Conflict and the Politics of Total Destruction*,

*1939–1945*', pp 137–56, edited by Roger Chickering, Stig Forster, and Bernd Greiner (Cambridge University Press, 2005).

Harrison, Mark, 'Economic Warfare and the battlefield on the Eastern Front, 1941–1945', draft chapter for Festschrift in honour of Hein Klemann, Department of Economics, University of Warwick, 2024.

Herman, Michael, 'What Difference Did It Make?', *Intelligence and National Security*, 26:6, pp 886–901, 2011.

Hill, Alexander, 'The Allocation of Allied "Lend-Lease" Aid to the Soviet Union arriving with Convoy PQ 12, March 1942 – A State Defense Committee Decree', *Journal of Slavic Military Studies*: 19:4, 2006, pp 727–38.

Hill, Alexander, 'British Lend-Lease Aid and the Soviet War Effort, June 1941–June 1942', *Journal of Military History*, 71:3, July 2007, pp 773–808.

Hill, Alexander, 'British Lend-Lease Tanks and the Battle of Moscow, November–December 1941 – Revisited', *Journal of Slavic Military Studies*, 22:4, 2009, pp 574–87.

Hill, Alexander, and Stahel, David, 'British "Lend-Lease" aid to the USSR and the Battle of Moscow in the Light of Soviet and German Sources', *Journal of Slavic Military Studies*, 34:4, 2021, pp 537–57.

Hinsley, F H, 'British Intelligence in the Second World War: An Overview', *Cryptologia*, 14:1, 1990, pp 1–10.

Hinsley, F H, 'The Influence of ULTRA in the Second World War', University of Cambridge Lecture, 19 October 1993.

Hinsley, F H, 'British Intelligence and Barbarossa', in John Erickson and David Dilks, *Barbarossa: The Axis and the Allies* (Edinburgh University Press, 1994).

Houghton, Frances, 'The Trial of Convoy PQ 17 and the Royal Navy in Post-War British Cultural Memory', *Twentieth Century British History*, 31:2, June 2020, pp 197–219.

Kohnen, David, 'Seizing German Naval Intelligence from the Archives 1870–1945', *Global War Studies*: 12:1, 2015, pp 133–171.

Lambert, Andrew, 'Seizing the Initiative: The Arctic Convoys, 1944–45', in *Naval Power in the Twentieth Century*, edited by N A M Rodger (Basingstoke: Palgrave Macmillan, 1996), pp 151–62.

Leutze, James, 'The Secret of the Churchill–Roosevelt Correspondence: September 1939–May 1940', *Journal of Contemporary History*, 10:3, July 1975, pp 465–91.

Levy, James, 'The Needs of Political Policy versus the Reality of Military Operations: Royal Navy Opposition to the Arctic Convoys, 1942', *Journal of Strategic Studies*, 26:1, 2003, pp 36–52.

Levy, James, 'Royal Navy Fleet Tactics on the Eve of the Second World War', *War in History*, 19:3, 2012, pp 379–95.

Lovelace, Alexander G, 'Amnesia: How Russian History has viewed Lend-Lease', *Journal of Slavic Military Studies*, 27:4, 2014, pp 591–605.

Ljunggren, Bengt, 'The Sleepy Sea Lord who was Churchill's Friend', *Surgical Neurology*, 18:5, November 1982.

Lytton, Avram, 'In the House of Rimmon: British Aid to the Soviet Union, June–September 1941, *Journal of Slavic Military Studies*, 26:4, 2013, pp 673–704.

Maiolo, Joseph, "'I believe the Hun is cheating": British admiralty technical intelligence and the German Navy, 1936–39', *Intelligence and National Security*, 11:1, pp 32–58, 1996.

Maiolo, Joseph, 'Anglo-Soviet Naval Armaments Diplomacy before the Second World War', *The English Historical Review*, 123:501, pp 351–78, 2008.

Maiolo, Joseph A, 'Did the Royal Navy decline between the two World Wars?', *The RUSI Journal*, Vol 159, No 4; p 18–24; August/September 2014.

Mastny, Vojtech, 'Stalin and the Prospects of a Separate Peace in World War II', *The American Historical Review*, 77:5, December 1972, pp 1365–88.

Neilson, Keith, '"Pursued by a Bear": British Estimates of Soviet Military Strength and Anglo-Soviet Relations, 1922–1939', *Canadian Journal of History*, XXVIII:2, August 1993, pp 189–222.

O'Hara, Vincent P, and Cernuschi, Enrico, 'Frogmen against a Fleet: The Italian Attack on Alexandria 18/19 December 1941', *US Naval War College Review*, 68:3, Summer 2015.

Perkins, John, 'Coins for Conflict: Nickel and the Axis, 1933–1945', *Historian*, 55:1, September 1992, pp 85–100.
Rahn, Werner, 'German Naval Strategy and Armament, 1919–39', in *Technology and Naval Combat in the Twentieth Century and Beyond*, edited by Phillips Payson O'Brien (London: Routledge, 2007).
Redgment, P G, 'High-Frequency Direction Finding in the Royal Navy – Development of Anti-U-Boat Equipment, 1941–45', in *The Applications of Radar and other Electronic Systems in the Royal Navy in World War 2*, edited by F A Kingsley (Palgrave Macmillan, 1995).
Roberts, Mervyn, 'Operation Countenance: The 1941 Invasion of Iran and the Clash of Propaganda Narratives', *Iranian Studies*, 52:3–4, 2019, pp 589–610.
Roblin, Sebastien, 'To Russia with Love: The British Valentine Tank in the Red Army', *Angry Planet*, 19 March 2020.
Robson, Maria, 'Signals in the sea: the value of Ultra intelligence in the Mediterranean in World War II, *Journal of Intelligence History*, 13:2, pp 176–88, 2014.
Rodger, N A M, 'The Royal Navy in the Era of the World Wars: Was it fit for purpose?', *The Mariner's Mirror*, 97:1, February 2011, p 272–84.
Sadkovich, James J, 'Understanding Defeat: Reappraising Italy's Role in World War II', *Journal of Contemporary History*, Vol 24, No 1, January 1989, pp 27–61.
Simpson, Michael, 'Force H and British Strategy in the Western Mediterranean 1939–42', *The Mariner's Mirror*, 83:1, 1997, p 62–75.
Sokolov, Boris, 'The role of Lend-Lease in Soviet military efforts, 1941–45', *Journal of Slavic Military Studies*, 7:3, 1994, pp 567–86.
Stadius, Peter, 'Petsamo: Bringing Modernity to Finland's Arctic Ocean Shore 1920–1939', *Acta Borealis*, 2016.
Stille, Mark E, 'The Influence of British Operational Intelligence on the War at Sea in the Mediterranean June 1940 – November 1942', *Naval War College* paper, 1994.
Sumida, Jon Tetsuro, "The Best Laid Plans': The Development of British Battlefleet Tactics, 1919–1942', *The International History Review*, 14:4, pp 681–700, 1992.
Sumida, Jon Tetsuro, 'British Naval Procurement and Technological Change, 1919–1939', in *Technology and Naval Combat in the Twentieth Century and Beyond*, edited by Phillips Payson O'Brien (London: Routledge, 2007).
Suprun, Mikhail N, 'Strength and Weakness of Totalitarianism in Wartime Soviet Union', *Septentrio Conference Series*, 2015 (4), pp 1–15.
Suprun, Mikhail N, 'Lend-Lease and the Northern Convoys in the Allied Strategy during the Second World War', *Journal of Slavic Military Studies*, 32:4, 2019, pp 574–80.
Syrett, David, 'The Last Murmansk Convoys, 11 March–30 May 1945', *The Northern Mariner*, 4:1, January 1994, pp 55–63.
Syrett, David, 'On the Threshold of Victory: Communications Intelligence and the Battle for Convoy HX-228, 7–12 March 1943', *The Northern Mariner*, No 3, July 2000, pp 49–55.
Tooze, Adam, 'Quantifying Armaments Production in the Third Reich 1933–1945', unpublished paper, www.adamtooze.com, June 2006.
Ulving, Lars, and Weierud, Frode, 'The Geheimschreiber Secret: Arne Beurling and the Success of Swedish Signals Intelligence', originally published as 'Geheimschreiberns hemlighet, Arne Beurling och den Svenska signalspaningens framgangar', in '*I Orkanens Oga, 1941 - Osaker neutralitet*', edited by Bo Hugemark (Stockholm: Probus Forlag, 1992).
Vego, Milan, 'Major Convoy Operation to Malta, 10–15 August 1942 (Operation Pedestal)', *US Naval War College Review*, Winter 2010, 63:1.
Vego, Milan, 'The Destruction of Convoy PQ 17, 27 June–10 July 1942', *US Naval War College Review*, Summer 2016, 69:3.
Waddington, Geoffrey T, 'Ribbentrop and the Soviet Union 1937–1941', in *Barbarossa: The Axis and the Allies*, edited by John Erickson and David Dilks (Edinburgh University Press, 1998).
Welbourn, Donald B, and Crichton, Tim, 'The Schnorchel: A Short-Lived Engineering Solution to Scientific Developments', *Transactions of the Newcomen Society*, 78:2, pp 293–315, 2008.

Wilton, George, 'The Royal Fleet Auxiliary and Post-War Change', *British Journal for Military History*, 8:3, November 2022.

*Unpublished theses and papers*

Austin, Douglas, 'The Place of Malta in British Strategic Policy 1925–1943' (unpublished doctoral thesis, University of London, November 2001).

De Ninno, Fabio, 'The Mediterranean Battle of the Convoys: Some revaluations', published 2021 on www.academia.edu.

Fancher, James Reagan, 'The Arsenal of the Red Warriors: US Perceptions of Stalin's Red Army and the Impact of Lend-Lease Aid on the Eastern Front in the Second World War' (unpublished doctoral thesis, University of Texas, May 2023).

Herrington, Ian, 'The Special Operations Executive in Norway 1940–1945: Policy and Operations in the Strategic and Political Context' (unpublished doctoral thesis, De Montfort University, Leicester, June 2004).

Jones, Ben, 'Ashore, Afloat and Airborne: The Logistics of British Naval Air Power, 1914–1945' (unpublished doctoral thesis, King's College, University of London, 2007).

Levy, James, 'Holding the Line: The Royal Navy's Home Fleet in the Second World War' (unpublished doctoral thesis, University of Wales, 2001).

Maiolo, Joseph A, 'Admiralty War Planning, Armaments, Diplomacy, and Intelligence Perceptions of German Sea Power and their influence on British Foreign and Defence Policy 1933–1939' (unpublished doctoral thesis, Department of International History, London School of Economics and Political Science, 1996).

Mann, Matthew, Christopher, 'British Policy and Strategy towards Norway, 1941–1944' (unpublished doctoral thesis, King's College, University of London, 1998).

Millar, Russell D, 'The Development of Anglo-American Naval Strategy in the Period of the Second World War, 1938–1941' (unpublished doctoral thesis, King's College, University of London, 1988).

Ryan, Joseph Francis, 'The Royal Navy and Soviet Seapower, 1930–1950: Intelligence, Naval Cooperation and Antagonism' (unpublished doctoral thesis, University of Hull, 1996).

Thornhill, Paula G, 'Catalyst for Coalition: The Anglo-American Supply Relationship 1939–1941' (unpublished doctoral thesis, University of Oxford, 1991).

Weir, Philip Anthony, 'The Development of Naval Air Warfare by the Royal Navy and Fleet Air Arm between the two World Wars' (unpublished doctoral thesis, University of Exeter, 2006).

*Websites*

The following have provided valuable information and in some cases access to primary documents. Where appropriate they are referenced in the footnotes.

forum.axishistory.com. Forum primarily devoted to the military operations and capabilities of the Axis states but much Allied material too. Covers all major war theatres.

www.armouredcarriers.com. Website devoted to the Fleet Air Arm armoured carriers, their aircraft and operations in the Second World War.

www.britishempireatwar.org. Forum for scholars interested in all aspects of the British Empire's war history.

www.cryptocellar.org. Managed by Frode Weierud. Contains much historical material on twentieth century cryptography but primarily the Second World War.

www.ellsbury.com. Contains much historical background on Enigma including the full texts of: Hugh Alexander, 'Cryptographic History of Work on the German Naval Enigma'; and, A P Mahon, 'History of Hut Eight'.

www.fleetairarmarchive.net. Excellent source of material on the Fleet Air Arm.

www.history.army.mil. Website for the US Army Centre of Military History. Contains a range of US Army publications and some documents in digital form relevant to the Second World War. Includes a full digital collection of the US Army's Official History of the Second World War.

www.ibiblio.org/hyperwar. Contains a useful selection of digitised original political, military and diplomatic documents relating to the Second World War. Includes some digitised official histories including volumes from the British Official History series.

www.intellit.muskingum.edu. Edited by J Ransom Clark, this is an excellent bibliography of published works on intelligence history.

www.Lend-Lease.net. Site primarily devoted to Allied Lend-Lease supplies to the USSR. Covers deliveries, deployment and Soviet views on performance and value.

www.measuringworth.com. Contains useful statistical data on the UK and US economies from 1800.

www.milspecmanuals.com. Contains a large range of digitised military and intelligence documents relating to the Second World War. The emphasis is primarily on American sources. Especially useful for sourcing Japanese Monographs and similar material. Includes a good searchable database.

www.naval-history.net. Provides a substantial collection of digitised original documents and naval history books across the whole twentieth century.

www.navweaps.com. Primarily focused on naval technology and weapons but also has order of battle and other material on key engagements. Useful papers on specific technical topics and weaponry of all types, including e.g. armoured flight decks and the Royal Navy High Altitude Control System (HACS) for anti-aircraft defence.

www.navypedia.org. Reference site providing construction data and basic order of battle of the main naval powers in the twentieth century.

www.nsa.gov/about/cryptologic_heritage/center_crypt. The historical section in the US National Security Agency website. Contains publications relating to the Second World War which can be downloaded in pdf format.

www.rnsubmusfriends.org.uk. Useful source of submarine material including a digital version of Vice Admiral Sir Arthur Hezlet's history *British and Allied Submarine Operations in World War II*.

www.royalnavyresearcharchive.org.uk. Virtual museum containing information relating to Royal Navy ships, establishments, units and personnel across the twentieth century. Five subsidiary sites including one on escort carriers.

www.secretintelligencefiles.com. Provides details of British government secret intelligence and foreign policy files, mainly sourced from the National Archives, from 1873 to 1953 with the majority in the 1930s and 1940s.

www.tankarchives.blogspot.com. Excellent source on Western tank supplies to the Soviet Union often drawing on rare Soviet sources.

www.uboat.net. Website dedicated primarily to U-boat operations in both World Wars but covers Allied boats too. Includes specifications, individual boat histories and causes of loss.

www.underwatertrust.org.uk. Excellent source on midget submarines and Chariots.

www.unithistories.com. Database providing a breakdown of individual units and biographical details of key individuals involved in the Second World War. Useful for checking appointments held by Royal Navy officers.

www.usnwcarchives.org. US Navy War college archives site records holdings and has important items in digital form, notably some war diaries for German Naval Staff Operations Division and Captain U-boats Norway.

www.vvsairwar.com. Excellent source for aircraft types, both Soviet and Western, deployed in the Soviet air force in World War II.

www.worldnavalships.com/forums. Searchable database and vast series of blogs covering every aspect of naval capabilities and operations in the Second World War.

www.ww2db.com. Database with useful reference material relating to the Second World War including copies of original documents.

# Index

2nd Air Fleet (Ge), 54, 156, 182
5th Air Fleet (Ge), 102, 128, 198–9, 210–12, 241–3, 250, 267–8, 270, 283–4, 290, 305–6, 308–9, 337, 351, 353, 355, 446–7
6th Air Defence Corps (Sov), 170–3
8th German Destroyer Flotilla, 150, 188, 196–7, 214, 221, 227, 249
10th Submarine Flotilla (Br), 51
30 Mission, 97–9, 106, 110–11, 113, 155, 174, 176, 233, 273, 407, 436

A-54, Czech agent, 94
Abadan, 129–30, 323, 477
ABC–1 staff talks, 5, 16, 22, 26, 28–9, 31–2, 34, 135, 160, 225
Abwehr, German military intelligence, 244–6, 283
*Achates* (Br) destroyer, 375, 379, 381, 383, 386
Admiralty, Western Atlantic escort savings 19, 1941 priorities 56–8, Fleet Air Arm 60, 62–4, Coastal Command 67, operational research 69, radar 71, 73, intelligence 74, fleet mobility 77, strategic reorientation end 1941 79, initially dismisses Arctic theatre but forced to reconsider 100, Murmansk 145, Arctic route challenges 147, *Tirpitz* sortie 202, 206, 208, Western Approaches support 215, convoy limits 222–3, 230–1, PQ 17 planning 271–6, intelligence developments and subsequent action 286–91, 298, impact of scatter order and lack of contingency planning 300–1, 304, reaction and accounting 310–11, 326–8, post PQ 17 suspension 321, 362, 365–6, winter 1942 series planning 370–1, future of German heavy ships 399, 412, March 1943 convoy suspension 409–10, Altafiord attack planning and Source 428, 433, autumn 1943 convoy resumption 437, *Scharnhorst* 450, post-Tungsten strikes on *Tirpitz* 468–9

*Admiral Scheer* (Ge) pocket battleship, 57, deployment to Trondheim 189, 196, 200, Narvik 238–41, 249, HX84 277, Rösselsprung 283, 286, 289, 293, 307, 309, Wunderland 339–40, PQ 18/QP 14 347, return to Germany 351, 119
Agnew, Captain William, 53–6, 390
Air to Surface Vessel (ASV) search radar, 5, 51, 53, 62, 68–71, 207, 447, 462, 465
Ajax, Autumn 1941 Trondheim attack plan 134, 185–6, 257
Albacore (Br) FAA TSR aircraft, 51, 62, 68–9, Petsamo 122–6, *Tirpitz* 207–8, Pedestal 342, 467
*Aldersdale* (Br) tanker, 272, 290, 305, 329
*Alexander Sibiryakov* (Sov) icebreaker, 339
Allen, Captain Gordon, Deputy Director Trade, 288
Allied Supplies Executive (ASE), 152–3, 155, 320–1, 471
Altafiord, Germans identify potential 244, 248–9, Rösselsprung 265, 268–9, Denham intelligence 270–1, British dispositions 273, 281, German deployment and implications 283–91, *Tirpitz* arrival 293–7, 300–1, Rösselsprung execution 305–9, PQ 17 aftermath 312, Hampden sortie 337, 352, PQ 18/QP 14 347–8, 351–3, QP 15 366, JW 51A 371–2, Regenbogen 373–80, 392, new Northern Task Force base 398–9, 409–10, 419, Source 422, 427–9, 431–5, Zitronella 430–1, *Scharnhorst* 441–2, 446, 449–51, 455–6, 458, Tungsten 466–7
Aluminium, Stalin emphasis and Soviet requests 25, 36, 100, 143, 167, 360, initial British supplies 36–7, 135, 143, 152, Soviet lost capacity 138, 141, Soviet production and Western contribution 1942–3 177–81, 183, 361, 492, First Protocol deliveries 357–8, losses 494
Ambrose, Commander Geoffrey, 112, 235

Anglo-American 1941 Moscow Agreement, 25–6, 139–42, 152, 166
Anglo-Soviet 1941 Agreement, 23
Anklet, British raid on Norway December 1941, 6, 186–8, 232, 245
*Anson* (Br) battleship, 58, 338, 375, 404, 467
Anti-aircraft ship, 50, 224, 240, 243, 261, 272, 274, 302, 353, 357
Arcadia, British–American summit in Washington January 1942, 6, 32, 85, 159–61, 165, 184–5, 254, 315, 318, 401, 488
Archangel, 8, 23, 37, 40, 98, 109, 112–15, 117, rail links 120–2, 127, 141, capacity 144–6, 164, Dervish 168, 174, 177, 211, 233, PQ 16 240, 243, 259, PQ 17 278, 299, 302, 304, 312, Wunderland 339–40, QP 14 353, independents 363, QP 15 365, British radio transmitters 407, RA 54A 441
Archery, British raid on Norway December 1941, 6, 187–8, 232, 245
Argonaut, British-American Summit in Washington June 1942, 314, 316–17, 401
*Argus* (Br) light carrier, 114–15, 125, 168, 260
*Ark Royal* (Br) fleet carrier, 39, 44–49, 51, 63–4, 70, 72, 78–9, 260, 343
Arnold, General Harold H (Hap), Chief of US Army Air Corps, 28, 32
Atlantic Charter, 18, 28, 33
Atlantic Convoy Instructions, 56. 277
Attlee, Clement, Deputy Prime Minister, 154, 229, 330, 459
*Audacity* (Br) escort carrier, 64–5, 70, 78, 336
Aurore, proposed *Lützow* North Atlantic raiding cruise January 1943, 6, 374, 380, 388, 399
Auto Barrage Unit (ABU), 50
*Avenger* (Br) escort carrier, 336–7, 342–3, 347, 349–51, 354–5, 405, 462
Avenger (Br) FAA TSR aircraft, 462, 464
Axis powers, 27, 30, 32–5, 39, 42, 45, 51–2, 54, 60, 74, 77, 85, 162, 235, 254, 320, 341, 343, 356, 364, 366, 368, 424, 495
Axis Tripartite Pact, 85
*Ayrshire* (Br) ASW trawler, 326

Bacon, Lieutenant Allon, 188
Bagration, Russian June 1944 offensive 6, 475–6
Banak, German airbase, 102, 211, 243, 248, 258, 286, 290
Barbarossa, German invasion of Russia 1941, 2, 6, 8, 10, genesis 80–2, alternatives 83–8, British intelligence on 88–92, implications 92–4, UK/US response to Eastern war 94–9, attack falters 106, Arctic element 115–18, German losses 132, 150, 156, 159
Bardufoss, 211–12, 238, 482
Barents Sea, Battle of the, 9, 380–8, 461, 499

Barracuda Enigma cipher key, 281
Barracuda (Br) FAA TSR aircraft, 62–3, 208, 467–8
Barrage fire, 47, 50, 483
Barry, Rear Admiral Claude, Admiral Submarines from 1943, 431
Bathythermograph effects, 465
Bear Island, location/status 105, British contemplate occupation 108, August 1941 landing 128, potential German threat March 1942 212
Beaufighter (Br) long-range fighter, 44, 51, 187, 261, 343, 419, 483
Beaufort (Br) torpedo bomber, 68, 262, 273, 337, 342
Beaverbrook, Lord Max, Minister of War Production, background and qualities 24–5, Riviera 27, Victory programme 135–6, Moscow supply conference 139–42, 157, ASE chair 152–4, motives for supporting Russia 154, 159, Ultra 155, replaced by Lyttleton 217
B-Dienst, German naval SIGINT division, 282–4, 307, 376, 387, 447–8, 451, 453
*Belfast* (Br) cruiser, 2, 444, 454, 467
Belomorsk, 117, 120–1
Benedict, British air defence of Murmansk, 168–9
Beria, Lavrentiy, Russian Minister of State Security, 155,
Beta convoy, 51–6, 69, 77, 277, 300, 390
Beurling, Arne, Swedish cryptographer, 270
Bevan, Rear Admiral Richard, SBNO North Russia, 112–13, 307
Bevin, Ernest, Minister of Labour, on Beaverbrook 24, 154, Russian aid 229
Bey, Rear Admiral Erich, 443, 445–6, 448–58
*Bismarck* (Ge) battleship, 18, 61–2, 70–2, 75, 77–8, 111, 189, 200
Björnstjerna, Colonel Carl, Chief Foreign Section of Swedish military intelligence, 269–71, 281, 372
Blackett, Professor Patrick, Admiralty Scientific Adviser, 69
Bletchley Park, GC&CS HQ, 12, 41, 74, 121, 151, 188, 206, PQ 17 281–2, 292, 294, 307, 309, 348, 355, 363, 366, 378, 392, damage to *Hipper* 399, 407, Cairncross 422, Zitronella 430, *Scharnhorst* 450
Blue, German southern offensive in Russia summer 1942, 6, 84, 159, 210–11, 250, 255, 278, 312, 325, 359–61, 401, 412
Bodø, 126, 186
Boehm, General Admiral Hermann, 150, 188, 192, 198
Bogen Bay, Ofotfjord, 207, 270–1, 283, 352, 372, 397–8

## INDEX

Bolero, US forces build-up in Britain, 6, 219, 223, 253, 311, 314–16
Bonham-Carter, Rear Admiral Stuart, 221–2, 226, 228–9, 231–2
Bortnowski, Colonel Leon (Perch), Polish intelligence representative Moscow 1941–2, 107
Bovell, Captain Henry, 207–8
*Bramble* (Br) minesweeper, 375, 380, 383, 388
Brauchitsch, Field Marshal Walther von, German Army Commander-in-Chief, 82–4, 118
*Bremse* (Ge) escort destroyer, 128
Brind, Rear Admiral Patrick, Assistant Chief of Naval Staff (Home), 289, 292–4, 297, 299, 301, 326, 365, 370
British Broadcasting Corporation (BBC), 96
Brivonesi, Rear Admiral Bruno, 52–3
Brooke, Field Marshal Sir Alan, Chief of the Imperial General Staff, on Beaverbrook 24, 141, 153, 'deception' and Ajax 134, as CIGS on Russia 153, 161, 184, 216, 230, Gymnast reservations 316, dismisses separate peace 369, 1943 German offensive 420–1, 'Unthinkable' 478, British 'softness' 491
Broome, Commander Jack, appointed to PQ 17 close escort and background 272, 274, 286, 288, air attacks evening 4 July 290–1, 298–300, response to scatter order 301–5, 309, aftermath 326–9, libel trial 331–4, PQ 18 338, Pedestal 341
*Brown Ranger* (Br) tanker, 45, 77
Bundy, Colonel Charles, US Army War Plans, 27, 30, 135
Burnett, Rear Admiral Robert, background and character 335–6, PQ 18 336, 342, 347, 353–4, Battle of the Barents Sea 371, 375–6, 378–80, 384, 386–8, JW 53 405, Golovko 443, *Scharnhorst* 445, 447–8, 450–8, 463
Burrough, Rear Admiral Harold, Halberd 48, Golovko 108–9, Anklet 187, 231, PQ 16 240, 242–3

Cadogan, Sir Alexander, Permanent Under-Secretary Foreign Office, Riviera 28, Stalin initial message 36, Barbarossa progress 106, Beaverbrook 141, Brooke 216, handling Stalin 411, 440
Cairncross, Captain John, NKVD agent, 422
Carls, General Admiral Rolf, 189, Rösselsprung 266–7, 306–8, Regenbogen 373–4, 389, Raeder succession 395, retirement 398
Casablanca summit, 27, 370, 399, 401–5, 408, 488–90, 495, 497
Catapult Aircraft Merchant (CAM) Ship, 224, 241–3, 247, 291

Caucasus oil fields, 83, 364
Central Interpretation Unit (CIU) Medmenham, 74
Cerberus, German Channel breakout, 6, 191–7, 221, 238, 295, 300, 389, 394
Chariot human torpedo (also Italian Siluro a Lenta Corsa), 424–6
*Chaser* (Br) escort carrier, 462–3
Cherbourg peninsula, 133, 218
*Chester Valley*, merchant vessel, 380, 384
Churchill, Prime Minister Winston, 10, Riviera 14–20, 23–5, 27–8, initial aid to Russia 36–7, 135–7, Barbarossa intelligence 88–9, and response 94, 96–7, 104, presses Ultra release 106, and naval support 114, 126, Iran 129, 131, Ajax 134, 185, Moscow supply conference 141–2, First Protocol and Beaverbrook 153–4, Moscow threat 155, Western aid for 'wear down' 159, Arcadia 161, Tovey 186, 188, 232–3, *Tirpitz* escape 207, centrality of Russia's role 217–18, PQ convoy capacity and risks spring 1942 223, raised with Stalin 233–5, 237–8, political concessions to Russia 251, Molotov visit 252–4, Eastern Front prospects mid-1942 256–7, Jupiter 257–9, Americans in PQ 17 escort 297, PQ 17 aftermath 313–14, 326–7, 330, lobbies Roosevelt on Torch 314–17, agrees American take-over of Iran route 322–3, August 1942 visit to Moscow 344–6, Torch driven suspension of convoys and impact on Stalin 362–4, resumption in December 364–70, Casablanca 402–3, Anglo-Soviet relations early 1943 406–7, 410, March suspension 411–12, presses to resume JW convoys autumn 1943 436–7, amidst further rows with Russia 439–40, success of winter 1943/44 convoy programme 470, Teheran 472–3, post Overlord convoys 475, 477–8, 'Unthinkable' 478, rationale for Arctic programme 488, 490–1
Churchill tank, 173, 175, 404, 415–17, 436
Ciliax, Vice Admiral Otto, views on Norway 194, 196, PQ 12 200–3, 206, 209, 238, 246, suggests Altafiord as base 249, 265
Citadel, underground Admiralty headquarters, 74, 282
Citadel, German offensive 1943, 6, 421–2, 472, 489
Clark Kerr, Sir Archibald, British ambassador to Russia 1942–5, 164, Churchill/Stalin meeting 345, 368, 406, 408, 436, 439
Claymore, March 1941 British raid on Norway, 186, 188
Clayton, Rear Admiral Jock, Head of OIC, 292, 296–7, 299–301

Coastal Command, 23, 67–9, 273, 281, 408, 419, 433, 447
Coke, Lieutenant Commander Charles, 72
Colthurst, Commander Anthony, captain of *Avenger* during PQ 18, 337, 350–1
Creasey, Captain George, Director of Anti-submarine Warfare 1941, 71
Crimea, 235, 252, 474
Cripps, Sir Stafford, British ambassador to Russia 1941–2, 37, 88–9, 92–3, 98–101, 104, 105, 107, 111, 130, 136–7, 141, 229
Crusader, British November 1941 North Africa offensive, 52, 54, 152
Cunningham, Admiral of the Fleet Sir Andrew, C-in-C Mediterranean 1939–43 then First Sea Lord, 29, Halberd 40–1, 43, 49, 52, Vian 108, replacing Tovey 232–3, 262, 277, Burnett 336, Roosevelt 346, destroyer training 390, Fraser 418, 459, escort carriers 462, *Tirpitz* 468
Curteis, Vice Admiral Albyn Thomas, Halberd 39, 45, 48, PQ 13 213, Harpoon 260–1

Dalton, Hugh, Minister of Economic Warfare, 99
Davidson, Major General Francis, Director of Military Intelligence, 155
Defence Committee, 28, 94–5, 100, 103, Spitzbergen 114, 127, Iran 129, 131, Moscow supply directive 139, Beaverbrook demands 155, Pound on air resources 216, Sledgehammer 220, Lyttleton review 229–31, 256, 262, cancels July 1942 convoy 311, 313, 343, November 1942 strategy 364–5, 367, 370, problems in Northern ports 406–7, suspends JW 54 409–10, 420, 437–8, 441, 459, 469
Defence Plan No 4, 19
Denham, Captain Henry, Stockholm naval attaché, Björnstjerna 269–71, Rösselsprung 276, 279, 281, 283, 285, 287–8, 291, 294, 297, PQ 18 335, 338, Wunderland 339, *Tirpitz* 352, 372, *Hipper* damage 399, Tungsten 428
Denning, Commander Norman (Ned), PQ 17 289, 292–301, 309, future of German heavy ships 400, 443, 497
Denning, Lord Tom, Master of the Rolls, 331–3
Dervish, initial Arctic convoy August 1941, 6, 26, 36, 114–15, 125–6, 143, 164, 168–9, 182, 239, 356, 471, 491
Destroyers for Bases Agreement 1940, 14, 58, 86
Dieppe raid August 1942, 96, 325
Dietl, Lieutenant General Eduard, 116, 118–19
Dill, General Sir John, 29, 97–8, 102, 134, 155, 161

Director of Military Intelligence (DMI), 155
Director of Naval Intelligence (DNI), 42, 110, 332
*Dithmarschen*, German supply ship, 249, 271
'Dog', US National Security Plan proposed by Admiral Stark November 1940, 29, 315
Dolphin Enigma cipher key, 73, 121, 151, 188, 196, 214, 279, 281, 290, 292, 295–6, 307, 309, 338–40, 352, 372, 399–400, 480
*Donbass* (Sov) tanker, 364
Dönitz, Grand Admiral Karl, Admiral commanding U-boats and from 1943 Chief of German Naval Staff, 2, 21–2, 65, 78, U-boats ineffective against Norway raids 188–9, resists build-up of Arctic force 198, presses redeployment 239, scathing assessment of PQ 16 operations 247–8, PQ 18 349, diverts boats to Atlantic late 1942 371–2, succeeds Raeder 395, future of heavy ships 396–7, changes senior personnel 398, risk management 398, Zitronella 429–30, *Tirpitz* damage 434, 468, *Scharnhorst* sortie 441–2, 446–50, 453, 455–6, 458, increases Arctic U-boat force early 1944 460
Donovan, William J, Presidential envoy and then Head OSS, 16
Double Cross network, 245–7, 275
Dowding, John, PQ 17 Convoy Commodore, 302–3, 305, 353
Drontheim, see Trondheim
Duff, Lieutenant Anthony, 432
*Duke of York* (Br) battleship, 58, 70, 159, 201, 226, 240, 272, 338, 443, 448, 450, 453, 456–7, 467
Dykes, Brigadier Vivian Dumbie, War Office Director of Plans, 27

Eccles, Captain John, Director of Operations (Home), 292–4, 297, 299, 301, 304
Eden, Sir Anthony, British Foreign Secretary, 36, Barbarossa warning 90, 93–4, despatch of Military Mission 98, Golikov visit 101, Iran 130–1, separate peace threat 137, underlines support for Russia 142, Beaverbrook 153, December 1941 Moscow visit 157, 190, 'wear down' 159, consequences of post PQ 17 suspension 311, 313, as ASE chair presses winter 1942 convoys 320–1, 365, 367, 370, Hampden crisis 407, March 1943 convoy suspension 410, October 1943 Moscow meeting 439–40
*Edinburgh* (Br) light cruiser, 39, 46, 48, 221, 224, 226–9, 231, 234, 239, 261, 371, 376, 443
Escort carrier, genesis and development 64–6, first Arctic deployment 336, availability

autumn 1942 343, preferred Arctic allocation 405
Falkenhorst, Colonel General Paul von, commander German Army Norway, 116, 119, 186
Fawkes, Captain Barney, 112
Faymonville, Colonel Raymond, US Lend-Lease representative, 92
Fighter Direction, 47, 49, 61–2, 70, 72, 464
Fighting Instructions 1939, 55–6, 277, 390, 499
Finland, Barbarossa planning 81–2, German/Soviet 1940 negotiations 85–6, Petsamo 100–2, negotiations with Germany early 1941 115–17, participation in Arctic operations 119–20, 153, 185, 189, 191–2, 233, 258, withdrawal from war 480
Firebrace, Lieutenant Colonel, later Brigadier, Roy, 97–9,
First Protocol, 140, 142, basic composition 143, transport options 144–7, delays 151–2, consequences of delays 162–7, Russian priorities 167, lack of cost/benefit 184, importance before German summer offensive 230, overall performance/impact 356–61
Fisher, Rear Admiral Douglas, SBNO North Russia, 307, 326, 459
Fleet Air Arm (FAA), 51, creation and development 60–3, 65–9, 71–2, Petsamo 116, 121–2, 124, 169, 498, 1943 new aircraft 208, fighter limitations 258, relative ASW effectiveness 462, Tungsten 466, 468, 499
Fleming, Lieutenant Commander Ian, 42
Fliegerkorps II, 54
Fliegerkorps X, 42, 54
Force H, 39–41, 45–7, 49, 72, 78, 225
Force K, 52–6, 77–8, 151, 300
Ford, Wilbraham, Vice Admiral Malta, 53
Foreign Armies East, German Eastern Front intelligence, 177, 211, 395, 413, 417, 445
Foreign Office, 89, 94, 97, 99, 132, 222
Fourth Protocol, 477, 490, 497
Franco, Spanish leader General Francisco, 83
Fraser, Admiral Sir Bruce, C-in-C Home Fleet 1943–4, 2 i/c Home Fleet 338, 404, appointed C-in-C and background/character 418, reviews resumption of JW convoys 419–20, Zitronella 431, Source 433, autumn 1943 JW series 438, *Scharnhorst* 441–4, 448, 450–1, 453–7, Churchill prefers as First Sea Lord 459, disputes Horton on U-boat priority 465, Tungsten 466–7, resists Cunningham on follow-up strikes 468
Fricke, Admiral Kurt, Chief of Staff, German Naval War Staff, 377, 389, 398
*Friedrich Eckholdt* (Ge) destroyer, 388

Frodesley, mini-submersible operation, 424–5
Führer Directives: No 38 54; No 18 83; No 32 84; No 21 86–7; No 37 119, 195; No 41 210; No 51 442, 461
Fulmar (Br) FAA fighter, 39, 44, 47–9, 61–2, 122–4, 260, 342–3, 483
*Furious* (Br) fleet carrier, 121–3, 371, 419, 467
Future Operational Planning Section (FOPS), 245–6
Fw 200 Condor (Ge), 64, 200, 202, 206, 211, 224, 296, 339

G7es (T5) *Zaunkönig* acoustic homing torpedo (also Gnat), 460–5, 481–2, 484
Geheimschreiber (Fish), German teleprinter cipher, 270
Gehlen, Colonel Reinhard, Head of Foreign Armies East Intelligence, 211, 395, 413, 417
German air force (Luftwaffe), 1, 13, 42, 64, 81, 96, 102, 113, 120, 122, 129, 150, 156, 158, 182, 187–8, 198–9, 209, 211, 218, 226, 241, 244, 258, 279, 366, 395, 430, 464, 465, 483, 498
German navy (Kriegsmarine), 9, 11, 13, 57, 73, 80, passivity 188–9, Norway redeployment 192, destroyer strength 196, oil shortage 197, air arm 199, 225, Dönitz command changes 397–8, Zitronella 429, damage to 470
Ghormley, Rear Admiral Robert, 16
Giffen, Rear Admiral Robert, 225
Glennie, Rear Admiral Irvine, 463
*Gneisenau* (Ge) battlecruiser, 57, 68, 189, 194, 201
Goebbels, Joseph, German Propaganda Minister, 22
Golden Comb (Goldene Zange), German torpedo attack concept, 350
Golikov, Lieutenant General Filipp, Head of Russian Military Intelligence (GRU), 98, 100–3, 105, 109, 118, 121, 133, 142
Golovko, Admiral Arseni, Commander Soviet Northern Fleet, 108–10, 112–13, 121, 125, 234–5, 429, 443
Gorkiy tank centre, 176, 360
Government Code and Cipher School (GC&CS), 12, Italian coverage 41–2, Dolphin 73–4, 188, Barbarossa warning 89–90, Eastern front coverage 105–7, 155, Shark 214, Wye Cottage 235, Abwehr 245, Swedish coverage 269–70, Naval Section and OIC 282, PQ 17 279, 281, 290, 292, 480
Gradwell, Lieutenant Leo, 326
*Greer* (US) destroyer, 20–1
Gross Domestic Product (GDP), 257
Group North German naval command, 188–9, 195, 197–8, PQ 12 199–200, 206,

209, 214, 227, 238, PQ 16 241–2, 244, 246, identification of Altafiord 248–9, Rösselsprung 265–8, 283–4, 289, 306–8, PQ 18 339, 347–9, 351–2, convoluted command 373, Regenbogen 376–7, 393, amalgamation with 'Fleet' 398, future of Northern Task Force March 1943 398, *Scharnhorst* 442, 446–8, 453
GRU, Russian Military Intelligence, 98
Gusev, Fedor, Soviet ambassador in London from 1943, 439
Gymnast, British–American invasion of Northwest Africa, later Torch, 6, 160, 162, 315–19

Hagelin C38m Italian cipher system, 42, 51, 60, 73
Hailsham, Lord, Lord Chancellor, 332
Halberd, Malta convoy, 6, 39–51, 56, 61, 64, 69, 216, 224, 260–1, 337, 341–3, 349, 351, 355, 483, 496
Halder, Colonel General Franz, German army Chief of General Staff 1938–42, 81–4, 88, 118–19, 177, 413
Halifax, Lord Edward, Foreign Secretary 1938–40, then British ambassador to Washington, 15
Hamilton, Rear Admiral Louis, Anklet 186–8, PQ 17 272, 274–6, 278, 282, 284–91, 292–305, 309, 325–33, JW 52 404
Hammerfest, 125, 238, 307
Hampden (Br) bomber, 187, 273, 337, 340, 343, 347, 352, 355, 406–9, 411
Hanko, 116–17
Hardboiled, British deception operation, 6, 245–6, 275
Harpoon, Mediterranean convoy, 259–61, 264–5, 274
Harriman, Averell, American presidential adviser and envoy, 25, 135–6, 139–40, 145–6, 157, 162–3, 252, 322–3, 346, 472–3, 491
Harvey, Oliver, Eden private secretary, 154
Harwood, Admiral Sir Henry, C-in-C Mediterranean in 1942, 262–3, 265, 277, 336
He 111 (Ge) bomber, 199, 211, 226, 231, 242, 290
He 115 (Ge) torpedo float plane, 199, 211, 242, 290, 366
*Henry Bacon*, merchantman, 483
*Hermann Schoemann* (Ge) destroyer, 227–8
*Hermione* (Br) cruiser, 39, 44–7, 49
High Altitude Control System (HACS), 50
High Frequency Direction Finding (HF/DF), 52, 65, 69, development 74–5, 227, 229, 404–5, 462, 464–5, 482
Hill, Colonel George, 107

Hinsley, Harry, Deputy Head GC&CS Naval Section, 292
Hintze, Captain Fritz Julius, *Scharnhorst* commander from October 1943, 445, 449, 454, 457
*Hipper* (Ge) heavy cruiser, 57, deploys to Norway 196, 213, 238, 240, Trondheim force with *Tirpitz* 265, Rösselsprung 266, 271, 286, 288–9, 307, returns to Narvik 338, redeploys to Altafiord 347–8, potential sortie against PQ 18/QP 14 351–2, independents 363, Regenbogen 374–8, 380–1, 383–4, 386–9, damage, decommissioning and return to Germany 396–7, 399
Hitler, Adolf, German Führer, 10, attitude to American intervention autumn 1941 21–3, U-boat transfers to Mediterranean 45, 51, genesis of Barbarossa 80–8, attitude to Arctic offensive 115–16, 118, 120–1, British threat to Norway 126, 128, 185, 188–90, naval reinforcement 191–3, 195–6, approves *Tirpitz* PQ 12 sortie 199 draws lessons 209–10, attitude to Blue offensive and Norway air reinforcement 210–11, Spitzbergen 212, prioritises Arctic convoys 222, fears PQ 16 heralds Norway attack 244, briefed on Rösselsprung 267, approves but with conditions 268–9, refuses *Scheer* Atlantic raid 340, action against PQ 18 352, rejects peace talks with Russia 369, reluctantly sanctions Regenbogen 377, risk appetite 388–9, 391, fury at Barents Sea outcome 392–4, scrapping of heavy ships and resignation of Raeder 394–6, Dönitz compromise 397, Citadel 421, repairs to *Tirpitz* 434, *Scharnhorst* sortie 446, 458
Home Fleet, 2, 9, 11, 41, 70, 78, 121, 125, 127, 151, 200–2, 206, 213, 217, 225, 241, 244, 247, 249, 258, 260, 272, 275, 286–7, 294–6, 298, 301, 305–6, 313, 338, 341–2, 350, 353, 355, 357, 370–1, 378, 399–400, 405, 409–10, 418–20, 430, 441, 457, 496–7
Hopkins, Harry, American presidential adviser and envoy, January 1941 visit to London 16–17, July visit to Stalin 23–5, Victory programme 26–7, 30, First Protocol deficit 161, 165–6, Marshall visit April 1942 219, Molotov visit 253, favours Gymnast 318, diversion to Iran route 322–3, Torch suspension 362–3, proposes halting Arctic deliveries at Casablanca 403, 490, 497, charge of falling under Soviet influence 490
Hopps, Group Captain Frank, 337, 352
Horton, Admiral Sir Max, C-in-C Western Approaches 1943–5, development of X-Craft as Admiral Submarines 424–6, 431, Arctic operations 464–5
Hungary, 98, 153

Hurricane (Br) fighter, 26, 36–7, 51, 61, 63, 114–15, 120, 125, 140, 146, 167–70, 172–3, 183, 200, 224, 233, 241–3, 255, 260, 291, 336, 342–3, 350–1, 361, 404, 414–16, 436, 471, 492, 495
Husky, Allied invasion of Sicily July 1943, 6, 402–3, 408–12, 418–22, 489, 495
Hvalfiord, Iceland, 240, 278, 339

Iachino, Admiral Angelo, Italian C-in-C, 46–8
Ickes, Harold, US Secretary of the Interior, 21
*Ijora* (Sov) merchant vessel, 203, 206
*Illustrious* (Br) fleet carrier, 72, 419
Imperial Japanese Navy (IJN), 56, 61, 68, 78
Ingersoll, Ralph, 107–8
Inskip Agreement of 1937, 66–8
Inter-Service Topographical Department, 466
Iran, 33, 35, 37, 128–31, 132, 158, 322
Iran supply route to Russia, 10, 13, 84, 130–1, 139, 322–4, 357–8, 363, 415, 477, 497
Ironclad, May 1942 British operation to seize Madagascar, 225, 250
Irving, David, historian and author, 330–4
Ismay, Major General Sir Hastings (Pug), Military Secretary to the Prime Minister, 141, 155, 220, 254, 408, 440, 473
Italy, 33, 39–40, 51, 54, 59, 83, 85, 199, 368, 420–1

*Jamaica* (Br) light cruiser, 371–2, 386–8, 443, 448, 467
Jan Mayen Island, 202, 241, 267, 270–2, 283–4, 347
Japan, 8, 18, 21, 30, 32, 34, 37, 56, 65, 78, 81, 85, 90, 130, 145, 156, 160, 316–17, 324, 369, 436, 472, 478, 490
Jeschonnek, Colonel General Hanns, German Air Force Chief of Staff, 268
Jodl, Lieutenant General Alfred, OKW Chief of Operations, 338, 340
Johannesson, Captain Rolf, commander German 4th Destroyer Flotilla, 442, 446, 449, 451, 454–5, 457–8, 461
Johansen, Torbjøhn, Norwegian SIS agent, 429, 435
Johnston, Tom, Regional Commissioner for Scotland, 17
Joint Board, US, 28, 31, 33, 35, 489
Joint Board Estimate of September 1941, 33, 489
Joint Intelligence Committee (JIC), 88–92, 95, 106, 110, 127, 132, 137–9, 145, 155–6, 158–9, 218, 256, 318–20, 369, 400, 412–13, 420–1, 432, 440, 473–4, 478
Joint Planning Committee (JPC), also joint planners, 97, 99, 114, 128–30, 134, 142, 159–60, 184, 218, 246, 253, 258–9, 262
Joint Staff Mission Washington, 27, 29

Ju 87 Stuka (Ge) dive bomber, 120, 123, 150, 211, 342
Ju 88 (Ge) bomber, 101, 120, 150, 199, 211, 226, 231, 241–2, 290, 350, 366, 479, 481–2
Jupiter, proposed British/Canadian attacks on northern Norway, 6, 257–9, 316, 362
JW convoys: adoption of new designation 356; JW 51A and RA 51 272; JW 51B 374–88; JW 52 404–5; JW 53 405–6; JW 54 initial cancellation 409–10, November 1943 sailing as JW 54A and JW 54B 441–2; JW 55A 443 and JW 55B 444–8, 451–2, 454; JW 56A and 56B 461; JW 57 463; JW 58 464; JW 59–66 477–84

Kaafiord, 124, 392, 428, 432–3, 449, 466–7, 469
Kadnikov, 168
Kandalaksha, 117, 120–1, 337
Kara Sea, 234, 339–40, 430
Karelia, 116–17, 170, 173
Kazan tank school, 174,
*Kearney* (US) destroyer, 21
Keitel, Field Marshal Wilhelm, Chief of OKW, 394
Kemi, Gulf of Bothnia, 100–1, 117, 119
Kennedy, Major General John, Director of Military Operations, 97, 106, 491
Kennedy, Joseph, US Ambassador in London, 15–16
Kennedy-Purvis, Admiral Sir Charles, Deputy First Sea Lord, 311
*Keppel* (Br) destroyer, 290, 302, 336, 341, 463–4
Kesselring, Field Marshal Albert, 54
Keyes, Admiral of the Fleet Sir Roger, Director of Combined Operations 1941, 96, 186
Kharkov, 166, 249–50, 252, 411, 414
Kharlamov, Admiral Nikolai, Head of Russian military mission in London and naval attaché 1941–4, 100–1
Kineshma, 168, 170
King, Fleet Admiral Ernest, US Navy chief of Naval Operations and Commander US Fleet, 29, 160–1, 165, 184, 219, 225, 237, 253, 313, 316–17, 321, 346, 362, 403–4, 487–8, 496–7
*King George V* (Br) battleship, 75, 201, 225–6, 228, 338, 371, 375, 405
Kinloch, Commander David, 381, 383, 390
Kirkenes, 102, 110–11, 117, 121–4, 126, 128, 133–4, 150, 190, 193, 196–8, 201, 211–12, 214, 227–8, 236, 238, 241, 243, 248–9, 273, 337, 456
Klüber, Rear Admiral Otto, Admiral Arctic 1942–4, 348–9, 353–4, 373–4, 376–81, 384, 387–9, 392–3, 398–9, 444, 447, 450

Knox, Frank, US Navy Secretary, 26
Kola Inlet, 8, 110, 120, 226, 233–4, 241, 371–2, 459
*Köln* (Ge) light cruiser, 338–9, 347, 371, 396–7, 399
Kolosjoki, 116, 121, 480
Krancke, Vice Admiral Theodor, Naval Representative at Führer Headquarters, 199, 267, 284–5, 289, 338–9, 348, 352, 373, 376–7, 391–4, 396, 398
Krivoi Rog iron ore fields, 138–9
*K-21* (Sov) submarine, 307, 309
Kuibyshev, Russian diplomatic capital following Moscow evacuation, 155
Kummetz, Vice Admiral Oskar, 238, 265, 267, 272, 293, 300, 348, 373–4, 376–8, 380–1, 383–4, 386–90, 392–3, 398–9, 430, 442, 445, 450, 458
Kursk, 417, 420–1, 437, 489, 493, 495
Kuznetsov, Major General A A, Commander Northern Fleet Air Force, 114
Kuznetsov, Admiral Nikolay, Soviet Navy Minister, 109, 235, 312, 314
KV-1 (Sov) heavy tank, 91, 173–5, 360, 416

LaGG-3 (Sov) fighter, 169, 171, 173
Lake Ladoga, 117, 170
Lambe, Captain Charles, Director of Naval Plans, 297, 299, 400
Land, Admiral Emory, Head of US War Shipping Administration, 144, 165–6, 471, 477
Langfiord, 428, 449–50
Larsen, Lief, Norwegian resistance leader, 426
Lawton, Sir Frederick, PQ 17 trial judge, 332
Leach, Captain John, 19
Leathers, Lord Frederick, Minister of War Transport, 471
Lend-Lease, 9–10, 13, 16, 26, 64, 86, 145–6, Soviet Union eligible but multiple demands on 162, minor contribution 1941 163, impact of American entry into war 164–5, 172, aluminium 180, provides vital surplus to Russia 256, 278, shipping waste 323, Stalin criticism to Churchill 345, Marshall judges still vital in 1944 475
Leningrad, 24–5, 36, 91, 93, 117, 121, 136, 139, 155, 160, 170, 173, 178, 182, 359
Linge, Captain Martin, 187
Litvinov, Maxim, Soviet ambassador in Washington from December 1941, 220, 223, 345
Litza, River, 118–19, 125, 480
*Llanstephen Castle*, 114, 168
Loch Cairnbawn, 428, 431
Lofoten Islands, 73, 115, 126, 186, 188, 207, 211–12, 271, 283, 285–6, 348, 446
*London* (Br) heavy cruiser, 286, 298, 303

Loukhi, 117, 119
*Lützow* (Ge) pocket battleship, 57, 68, 196, 238, 241, 283, 286, 288–9, 293, 338, 340, 372, 374–8, 380–5, 387–9, 392, 397, 399, 409, 422, 427–8, 430, 433, 437, 441, 443, 445
Lyster, Rear Admiral Lumley, Fifth Sea Lord, 65–6
Lyttleton, Oliver, Minister of Production from 1942, 217, 222, 229–30, 437, 470

Macmillan, Harold, 154
Macready, Lieutenant General Gordon, Assistant Chief of General Staff, 141
Malaya, 34, 78, 183, 260
Mannerheim, Field Marshal Carl, Finnish leader, 120
Margesson, David, British Secretary for War, 101
Maritime Commission (US), 144, 163
Marrow, December 1941 Russian proposed joint Petsamo attack, 6, 191, 259
Marshall, General George C, US Army Chief of Staff, Dill 29, Philippines 32, Joint Board strategy 35, advocates cutting Russia aid 160–1, 165, April 1942 London visit and Sledgehammer 219–20, Molotov visit 223, 252–3, opposes Gymnast 316, 317, British deceit and shift to Pacific 317–18, reluctant acceptance of Torch 318–19, queries cost/benefit of Arctic convoys at Casablanca 403, but early 1944 sees Western aid still crucial to Soviet victory 475
Martel, Lieutenant General Giffard, Head of 30 Mission 1943, 436
Mason-Macfarlane, Major General Noel, Head of 30 Mission 1941, 97–9, 101–3, 105–7, 110, 132, 191, 216, 237, 273
Matilda (Br) tank, 173–6, 183, 200, 221, 249–50, 360, 415, 417
Matochin Strait, 304, 307
Maund, Captain Guy, SBNO Archangel, 112
McGrigor, Rear Admiral Rhoderick, 469, 481–2
McNaughton, General Andrew, commander of Canadian forces in Britain, 259
Me 109 (Ge) fighter, 101, 123–4, 171–2, 177, 211
Me 110 (Ge) fighter 123
*Mein Kampf*, 80
Meisel, Admiral Wilhelm, Chief of Staff German Naval War Staff from March 1943, 398, 448–9, 458
Menzies, Sir Stuart, Chief of SIS or 'C', 106, 111
Michela, Major Joseph, US Army attaché in Moscow, 92
MI5, Security Service, 245–6

# INDEX

MIG-3 (Sov) fighter, 91, 169, 171, 173
Mikoyan, Anastas, Soviet politburo member for war supplies, 163-4
Miles, Rear Admiral Geoffrey, Head of 30 Mission 1942, 98, 108-9, 111, 234-5, 273, 312
Ministry of Aircraft Production (MAP), 62
Ministry of Economic Warfare (MEW), 116, 137
Ministry of War Transport, 152, 404, 494
MI6, see SIS
Molotov, Vyacheslav, Soviet Foreign Minister, Berlin visit November 1940 85-7, 30 Mission 98, abandonment of Moscow 155, convoy reductions spring 1942 223, visits London and Washington 251-5, Churchill visit to Moscow 345, Hampden crisis 408, resumption of convoys autumn 1943 436-7, Eden meeting pre-Teheran 440
Montagu, Commander Ewen, NID staff, 246
Moore, Vice Admiral Sir Henry, Vice Chief of Naval Staff 1941-3, then deputy commander Home Fleet, 69, Lyttleton review 222, PQ 17 297-9, 310, 326, Tungsten 466-8
Moran, Sir Charles, Churchill's doctor, 17
Morgenthau, Henry, US Treasury Secretary, 165-6, 253
Moscow, 25, 36, 54, 81, 91-4, 98, 106-7, 109-10, 117, 121, 130, 138-41, 145, 152, 155-7, 160, 168, 170-1, 173-4, 176-7, 180, 182, 185, 210, 320, 344, 359, 439, 478, 493
Moscow Air Defence Region, 170, 172-3
Moscow Supply Conference, 135, 137, 139-42, 488
Mountbatten, Vice Admiral Lord Louis, 186, 259, 315-16
Murmansk, 8, 25-6, proposed joint operations 100-3, Vian visit 109-11, initial German operations against 113-21, 126, 1941 capacity 144-5, German attitude to 150, and intervention 151, Benedict 168-9, 182, primitive facilities 231, German bombing mid-1942 278, 312, unloading problems early 1944 459, 464
Murrow, Edward R, 16-17
Mussolini, Benito, Italian Duce (leader), 369

Narvik, 116, 124, 126, 133-4, 185-6, 188-9, 192-4, 196, 198, 201, 206, 238-42, 244, 249, 258, 265, 269, 281, 286, 289, 338-40, 348-9, 352, 372, 392, 397-9, 409-10, 427, 433, 447, 460, 479-80
Naval Intelligence Division (NID), 74, prewar Russian coverage 92, Trondheim U-boat shelter 196, PQ 13 assessment 215, *Trinidad* attack 231, Headache technique 240,
Rösselsprung 269, 271, 282, German heavy ships 1943 419, *Tirpitz* damage 435
*Nelson* (Br) battleship, 39, 45-7, 58, 98, 344
Neutrality Acts, 22
Nicolson, Harold, 97
NKVD, Soviet Intelligence and Security Service, 107
Noble, Admiral Sir Percy, C-in-C Western Approaches 1941-2, 57, 272, 328
Northern Fleet (Russian), 91, British priority to avoid German seizure 100, accepts British liaison 111, defensive mindset 113, 115, value of British support 358, German view of 117, exaggerated successes 234
Northern Fleet Air Force, 168-9, 170, 216, 337, 416
Norway, 8, 10-12, Hitler's 'zone of destiny' 126, Ajax 134, parallel British/German perceptions 185, British raids 185-91, German reinforcement 192-5, Hitler's Trondheim vision 195-6, March 1942 OKW directive 210, British deception operations 245-6, Jupiter 257-8, 362, SOE and Linge 426, strategic importance to Germany 1944 479
Novaya Zemlya, 299, 304, 307, 312, 336, 339-40, 347-8, 351, 353
*Nürnberg* (Ge) light cruiser, 372, 409
Nye, Lieutenant General Archibald, Vice Chief of the Imperial General Staff, 157, 161, 184, 190-1

*Obdurate* (Br) destroyer, 379, 381, 386, 389-90, 461
*Obedient* (Br) destroyer, 379, 381, 383, 386-7, 390
Oberkommando der Wehrmacht (OKW), 80, 84, 115, 119, 128, 185-6, 188, 192, 210-12, 213, 244-5, 250, 289, 338, 394-5, 444
Obersalzberg, 80, 82, 84, 87
Obozerskaya, 121
O'Brien, Lieutenant (later Admiral) William, 303, 331, 333
Office of Strategic Services (OSS), 16
Onslow, Commander Richard, 240, 242-3
*Onslow* (Br) destroyer, 349, 375, 381, 383
Oktyabrskii, Vice Admiral Filip, Soviet Black Sea fleet commander, 112
OKW Survey August 1941, 84-5
Operational Intelligence Centre (OIC), 73-4, 206, 208, 282, 286-90, 292-3, 299-300, 307, 309, 337-8, 340-1, 352, 363, 366, 372, 378, 392, 399-400, 419, 430, 435, 448, 450, 461, 463, 466
Operational Research, 69
Ōshima, Hiroshi, Japanese ambassador in Berlin 1941-5, 90

Ostfront, *Scharnhorst* sortie 25 December 1943, 448–50, 453, 458
Overlord, 6, 440, 459, 470–5, 477, 489–91, 497

*Palomares* (Br) anti-aircraft ship, 272, 290, 306, 353
Pan-American Security Zone, 19
Pearl Harbor, 22, 164–5, 184, 358
Pedestal, August 1942 Malta convoy, 6, 49, 63–4, 321, 325, 341–4, 355, 357, 470, 496
Peters, Captain Rudolf, commander Arctic U-boats 1943, 447, 450, 453, 458, 460, 462
Petsamo (also Liinahaman), strategic importance to Germany and perceived Russian designs on 86, 116, status in 1941 100, Golikov advocates joint operation against 101–2, German occupation 118, FAA attack 121–4, 158, 169, Germany perceives continuing threat 185, 193, 210, 339, new Russian proposal 190, airfield 211–12, 243, Jupiter 254, 258–9, German withdrawal 480
P 54 (*Unshaken*) (Br) submarine, 307, 309
P-40 Tomahawk (US) fighter, 25–6, 36, 114, 168–70, 172–3, 200, 471
Phillips, Vice Admiral Sir Tom, Vice Chief of the Naval Staff, 101
Pika, Colonel Helidor, Czech military attaché in Moscow, 107
Placentia Bay, 14–16, 488
Ploesti oil complex, 84, 86, 116
Poland, 88, 251, 470, 473, 478
Polyarnoe, 109–10, 112, 114, 117, 124, 233, 235, 273, 407
Portal, Marshal of the Royal Air Force Sir Charles, Chief of Air Staff, 114, 161, 169, 218–19, 368, 422
Pound, Admiral of the Fleet, Sir Dudley, First Sea Lord, opposes Force K 51–2, 54, 79, Beta precedent 55, Petsamo 100, 114, initial coolness to Russia 101–3, 153, Vian 108, Ajax 134, Norway raids end 1941 188, *Tirpitz* escape 207, and faith in Admiralty direction 208, convoy cost/benefit 215–17, 225, 232–3, 236–7, supports Tovey 233, PQ 17 274–7, 288–9, scatter decision 292–301, 304, 309–11, 326–31, Maisky 313, future convoy policy 321, 343, 346, winter 42/43 series 365, 369–70, Casablanca Arctic discussion 399–404, March 1943 suspension 410, 412, 415, Fraser 418, doubts new Atlantic breakout 419, Trident 422, *Tirpitz* bombing 423, death 437, Arctic stance 490, 495–7
Pownall, Lieutenant General Sir Henry, 97, 154

*Pozarica* (Br) anti-aircraft ship, 272, 291, 302, 333, 353
PQ convoys: PQ 1 and series naming 37; PQ 2 – 11 147; PQ 12 164, *Tirpitz* sortie and British protection 199–202, convoy progress 202–3, and Map 3 204–5, respective conclusions 208, 213; PQ 13 213–15, 231, 264; PQ 14 215, 221–2, 226; PQ 15 221, 223–9, 236–7, 240–1; PQ 16 237–8, 240–5, 247–51, 255–7, 259, 264, 268, 270, 272–3, 278, 282–3, 311, 354, 494; PQ 17 – see below; PQ 18 11, 224, 279, postponement 311, 313–14, 319, 321, 325, planning/preparation 335–40, Pedestal 341–3 and Torch 346–7 factors, execution 347–52 and results 354–6
PQ 17, 1–2, 9, 12–13, 55, 209, 244, 247, 260, Rösselsprung 265–8, British threat intelligence 269, 271, 279, 281–2, 286–8, German intelligence 282–3, British planning 272–7, composition and progress 278–9, 285–8, Map 4 280, German surface deployment 283–5, Hamilton's cruisers 288–90, 4 July air attacks 290–1, Ultra evening 4 July 292–6, Pound's decision to scatter 297–300, and its communication 300–1, implementation 301–5, German reaction and *Tirpitz* sortie 305–9, immediate aftermath 310–14, in national memory 325–34
*Prince of Wales* (Br) battleship, 14–15, 18–19, 25, 39, 45, 47–8, 50, 71, 78, 151, 207, 330, 386
*Prinz Eugen* (Ge) heavy cruiser, 57, 189, 194, 196–7, 200, 283, 372, 394, 396–7, 400, 419, 458
P-39 Airacobra (US) fighter, 168–9, 200, 255, 414, 492
*Punjabi* (Br) destroyer, 225, 228
Purple Japanese diplomatic cipher system, 90
Putin, Russian President Vladimir, 10, 488
PVO, Soviet Home Air Defence Force, 170–2, 255, 416

QP convoys: QP 2–7 147, 150; QP 8 202–3, 213; QP 9 213, 214–15, 264; QP 10 217, 221–2; QP 11 224, 226–8; QP 12 241, 243, 247, 264; QP 13 272–4, 279, 283, 286; QP 14 335–6, 347–9, 351, 353–5, 362; QP 15 365–6, 370, 373
Quebec summit, 472

RA convoys: RA 51 372; RA 52 405; RA 53 405–6; RA 54A 441 and RA 54B 442; RA 55A 444–5, 447–8, and RA 55B 448; RA 56A 461–2; RA 57 463; RA 58 464, 469; RA 59 469; RA 59A – RA 66 481–5

## INDEX

Raaby, Torstein, Norwegian SIS agent, 429, 435, 466
Radar, 1, Somerville role 41, 1941 Mediterranean experience 44–51, Force K and Beta 52–3, 55, RN air operations 61–3, escort carriers 64–5, ASV 68–9, RN radar development/deployment 1938–41 69–73, provision to Russians 113, 183, 357–8, 492, 151 Wing lacks 169, *Tirpitz* avoids use 202, *Trinidad* and Z 26 214–15, application to AA ships 224, *Palomares*' PQ 17 air warning 290 and *Pozarica* 291, adopted by Fw 200 339 and BV 138 447–8, Pedestal sets radar direction standard 342–3, PQ 18 and *Avenger* 350, Barents Sea 383–4, 386–7, *King George V* and JW 53 405, Germans perceive British superiority 443, 446, 455, 457–8, *Scharnhorst* sortie 452–7, final convoys 462, 465, 481, 483
Raeder, Grand Admiral Erich, Chief of German Naval Staff, 21–2, 45, Sealion 80–1, Mediterranean strategy 83–4, 87–8, 1941 Arctic operations 117–18, 121, threat to Norway 126, 189–90, 192–4, Trondheim 195, fuel shortage 197–8, U-boat deployment 198, air power 199, *Tirpitz* and PQ 12 199, 209–10, 222, 246, Rösselsprung 266–9, 284, 306, 308, 338, 340, PQ 18 347, 352, 372, Regenbogen 373–4, 376–7, 384, 389, 391–3, heavy ships and resignation 393–9, 497
Ramsbottom-Isherwood, Wing Commander Henry, 167–8
Rankin, scenario for unopposed Western military deployment into France, 6, 474
RDF, see Radar
Reche, Reinhard, commander *U-255* and top Arctic ace, 406
Red Enigma key, 105, 151, 279
Regenbogen, German navy plan for winter 1942 surface attack on Arctic convoy, 6, 374, 376–7, 380, 384, 388–9, 391, 442
Reinicke, Commander Hansjürgen, 238, 445
*Reuben James* (US) destroyer, 21
Reykjavik, 200, 202, 213–16, 241, 272, 347
Reza Shah, Iranian monarch, 129
Ribbentrop, Joachim von, German Foreign Minister, 83, 85, 87
Riccardi, Admiral Arturo, Italian Chief of Naval Staff, 46
Riviera, British–American summit in Placentia Bay August 1941, 6, 16–28, 31–7, 39, 45, 56, 85, 95, 131–3, 135, 160, 254, 318, 488–9
*Rodney* (Br) battleship, 39, 47–8, 70, 72, 336, 344
Rokossovsky, General Konstantin, 174
Romania, 84–6, 112, 116, 136, 153, 197
Roosevelt, President Franklin D, 8, 10, 14, early correspondence with Churchill 15–16, Hopkins 16–17, Riviera and outcomes 18–30, 32–3, Joint Board estimate 33, commits to aiding Russia 104, 135, 144, Arcadia 160, agrees Lend-Lease status for Russia 162, and expedites aid 165–6, 'second front' 220– , 223, handling Stalin 222, invites Molotov 223, approves Task Force 39 225, Molotov visit 252–3, insists Russia's survival critical 253, agrees PQ 18 suspension 313, Argonaut and Gymnast 315–18, takeover of Iran route 323, insists PQ convoys have equal priority with Torch 346, but accepts temporary pause 363, while denying naval assistance 367–8, reaffirms support for Russia at Casablanca 401–3, accepts cancellation of JW 54 411, early 1944 insists aid still of paramount importance 473, reflections 488, 490–1
Roskill, Stephen, naval historian, 330–1, 334
Rösselsprung, German plan to attack convoy PQ 17, 265–73, 283, 289, 306–9, 349, 426
Rostov, 156, 256
Roundup, British–American invasion of France subsequently Overlord, 6, 219–20, 315–20, 346, 420–1, 489, 491
Rovaniemi, 100, 117
Royal Fleet Auxiliary (RFA), 77
Russia Liaison Group, 98–9
Rybachiy peninsula, 102, 113, 118, 214
Rzhev, 170–1

Salla, 117, 119
*Scharnhorst* (Ge) battlecruiser, 2, 9, 12, 57, 189, 194–5, 201, 209, 372, 394, deploys to Norway 396–9, 400, 404, 409, 422, 427–8, Zitronella 429, 432–3, 438, final sortie 441–58, 459–60, 498–9
Schofield, Captain Brian, 29
Schmundt, Rear Admiral Hubert, Admiral Arctic 1941–2, 198, 227, 238, 266–7, 284, 289, 296, 348
Schniewind, General Admiral Otto, 246, 249, Rösselsprung 265–7, 269, 271, 275, 283, 285, 289, 293, 306–9, 338, 348, Regenbogen 373–4, 393, 395, absorbs Group North 398, 430, *Scharnhorst* sortie 442–3, 445–7, 450, 455, 457–8
Schnorchel or snort fitted U-boats, 460, 479–80, 482–3, 485
Sealion, German plan to invade Britain 1940, 80–3, 87, 89
*Sealion* (Br) submarine, 124
*Seawolf* (Br) submarine, 124, 203, 224, 273
Second Protocol, 180–1, 230, 253, 257, 279, 320–5, 344, 356, 362, 365, 402, 415, 475, 491, 495

Sengwarden, Group North headquarters, 268
Shaposhnikov, Marshal Boris, Chief of Soviet Army Staff from July 1941, 190–1
*Sheffield* (Br) cruiser, 39, 46, 48, 70, 72, 371–2, 384, 386, 388, 404–5, 444–5, 467
Sherbrooke, Captain Robert, commander of JW 51B close escort at Battle of the Barents Sea, 375, 379, 381, 383, 386, 388–90
Sherman (US) tank, 174, 414, 417, 471, 476
Shinwell, Emanuel, Labour MP and postwar Minister of Defence, 326–8, 330
Sicily, 40, 43, 47–8, 260–1, 341–2, 402, 420–1
Signals Intelligence (SIGINT): British 40–2, 49, 73–4, Barbarossa 88, 90, 107, Petsamo 121–2, threat to Moscow 155, Wye Cottage and Black Sea 235–6, Hinsley 292, Mediterranean mid-1942 341, German air withdrawals 366, *Scharnhorst* and *Prinz Eugen* deployment 396–7, Russian threat to intercept sites 408, support for Citadel 422, *Tirpitz* 423, Altafiord berths 428, Source transit support 431, and warning of heavy unit departure 433, Tungsten 466; German 125, 282–3, Regenbogen targeting 374, Zitronella objective 439; Italian 53; Russian 236; Swedish 281, 352, 372
Siilvarsuo, Finnish Major General, 119
Sikorski, General Wladyslaw, Polish prime minister in exile, 139
Silver Fox, German Arctic theatre Operation, 116–18, 121, 142, 150
SIS, Secret Intelligence Service, also MI6, 6, 12, 89–90, 106–7, 111, 196, 201, 281, 399, 428–9, 435, 466
Sladen, Commander Geoffrey, 125, 196
Sledgehammer, limited attack on Cotentin peninsula 1942 or 1943, 6, 217–21, 224, 229–30, 245, 250, 252, 257–9, 314–20, 344–5, 367, 402, 489, 491
Smuts, Field Marshal Jan, South African premier, 364
SOE, Special Operations Executive, 96, 99, 107, 111, 187, 424, 426–7
Somervell, Lieutenant General Brehon, Head of US War Supplies, 403
Somerville, Vice Admiral Sir James, commander Force H 1941, background and qualities 41, 233, 418, Halberd planning 39–44, 46–7, intelligence 41–3, counters Italian fleet 48, achievement and lessons 49, 261, 341, 351, 355, 496, radar contribution 71, cruiser policy 228, interwar destroyer training 390
Spain, 30–1, 83–5, 132, 140, 160, 315, 320
Spider, British deception operation, 246–7
Sørøya Island, 432, 434, 451, 456
Source, midget submarine operation against *Tirpitz*, 6, 422, 427–35, 437, 468

Spitfire (Br) fighter, 63, 115, 140, 177, 225, 281, 286, 337, 343, 352, 363, 429, 431, 436, 466, 477
Spitzbergen, location and status 105, Allied occupation considered 108, 114, 126–7, Operation Gauntlet destroys facilities 127–8, German plans 128, 212, 236, both sides establish small meteorological facilities 212, PQ 18 fuelling 336, 338, 347, independent wrecked 363, Zitronella raid 429–30
Stalin, Soviet leader Joseph, Hopkins visit 24–5, September 1941 Churchill message 36–7, Germany negotiations late 1940 85–7, Barbarossa warning 89, Ingersoll 107–8, first message to Churchill 109, 135–8, Iran 130, Moscow Supply Conference 140–1, starts 'second front' campaign 153, December 1941 Eden visit 157, 179, 183, Mikoyan reviews First Protocol deliveries 163–4, Clark Kerr arrival 164, Moscow air defence 170, aircraft design 171, Zhukov and holding Moscow 176, Marrow 190–1, Roosevelt invites Molotov 223, increasing threat to PQ convoys 234, 237–8, 1942 Molotov visit 251–3, demands more fighters 255–6, but agrees diverting A-20s to Egypt 312, responds sharply to suspension of PQ 18 313–14, 319, Churchill's Moscow visit 320, 344–7, German aircraft production 360, anger at Torch convoy suspension 364, peace feelers 369, 413, criticises Torch progress and disappointment at March 1943 convoy cancellation 411, aggrieved over broken supply 'contracts' and 'second front' promises 436, 439–40, but appreciates overall winter 1943/44 convoy programme 460, 470, Teheran summit 473, Japan commitment 478, reflections 486–7, 498
Stalingrad, 255–6, 320, 323–4, 359, 362–4, 366–7, 369, 377, 392, 394–5, 401, 406, 411, 477, 487, 489, 493, 495
Stange, Captain Rudolf, 380, 383–4, 387, 389–90, 392–3
Stanley, Colonel Oliver, Head of FOPS, 245
Stark, Admiral Harold (Betty), US Chief of Naval Operations, 20, 29, 32, 35, 315
Steinhardt, Laurence, US ambassador in Moscow 1941-2, 24
Stimson, Henry, US Secretary for War, 26–7, 160, 165, 316–17, 401
Strelow, Siegfried, commander *U-435*, 354
Struszynski, Waclaw, 75
Stumpff, Colonel General Hans-Jürgen, Commander German 5th Air Fleet in Norway, 102, 212
Sturmovik (Il-2) (Sov) attack aircraft, 91, 171, 178

INDEX 573

Substance, Malta convoy, 41, 43–6, 49–51, 124, 261
*Suffolk* (Br) cruiser, 37, 70, 72, 121–2, 125
Suhren, Captain Reinhard, commander Arctic U-boats from late 1944, 481, 483–5
Svalbard Treaty, 105
Svir river, 121, 145
Sweden, 115–16, 134, 185, 189, 193, 196, 413–14, 426
Swordfish (Br) FAA TSR aircraft, 39, 44, 48–9, 51, 62, 65, 67–8, 122, 124, 260, 336, 349, 353–4, 462–4, 467, 469, 481
Syfret, Vice Admiral Neville, Vice Chief of Naval Staff, 437–8
Symbol, British–American summit at Casablanca January 1943, 6, 401, 488–9

T5, see G7es
T-34 (Sov) medium tank, 91, 173–5, 178, 250, 322, 360, 416–17, 422, 492
T-60 (Sov) light tank, 250, 322, 360
T-70 (Sov) light tank, 173, 176, 360, 416
Tanafiord, 456
Task Force 39, later 99, 225–6, 494
Tedder, Air Marshal Sir Arthur, Air Commander Middle East, 262–3
Teheran summit, 164, 439, 470, 472–3, 498
Third Protocol, 180, 436–9, 459, 472, 475
*Tigris* (Br) submarine, 114, 124, 126, 348–9, 353
Timoshenko, Marshal Semyon, Soviet Defence Commissar, 85
Title, Chariot operation against *Tirpitz*, 426–8
TNT, 181–2, 347, 358, 493, 502
Tobruk, 52, 99, 316, 325, 344
Toluene, 181–2, 358, 493, 502
Torch, Operation, previously Gymnast, 2, 6, 32, 259, 318–21, 325, 344–7, 354, 362–3, 366–8, 371, 373, 401, 403, 406, 417, 489, 495
Tovey, Admiral Sir John, C-in-C Home Fleet 1940–3, 71–2, Vian 108, Petsamo 122–4, Spitzbergen 127, challenges of Arctic route 147, Ultra 151, Anklet 186–8, PQ 12 201–3, 206–8, PQ 13 215, PQ 15 225, *Edinburgh* loss 228, and *Trinidad* 231–2, difficulties with Churchill 232–3, PQ 16 243, deception operations 246, PQ 17 planning 271–7, execution 286–91, 308–9, aftermath 303–5, 325–30, 333, PQ 18 planning 335–8, 342–3, *Scheer* and *Ulm* 340–1, QP 15 365, winter 1942/43 convoy series 370–1, 405, Barents Sea engagement 387, 404, relieved by Fraser 418, 490
Trans-Persian Railway, 130–1
*Trident* (Br) submarine, 114, 124–6, 196, 273
Trident summit, Washington May 1943, 6, 420–2, 436
*Trinidad* (Br) light cruiser, 213–15, 221, 231–4, 236

Tromsø, 123–5, 133–4, 150, 188, 203, 206, 211, 238, 281, 289, 301, 429, 433, 448, 463, 469, 480
Trondheim, 118, Ajax 134, German navy redeployment 192–7, Hitler's 'Drontheim' vision 195–6, U-boat base 198, 239, 460, 480, *Tirpitz* 200–1, 203, 206–7, 371–2, 422, 424–6, Fw 200s 211, *Hipper* 213–14, communications via Sweden 269–70, British PR cover 281
Tungsten, April 1944 FAA attack on *Tirpitz*, 6, 466–8
Turkey, 84, 129, 132
Turner, Rear Admiral Richmond (Kelly), US Navy Director of Plans 1941, 29
*Tuscaloosa* (US) heavy cruiser, 14, 225, 301, 340–1
Type XXI U-boats, 2, 479–80
Typhoon, October 1941 German Moscow offensive, 6, 54, 140, 155–7, 440

U-354 (Ge) 376, 378–80, 384, 392
*Ulm*, German minelayer, 340–1
Ultra, British codeword for sensitive SIGINT, 2, 12, Italian Hagelin 42, 51–4, 77–8, Barbarossa insights 89–91, German Red and Vulture keys 105, sharing with Russia 106, FAA Petsamo attack 121–2, 124, submarine operations 124, and 1941 threat to Moscow 155–7, 159, Cerberus 194, German fuel shortage 197, 216, Norway reinforcement early 1942 201, *Tirpitz* PQ 12 sortie 203, 206, German interest in Spitzbergen 212, German order of battle 213–15, *Trinidad* sinking 231, targeting of Kola and White Sea 233, PQ 16 240, deception operations 246, June 1942 JIC Eastern Front assessment 256, PQ 17 269, 273, 275, 279, 282–3, 286–7, 290–1, 293, 295–8, 300–1, 305, 307, 309, 326, 329, 331, German air strength summer 1942 337, PQ 18 search 339, *Ulm* 341, PQ 18 349, 353, German aircraft production 360, Stalingrad 369, JW 51A 372 and JW 51B 378–9, Zitronella 431, *Scharnhorst* sortie 443–4, 450, final convoys 482–3
Umansky, Konstantin, Soviet ambassador to the United States 1941–2, 23–4, 220
Unthinkable, hypothetical British 1945 operation to impose West's will on Russia, 478
Ural mountains, 34–5, 138, 178, 278, 322, 493
Uranus, Soviet Stalingrad counter-offensive November 1942, 6, 359, 366

Vaenga Bay, 109–10
Valentine (Br) tank, 173–6, 183, 200, 249, 322, 360, 415–17, 436, 471–2, 492–3

Varanger Fiord, 101, 110, 121–2, 234
Vardo, 109
Varley, Commander Cromwell, 425
Vest Fiord, 126, 186, 188, 206–7, 248, 283–4
Vian, Rear Admiral Philip, 108–10, 113–14, 119, 121, 126–8, 260, 262–3, 277, 309, 375, 418
*Victorious*, British fleet carrier, 121–3, 125, 201, 203, 207–8, 240, 272, 298, 308, 341–3, 371, 418, 467, 496
Victory Programme, 27, 32–3, 35
Vigorous, Mediterranean convoy, 259–65, 274–5, 277, 298, 309, 336, 357, 496
Vishinsky, Andrey, Soviet Deputy Foreign Minister, 89
*Vizalma* (Br) ASW trawler, 375–6, 380, 384–6
Vladivostok, 131, 139, 144–5, 161, 166, 180, 324
Volga, River, 34, 131–3, 138, 168, 256, 364, 493
Vologda, 145, 168, 177
Voronezh, 250, 256, 417
Vulture cipher key, 105, 155, 157

*Wainwright* (US) destroyer, 290–1
Wake-Walker, Rear Admiral Frederick, 121–5, 272, 466
Walker, Commander later Captain Johnny, Escort Group commander, 247, 464–5
War Office, 96–7, 99, 110, 152
War Shipping Administration (US), 144, 477
Washington, 8, 20, 26–7, 29, 92, 135, 158–60, 185, 219, 221–3, 250, 251–3, 288, 314, 317, 319, 345–6, 368, 401, 410, 420, 488, 490, 497
*Washington* (US) battleship, 225–6, 240, 272
*Wasp* (US) light carrier, 225
Watson-Watt, Sir Robert, 41

Wavell, General Sir Archibald, C-in-C India, 130, 491
Weichold, Vice Admiral Eberhard, German naval representative Rome, 54
Welles, Sumner, US Assistant Secretary of State, 28, 104
Wellington (Br) medium bomber, 51, 53, 67–8, 262
Western Approaches Command, 57, 67, 74, 215, 272, 338, 410, 442–3, 480
White Sea Canal, 118, 120
Winn, Commander Rodger, 29, 294–8
Wright, Charles, Director of Naval Scientific Research, 73
Wunderland, German raider operation in Kara Sea, 339–40, 351–2
WW1 strategy paper, 160
Wyburd, Commander Derek, 112
Wye Cottage intercept site, 235

X-Craft midget submarines, development 424–5, 427, and Source 428, 431–4

Yak-1 (Sov) fighter, 91, 169, 171
Yeaton, Major Ivan, US Army attaché in Moscow, 92

Z 26 (Ge) destroyer, 150, 214–15, 221
Zaporozhe aluminium refinery, 138
Zar, German minelaying operation August 1942, 340
*Zaunkönig*, See G7es.
Zhukov, General, later Marshal, Georgy, Russian Chief of the General Staff 1941, 98, 176, 190, 487, 493
Zitronella, German raid on Spitzbergen September 1943, 429–30